PRAISE FOR

The MAJIC BUS
An American Odyssey

"This joyous adventure in the rediscovery of America not only makes a wonderfully readable book, it also shows our schools and colleges exciting new ways of teaching our children about their country and its history."

—Arthur Schlesinger, Jr.

"Brilliantly revealing . . . *The Majic Bus* reads like an engaging travel book, filled with the author's wide-eyed wonder at the cultural depth and diversity of his own country. Brinkley is a super writer who can capture the enduring allure of Route 66 without resorting to cliché."

—*Toronto Globe and Mail*

"*The Majic Bus* is one part history, one part memoir, one part travelogue and one part literary criticism. Taken together, it is a moving tribute to the evolving culture of America, from Walt Whitman to Jack Kerouac, from Thomas Jefferson to Martin Luther King, Jr.— and more testimony to how much we owe our past."

—*Dallas Morning News*

"This is a marvelous book, a veritable love song to America. Doug Brinkley knows more about American popular culture, how teachers ought to relate to students, the great American novels, the diplomatic history of the Cold War, what are the important historical sites and why every American should visit them, than anyone else I know."

—Stephen Ambrose

"*The Majic Bus* is an entertaining volume whose tone is unabashed idealism and nationalism, a celebration of the American landscape—geological, cultural, and historical."

—*The Chronicle of Higher Education*

"What a marvelous idea—teaching students about America by letting them experience it on the road in all its glory, its shabbiness, its wonderful enthusiasms and beauties, its unfulfilled promises and ugliness, its incredible diversity and richness. This is one recent book I wish every American would read. It will inspire any breathing American to travel the open road with eyes that see and a heart and mind that try to feel and understand this vast and great land of ours."

—George McGovern

"This enjoyable book by Professor Brinkley will almost certainly inspire students in other universities to suggest similar courses in what clearly proved a most commendable experiment. The text is far more than a straight explanatory travelogue. You may no longer be a student, but you will learn a good deal from this book about American travel and travel writers you never knew before."

—*The Barkham Reviews*

"Poised somewhere on the American landscape between Jack Kerouac and Charles Kuralt, these students, the tamer 1990s heirs, perhaps, to Ken Kesey and the Merry Pranksters of the 60s, say they have had enough of the malls and landscaped lawns in and around their campus and are mad to experience a different America."

—*New York Times*

"*The Majic Bus: An American Odyssey* [is] an exuberant, celebratory, energetic, optimistic, activist, jam-packed 500-page account of a professor with seventeen students in a chartered bus who set out to discover America."

—*English Journal*

"As the heritage of America's Beat Generation Road appreciates in human understanding, this *Majic Bus* tour exemplifies many joys of Kerouac's legacy—the old openhearted enthusiastic non-chauvinist American spirit of compassion to Person, Earth and Heaven expands toward this millennium's end."

—Allen Ginsberg

"An offbeat travelogue that will keep readers interested from start to finish."

—*Milwaukee Journal*

"Want to fall in love with America, all over again? Want to experience, albeit vicariously, the enjoyment of an event-crammed cross-country bus tour with 17 bright and eager college students and their youthful, inspiring, supremely intelligent professor? Want a refreshing refresher course in American history and culture that's an absolute hoot to boot? Then this book is for you, and it's one you'll read and enjoy again. Even better, it may inspire you to go so far as to get out and see this great country in a similar fashion."

—*Tampa Tribune and Times*

"This excursion is much more than a travel book. As he did to members of the tour, Brinkley elaborates to the reader on the various places visited discussing American history, geology, literature, architecture, art and social concerns. Readers may not receive the six college credits that the participants did, but they certainly will get an education from their own ride on *The Majic Bus*."

—*Cleveland Plain Dealer*

"A folksy omnibus of a book . . . And for those who thrive on trivia, *The Majic Bus is* a treasure trove of Americana for the 1990s."

—*The Press Democrat* (California)

"Tests in hotel rooms, lectures in restaurants. Cross-country field trips. What in the name of education is going on here?"

—*USA Today*

"Douglas Brinkley, the indefatigably eager guide for this Magical History Tour, rediscovers the American past in the American landscape. Along the way, Thomas Jefferson and Elvis Presley, Malcolm X and Mark Twain, Robert Johnson and Dr. King, and a hundred others come alive again for a new generation, linked to the places they lived, the country they changed."

—Geoffrey C. Ward

"*The Majic Bus* is a slapdash travelogue as well as a carefully routed historical, literary tour. It is full of information on everything . . . jazz, art and the natural world . . . If you have been anywhere along their route, you will see it through different eyes. If you have never traveled where they traveled, you may frequently feel as if you'd been there. It is a book of new perspectives on old history, a book to revive memories and forgotten dreams, to remember what it is like to be young."

—*Bismark Tribune*

"*The Majic Bus* is a packed multifarious guide to armchair travelers with short attention spans. A loose assemblage of notes on American literature, music and history, it's the kind of book that makes you feel envious and proud of our country's staggering diversity, oddity and potential."

—*San Antonio Express*

"*The Majic Bus* has such vitality, force and power that it left me breathless, wishing I could be a student again, a member of Doug Brinkley's class, a party to this incredible journey into America's past."

—Doris Kearns Goodwin

"What the reader gets in *The Majic Bus* is part travelogue, part history lesson and part polemic on the nature of present-day history teaching . . . For a generation that may never have read *On the Road* or stayed awake in geography or history classes, Brinkley's affectionate collage of this country, its expansiveness, its grandiosity, could lather the curiosity."

—*Kansas City Star*

Douglas Brinkley

The MAJIC BUS
An American Odyssey

There is no truth but in transit.

—RALPH WALDO EMERSON

ANCHOR BOOKS
DOUBLEDAY
NEW YORK   LONDON   TORONTO   SYDNEY   AUCKLAND

All the author royalties for this paperback edition will be given to the following nonprofit organizations in the business of making a difference:

Thomas Wolfe Memorial
  Advisory Committee
P.O. Box 7143
Asheville, NC 28802
(to build a visitors' center)

Robert F. Kennedy Memorial
Action Corps Program
1206 30th Street
Washington, DC 20007

Sierra Club
Student Coalition
730 Polk Street
San Francisco, CA 94109

The Delta Blues Museum
A Division of the Carnegie Public Library of Clarksdale,
  Mississippi
114 Delta Avenue
Clarksdale, MS 38614

AN ANCHOR BOOK
PUBLISHED BY DOUBLEDAY
a division of Bantam Doubleday Dell Publishing Group, Inc.
1540 Broadway, New York, New York 10036

ANCHOR BOOKS, DOUBLEDAY, and the portrayal of an anchor
are trademarks of Doubleday, a division of
Bantam Doubleday Dell Publishing Group, Inc.

The Majic Bus: An American Odyssey was originally published in hardcover by Harcourt
Brace & Company in 1993. The Anchor Books edition is published by arrangement with
Harcourt Brace & Company.

Permissions and credits appear on page 523.

Library of Congress Cataloging-in-Publication Data

Brinkley, Douglas.
    The majic bus : an American odyssey / Douglas Brinkley. — 1st
Anchor Books ed.
        p.   cm.
    Originally published: New York : Harcourt Brace, ©1993. With
updated and rev. introd.
    Includes bibliographical references.
    1. United States—Description and travel.   2. United States—
Civilization—1945–   I. Title.
[E169.04B75   1994]
917.304'928—dc20   93-45878
                                                        CIP

Printed in the United States of America
First Anchor Books Edition: July 1994

10   9   8   7   6   5   4   3   2

DEDICATED TO THE MEMORIES OF:

Jack Kerouac	The Lonesome Mystic Highway Saint of America
Thomas Wolfe	For *Look Homeward, Angel, You Can't Go Home Again, Of Time and the River*, and *The Web and the Rock*
Stephen Foster	For "My Old Kentucky Home," "Hard Times Come Again No More," "Old Folks at Home," "O Susannah," and many other national musical treasures
Miles Davis	For defining "cool" by playing it
Robert Kennedy	For rolling up his shirtsleeves and caring

SAVE THE MOJAVE DESERT

The legislator's rule of thumb is that one letter represents one hundred voters. The California Desert needs a continual outpouring of letters in which citizens, young and old and from every state, write their congressmen and their two senators and say: "We need three parks in the California Desert. Please vote for the California Protection Act."

The address of all congressmen is:	House Office Building Washington, DC 20515
The address of all senators is:	Senate Office Building Washington, DC 20510

Seattle, WA
(Mt St Helens Ntnl Volcanic Mnmt)

Spokane, WA

Medora, ND
(Theodore Ro...
Ntnl Pk)

Crow Agency, MT
(Little Bighorn Battlefield Ntnl Mnmt)

Amidon, ND

Portland, OR

Missoula, MT

Billings, MT

Deadwood, SD
(Mt Rushmore Ntnl Mem)

Mitc...

Eugene, OR
(Jedediah Smith Redwoods St Pk)

Pleasant Hill, OR

Rapid City, SD
(Badlands Ntnl Pk)

Fortuna, CA

Eureka, CA
(Redwood Ntnl Pk)

Ferndale, CA

(Humboldt Redwood St Pk)

Estes Park, CO
(Rocky Mtn Ntnl Pk)

Boulder, CO

Oakley
(Monu...

Mendocino, CA

Glen Ellen, CA

Central City, CO

Denver, CO

San Francisco, CA

Grand Junction, CO

Monterey, CA

Salinas, CA

Telluride, CO

Cheyenne Wells, CO

Carmel, CA

(Boulder Dam)

(Grand Canyon Ntnl Pk)

Cortez, CO
(Mesa Verde Ntnl Pk)

San Luis Obispo, CA

Las Vegas, NV

Solvang, CA

Taos, NM

Santa Barbara, CA

Williams, AZ

Santa Fe, NM

Flagstaff, AZ

Gallup, NM

Albuquerque, NM

Sioux Falls, SD

Chicago, IL

Cleveland, OH

New York, NY

Hempstead, NY

e, KS

Kansas City, MO

Springfield, IL

Charlottesville, VA

Washington, DC

Independence, MO

St. Louis, MO

Cherokee, NC

Asheville, NC

Memphis, TN

Clarksdale, MS

Oxford, MS

Atlanta, GA

Montgomery, AL

New Orleans, LA

Biloxi, MS

1992
Itinerary

I would rather be ashes than dust!
  I would rather
    that my spark burn out in a brilliant blaze
    than it should be stifled by dryrot.
  I would rather be a superb meteor,
    every atom of me in magnificent glow,
    than a sleepy and permanent planet.
  The proper function of man is to live, not to exist.
  I shall not waste my days trying to prolong them.
  I shall use my time.
                    —Jack London, "Credo"

The Open Road. The great home of the soul is the Open
Road. Not heaven, not paradise. Not "above." Not even
"within." It is a wayfarer down the road.
                    —D. H. Lawrence, "Whitman"

If I don't use the cork
  I may spill the wine—
But if I do?
                    —Jack Kerouac, "Pome"

Contents

Contents

Preface
TO THE ANCHOR EDITION
NEW IDEAS, NEW UNDERSTANDING, NEW HOPE

Resurrect yourself with a strong cup of coffee
shake off the dust of the grave and start sweeping.
Beneath the rubble of exhausted culture
you may catch a glimpse of something gleaming.

—ROBERT HUNTER
from *No Apocalypse*

Hey ho, let's go . . .

—THE RAMONES
from "Blitzkrieg Bop"

WHEN *THE MAJIC BUS: AN AMERICAN ODYSSEY* WAS PUBLISHED IN early 1993, I had no idea what kind of response to expect. I knew *why* I wrote the book: to ignite (or reignite) an intense passion for the United States in high school and college students, their parents, and educators who, like me, viewed teaching as a privileged calling. I hoped an account of my Hofstra University course "American Odyssey: Art and Culture Across America" would capture the whirlwind spirit of our raucous educational adventure by sleeper bus to thirty states in six weeks and whet student appetites for learning by presenting our national historical and literary heritage in a contemporary, information-packed fashion. I wanted to write a book students might actually read for fun as a first step to understanding what Thomas Wolfe called "a billion forms of America," and more important to recognize that the past belongs to them too. I wanted to help bored and jaded students develop a sense of democracy's potential and of community responsibility, to develop an enthusiastic understanding of what it means to be a civic-minded American. I wanted students to love and cherish learning for its own sake, to open minds, broaden experience, think hard, value cultural diversity, plunge into books, acquire subculture tolerance, and take calculated risks on what Walt Whitman calls "The Open Road."

From my rather youthful vantage point, I realize that with today's severe educational crisis, teachers cannot merely preach at powerless students about corrupted virtues and misguided values; they must "walk the walk and talk the talk." Young people have learned from their parents—and from the job market—that history and literature and geography aren't especially important. Nearly ninety million adults (one in four) are, according to the Department of Education, either illiterate or functionally illiterate. Undergraduate education is not faring so well either. The 1993 Brock study's final report stated that our undergraduate education system is a "prescription for decline" and found that four in ten college graduates earned a degree without studying English or American literature and one in four graduated without taking a single history course. Even many of our most highly educated citizens know next to nothing about our country's past or, for that matter, about any country's past. College enrollment in humanities continues to decline at an alarming rate while the "money-making" majors of business and management flourish. For example, in 1991 over 250,000 bachelor degrees were awarded in business, compared with 7,300 in philosophy and religion combined. How can caring humanities teachers make an end run around such seasoned indifference and monetary motivation, especially when the liberal arts are so little valued in the marketplace? What would I as one lone teacher do?

I knew what I would *not* do: join what has become a cottage industry of complaint led by cynical educational naysayers such as Dinesh D'Souza *(Illiberal Education)* and Allan Bloom *(The Closing of the American Mind)*. When was the American mind ever open? Certainly not when Jim Crow reigned in the South and when Ivy League schools and the University of Chicago taught "Great Books" to an elite few. Nor would I prepare an arid checklist of "facts" that every "educated" person should know. Instead, I would develop a course on American literature and history to meet my students on their terms, not on mine. My simple modus vivendi: respect your students and they will respect you in return. *The Majic Bus* tells the story of that effort. Like my Hofstra course, it was meant to teach young people about their America by making our national heritage exhilarating and relevant, joyous and meaningful, not a dose of puritanical castor oil. Between 1990 and 2005, one out of every three students with a baccalaureate (including business majors) will have to undertake mundane, unfulfilling employment, such as working for the post office or making pizzas or passing out flyers in the mall—what novelist Doug Coupland calls "McJobs." Why bother? Why take out student loans, or put your parents in terminal debt, to work at the local car wash—if you are lucky? It is that question we have to help students find an answer to, and they can't find answers if they feel hopeless and cheated. The time has come for college presidents to start celebrating ideas and knowledge, to stop recruiting vulnerable high school students with misleading Madison Avenue slogans like "We teach success."

Today's young people, so many of whom come from broken homes or homes in which both parents must work to stay afloat financially, don't need to be hoodwinked into college or blamed for all our society's social ills. More than ever, today's students need honesty and inspiration and encouragement, time and attention, civility and empathy, and—most important—adult role models, not finger-pointing education theorists with a laptop full of woeful statistics about our children's inevitable doomed future. From preschool to university, teachers and administrators must start spreading optimism, nourishing imaginations, and demonstrating the value of sustained effort to gain knowledge. If we put our collective energy and capital and faith behind our schools, we might get them—and America—back on track. "A person without faith is like a walking corpse," Bob Dylan recently reflected. "And people have to fight to get faith back."

So now you know the why of *The Majic Bus*. How was it received? Because the book was based on a real classroom journey into America, filled with honest and good intentions in the simple pursuit of revelatory knowledge about our national heritage, it was popular with the very audience I intended to reach. Dozens of college students wrote to me asking how they could take part in a similar course at their own schools. Other students sent me original poems and music cassettes, wall posters and T-shirts, drawings and environmental pamphlets, as gestures of appreciation for not putting their generation down, and for trying to make learning interesting and accessible. Instead of mocking American pop culture—rock and roll, alternative newspapers, fast food, and the rest—I celebrated it. "I just wanted to tell you how much I enjoyed *The Majic Bus*," wrote Anne Meyer of Plymouth, Minnesota:

> I never thought it was possible to fit Etta James (my idol), Little Willie John, Thomas Jefferson, Heritage U.S.A. (not my idol) and the Corn Palace all into one book! My main interests are literature/history/pop culture/art history, though I have so far been unsuccessful explaining to anyone how they are related! I'm temporarily a college drop-out, but after your book, I am planning to go to a school in my state that is known to encourage independent study and flexibility in learning techniques, which are vital to what I consider an excellent education.

Lee Laskowski, a student at Central Connecticut State University, wrote that the book "has inspired me to read more, write more, and not just sit here and waste an entire summer, but to get out and see the country." Clarence Felton, a sixteen-year-old from California, wrote: "After reading *The Majic Bus*, which my mom gave me, I now love America in a way I never dreamed possible." These are the responses I was hoping to elicit.

I was also pleasantly surprised by all the enthusiastic mail that poured in from teachers and educators all over America, most of whom supported my assertion: "With our current education crisis it is not so important *what* students read as long as they read *something*." Richard T. Handley of St. Ojai, California, wrote that the book "inspired me to take my students on a history scavenger hunt." Nancy Scott, a teacher in the Windthorst Independent School District, described her own "Texas Odyssey," in which she took her seventh-graders around the Lone Star State. Gioia Ottaviano wrote, "I recently finished forty-five years teaching in the elementary grades in Schenectady, New York, and applaud *The Majic Bus* and your enthusiasm to make education meaningful for your lucky students." Randall Doyle, a history professor at the University of Idaho, read the book and put together his own "Pacific Northwest Odyssey," with a busload of students in tow. Beverly Wilson Palmer, coordinator of writing programs at Pomona College in California, had her class write me long letters recommending historic sites for the Majic Bus's next journey. (I've already incorporated suggestions from Bridgette Craig, Don Flores, Diana Curiel Hidalgo, Brian Fisher, and Shirin Malekpour into my 1994 itinerary.)

Edythe Holbrook, the director of the American-Russian Youth Orchestra, invited me to Yale University to discuss the book with over eighty talented, young classical musicians from both nations who were touring the United States. Judy M. Edelhoff of the National Archives was so taken with *The Majic Bus* that she sent me huge rolls of colorful historic posters to distribute to my students. The Association of Independent Michigan Schools invited me to be a guest educator at their fall convention at the picturesque, serene Cranbook School; over five hundred educators attended. Universities and colleges invited me to read from *The Majic Bus;* my visits ranged from West Chester University in Pennsylvania to Georgia Southwestern to the University of Louisville. Librarians from King of Prussia, Pennsylvania, Garden City, New York, and Texas A&M wrote letters of encouragement. Three different senior-citizen homes asked whether I might be persuaded to take them on a "Rocking Old Folks Tour of America," as one ninety-two-year-old put it. In fact, what astonished me most about the reception accorded *The Majic Bus* was how varied the enthusiasts were: professors from M.I.T. and Harvard, a U.S. Navy nuclear engineer, park rangers, New York City police officers, a Georgia congressman and a former Arkansas senator, local historians and a Pulitzer Prize–winning poet, Jesuit priests and born-again Christians, rock musicians Bob Geldof and Joey Ramone, and RV'ers and Teamsters from almost every state gave American Odyssey the thumbs-up. As eighty-three-year-old Eleanor Harland of Pushford, New York, wrote, "Traveling while reading and seeing is wonderful education and *much, much more.*" Some twenty college radio stations asked me to chat with students on the air about

American history and to rev up their listeners about their boundless futures. Brian Lamb, the founder, chairman, and CEO of C-SPAN, was so excited about *The Majic Bus* that he had me speak to his board of directors about it in Washington, D.C. He surprised everyone present by announcing that a bright yellow forty-five-foot custom coach, to be called the C-SPAN School Bus, would crisscross America for the 1993–94 academic year, with television journalists and political analysts, talking to teachers and students and ordinary citizens in communities across the country.

One invitation had a particularly profound effect on me. I was chosen to be Yale University's Lustman Fellow at Davenport College to lecture on *The Majic Bus*. Dr. G. E. Thomas, the second African-American admiral in United States history, President Reagan's ambassador to Kenya and Guyana, and currently master of Davenport College, had read the book and wanted me to discuss with his students and peers my perspective on "the state of the nation," the American Road, and the possibility of other American Odyssey courses in the making. Shortly after my arrival in New Haven, I passed through the gargoyled gate that led to the cloistered Davenport College and went up to a second-floor suite that was to be my quarters for two evenings. The decor was Yankee sparse and Tory elegant, complete with a hard bed, an oak desk, a cold bathroom, and a fine view of the nonstop bustle of York Street. The walls were filled with signed photographs of dour-looking former masters, autographed for posterity with a word or two of wisdom on the essence of a Yale education. The library at my bedside was composed of bound leather antiquarian editions of the classics, heavy on complete sets of Horace Walpole and Samuel Coleridge. The collection had a decidedly Anglophilic bent, which made me expect cucumber sandwiches, scones, and Earl Grey tea for lunch. There was no Melville or Whitman here, no Du Bois or Faulkner. Out of this one-thousand-book collection only Emerson and the Mathers (Cotton and Increase) were deemed worthy. There was, of course, a Yalie section: Timothy Dwight's *Memories of Yale Life and Men* and Eugene H. Kone's *Yale Men Who Died in the Second World War*, for example, but no signs of Sinclair Lewis, Yale Class of 1908 and America's first recipient of the Nobel Prize for literature.

My eye fell on a slender brown volume, Thornton Wilder's *Our Town*, published in 1938. It was a first edition of the Pulitzer Prize–winning play, Wilder's great hymn to everyday living and its potentialities. The inside cover was simply illustrated by A. E. Fisher with symbols of the idyllic, fictional, turn-of-the-century Grover's Corners, New Hampshire: Presbyterian church steeples and manicured graveyards, a one-room schoolhouse with wing-spread birds soaring high above, smokestack factories and an imposing train depot, modest Victorian-era houses, and a meandering stream with covered bridge.

I was thrilled to see on the first page that Wilder had also been a Davenport Fellow and had inscribed *Our Town* personally for the library in May 1938. Underneath his signature he wrote, "All that education for nothing," with a note to see page thirty-eight. There, Wilder furiously underlined, almost incising the page, the following: "Joe was a bright fellow. He graduated with honors and got a scholarship to Boston Tech— M.I.T., that is. But the war broke out and Joe died in France. All that education for nothing." Written at a time when great nation-states moved inexorably toward worldwide conflagration, Wilder clearly wanted his young Yale readers to contemplate the grievous consequences of war. But what would most concern Wilder, a teacher as well as a writer, if he were alive today?

Perhaps he would see what I and many others see: the war is right here in our own cities and towns. Our ravaged inner-city schools are literal combat zones, where youngsters arrive at school armed against predators, where random violence is the outgrowth of the death of community, while in so many of our suburbs, there is a trenchant sterility stemming from toxic boredom for the want of a larger purpose. "What do you say, for instance, about a generation that has been taught *rain is poison* and *sex is death*?" Dr. Hunter S. Thompson gloomily asks in *Generation of Swine*. "If making love might be fatal and if cool spring rain on any summer afternoon can turn a crystal blue lake into a puddle of black poison scum right in front of your eyes, there is not much left except TV and relentless masturbation" (and, of course, joining a neighborhood gang or bringing Uzis to school or selling crack on street corners). Today, the name of the school learning game is survival. According to the Children's Defense Fund, every other hour in America a youngster is shot to death with a handgun. As President Clinton recently put it in a moving, heartfelt speech in Memphis, "If Dr. Martin Luther King, Jr., were alive today, he would tell his followers: I did not live and die to see thirteen-year-old boys get automatic weapons and gun down nine-year-olds just for the kick of it. I fought for freedom, but not for the freedom of people to kill each other." No doubt about it, as poet Lou Reed sings, in today's debt-ridden, violence-prone America, young people need "a busload of faith to get by."

That evening at Davenport College, with a giant portrait of John Davenport, one of the Puritan founders of the New Haven colony and the man who first invisioned Yale, gazing from behind the podium, I spoke about my American Odyssey course, the great fun I had teaching college on the road in 1992 and 1993, and my belief in the importance of a liberal arts education. Afterward, a graduate student working on his Ph.D. in postwar literary deconstruction theory asked: "Aren't you a trained historian? What gives you *the right* to teach literature? Do you help students deconstruct these texts on the road?" My response was that I know how to celebrate great poetry and literature, to make texts come alive, to make them "like a ripe red tomato, so juicy that when you bite into it the text sprays all over the place," in novelist Tom Robbins's words. Not satisfied by my answer, he pressed further: "Just what is your pedagogy for teaching that you try to convey in *The Majic Bus*?" My answer? All that education for *something*.

THE HUMMING BIRD GRILL
New Orleans
December 31, 1993

Introduction

One man can make a difference and each of us should try.
—ROBERT F. KENNEDY

THOMAS WOLFE ONCE WROTE, "I BELIEVE THAT WE ARE lost here in America, but I believe we shall be found. And this belief, which mounts now to a catharsis of knowledge and conviction, is for me— and I think all of us—not only our hope, but America's everlasting dream." Like Wolfe, I believe we are losing our national heritage while too many scholars, pundits, and politicians sit back idly clucking their tongues and using their pens not like swords but like word processors—spawning billions of bits and bytes about our rapidly disintegrating public school system but taking no direct, uplifting action to improve the situation. Although the roots of our national educational crisis can be traced to the primary and secondary schools, owing largely to a lack of federal commitment and funds during the past two decades, college professors and administrators

1

also deserve a share of the blame. Administrators by the very nature of their role tend to focus on the business side of running a university, as interested in turning a profit as in looking after the intellectual development of students. With professors the problem lies in a flawed set of values. Too often professors consider teaching to be menial work, infra dig, an annoying distraction from our true mission: research and writing. Tenure is rewarded for scholarship; the art of teaching garners little respect or homage. Students become a necessary nuisance, and we can blame their deficiencies on the sorry state of the public school system and be relieved of any obligation to do something about it. In an American historian the situation engenders acute despair, for more students than one can imagine graduate from college without the most rudimentary knowledge of their nation's history and geography. Last year I asked a class of thirty college students who Andrew Jackson was, and not a single one had even the foggiest idea. (For starters I told them to check out a twenty-dollar bill.) I asked another class to name a major city in Kansas; not one of them could come up with Topeka or Wichita or even Kansas City. Over cocktails at professional meetings, history professors from all over the country, be they from the Ivy Leagues or the junior college system, share their own favorite stories from the teaching trenches where the student is always lazy and illiterate. This may be therapeutic, but it does nothing to change a terribly defective educational system.

In recent years many important books have been written about how to teach American history—with Arthur Schlesinger, Jr.'s brilliant *Disuniting of America* leading the pack—but until now the debate has been centered around multiculturalism and ethnocentrism and canonizing literature. *The Majic Bus: An American Odyssey* is not one of those books. I do not intend to ridicule the dull academic prose or to debate the animadversions of Dinesh D'Souza, Allan Bloom, and E. D. Hirsch, for by focusing on texts and blaming Generation X they seem to have forgotten about the teaching side of the education equation. With our current education crisis it is not

2 so important *what* students read, but that they read *something*. Martin

Anderson's provocative *Imposters in the Temple: American Intellectuals Are Destroying Our Universities and Cheating Our Students of Their Future* (1992) is an engaging blueprint for anyone interested in how to restructure universities for the nineties, but even he goes astray when he starts moralizing about the lack of academic integrity. There is too much sanctimonious and self-righteous integrity floating around our universities, and not enough anarchy and caring. Unlike these well-intentioned commentators and their equally well-intentioned cultural critics, I offer no magical solution or comprehensive philosophy of education except to urge university professors to start caring about undergraduate education again, to make scholarship secondary to what takes place in the classroom. I've given up on the boards of trustees, university presidents, and other administrators to remedy the situation. Individual professors with reformist inclinations must seize the day themselves. Urgent action is required, for the situation is not improving. "Caution," Woodrow Wilson noted, "is the confidential agent of selfishness." I have grown tired of playing by the rules and remaining voiceless while America is being lost: It is time to reclaim it with pure, unadulterated energy, commitment, enthusiasm, and hope. "I am an idealist," Carl Sandburg once flatly stated. "I don't know where I'm going but I'm on the way." Until every college student in the United States knows the difference between Idaho and Iowa, the Mississippi and Missouri rivers, the Sonoran and Mojave deserts, the Cherokee and the Sioux, the Everglades and the Okefenokee Swamp, blues and jazz, William Henry Harrison and Benjamin Harrison, Yellowstone and Yosemite national parks, Thomas Wolfe and Tom Wolfe, history professors should ban the use of such gaseous concepts and theories as "neo-post-revisionist corporate synthesis," "fratricide of the paradigms," and "operational code." It is time to cut the bull, ship the excessively arcane language back whence it came, and get on with igniting flames of enthusiasm about American history in our classrooms and communities.

It has been my observation that as scholars work to obtain their Ph.D.'s in American history, somewhere along the line they lose the spirit of America, either drowning in a sea of newly acquired social science jargon or becoming seduced by the power of the obscure footnote. "The average

3

Ph.D. thesis is nothing but a transference of bones from one graveyard to another," Texas folklorist J. Frank Dobie once noted. But today's students deserve the drama, the flesh and blood of their inherited past. A start in the right direction would be an attitudinal sea change: History should be considered not a social science but a jewel in the crown of the humanities. Such statements sound bold, but they are futile. It is one thing to prescribe broad-minded remedies for the profession, but what sort of immediate, concrete action can a professor take?

After an overdose of academic trivialists, cynics, and preachers of negativism, the only temporary solution I could think of was to escape the classroom with my students to discover America by sleeper bus. "Movement is always to be preferred to inaction," Norman Mailer has observed. "In motion, man has a chance." Instead of passing the buck, ignoring the problem, or delivering yet another boring black-hole historiography conference paper on the state of the profession, I would teach American history and literature on the road. My students would read Mark Twain in Missouri; Carson McCullers in Georgia; William Faulkner in Mississippi; Hunter S. Thompson in Las Vegas; John Steinbeck and Jack London in California; and Jack Kerouac, Langston Hughes, and Walt Whitman everywhere. Together my students and I would try to discover our American heritage. Instead of sitting in a Long Island classroom reading about Abraham Lincoln's Illinois, Jimmy Carter's Georgia, Harry Truman's Missouri, or Thomas Jefferson's Virginia, we would visit those states ourselves on a historical exploration of America. It would be a physically grueling, high-risk venture, but as Ken Kesey has written, "It is better to fail with faith than to succeed with security." Our goal was to turn a bus into a classroom, our mission to learn about America 1992, wage war on apathy and win, discover unknown aspects of ourselves, and make the study of our nation's heritage more fun than television—for America may be many things, but dull is not one of them. We wouldn't simply study America, we would grab it by the scruff of its neck.

Here's what we did: watched the sun set over Monticello, prayed for mercy at Ebenezer Baptist Church in Atlanta, and followed the ghosts of Tennessee Williams and Louis Armstrong around the French Quarter. Together we got dizzy in the high altitude of the snowcapped Rockies, sunburned on a Santa Barbara beach, and shaken up in a 7.1 earthquake while camping in California's Humboldt–Redwood State Park. We lost money on the altars of Las Vegas, cooked breakfast on the side of the road next to our broken-down bus in Oregon's Willamette Valley, got soaked rafting the turbulent white waters of the Rio Grande near Taos, shared a night's sleep perched high in the ancient star-bright sky of Mesa Verde, and walked down the back alleys of a lonely and windy Chicago flypaper night.

Together we spit out our spontaneous prose poems in Colorado; practiced lotus-style meditation at a Buddhist institute in Boulder; shouted Vachel Lindsay's "Bryan, Bryan, Bryan, Bryan" out loud on his rickety Springfield, Illinois, front porch; and sang the Blind Willie McTell blues in the Mississippi Delta. We spent a light afternoon with the dark William S. Burroughs in Lawrence, Kansas, and a fog-shrouded dusk with Ken Kesey at his farm in Oregon, dressing in Day-Glo rain gear to whiz around the misty Bigfoot countryside in the psychedelic bus, "Further." Collectively we prayed for salvation at Our Lady of Guadalupe Church in New Mexico; spent Passover in a Las Vegas hotel, Easter Sunday on a California beach; talked to a Crow medicine man who resides on the site of the Battle of the Little Bighorn; and ate cafeteria food with Mormons at the Grand Canyon in Arizona. We stood together at the top of the Saint Louis Gateway Arch and pondered Thomas Jefferson's Louisiana Purchase; discussed Jimmy Carter's Atlanta Project as we walked Dr. Martin Luther King, Jr.'s, Historic Auburn District; drifted along the Sangamon River in Illinois and realized it actually was the Land of Lincoln, as the license plate says; honored the grave of Harry Truman and wished he were still with us; watched the buffalo roam in the North Dakota Badlands; thanked Theodore Roosevelt for his conservation efforts; and stared in awestruck wonder at the faces on Mount Rushmore.

We listened to Bourbon Street jazz in New Orleans, Son Seals's electric guitar blues in Chicago, Elvis Presley at Graceland, Carlos Nakai's wind flute on the Ute Indian Reservation, Chuck Berry in Saint Louis, and the Grateful Dead in San Francisco, and we saw Bob Dylan perform at the Paramount Theatre in Seattle. We gaped at herds of elk and bighorn sheep in Colorado, heard the sea lions bark at Big Sur, and on May Day branded cattle—mountain oysters and all—at the Bar-7-Bar Ranch in South Dakota. We were poets and rappers and pilgrims in search of the soul of the U.S.A., racing against the wind, learning to be free by filling our minds with hands-on knowledge and our lungs with the glorious delirium of fresh American pine.

All this was part of a six-week experimental course I offered at Hofstra University during the spring of 1992. It was called "American Odyssey: Art and Culture Across America." I took seventeen students, mainly seniors, on the journey. They were assigned twelve seminal books to read, took exams in a Las Vegas casino and a San Francisco motel, and submitted a journal on their return to New York. We visited thirty states and a dozen national parks. It was a smash success, and this book tells the story of our six-week odyssey crisscrossing America in search of our country, our heritage, ourselves, and, of course, a helluva good time.

This book is about one professor trying to make a difference, as Bobby Kennedy asserted we should, not about armchair complainers. Jack Kerouac once told Allen Ginsberg, "I have no time for your negativity: I'm not anti-anything." That is the posture I try to adopt in this book, except when it comes to racists and certain corporations and individuals who are ravaging the American landscape and debilitating our ability to act as a unified nation—then I'm anti-. Look upon this book as a good old-fashioned story with a happy ending, imperfectly written and told, but bursting with energy, filled with hope, and as American as Little Rock, Arkansas, and Little America, Wyoming. It is not about a professor "observing" his seventeen students for six weeks, scrutinizing their personal deficiencies and inner selves and reporting on them as if they were B. F. Skinner's lab animals. It's about an imperfect expedition through America by all twenty of us (driver and administrative assistant included) as a cohesive unit, out to discover our country collectively, leaving television and blackboards behind in our bus exhaust. Naturally we had our differences and feuds, even an occasional angry altercation—that was all part of the education, all part of life. But what was extraordinary was how close we all became, how much uplifting fun we shared, what a special group solidarity we achieved. When the Majic Bus returned to Hofstra after six weeks on the road, we didn't want to say good-bye. We felt like warriors—that no one else would ever be able to understand what we had gone through, what we had accomplished, what we had discovered, and what we had failed to do.

This brings me to the history of why and how this book was written. An American Odyssey: Art and Culture Across America generated an unanticipated outburst of enthusiastic media attention. The *New York Times* ran a story on us that was picked up by the wire services and reprinted in dozens of newspapers across the United States. "Good Morning America" filmed us live for sunrise at the Grand Canyon, and on our return they had us all in the New York studio to recount to the nation our road experiences. National Public Radio featured us on two different occasions. Wherever we went the great people of America embraced us. Aside from its inherent human-interest value, the American Odyssey course garnered widespread attention because of its alternative, action-based approach to traditional education. The motto of the course came from Davy Crockett: "Be sure you're right, then go ahead." This attitude instinctively appeals to America.

When we returned from the journey in May 1992, I was greeted by two-hundred-plus enthusiastic letters wanting to know about my American Odyssey course, and letters continued to arrive well into autumn. Many were from high school teachers and college professors wanting to know how they could create such a course.

I was asked to write about our experiences. Although I had taken sporadic notes on the road and had the student journals in my possession, I was reluctant at first. How could I write about my own students without breaking bonds of trust? Being a teacher is like being a doctor. One must protect students' privacy, dignity, and confidences as doctors do with their patients'. Several publishers suggested using pseudonyms, but this seemed a cowardly cop-out; besides, it would have devalued the whole bold educational experience. The students themselves urged me to go ahead and use their names, and they promised moral support, personal memories, and photographs to fill in any gaps. With their encouragement I decided to try to write a book based on our journey, using their journals and debriefings as the grist.

What book would I write? One book I knew I could not write was a litany of flaws and foibles. All of us have our darker moments, when we say and do stupid things. I have chosen to focus on the light and bright—that is, the redeeming qualities of each student and our experiences together. While this distinction has the disadvantage of making it impossible to draw full-blooded, true-to-life portraits of the students, I rest easy knowing that thirty years from now they can pull this book off the shelf and be proud of how they are portrayed, perhaps even bragging about it to their children, grandchildren, and neighbors. They are all friends, and like all youth, they are, as Jack Kerouac said, "angels of pure future."

When it became time to find a publisher I turned to Harcourt Brace & Company. They understood what was driving this enterprise and promised to advertise the book and the ideas it contains. Harcourt had one proviso: They insisted I deliver the manuscript by Christmas if they were to have the book edited, printed, and distributed by March, to coincide with the departure of American Ódyssey II. This time we would be heading to the vast forests of Alaska; reading John McPhee, Joe McGuinness, Jack London, Harry Crews, and Ken Kesey in the Arctic tundra; hiking Mount McKinley by morning, dogsledding the Yukon by day, gazing at the aurora borealis by night. This necessitated the book being written in four feverishly short months, from September to December 1992, while I was teaching two courses at Hofstra.

There was one final issue. I felt uneasy about making money from an educational venture that so many people helped make possible and that wasn't conceived for profit. An agreement was reached with the publisher: I would deliver the manuscript within the stringent deadline, Harcourt would rally behind the book, and I would give author proceeds to nonprofit organizations.

The Majic Bus: An American Odyssey is meant to be only an indirect participant in the national debate on how to teach American history in an ethnically diverse society. Can we still honor George Washington and Thomas Jefferson even though they were slave owners? How can Buffalo Bill be a folk hero in the era of the Endangered Species Act? Should Andrew Jackson remain on the twenty-dollar bill when one considers the Trail of Tears? I say that these questions pale into insignificance when students don't even know about Washington's and Jefferson's revolutionary accomplishments or Buffalo Bill's contribution to the building of the transcontinental railroad or what is meant by Jacksonian democracy. If we are to exist as a nation we cannot hold history up to today's standards, thereby reducing our folk heroes, artists, and public servants to scoundrels. William F. Buckley, Jr., has noted that "history selects its heroes and its villains, and few of us resist participation either at the parade or at the guillotine." Today in America the only history we celebrate is the beheading; this needs to change.

Why has this historical reductionism come about? Because we have failed to teach American history in our high schools and universities and let the sleazy tabloid merchants, television talk shows, and monomaniacal psychobiographers do the job for us. Our national fixation on the sex lives of the long dead, as well as those of our current political leaders, drives out any sense of proportion or judgment of a whole life and the era in which it was lived. Ask almost any college student about Martin Luther King, Jr., and John F. Kennedy, and they can tell you of their sexual exploits but are clueless as to what the Montgomery Bus Boycott was all about or what the Alliance for Progress was. Under the Faustian mantle of digging for the truth, we have turned popular history into the study of scandals and conspiracy theories. The solution is to get back to teaching the basics. In order to obtain a high school diploma it should be a requirement to have memorized (yes, memorized) the capitals of the fifty states, be able to name the presidents in sequential order, and be able to fill in correctly a blank map of our nation with not only the states but all the important lakes and rivers, right down to the Yockanookany and the Wapsipinicon. It is just as important for students to learn how to spell and pronounce and to understand the historical significance of Chickamauga and Appomattox, and be able to locate them on a map, as it is to learn foreign languages and how to program computers. Facts before formulas is what history must be about— teaching people that they exist in time and space.

This book also tries to discover what's "going down" across America and report on it, more like John Gunther's 1948 classic *Inside USA* and Charles Kuralt's engaging *Life on the Road* than William Least Heat Moon's fine travel book *Blue Highways*. Instead of relying on formulaic media reports about America in decline, we went to discover for ourselves. Another objective of both the course and the book was to offer a compendium of local history and pop culture in 1992. Wherever we traveled, the past wasn't far behind. As William Faulkner noted in *Requiem for a Nun:* "The past is never dead. It's not even past."

It is my hope that *The Majic Bus: An American Odyssey* will become a favorite with students and travelers hoping to discover their country, a resource for parents who want their children to experience America, and an inspiration for educators looking for alternative approaches to teaching American history and literature. A course like American Odyssey is not meant to supplant the traditional classroom education; it is meant to complement it. Many professors, because of their temperament, family obligations, or age, may not be suited to life on a bus for months at a time, but they can encourage those who are interested in undertaking such a hands-on approach to education. The end of the Cold War and election of Bill Clinton to the presidency signifies that we as a nation are entering a period of rethinking who we are and what we stand for. As a "road" book, *The Majic Bus* is concerned with the tensions between obligation and freedom, creativity and convention, between America-as-it-is and America-as-we-want-it-to-be. It is meant to be an enjoyable read, a public service message that even with all our national problems, we are still a nation on the rise. We may be lost, but I believe, along with Thomas Wolfe, that we shall be found. America has a genius for cyclical renewal, and we're perched on the eve of our greatest yet. Bill Clinton and Al Gore—their own 1992 bus tour of America under their belts—are ready to provide the leadership. So quit that finger pointing, roll up your shirtsleeves, and start working to make a difference.

Now get ready for the bus ride into the great wide open, and remember, write your senators and representatives in support of the California Desert Protection Act. Let's save the Mojave Desert from ecological destruction while we still can. Keep the faith, and remember that the true discovery of America is before us.

LOCUST VALLEY, NEW YORK
January 1, 1993

1

There is No Truth But in Transit: The Making of "An American Odyssey"

We are restive entirely for the sake of restiveness. Whatever we may think, we move for no other reason than for the plain, unvarnished hell of it.

—JAMES AGEE

THE NOTION OF TEACHING AMERICAN HISTORY AND LITER-
ature on the road has its roots in my childhood, in vivid memories of family vacations in which my mother, father, sister, and I crisscrossed our nation in search of our past, present, and future. A blue Pontiac station wagon was our horse, a twenty-four-foot pale cream Coachman trailer our wagon, our "Buckeye Buggy," as we named it. Trip planning traditionally began in late winter. There was something magical about deciding where our summer journey would take us—a grim, gray Ohio flannel-pajama winter evening became pregnant with possibility. Which awesome canyon would be ours, which campground our temporary home? My father and I would sit at our kitchen table, a well-worn road atlas and a KOA Kampground guide in front of us, and together plot our route in

exact detail. He was Lewis and I was Clark, as we made preparations for that big July day when sweet America would open up in front of us.

Memories of these journeys over the years stand out in my mind: a fast-food-loving Smoky Mountain black bear chasing us from our streamside Kentucky Fried Chicken picnic; meeting baseball legend Ted Williams in a Miami hotel lobby; staring in childish innocence at Plymouth Rock, believing that it was staring at me; the sun slowly rising over a saguaro cactus desert outside Tucson as a Tom Mix cowboy on a long-maned stallion rode away toward the purple-pink horizon; viewing my first alligator as it coyly floated on the murky mosquito waters of the Everglades, the terror of its jaws not a whit less scary because it was a potential handbag; gazing out over Lake Michigan from the ninety-eighth floor of the tapering brown John Hancock Building in Chicago and realizing for the first time, as the building swayed, that I was insignificant in the scheme of things; standing with my family, hands clasped, at the tomb of John F. Kennedy in Arlington National Cemetery and vowing to make sure his eternal flame never went out; watching a man with slicked-back hair and a red carnation in the lapel of his pin-striped suit win ten thousand dollars at a Reno slot machine, and my mother, aghast, pulling me away, insisting life wasn't that easy; a post-thunderstorm rainbow draping the Grand Canyon in colors so dazzling that tears rolled down my cheeks; observing Gene Rayburn host the quiz show "The Match Game" in a back-lot Burbank studio with APPLAUD blinking on and off and recognizing then and there what a sham television was; seeing Lincoln's boyhood log-cabin home outside White City, Kentucky, and immediately comprehending the source of his native humility and humanity; getting a severe case of goosebumps when the troubadour died and the chorus launched into "Beautiful Dreamer" at a summer-stock production about the life of Stephen Foster in his hometown, Bardstown, Kentucky; inspecting my first moon rock at the Neil Armstrong Air and Space Museum in Wapakoneta, Ohio, and deciding that an astronaut's life was not as exciting as my Johnny Quest—cartoon imagination had led me to believe; trying to float in Utah's Great Salt Lake, only to get sticky and nearly drown . . . It is such memories that are the wellspring of the educational experience I wanted for my students.

———————

Besides the events themselves, there was another essential element to those expeditions across America: the long summer days we spent as a family in motion. As much as I enjoyed the wax museums and miniature golf courses, the Parrot Jungles and Sea Worlds, the towering monuments to George Washington and our Civil War dead, the amusement rides at Cedar Point in Sandusky, Ohio, and the robotic attractions of Disneyland, the sheer sensation of traveling down the open road in the back of the station wagon, letting America engulf, electrified my youthful heart. It was the constant movement that excited me; the destination was secondary. Later, when I discovered Walt Whitman, I was thrilled to find my boyhood sentiments had already been perfectly expressed by our national poet: "O public road," Whitman intoned in his *Song of the Open Road*, "you express me better than I can express myself."

And so I became an apostle of the open road. But what America did I want my students to discover? Nowadays, because of the success of William Least Heat Moon's *Blue Highways*, searchers of America feel they must uncover the forgotten hamlet, the rusted moonshine still, or the black-dirt farmhouse on a rural back road to find plurality and drama in a rapidly disappearing "authentic" America, a nation overrun by the proliferation of McDonald's and their spawn and the gospel of sameness. Although I have some sympathy with this sentiment, by and large I think its source is a misguided and intellectually trendy nostalgia, not a genuine American dilemma.

The doctrine I wanted to teach is that if you wish to find America, look within. Discover your affinity to movement for movement's sake, and then take to the road you want rather than exist in your inertia. Whether it is a congested, multilane superslab, such as I-95 to Florida, or a nameless, one-lane West Virginia mountain road to nowhere makes no difference because the America you're looking for can never be found—it's always somewhere just over the horizon, around the next bend. To find liberty in America—that notion enshrined in our nation's birth announcement, that sought-after sensation of freedom—hop in your car and drive in any direction for five hours, at any speed on any highway or road, with no objective, no one to meet, alone behind the wheel. Then, when the tank nears empty, fuel up at a gas station, look into the sky, feel the wind, sun, rain, or snow in your face, and freedom is yours. If you don't have a car, a Greyhound will do, provided you keep your nose to the glass and don't doze off. The road unshackles the American psyche like nothing else. In Flannery O'Connor's short story "The Life You Save May Be Your Own," Mr. Shiflet declares: "The body, lady, is like a house: it don't go anywhere: but the spirit, lady, is like an automobile: always on the move, always." James Agee, in a 1934 *Fortune* article, "The Great American Roadside," described the essence of America's soul:

> God made the American restive. The American in turn and in due time got the automobile and found it good. The war exasperated his restiveness and the twenties made him rich and more restive still and he found the automobile not merely good but better and better. It was good because continually it satisfied and at the same time greatly sharpened his hunger for movement: which is very probably the profoundest and most compelling of American racial hungers. The fact is that the automobile became a hypnosis.

Sometimes the road imagery of the American experience is solitary, an abandoning of domestic ties. But for me the road has always been collective and familial, although my family was unaware they were harboring in their midst a potential outlaw hungering after the faintly illicit, the potentially dangerous, a walk on the wild side—but not too wild. I grew restive whenever we were rooted, even for a day, in our trailer home. I could hardly wait for the moment when the jacks were unscrewed, the sewer hose and electrical wire disconnected for us to flee the campground for some new, unknown highway. I was a young renegade in the bosom of an intimate, shared family experience, for whom being on the road always meant new possibilities and new adventures: a summer hailstorm in Wyoming; a pink tornado in Illinois; a roadside armadillo family in Louisiana; a Missouri raccoon who washed the sugar cube we gave it in a stream so thoroughly it disappeared; the tragedy of turtles in an East Texas flash

15

flood, who necked their way onto the highway to escape drowning, only to be run over by oncoming eighteen-wheelers.

On the road during those long-ago summers I often took a siesta in the back of the car. Wedged between a blue cooler and my warm dog, Hector, I nodded off to the hollow hum of engines and the muted echo of tires against pavement, always half-alert for the raw, throaty roar of a motorcycle, hoping against hope it was a "Hog"—a big, bad, and bodacious Harley-Davidson—ridden by a man in Gothic drag on his way to perform some mysterious rite, on the same road as our wholesome family station wagon. No highway sight excited me more than a 1200-cc fully rigged Hog. Even at a young age I knew my Harley history. It was a Harley, heavy with chrome and pulsating with power, that chased Rommel through North Africa during World War II. It was a Harley that Dennis Hopper drove to New Orleans in *Easy Rider*. Harleys were synonymous with cool, an essential part of the American road. Rock poet Lou Reed, who wrote the song "Walk on the Wild Side," once said, "When it comes to pleasuring the major senses, no motorcycle on earth can compare to a Harley. That's why I've tattooed my Harley's name on the inside of my mouth." Even President Ronald Reagan got on the bandwagon when he visited a Harley factory in 1987 and declared: "We're on the road to unprecedented prosperity in this country, and we'll get there on a Harley." Someday I'm going to rent twenty Harley 883 Sportsters, a bike per student, and teach American Odyssey the way it should be taught—twenty-seven inches off the highway.

Being on the road in America means communicating the journey through journals, photos, or video. There needs to be a record, and this is an essential element of the student experience. My mom knew that intuitively. She never knew of the Jack Kerouac – Neal Cassady taped conversations about America; or Allen Ginsberg's taped poetic meanderings across our nation from 1965 to 1971; or Ken Kesey and the Merry Pranksters driving from California to New York in their 1939 International Harvester school bus, Furthur, filming their entire "unsettling" of America for posterity; or of John Steinbeck's intimate communion with himself, his poodle, and our nation, which he published as *Travels with Charley*. She simply had the marvelous idea of chronicling our family vacations on a small, portable tape recorder.

As Mom's tapes underscore, the road is inextricably bound up with song. Now, twenty years later, it is an odd sensation to hear my squeaky voice singing "The Ballad of Davy Crockett," boyishly imitating a frontier twang as we drive through the Blue Ridge Mountains, so titillated by the line "killed him a bar when he was only three" that I repeat it endlessly, an anthem to empowered children everywhere; chanting Ray Charles's "Hit the Road, Jack," a Brinkley classic performed, with little prompting, in Ray·Ban sunglasses in roadside restaurants across America; and singing Jimmy Webb's "Wichita Lineman" and "By the Time I get to Phoenix" in both places *in situ*. I am not alone when it comes to vocalizing. My father debuts with a sanguine rendition of "Sixteen Tons," as if he were Tennessee Ernie Ford himself; my sister recites the Beach Boys' "California Girls" as we drive up Highway 1 north of LA, the mighty Pacific surging on our left; my mother sings Yip Harburg's "Somewhere Over the Rainbow" as we drive through a Kansas lightning storm, trying her best to sound like Judy Garland, her offspring chorus humming like little cherubs in the background.

The odd thing is that these tapes have created a new music, something beyond the solos and duets that are replayed time and again. All the words and sounds of my mother's tapes combine to make our family hymn, our remembrance of things past, a tender song of ourselves and our nation. The late minimalist composer John Cage once asked me, "Did you hear the crack in the air?" All I had heard was silence. "You must be more aware of sound," he told me. "Forget the obvious, listen for the pulse." It took me a while to recognize that this cryptic comment applied to our primitive family recordings as to a great stage musical—the Brinkleys' Aaron Copland symphony—the opening of a bag of Doritos our percussion section, the sounds of the whizzing trucks our horns, the incessant hum of wheels completing our family's road composition. When you're moving down the highway in America, all sounds mesh to compose an orchestral arrangement with guest soloists—the frantic cry of migratory birds or the simple sound of a distant siren—part of the excitement being that you never know who will be performing with your orchestra. So, as the American Odyssey was creating its own symphony, I knew that pop music, blues, and jazz would be integral parts of the journey, as well as truck horns and soda-can openings in the night.

There was a downside—if you can imagine it—to all these family excursions, to learning every aspect of my country, from the leading industries of each state to how to distinguish a soybean field from a potato field, a sycamore from an oak. It was awfully hard to return to school every September. At an early age it was already apparent to me that the story of America was too large to be taught in a classroom—our history too dramatic and fluid, our people and geography too diverse and varied, and our spirit too restless and ever-changing to be shackled to desks in a blackboard bunker. How I used to fidget and daydream, wishing I were Huck Finn floating down the Mississippi River or Billy the Kid shooting a tin can off the needle of a cactus—anyone but the boy imprisoned in the glass bubble of civics and history class. Since I had been taught that movement and restlessness were our national traits, epitomized by all the migrations from Europe, followed by western expansion to settle America, creating a nation from sea to shining sea, why, I wondered, did teachers always try to suppress this rambling instinct in young people?

When I turned sixteen, got my driver's license, a two-hundred-dollar green 1966 Pontiac Catalina with an eight-track tape deck, complete with *The Best of Buffalo Springfield* permanently stuck inside, and a minimum-wage job as a porter at the local Holiday Inn, family journeys came to an abrupt end. At that age it was too embarrassing to be seen with one's parents at the mall, let alone vacation with them. America was temporarily out of my mind, but it never left my vision.

Northwestern Ohio is, of course, part of America. I was surrounded by its sturdy rural qualities: the frozen cornfields in winter; the echo of an axe on Christmastime wood; the smell of slaughter at the turkey farm each November; the tap dance of pool balls breaking at the Corner Bar; bass fishing in the Maumee River every spring; collecting muddy jars of tad-poles from Tile Pond; Fourth of July pig roasts at "The Farm" with Toad, Giles, Gunner and Rob; postprom parties at Fort Megis; talking local politics with Mayor Niederhouse as he pumped gas into my Pontiac Catalina at his Gulf station; and the V of Canadian geese honking in the graying autumn skies. All this made me love Ohio while its unvarying sameness simultaneously fueled a longing to escape, to find my way to a new and surprising land. Cars were not exactly freedom tickets, for my friends and I seldom left Wood or Lucas counties, for fear of parental reprimand and for lack of gas money. There was also a growing distance between me and my high school friends: In the final analysis most of them never wanted to leave Perrysburg, happy to live circumscribed lives, never venturing farther than Michigan or Indiana, and then only for a wedding.

One random day I had a minor epiphany at the Holiday Inn—an event that changed both my young life and everything I looked at in and thought about America. I had brought breakfast to a couple from Pennsylvania, and I must have revealed my suppressed longings to leave, although I have no memory trace of our conversation. Perhaps they sensed a budding fellow restive, but as I turned away, they handed me a tattered copy of Jack Kerouac's 1957 novel *On the Road* as if it were the Gideon Bible, and instructed me to read it.

And thus were laid the intellectual underpinnings of the American Odyssey course. I had never heard of Jack Kerouac, the man most associated with the Beat Generation, to use the media catchphrase for the disaffected intellectuals of the Eisenhower era. I couldn't even pronounce his name, but the paperback cover immediately caught my eye—a ribbon of America's highway disappearing into a blinding orange sun. Underneath was the boldly lettered claim "the book that turned on a generation." From the first page I was hooked. Here was the book I had intuited and craved, just as an earlier generation needed *The Sun Also Rises* and *The Great Gatsby*. I wasn't sure what Kerouac meant by "the mad road, keening in a seizure of tarpaulin power," but I sensed in his writing a quest for the heroic, founded in action, and a manic desire to find the key to life's meaning by putting the accelerator through the floorboard. His use of language was exhilarating, the way the words rushed like a river, freely flowing across the page. I finished *On the Road* in two sleepless nights, wishing I were Dean Moriarty (Neal Cassady) or Sal Paradise (Jack Kerouac), blazing across America in a big, shiny, tail-finned car listening to Lester Young jazz, eating apple pie à la mode in Iowa, talking about the Old West with farmers in Nebraska, gassing up in Texas, parking cars for cash in Manhattan, shooting pool in Denver, reading poetry in San Francisco's Chinatown, working as a migrant laborer in California, drinking *cerveza*s in Old Mexico, basically searching for "It"—what Kerouac called "the moment when you know all and everything is decided forever."

The character of Dean Moriarty permanently changed my lifescript, for his vagabond antics made me realize that in order to survive, I had to escape Perrysburg. I knew my life would be an insurgency of sorts— against what, I wasn't sure. There was a perverse element to my rebelliousness. After all, I had grown up and been nurtured by a family of adventurers who had discovered a socially acceptable outlet for their wanderlust. Dean simply threw salt on the niggling wounds of my life in Perrysburg—exacerbating my feeling that I was like one of Pavlov's dogs, responding to the high school bell signaling me that it was time to move on to the next cage, the inherent monotony of punching the time clock at the motel.

Kerouac offered more than mere rebellion against the status quo, the mundane, the routine, the trivial, the conventional. One passage in particular grabbed me by the throat, captured my lust to meet all kinds of people, to see storybook cities, a clarion call to burst out of Ohio, passport in hand: "The only people for me are the mad ones, the ones who are mad to live, mad to talk, mad to be saved . . . the ones who never yawn or say a commonplace thing but burn, burn, burn like fabulous yellow roman candles." I, too, wanted to know all the crazy saints who never yawn or say a commonplace thing.

How could I be a great bop wanderer, a mystic in search of ecstasy, a hobo scribbler of haiku and jazz poems, somehow discovering, in Kerouacian terms, how to "dig" life in the divine world to the fullest? I can only say that the stolid, tough-minded values of Perrysburg probably helped to save me from acting precipitously on these wildly romantic notions. Many of the Beats were "remittance men," their adventures funded by monthly checks from home. Although I didn't know it at the time, I must have had an inkling that it took some money to support the road. My parents didn't raise no fool, and so I stayed on track, dutifully sitting in the cage and punching that old clock, life infinitely sweeter now that I had a vision of a different future.

There is no doubt that *On the Road* was the seminal book of my coming of age. What I didn't know then is that it had turned millions of others around the world on to Whitman's America. During the Cold War it was not the so-called Voice of America, Treasury-hemorrhaging military expenditures, Foggy Bottom's diplomatic cunning, CIA cloak-and-dagger derring-do, or even democracy American-style that fueled the young intellectual radicals and freedom fighters of Eastern Europe and the Soviet Union. The voice of America they heard was Walt Whitman's—the voice of the Mississippi Delta blues, spontaneous jazz, reckless rock and roll, Bob Dylan protest songs, William Burroughs's *Naked Lunch*, Allen Ginsberg's *Howl*, and Jack Kerouac's *On the Road* supplemented with images from Hollywood and later from MTV. From the Molotov cocktail–throwers of the Hungarian Revolution of 1956, to the underground legions of young intellectuals avoiding jazz police during the Prague Spring of 1968, to East German John Henrys swinging their sledgehammers for freedom in 1989 as the Berlin Wall came tumbling down in our CNN living rooms, the Eastern European youth movement against totalitarianism was not seeking democracy per se: They were demanding jazz, rock and roll, Hollywood, and Beat poetry, and Jack Kerouac's *On the Road* was an important catalyst. "Kerouac opened a million coffee bars and sold a million Levi's to both sexes," William Burroughs has said: "Woodstock rises from his pages." So does the Velvet Revolution. Indeed, as columnist George Will has commented, it was John Lennon—a student of American pop and counterculture—and not Vladimir Lenin whom these young people emulated. (I find it incredible that the CIA was caught by surprise when the Berlin Wall was struck down in August 1989, for that June in New York City's alternative East Village music clubs, such as CBGB's and the

21

Continental Divide, young underground poets and rockers were matter-of-factly discussing the August teardown over beer, wondering if they could scrape together enough cash to lend a hand. What Bob Dylan sang in 1965 applied in 1989: "Something is happening and you don't know what it is, do you, Mr. Jones?" Even the teenage tank resisters of Tiananmen Square had traded in Mao's *Red Book* for smuggled copies of Ginsberg's poetry and recordings of Thelonious Monk's *Mysterioso* and Charlie Parker's *Ornithology*.)

I managed to make my escape from Perrysburg in time-honored fashion: I went *away* to college. Away wasn't very far—to Ohio State in Columbus—but it was a start on the road. Kerouac admirers will understand when I say I applied the "Kerouac test" to sort out the cool from the uncool. Those who had never heard of Kerouac were dismissed as boring. Those who passed became fast friends and remain so to this day, although many left Kerouac behind as they entered their thirties, saying he is a writer for the young. In fact, the opposite is true. Kerouac is best understood when you are older, for after all the hitchhiking and madcap driving and zany adventures, his despair lingers. America can never be the Big Rock Candy Mountain, our city on the hill. His final message is that you've got to get out and look for America—both within yourself and on the road—and no matter what you find, you are better off than sitting in a cage.

Although American fiction was my passion, I somehow ended up a history major, with the labor movement my specialty. Joe Hill, John Reed, Emma Goldman, Mother Jones, Terence Powderly, Wild Bill Haywood, and Woody Guthrie snatched my soul. How I loved the larger-than-life Wobblies, labor heroes who were fearless and unfazed by adversity, who could joke in the face of calamity. At first it didn't matter to me whether all this was true. Then, as I went on to earn my undergraduate degree in history, one by one all these labor heroes, with a few frontiersmen to boot, were reduced to mere mortals, devalued of their grandeur. When I began contemplating law school, Warren Van Tine, a labor historian at Ohio State, gave me the best advice ever. Recognizing my instinctive love of history, he suggested forgoing law school, at least for a while, and getting an M.A. in American history. Van Tine's advice had an additional virtue: I hopped from the capital of Ohio to the capital of America. The momentum was picking up; my life had not soared into a Kerouacian realm, but there was more progress and a new and bigger stage on which to act. I went on to earn an M.A. and a Ph.D. in diplomatic history at Georgetown University, my dissertation a biography of Dean Acheson as elder statesman of the Cold War.

In graduate school I began to be more ambivalent about history as a profession. The price for becoming a professional was high: cynicism and narrowness. A belief in heroes was tantamount to membership in the Flat Earth Society. Nearly everybody I encountered was cynical, enjoying criticism for its own sake. Heroes were impermissible; it was socially unacceptable to admire and respect any historical subject, even Jesus Christ. One became a Kitty Kelley with footnotes, unearthing and documenting deficiencies and flaws in reparation for the hagiographies of predecessors. Worse yet was the academic obsession with specialization. It was, and is, impossible to be an American historian—one specializes in the Jacksonian Era or the Progressive Era or American gender history. And so, as a biographer of Dean Acheson, the master architect of the Cold War, I was fitted into the Cold War historian slot. For the rest of my career I was expected to view myself and American history through this single lens. Well, it beat rural Ohio, and I was certainly getting to meet fascinating people up and down the East Coast.

After brief teaching stints at the U.S. Naval Academy and Princeton University I landed a job in the history department of Hofstra University. Hofstra—located on Long Island, a short commute to the cultural capital of the United States, New York City—offered new avenues to explore. Although I enjoyed teaching my Cold War specialty, something was missing—the passion for America I had experienced as a boy on our family travels: The fires ignited by *On the Road* had been extinguished. Teaching

American history in a classroom, day in and day out, was not the way to foster a lifelong love of learning in students or professors. But Hofstra had an alternative: New College, one of Hofstra's five degree-granting units.

Founded in 1959, New College is a small, interdisciplinary liberal arts college with about 450 students. The small size is deliberate, to help students and faculty forge effective academic relationships, to maintain flexibility within the interdisciplinary curriculum, to facilitate individualized study, and to allow students to work at their optimal pace. The unwritten motto of New College was given to us by Emerson: "The secret of education lies in respecting the pupil." New College professors can create their own courses, teach their current passion even when it branches away from the roots of their specialized expertise. Classes are small, and daily faculty interaction with students is encouraged. At New College teaching is primary, although scholarship is also important. The college is organized into four areas of inquiry: humanities, creative studies, social sciences, and natural sciences. Organization by areas gives undergraduate education at New College a strong interdisciplinary focus. The philosophy of New College is well summed up by political scientist Linda Longmire: "The task of learning implies relationships—not just between ideas but between people."

At New College I could still teach my specialty courses on the history of American foreign policy, but I could also create courses of my own choosing. During my first year I devised a course called "The Beat Generation and Counterculture in America." It was the most energizing course I had ever taught because it attracted students highly motivated to learn about Jack Kerouac and Thomas Pynchon, Charlie Parker and Jackson Pollock, Joan Baez and Gloria Steinem, Phil Ochs and the Chicago Eight, James Baldwin and James Brown. Allen Ginsberg was a guest lecturer and performed poetry, accompanying himself on his harmonium; we took field trips to see Lou Reed and John Cale perform *Songs for Drella*, a tribute to Andy Warhol; and we heard Norman Mailer speak at a tribute to Bernard Malamud at Cooper Union, in the East Village. The course was so much fun to teach, and most students couldn't wait to come to class—learning had become more fun than slacking off or watching television. The success led to an upper-level seminar, called "Jack Kerouac," the next year. The course was filled overnight, with auditors attending just out of the pure desire to learn about the Beat bard.

For the Kerouac course we had a very special guest speaker, the abstract painter Stanley Twardowicz. Kerouac had spent 1961 through 1964 living with his own mother in Northport, a fishing village on Long Island Sound, writing haiku, shunning publicity, and trying to drink away his pain at Gunther's Bar, often in Twardowicz's company. The two became close, downing Jack Daniel's boilermakers late into the night and sometimes taping these marathon sessions, in which Kerouac can be heard singing the Sinatra repertoire and talking in blues rhyme. Kerouac died in 1969, but Stanley Twardowicz is alive and well in Northport, painting his huge abstract canvases in his studio-garage. Stanley and I became friends, for I am an ideal audience for his Kerouac stories and appreciate his Beat counsel to "never enter a club that has velvet ropes in front." Stanley's life is right out of Kerouac's *Lonesome Traveler:* Golden Gloves boxer, world-class hitchhiker, semipro baseball player in Detroit, railroad hobo, Delaware cornhusker, Cedar Tavern denizen, art teacher, New York School painter in the 1950s, and best man at Roy Lichtenstein's wedding. Stanley would make guest appearances in my Kerouac class, in his paint-spattered shoes and trademark fishing hat, and the students loved him. Meeting Stanley Twardowicz was education at its best, for he spoke of the real Kerouac, not the mass-market one. We got to know the Kerouac who never drove a car, who shopped at the Walt Whitman Mall, and who was an admirer of William F. Buckley, Jr.

The class also journeyed to Kerouac's beloved redbrick, working-class Lowell, Massachusetts, visiting his birthplace at 9 Lupine Road and the Kerouac Commemorative, in a small downtown park, in which selected passages from his various books are engraved on eight marble columns on the bank of the Merrimack River. On this trip we also visited Thoreau's Walden Pond, but it was the Merrimack River in pre-Christmas twilight condensing toward darkness that caused us to shudder, to feel the shroud presence of Dr. Sax, from Kerouac's eponymous novel, whose mysterious spirit still seems to pervade Lowell, to understand at last that *On the Road* was not a novel but a religious poem for America, a gift to us all.

This journey to Lowell had made our class comfortable and cohesive; we had become friends. At our last session, Alex Sirotin, a brilliant student and recent Russian-Jewish immigrant who lived with his father at Brighton Beach, Brooklyn, asked directly: "Why do we have to learn about America from a classroom on Long Island? Why don't you teach us on the road?" When the pandemonium of student yeses finally died down, I thought, Why not? My family travels across America had taught me so much about my country, it was a privileged education to be shared. Most Hofstra students have never been far outside the tristate area of New York — New Jersey — Connecticut. Teaching on the road would be an opportunity to put some juice and energy back into education. I encouraged Alex to flesh out the idea in writing for a more detailed proposal to the dean, David Christman, an art historian whose passion for jazz would, I hoped, make him open and receptive to such an unconventional course.

When I approached Dean Christman about teaching American history and literature on the road, in either a giant Winnebago or a rock-and-roll tour bus, he chuckled, shook his head in disbelief, and carefully lit his pipe. After a few contemplative puffs, he said, "If you're serious and up for it, so am I." I was up for it, all right, still blissfully ignorant of the many obstacles that lay ahead. One difficulty of which I was not ignorant was the vicissitudes of group travel. For the past two summers Linda Longmire and I had shepherded twenty Hofstra students abroad for a month of classes on U.S.–Dutch relations at the Roosevelt Study Center in the Netherlands, and I knew only too well both the joys and frustrations of that kind of educational venture. Living for six weeks on the road with a bunch of students would be even more intense. Unlike in Europe there would be no reprieve away from the students, no personal space, and little time to myself. When Dean Christman and I brainstormed over the next few weeks, these concerns became secondary as we worked to transform the road course we were calling American Odyssey into a reality.

Price comparisons revealed that traveling by bus would be the most cost-effective, but the cost of leasing a bus from major operators was astronomical, primarily because the driver had to be paid hourly union rates. We focused on finding an independent owner-operator who would take us anywhere in America for six weeks, little realizing that when we found "Mr. Right" he would become such an integral part of the educational experience. There were many other wrinkles to iron out: student insurance policies, empty dorm rooms, how many credits to award, how much money it would cost students. But Dean Christman and I had grown steadfastly committed to making American Odyssey happen, and the rest was elbow grease.

As word of the American Odyssey course offering spread through the Hofstra campus, my office became a virtual wailing wall of student petitioners. Everyone had a reason why he or she *had* to go on the trip. Pundits may brood that we are producing a generation of inarticulate, unmotivated young people, but if we were to use lobbying skills as a measure of fitness, today's young Americans hold their own. Persistent begging was the most common tactic, with crying and bribery close seconds. Obviously some sort of objective academic-performance criterion was needed to help select who went. A selection committee was created. It was agreed that graduating seniors with a 3.0 or better GPA would get priority, and that the group would comprise equal numbers of men and women. A few slots would be left open for "special cases."

The dramatis personae of American Odyssey slowly began to develop. Here is a rundown of some of the students; the reader will meet the rest later on:

Alison Andrews was clearly one of the special cases. I will never forget the day she flew into my office, clutching a copy of *Blue Highways*, a cry from her heart bursting forth that she had to escape Long Island. I recognized that feverish need, and once she calmed down she emerged as a sensitive, poetic being, headstrong and animated, with an appetite for travel. She was only a junior, but she brought a proper road esprit to the venture. Alison represented one end of the spectrum of our developing group. A sincere outdoor enthusiast with an Earth First philosophy, her pressing concern was for us to climb the highest peaks in Colorado and camp out in remote parts of Montana, "regardless of weather conditions." A corollary was her insistence that we avoid urban centers, for they spelled crime and congestion. We did not always meet Alison's expectations, but she was a good sport throughout. I remember her as our overanxious energizer, always trying to lift group spirits, a human firefly who tried to lead us through the dark forests of the West in a wistful zigzag looking for an elusive America she never quite found. Without her I never would have discovered the music of Shawn Colvin or Richard Linklater's cult film *Slackers*, about a generation of young downwardly mobile idlers in Austin, Texas.

Another special case was Aíne Graham. While Aíne was an outstanding graduating senior, she had not finished her coursework in one class. In principle she was ineligible, but bureaucratic rules should always be broken when the human spirit is concerned. Aíne was determined to be a part of American Odyssey, and Dean Christman and I awarded her an Oscar for best lobbying. Here was a bright, articulate woman blessed with an eager curiosity and a friendly disposition who reminded us daily that her "lifelong dream," ever since she watched "The Partridge Family" on television, was to see America by bus in a communal, freewheeling fashion. She promised to take care of her incomplete and said she was willing to do extra-credit work, read extra books, and write extra papers if only she was given the opportunity to enroll. Only Scrooges would thwart a "lifelong dream"; so we said, "Welcome aboard!" As it turned out, Aíne became the undisputed group leader of the journey, friendly with everybody, never complaining, and learning "more about the United States in six weeks on the road than I had in four years of college"—at least, that's what she said during an interview on "Good Morning America."

The core of American Odyssey was formed by two graduating seniors whom I knew well from having them in a number of classes: Kenny Young and Stefanie Pearlman. Both were A students with an insatiable appetite for learning mixed with a healthy disposition toward fun. Both are now in law school—Kenny in Delaware and Stefanie in Missouri. My advice to readers is to remember their names: In a few years you may be able to retain them!

Kenny, one of the most personable people I've ever met, is a born advocate with a happy-go-lucky smile permanently fixed to his face. In many ways Kenny is what Eisenhower era students called "a big man on campus." He knew everyone, and everyone liked him. He had made an appointment to see me just as the American Odyssey course offering was being officially announced to the student body. He came not to plead for himself, as he had an assured slot, but to make the case for two of his fraternity brothers in Kappa Delta Rho (hereinafter referred to as KDR) whom he thought merited consideration: Matt Price and Justin Buis. Kenny was already in the lawyer mode, presenting his clients in their most favorable light. I did not know Justin, but I was well acquainted with Matt—at six-three and 220 pounds, he was hard to miss. A Reagan-Bush Republican with a flag-waving, patriotic disposition toward both America and Israel, he would have been perfectly cast as a bodyguard to former Israeli Prime Minister Yitzhak Shamir. It was always fun to have Matt in a class because he spoke his mind, heedless of what was politically correct—although goading liberals had become a recreational sport for him. Add to this Matt's Grateful Dead obsession, centered around collecting bootleg tapes—this born bar bouncer can best be described as an interesting mix. What I didn't know was that Matt was also a superbly adept video artist. He was to sign on later with a special assignment—to record our journey with his videocam. (The reader might as well know at the outset that he did a spectacular job.) Justin was also to sign on, and I would learn more about his unusual life—living on an Arkansas commune with his mother and riding motorcycles with his father—as we traveled the country together.

Meanwhile Stefanie began to help organize the trip. In addition to bringing her good friends Shari Berkowitz and Darlene Dudash on board, she was an active contributor to discussions on which routes to take and what books would be most appropriate. Unlike Alison, who wanted to rough it, Stefanie reminded me that the cosmopolitan side of things had its place, too, and that seeing Robert Rauschenberg's art in Chicago should have as

29

great a priority as watching a Steller's jay hop at the Grand Canyon. If Alison was our Annie Dillard, Stefanie was our Kitty Carlisle. Every day Stefanie checked in simply to see if she could help. We added Saint Louis to the itinerary because Stefanie's parents had promised us a home-cooked meal and we would not violate the first rule of travel: Never turn down hospitality. As we pondered a map together, it became clear that we couldn't go everywhere we wanted. Since New England was so close to home, we decided to skip it altogether. Although many students wanted to head straight west—first to the Rockies, then to the golden beaches of California—I had other plans. We would go south first, to the warmer climates, with Washington, DC, Atlanta, and New Orleans our central stops. Then we would follow the Mississippi River to Memphis and Chicago, where I was to participate in a panel discussion, "The United States and European Integration, 1947–1955," at the Organization of American Historians Conference on April 4. The students would attend selected sessions and write about them in their journals. From Chicago we would visit Stefanie's parents in Saint Louis, stop briefly in Independence to visit the Harry Truman Library, pay our respects to William Burroughs in Lawrence, and then head to Boulder, where we would be guests of the Jack Kerouac School of Disembodied Poetics. From Boulder onward, it would be an all-west-of-the-Rockies affair, with spontaneity governing which fork in the road we'd take. With the exceptions of Stefanie and Justin, most students had never traveled America, although a few had been to Europe or Israel.

Since we hadn't yet found a bus, Dean Christman and I thought hard and came up with a flat fee of one thousand dollars per student. This meant we had seventeen thousand dollars in our coffers to pay someone to take us anywhere we wanted for six weeks, diesel and tolls included. Since most students lived in dormitories, we were able to have their dorm fees prorated. This meant that if they vacated their rooms in mid-March, they would be refunded almost a thousand dollars each. The numbers were falling into place. The dorm refunds could go toward paying the driver, and since we were sleeping on the bus, student outlays would be limited to tuition, food, and incidentals. If they budgeted their money carefully, it would cost them approximately the same to travel and study all over America for six weeks as it would to stay back at Hofstra. This educational bargain is one more factor that makes American Odyssey so special.

Concerned that weeks of sleeping in cramped quarters might make us stir-crazy, I canvassed the marketing offices of major hotel chains to cadge some free rooms in the larger cities we would be visiting. My approach was that the students and I were embarking on an important historical and educational journey across America, and if they would give us free rooms—in essence, help to sponsor us—we would promote them wherever we went. This impeccable logic fell on deaf ears until I reached Buffy Jones at Best Western's corporate headquarters in Phoenix. Her response—"I wish they'd offered a class like this when I was in college"—was one we were to hear wherever we went. Because most Best Western Inns are individually owned, corporate headquarters could not give away free rooms, but Buffy arranged for me to use the corporate seal of approval when contacting the inn owners directly. After days of faxing and phoning, I was able to negotiate free rooms in Chicago, Las Vegas, and San Francisco. Elsewhere we would either sleep on the bus or camp under the stars in national or state parks.

An American Odyssey: Art and Culture Across America would be offered in Hofstra's New College Session IV (March 17 – May 7), giving its seventeen students a mosaic of all that is American, from poetry to fiction, from music to architecture, from history to current events. Dean Christman and I decided that spring would be the best time for our trek because we would be able to get into the High Rockies without getting snowed in. We also decided that each student who passed would earn six credits. They would be responsible for reading the assigned literary texts, taking two exams, and keeping a daily journal. I assumed that all students had already read Kerouac's *On the Road,* so two of his other books were required: *Mexico City Blues* and *The Dharma Bums.* After a great deal of debate over which American classics to teach, I chose Walt Whitman's *Leaves of Grass*, Mark Twain's *Adventures of Huckleberry Finn*, Willa Cather's *O Pioneers!* Carson McCullers's *Ballad of the Sad Cafe*, Langston Hughes's *Selected Poems*, Larry McMurtry's *Last Picture Show, Black Elk Speaks* (edited by John Neihardt), Hunter S. Thompson's *Fear and Loathing in Las Vegas*, Jack London's *Call of the Wild* and *White Fang*, and John Steinbeck's *Wayward Bus*. These texts would be supplemented by on-the-road history lectures plus occasional handouts of additional readings. In making out this rigorous reading list I failed to consider the difficulty that some students experienced trying to read while in motion, and so some students were able to read more than others were.

Nevertheless, what I found particularly satisfying as a teacher was that some of the students were so turned on by meeting authors William Burroughs, Bobbie Louise Hawkins, Ken Kesey, and Josephine Humphreys that on their own they purchased many of their works. After visiting Jack London's ranch in Glen Ellen, California, Justin began reading *Martin Eden*, the first time in his life he had ever read a book that was not assigned. A day after the thrill of traveling around Oregon with Ken Kesey in his new psychedelic bus, Further, our bus became weighted down with copies of *Sometimes a Great Notion* and *One Flew Over the Cuckoo's Nest*. There is no more satisfying sensation for an educator than to point to the door of learning and have the students kick it open and step inside.

Aside from the bus driver, the final piece of the crew puzzle was Dean Christman's assignment of his administrative assistant, Beth Neville, to join us on American Odyssey. Her job was to collect receipts, budget money, and serve as daily telephone liaison with Dean Christman, who — like a concerned parent — was anxious to keep tabs on his charges. Today Beth is the bright star of Hofstra's admission office, where her exciting American Odyssey stories have become her most effective recruiting tools on the high school circuit.

———

Since I was unable to locate an affordable bus with an unstuffy driver who didn't wear a uniform, the task was assigned to Beth. She unearthed the perfect fellow at the Nassau Coliseum RV show. He was handing out business cards denominating him "The Buffalo Bill of Busing," as he was respectfully referred to on Long Island. In my mind I wanted someone who was a combination of the two contradictory impulses that had spawned American Odyssey in the first place: the educational intimacy of my family highway sojourns and the wild Dionysian frenzy of *On the Road*. We needed a hybrid of Dad and Neal Cassady, someone who didn't do drugs but had a restless sense of adventure, someone who would help maintain order but didn't mind loud, nonstop rock and roll blaring from the speakers, someone who shared my sense of passion for learning about America but wasn't a stuffed shirt about it. Someone who, as James Agee says, was "restive for the sake of restiveness," who liked traveling for the "plain, unvarnished hell of it." Someone who didn't like to live by an itinerary or be on a schedule. Sound hard to find? It was for a while, and then we discovered Frank Perugi and it was all systems go. American Odyssey was ready for takeoff.

2

Frank Perugi and "The Majic Bus"

I may be goin' to hell in a bucket, babe,
But at least I'm enjoyin' the ride.
—GRATEFUL DEAD

FRANK PERUGI HAS PUT IN SO MANY DIESEL HOURS ON America's highways and byways that he can identify which state he's in just by tasting the tap water. And, if the old adage of elephant hunters holds true——that when you go to heaven, God doesn't look you over for degrees or medals but scans you for scars——then God is going to get an eyeful with Frank Perugi.

The second of seven children, Frank was born in Brooklyn on June 6, 1955, the year James Dean's road life ended. His father logged thirty-five years with Grumman, a major aircraft manufacturer on Long Island, while his mother, from Newfoundland, had her hands full raising Frank and his six siblings. The Perugis came from Tuscany, where, for centuries, they had been marble carvers. Proud of his heritage, Frank still keeps a slab of marble, used as a tabletop, at his home in Franklin Square, New York, and positively beams when he speaks of his grandfather's stonework, which can be seen in Saint Patrick's Cathedral.

Life in the Perugi family was normal until 1968, when Frank's older brother Randy, who was walking along the road, was killed in an automobile accident. He was hit by an off-duty cop drag-racing his brother-in-law down a back road, traveling so fast that he left skid marks one hundred feet long. Grief-stricken by his brother's death, one of fifty thousand U.S. traffic deaths annually, Frank was also outraged that his brother's killer was charged merely with vehicular manslaughter and faced only a one-year suspension from the force. The reckless cop who ended Randy's life never spent a day in jail: "When you're a nobody, you just get turned over like one," Frank concluded bitterly.

The Perugis' American dream began to unravel that day. Frank's hard-working father lost his sense of purpose, and the whole family unit started disintegrating. They had spent six pain-filled years trying to come to terms with Randy's senseless death when disaster struck once again. On a chilly November evening in 1974 a diesel semitruck barreling down Route 111 in Smithtown, Long Island, with a full-throated roar, bulldozed right over Frank's mother's 1959 Ford, instantly killing her and his little brother Joe. He could scarcely process the news: his mother and brother dead, the innocent victims of a despondent, burned-out trucker who was not paying attention to the road. The exhausted driver never even saw their car, never even put on the brakes, just smashed it like an accordion. Frank was devastated beyond words. To Frank his mother was a saint. She did charity work at Saint Catherine's, and the local nuns could always count on her to take them grocery shopping every week. After Randy's death she was not bitter, she simply went on in her devotion to family and church, helping junkies and handicapped people. And in an instant this devout believer and dedicated mother was obliterated, only her spirit remaining.

Frank, the eldest son, at nineteen, didn't know which way to turn. He finally said to hell with it and told his father that he had to escape the pain. Quitting his job as a machinist at Grumman, he bought a Honda

35

350 motorcycle, cleaned out a stack of canned food from his mother's cabinets, grabbed some blue jeans and T-shirts, and hit the road for the American West, less than a hundred bucks in his pocket. For his two male traveling companions, also on bikes, the ultimate destination was California; for Frank it was anywhere but Long Island, anyplace where he could numb his mind to all those deaths and bury, at least for a while, all the pain. Frank was on a personal odyssey. He knew he couldn't return until he had some explanation for all this pain—some means of soothing his despair and channeling his rage. He let his hair grow long, not to express anti–Vietnam War sentiments or to be fashionable, but as a sign of no longer being owned by Grumman or the police or the government or anyone else.

Frank never forgot the exhilarating sense of liberation he felt when he bolted from New York City on his bike, leaving behind six years of trouble and woe. The farther from New York he got, the better he felt. The wind against his face was therapeutic, life affirming. Things were going well as he and his companions biked through the fertile soil, wholesome towns, and agricultural abundance of Pennsylvania, Ohio, Indiana, Illinois, and Wisconsin. In Minnesota, however, they hit a ferocious head wind and were unable to reach even thirty miles an hour. They decided to quit fighting the wind and pulled into a campground in Fairmont. The guys decided to turn this delay into a party and bought some Mad Dog 20/20 and a six-pack of Old Milwaukee. Storm clouds were looming, so they quickly assembled tents, fortified by swigs of Mad Dog to kill the chill in the air. When rain arrived, the men were in a rowdy, carefree mood, popping wheelies down the gravel drive. Frank hit a pothole and flipped over, breaking his collarbone. One of Frank's comrades strapped him, in wrenching pain, to the back of his bike and zoomed him to the emergency room at Fairmont Hospital. Frank was no longer able to bike it across country, so his friends wished him a speedy recovery and raced off for California without him. Frank traded his Honda for a neck brace and a one-way bus ticket to Los Angeles.

The trip was a good one, he recalled, partially because "the girls on the bus were pretty sympathetic, always puttin' powder on my neck for me and stuff," but, more important, for combatting his grief. His sadness turned to awe at seeing for the first time the vastness of the Great Plains, the majesty of the Rockies, the unearthly dead zone of the Mojave Desert, and the sunny blueness of the Pacific. His Brooklyn jaw was perpetually agape. There was no touring or sightseeing on that Greyhound, just a fifteen-minute cigarette stop and a cup of coffee every hundred miles or so at a bus depot. Nevertheless, to this day Frank remains in debt to Greyhound for allowing him to discover not only America but himself, for "gettin' the road movin' past me, and gettin' the sights and sounds of this great country into my head." He now wanted to wake his fellow country-men to the fiery glaze of the desert stars, to the holiness of the praying Joshua trees, to the miracles all about them that society had conditioned them to ignore lest they ask themselves why they submitted to the daily regimentation of their mundane lives. He was done feeling sorry for himself; he was going to jam some excitement into his life and others' while he could still breathe. Life was a carnival, humor the only medicine with the power to heal, the engine for self-transformation.

In LA Frank made his way to the Sacred Heart Seminary, where a priest who was a family friend put him up. With the church as his base, Frank would hitchhike a day at a time, usually into the Mojave Desert, just to wander around, getting acquainted with miners and hippies, ranch-ers and hermits, tubercular convalescents and real estate speculators. He spent some time in Palmdale and then hitched his solitary way up the rugged Pacific Coast to Vancouver, Canada, where he stayed with his cousin on a fourteen-acre farm. Fancying himself a drifter, Frank lived his life on the road with these guiding principles: Moss will never grow on this razor's back; better to burn out than rust away; and don't look back. Frank roamed around America, always looking for minimum-wage work and the heart of Saturday night. He also saw so much that disturbed him: a black man beaten to a pulp in Denver for no reason but the color of his skin; men in Chicago who died nameless in the gutter; migrant workers picking grapes near Fresno until their fingers bled; the prostitutes in the back alleys of New Orleans shooting heroin after turning a twenty-dollar trick. As he hitchhiked right on through all the little one-blink towns, Frank wondered whether all the church crucifixes he saw really stood for forgiveness and mercy. And most of all he wondered about himself. Now that he had jettisoned all the baggage of the past, how could he get his life together, acquire the discipline and direction to turn his new outlook into action?

Back in New York, he decided—for reasons he can't quite explain today—to become "a shaved one"—no, not a Hare Krishna but a U.S. Marine. Not surprisingly it was the wrong decision. After a few months of one-handed push-ups and yessir this and yessir that at Parris Island, he wanted out. Frank's thoughts were of yodeling on top of Pikes Peak, surfing Malibu waves, and watching the fishing boats return with the daily catch, a flock of hungry seagulls trailing. He was, he realized, too independent of mind for the military, too much the dream weaver. Luckily he was able to finagle an honorable discharge and headed straight to Myrtle Beach, South Carolina, to spend a month with his cousin, fishing for large-mouth bass and whistling the theme song from "Mayberry R.F.D.," happy just to be out of the marines. Once he got some money together, he bought a Greyhound ticket, this time to San Diego, where he hung out in Oceanside for more than a year, shooting pool with a flock of lost souls from the sixties—some hippies and some "wanted" barroom rounders with a countenance half horse and half alligator—just killing time, wondering what the next move was.

One afternoon Frank was sitting under a palm tree, watching the ocean roll, when a beachcomber carrying a kit of needles and dye asked whether he wanted a tattoo. Ever since he had seen an elegant unicorn tattooed on the back of a Marine friend, Frank had wanted one, too, but he never had the money or the time. Frank had no hesitation as to subject. From age thirteen he had carried the moniker "Fritz the Cat" and kept a good-luck picture of the X-rated cartoon character in his wallet. And now serendipity was knocking; here was his chance, and it was inexpensive to boot. An hour later Frank had a large green image of Fritz the Cat on his right forearm, while on his left was Shorty, the disheveled cartoon character from the movie *Fritz the Cat* who has no legs and travels everywhere on a skateboard.

A few days later, the bandages off, Frank headed back east to visit his Dad, showboat his arty new forearms, and start a summer job as a cook in Montauk. On the way he stopped in Arizona, where he got his ear pierced, purchased some turquoise jewelry, began wearing his fashion-signature bolo tie, and got himself a black Stetson and a jazzy pair of Tony Lama rattlesnake-skin boots. He was now the High Plains Drifter with the True Grit of Rooster Cogburn, eager to display the new western-ized Frank in New York, to show off his dark California tan, Harley-Davidson belt buckle, and new duds that would make even the folk-sing-ing Brooklyn cowboy Ramblin' Jack Elliot green with envy. And though he had no Pecos Bill tales of digging the Rio Grande with his bare hands, Frank had done some hard travelin' and knew how to spin a yarn.

It was now the summer of '76, two hundred years after the American Declaration of Independence was signed and two years after Frank's personal Declaration of Independence. Apple-pie Bicentennial celebra-tions were exploding across the nation when Frank visited his father for a week. Frank's father was decidedly underwhelmed by his son's new Easy Rider, gun-for-hire look. Ignoring the disapproval, the prodigal son did some guilt-assuaging yard work, signed his John Hancock to a number of U.S. government documents that officially released him from the marines, and split for the wind-battered Montauk beach with only a bedroll under his arm. Frank had just turned twenty-two. For the past two years he had journeyed through America in search of himself, a nomadic jack-of-all-trades, definitely master of none, in quest of a way to make a difference.

On July 4 Frank took his newly acquired Kawasaki for a spin to the Montauk Point lighthouse, on the farthest eastern tip of Long Island. He was leaning against his bike, soaking up the afternoon rays, when a 1938 Brill City bus came chugging past. The driver, a middle-aged hippie with long hair and a beard that would make Jesus proud, flashed him the biker's sign of greeting, which is a fisted forearm in the air. Amused by this psychedelic bus-man and his far-out vehicle, Frank returned the sign. Frank correctly inferred that the hippie wasn't headed to Woodstock but to a big Fourth of July keg party just down the road, an all-night bash the local rock stations were advertising as the blowout of the summer. He decided to follow, although he wasn't sure why. Frank thought of himself more in terms of a bad-ass biker than a hippie; he was an old-fashioned American outlaw patriot, not a pot-smoking, flag-burning peacenik. The Fourth of July was a time for him to blow off some fireworks, not blow a joint. But though Frank had no great truck with hippies, he sure did like this particular hippie's vintage 1938 bus. At the party he found the bus parked under an old oak tree, its owner sitting on a blanket with another Jesus look-alike, making beaded necklaces and horsenail jewelry. Frank introduced himself as Fritz the Cat, the men introduced themselves as Hippie John and his open-field sidekick, Tom.

Conversation immediately turned to buses, and John told Frank about the "Green Tortoise," a semicounterculture bus, owned and operated by the offbeat, buckskin-and-braids Oregonian Gardner Kent, designed to take people cross-country from New York to San Francisco in what amounted to transcontinental minitours. The Green Tortoise was a low-budget, low-maintenance enterprise. The bus's interior had been gutted, foam cushions were tossed haphazardly on the floor, acid-rock music blared nonstop as the chassis throbbed violently mile after mile. Everything was painted snapping-turtle green, except for patches of youthful graffiti, and pets were permitted. Passengers sat on cushions against the sides, facing the center, and off they rattled to see America, stopping along the way to hike, raft, and enjoy the hot springs.

Frank was hooked by tales of the fabled Green Tortoise and arranged to take the bus's next cross-country trip. Boarding in Manhattan with only a gym bag full of clean clothes, Frank was excited about the great gypsy adventure that awaited him. A mere two hours later, enthusiasm had turned to disgust. The Green Tortoise was a noisy, dilapidated, chaotic rust bucket with no rules, no bathroom—just a bunch of kids getting sacramentally wasted on grass and booze. He was repulsed by the behavior of his fellow travelers throwing litter out the window, fighting over who would get the funnel next to be able to pee as neatly as the rattling bus would allow, through a hole in the floorboards—women included.

Out of the Green Tortoise chaos, Frank found a calling. He would turn people on to America in his own safe, squeaky-clean bus that reflected him and his ideas. It took no time to think up a name, it was instantaneous. He would call it the "Majic Bus," after the Who's song "The Magic Bus," about a stationary double-decker in Amsterdam—that most libertarian of cities—that served as a coffee shop and smoke emporium. Frank changed the *g* to a *j* so people didn't think he was ripping off the British rock group. Upon his return to New York, Frank had promotional T-shirts made for his dream, MAJIC BUS: X-RATED TRUCKERS in gold lamé lettering on the back and Fritz the Cat on a couch with a female cat in front. Frank handed them out by the hundreds to friends, as a hook to solicit money for a deposit on a bus, giving a decidedly macho tone to his budding enterprise. To test the waters, Frank borrowed from a family friend a 1967 Silver Eagle bus, a quality sleeper, and drove it to Montauk to test-market friends and young beachsters for what kind of response he would obtain if he said, "How many want to go with me to California?" Fifty-plus adventurer wannabes were ready to drop everything and join Frank in crossing America. Encouraged by this display of enthusiasm, Frank admitted they'd have to wait a spell until he raised enough money to buy his own Majic Bus and take them in style.

It took Frank ten years, driving more than three thousand miles a week, to achieve his dream. He raised the cash by trucking every corner of America, sometimes picking up antique cars for a wealthy New York tycoon who opened a museum of vintage autos, other times diesel trucking every cargo imaginable, from Swanson TV dinners to Topps baseball cards. During that decade Frank grew sick of the business. Only his dream kept him going. It was grueling work, and most truckers he met had to work two jobs just to break even. Along the way Frank fell in love and married a woman who shared his Majic Bus dream. He tried to be a responsible husband and later, father, all the while clinging to his dream of the Majic

Bus. The more time he spent on the highways, eating soupy chili at truck stops, copping Zs in rest areas, drinking bad coffee with Cremora instead of cream, the more frugal he became in order to save money. Over the decade Frank also witnessed the decline of the Teamsters, who had at one time been family men, owner-operators of their own rigs. Now they were leased like servants to many different companies, their pride and dignity traded for speed like black beauties and animal tranquilizers just to drive alive. To Frank, the trucker's world, glorified by country singers Jerry Reed and Red Sovine, had all but vanished; it had become a business of blisters and bloodshot eyes. He got rid of his CB, fed up with all that "breaker, breaker" nonsense, preferring to just keep shifting gears and talking to the windshield.

In 1987 Frank finally put together the twenty thousand dollars needed to buy the GMC bus he wanted from Oklahoma Transit. It was not the Majic Bus of his dreams because it was not a fully equipped sleeper, just a regular tour bus with rows of passenger seats and unspeakable miles on the odometer, but it was a start. He said good-bye to trucking; he was going to run his own company, The Majic Bus, Inc. (A fringe benefit, Frank once confessed, was that "truckers have to load and unload their cargo; passengers load and unload themselves.") So, with his wife, Mary Alice, handling the paperwork and monitoring the Majic Bus 800 phone number from their home-office in Franklin Square, New York, Frank started marketing, initially for conventional touring, but with an unconventional difference: Frank Perugi's own personal touch, even for day trips, which included barbecuing food, taking scenic back roads, telling stories, doing whatever it took to make the trip a little extra special. He made business cards, advertised in newspapers, and showed the Majic Bus on the RV-show and rock-concert circuit in hopes of finding customers. He found just enough to stay afloat. People weren't ready yet for cross-country treks, but he did well with short jaunts to Atlantic City casinos, ski trips to Hunter Mountain and Lake Placid, summer excursions to a Great Adventure amusement park, Jersey Shore metal bands that wanted to show up at their Hoboken gigs in style, prom nighters who wanted to graduate with champagne without worrying about DWI, college students who wanted to see Bruce Springsteen at the Meadowlands or the Grateful Dead in Saratoga Springs, and Manhattan office workers who wanted to see the Yankees play but were afraid to drive into the Bronx. Business never boomed, but it was steady. Besides, instead of leaving his wife and daughter, Colleen, for months at a time, as he did as a trucker, now he was only gone for long weekends.

After a couple of years of penny pinching, Frank had saved enough money to purchase a second bus, Majic Bus #2, an old, beat-up New York City Transit vehicle that had been retired in 1990. No sooner had Frank paid his thirteen thousand dollars for the bus at the ShortLine Terminal Agency, a sort of used-bus dealership in New Jersey, than off he went to Tulsa, Oklahoma, with a tape of the unique piano blues of Leon Russell as his companion the whole way. He reached Service Enterprises, an outfit that converts buses into dormitory-style motor homes, late one evening, raring to start construction of his dream sleeper, his *Spruce Goose* on wheels. With the help of Service Enterprises, Frank was going to transform a superannuated New York City Transit bus into a highway hotel. Step one was a large, stainless-steel MAJIC BUS sign for the front, complete with a lightning bolt to energize his passengers. Next he painted the outside royal blue and had the words MAJIC BUS stenciled on the sides. Finally he made a detailed design of how he wanted the interior: four private sleeping compartments, all with bunk beds; a living-room area that could accommodate a TV-VCR; a bathroom complete with toilet, shower, and sink; a wet-bar area in front, along with a small refrigerator; a sunroof in each room so passengers could feel the wind in their faces; and windows—plenty of glass—so passengers could see America flashing by. The bus would be carpeted throughout and have central air-conditioning to keep people comfortable in the humidity of the bayous and cool in the sweltering dry sun of the Sonoran Desert. Smoking would not be allowed. A stereo system would blast the music of choice: Willie Nelson in Texas, Ray Charles in Georgia, Janis Joplin in San Francisco, B. B. King in Chicago, Smokey Robinson in Detroit. Just thinking about the music made

Frank eager to get the Majic Bus on the open road. But the thirteen thousand dollars had drained Frank's cash reserves. He had to leave the bus in Oklahoma and send Service Enterprises an additional twenty-four thousand dollars to proceed with the repairs and remodeling on a pay-as-you-go basis.

For nearly two years Frank sent whatever spare cash he could scrape together to Oklahoma, hoping to make his first transcontinental trip in spring 1992. Money worries aside, Frank had an even bigger problem: finding a group bent on discovering America via his Majic Bus. And then, in January 1992, on Beth Neville's suggestion, Frank got a call from me. After a five-minute phone conversation with Frank, I knew I had found my man. He was our Neal Cassady—albeit a more sedate, 1990s version—and his Majic Bus would be our drug-free version of Ken Kesey's "Furthur," the real star of Tom Wolfe's *Electric Kool-Aid Acid Test*.

Frank was a philosopher-trucker, and that was what I liked most about him. He had an endless repertoire of maxims for every occasion, for example: "When you're over the hill, you begin to pick up speed," or, "There is nothing wrong with America that a good cup of coffee and morning prayers can't fix," or, "We're hopelessly lost but making good time." And talk about knowing the country, Frank is a walking instruction manual of America's highways and byways, of truck-stop cuisine, and of how to make bad cowboy coffee.

"You never know when you're making a memory," he said at our first meeting with Hofstra Dean David Christman, during which we officially hired Frank and his Majic Bus for seven weeks. We shook hands on the deal, and Hofstra signed a contract with Majic Bus, Inc.; there was no turning back. New College course SGG 19, American Odyssey: Art and Culture Across America, was born. Frank's parting question to me that day was, "What do you want to name the bus?" The Majic Bus had a marquee in front to inform would-be passengers of its destination. I said, How about "Dire Wolf"?—my favorite Grateful Dead song from *Working Man's Dead*, an appropriate symbol for the economic and environmental problems America faces. Besides, Jack London's *Call of the Wild* and *White Fang* were assigned course texts, and wolves were my favorite animal. Frank liked the name and agreed to see what he could do about making the sign.

Frank left Hofstra elated. But there was no time for breaking out the champagne. The Majic Bus sat marooned in Tulsa, still needing lots of work before it was road-ready. Within a week Hofstra cut Frank a check for ten thousand dollars, and he immediately sent it on to Tulsa. Since we were buying sight unseen, I was eager for the remodeling to be finished as quickly as possible and the Magic Bus to arrive in New York.

It was now late January, and many travel and accommodation details still had to be ironed out. The next eight weeks were jam-packed with preparations and answering a nonstop barrage of questions: what clothes to bring, how much spending money to carry, whether to expect rain (maybe yes, maybe no, it depends), and whether we would have a telephone on the bus. I was more than ready to take off by the time our March 28 departure date rolled around. As the day approached, everything seemed under control. The preodyssey week of organized class discussion and lectures on American immigration, Native American cultures, Ralph Waldo Emerson and Henry David Thoreau, Manifest Destiny, Walt Whitman's *Leaves of Grass*, Frederick Jackson Turner's frontier thesis, and American folklore went well. The students asked many pertinent and challenging questions, all of which served to help ground us in the basics of American history and literature before we embarked cross-country without the rigid scaffolding of traditional classes. My only real concern was the Majic Bus itself. Frank's land yacht, as he referred to it, had yet to make its New York debut, and now there were only days to go. On the Friday morning before our 6:30 A.M. Saturday departure Frank called from Tulsa. For the past week he had been out there, drill and hammer in hand, getting the bus ready for our March 28 launching. The Majic Bus was in tip-top mechanical shape, but the promised bunk beds, television, and wet bar were not yet in place. Frank wanted to postpone the departure by two days. Impossible, I said. All the students were packed, the PR wheels were in motion, and a delay would kill morale. Many parents had come

45

to Hofstra for the weekend expressly to wish their offspring a bon voyage. The local press and television stations were scheduled to be there for our 6:30 A.M. takeoff. Saturday's *New York Times* would feature a major story about this innovative American Odyssey course, announcing to millions our departure that morning. It was physically impossible to make 6:30 A.M., Frank said; the best he could do was noon. Come hell or high water, I insisted the Majic Bus had to be at the Hofstra Student Union at high noon *sharp*. Frank replied, "You got it. See you then, Captain." I put down the phone and crossed my fingers anxiously.

It was a long, restless night for me, tossing and turning with nightmares of the entire American Odyssey enterprise crumbling like a sand castle. Usually a good judge of character, I started having midnight doubts about Frank. I could only hope I had not been hoodwinked. The finale to my longest night was waking up to thick patches of morning fog. Two giant cups of 7-Eleven coffee, an egg-and-cheese sandwich, and a therapeutic thirty-minute drive to Hofstra in my Chevy pickup, listening to the Byrds singing Dylan's "My Back Pages" and "Chimes of Freedom," banished all the night fears. A rush of excitement swept over me at the mere thought of Montana.

I had bought a Saturday *New York Times*, and the article by Josh Barbanel about our "mad dash by sleeper bus to celebrate America" was terrific. Barbanel had captured the spirit of American Odyssey, which he described as a cross between Jack Kerouac and Charles Kuralt, seeing us as "the tamer 1990's heirs to Ken Kesey and the Merry Pranksters." The article, including a picture of some of us studying a map of the United States, also contained a few student observations, like Alison Andrews's acerbic rationale of why she was getting out of Long Island: "When people start mistaking landscaping for nature, you know you've been in a place too long. Apathy and ignorance is all I see. This is my last chance to restore my faith in America and Americans."

Beth had called all the students the previous evening to inform them of the noon departure. No sooner had I walked into my office than the phone was ringing. It was Frank calling from Columbus, Ohio, saying the Majic Bus was on the way, but he wouldn't make Hofstra until 3:00 P.M. Cheered by Frank's progress, I phoned students to alert them to this new delay. Student patience was running thin but much assuaged by the *Times* coverage, which had them all abuzz. I called *Newsday* and a local television news team and told them not to come. For the next five hours I sat in my office making last-minute phone calls and listening to Hank Williams utter poignant country syllables to the strain of a steel guitar. At 2:00 P.M. I went out to the Student Union, where parents' cars were lined up, the passengers all smiles and waves. It had stopped raining, but a chilly March wind was blowing. I was astonished at student cleverness at circumventing the one-bag rule—there were giant army-surplus bags and gargantuan pieces of luggage about the size of a VW bus everywhere I looked. Alan had purchased corned-beef and turkey sandwiches from Ben's Kosher Deli, and many students were chowing down in eager anticipation. Jared had his giant "portable" CD player, which was larger and heavier than most nonportable stereos, playing Tom Petty's new *Into the Great Wide Open*. From that moment on, the title track and "Learning to Fly" were the official American Odyssey anthems. I spoke to parents, apologizing for the delay, but nobody seemed to mind. They, too, were impressed by the *Times* coverage.

Three o'clock came and went, and still no Majic Bus. Finally, at 4:30 P.M. a big blue-and-silver bus, BIG BAD WOLF, not DIRE WOLF, pulsating red on the marquee, came barreling down the road like an enraged bull charging for the matador's cape. We erupted into a thunderous standing ovation, hooting and hollering. Our adrenaline was working kinetic overtime as Frank and his friend from Tulsa, Joe McDougall, whom he had shanghaied to help with the driving, bounded off the bus. In a loud, authoritative voice Frank announced, "Load em' up," adding a menacing, "The Big Bad Wolf has arrived." I had the students stay put until I could study the interior and decide where each would sleep. This was the first time I had seen the Majic Bus, and boy, was I in for a surprise. No bunk beds had been constructed, so, Green Tortoise–style, the students and I would have to sleep on floor mattresses; the TV and other amenities were nowhere to be found; and the quarters were much more cramped than I had supposed. The Majic Bus was not the "luxury liner" I had envisioned, although the all-important rest room was squeaky clean. Frank saw the shock register on my face and said, "Sorry, but we had to take off before the bunk beds were constructed. I'll build them as soon as we get a free day on the road." It was too late for the professor to panic. One by one I called the students in and assigned them spots.

Darkness was setting in as we loaded the last duffel bag into the luggage bay and exchanged traditional bear-hug good-byes with families and friends. Then we made a horn-blowing getaway, everyone thinking, Let's get out of Hofstra fast. There was no sentimentality in leaving, only the stark realization that for the next six weeks the Majic Bus was to be our home. We had been on the road less than a minute when Jay, our music director for the trip, handed me an Allman Brothers tape to play. Right on cue "Ramblin' Man" burst forth from the speakers, and the odyssey had begun, heading off to what Thomas Wolfe called "a billion forms of America," our first destination Washington, DC.

The front of the bus, where I spent most of the trip, was known as the porch—a carpeted-platform open space in back of the driver that could hold seven people. Frank, who seemed to have a motor mouth without an off switch, was at his best when the porch was packed. We could all look out the front windshield together; swap stories; talk history, literature, music, or religion; and listen to Frank's highway yarns. For me those animated porch gatherings were a particularly memorable part of American Odyssey. The bus rules boiled down to three: no smoking, drugs, or excessive messiness. Frank was a relentless enforcer of all three.

It was dark as we entered the heavy flow of traffic on the Cross Island Parkway and inched past Belmont Park racetrack, where horseracing legends permeate the air, past the worn-out redbrick factories and Archie Bunker row houses with their BEWARE OF DOG signs posted on the fenced-in front yards, giving Queens its decidedly charmless quality of dogged survival but nothing more. In a sign that collegians of the nineties were different from those of the eighties, the first heated porch debate concerned taxes, a five-letter word that had been of no concern to me at age twenty. April 15 would soon be here, and we discussed the financial hoop jumping everyone had to endure filling out tax forms in the United States. Alan Mindel, who always talked emphatically about politics and brought to the trip refreshing candor and wit, launched into a tirade of disgust about the IRS. "The IRS behaves like a pack of bloodsucking Big Brother bandits," he offered up, in that inimitable way he has of opening a discussion. Since I myself was in the difficult midst of gathering all the receipts and numbers that represented my fiscal 1991, I wasn't too amenable to steering the debate into a more analytical and less scornful direction. We agreed it was a pity people had to work hard all year long and then simply be forced into a confusing paper game with a government agency that exempts itself from the Bill of Rights as a matter of daily routine and judges good citizenship solely on the ability to abide with its many abstruse and arcane rules. Too bad, we thought, that someone more electable than Jerry Brown wasn't pushing for the straight 13 percent flat tax, recognizing deep down the impossibility of scrapping our present loophole-ridden system. Frank and his buddy were detailing a new approach to taxes—pay none—as we passed the sign for Coney Island, which elicited the first shouting onslaught of "Professor Brinkley, let's stop!" this time from Justin, who wanted a Nathan's original foot-long hot dog. I demurred, since we weren't even off Long Island yet. (Before long the formal "Professor Brinkley" would be replaced by just "Doug.")

It was raining as we bounced over the Verrazano Narrows and Goethals bridges, the swarming rock of Manhattan glowing behind us in the rear-view mirror. As we listened to the Traveling Wilburys sing "Tweeter and the Monkey Man," a sign welcomed us to the Garden State. Frank grabbed the New Jersey Turnpike toll ticket from a small, mean-looking machine that would spit out computer cards twenty-four hours, 365 days a year, long after we were dead and gone. We were on our way! The students were too hyper to sit still in their compartments, so they crowded either into the party room in back or into the porch up front. The group pulse was upbeat. Jay had brought a case of personally selected rock-and-roll road cassettes for the journey. What a fantastic collection it was, the emphasis on stinging electric Texas roadhouse blues guitar greats: Johnny Winter, T-Bone Walker, Albert Collins, Freddie King, Johnny "Guitar" Watson, and Johnny Copeland dominating, plus a special row for Stevie Ray Vaughan. In the earliest months of American Odyssey planning, I had promised Jay we would visit Stevie Ray's grave in Austin, Texas, but it was a promise I was unable to keep as the itinerary got more and more jammed. As concrete plans replaced wannas, the Lone Star State had to but cut entirely. This was a pity, because the Alamo in San Antonio is one of a handful of must-see historical American landmarks, and I felt regret at its omission, but we couldn't do EVERYTHING. As it was we were visiting more places than was rational in such a short span. The Majic Bus was not traversing America but trailblazing across a nation.

For the next two hours the students chattered excitedly about the expedition and began working out congenial sleeping arrangements. Without bunk beds, the sleeping quarters were indeed tight. To forestall complaints I played martyr by claiming the hallway as my six-week bed. It would be hard for students to gripe about sleeping space, for they at least had mattresses, while their poor professor was enduring the hard bus floor. Frank kept assuring us he would build bunks as soon as he had a chance. As we cruised down the New Jersey Turnpike, we collectively wondered how we would survive without killing each other in such a compressed space. Although our doubts were unexpressed, Frank, intuiting our concerns, kept saying not to worry, the bus would get bigger every day: "You're all gonna trim down." The students discounted his words as an attempt to placate. But Frank was right. By the end of the trip, the inside of the Majic Bus had grown; it was no longer confining. After a month or so of our being cooped up, the space grew into a universe of its own. This lesson had the bizarre side effect of making me appreciate Emily Dickinson's backyard Amherst poetry more than ever before.

50   We began to focus on "roadness" for the first time as we crossed the

Delaware Memorial Bridge, with its hulking green towers, the Delaware River, of George Washington—crossing fame, rushing underneath us, the Du Pont chemical facilities intruding on the banks like weeds. On the other side of the bridge a sign read, WELCOME TO DELAWARE, THE SMALL WONDER, with the subheading THE FIRST STATE. Delaware may have been the first state to ratify the Constitution, but a superficial acquaintance places it among the last states one would describe as a wonder. The old joke goes that on meeting someone from Delaware, one never asks what town they're from but what exit. This, of course, is unfair, as anyone knows who has visited the splendid Winterthur Museum or spent any time on the clean and expansive beaches of Rehoboth. Nonetheless Delaware tends to be a state to drive through, not a destination in itself, unless of course you are seeking shelter under the generous umbrella of its corporate law, in which case you break ground, lay a foundation, hang up a sign, acquire a toll-free 800 number, and call "the First State" home.

At 8:00 P.M., with Neil Young's "Rockin' in the Free World" blasting through the bus, Frank and his buddy, Joe, loudly swapping Oklahoma bus stories over the music, and general road fever pandemonium exploding throughout the bus, Delaware was the last thing on my mind. Now that I had the chaos contained, my next worry was time. We were behind schedule. I had promised my friend Jennifer Herman, who, with Vivian Brown, owns the Francis Scott Key Bookstore in Washington, that the Majic Bus would pull in front of their literary landmark at 9:30 P.M., where they would feed us pizza and let us spend our first night sleeping on their store floor. It now looked like it would be closer to midnight. As we whizzed past a silly welcoming sign that read, TREE-MENDOUS MARYLAND, I explained our time problem to Frank, who promised to pull off at the next service plaza so I could call Jennifer. When we saw the large sign that said, MARYLAND HOUSE, with its brightly colored logos of Roy Rogers, Sbarro Pizza, Bob's Big Boy, Shell, and Exxon beckoning hungry travelers and their equally hungry gas tanks, we made a quick pit stop. I shouted the first of what would become the Brinkley litany: "Everybody back on the Majic Bus in five minutes!" We trotted into a faux-colonial Mount Vernon structure with a plastic banner in front: MEAL VALUES AHEAD. Most of the students made a beeline for the rest rooms, not yet accustomed to our own more humble bus facilities, not yet acquainted with the unforgettable sound of the toilet flushing and the stained aluminum pan at the bottom opening up and yawning into our septic tank. Justin, Matt, and Kenny—hereinafter known as the KDR frat boys because they were nearly inseparable "brothers"—headed straight for the self-serve soft-drink dispenser at the Roy Rogers and proceeded to guzzle down cups of Mountain Dew. After phoning Jennifer about our delay and asking her to keep the pizza warm and the beer and soda cold, I returned to the bus for my first head count, not a frivolous exercise in this instance. We were one short. Everyone was aboard except Kevin.

More than any other student on the trip, Kevin personified the media's twenty-something-generation stereotype, for he was a devotee of MTV, *Spin*, and Lollapalooza, with an encyclopedic understanding of the world beat and industrial noise that made him a "happening guy" at the ecstasy clubs in Manhattan but was of little benefit when trying to escape the monotonous McJob employment cycle. With his pierced ear and quasi-punk clothes Kevin was just a week behind Johnny Depp and Luke Perry when it came to fashion. While he was crazy about Chuck Berry and Elvis Presley, he had little use for Dead Head retreads who continue to glamorize the Haight-Ashbury of the sixties, a place in time when people actually bragged about not showering and not clipping their nails. Christian Slater in *Heathers* was closer to the effect Kevin was after, and if he had to listen to Frank's sixties ramblin'-man rock, then he preferred it with a nineties chain-saw edge, like the Rollins Band covering Canned Heat's "On the Road Again."

I found the missing Kevin inside playing the "Street Gunner" video game. The objective is to stop the evil plot of STRUM, an international terrorist organization, by firing nine Hammer Twin–1022 missiles. "Kevin, we're leaving!" I shouted. "Just a minute. Give me a minute," he responded without looking up, as he continued to fire away. I watched as he unloaded his last round. I waited until we were out of the video arcade to issue a reprimand, wanting to ensure I had his full attention. It occurred to me that for the next six weeks my primary role would not be that of guide, professor, or authority figure but that of shepherd. And shepherd I was for the duration of the American Odyssey journey.

Later, as we approached Baltimore, we had our first experience with interbus camaraderie. An old clunker ID'd as "Mt. Pleasant Baptist Church, 1801 E. Preston St., Balt., MD" pulled alongside, beeping its horn and flashing us the peace sign. The driver held up a sign that read, YE MUST BE BORN AGAIN (JOHN 3:57). We gave them the thumbs-up and took it as a sign that we should eject the *Never Mind the Bollocks, Here's the Sex Pistols* tape and plop *Al Green's Greatest Hits* in its place.

As we drove through the long, greasy Baltimore Harbor Tunnel, Jared joined the front-porch gang, discussing at length—very great length—how Baltimore Memorial Stadium was being torn down, how the new stadium, Oriole Park at Camden Yards, would be the best in baseball, and how Earl Weaver was one of the greatest managers ever. One might think that this outpouring meant Jared was a Baltimore Orioles fan, but not so. Jared's a sports fanatic the likes of which I had never met before. As a starting point in his hopeful career as a sportscaster, Jared Max Goldman helps pay his way through college by working as an announcer at Sports Phone, where he is known simply as "Jared Max" to the sports addicts and compulsive gamblers who call for up-to-the-minute scores and to talk through the trauma when their team loses or fails to cover the spread. As we emerged from the tunnel, I realized just how far gone Jared's sports mind was. He was now taking what he called an informal survey of who was the greatest third baseman: Brooks Robinson, Ron Santo, or Eddie Mathews. His enthusiasm was undiminished by the sneering "What's your problem?" from the KDR boys or the dismissive "Sit down, Jared, and look out the window" from Stefanie and Shari. Changing tack, he asked an open-ended question: "Do you guys think baseball will come back to Washington?" Nobody paid it any attention as we whizzed on by the bedroom suburbs of Columbia, Scaggsville, Beltsville, and Suitland that punctuate the ring road better known as Washington's Beltway; gawked at the icy white Mormon temple that looms over the interstate, a displaced palace from another galaxy; and got off at Wisconsin Avenue, which would take us straight into Georgetown.

For the students Georgetown conjured up visions of gracious dinner parties where Washington's elite toast the success of the GATT or some such treaty with Merlot sipped from Waterford crystal. Tom, an avid history buff, said he associated Georgetown with President John F. Kennedy, with the mystique of Camelot, and hoped to visit the N Street address where the Kennedys had lived just before their move to the White House. But as we approached the intersection of Wisconsin and M Street, the main commercial strip, there was no sign of Washington, no Pamela Harriman or Katharine Graham or Claiborne Pell out for an evening stroll, just throngs of preppie Georgetown and George Washington University students, buzzed Fort Myer jarheads searching for neon-studded honkytonks; European tourists about to experience overpriced American jazz; nervous underage Maryland teenagers fortified with recently laminated fake ID's so they could drink with the big guys; gawkers from mid-America who believed they had found East Coast culture in boutiques such as Condom Rageous or Commander Salamander's; and residents from every other part of Washington who wanted to promenade and be a part of all the carnival commotion. Weekends in Georgetown have become one nonstop street party, a Mardi Gras every Friday and Saturday night. When Richard Nixon became president there were 13 places licensed to serve alcohol in Georgetown; by the time Bill Clinton moved to the White House, there were more than 125. That statistic says it all. Needless to say, weekend traffic has become a nightmare, and the Majic Bus was in the thick of it. Eventually we made our way to the Francis Scott Key Bookshop at the corner of 28th and O streets, NW, in the residential part of Georgetown, illegally parked the bus out front, and thronged into the favorite haunt of Washington's better-known bibliophiles for just-delivered Geppetto's Pizza. We brought our sleeping bags along, for our first night would be spent on the sixteen-foot-wide bookstore floor. The students couldn't get over the fact that we were actually going to sleep in a bookstore.

As we stood around and ate, Jennifer told the students the history of the shop, which opened in 1937. She and Vivian acquired it in 1990 after the death of the venerable founder, Martha Johnson. The shop's connection to a half century of Washington life includes two-time Democratic presidential nominee Adlai Stevenson, who lived in the apartment above the store and could often be found browsing through the stacks. Alice Roosevelt Longworth used to arrive, her chauffeur in tow, every Friday afternoon to buy her reading material for the next week. When John Foster Dulles was ill with cancer, his wife purchased all the Nero Wolfe mysteries missing from his home library. Over the years such powerful Washington figures as Dean Acheson, Joseph Alsop, Felix Frankfurter, Averell Harriman, Henry Kissinger, and authors E. B. White and Larry McMurtry were among its clientele. Today members of Congress, judges, CIA operatives, cabinet members, journalists, and assorted think-tankers are regular customers. Jennifer spoke about why she loves Georgetown—the brick-and-cobblestone streets, the grand old trees rising up from green backyards, the beautiful foyers in the stately Federal-style mansions, and the colorfully painted Queen Anne and Victorian dwellings. She also acknowledged the tensions between residential and commercial Georgetown, symbolized by the battle many residents are waging against a proposed Georgetown subway stop and the "undersirables" it might transport to their neighborhood. Having my own Georgetown history, as a former graduate student at Georgetown University who lived in the village for five years, I was able to add other aspects of local history and lore, such as the construction of the C&O Canal, begun in the 1820s, and how the New Deal and World War II brought a flood of diplomats and bureaucrats to town. The next morning the students would get to explore Old Georgetown on their own.

Their history lesson over, they were free to sleep, read, or wander about town; the only stipulation was a 2:00 A.M. curfew. The KDR boys, thirsty for a beer, wanted to scout out "the local talent," so I suggested the Old Martin's Tavern, where some of FDR's cabinet hammered out the intricacies of the New Deal and where Senator Lyndon Johnson devoured steak for dinner. Jennifer and I took off for a drink at Clyde's saloon.

It was midnight when we began our brisk four-block walk, chatting about the upcoming presidential election. We were only a few yards outside her store when we sensed someone's presence behind us. Out of the corner of my eye I saw a demented-looking man move alongside. In an instant he had pulled a .38 from his raincoat, held it to my head, and demanded, "Give me all your money." Jennifer replied that she had none, and he pushed her aside. He ordered me to lie down spread-eagled on the sidewalk. He leveled his gun at my head and began digging through my pockets as I tossed my wallet onto the brick sidewalk. He was a tall, barrel-chested Hispanic in his midtwenties, wearing a blue ski hat, his stubbly, unshaven face had angry, desperate eyes that flashed: Volatile, dangerous crackhead. Never before had I felt so helpless—one pull of the trigger and I'd be history. After frisking me down for ten seconds that seemed like eternity, he took off, running for the dense natural cover of nearby Rock Creek Park, my wallet and loose change in hand. For a minute I lay on the sidewalk stunned, trying to process what had just transpired. Jennifer and I checked again and again with each other to make sure everything was all right. Then I stood up, dusted myself off, and together we walked back to the shop to call the police. My main concern was how to avoid alarming the students unnecessarily. Even though my stomach was doing somersaults, I would have to downplay the incident to prevent a wave of student paranoia before the trip even got going. Although the mugger had gotten away with all my credit cards, my driver's license, and seventy dollars, he had missed the ten crisp one-hundred-dollar bills in an envelope in my sport coat. I tried to be Mr. Positive, thinking how lucky I had been, meanwhile stuffing the thousand bucks into my shoe in case there was a next time. Only later that evening, as I was trying to sleep, did the haunting apparition of my attacker's face and the memory of the cold barrel of his gun against my warm forehead bring on feverish nausea.

Within minutes of my calling the police, two patrol cars arrived at the shop, as well as an undercover detective on foot. Jennifer and I told them what had happened. When I reported that the mugger only got seventy dollars, one of the officers snickered, "Only seventy! They'll kill you for five if they're desperate for crack." We got into a police car and went cruising for the suspect. We followed a trail of my business cards, rifled from my wallet, that led us directly to the entrance of Rock Creek Park.

Simple geography, namely Rock Creek Park, has long divided Washington into two different worlds—one the world of impoverished inner-city realities and drug-related violence and the other the elegant high life of a great world capital. There is little sign that the enormous cultural and social distance between northwest and southeast Washington is narrowing. Only now the violent crime has leapt the firebreak into the wealthier enclaves such as Georgetown. Crack addicts, like bank robbers, are going where the money is, for a quick, easy hit on the affluent. In 1987, when William Colby, the former director of the CIA, was mugged at gunpoint while walking near his Georgetown home, the occurrence carried an even heavier freight of symbolism when Colby commented, "I've been shot at all over the world, but never mugged." Rock Creek Park is no longer solely a barrier between races and classes but a getaway route out of Georgetown for crack criminals. The 1,750-acre park has become Sherwood Forest, where the criminals steal from the rich not to give to the poor but to inject, inhale, sniff, or smoke their lives away with no prospect of a way out. "Once they hit the park it's hard to find them," an officer said, stating the obvious, as they shone a searchlight into the brush. Back in the patrol car we heard a crime in the making over the radio—a gang shooting taking place. "We'll pretend we didn't hear that," he said. "I'm not getting involved in that mess." They took us back to the bookstore, where wide-eyed students were anxious for all the details. To put the mugging in context, I told them I had lived in Washington for five years and had never been a crime victim. I spoke factually about the changes that had occurred in Washington. In the three decades since President Kennedy wittily described Washington as a city of Southern efficiency and Northern charm, it has been transformed into a virulent mutation of Dodge City. Our nation's capital has also become the murder capital of America, with an average of one murder every sixteen hours. Officials estimate that 80 percent of the city's shootings and murders are drug related. As in other U.S. cities, the spread of crack cocaine is the fuse that has ignited this wave of violence.

While all this was happening, I learned later from Frank, he had got his friend, Joe, off to National Airport and driven up Wisconsin Avenue to the "Social Safeway," so known because people shop there hoping to meet new, well-placed contacts. Frank was uninterested in contacts, he only wanted the Safeway parking lot to sleep for what remained of the evening; there was no space for the Majic Bus on the narrow Georgetown streets. He was too exhausted to worry that the police might bang on his door in the middle of the night demanding that he shove off. With the bus empty, Frank made an inventory of urgently needed repairs. He stalked each compartment with a roll of duct tape, taping up hanging wires and covering sharp metal edges. Of all the fancy tools he brought along, he knew that in the end a simple roll of duct tape would be his most reliable friend.

Next Frank opened the secret storage compartment above the driver's seat and pulled down three objects he considered essential for our journey: First, a small black-and-white framed photograph of a sneering Clint Eastwood—Frank's only real hero—from the movie *The Good, the Bad and the Ugly*, which Frank placed behind the driver's seat. A framed poster of a hanged cowboy, dangling from a tree, only his spurred boots and pants legs showing, with the caption NEVER STEAL A STETSON—which Frank displayed prominently on the side door as a deterrent to anyone so much as touching his hat, much less having the audacity to try it on. Finally he pulled out a giant Rand McNally road map of the United States, which he unrolled with all the dignity and respect of a Talmudic scholar opening a sacred scroll. Spreading it out, he attempted to smooth the creased edges and wrinkles with the sleeve of his jeans jacket, but he realized it would be impossible to keep a working map in mint condition. America would be there for the students, large and durable if slightly worn at the edges, nothing a little Super Glue couldn't fix. He wrestled the map, in all its glory, into place right next to Clint Eastwood. He was proud of the map; with it the Majic Bus could go anywhere. Without it the Majic Bus was just a common carrier whose horizon would stretch only from point A to point B.

With the map up, Frank's Majic Bus dream was now officially a reality. He grabbed a black marker and drew a straight line down I-95 from New York to Washington, adding the date 3/28 with a circle around it. The students would be able to chart our daily progress. Frank told me the next day that as he stared at the map, tears welled up in his eyes; his dream had come true. Embarrassed by the map's symbolic power and the up-surge of emotion it elicited, he thought of his stint in the marines, where one is made to salute a government-supplied symbol, the flag. Now Frank had his own symbol of America, his map. In mock imitation of his Parris Island days, he smartly clicked his cowboy boots together and offered Rand McNally his heartfelt salutation. Exhausted from his nonstop dash from Oklahoma, his body still functioning on Tulsa time, followed by the pressure-cooker drive from New York to DC, Frank collapsed on a mattress in the front sleeping compartment and immediately dropped off to sleep to the distant wail of sirens, his beloved Stetson pulled over his eyes.

3

Virginia Is for Lovers of Thomas Jefferson and Sam Shepard

The road's what counts. Don't worry about where it's goin'.
—SAM SHEPARD

GEORGETOWN ON AN EARLY SUNDAY MORNING—THAT glorious time of the week when there is no traffic, just untouchable silence—helps transport back in time the cobblestone streets, redbrick sidewalks, and Federal, Queen Anne, and Victorian dwellings for a few, all-too-brief hours. Without the crush of weekend invaders and midnight shadows who descend on this Washington town-unto-itself, Georgetown once again becomes a serene, small-town urban village of storybook homes and lovely gardens. On this particular late-March morning the giant brass doorknobs of the homes glinted seductively, gateways to hidden historical treasures within. Birds were chirping, cats were lolling, and wary watchdogs were wagging their normally suspicious tails. Even the shards of brown and green bottles, remnants of Saturday night's debauch, scattered

60

over the warm red bricks glistened jewellike, showing off their jagged prisms as they basked in the sun.

I was one with the cats, dogs, and shards, especially grateful to have survived the mugging, whistling "Zip-a-Dee-Do-Dah" to rekindle my normal disposition as I brewed good-morning pots of coffee for the still-sleeping students. When the coffee machine sputtered its last drop and hissed, I roused them out of their sleeping bags with an offer they couldn't refuse: a mug of java and a picture-perfect day. They were ebullient— the night in the bookshop apparently a tonic—and anxious to begin an afternoon of sightseeing. Independently they consulted maps and guidebooks, picked destinations, splashed water on their faces, and bolted out to explore Washington. I had made it course policy to encourage individual students to visit whichever historical sites and museums interested them most when we were in major cities. They would get enough group touring on the road, and it was equally important for students to pursue personal passions and interests on their own. The only stipulation I imposed was that they record what they saw and learned in their journals.

Dan was especially keen on photographing the town houses and shop facades of Georgetown, seeing the charming redbrick community as a repository of fascinating architectural photo ops. He produced some classic magazine shots—the entrance gates of Dumbarton Oaks, the early-nineteenth-century Georgian-style mansion in which the groundwork for the UN was laid in 1944; Georgetown Pharmacy on Wisconsin Avenue, for years a formal gathering spot for some of Washington's most celebrated luminaries, like Art Buchwald and David Brinkley; the Scott-Grant House on R Street, in which President Ulysses S. Grant summered to escape the steamy heat of the White House; the wall behind Evelyn Nef's home on which her artist friend Marc Chagall had created a mosaic; the Old Stone House, Washington's only surviving pre-Revolutionary building; Mount Zion Church on 29th Street, the first black church in the city and once a stop on the Underground Railroad; and the colorful doors and fascinating flower boxes of the town houses surrounding Georgetown University, the oldest Jesuit school in the country. Assigned the role of trip photographer, our "collector of images," Dan took on his assignment with a zeal and passion worthy of Dorothea Lange and Robert Frank—or should I say Matthew Brady, since we were in Washington. Only twenty-two, Dan is already one of the most promising photographers in America. He had almost not taken the American Odyssey course because he would miss free-lance filming the April 5 march from the White House to the Mall near the Capitol in support of abortion rights, which he had helped to organize. Dan, who often wore pro-Choice and Year of the Woman T-shirts, claimed that the Washington march would draw at least a half million people; he was right. A graduating senior, Dan ultimately decided to forgo the march, because "there will be other marches, but I'll never have another chance to take American Odyssey." The upcoming march was a central concern for Dan, Alison, and some of the other students, who worried that *Roe* v. *Wade*, the 1973 Supreme Court decision recognizing a constitutional right to abortion, would soon be reversed by right-to-life groups.

I was glad that my students were committed activists, but it was equally gratifying to watch Dan's professionalism as he spent every waking moment angling his camera for the perfect shot, sometimes lying on streets or sidewalks or atop the Majic Bus to capture the soul of America.

Since many students had already visited Washington either with their parents or on their own, we decided not to spend much time on a standard tour of our nation's capital. We would go past the Washington Monument, the Vietnam Memorial, and the White House collectively on our way out of town, enjoying the cherry blossoms in all their pastel glory. Of those who had spent the afternoon at the Mall, most were drawn by the Lincoln and Jefferson memorials and the massive Federal Triangle complex, a monument to anonymous thousands of government officials. At the Lincoln Memorial student interest focused more on the reflecting pool and the site where more than two hundred thousand people had gathered to hear Dr.

Martin Luther King, Jr., deliver his famous "I Have a Dream" speech in August 1963 than in the statue of arguably our greatest president.

Tom Tolan, an impassioned history buff, couldn't understand why there was no monument to Franklin Delano Roosevelt, the four-term Democratic president who steered the country through the depression and World War II in the face of his own personal struggle with crippling polio, which left him in a wheelchair. It gave me great joy to inform Tom that after thirty years of squabbling over the matter on Capitol Hill, money had finally been appropriated and ground broken for a long-overdue tribute to FDR to be erected on the Tidal Basin in 1995. Thanks is due in part to Democratic Congressman Claude Pepper, a veteran of the New Deal and to his dying breath a consummate lobbyist and representative of his elderly Floridan constituents. On his deathbed Pepper extracted a promise from that lapsed Democrat, then-President Ronald Reagan, to build a memorial for FDR. It took the relentless lobbying efforts of William J. vanden Heuvel, president of the Franklin and Eleanor Roosevelt Institute, to finally make this dream into a reality.

Washington, our first stopover, brought home to me an important lesson: Student interests vary and need to be respected. Nothing illustrated this observation more clearly than a summary of the destinations various contingents chose for their afternoon in DC. Besides seeing the monuments, one group headed to Ford's Theater, the site of Abraham Lincoln's assassination by John Wilkes Booth on April 14, 1865, as the president watched a production of *Our American Cousin*. Another was off to the Phillips Collection for the paintings of such American modernists as John Marin, Georgia O'Keeffe, and Arthur Dove. Still others were content to hang out and stroll around Georgetown, browsing the shops; relaxing among the flowers, shrubs, and trees of Dumbarton Oaks; or taking in the mausoleums, crosses, and gravestones of Oak Hill Cemetery's amphitheater of the dead on a hill overlooking Rock Creek Park. There they could pay special homage at the resting place of playwright and diplomat John H. Payne, remembered today primarily for his song "Home Sweet Home," expressing a sentiment that had no perch in student memory for the next six weeks. Their home now was the Majic Bus, a fact of life they would soon comprehend in all its implications.

Frank was to pick us up at precisely 3:00 P.M. for the ride to Monticello, Thomas Jefferson's home in Charlottesville, Virginia. As the students congregated back at the bookshop I heard all their tales. Darlene Dudash had caught Potomac fever, ready to join that Washington tribe known as the Hill People, a subculture of recent college graduates who hold many of the nineteen thousand staff jobs in the offices of senators, representatives, and congressional committees on Capitol Hill. First she was going to law school in Ohio, then to return to her native New Jersey and she would enter politics after passing the bar. Then she would return to Washington as a Hill Person, all right—as a congresswoman. She wanted to become a public servant, to improve people's lives through government. If she couldn't become Darlene Dudash, New Jersey congresswoman, she'd find some other way to serve the people, probably as a district attorney.

Tom Tolan, the class political history maven, also wanted to enter public service after graduation, though his current goal was not so lofty. All he wanted was "a job. I just want to be one of the three hundred thousand bureaucrats in the federal government's Washington work force." To Tom living inside the Beltway was something devoutly to be pursued, a mark of distinction in itself. But lack of money might keep him from achieving even that modest dream, for the only "jobs" he could find were nonpaid internships. Entry-level positions in Washington are now often unpaid, not only in government but in the press and lobbying organizations as well, effectively limiting the flow of applicants to those families wealthy enough to be able to subsidize an apprenticeship to get their kids on track. Tom didn't have that luxury and wondered how he was expected to survive in an expensive city like Washington without a paying job. Blind ambition was not goading Tom; he had no burning desire to get rich; he simply wanted a meaningful eighteen-thousand-dollar Beltway starter job, and if he found one he'd be only too glad to pay his share of taxes.

Kevin had heard about a local outfit called Gross National Product that conducted scandal tours of DC's more outrageous landmarks. He asked whether we could take their tour and skip Charlottesville. The twenty-seven-dollar itinerary includes watering holes where John Tower drank to excess, the alley adjacent to Gary Hart's house in which Donna Rice made her backdoor debut, the building in which Fawn Hall shredded documents for Oliver North, and the spot on which first Secretary of the Treasury Alexander Hamilton was blackmailed by his lover's husband. I convinced Kevin to purchase a copy of *The Quayle Quarterly* instead, to fulfill his need to make politics into theater of the absurd, little realizing that spring day that Kevin was purchasing what would in November become a collectible, when its subject lost the election. Feeling shortchanged, Kevin's only response was, "Denial ain't just a river in Egypt."

One of the more remarkable contributions the Bush administration made to American culture was giving us Dan Quayle as vice president. Quayle's meteoric rise, it seemed to me, eradicated two centuries of divisive ethnic jokes and slurs by making him an all-purpose whipping boy of American humor. The nation took up the now-departed veep as a national pastime. Quayle's latest gaffe took the place of the typically crude ethnic campus jokes that once made the rounds. His classic misrendering—"What a waste it is to lose one's mind"—is a shoe-in for inclusion in future dictionaries of quotations under "nincompoop." All my students, even the Republicans, had a favorite Quayle howler. My own personal favorite was his attempt to persuade the Japanese to remove trade barriers to American rice: "Japan," he said, "has to put some rice on the table." A believer in the people-living-in-glass-houses theory of compassion, I am careful not to sit in judgment of anyone misspelling *potato*, but when the man from Indiana who was just a heartbeat away from becoming president misspelled the word and had to be corrected by a fifth-grader, it occurred to me that Quayle's great contribution was to demonstrate that one of

America's fundamental myths was still alive: Anyone can become president of the United States.

Just as the last students straggled in, Frank pulled in front of the bookshop with the bus. While we were traipsing around Washington he had been busy duct-taping and rearranging. A new and sensible rule had been enacted: From now on only a sleeping bag and a small book bag would be allowed aboard the bus. For the sake of sanity and space, all other bags would be stored in the luggage bay. Frank beamed like a proud new father as he showed off the mounted icons: his Rand McNally map of America and his beloved Clint Eastwood mug shot. Time was working against us if we were going to make Monticello before closing, so we offered our generous host, Jennifer, warm thanks and piled onto the bus. Frank gave us the first of his many cleanliness lectures, admonishing against leaving the toilet lid open or letting food crumbs fall on the floor. It was difficult enough living together in close quarters, and garbage would attract maggots, roaches, and ants, he warned, and we would itch our way across America. This was a spiel we were to hear every so often from Frank, for our Neal Cassady turned out to be obsessed with cleanliness— not without reason.

As we were pulling out, Tom complained we hadn't spent enough time in Washington. He was right, of course, but I jokingly replied that Washington was a city of transients and we were just doing what everyone who comes to DC does—coming and going. Allen Drury, who wrote of Washington in his Pulitzer Prize–winning novel *Advise and Consent,* said it best: "It is a city of temporaries, a city of just-arrived and only-visitings, built on the shifting sands of politics, filled with people just passing through." Tom's complaint would be voiced many times throughout the American Odyssey course. My stock response: "Well, you've just had a taste. Now come back on your own and eat a meal."

———

Our "Sunday drive" route out of Washington was the Arlington Memorial Bridge, the Potomac River flowing beneath our wheels, our eyes fixed on the Custis-Lee mansion, owned by Robert E. Lee until the federal government confiscated the property and turned it into Arlington National Cemetery. The long rows of simple white marble gravestones caused a spontaneous moment of silence as we passed. While portions of Washington have deteriorated, the suburbs have been the beneficiary of an economic boom that has transformed metropolitan Washington into an archipelago of shiny high-rises and miniurban centers stretching from Tyson's Corner to Silver Spring, Maryland. All is not rosy in suburbia, though. If Washington has homeless people, its overbuilt suburbs of Arlington and Rosslyn have peopleless buildings. Sterile new office buildings and high-rise apartments, depressing enough in their banality, are doubly so as they beg for tenants.

But at least the welcoming sign, KEEP THE FREE STATE LITTER FREE, was an improvement over TREE-MENDOUS MARYLAND. As it turned out, however, we didn't need a sign to tell us we were in the oldest, largest, and wealthiest of the original American colonies—the state that has produced more U.S. presidents than any other—for we were surrounded by a sea of cars with bumper stickers that read, VIRGINIA IS FOR LOVERS. We just went with the flow. As we passed Patrick Henry Drive, a slick, modern brown Metro car rode above ground paralleling us, dropping crowds of Sunday escapees back at antiseptic concrete stations. Lest Sunday prove too liberating to these lovers of conformity, they can shuck off any notion of vitality or creativity by hopping back into their assembly-line cars and driving to their prefab homes for a microwave dinner on TV trays as "60 Minutes" drones on. Signs posted on the Metro stations warn: DANGER: HIGH VOLTAGE—NO TRESPASSING. There was no voltage as far as we Hofstra University escapees were concerned. The suburban life-style was the last thing we wanted to trespass on. We were headed into the South, to the foothills of the Blue Ridge Mountains, to Charlottesville and the surrounding horse country, and then smack into Asheville, North Carolina, and the Great Smoky Mountains and Atlanta, until we arrived in

New Orleans ready to dance till dawn to the sounds of Dr. John and Professor Longhair.

Although most people associate Charlottesville with Thomas Jefferson's Monticello and the University of Virginia, it is also home to America's greatest living playwright—a man whose literary output is on par with that of Eugene O'Neill, Tennessee Williams, and Arthur Miller—Sam Shepard. His unique gumbo of styles—using mythical American heroes, rock-and-roll music, poetically unconventional language—and his ability to create surreal, dreamlike American landscape images set Shepard apart from more traditional American dramatists. No other American playwright has won more than two Obie awards. Shepard has collected ten, plus a Pulitzer Prize for drama for his *Buried Child*. Raised in Duarte, California, which is not much more than an avocado grove, Shepard has written of the sensation he always experiences driving to the Deep South, a sensation I share: "Now I am heading in the right direction. Away from the quaint North. Away from lobsters and white churches and Civil War graveyards and cracker-barrel bazaars. Toward the swamps, the Bayou, the Cajuns, the crocodile." Sam Shepard was on my mind a great deal during those six weeks. When that gun had been pointed at my head by a man looking for a "hit" of crack, I had thought of the hit man, Hoss, in *The Tooth of Crime*. "I think there's something about American violence that to me is very touching," Shepard told Michiko Kakutani of the *New York Times* in a 1982 interview. "In full force, it is very ugly, but there's also something very moving about it because it has to do with humiliation."

In the sober post-mugging aftermath I actually began to feel sorry for the man who had robbed me, for a fellow citizen who had sunk to such depths of violent desperation. I imagined him crouched, wild-eyed and paranoid, in some cold-water, rat-infested squatters' flat in southeast DC, nerves shattered, neurons firing at random in his coked-out brain, staring at my driver's license photo, hating my tie-wearing whiteness, racking the dregs of his brain for some way to score some quick cash from the license, perhaps by selling it to some underage bicycle bandit for a few bucks or for a fake Rolex or for a couple hits from a crack pipe. What a way to go through life—helpless, hopeless, in abject poverty in an unpredictable assassin's world, living hour to hour for the next angry fix, unable to get a firm grip.

The robbery had the unanticipated side effect of kicking me into a more frivolous, carefree mood, a hunger for now, not tomorrow. Sure it was important for the students to learn about America, but life's fragility made me decide that it was equally important for them to have fun, to loosen up, to scream into the night air, to jam our six weeks full of enough joyous memories to fill a lifetime. No longer would I verbally or mentally put down the students for what they didn't know. Life was too short. I would accept them for who they were now. I would refrain from imposing my political views on them, and I would not try to make them adhere to overly strict regulations. I had important things to learn from them.

After only a day on the road, one of the most important things I had learned was just how deep the resentment and bitterness of the recession-squeezed Yo generation runs; by *Yo generation*, I mean the post-baby-boomers now in their twenties who face a bleak job market and possess attitudes of apathy and cynicism toward the America of their parents and the future of civilization on planet Earth. "Boomerangers," as Kevin calls them—the first generation in America that is leaving the home nest only to return a few years later. They see themselves saddled by a five-trillion-dollar debt plus a plethora of economic problems, not of their own making, that defy solution: a declining standard of living, a longer workweek, the end of the American dream of upward mobility. Urban ills have compounded: homelessness and violence, town-hall corruption, battered women, cops on the take, garbage-strewn boulevards, syringe-littered playgrounds, handgun hellos, elementary schools equipped with metal detectors, broken billboard boasts, dingy day-care centers, polluted air, hazardous waste dumps, and growing racial hatred and animosity. Thanks for the inheritance, folks, is a recurrent theme. To the Yo generation, it wouldn't be quite so bad if their elders just admitted they'd screwed up, asked for forgiveness, and passed the plague torch, but no, they add to the sins of profligacy an insufferable self-righteousness and arrogance. The Yoers look at their "hypocritical" parents as representatives from the only generation ever that took what they inherited, skimmed the cream, left America in worse shape than ever before, and then had the greedy gall to hurl insults at their "lazy" latchkey children. The Yo generation believes that action counts and winsome words mean next to nothing.

As we bounced along on the Majic Bus and the road began to take on a little altitude, I jettisoned any notion of the search for deeper meaning or spiritual quest and all the psychobabble that flows so freely from the lips of paunchy New Age professors. We would work hard and play hard. And though we would study Bill Moyers's America, we would live like Evel Knievel flying over Snake River Canyon on his motorcycle. We would make a memory.

I looked around at the students talking and chatting, and I imagined them as wrinkled, parchment-skinned ninety-year-olds existing in old folks' biospheres or waking one morning, peering out of the blinds at the falling leaves of autumn, taking inventory of days long gone, a videotape of ghosts fast-forwarding through their consciousness. Freezing the frame on their college days, they would recall some Majic Bus adventure, and a frisson of pleasure would ripple through them, and they would smile. It would be 2062; their grandchildren would listen to their tall tales of a magic time when a diesel-fueled Majic Bus roamed America, igniting a brief, sweet moment—perhaps the only moment when their hair blew defiantly in the wind and America stood receptive at their feet.

In another fundamental way, too, Sam Shepard helped me understand a side of America I tended to dismiss with intellectual disdain. From the vantage point of a mobile home in Duarte, Shepard fills his America with mobility, choices, options, however vulgar they may appear to the effete

70

classes: skies studded with illuminated logos of fast-food restaurants, strip shopping centers, air-conditioned malls with planted asphalt seas, Holiday and Ramada inns, twenty-four-hour restaurants, multiplex cinemas, garden apartments, discount stores, factory outlets, and deposit-and-run banks. It's easy to dismiss this side of America as banal and common—which, truth be known, was my "intellectual" reaction before reading Shepard. He convinced me I was out of touch with the majority of the American people when I mourned the closing-down of a ma-and-pa store because a Wal-Mart had come to town. The Wal-Mart is a sign of local status, not decline. According to Tom Wolfe, these franchise signs are "the new landmarks of America, the new guideposts, the new way Americans get their bearings." Shepard's insight into the franchising of the American landscape has become mine: The franchised sameness and subdivisional sprawl are to be viewed as "magical, mystical junk." Midas Mufflers and Jiffy Lubes, Hardees and Fuddruckers, Sears and J. C. Penneys, Kmarts and Wal-Marts, 7-Elevens and Stop and Gos, Dunkin' Donuts and IHOPs, Bob Evanses and Denny's, Dairy Queens and TCBYs, Red Lobsters and Steak and Ales, Pizza Huts and Little Caesars, the Jehovah's Witnesses and the PTLs are magical, mystical businesses that nourish the American psyche. Once the magic and efficiency are acknowledged, it is easier to swallow, to tolerate, to enjoy. American intellectuals should ignore the European critics and loosen up. They need to read the Book of Mormon in a Taco Bell and get in groove with the funky side of America—the side they tend to dismiss as pop trash and wrongly malign as evidence of our national decline. I made a pact with myself: Only an occasional easy cheap shot at America's great magical, mystical junk strips, now the heart of nearly all cities and towns. And I adopted a joking maxim: Never trust anybody who doesn't eat fast food or has never set foot in a pastel-painted Clifford May ranch house.

All this was crossing my mind as we drove through Fairfax County, Virginia, the new capital of magical, mystical junk. We left State Route 66 (not the famous Route 66 that used to run from Chicago to Santa Monica) and got on 29 south to Charlottesville. A red-and-yellow sign, GUNS AND SOUVENIRS 29 MILES, stood comfortably alongside a Wendy's

71

with the same color scheme, a giant inflatable Frosty Cup balloon tethered to the roof. A handpainted plywood sign offered peaches at a roadside stand with a rusted, corrugated-steel roof straight out of a Walker Evans photo from *Let Us Now Praise Famous Men.* Following close on was an official sign, produced by some poor sod at some Tidewater penitentiary, for the JAMES MADISON HIGHWAY (SEMINOLE TRAIL), and a white wooden shed peddling BASEBALL CARDS 1–8 DAILY.

The farther away from metropolitan DC we got, the nicer the natural scenery. Soon our eyes took in rolling green pastures with white picket fences and staggered bales of hay punctuating the scattered aluminum-sided split-level houses with long gravel driveways, plastic lawn furniture, mowing machines, rusted TV antennas, and an occasional satellite dish— evidence that we were leaving urban congestion and that something more substantial, like the Blue Ridge Mountains, lay ahead. John Mellen-camp's *Scarecrow* cassette—a meditation on bank farm foreclosures— poured out of the speakers. The porch was brimming with students staring out the windshield. As we crossed the Rappahannock River a steady rain pounded against the sheet-metal roof, producing an eerie lonesome sound that caused a cozy camaraderie to emerge, no longer driver, professor, and students, but all riders in the storm. As Mellencamp's grandmother sang "Grandma's Theme," an old-fashioned lullaby to introduce "Small Town," we were rolling by large white barns with silver silos; RABBITS FOR SALE signs; rock shops; old wooden churches turned country antique shops; shooting ranges; the Pig 'n' Steak Restaurant (pit-cooked); PAT ROBERTSON FOR PRESIDENT signs; Willie's Auction House, marked by a Confederate flag in front; the new cinder-block "Jesus Is Lord" Family Worship Center, austere in the extreme; and an advertisement for Rebel Yell Whiskey. We knew we were in Dixie. Alan broke the mood by asking me whether I was a "Star Trek" fan. My answer was no, which did not deter him from a lengthy and learned discussion of both the movies and the TV episodes. Not only did Alan know all the plots backward and forward, but he had memorized large chunks of dialogue. His favorite Captain Kirk saying, "You Klingon bastards, you killed my son," was mercifully short.

Janine Hayes, soon to be nicknamed Darkstar because of her penchant for "Star Trek" and the Grateful Dead, and a belief in reincarnation, fortune-telling, and other forms of mysticism, was sitting quietly on the porch, keeping mainly to herself. She concurred with Alan's detailed analysis of why the starship *Enterprise* would never have survived had it not been for "Bones" McCoy's medical cunning. For Janine, unlike most of the other students, journal writing was not a course assignment but rather a form of therapy that was already an important part of her life. At course end, when students turned in their journals for grading, hers was a unique piece of writing, shrewdly observant, portions deserving a wider audience. But on the way to Charlottesville, I had no sense yet of her intellectual depth. Our first conversation was about folk music and the women's movement. Before long, she shyly asked—with a bit of a Diane Keaton nervous flutter—whether she could play the tape resting unnoticed in her lap. Out came the voice of Melanie, a folk sensation of the sixties who had long ago been relegated to the cutout bins without even a last hoorah in the "nice price" category, singing "Look What They've Done to My Song, Ma"—resurrected by a nineteen-year-old Hofstra student. "Melanie and Joni Mitchell are two of my favorites," Janine volunteered. And so, as we headed to Charlottesville in the rain, it was Melanie setting the mood, her defiant, liberating voice banishing from memory my cluttered desk, academic pettifoggery, tiresome bureaucrats, phone machines, television, and karma killers of all sorts. All the people and things that were jammin' me had been left behind, erased by the power of song.

We were now in Madison County, home to our fourth president as well as to the Wonderful World of Miniature Horses emporium, with its profitable sideline of Vietnamese potbellied pigs—the trendy pet of 1992— popular because the small critter can be taught tricks and to use a litter box and, when the novelty wears off, provides a little nouvelle-cuisine pork chop.

The sight of a Jefferson National Bank reminded me of my teaching duties, and as we rode along, I began lecturing on the genius of Thomas Jefferson. When it came to a giant like Jefferson, my voice changed to one of utmost respect.

Elected to the Virginia House of Burgesses in 1769, in 1767 he became a delegate to the Continental Congress, where he was appointed to a committee to draft a Declaration of Independence. Jefferson, reflecting the Enlightenment philosophy of John Locke, wrote the first draft, which asserted that all men are created equal and are endowed by their creator with certain "inalienable rights." To condemn the Declaration because African-Americans, Native Americans, and women were excluded from the polity is not only to sit in judgment in hindsight, using modern standards, but also to miss the prodigious seeds Jefferson planted. Given typical eighteenth-century values, it was a compelling argument for democracy—that each person is entitled to the protection of the law and that governments exist only with the consent of the governed. Although only a few students knew much about Jefferson the scholar, author, farmer, natural scientist, and architect, they all knew he was a slave owner who fathered illegitimate children with one of his slaves, Sally Hemings. That a man like Jefferson, an American hero in so many important ways, has been reduced to a slave-owning misogynist whose face is on the nickel pains me greatly, although I can understand that for those whose ancestors might have been Jefferson's chattels his image is irrevocably tarnished.

I bit my tongue at student unfamiliarity with Jefferson and simultaneously realized it was going to be a lot harder to stop sitting in judgment than I had imagined. I lectured at some length about his multifaceted career: his stints as minister to France and as the first U.S. secretary of state; his fear of the possibility of tyranny under a strong federal government; his constant conflict with Alexander Hamilton; his role in organizing the Democratic-Republican party in opposition to the Federalists; his difficulties as vice president under John Adams; the 1801 electoral tie with Aaron Burr and Jefferson's consequent selection as president by the House of Representatives; and his most important act as president—the Louisiana Purchase, in 1803. Jefferson, known for his wit, comes in handy when people call me lucky. I spout Jefferson back at them: "I'm a great believer in luck. The harder I work the more I have of it."

Soon we would be touring Monticello, the home he designed, but as we turned off 20 South and headed up a hilly, tree-lined road known for sharp turns and the Historic Mitchie Tavern, luck wasn't with me (I had no Jeffersonian saying to cover this situation). To my dismay and embarrassment the gates to Monticello were closed. It was 4:45 and although people were still milling about, no more tours were offered. Determined to get in somehow, Kevin and I jumped the gate and went looking for a park ranger to negotiate with as the daylong drizzle turned to snow flurries at the high altitude. We didn't have to look very far for a ranger, as one came charging right at us. I explained our situation. Although he sympathized with our plight, a rule was a rule: Monticello was closed. But he had a tip, which he said he would disavow if we were caught: Cross the road to the sign for Mountaintop Farm, disregard the PRIVATE, KEEP OUT warnings, and climb straight to the top. To the east we would get an awesome view of the Virginia Piedmont farmlands that form what Jefferson called his "sea view," with the site of his birthplace, Shadwell, in the foreground. To the west we could spy on the city of Charlottesville; the University of Virginia, which Jefferson founded and made the "hobby" of his old age; and beyond it the foothills of the Blue Ridge Mountains. "The kids will get a kick out of it," he told me. "The view from Mountaintop Farm is what you get on the nickel, and none of the tourists ever get to see it because of the NO TRESPASSING signs posted."

Disappointed that Monticello was closed, I chose the consolation prize and made the most of it, telling the students to follow me up to Mountaintop Farm. The moist flurries, the encroaching darkness, the strenuousness of the furtive climb left many students back at the bus, but ten of us were gone like wild geese in winter, determined to climb Mountaintop no matter how steep. Dan and Alison led the way. All I can say is, What a view. From that vantage point, the site of Jefferson's Monticello and its flower and vegetable gardens and budding dogwoods and rolling crests is enough to snatch what is left of your breath. There is something noble about Jefferson's domed Palladian home, something that strikes to the heart of what it means to be an American. This sentiment wasn't limited to a romantic history professor, for all the students perched on the mountain felt the same lump in the throat. No other moment during the entire American Odyssey elicited such a wave of patriotism, although perhaps *patriotism* is not quite the right word. Only on top of this mountain did we instinctively understand that America was and still is a dream, a process. The American experience is unique and it is ours. America isn't in decline, it is just being born. Dan looked at a nickel to make sure the ranger was right, and we lingered awhile longer. Alison rubbed mud on her face, anointing herself with a little bit of Jefferson's America. I finally broke the silence, indicating the need to retreat down the mountain back to the bus.

For those who had made the climb, American Odyssey had already hit a peak experience that would be with us forever. I thought about what Frank had said weeks ago back at Hofstra: "You never know when you are going to make a memory." I now also understood what John Steinbeck meant in *Travels with Charley* when he said that the first rule of traveling is to throw all plans out the window. I would take John Steinbeck's advice. We would try to stick to our itinerary, but if something came up we would ditch the scheduled event and go with the flow. From now on we would be lawless as snowflakes, in Walt Whitman's words, no more being held hostage to a piece of paper.

We stopped in Charlottesville at Mr. Jefferson's University of eighteen thousand students (in a town of forty-three thousand) to stroll around the grounds and admire the neoclassical architecture. During the Civil War, Charlottesville was spared much of the destruction that leveled so much of the South. The well-to-do postwar settlers scattered themselves throughout the idyllic Albemarle County horse country, attracted by its natural beauty. Settlers are still coming. Charlottesville and environs, in my opinion, are home to more essential creative writers than any other city in the United States—with the obvious exceptions of New York, New Orleans, San Francisco, and Los Angeles. But I write this with hushed pen because Sam Shepard, Peter Taylor, Ann Beattie, Rita Mae Brown, and Mary Lee Settle want to keep their secret quiet. In recent years refugees from Hollywood have also been arriving: Lee Majors, Kate Jackson, Sissy Spacek, Maxwell Reid (Venus Flytrap on "WKRP"), and Jessica Lange are the most prominent. Muhammad Ali, the Heavyweight Champion of the World for Eternity, considers the Charlottesville area home. No one has bothered to make a list of the industrialists, business executives, and financiers who have retired to Charlottesville or escape there on weekends, but a short list would include a Bronfman of distillery wealth, a Busch of the brewery family, and an heir to the Scripps-Howard publishing fortune.

But, as the Majic Bus pulled up to a Bonanza Steakhouse for an all-you-can-eat buffet dinner, the world of pheasant under glass and fox hunts was far removed from our reality. Frank had selected Bonanza "because the food was cheap, steady, and plenty." Besides, there was a sewage drain behind the kitchen where Frank could drop a hose and empty our already full septic tank.

After dinner we prepared for our first night on the bus. We had forgone the Skyline Drive through the Shenandoah National Park for the sake of time. Now we would also have to bypass some historical sites, such as Woodrow Wilson's birthplace in Staunton and Stonewall Jackson's house in Lexington, since it was way past closing time. Instead we made a quick stop at the Natural Bridge, just off I-81 south of Lexington. Dubbed one of the Seven Wonders of the World by somebody, the stunning rock formation, known to religionists as the Bridge of God, is one of Virginia's must-see sites. In addition to its natural beauty, the rock formation served an important and functional role in the Revolutionary War. American soldiers poured molten lead from the top, and as the drops fell, they were shaped into spheres by gravity and cooled in the waters below. Troops harvested the spheres for bullets in their battles against the redcoats. (In 1774 Thomas Jefferson had petitioned King George III for a grant of land that included Natural Bridge, and the king acceded on July 5, 1774—two years almost to the day before the signing of the Declaration of Independence—perhaps thinking he was forestalling trouble by buying off the colonists.)

Natural Bridge's historical role is lost, however, on the hordes of modern-day pilgrims who flock there to watch the so-called "Drama of Creation," a light show with classical music, depicting the Book of Genesis. Over the loudspeakers the narrator, in an appropriately deep, patriarchal voice, intones as solemnly as if he were the basso profundo Lord himself. Natural Bridge has become a mecca for Christian fundamentalists seeking the Lord in rock, with the help of a laser performance to show them the way. They claim that on the highest portion of the rock arch, shadows at sunset replicate a large image that resembles the American coat of arms—indisputably an interesting and beautiful natural phenomenon. Still, the privately owned Natural Bridge seems more like the handiwork of a Hollywood set designer than that of the Almighty. It was especially hard to imagine God in the giant gift shop with its religiomechanical gizmos.

On our way back to the bus, a Bible-thumping minister and a young helper in a T-shirt that read, RICHMOND: OUR NATION'S CAPITAL, handed us pamphlets headlined: "If your rock is dark let Jesus provide the spark." When Kevin mentioned that we had been having an off day—unable to tour Monticello, Stonewall Jackson's House in Lexington, and "some other historical home in Staunton"—the padre flinched in empathetic anguish, saying, "Oh, no! You missed the Statler Brothers Complex in Staunton." It turns out that the elementary school attended by the famous country-gospel quartet has been converted into a museum of Statler Brothers Bible-singing memorabilia. When I indicated that it was Woodrow Wilson's birthplace we had wanted to visit, he responded, "I didn't know Wilson was from Virginia, let alone Staunton, and I'm in town all of the time. But that Statler collection would really have been something for the kids to see." (Well, at least the guy knew Woodrow Wilson had been president.) As we were departing, the soul saver asked for ten dollars for the pamphlets he had voluntarily handed us. One of the curmudgeonly H. L. Mencken truisms came immediately to mind: "Perhaps the most revolting character the United States has ever produced was the Christian business man."

The rest of the evening was like a giant slumber party: The rowdiness and first-day jitters had evaporated, and we just relaxed listening to Blind Faith's "Presence of the Lord" over and over again, a healing antidote to those religious rascals. Shari Berkowitz and I talked a lot about the Civil War that evening, her favorite subject. Throughout our journey Shari could always be counted on for three things: unwavering optimism, serious historical discourse, and a mean game of pool. When Shari spoke authoritatively about the Confederate partisan rangers John Hunt Morgan, John Singleton Mosby, and William Clarke Quantrill, you listened. And when she said, "Rack 'em up," you knew you were in for a licking.

One by one students dropped off to sleep sprawled on floor mattresses, five to a compartment. I overheard persistent student grumblings about the promised bunk beds, TVs, and other luxuries. The next day I gave my charges a choice: Either they quit grousing or I would personally purchase them a train ticket home. I said I felt that former Secretary of State Dean Acheson had been right when he said, "Complaints are a bore and a nuisance to all and undermine the serenity essential for endurance." The students chose to shut up and stick with the Majic Bus. A few days later Beth found a NO WHINING sign and posted it next to Clint Eastwood, another addition to our portmanteau of American Odyssey maxims.

Frank's plan was to drive us out of midatlantic Virginia on US-77 and catch I-40 in North Carolina, staying awake with the aid of a thermos of Dunkin' Donuts coffee. Somewhere near Asheville he would find a truck stop, park, and catch a few hours' sleep. After many uneventful hours whistling Dixie, he eventually pulled off at Hungry Homer's twenty-four-hour truck stop; inhaled a late-night grilled-cheese sandwich and ketchup-covered fries at Shirin's Restaurant; dieseled up at the Phillips 66 pumps; pulled off his lizardskin boots; put his sweaty, white-socked feet on the dashboard; and tilted back in his seat, content with just a few hours of trucker shuteye before the sun rose and he coffeed up once again, to start another new morning in America.

4

In Thomas Wolfe Country with Georgia on Our Minds

I think the true discovery of America is before us. I think the true fulfillment of our spirit, of our people, of our mighty and immortal land, is yet to come. I think the true discovery of our own democracy is still before us. And I think that all these things are certain as the morning, as inevitable as noon.

—THOMAS WOLFE

VEILED MOUNTAINS WERE AHEAD, AND DARK NORTH Carolina spruce forests, lining both sides of the highway, greeted me as I stood up in "bed"—the turquoise-colored hallway I called home—awakened by the hum of the wheels. The spruces immediately struck me as providential stalwarts, courageous protectors of the unspoiled wilderness from encroaching civilization, fortunate to have survived, a mere ax swing away from being sacrificed to the great god Interstate. The morning sun was just starting to shimmer off its drizzle-filled sleep, ready to artfully ward off the dark, ominous clouds that promised rain a county away. Frank had been burning up the road for an hour, listening to the Rolling Stones' *Exile on Main Street*, hankering for someone—anyone—to wake up and ride shotgun with him. I rolled up my sleeping bag; smiled at

Beth, who was stretching as she fumbled for the cigarettes she was not allowed to smoke, and I went digging for toothbrush and paste so I could start the day with at least a portion of my person peppermint fresh. "When you start seeing runaway-truck ramps, you know you're heading into the Great Smoky Mountains," Frank, ever the roads scholar, told us in a ruminative mood as he offered us his thermos of coffee, knowing full well that without it we would be zombies in no mood to talk. A small home-made billboard flashed the lure DEER BOWHUNTING, with an arrow directing deer-hunting motorists who wished to avoid the taste of gunpowder in their venison. The sign prompted Frank to launch into stories about Michigan rocker Ted Nugent—the Motor City Madman—as a bowhunting fanatic. Our lack of enthusiasm about bowhunting didn't slow Frank down.

After our late departure from Hofstra, the Georgetown mugging, the Washington whirlwind, and running behind schedule in Virginia, it felt great finally to be right on track, not a mile out of step. I was determined to stay on schedule for the day's three main events: Thomas Wolfe's House, the Biltmore Estate, and the Cherokee Indian Reservation.

Frank noticed our grimacing efforts to swallow his poisonous, more-potent-and-reprehensible-than-cowboy coffee and asked whether we wanted to get a "real" cup at the next exit. I leapt at the chance, particularly because Exit 65, Black Mountain, North Carolina, was home of a celebrated experimental arts school of the 1950s. Beth and I raced into the Black Mountain Family Restaurant for coffee to go, planning to inquire about the location of what once was Black Mountain College, an educational community active from 1933 to 1956, hoping we might be able to pay the grounds an early-morning visit. I asked a tobacco-chewing old-timer in overalls and a Braves cap—Milwaukee, that is—whether he knew its location. "The only Black Mountain school I know is the primary school across the street," he snorted, scratching a U.S. Navy anchor tattoo that took up a good portion of his right arm. From his loutish, unforthcoming, unfriendly reply, he immediately struck me as a person free of prejudice, despising all humans equally. Nonetheless I persisted, providing a brief précis of the famous experimental college where poets could study with Charles Olson, Robert Duncan, Ed Dorn, and Robert Creeley, where Franz Kline and Robert Rauschenberg taught painting, where John Cage and Robert Tudor taught music and Merce Cunningham taught modern dance. A dim bulb lit in the old-timer's memory palace, and at last he gave evidence that he understood what I was asking about. "We ran that bunch of crazies out of here forty years ago," he intoned as he spit tobacco juice into an empty jelly jar. "You won't find none of them fruitcakes around here. They're all dead from AIDS or are in prison, I'm sure," raising his voice loudly enough to burnish his well-established reputation as a local kingfish and a Jesse Helms follower.

I had been set up for this performance. When I pressed him further, he snarled, "Listen, Frostbelter, Black Mountain is the land of the sky, not the land of the high anymore." The sound of this living cartoon of a redneck putting down the extraordinary achievements of the Black Mountain School made me wonder how such enormous talents survived as long as they did in such a poisonous atmosphere. But I quickly reminded myself not to judge a town by the first—and in this case, the only—person we met.

The Land of the Sky, as the old-timer had called this region of western North Carolina, located on the losing side of the Mason-Dixon Line, is today filled not only with a handful of roadside rednecks who make a living selling mud coffee and tacky souvenirs but, more importantly, with some of our nation's finest artisans—weavers, woodworkers, and ceramicists as well as environmental activists living alongside the traditional, hardworking, and hard-luck mountaineers. The region is also the Appalachian home and spiritual wellspring of one of America's finest novelists: Thomas Wolfe. The Majic Bus was not simply visiting Asheville, the home of Thomas Wolfe—we were making a pilgrimage.

The Land of the Sky has a plenitude of other attractions for those without literary interests. For sportsmen the region is cherished for its fine fly-fishing and hunting, for its fast-flowing trout streams, and for the legendary black bears found on its scores of hiking trails. For senior citizens, Asheville, where the Blue Ridge meets the Great Smokies, is retirement heaven, at least according to Rand McNally, who rated it number one in the nation a few years ago. For children it is known for its summer nature camps, wildflower walks, and field schools. Tourists often visit the area to admire one of the artifacts of the robber-baron legacy of George Vanderbilt, who in 1895 erected a 250-room neo–French Renaissance château he called the Biltmore. For Civil War buffs, Asheville was the home of Zebulon B. Vance, North Carolina's dynamic governor during the War Between the States. But for me Buncombe County—in fact, the entire state of North Carolina—means Thomas Wolfe country.

With the students finally awake, Frank maneuvered into a wooded trailer park outside Asheville so we could take hot showers, make phone calls home, and do some toe-touching and stretching exercises. The campground owner, somewhat put off by our Big Bad Wolf marquee, allowed us to shower for two bucks a person. The students on tight budgets vied for free ones on the bus. As we sat around the desolate trailer park among scattered spruces, hemlocks, and firs, and cackling crows and winter wrens, all of us taking turns showering, Jay, who plays blistering lead blues guitar for a rock band on Long Island, broke out his acoustic six-string and launched into Stevie Ray Vaughan's "Empty Arms" and the Allman Brothers' "Melissa." I borrowed his guitar and followed with the Grateful Dead's "Friend of the Devil" and Steve Miller's "Joker." Although I am by no means in the same string league as Jay, as either a picker or a grinner, many students were nevertheless amazed to find that their professor could at least play with such reckless abandon while trying to approximate Bob Dylan's nasal twang. I later overheard one student remark, "Professor Brinkley would be good if he didn't sing like a wounded hound dog." Instead of letting this stinging assessment deflate my musician's ego, I chalked up the ill-considered opinion of an untutored student too brainwashed by Top Forty radio to appreciate that their professor was trying to sound like a mix of the hillbilly and country geniuses Hank Williams, Roy Acuff, Woody Guthrie, and Dylan himself. Self-justification is such a marvelous coping device: Truth be told, I have rhythm but I can't carry a note.

Six of us passed the time playing Nerf football—two-below-tap, two completes a first down—a game we perfected over the next six weeks, launching long, wobbly passes all across America—in truck stops, grassy fields, art-museum parking lots—occasionally wiping out with arms stretched in hopes of catching the sponge spheroid on gravel, grass, or asphalt. The hungrier students hoofed the half mile downhill for a Shoney Big Boys buffet breakfast—a repellent restaurant, according to the returnees, who were apparently unaware of humorist Roy Blount's first law of good fast food: "Avoid scrambled eggs assembled in vat-sized proportions." Other students lounged on a picnic table reading selected short stories from Thomas Wolfe's *From Death to Morning*, in preparation for touring his home in Asheville. Stefanie chatted with a retired couple from Chattanooga who were "doing" America in a weathered, primordial 1950s Elkhart, Indiana, RV tin-can special that called to mind a Steinbeck description in *The Grapes of Wrath:* "Half passenger and half truck, top-sided and clumsy." They advised Stefanie to tell her professor that no matter what else we did we must not miss the "amazing" Biltmore mansion. We didn't. While we showered and ate, Frank played Sherlock Holmes, trying to locate a mysterious oil leak. Wrench in hand, he emerged triumphant from under the bus, a Franz Kline abstraction of greasy black grime all over his face and arms, on which were also caked the white powder from several doughnuts. When Matt teased him for being a motorhead and a grease monkey, Frank shot back, "You can't analyze dirt unless you taste it."

Justin Buis, who smoked more cigarettes and ate more food during the journey than the rest of us combined, turned out to be a soulmate of Frank's and his stalwart mechanical assistant throughout the trip. While the other students came to appreciate the Majic Bus as their home away from home, Justin instinctively appreciated it as a machine. In his sophomore year at Hofstra, Justin opened his own business called Tender

Loving Care, an automobile-detailing service, which quickly attracted a diverse clientele ranging from Rolls-Royces to Pintos. Justin worships motorcycles and automobiles, the sound of a vehicle accelerating as sweet to his ears as bagpipes to a Scotsman. Like Hazel Motes in Flannery O'Conner's *Wise Blood,* Justin believes that "nobody with a good car needs to be justified." In high school, when other students studied Spanish or science or dreamed of beach parties or getting rich quick, Justin studied carburetors—and even dreamed about them. While the other students toured museums and historic homes, Justin's personal odyssey consisted of hanging out with Frank by the road, gossiping about various vehicles, guessing the age of a muffler by the rumble it made as it passed them, or analyzing and reanalyzing the stock-car-racing feats of Richard Petty— King of the Road, as Frank called him, for Petty had won the prestigious Daytona 500 seven times. I used to tease Frank that Richard Petty was a rank amateur compared to Junior Johnson, who had learned his driving skills while running moonshine in the hills of North Carolina, evading the meddlesome federal agents who put his daddy in prison. In his *Esquire* profile of Junior Johnson—"Great Balls of Fire"—Tom Wolfe described the auto bandit's white-lightning feats, calling him "the last American hero." Frank insisted that Junior Johnson was a figment of my television-watching imagination: "He sounds just like Luke and Bo Duke of 'The Dukes of Hazzard' driving the 'General Lee.' I'm sure that's where you're conjuring up this character from," refusing to believe it was the other way around.

Before we left the campground for Asheville, I lectured on Thomas Wolfe. Most of the students had confused the long-dead Thomas Wolfe (1900–1938) with the very-much-alive Tom Wolfe, whom they knew either from reading *The Electric Kool-Aid Acid Test* or *The Bonfire of the Vanities* or from seeing the movie version of the latter. Clarifying the common mix-up, I told them of Wolfe's creative genius, of his larger-than-life autobiographical manuscripts that editors Maxwell Perkins and Edward C. Aswell helped to shape into some of the most important pieces of literature ever produced in America. Wolfe worked as a writer and teacher in New York City and traveled all over the United States and Europe but never forgot his beloved Asheville and chronicled the town's headlong rush toward becoming a tourist and retirement center. I spoke of Wolfe's unsurpassed poetic sensitivity to the people and sounds of America and the South; his incredible pocket notebooks, which serve as an unsurpassed social history of the 1920s and 1930s; and his short and troubled life, which culminated in his early death at age thirty-eight. I mentioned Wolfe's passion for this country in all its glory and in all its loneliness. Not since Walt Whitman had an American poet or writer captured in words the essence of this big, lonely, vast continent in prose poems. As Wolfe wrote in *You Can't Go Home Again:* "We are so lost, so naked and so lonely in America. . . . Immense and cruel skies bend over us, and all of us are driven on forever and we have no home." I think about these words often, usually when I'm alone, driving down some highway at night, and they make me shiver and swallow hard. Wolfe's words are like listening to Hank Williams wail, "I'm so lonesome I could cry," while blues-drinking away sorrows in a smoky juke joint or noisy honky-tonk, the neon beer sign blinking eternally on and off, on and off. Wolfe's lyricism isn't rooted in nostalgia, for nostalgia is death. He feels the loneliness of America in his soul but presses on with healing optimism and hope for his country's redemption and never-say-die future: "I believe that we are all lost here in America, but I believe we shall all be found. . . . I think the true discovery of America is before us."

Some critics tend to belittle Thomas Wolfe's immense, landmark literary achievement, often by calling him an adolescent writer or an American primitive. Those deluded critics say that just because he was possessed of genius doesn't mean he wrote great novels. They point out the rambling, uneven passages in his prose and ridicule his giantism, formlessness, and rhetorical extravagance, saying that his novels lack compactness of statement and labeling his organization crude and unwieldly. But these supposed deficiencies are exactly what make Wolfe our native prose prodigy and his achievement so important—exactly why, like Whitman's, his "song of himself" is the song of America. As a writer Wolfe's strengths are America's strengths; his weaknesses are America's weaknesses. In an age when Hemingway reigned and modernists wanted simple, unadorned-statement prose, Wolfe was a postmodernist whose literary cup ranneth over in extravagance, just like America itself. "You want to make a perfect thing," he told John Hall Wheelock, "but I want to get the whole wilderness of the American continent into my work."

Thomas Wolfe is to American literature what Leo Tolstoy is to Russian literature—both great bards left over from the days of spoken literature. And as for purity of prose and common sense, no American writer has written more masterfully and with more ecstatic energy about both sides of the track—small towns and big cities, rich folk and poor folk—than Wolfe. In *You Can't Go Home Again*, Wolfe's last novel—the odyssey of an American in search of himself and in search of his native land—he asserts that every American ought to be required by law to read Emerson's wonderful essay "Compensation." It is my brash contention that every American ought to be required by law to read *Look Homeward, Angel* and *You Can't Go Home Again.* Fortunately I did not have to resort to legalism with several students, for I was able to inspire them to become interested in Wolfe by saying how much Kerouac had been influenced by the vitality of Wolfe's prose, modeling his first novel, *Town and the City*, on Wolfe's style. I also pleaded that if they read only one book in their twenties it should be *You Can't Go Home Again*—a masterful achievement only Norman Mailer and Tom Wolfe have had the courage to attempt to surpass in contemporary times. So, with Thomas Wolfe on the tip of everyone's tongue, instead of a bell sounding at the end of class we loaded onto the Majic Bus for downtown Asheville to visit 48 Spruce Street—which his mother called "The Old Kentucky Home"—the birthplace and boyhood home of this oversize genius of American letters.

Built in 1880 in Queen Anne style, Wolfe's white, shingled home, formally known as the Thomas Wolfe Memorial State Historical Site, is one of the oldest houses in downtown Asheville. Family pictures, clothing, and original furnishings fill the house, and eye-catching stained-glass windows abound. Wolfe's mother ran a boardinghouse here for years, and he used it as the setting of the autobiographical *Look Homeward, Angel*, in which he called Asheville "Altamont" and the house "Dixieland." Wolfe was represented by the book's protagonist, Eugene Gant. Indeed, *Look Homeward, Angel* abounds with identifiable locals throughout, given life eternally through Wolfe's fiction. In fact, around North Carolina they call it *Look Inward, Asheville*. The novel's title comes from a line from Milton's great poem "Lycidas," but Wolfe also had in mind real stone angels, imported from Italy by his father, that stood in the monument shop yard. Frank was thrilled to learn that Wolfe's father was a stone-cutter just like his grandfather. Wolfe is buried in Riverside Cemetery in the historic Montford District of Asheville, as is that master of the short story William Sydney Porter (O. Henry).

While I rocked on the porch swing of The Old Kentucky Home, the students went off on their own to explore Asheville, with instructions to meet back at the bus in two hours. The student expeditions that afternoon included strolling down Thomas Wolfe Plaza, visiting the Asheville Community Theatre, sipping cappuccino in an authentically hip "unredneck" coffeehouse, and photographing Highland Hospital, where Zelda Fitzgerald—wife of author F. Scott Fitzgerald and a writer as well—was institutionalized after her famous "crack-up." She died there in a fire in 1948. Zelda had heroic dimensions for women on the trip, for she had lived in the flapper fast lane, rejecting the role of domesticated passivity of the traditional woman and boldly embracing that of the modern "New Woman." Alison saw Zelda as "the Madonna of the 1920s." Many of the other students had grabbed lunch at Burt 'n' Harry's New York Deli, directly across from The Old Kentucky Home, still unable to let go of the corned-beef comforts of home. Meanwhile Jay and Dan, whom people often confused, mainly because they both have long, curly black hair, had an odd Asheville experience. As they left the cappuccino café they asked a street wino directions to Thomas Wolfe's home. "Come with me, boys," he replied, with a weird glint in his eyes. "I'll show you. Don't be afraid, I won't rob you." For reasons still inexplicable even to themselves, like sheep they followed this besotted shepherd down a back alley. When he turned around to look at them, wolf-eyed, as if they were lamb chops ready for the grill, panic struck and they fled in terror of real or imagined consequences. How could they have been so dumb, they asked themselves, walking down an alley just because some crazy led them there?

With the still-ashen Jay and Dan the last to return, we left downtown for the Biltmore estate to the spontaneous performance of a talkin' blues song called "Down the Alley" they composed to immortalize their homeboy stupidity. The robber-baron legacy was alive and well at the privately owned Vanderbilt estate, with an admission price of $18.95 for adults and no college discounts, making it an expensive proposition for students. They had seen mansions before and were dubious about blowing three days' worth of food money just to tour "the nation's largest private residence." I agreed the admission was steep but promised it would be a worthwhile investment. Reluctantly they dug into wallets to fork over the cash; none left disappointed.

George Washington Vanderbilt (1862–1914), the grandson of the great steamship and railroad financier Cornelius Vanderbilt, fell in love at first sight with the blue-tinted mountains of western North Carolina. In 1887 he began buying land south and west of Asheville, eventually acquiring 130,000 acres, including Mount Pisgah (5,749 feet), one of the most beautiful peaks in the Appalachians. George Vanderbilt was a dreamer and a doer, and when he boldly declared that he was going to build the finest country home in America, few doubted him. He immediately immersed himself in the study of architecture, forestry, and landscape gardening in preparation for the endeavor. Working with architect Richard Morris Hunt on the blueprints, Vanderbilt poured three million dollars into the construction, modeling his mansion on châteaus in France's Loire Valley. He spent millions more on improving the grounds. Frederick Law Olmstead, the designer of New York's Central Park, was Vanderbilt's landscape architect.

Vanderbilt may have been an extravagant fellow, but he also had a pragmatic side that proved beneficial to our nation, for he became a scientific farmer and stock breeder, as well as a pioneer in the science of forestry. When G. W. Vanderbilt showed off a pedigreed hog, it was an event of national importance. When he bred a prizewinning Jersey cow, it broke all records for milk production. When he built roads and trails through the great forest areas, they were models for what would become our national parks. In fact, Gifford Pinchot, Vanderbilt's superintendent of forests, went straight from the Biltmore to head the U.S. Division of Forestry in 1898.

On this particular afternoon fog hung over the Biltmore in little smoky clusters, the only ostensible source of moisture in the sodden air. It wasn't raining, but we were all damp. Since it was still early on the road, student cameras were poised for action, and they scrutinized the grounds for the most grotesque gargoyle or the perfect rosebush. Though we all took the guided tour of the mansion, we spent more time in the most beautiful walled garden imaginable. Inside, students tended to be more interested in the rare first editions in the twenty-thousand-volume library, the skylit court of palms filled with giant tropical greenery, and the indoor racquet courts, bowling alley, swimming pool, and mile-long kitchen—which must have had more pots, pans and knives than all the Williams Sonoma outlets in America combined—than in the Oriental rugs, Early American furnishings, and countless Vanderbilt family portraits.

Mitch Bernstein was especially attuned to the George Washington Vanderbilt saga. A businessman by instinct, Mitch thinks Madison Avenue, breathes Wall Street, and has a heart John D. Rockefeller would be proud of. Mitch is obsessed with amassing piles of money—partially for the challenge, to prove his cunning, and partially to create for himself the role of generous benefactor à la Rockefeller. Unlike some of the other men on the trip, Mitch's boyhood heroes were not Michael Jordan or Bruce Springsteen but Ted Turner for creating CNN, Phil Knight for building Nike into a shoe empire, Leon L. Bean for his clothing catalog business, Ray Kroc for McDonald's, and Bill Gates for Microsoft. The brightest star in this galaxy of entrepreneurs, the person he revered most, was Sam Walton, the founder of Wal-Mart, whom Mitch referred to in worshipful tones as the "greatest guru of merchandising." Even though George Washington Vanderbilt had inherited all his money, a strike against him in Mitch's pantheon, he was redeemed by his creative, innovative, and entrepreneurial risk taking. Mitch admired the bootstrap entrepreneurs, the gutsy Horatio Algers with empty pockets and burning ideas who through sheer will transformed a mere scheme into an empire. A business major at Hofstra, Mitch has been selling since he was a boy, from candy on his front lawn to watches at flea markets—apprenticeship exercises, he hopes, for the big payoff, the moneymaking scheme that will spell bonanza, the rainbow he can ride like a leprechaun right to his pot of gold. Other students took the American Odyssey to discover America; Mitch enrolled to discover "how and where to make money and live best in America." The Biltmore and George Washington Vanderbilt Mitch found mildly inspiring—they got his moneymaking wheels turning—but it was in Portland, Oregon, when he visited Nike Town, that Mitch came up with an idea he believes could someday make him a millionaire or, who knows, even a billionaire. As Arthur Miller has Willie Loman say in *Death of a Salesman*, "A salesman has got to dream, boy. It comes with the territory."

We returned to the Majic Bus to continue our drive through the Biltmore grounds, stopping, under student pressure, at the Vanderbilt state-of-the-art winery, which advertised "free tastings." Concerned about wasting too much time, I made the students do a quick march through the wine-making museum and aimed them straight at the bar. Although I can't say Mr. Vanderbilt makes a good wine, it isn't bad. While we all leaned against the wine bar, sampling five different North Carolina vintages, cleansing our palates with Goldfish crackers between sips, Mitch was nosing around the gift shop, taking mental notes, astounded at the queue of people anxious to purchase anything from bleu cheese wheels to barbecue bibs with the Biltmore insignia on them. Feeling a tad lightheaded from our midafternoon indulgence, we floated our way back to the bus, ready for the Cherokee Indian Reservation.

Christine Morga was particularly looking forward to setting foot on what she regarded as sacred soil. With a soft, saintly disposition and an instinctive outrage at the industrial barbarism perpetuated by white European males on Native Americans under the guise of human progress, Christine felt an affinity for Indians that was grounded more in myth, an active imagination, and a romantic bent than in historical reality. She first became engrossed with their ritualistic life-style after seeing *Dances with Wolves.* Her friends may have swooned over Kevin Costner, but she fantasized about falling hopelessly in love with a sleek, muscular modern-day warrior—the tall, silent type who rides horses bareback by day and a Harley by night. She was put off by all the money-hungry, preppy poseurs and dumb jocks at school and yearned for a rebel with a cause as a matter of birthright. She wanted an Indian resistance fighter who tied his long hair in a ponytail, just like Axl Rose of Guns N' Roses and Anthony Kiedes of the Red Hot Chili Peppers, who she knew also had tattoos of Chief Joseph and Sitting Bull on his arms and wore ripped jeans and dangling feather earrings. If she could find a guy like this, she would run off with him. Money was of no consequence; finding someone in tune with himself and nature was. She might even change her name to Chesapeake or Cheyenne, "tons" more romantic than her ordinary, run-of-the-mill, suburban *Christine.* So as we headed to Cherokee, North Carolina, Christine was in a dreamy mood; by evening's end reality had intruded.

To get to Cherokee we angled west for thirty-one miles, through the scenic mountains of Nanthala National Forest. Plant life here and in the adjacent Great Smoky Mountain National Park is more varied than anywhere else in the world's Temperate Zone. There are nearly two thousand plant species, some 150 different trees—half as many as in the entire continent of Europe. Recently the red wolf was reintroduced into the Smokies with hopes that by 1993 there might be as many as seventy-five in the park. The reintroduction of river otters has already been a resounding success. Yet, sadly, the haze over the Smokies today is partly acid rain, mostly from nearby coal-fired power plants. I put on a Roy Acuff tape purchased at the Asheville Goodwill, anxious to expose the students to his quivering, emotional songs of primitive faith rooted in rural values that made him the King of Country, a title first given to him by Dizzy Dean. For the decade starting in 1938, Acuff and his Smoky Mountain Boys were country music superstars, with a long list of hits like "The Great Speckled Bird," "Wreck on the Highway," "Low and Lonely," "Fireball Mail," "Wabash Cannonball," "The Precious Jewel," "Pins and

Needles (In My Heart)," "Freight Train Blues," and "Streamline Cannon-ball." I had once driven all the way to Nashville from Annapolis just to hear Roy Acuff play at the Grand Ole Opry—if I wasn't yet alive for Hank Williams, I sure in hell wasn't going to miss Roy Acuff, the country fiddler who in 1948 had even run for governor of Tennessee as a Republican. According to legend the Japanese banzai attack on Okinawa had a sticks-and-stones aspect, taunting Americans with such morale killers as: "To hell with Roosevelt; to hell with Babe Ruth; to hell with Roy Acuff." When Roy Acuff, a true American original, died of congestive heart failure on November 23, 1992, I mourned, taking it as a real personal loss. So as we were driving past pines and spruces, a flock of wild geese overhead winging their way northward, Roy Acuff set the mood for the students' first sojourn out of the emerald valley and into the Great Smokies.

On our climb high into the mountains, Alison noticed a billboard for HILLBILLY GOLF, featuring gnomelike creatures with orange beards and red freckles and moonshiny eyes: cartoon depictions of the feuding Hatfield and McCoy clans. We were in corncob-pipe alley of the Blue Ridge Parkway, where the hillbilly is king and the dollar rules, or better yet, the Confederate dollar, a much sounder currency. You see, a one-dollar bill printed in Richmond from 1862 to 1864, bearing the por-trait of Clement Clay, in "average circulation condition" is worth about ten times a comparable U.S. dollar. Humorist John Shelton Reed, a self-proclaimed semipro curmudgeon who tracks the decline of the West and the rise of the South from his office at the University of North Carolina at Chapel Hill, has written: "As the Yankee dollar is eaten away by infla-tion, Confederate money should begin to attract not just currency specu-lators but ordinary Americans looking for a sounder currency in which to hold their savings." In *Whistling Dixie: Dispatches From the South*, he asserts that "they couldn't do better. Since 1965, the Confederate dollar has outperformed even such blue chips as the German Mark, the Swiss Franc and the Japanese Yen." But beginning with the comic strips "Snuffy Smith" and "Li'l Abner" and the films of Ma and Pa Kettle, the real fortune to be made from the Southern heritage has not been in Confederate money but in marketing hillbillies—the entertainment megabucks of Nashville and Hollywood.

When Northerners cross the Mason-Dixon Line, the issue of stereotypes is inevitably raised. As a Southerner by birth and a Northerner by choice, I was mildly surprised—although perhaps I shouldn't have been—that its first manifestation was the students' stereotyping of Southern whites. The students carried with them an indelible stereotype of Appalachian rural folk from television and movies. Etched in their minds are images of crude, ornery, and oafishly backward rural folk: Jim Nabors as Gomer Pyle, the warm-hearted, inept, hayseed marine; Don Knotts as Barney Fife, the goggle-eyed and foolish small-town law officer; and Flo, the spunky waitress whose favorite riposte is "Kiss my grits!" The stars of "Hee Haw"— Roy Clark, Buck Owens, and Minnie Pearl, known for the price tag dangling from her hat and her hearty "Howdy!"—portray stereotypical rural Southerners all the way to the bank. The cruel South, "The Land of the Lost Cause," was best known to students not from D. W. Griffith's *Birth of a Nation* or Alex Haley's *Roots* but from the movie adaptation of James Dickey's novel *Deliverance*. The now-notorious words "squeal like a pig" automatically make faces grimace in imagined pain when uttered. But the show that truly fixed how students viewed Appalachian mountain people was "The Beverly Hillbillies." The story line is well known. Jed Clampett, the family's patriarch, discovers oil on his impoverished homestead, becomes a millionaire, and to use the words of the sitcom's hit theme song, "moved to Beverly . . . Hills, that is—swimming pools, movie stars." It's been said that America is a country where everyone knows the words to the "Beverly Hillbillies" song but can't remember their own blood type, and that's about right. Unless you travel the blue highways of America and meet real rural folk, it's the TV images and pop-song lyrics that linger.

In particular, I remember an episode when Jed Clampett, played by Buddy Ebsen, thought "golfs" were animals to be clubbed to death with an elaborate collection of woods, irons, and a putter. It is not surprising that even in rerun these TV images left lasting impressions on the students, but it's still a shocker that the combination of "Hee Haw" and "The

Beverly Hillbillies" has shaped the negative country-bumpkin way in which merchants along this road into the Cherokee Reservation choose to depict their own culture. As film executive Joseph Levine once noted, "You can fool all the people all of the time if the advertising is right and the budget is big enough." When I mentioned to Alan that during its heyday in the early sixties "The Beverly Hillbillies" had an estimated audience of sixty million and was an important sociological pop Americana document, he said, "Oh yeah, for sure, it led to the spin-offs 'Green Acres' and 'Petticoat Junction.' " Alan knew his hillbilly history, and perhaps all those media stereotypes prevent us from seeing the self-mockery inherent in Hillbilly Golf. But, any way you slice it, Norman Mailer is right: "Television pollutes identity."

By the time we arrived in Cherokee it was dark. The small town sits astride the southeastern entrance of the fifty-thousand-acre Great Smoky Mountains National Park, the most popular national park of all, with as many visitors annually as Yosemite, Yellowstone, Grand Teton, and Rocky Mountain national parks together. It is the center of Cherokee culture, a place where old ways are perpetuated in classes and religious ceremonies, and yet it is a place that oozes repellent tourism of the worst sort. All manner of "redmen" souvenirs are peddled in trading posts: rubber tomahawks, feathered headdresses, Pocahontas dolls, cardboard drums, fake scalps, plastic peace pipes, and hundreds of other "authentic Indian" sourvenirs and fripperies (including Jesus and Elvis felt paintings) imported direct to Cherokee from the sweat factories of Hong Kong and Taiwan.

Today only eight thousand Eastern Cherokees survive, compared to the twenty-nine thousand Cherokees who used to populate the conifer and broadleaf forests of the Smokies before the U.S. Army rounded them up in 1838 and forced them to march to a reservation in Oklahoma, a march they call the "Trail of Tears." It left Christine on her own trail of tears to see one of the Five Civilized Tribes — once a proud nation who called themselves *Yuniwaya*, or "the real people"; who spoke an Iroquoian language with at least three different dialects; who gave women positions of respect within the tribe; who were led by shamans known as *adawehi*, who had years of training in the use of medicinal plants and were adept at curing—now reduced to penny-ante capitalism and debased free enterprise, surviving in the twentieth century by selling fake beads and moccasins, attracting tourists into their shops by performing their sacred Green Corn Dance and Eagle Dance on asphalt parking lots with outrageous war bonnets on.

Christine was aghast, too, at a brochure she picked up at a trading post for the Cyclorama Wax Museum, which said, "See the vast empire of the Cherokee Nation fade away on large scaled electronic maps." What disturbed her most was that these tourist enterprises were owned and operated by Cherokees. How could this be? In his book *On the Spine of Time: An Angler's Love of the Smokies*, Harry Middleton cites the bitter assessment of his Cherokee merchant friend Bob Winterwolf Dougal, who refers to the whites who buy Indian souvenirs as snowflakes: "They come by the thousands, let me tell you. By herds, fat and docile, every one of them ready to empty their wallets for sight of an Indian walking about in a loincloth, a bloody knife in one hand and a bottle of hooch in the other. Yessir. As long as there is wampum and wigwams, they stand in line to lay their money down." And that's exactly what our group of Long Island snowflakes did.

Parking the Majic Bus at the reservation's McDonald's, where teenage tourists pull up to the window for "buffalo burgers" or ask whether their hamburgers are "genuine red meat," we crossed the bridge over the Oconaluftee River and headed straight for the souvenirs at Saunookes's Trading Post to lay our wampum down. Many of the students bought some banal rubber snake souvenir, but Frank acquired a twenty-dollar white-feather good-luck medallion—promptly hung right next to his icon of Clint Eastwood—an Indian artifact from Hong Kong that Frank claimed would keep the Majic Bus safe from bad luck and evil spirits. Since it wasn't my twenty bucks, I could only hope Frank was right. Kevin found it fun to chat with the two roadside "chiefs" he encountered, dressed in full warrior regalia, shills for the high-stakes reservation Bingo featuring five-figure cash jackpots, at the local parlor. Christine was disheartened. It wasn't just Cherokee's Santa Land, where, in some weird equivalence, Geronimo and Kris Kringle both hand out lollipops to the kids; or the collared baby black bear cubs in the pits behind Saunookes's Trading Post, or the FIVE DOLLARS TO MEET A REAL INJUN sign that so dejected her, or even that people paid money to participate in such commerce. As we headed to the Dairy Barn for corndogs and milkshakes, Christine spied some local Cherokee boys in Bugle Boy jeans, NBA basketball T-shirts, and Nikes. These typical American teenagers brought home to her the extent of her Native American fantasies, and she was embarrassed. Fueled by *Dances with Wolves,* she had envisioned the Cherokees as mighty warriors chanting sacred songs and swapping animal stories by a roaring fire. She wanted them to be riding horses, not driving Chevrolets. Instead, as we moved away from the profane trading posts and the world of performance for tourists, the young Cherokees on the reservation were no different from the kids back on Long Island. And why should they be? They were American rock-and-rollers just like the rest of us. Yet she was shocked to learn that one Native American teenager in six has attempted suicide, a rate four times that of other teenagers. She now understood the flaws in her romantic excess—a milder form of racism. It also astonished Christine that she was not a whole lot different from the Santa Land "snowflake" tourists whom she despised, imposing a version of what Indians should be. By the time Christine saw the poverty of the Crow in Montana and the Sioux in South Dakota on our American Odyssey, her romanticism had been abraded by the growing awareness in her young soul. She realized that much of America, regardless of color or past history, is about making money, and if the Cherokee knew how to turn a bonnet into a buck, that spoke highly of them—sort of. She knew the Cherokee Reservation had taught her an important lesson but she didn't quite know how to digest it. The truth is none of us did, except Frank, who took it for what it was. He was happy that the Majic Bus had now been blessed by a Cherokee shaman—the end to the pesky oil leak, he hoped.

Pulling out of Cherokee, we inadvertently entered the Great Smoky Mountain National Park while looking for the best route to Atlanta. Backtracking to Cherokee, I hopped out to ask directions in a reservation convenience market. What I didn't realize was that Jared Goldman had followed me inside for sweets. Jared was the only freshman on American Odyssey, his fresh young mind finding the traditional classroom setting tedious and unstimulating. In addition to having an obsession with sports, a fine writing style, and penchant for witty repartee, Jared was a candyholic. Jared went through Chuckles, Red Hots, and Good & Plentys the way a chainsmoker goes through a carton of Camels. After getting directions I sprinted back to the bus, unaware I was leaving Jared behind with an armload of Bit o' Honeys. Soon after, Stephanie noticed Jared was missing, and we immediately turned around, only to see him in the back of a Ford pickup, frantically trying to wave us down. We burst into hysterical laughter. When the resourceful Jared realized we had left, he quickly asked two Cherokee playing Pac-Man for help in catching up to the Majic Bus. Catch up he did, but Jared stalked on board as angry as a hornet, a mood made worse by the mock ovation accorded his entrance. It was a lesson for the students to watch out for themselves, and for me always to take a head count. We teased Jared for the rest of the trip about the incident. After a night's sleep he learned to take the ribbing with a smile.

Frank eventually found his way out of the Smokies (sixteen peaks that reach over six thousand feet) as the students read, played cards, or just relaxed and chatted among themselves. I was looking forward to Georgia, the state of my birth, and played a Peach State mix of songs including the B-52s' "Love Shack," Otis Redding's "Sitting on the Dock of the Bay," Ray Charles's "Georgia on My Mind," Little Feat's "Oh Atlanta," James Brown's "Please, Please, Please," REM's "Losing My Religion," Little Richard's "Tutti-Frutti," Kris Kristofferson's "They Killed Him," and my favorite, Gladys Knight and the Pips' "Midnight Train to Georgia." When

I was growing up in Decatur, an Atlanta suburb, in the 1960s, the South was in a battle over desegregation, a battle to which I was largely oblivious. While Governor Lester Maddox was wielding an ax handle, refusing to serve blacks in his fried-chicken restaurant, I thought nothing of worshiping Robert E. Lee, whose chiseled, motionless stare intruded on my daily consciousness from his position—mounted on his horse, carved Mount Rushmore-like—high up on Stone Mountain, only a few crow-flyin' miles from my bedroom window. In my youth Lee represented the epitome of a dignified underdog, the gray fox of the American Civil War whose sheer, unsullied integrity turned surrender at Appomattox Court House into victory of the Southern gentlemen over the scorched-earth barbarians of the North. How I resonated with drummer Levon Helm of The Band singing "The Night They Drove Old Dixie Down," a poignant, instinctive folk ballad of the Civil War South. The line "Virgil, quick come see, there goes Robert E. Lee" vibrated within me, a highly visible, moving historical myth. As a child I could imagine the electricity that must have charged through the war-ravaged countryside when Robert E. Lee, in an immaculately pressed gray uniform, rode his white mare through town, his polished sword gleaming silver at his side. Lee was the living embodiment of the Confederacy, a noble man larger than his legend. Every Sunday after church I'd beg my parents to be taken to Stone Mountain to gaze at General Lee, Stonewall Jackson, and Jefferson Davis, whose carved images still proudly uphold aspects of a Southern heritage that is in retreat, partially because of the Civil Rights Act of 1965 and the coming of CNN internationalism and global village economics.

It was only years later that I realized how warped it was to revere Confederate leaders, how Stone Mountain was not simply a benign monument to the Southern heritage but also where the Ku Klux Klan was revived in 1915. So the Majic Bus would bypass Stone Mountain for the New South, the Atlanta now known as "the world's next great city," the city of the Martin Luther King, Jr. Center for Non-Violent Social Change and the Jimmy Carter Center—a city Scarlett O'Hara would not recognize.

By the time we made it to I-285, Atlanta's beltway, known as "the Big O around the A," it was after midnight and we had no place to stay, only a 10:30 A.M. appointment with Donald Schewe, the director of the Carter Library, the next morning. A handful of the students, complaining of sore backs, wanted to sleep in a motel for the night. We found a Red Roof Inn where nine of the students crashed, in clean-sheeted comfort, three to a room. The rest of us slept on the bus, which Frank parked behind the motel.

The motel had the added advantage of being just a stone's throw away from a Waffle House, and I dozed off with visions of syrupy pecan-waffle delights dancing in my head. Beth and I woke up early, and rubbing the grit from our eyes, carried our Dopp kits up a flight of stairs, pounded on the doors of Rooms 220 and 222, respectively, intent on taking hot showers. In Room 220, Dan, Jay, and Alan were already swigging down sodas to kill their morning breath while staring blankly at Rod Stewart's "Broken Arrow" video on MTV. The bathroom looked more like a steamroom, having hosted three marathon showers, the sopping white motel towels heaped on the tiles. After a vigorous soaping session I headed over to the Waffle House with Dan, Alan, Alison, and Beth.

Without a doubt Waffle House is the best franchise in America. Where else can you find waitresses who exude maternal attentiveness and the sweet smile of Raphael's Madonna and can bark out to the kitchen, like marine drill instructors, "Give me some spuds scattered, smothered, covered, chunked, and topped," with hairdos piled as high as an order of lumberjack pancakes, ozone-layer destroyers one and all. The jukebox in the meantime blasts out such favorites as Eddie Middleton's "Waffle Doo-Wop" and Mary Welch Rogers's "Waffle House Thank You." The nation's short-order cooks should be required to take egg-cooking lessons from any Waffle House in the South as a requirement to practice their craft. Be

101

they scrambled, over easy, sunny-side up, fried, poached, or basted, Waffle House does eggs your way. And they don't dump onions in your hash browns—they ask whether you want cheese or onions in them. *Ask* is the operative word here. (In New York hash browns come with onions mixed in. Onions, those nutritionless bulbs, are the fruit of Satan and should not be forced on the unwary.)

At the counter Alan entered into animated conversation with a good ol' boy from Griffin, Georgia, who asked Alan out of the blue whether he liked "The Cosby Show." When Alan feigned indifference, the trucker offered his own unsolicited critique: It was "nigger trash." Here I'd been telling my students that the South is unfairly maligned in the North as the land of lynchings, cross burnings, chain gangs, and the Scottsboro trials. Racism was on its way out, I asserted, and progressivism, Jimmy Carter / Bill Clinton–style, had replaced it, and now the first Georgian they met had a neck so red it was blistering.

Still the guy was the only outspoken racist we met in the South, where the reputation for Southern hospitality was an actuality. After spending time in Atlanta and New Orleans, we all concluded that it is conceivable that the North could learn a thing or two about race relations from these progressive American cities. But when you stumble upon the species of Southern racists who sound like Lester Maddox, the impulse to pick up an ax handle yourself is hard to resist.

5

Back from the Wind: Atlanta and New Orleans

America is woven of many strands; I would recognize them and let it so remain. . . . Our fate is to become one, and yet many—This is not prophecy, but description.

—RALPH ELLISON

WE ARRIVED AT THE JIMMY CARTER CENTER ONLY A FEW minutes late, with the electric blue sky above us blotting out our exasperation at clogged traffic and wrong turns. Atlanta's famed azaleas and dogwoods were everywhere throughout the center's grounds, their explosive pink petals in full bloom. Only the mild humidity and unbroken sunshine signaled summer's heat waiting in the wings. The Atlanta tradition of sitting on the front porch on a sweltering afternoon sipping Coca-Cola— begun in 1886, the year Atlanta resident Dr. John Pemberton concocted a syrup in his backyard for a soda he planned to sell for a nickel a glass—has disappeared in the age of air-conditioning, probably to no one's regret except the incurably romantic's.

In front of the center stood a huge concrete slab, a chunk of the Berlin

103

Wall on tour, the in-vogue souvenir of the early 1990s. This artifact, the work product of nearly a half century of Cold War, now sitting on display in the warm Georgia sun—this cement symbol of repression, now sanitized into found art—to me clearly stood for the unambiguous triumph of freedom, hope, and justice, the futility of walling in and walling out the human spirit. Colorfully spray-painted with urgent graffiti on the Western side, totalitarian gray on the Communist, this Cold War remnant was an immediate topical conversation piece. For some of the Jewish students, the positive symbolism was not so apparent, for they were terrified by the neo-Nazis of the new unified Germany, who routinely attack immigrants. Ripped from its context, the abstract chunk of the wall was not even an *aide-mémoire* to remind us of CNN's extraordinary images of earnest German teenagers chipping away like craftsmen, picks in hand; the slab was more like the side of a building blown up by industrial explosives. But we all dutifully posed in front of it for photos, not sure just what to make of it—it was a slab of the Berlin Wall and that was enough.

We entered a long walkway that led into what has been called the most beautiful of our nation's ten presidential libraries. The Carter Library—which is adjacent to the nonprofit Carter Center facilities—highlights our thirty-ninth President's White House years with photos, memorabilia, state gifts, a re-creation of the Oval Office, and audiovisual presentations. Like all presidential libraries, it is also the depository of the president's governmental papers. Set quietly in the shadow of Atlanta's shiny downtown skyscrapers, which seem to have leapt from the architect's brain straight into reality, the center's UFO-style circular buildings are surrounded by Japanese gardens of azaleas and sunflowers, a pond brilliantly colored by koi that animate the water like bright orange darts, and a cascading waterfall. Donald Schewe, the director, welcomed us and explained the exhibits and the library's various projects. Tom, hoping he might actually get to meet President Carter, asked how often he visited the complex. We learned that the Carters maintain an apartment there and occasionally spend the night, usually when he is conducting an international conference, but Tom was out of luck; we would not bump into them during our visit.

Many of the students on American Odyssey, especially the Republicans, thought I exaggerated Carter's strengths, their opinions shaped only by media memories of his paste-on smile, his buffoonish brother Billy, the "killer rabbit" incident, the *Playboy* "lust in my heart" interview, the Iran hostage crisis, and his boycott of the Moscow Olympics after the Soviets invaded Afghanistan. By the time we left the Carter Library and Center their estimation of Jimmy Carter as both president and humanitarian was way up on the charts. Although they laughed at the sight of his "Peanut Brigade" campaign paraphernalia and his brown cardigan fireside-chat sweater exhibited under glass, they were deeply impressed by the display on Menachem Begin, Anwar Sadat, and the Camp David accords. They were even more moved by something that can't be categorized, labeled, and put in a display case: the exemplary courage Carter has demonstrated as a moral force and a civic leader in a series of humanitarian initiatives here in Atlanta and throughout the country and the world.

Since leaving the White House in 1981, Carter has crisscrossed the world monitoring free elections, mediating overseas disputes through the Carter Center, helping Habitat for Humanity build houses in impoverished urban neighborhoods and rural byways all across the United States and abroad, and financing research on improving agriculture and health care worldwide through the center's Global 2000 Program. What impressed the students about Jimmy Carter is his relentless single-mindedness in tackling seemingly unsolvable problems. The students found this quite simply refreshing: If people are homeless, build homes; if they are hungry, feed them. Already some historians who (like Arthur Schlesinger, Jr.) were critical of Carter as president are touting him as America's best living ex-president. And if there is any justice in Stockholm, he will win the Nobel Peace Prize for his prodigious efforts to improve living conditions around the world and to make it a better, more equitable place to live. As for Carter's presidency, the revisionism is just beginning and his stock is rising. Carter will never be considered a "great" president in the sense of Washington, Lincoln, or FDR, but he deserves high marks for his progressive and enlightened civil rights and environmental policies, for the Camp David accords and the Panama Canal treaties, and for his human rights and energy policies. Any way you slice it, Jimmy Carter is a remarkable public servant to whom all Americans are indebted; he is an honest, tireless reformer and a national treasure.

We learned about the Carter Center's ambitious program of urban renewal, the Atlanta Project—intended as a model for other cities—a new nonpartisan community effort aimed at eradicating the city's seemingly intractable poverty and crime. Carter himself, tenacious as ever, is marshaling community resources to wipe out joblessness, lack of health care, drugs, illiteracy, teenage pregnancy, and the lack of housing in the premier city of the South. This effort will gather a cadre of volunteers—Oprah Winfrey has donated fifty thousand dollars and Jane Fonda has signed on to teach exercise classes—committed to helping people help themselves in twenty "cluster" neighborhoods in Fulton, Dekalb, and Clayton counties—a sort of domestic Peace Corps.

Why, one might ask, is Carter, at sixty-nine, undertaking such an unprecedented project? Perhaps one reason is the irony that Atlanta, in many ways a model of racial harmony and professional opportunity for some of its black residents, has left so many others hopelessly behind. Fortune magazine recently hailed this corporate and cultural hub as the best place to do business in the United States. Thanks to its unquenchable boosterism, it will host the 1994 Super Bowl and the 1996 Summer Olympics in its brand-new Georgia Dome, which games bring with them a myriad of economic opportunities. Yet, despite its success, Atlanta repeats the pattern of Washington, DC—islands of wealth and opportunity in a sea of poverty, crime, and homelessness. But what makes Georgia's showcase city different is the unflagging belief of its citizens that they can whip these social and economic ills by working together as a community. Rev. Jesse Jackson sets the tone in Atlanta with his "Keep Hope Alive," stirring words that have struck a chord in young people. With that message reverberating, civic spirit has swept Atlanta like wildfire, inspiring Jimmy Carter to bridge the chasm between the haves and the have-nots right in his own state. "Somewhere in God's world we need to demonstrate that progress can be made," Carter says with simplicity and determination.

Carter is not merely lending his name, prestige, and political rhetoric to the Atlanta Project, he is investing most of his time and energy in what he envisions is not just a Great Society War on Poverty, but an absolute victory over it. "The Atlanta Project has aroused a high level of interest and support because it is grand in scope, idealistic, challenging, adventurous, and potentially gratifying," Carter has noted. Part of what fuels Carter's hope that we can actually lick poverty is his personal contact with poor people, building homes for Habitat for Humanity. "We worked side by side with them and found them so eager, ambitious, and competent," Carter said recently. "We have underestimated these people, and I have seen them just after they move into a decent house, start talking about what college they want their children to go to. It is almost a chasm for some of us to cross, but with an adequate degree of groundwork and acculturation it can be done." There are, of course, those who mock Carter's bold—some say preposterous—plan to eradicate poverty in Atlanta by 1996, calling him hopelessly idealistic and "in over his head." But most of those naysayers are the same seventies cynics who said the idea of a one-term Southern governor who thought he could be U.S. president was absurd. They fail to understand what Jimmy Carter is all about.

To those familiar with Carter's superb record of social liberalism as president, the Atlanta Project comes as no surprise. Since his days as Georgia's governor, in fact, Carter has displayed a genius for creating public-private partnership ventures. But of all Carter's reform efforts, the Atlanta Project is his most enterprising. If he can succeed in ending homelessness, improving education and health care, and smashing poverty in Atlanta, it will encourage other cities in America to start a similar grass-roots effort. From "the city too busy to hate," Atlanta will have been transformed into the first American city in which Martin Luther King, Jr.'s "I Have a Dream" words have leapt from the annals of oratory into the kingdom of earthly reality.

After several wonderful hours in the Carter Center, the Majic Bus was off, this time to the Martin Luther King, Jr., Center for Non-Violent Social Change, located in the historic Auburn Avenue District. On our way we drove past blocks of boarded-up homes with broken windows, smashed storefronts, and garbage piled up in back alleys, a stark and squalid contrast to the glitzy glass towers of downtown, which at their haughty remove seemed almost to gloat at the disparity of wealth (one could only hope that the three low-income neighborhoods of Summerville, Peoples-town, and Mechanicsville would get treated with care when the Committee for the Olympic Games prepared to build their shiny new stadium). But we did not lose heart; we had left the Carter Center true believers in the Atlanta Project; we had faith that the wheels were in motion. As Jack Kerouac reminded us, "Walking on water wasn't made in a day."

We parked the bus across the street from the King Center, right next to the redbrick Ebenezer Baptist Church, the spiritual center of the civil rights movement. There, from 1960 to 1968, Martin Luther King, Jr., was copastor with his father. Since her husband's assassination in 1968, Coretta Scott King has been the keeper of "the Dream." Now she may finally be gaining recognition for her own significant achievements in promoting racial equality and social justice, for keeping hope alive. She has raised more than $10 million for the Martin Luther King, Jr., Center for Non-Violent Social Change (known in Atlanta as the King Center), which from the early planning stages had been a mandatory stop for the American Odyssey course. It was Coretta Scott King who insisted that "non-violent" be part of the center's official name, and we quickly realized why this was so important, for the King Center is not simply a memorial to the slain leader but a living, action-oriented monument to nonviolent social change via educational and community action programs. Founded in the basement of Mrs. King's Sunset Avenue home in Atlanta in 1968, under her stewardship the center has grown into a sprawling multicomplex with an annual budget of $3.2 million, and sixty-three employees.

108   As the students filed out of the Majic Bus to the center entrance, we

stopped in our tracks. There in the middle of a reflecting pool was the white marble crypt—with its eternal flame—that contains the body of Dr. King. There is something simultaneously noble and humble about the crypt. We watched the water ripple into growing concentric rings as two young African Americans kissed pennies, made wishes, and tossed their coins into the pool. What were their wishes? I wondered. We would never know, but the gesture made us uncomfortable, partially because we were cloaked in white skin but also because we now realized we were entering a sacred shrine. There was also a sense of guilt. It made me think of what Archbishop Desmond Tutu once said: "Thank God I am black. White people will have a lot to answer for at the Last Judgment."

As we toured Freedom Hall, with its exhibits from the civil rights movement, ranging from Dr. King's small travel kit to the Nobel Peace medal awarded him in 1964, and viewed a movie called *Sweet Auburn*, about the history of one of Atlanta's premier black residential and business communities, we felt out of place. Sitting in the auditorium, the only white faces in a somber audience of fifty African American high-schoolers, my students experienced for the first time what James Baldwin had learned as a boy: "It was a great shock at the age of five or six to find that in a world of Gary Coopers you are the Indian." In the world of African American history, we were more than tourist snowflakes—we were the bad guys, the progenitors of plantation beatings, chattel slavery, Jim Crow laws, and ongoing racial discrimination. But the people at the King Center were glad we had come, pleased that a busload of white college students were paying their respects to their martyred hero. Since half the American Odyssey students were Jewish, it was an especially meaningful encounter, for in the Crown Heights area of New York City tensions between African Americans and Jews had recently reached a boiling point. Alan in particular was heartened to learn that Coretta Scott King, asked in 1991 how her husband would have responded to the anti-Jewish sentiments expressed by some African American leaders, such as Louis Farrakhan and Al Sharpton, answered: "To tolerate anti-Semitism is to cooperate with the evils of prejudice and bigotry that Martin Luther King, Jr., fought against. In a speech he delivered one month before he was assassinated, my husband said, 'For the black man to struggle for justice and then turn around and be anti-Semitic is not only a very irrational course, but it is a very immoral course, and wherever we have seen anti-Semitism we have condemned it with all our might.' "

We walked down the street to 501 Auburn Avenue, where Martin Luther King, Jr., was born on January 15, 1929, in a two-story Victorian house. The King home exuded a sense of family struggles and closeness as we saw the piano at which Dr. King's mother taught her three children gospel music; the dinner table, set with original china, where his father used to hold court and talk politics; sets of Chinese checkers and Monopoly, which the young Martin is said to have played with a "Boardwalk" and "Park Place" vengeance.

The story of how Dr. King came to symbolize the struggle of black Americans for full and equal participation was well known to the students. In 1986, when his birthday was declared a national holiday, Americans were forced to pay closer attention to his philosophy of nonviolent activism, primarily because of the media blitz. Most remembered seeing Ebenezer Baptist Church on the nightly news every January 15. Ronald Reagan or other politicians would be fidgeting and vaguely standoffish in the predominantly black congregation; standing at the altar with Jesse Jackson, Coretta Scott King, Martin Luther King, Sr., Andrew Young, and Maynard Jackson; or singing and swaying to "We Shall Overcome," hands linked in honor of the great civil rights activist. A tour guide told us that every day for eighteen years a relentless Coretta Scott King had lobbied presidents, cabinet officials, and members of Congress until she finally succeeded in establishing a national holiday for her slain husband.

Ironically, through the granting of a national holiday to Dr. King, he became government sanctioned, losing his antihero status with the young. There was no longer any risk in admiring him, now that even Ronald Reagan had agreed that he was a hero suitable for inclusion in textbooks. As a consequence such seventies pop stars as Stevie Wonder and Quincy Jones could sing "Happy birthday, Dr. King," until they were hoarse, and Bill Cosby and Harry Belafonte could hit the talk-show circuit, reminiscing again about their civil rights marches with him, but the net result, among both blacks and whites of the Yo generation (or Generation X), was a turning away from Dr. King's Christian turn-the-other-cheek philosophy.

Dr. King now represents the status quo as embraced by the media mainstream and reflected in James Earl Jones—narrated documentaries about social responsibility. To many African Americans Dr. King was a lackey of white power while Malcolm X was the fearless black revolutionary. Similarly, for the generation ruled by Madonna, not Helen Reddy; Camille Paglia, not Gloria Steinem; Sister Souljah, not Joan Baez; KRS-One, not Peter, Paul, and Mary; Martin Scorsese, not Robert Redford; Rap, not Rod McKuen; AIDS, not Free Love; an Uzi, not a Peace Symbol; and *Naked Lunch,* not *Zen and the Art of Motorcycle Maintenance,* it only made sense that it would be Malcolm X, not Martin Luther King, Jr., who spoke to them—and Malcolm X they got.

Although Spike Lee's thirty-three-million-dollar Warner Brothers blockbuster hit the screens after our American Odyssey journey, the promotional tidal wave of Malcolm X mania had already hit Generation X with a proliferation of posters, T-shirts, trading cards, caps, car fresheners, and CDs of his "blue-eyed devil" speeches. At the King Center we must have seen a dozen young African Americans sporting X caps of various colors, as well as one teenager with an X haircut. Many of these young people had never read *The Autobiography of Malcohm X* and/or knew little about his real life. But that large, anonymous X seemed to speak directly to them: It marked their refusal to be pigeonholed, defined, or vilified by others. The more serious Malcolm worshipers even managed to learn the universal Muslim greeting, *as-salam-alaikum,* without knowing what the Koran was, let alone reading it. They were responding to the young Malcolm—the promoter of black separatism, as interpreted by Chuck D of Public Enemy—not the later Malcolm X, who after his trip to Mecca philosophically aligned himself closer to Dr. Martin Luther King, Jr. They were the alienated X generation, believing that nothing really mattered—regardless of color, we're all enslaved by other people's conventions. The letter X was liberating, a self-declaration of independence, a symbol of self-love, a

111

lonely rage, and a demand for respect "by any means necessary." In urban America today, when three African American males strut down the avenue with their X caps on, they're no longer Ralph Ellison's "invisible men"; they're Malcolm's kids, who're saying, "Jump back, whitey, and take notice." No one understands this better than that innovative filmmaker Spike Lee, whose movie Malcolm X is more than a tribute to the Black Muslim revolutionary: It is a generational manifesto. The Yo generation eschews reading, so it took a movie to transform Malcolm X into a youth-cult figure. Now young people have finally found someone they want to read about, and *The Autobiography of Malcolm X* has reemerged explosively on the American scene as number one on the *New York Times* and other paperback best-seller lists. Spike Lee may have turned Malcolm Little into Malcolm Megabucks, but he had also exhorted American youth to read, to think about their heritage. It is Spike Lee who will help define African American youth culture in the 1990s, and he'll do it by making white America pay attention.

After three stirring hours at the King Center we met up again with Frank, who was doing his own share of reducing the unemployment rate by giving two homeless teenagers twenty bucks to help him wash the Majic Bus. As we emerged from Ebenezer Baptist Church, there they were— Frank and two street kids, having ferried buckets of hot soapy water from a nearby gas station—scrubbing away at the mud-splattered bus and dancing as they worked to the music of Bobby ("Blue") Bland.

We sat on the sidewalk to discuss Martin Luther King, Jr., and black-white relations in the United States. Suddenly two African American men in their thirties appeared before us—one with an extended Chicago White Sox cap—announcing that for one dollar they would sing us a song. Aíne immediately produced a dollar, and our two street minstrels in sweat pants and leather jackets broke into an *a capella* rendition of Percy Sledge's "When a Man Loves a Woman." Perched on the sidewalk, Ebenezer Baptist Church as our backdrop, listening to Little Sparrow and Cricket Heels (as they called themselves) sing, was a moving experience. The spontaneous musical happening, in the place that was the heart and soul of America's civil rights movement, linked us emotionally to the black experience in America with an intensity and immediacy that could not be garnered from sanctioned symbols and predigested displays, no matter how well intended. For a moment we were connected to a living tradition. Matt immediately began filming, which intensified their street jive. Little Sparrow dropped to his knees, James Brown–style, and started shouting, "Please, please, please," in an attempt to cadge another play. We appreciatively forked over more dollars and were rewarded with a string of Al Green hits. Then Little Sparrow shouted, "Are you ready?" We howled back, "Yes," and he launched into the Impressions' 1968 Christian soul classic "People Get Ready," with a voice as silky as Smoky Robinson's: "People get ready there's a train a-comin' / Don't need to ticket you just get on board." It was perfection. The youngsters helping Frank scrub the bus sang along with them as a small crowd gathered to listen, everyone snapping fingers and swaying in response. They closed with Dion's "Abraham, Martin, and John," shook hands with us, said, "Keep the faith," and headed down the street singing and jiving, enjoying their seemingly random lives. We just turned around and they were gone.

It was late afternoon by the time we left the King Center, and we hadn't had lunch yet, so after a quick stop in front of the Big Bethel African Methodist Episcopal Church, with its JESUS SAVES sign dominating the steeple, and the nearby Royal Peacock Night Club, a historic showcase for black musicians, now closed, looking like an exhausted, smash-faced boxer who had taken one punch too many, we headed to the Varsity, a sprawling, 1950s-style diner near Georgia Tech to indulge in their unbeatably greasy delights. The Varsity, home of America's best hot dog and orange frosty, has a lingo all its own: "One naked dog, walking, and a bag o' rags" gets you a plain hot dog and french fries to go. We chowed down on our way to Grant Park, where students could either spend an hour at the Atlanta Zoo to check out the new Birds of Prey Amphitheater, Flamingo Lagoon, and African Rain Forest, or visit the adjacent Cyclorama, a huge circular painting (42 feet by 358 feet in circumference) depicting the Battle of Atlanta. Shari, our resident Civil War buff, led a group of us into the Disney prototype, painted from 1885 to 1886 by a group of Polish and German artists. It still remains an entertaining way to learn history, even if that history isn't accurate.

Spectators sit inside the circle of the painting and the viewing platform slowly rotates while they watch, seriatim, General William Tecumseh Sherman burn Atlanta to the ground and then set out on his notorious "march to the sea." By the time we rotated through 360 degrees of battle it was clear to one and all that Sherman had not been exaggerating when he wrote, "Behind us lay Atlanta, smoldering in ruins, the black smoke rising high in the air, and hanging like a pall over the ruined city." It was disconcertingly dysfunctional after an intense afternoon at the King Center to see the Cyclorama of Civil War Atlanta burning, with not a single Negro slave represented in the entire painting. With the openness of youth, Shari asked the African American woman who narrated Cyclorama whether this omission didn't strike her as exclusionary, if not downright racist. "No," the narrator responded evenly. "Times were different when this was painted; we weren't considered people then," clearly unwilling to risk her livelihood by discussing the bad old days. Shari mulled over the response for the rest of the evening.

As the zoo contingent rejoined the Cycloramans at the Majic Bus, we opted for a quick game of football to burn off some of those Varsity calories. After we worked up quite a sweat, a blind vendor in a seersucker suit sold us shaved ice snowballed in a cone-shaped cup and topped with fruit-flavored syrup, his aged German shepherd growling softly and flashing us incisors to ensure that its owner wasn't cheated. Matt muscled his way to become the only person to take a shower, before Frank drove through downtown Atlanta. We parked in front of the blue-bubbled Hyatt Regency, and the students bailed out for four hours on their own. One small contingent immediately headed to the hyperactive underground Atlanta, the reincarnated six-block entertainment-shopping district opened in 1989, which now accommodates one hundred specialty retail shops, twenty food-court vendors, and twenty-two restaurants and nightclubs on three levels. Besides having dinner, they made a pilgrimage to the World of Coca-Cola Pavilion, a fifteen-million-dollar museum, shrine, and tasting center for what the company modestly calls "the most successful product in the history of commerce." In front of the pavilion they watched a teenager lose ten dollars at three-card monte to a street hustler with a plastic hospital bracelet on each wrist. Another group, which I led, strolled around downtown and had a drink atop the Hyatt's dimly lit, revolving Polaris Restaurant, the peach sky just bruising into evening as we arrived at sunset, right on cue. Of course we didn't dine there, perched high in the sky, for we had all learned the first rule of travel: "Never eat while spinning."

Reconvening back at the bus, we swapped stories while cruising down Peachtree Street, one of America's grand historic thoroughfares. As Frank hunted for a way out of Atlanta, I gazed at Peachtree, thinking how different European streets are from America's. European streets typically end—or begin—in an enclosed communal space: a *piazza*, a *place*, an *agora*, a *forum*. The straight streets of the American city extend on into the infinite horizon. The old adage that all roads lead to Rome applies to all the great European capitals: In Paris, Rome, and London, all roads converge in the city. But the American urban grid disperses the city outward, which is perhaps not surprising when most of our forebears found it preferable to abandon everything and everybody they knew for the unknown of the New World. And so Peachtree does not run into Atlanta, but out to the sleepy suburbs and their industrial parks and on into the countryside, to little red-clay farms and brier patches, to peach orchards and cotton fields, to the Georgia coast and into the Appalachians, to the submerged alligators of the Okefenokee Swamp and the flying golf balls of Augusta National.

Springtime had given birth to crocuses, dogwood blossoms, and a fine crop of peachfuzz hot-rodders zooming down Peachtree, socialized enough not to run red lights but taking fiendish delight in putting the pedal to the metal for a block and then slamming on the brakes to a screeching halt. Held at bay by a red light in front of the Peachtree Arts Theatre, a red

Camaro with four college-age guys—looking not for trouble but for display opportunities, like peacocks fanning their tails—squealed to a halt next to us, Lynyrd Skynyrd's "Freebird" exploding from their chariot of fire. A red-haired mother with two preschool children scurried safely across their path, glaring at the Camaro for menacing her precious ones. The scene brought to mind novelist Margaret Mitchell, who was run over by a drunk driver racing down Peachtree. Mitchell died five days later in Grady Hospital. The driver, who had twenty-three prior traffic violations, was charged with involuntary manslaughter. As I told the story to Frank, topping it off with a tasteless "and she was gone with the wind" quip, he grew uncharacteristically silent, even somber. It was only later in our journey that he told me of the tragedies he and his family had experienced at the hands of reckless drivers.

While I was in auto-fatality mode, it was a small leap to Bessie Smith, so I told the students all about the legendary Empress of the Blues. After making her first recordings in 1923, she became a regular attraction at Bailey's 81 Theatre in Atlanta. She rose from the fog of obscurity to such a pinnacle of fame that her appearances caused serious traffic jams from Detroit to New Orleans. Of all the female blues and jazz singers Bessie reigned supreme. Her 156 album sides, recorded for Columbia Records, saved the company from almost certain bankruptcy. Then in 1937 an authentic American tragedy struck, best remembered now from Edward Albee's play *The Death of Bessie Smith*. One evening, on her way from Memphis to a performance in Clarksdale, Mississippi, she was in an automobile accident. Because she was black, the angels of mercy who ran the nearest hospital, which was for "whites only," wouldn't allow her in, so she bled to death. We elected to hold a Bessie Smith memorial festival right then and there; in addition to dozens of her songs, we listened to The Band's tribute to her, called simply "Bessie Smith."

When Frank found I-85 South it was Bessie's unmistakable husky voice that set the mood, the sound accompanied by the whoosh of trucks passing in the night, an occasional horn, the rattle of undetectable loose metal, the rush of cool night air whistling through the roof's portholes, and the idle chatter and laughter of youth. It was as if we were floating down the Georgia interstate, a part of some buried child's dream. For the next five weeks we would shuck off our old regimented lives—movement would be our permanent condition, community our mode of expression.

We cheered as we entered Lynyrd Skynyrd's "Sweet Home, Alabama"— home to us not because of racist former governor and Democratic presidential candidate George Wallace or the collegiate football strategies of Bear Byrant but because of those Alabama natives Booker T. Washington, George Washington Carver, Helen Keller, and Nat King Cole.

We reached downtown Montgomery, cradle of the Confederacy, about an hour later, in quest of cold beers and a boogie-woogie jukebox. Everything was silent and shut, except for the fly of a vagrant peeing on the sidewalk in front of the white-domed State Capitol. Less than a block away, four policemen were shooting the breeze, standing outside their patrol cars, sharing a box of doughnuts while they were in all likelihood swapping tall tales about who was the best crime fighter, oblivious to the urinary impropriety being committed nearby against the great state of Alabama (as they say at political conventions). We paused for a moment at the corner of Rosa Parks Avenue (named after the woman whose refusal to give up her seat in a "whites-only" section of a Montgomery bus sparked the Montgomery bus boycott in 1955) and West Jeff Davis (named after the Civil War president of the Confederacy), an ironic and symbolic intersection that seemed to sum up the two Souths: the Sunny South versus the benighted one, *Uncle Tom's Cabin* versus *Birth of a Nation*, *Gone With the Wind* versus *Roots*. Bessie was still going strong as, mellow but high spirited, we left Montgomery. Only now, with no beer in prospect, one by one we all dropped off to sleep in a state of blissful forgetfulness, all except Frank, of course, who drove by the guitar-strumming Hank Williams statue in town, tooted his horn, and listened to Bessie all the way to Biloxi, where he finally got a few hours' sleep.

Frank had parked the Majic Bus right on the beach, and we awoke the next morning with the sun shimmering on the blue-green Gulf of Mexico, a Caribbean breeze wafting the smell of salt air and tropical fish over us as it rustled a few tattered palms into swaying ever so slightly. Curious seagulls, sensing the possibility of handouts, strutted around the bus as though it were a can of sardines they hadn't quite figured out how to pry open. A small one-engine plane flew overhead, trailing a sign advertising wind-surfing lessons to the yet-to-arrive hordes of spring-break collegians. As we poured out of the bus and adjusted our eyes to the bright morning sun, ready for a wake-up splash in the gulf, we were greeted by the sight of three very dead, very water-logged seagulls lying at water's edge, flies and other scavenging insects feasting on their partly devoured carcasses with all of nature's indifference. The sight turned us off to the swim, so we opted instead for a hearty pancake breakfast at which nobody ordered eggs or anything even vaguely associated with fowl. Justin asked the cashier—a weathered old salt with sunburned eyes—about the possibility of taking a deep-sea shrimp boat out into the gulf. After a two-minute monologue, obviously committed to memory by a lifetime of retelling, about how he "won the battle of his life" reeling in the stuffed blue marlin prominently displayed above the register, he offered to take us shrimping for a "reasonable group fee." Although it was doable, I nixed the idea, not wanting to spend too much time in Biloxi, anxious to make New Orleans for lunch. In *The Air-Conditioned Nightmare*, a caustic, bitter critique of the American scene published in 1960, Henry Miller said that Biloxi was the most pleasant surprise of his trip. He must have seen something we missed. Though the sultry sea breeze was pleasant enough, and though the town has plenty of Old South architectural gems, Biloxi itself reminded us of a decaying Jersey beach resort minus the boardwalk. What makes Biloxi—as well as nearby Ocean Springs, Bay Saint Louis, and Pass Christian, Mississippi—so fascinating is that plantation-style architecture has been transplanted to the leisurely Old South beachfront, giving these communities a distinct antebellum charm, although all have been sadly overwhelmed by commercial ventures and high-rise condos.

After breakfast we strolled back down the beach, which for nearly two centuries has been a popular resort area for residents of Natchez and New Orleans to escape the sweltering heat and cool out in, we gritted our teeth and waded into the gulf, which was as warm as blood. We didn't stay in for long. As we walked on, we ran into an old man named Hale dressed in full safari getup, scavenging in the sand with a metal detector for "lost treasure." He said he once found a Purple Heart right where we were standing, which he sold to "some fool survivalist for fifty dollars." Told of our cross-country trek, he wailed that we were giving Biloxi short shrift and invited us back in February for a "real Fat Tuesday" Mardi Gras celebration. New Orleans, he said, had shamelessly let its chamber of commerce transform Mardi Gras into a "queer carnival" full of druggies and "freakish undesirables." In Biloxi, he bragged, Dixie Mafia kingpins organize Mardi Gras, and "let me tell you, kids—gangsters, *they* know how to throw a party! Patriotic, not like all that New Orleans sissy stuff." Kevin asked what he recommended we do while in Biloxi. It took him all of a second to respond: "If I were you fellas, I'd run over and see the tittie show at the Golden Nugget or the Dream Room. You can't miss em'. They're shinin' pretty, across from the Krispy Kreme right on the old Scenic Highway."

Ignoring the treasure hunter's tip, we loaded onto the Majic Bus and headed off for a brief planned stop at the Jefferson Davis shrine in Beauvoir; then we would shoot straight for the French Quarter. Students, particularly the would-be shrimpers, were now grousing about wasting precious New Orleans time for yet another dull Confederate memorial. Bourbon Street jazz, Mississippi River paddleboats, and Creole gumbo were on their minds, not Jefferson Davis's goatee and rusted swords. Suddenly I realized it was April 1, and my prankster wheels started to spin in overdrive. As we drove I mentally weighed an array of historical shenanigans. Inspiration struck when we passed a small, lighted baseball stadium with fold-up metal bleachers and permanent dugouts. I asked Frank to pull over. "Everyone out!" I shouted. "We're stopping to see Ty Cobb's grave." (Here was my moment for April Fool's Day revenge.) The students

119

assembled on the grass and I gave a brief lecture on the Georgia-born (and -buried) Ty Cobb. (Arguably the greatest baseball player ever, he retired with an astonishing lifetime batting average of .367.)

"See that mound of dirt behind the left-field fence?" I pointed, like Babe Ruth, to where I was going to hit one out of the park—metaphorically—and then ad-libbed, "That's Ty Cobb's grave. There's no tombstone because he was a humble man and wanted to be buried in an unmarked place, inside the shape of a pitcher's mound." When Jared, our sports maven—in cahoots with me on the prank—confirmed that Cobb was truly buried behind the left-field fence of a Little League park, they bought it. Off they marched to the unmarked mound while Frank, Jared, Beth, and I stayed behind, trying not to split our sides with laughter. They all dutifully snapped photos of the mound, and one student wrote in his journal that it had been a "moving experience." Some of the students even brought back a handful of dirt from the mound. In the face of later skepticism, I insisted that Ty Cobb was buried there. Gradually, as the day wore on, some students realized that it *was* April Fool's Day, and Ty Cobb's grave *had* been created out of thin air. But many never figured it out. If W. P. Kinsella and Ring Lardner could make up baseball stories that seemed authentic, so could I; especially on April first.

We had a pleasant drive to New Orleans, along beautiful bays and artificial beaches, clear enough to see the outlines of the Gulf Islands National Seashore to the south, protruding upward from the green-brown swirl of water, and the giant arching oaks and crape myrtle trees in front of plantation-style houses with columned porches to our north. Yards were bursting with camellia, cape jasmine, and even an occasional fig, lemon, or pomegranate tree. As we entered Louisiana bayou country, alligator stories made the rounds on the porch: Kevin told of a man from Tallahassee who showers with one; Christine reported how the Seminole Indians of Florida revered them; Frank revealed the Cajun superstition that an alligator crawling under the house is a portent of death; Janine mentioned that Southern folk medicine uses alligator teeth and oil to treat certain ailments; Alan told us the old saw about alligators in New York sewers; and I added that alligator wrestling has been a popular sport in Louisiana for two hundred years. When we had exhausted the topic of alligators, Alison brought up Anne Rice's vampire novels, set largely in New Orleans. Apparently most of the students had read at least one of them.

Time flew by as the raucous zydeco music of Clifton Chenier and the Louisiana Hot Band entertained us straight into the embrace of the Crescent City. Frank exited the interstate by the ultramodern Superdome, searching in vain for a parking spot close to the French Quarter. As William Faulkner noted in his 1927 novel, *Mosquitoes*, traffic in New Orleans "inched forward, stopped, inched forward again." Eventually, after a fruitless half hour searching not only for a parking place but also for a glimpse of the maddeningly elusive Mississippi, hidden from sight by a levee, Frank let us all disembark with orders from me to congregate at the Sheraton New Orleans on Canal Street at 3:30 P.M. sharp. Tardiness would not be tolerated, for we were expected at the University of New Orleans for a guest lecture by Professor Steve Ambrose on his favorite subject besides D-day and Eisenhower—the Lewis and Clark Expedition of 1804 to 1806, with an emphasis on Meriwether Lewis.

No sooner were we out of the bus and into the French Quarter than rollicking, good-time jazz from nearby Jackson Square filled our ears. What we thought was one jazz band turned out to be three separate, cacophonous groups playing completely different styles of music in the public space, all vying for tourist attention and dollars. While one band played traditional Dixieland, another played crazed, Cajun-accordion zydeco, while yet another played rhinestone-cowboy country kitsch. The competition was stiff, for besides musicians there were white-faced mimes, fire eaters, jugglers, tambourine men, gypsy tarot-card readers, voodoo merchants, break-dancers, puppeteers, portrait artists and cartoonists, hippie jewelry makers, Indian bead makers, and born-again Christians preaching salvation. Jackson Square—site of the ceremony marking the Louisiana Purchase, and dominated by a large equestrian statue of General Andrew Jackson, who defeated the British in the Battle of New Orleans—was the carnival the students always imagined it would be, full of noise

121

and pulsating rhythms, except that the Spanish-style Saint Louis Cathedral was more awesome and the square more commercial than they had supposed.

Dan and Jay had made a solemn pact to hear as much music as they could while in New Orleans. They started in search of authentic jazz—which struggles to maintain visibility in the age of MTV, hip-hop, and rap music—by following a haunting sound from the levee. There they got not only to inhale their first view of "Ole Man River" but to watch and listen to a young African American trumpet player, no more than twelve, blow his untarnished soul and mind out into his tarnished horn, playing not so much for money as for the dream of being the next Louis Armstrong, who also began on the levee.

Dan and Jay were far from being jazz purists. New Orleans's funky music heritage was special to them because it conjured up not only images of the piano jazz master Jelly Roll Morton, the soprano sax and clarinet of Sidney Bechet, and the trumpets of King Oliver and King Louis, but also the late rhumba-blues saint Professor Longhair warbling the comical "Bald Head," or the socially conscious Neville Brothers harmonizing to "Yellow Moon" and Fats Domino pounding out R&B thrill after thrill, singing his 1949 cut "The Fat Man" with the same thick regional accent he had into the 1990s. Whether it was hard-pressed jazz soloists wailing notes on the levee; fast-paced blues tunes being sung and played on a Chartres Street tin cup with spoons; the battered horns of Bourbon Street bands blaring away through open doorways of dance halls; or institutionalized Dixieland drifting out of the musty, weathered walls of Preservation Hall, Dan and Jay were listening avidly. Sure, the French Quarter had become a tourist trap, and Bourbon Street, named after French royalty, was now ruled by the "adult entertainment" sleaze merchants. But still to be found were the drunken, one-eyed notes of Jean Laffitte—era sea chanteys dangling in the air of Pirate Alley, dirges pouring out of the voodoo-tomb mouths of the Buddy Bolden and Marie Laveau black-magic dead, and music history swirling around every bend, from the fat crickets in the mausoleums of Saint Louis Cemetery to the midnight jazz mass at Our Lady of Guadeloupe Catholic Church, whose once-mossy walls, now scraped clean, still seemed to vibrate with an eerie percussive quality—the echo of slavery's whip.

While other students spoke with craft vendors and storekeepers, munched crayfish *étouffé* and alligator-sausage po' boys and savored bananas Foster and pralines, Dan and Jay hunted for sound. And they found it: a woman bigger than Etta James singing Shirely Caesar gospel on the steps of the Second True Love Baptist Church; a young Scat Man Crothers, with his top hat extended, singing "Bye Bye Blackbird" in front of the place where William Faulkner wrote his first novel, *A Soldier's Pay*; a group of dread-locked rastamen chanting Haile Selassie speeches to the beat of bongos, helped along by hemp; a ragtag band of young, colorfully attired Haitians demonstrating for open immigration, singing "America the Beautiful" in Franglish in front of the old U.S. Mint, where "a streetcar named Desire"—one of the cars from the old Desire line—is on display; a college kid from Tulane with long sideburns, dressed like the young Elvis, strumming and shouting "Suspicious Minds" for the steady flow of Japanese and German tourists disembarking from buses in front of the Mardi Gras Museum in search of Americana; an old drunk who looked like a disheveled Al Hirt, mumbling Mother Goose rhymes in a gravelly hipster voice in Louis Armstrong Park, demanding handouts simply for being the lost soul that he was; a woman playing her portable keyboard in front of the Palm Court Jazz Café on Decatur Street, in the belief she would have been as famous as Harry Connick, Jr., had she been born male; a satin-jacketed black street gang making music of sorts just by arguing among themselves like a swarm of killer bees; a hometown banjo man slowly picking "Fair and Tender Lady" in painful anguish; a yazoo con man, hum-buzzing "When the Saints Go Marching In," who figured out years ago that tourists don't know the difference between him and real musicians and tip the same; and a woman named Roxanne, in a sequined outfit with pom-poms, who for five bucks cheerleads fight songs on request in front of Johnny White's Sports Bar and makes more money in an hour than the other performers do in a day.

It didn't take Dan and Jay long to decide that Storyville might be dead but New Orleans was happening, and they wanted to be a part of it. Jay now realized for the first time that he, too, was a real musician; his guitar playing wasn't merely an avocation. It was a trade, a skill, a meal ticket. If all else failed, he could take to the lost highway and play the tortured Delta blues, starting at the "crossroads" junction of Highways 61 and 49 in Mississippi, then drifting up and down America's byways, using New Orleans as his base and Robert Johnson as his mentor. What would he be missing, anyway? Insurance policies, pension plans, and income taxes? New Orleans got his mind spinning like the paddlewheel of a steamboat, for now he had experienced the ethnic gumbo of New Orleans. By comparison even New York seemed bland. Jay instinctively felt the clash of two cultures, the Latin-Mediterranean-Catholic influence and the WASP South, and he understood why author Walker Percy called New Orleans the only "foreign city in the United States." In New Orleans he could be frivolous and stand on a pedestal, he could be carefree as the talking-blues-man Harmonica Frank, whom he read about in Greil Marcus's book *Mystery Train*, singing "Rockin' Chair Daddy": "Rock to Memphis, dance on Main / Up stepped a lady and asked my name / Rockin' chair daddy don't have to work / I told her the name was on the tail of my shirt!"

I spent my time away from the students in search of two very specific items: a signed common first edition of *A Confederacy of Dunces* (signed by either his mother or Walker Percy), the only novel by New Orleans's native son John Kennedy Toole, who committed suicide at age thirty, and a box of Sister Mary's homemade pralines, available only at Saint Clare's Monastery, which I had foolishly promised to bring home to a friend in New York. Believe it or not, the signed novel was easy to find; I just headed over to Beekman's Books, which has two entire floors of used editions, and plucked it off a shelf for a fairly hefty fee.

Pralines were another matter. Pralines are a roundish, freeform candy patty about three inches in diameter and a half-inch thick, made with pecans, milk, butter, and lots of sugar. A good, fresh praline should melt in your mouth. Pralines are not difficult to find in New Orleans; in fact they abound in candy and souvenir shops all over the French Quarter. But finding Sister Mary's pralines was another matter entirely. Before I left New York, my friend—who grew up in New Orleans—brought me *au courant* on praline history. It seems that a recipe for an almond candy had been brought to New Orleans from France by Ursuline nuns in 1727. Finding no almonds but plenty of pecans, the cooks improvised, thus the birth of pralines. For generations the special "original" recipe has been passed down from nun to nun, and today a box of Sister Mary's pralines are a delicacy to die for. The problem is that they are hard to come by: Demand outweighs the monastery's output. Uncertain of my chances of success, I decided nonetheless to give it a try. Worried I'd get lost traveling by streetcar, I splurged for a taxi and headed to Audubon Park, where Saint Clare's is located. A handwritten cardboard sign on the monastery shop window read, YES—WE HAVE SISTER MARY'S PRALINES. I purchased twenty-four for nine dollars. By the time the Majic Bus hit Memphis they were all gone. Only the receipt was left as proof to my friend that I had fought the good fight against everything but temptation.

As we congregated back on the Majic Bus, the party-revved students were bubbling over at the prospect of a crazy evening in the Big Easy, where "the night life is the right life." Everyone had a different story to tell. Kevin had gone to an old-fashioned, Ring Lardner–style barbershop and got a crew cut; Darlene had gone to the New Orleans Steamboat Company to make dinner cruise reservations for ten on the authentic steamboat *Natchez*; Alan had gone looking for spots filmed by Oliver Stone in *JFK*; and the KDR boys had eaten po' boys and muffuletta sandwiches at the Napoleon House courtyard, where Mozart or Haydn or one of those wigged guys was playing, and then washed down the sandwiches with Dixie Beers at a nearby bar. Everyone had spent some of their time strolling and gawking at the never-ending street theater of the Vieux Carré (the old square), with its mad cast of characters and centuries-old buildings dripping fancy black cast-ironwork as if they were a stage set. Aíne, Janine, and Christine had sat along the riverfront, enjoying the sultry spring day, listening to the sounds of the calliopes on board the docked steamboats. Tennessee Williams's favorite city had become ours in only a few hours.

We arrived at the University of New Orleans, which sits on Lake Pontchartrain, about fifteen minutes late, greeted by Steve and Moira Ambrose and a journalist from the *New Orleans Times-Picayune* who ended up writing a terrific story about the American Odyssey course. Historian Steve Ambrose, a star pulling guard and middle-linebacker during his student days at the University of Wisconsin, has long been an inspiration to me. Besides writing such American history classics as *Crazy Horse and Custer: The Parallel Lives of Two American Warriors*, a two-volume biography of Dwight Eisenhower, and a three-volume biography of Richard Nixon, he has a genuine gift for teaching young people and an insatiable mountain man's instinct for exploring the Rockies. Often during the summer when he is not writing a book in his Wisconsin cabin, he takes groups of young people down the Lewis and Clark Trail, reading selected passages from the *Journals* out loud in the exact spots described.

Ambrose regards Meriwether Lewis as the epitome of the authentic American hero, for Lewis possessed a rare combination of talents—for military leadership, exploration, scientific observation, and mapping, and an extraordinary literary gift—that together made him the perfect buckskin scout to open the American West. As a demonstration of his devotion to Lewis, Ambrose once spent the night in a cemetery in Tennessee, sleeping beside Lewis's grave, not to commune with his spirit but simply because he wanted to. After we all sat down in a large classroom, Ambrose gave a brilliant, booming lecture on Lewis and Clark and their companions, who from 1804 through 1806 became the first white men to cross the western half of North America, in what is now the United States. As always, Ambrose spoke to the students, not at them—the sign of a real teacher. Using slides he had taken along the trail to augment the lecture, Ambrose talked about the complementary abilities of the two men, although Lewis was the ultimate authority in every aspect of the expedition. The students learned just how significant an achievement this twenty-eight-month, eight-thousand-mile trek really was. Beginning in Saint Louis, the expedition traveled up the Missouri River, crossed the Rocky Mountains, and by way of the Clearwater, Snake, and Columbia rivers reached the Pacific Ocean. On that entire journey only one man lost his life, probably from a ruptured appendix. For the remainder of American Odyssey we would time and again cross paths with Lewis and Clark and recall various points Ambrose had made.

After lecturing, Ambrose opened things up for a question-and-answer period. Although most questions pertained to Lewis and Clark, Stefanie asked about the popularity of ex-Klansman and former gubernatorial candidate David Duke, who had only months earlier grabbed headlines all across the United States with his outspoken white-supremacist beliefs. Ambrose tried to assure the many Jewish students that they had nothing to fear in Louisiana but admitted that the politics certainly differed from New York's—a fact he underlined chillingly by telling us about a New Orleans neighbor who flies a Nazi flag daily. He explained about Cajuns, actually Acadians, French-Canadians who were expelled from Nova Scotia by the British and migrated to Louisiana. He said we could find their descendants living a little to the west of New Orleans, still engaging in farming and trapping, still speaking their unique brand of French in low-lying and boggy bayous, and still proud to call themselves Cajuns. His parting advice to the students was to try jambalaya for dinner, a spicy rice dish cooked with stock and chopped seasonings and made with a number of ingredients, including sausage, shrimp, ham, and chicken.

That evening I dined with the Ambroses at a local Creole café on crayfish, oyster stew, and history talk. Frank dropped the students in the French Quarter for dinner, followed by hours for fun on their own. We would pull out of New Orleans at 2:00 A.M., heading first to Oxford, Mississippi, to visit William Faulkner's house, and then on to Graceland, the home of Elvis Presley in Memphis. Chicago was next, where we could at last grab a night of bed sleep courtesy of Best Western hotels. Given tight student budgets, expensive Cajun restaurants like K-Paul's Louisiana Kitchen were out of the question, but the moderately priced Olde N' Awlins Cookery wasn't. Many of the students dined there, eating hot and spicy "blackened" Cajun food and trying alligator sausage as an appetizer.

Darlene led her delegation to the Toulouse Street Wharf to board the *Natchez*, a marvelous three-deck sternwheeler docked at the wharf behind the Jackson Brewery, which took them on a two-hour cruise down a small section of the world's third longest river. The students had just started reading *The Adventures of Huckleberry Finn*, and simply seeing the brown muddy water foam in the paddlewheel with a Dixieland jazz combo playing on board was a rush, as the guide on the intercom told them that the Mississippi and its tributaries linked thirty-one states to the gulf. They were amazed to learn that so much tonnage passes along the river that the Port of New Orleans surpasses New York in shipping. A single tank barge, of which they saw and heard many, bleating like lost sheep, can be more than a thousand feet in length, and its nine-million-gallon capacity exceeds that of a thousand railroad tank cars. But what interested them more were the commercial fishermen scouting catfish and the one-room shacks perched on stilts over the Mississippi: They wondered who lived in them and how often their makeshift homes were flooded.

After the river cruise, the *Natchez* group took to Bourbon Street with a madcap vengeance. While Dan and Jay listened to rarefied jazz, rhythm and blues, and zydeco music in various uptown bars like Tipitana's (home of Professor Longhair) and the Maple Leaf, most of the other students were content with a flaming drink at Pat O'Brien's and a dance down Bourbon Street to whatever brass band jammed the loudest. Stefanie and Alison were in a particularly vibrant mood. Something about the air of New Orleans made them lose their inhibitions, and when they heard a small jazz combo launch into "Hello, Dolly!" they grabbed Kevin and started dancing in the middle of Bourbon Street. They went shake, rattle, and rollin' away, their cheeks flushed red as streams of sweat rolled down their faces. Then, just as the band started playing "Hang on, Sloopy," Stefanie's ankle popped out, and she collapsed on the street in excruciating pain.

Kevin helped her up, but she was unable to walk properly. By the time she got back to the Majic Bus, her ankle was badly swollen. We got some ice and tried to make her as comfortable as possible, but she was concerned about being an imposition on us. Our stoical trooper called her parents in Saint Louis and decided to leave us for a few days to get X rays, an Ace bandage, and crutches. Since we were heading north to Chicago after Oxford and Memphis, we decided to drop her off in Saint Louis and pick her up on our way back down.

We were all exhausted as we left New Orleans—all except Frank, who had taken a six-hour nap. I remember nothing else about the evening except hearing Little Milton sing his number one R&B hit "We're Gonna Make It" as I drifted off to sleep. We were headed into the heart of the Mississippi Delta.

6

Into the Mississippi Delta

Ah, just act the way you feel.

—ELVIS PRESLEY

M-I-S-S-I-S-S-I-P-P-I.   IN   ELEMENTARY   SCHOOL   MOST
Americans learn how to spell it rote fashion, but do we really ever have
a cohesive vision of one of the nation's poorest states? In high school
history classes Mississippi is remembered as a battleground of the civil
rights movement of the 1960s. To a score of Bob Dylan singing "Oxford
Town," thirty-year-old black-and-white film footage flickers through our
collective conscience as James Meredith courageously challenges segregation, entering class at Ole Miss surrounded by federal marshals. In
college literature classes Mississippi is the sacred soil of the Literary
South, nourishing storytellers William Faulkner, Eudora Welty, and Willie
Morris. And outside our formal institutions of learning, there is yet a third
important cultural stream, split into many currents: America's musical

130

heritage. To millions of inhabitants of the Bible Belt (geographical and coaxial), rock-and-rollers, and pop-culture mavens, the northeastern Mississippi town of Tupelo is our nation's Bethlehem—the birthplace of Elvis Presley. For a smaller but no less enthusiastic cult, it is the fertile alluvial floodplain of the Mississippi Delta that is sacred—the fount of Delta blues.

We awoke at 6:00 A.M. in perishing darkness in Clarksdale, the first major Mississippi Delta town south of Memphis. Clarksdale had once been the center of the Delta Blues, and the Majic Bus was in pursuit of the animating spirits of Robert Johnson, B. B. King, Charley Patton, Howlin' Wolf, Son Thomas, John Lee Hooker, and Muddy Waters. It was a sentimental and foolish quest—especially at that predawn hour, for the Delta blues is night music. Besides, I don't know what we expected to find. Life in the rural Delta was always hard for its poor inhabitants, especially during the Great Depression—the heyday of the Delta blues. Perhaps the only lesson to be gleaned was not to romanticize rural poverty. Until the 1940s there were more black people in the Delta than in all the New England states combined, and today whites remain a clear minority in the region.

Only Frank, Beth, and I were awake as the dark sun began to rise and bugs splattered against our windshield like hail; the students were clearly not in an early-morning mood after a night in New Orleans. We drove past the Delta Blues Museum, housed in the large redbrick Carnegie Public Library, only blocks from the Sunflower River. Fellow early birds— two barefoot black boys—bounced tennis balls off the wall of Clarksdale Baptist Church, across the street from Saint George's Episcopal Church, where Tennessee Williams's grandfather was rector and the budding playwright grew up at the rectory next door. In his best works Williams used Clarksdale and Delta place-names and personal names to give his dramas a ring of Southern authenticity. We also paid our respects to Bessie Smith at the Riverside Hotel—in 1937, the black hospital where she died. The tangible signs of Clarksdale's rich blues heritage were somehow evident in the closed shops and silent churches without being noticeable, as if an

131

entire historical drama had been acted out over many years and we were glimpsing a split second of the final act. "This briefly, is the Mississippi Delta," David L. Cohn wrote in his lyrical 1948 memoir, *Where I Was Born and Raised*. "Under these conditions, against this background, and in this environment nearly one hundred thousand whites and three hundred thousand negroes live and have their being. It is a strange and detached fragment thrown off by the whirling comet that is America."

The Delta, that strange, flat and haunted region, a great agricultural garden of cotton, soybeans, and rice, lies between Memphis and Vicksburg. As Big Daddy says in Williams's *Cat on a Hot Tin Roof*, the Delta "is the richest land this side of the Valley Nile." William Faulkner described it in one of his books as "five thousand square miles, without any hill save the bumps of dirt the Indians made to stand on when the river overflowed." At my instigation we were making an early-morning pilgrimage to a sacred spot. We drove past a few rusting stop signs and abandoned tractors to the junction of Highways 61 and 49, just outside of town—not far from serene Moon Lake, made famous by Tennessee Williams in *A Streetcar Named Desire* and where Deacon Fred Davis still performs his highly ritualistic baptismals. This junction is known to music lovers as the crossroads made notorious by the enigmatic Robert Johnson, King of the Delta Blues. Blues mythology has it that at this crossroads Johnson sold his desolate, desperate soul to the devil to play the meanest blues guitar in the region. Some say Johnson, who went on to record twenty-nine seminal blues songs, got the best of the bargain, although he died young in 1938, his death shrouded in black-magic rumor. According to one version, he died in agony after being fed lye by a jealous girlfriend. According to another, he was stabbed (or possibly poisoned) in a juke joint by a jealous husband. Without Robert Johnson, rock and roll would not have been possible. "The blues had a baby and they called it rock and roll," legendary Rolling Forks, Mississippi, bluesman Muddy Waters once noted.

I had Frank stop at the crossroads, the tape deck moaning Johnson's "If

I Had Possession Over Judgment Day." Outside, a single-engine plane dusted the vast cotton fields surrounding us, its mission the slaying of the insatiable and marvelously adaptable insect hordes. As I stood on Highway 61—the road that carried migratory blacks from New Orleans to Memphis to Chicago in search of the promised land that has yet to be—a chill swept over me, as if the Delta sky were heaven and the crossroads a crucifix and Judgment Day upon us, upon our nation. The feeling was self-induced by years of imagining myself standing there, and I wanted it to linger.

I looked out over the cotton fields. There was cotton as far as the eye could see. The soil here is dark Delta silt, the finest crop-growing dirt anywhere. Dozens of plump, damp night crawlers, evidence of last night's crackling thunderstorm, slithered onto the wet asphalt of Highway 61. Bloated in the middle like tiny pythons from gorging on the soil's abundant nutrients, they bore witness to the land's fertility. Even though it was a warm, pregnant-possum spring morning, the air lay heavy, more like a Delta winter dusk, in which all is a sullen, sorrowful gray. There were no historical markers at the crossroads, no trace of Robert Johnson's pact with the devil, except for a cracked black plastic Gibson guitar pick I found, a sign that a fellow pilgrim had inadvertently—or intentionally—left a piece of himself behind. Highway 61 has become a new route of return, as people flock to the Delta in search of the roots music and the great literature that sprang from this most improbable garden. Yet there was no Edenic sign of life at the crossroads, only the promise of stormy weather and the fading buzz of the solo crop duster that controlled the morning skies.

As we headed back to Clarksdale, the town's faint streetlights seemed happy the night shift was over. Soon Jim O'Neal, founder of *Living Blues Magazine*, would flip the sign on his shop, Sunflower Avenue Stackhouse Records, from CLOSED to OPEN; Wade Walton would start singing the blues as he cut hair in his shop; and Mayor Aaron Henry Espy, the brother of

133

Bill Clinton's secretary of agriculture, would begin another slow-paced day at City Hall. But it is when darkness prevails, when demons and spirits reign, that the bottle caps at Margaret's Blue Diamond Lounge are popped and guitars are tuned in tandem lament like front-porch-dirge crickets after the first October frost. It's the tuning of guitar strings over the relentless insect obbligato—not "field hollers," Sunday preachers, and harmonicas—that is the taproot of black music in America and that still survives in the old form in the Delta. Many of the other old ways no longer survive, however, replaced by magical, mystical junk strips with a Wal-Mart instead of the main square as the town center. The sharecropper shotgun shacks are abandoned; the African American churches that accent the landscape are in disrepair; the continual river floods are no longer contained by the dirt levees; and many new plantation owners live in faraway places like Britain, Japan, and the Middle East; but Robert Johnson's guitar of unrequited love can still be heard in the Delta juke joints.

Since most of the students were still sleeping, we decided to head down Route 6 for sixty miles so we could all breakfast in Oxford, the model for William Faulkner's "Jefferson," the heart of Yoknapatawpha County. Faulkner, who was born in New Albany, Mississippi, in 1897, lived from 1930 until his death in 1962 in Rowan Oak, his intricate antebellum home at the bend of Old Taylor Road on the southern edge of town; and the Majic Bus was going to pay it a visit.

On our way to Oxford we all seemed to get a mild case of the blues. Frank was complaining of hand cramps from gripping the wheel so tightly, while our tired, gritty eyes gazed blankly at the cotton and soybean fields, railroad tracks, shiny farm equipment, shacks barely standing, tree-eating kudzu vines choking the Mississippi hills, and hidden mossy ponds, where, it is said, catfish grow as big as crocodiles and "mooskeeters" the size of bats. Before we parked for breakfast in downtown Oxford, I had Frank pull in front of the Lyceum at the University of Mississippi—Ole Miss—

which opened in 1848 with eighty students and remained whites-only until James Meredith's integration breakthrough in September 1962.

Meredith's admission to Ole Miss climaxed eighteen months of legal and political resistance from both university and state officials—particularly Governor Ross Barnett, who physically barred Meredith's admission on two occasions. The federal government, in an effort to avoid rioting, ensconced him quietly on campus amid a phalanx of federal agents, but when it was discovered that Meredith was there, rioting ensued that left two dead and hundreds injured. Eventually the racial tension that accompanied Meredith's admission subsided, and he graduated in August 1963. My students loved hearing that when he received his diploma at the graduation ceremonies he wore a NEVER badge, Ross Barnett's segregationist motto, turned upside down.

Ole Miss is a remarkably beautiful campus. Sitting on a lawn of the serene, tree-shaded campus—whose 1992 student body in large measure resembled that of a typical Northern college—it was hard for students to imagine the racial hatred evoked by the mere presence of a black person. I mentioned that James Meredith, who lives in Cincinnati, believes that nothing has changed since 1962: Whites still treat blacks as second-class citizens. Meredith feels the best solution is for all blacks to move to Mississippi, form a nation, and secede from the Union. When students expressed dismay at this separatist view, I decided it might be apropos to run through a brief who's who of a few non-Baptist black leaders of the sixties: former Black Panther Bobby Seale, writing barbecue cookbooks in Philadelphia and helping the poor; comedian-activist Dick Gregory, a self-anointed diet guru with his own slim-trim-powder line; author of *Soul on Ice*, Eldridge Cleaver, writing for William F. Buckley, Jr.'s *National Review*; James Forman, advocating some kind of back-to-Africa movement; Stokeley Carmichael (now Touré), the warm-up act for Louis Farrakhan, head of the Nation of Islam. We could draw no useful generalization from this where-are-they-now? exercise except a reminder that the African

135

American community was not a monolith in the sixties, and it is not a monolith now. There is a broad spectrum of voices—from Angela Davis, who ran for vice president on the Communist party ticket, to Associate Supreme Court Justice Clarence Thomas—but there is no question that all these disparate individuals share one thing in common: a burning desire to end discrimination against blacks by white America.

After my lecture we trooped to Smitty's Restaurant for a home-style Southern breakfast featuring grits and redeye gravy, biscuits with blackberry preserves, fried catfish, chicken and dumplings, and cornbread and black-eyed peas. It was the relaxed Southern rhythms of Smitty's, not the food, that the students hoped to connect with. But our large, somewhat grungy group caught the immediate attention of the locals—as it would in any small-town restaurant—and we were the object of stares and some titters. The intrepid Jared nevertheless decided to interview two beefy, thick-necked old men wearing caps advertising a local fertilizer company. He asked whether they admired their town's literary great, William Faulkner. "You mean ol' Count No 'Count?" the less beefy one replied in a thick drawl. "Nobody reads him aroun' here 'cept the college kids. Why should I care about what a lazy drunk with high-falutin' airs thinks about Mississippi?" Asked what author they liked, they took awhile, but they both chose Stephen King—putting them in good company with many Americans. The students were amazed to find that Smitty's sported a framed photo of Dan Quayle on the wall, a tribute to the patron saint of the Republican right. In their small world, defined by the college campus, the only photos of the then–vice president they had seen were graffiti sketches on dorm walls. Despite Jared's effort to make contact with the locals, we decided it was perhaps best to keep a low profile, even though the menu at Smitty reads: "If you need anything that ain't on here, holler at the cook!" If looks could have killed, the late-breakfast crowd at Smitty's would have made mincemeat out of what they considered a noisy, disheveled crew from New York. But the food was finger-lickin' good, and after a while the hostile glares tapered off.

Breakfast over, the students roamed around Oxford for an hour or so.

Many of us headed over to Square Books, one of the South's finest book-shops, where some students, without the compulsion of an assignment, purchased such Faulkner classics as *The Sound and the Fury* (1929), *As I Lay Dying* (1930), and *Absalom, Absalom!* (1936)—all novels that for-ever altered American literature. The pleasantest surprise was that Frank purchased a cassette of Faulkner reading his own fiction. Since Frank had never gone to college, never formally studied the country he loves so much, he was immensely open—even more so than the students—to the educational opportunities American Odyssey presented, especially Lewis and Clark and the great American writers we were studying. So, while Frank taught me about truck stops, juke joints, and highway vernacular, I reciprocated with stories about our country's history.

We all met back at the bus for a ten-minute hike through lush Bailey Woods to Faulkner's secluded Rowan Oak—the house where he created the world of the Compson brothers and Flem Snopes—preserved as it was the day he died in July 1962. Sitting in Faulkner's backyard, I lectured to the students about why this high-school-dropout-turned-Nobel-Prize-winner chose to set his nineteen novels in this northern Mississippi town, which he called "my own little postage stamp on native soil." If Faulkner meant the postage stamp to be a symbol of sovereignty and control, that was surely not the case in his Mississippi.

Faulkner came of age at a time when Mississippi and the South were changing rapidly. He grew up a part of the post–Civil War culture, which was dominated by memories of the Old South and the war at the same time as the region experienced the modernizing forces of twentieth-century Northern industrialism. (Had Faulkner lived another month he would have seen James Meredith integrate Ole Miss). Faulkner valued community—at least in the abstract—as the source of history, custom, tradition, and myth, and this is expressed also in his obsessive efforts to restore Rowan Oak to its antebellum grandeur.

But a postage stamp also means communication. And blasting their way into Faulkner's love of his Southern past were the works of such modern-ists as T. S. Eliot and James Joyce. Although Faulkner saw modernism as a sweeping away of the past, a destruction of history, and an assertion of the primacy of the individual over community, he nonetheless transplanted their literary techniques to his native soil, in an attempt to divorce modernist style from modernist content. And thus, as F. Scott Fitzgerald so acutely noted, it was Faulkner's complex fate to struggle to hold these two opposing ideas in his mind at the same time and still somehow retain his ability to function.

The ironies of Faulkner's situation are rampant. As Jared had discovered from his research at Smitty's Restaurant, Count No 'Count was never really accepted in Oxford, even though the frail writer tried manfully to don the good ol' boy mantle—shooting quail, fishing for catfish, and drinking corn liquor with the locals, who all the same thought writing was an effeminate occupation. Faulkner spent his entire productive literary life in Oxford, in a shoe that didn't quite fit, unable to function effectively elsewhere.

And so he was a deeply conflicted man, obsessively restoring Rowan Oak to its antebellum glory in a world in which Rowan Oak was an absurd anachronism, and writing in a language of disintegration, not restitution. Faulkner was torn between his longing for the Old South, which was rapidly disappearing under the onslaughts of Northern industrialism and modernism, and his willful dedication to anarchistic innovation, using such avant-garde techniques as nonlinear narration, abstraction of character and place, and shifting points of view. Faulkner was our greatest literary retriever, drawing on the folklore of the South and Oxford and reconstructing it as myth.

Reading Faulkner gives a clear sense of the predicament faced by the post–Civil War South, as well as a clear understanding of the United States as it entered the turbulent twentieth century. Sitting on the lawn of Rowan Oak, I regretted not having assigned the students any Faulkner, but this did not deter me from telling them Faulkner tales. The students' favorite was of his disastrous time as University of Mississippi postmaster, from 1921 to 1924. He was forced to resign following accusations by officials that their postmaster preferred to read rather than attend to patrons, tossed mail in the trash can, and played golf during official hours—

among a long list of other derelictions. Eudora Welty once imagined what a postal patron during Faulkner's tenure might have found:

> We've come up to the stamp window to buy a 2-cent stamp, but we see nobody there. We knock and then we pound, and then we pound again and there's not a sound back there. So we holler his name, and at last here he is. William Faulkner. We interrupted him. . . . When he should have been putting up the mail and selling stamps at the window up front, he was out of sight in the back writing lyric poems.

Later, as we walked through the lovely oak-lined residential streets of Oxford and back to downtown, with its wonderful ambience and charm, I thought about Faulkner and all that he represented: the culture of the romantic Old South and the impossibility of disentangling it from the economic and social bases of slavery and Jim Crow that had made it possible.

If we use the most telling evidence of the death of the Old South and the triumph of the New—Bill Clinton's choice of another Southerner as his vice presidential running mate (defying the conventional strategy of using his choice to give the ticket geographical diversity)—we can see William Faulkner as the last modern intellectual to carry the literary burden of the Old South like an albatross around his neck—the Civil War and the race issue always nipping at his heels like baying hounds. Faulkner was a literary vessel for the wilting-away of the Southern magnolia, his mythical Yoknapatawpha County—the last bastion against the rapid waters of Yankee industrial progress, the Snopeses, and the U.S. Constitution finally rushed through Oxford in a flash flood, drowning the last remnants of a time-honored tradition. Of course, Faulkner's Old South can still be found in Oxford and elsewhere, in the archives and museum of the Center of Southern Culture at Ole Miss and in the voices of the men at Smitty's who called Faulkner Count No 'Count—voices Faulkner treasured nonetheless because they had survived for a hundred years, though their death certificate had been signed at Appomattox Court House.

As we picked up I-55 for the hour-long drive to Memphis—the city where nothing ever happens and the impossible always does—Elvis Presley was on our minds because we were heading to Graceland, Memphis, Tennessee. In the bland world of airlines, pilot chatter is limited to stating weather conditions, pointing out the Grand Canyon on your right, the Golden Gate Bridge on your left. But when a pilot about to set his passengers down in Memphis gets on the intercom, there's a special warmth to the announcement, a tone reserved for personal heroes: "Welcome to Memphis, the home of Elvis Presley, the King of Rock and Roll." But we were driving to Memphis. How should we get in the Elvis mood? Rock artists Paul Simon and Warren Zevon have sung about the meaning of driving to Graceland, but we weren't that introspective and decided to listen to the King himself.

We were rocking out to his 1950s Sun Record hits as we killed time debating which Elvis should be on the commemorative stamp planned by the U.S. Postal Service: the fresh-faced young man in his twenties or the obese fellow he became. On the Majic Bus the choice was unanimous for the young Elvis—as it proved to be, by a three-to-one margin, for the rest of America. Our only major complaint for the Postal Service was that it had taken so long to honor the King; after all, there is a stamp for Jan E. Matzeliger, inventor of the shoe-lacing machine. We knew that Tanzania had resolved the "Which Elvis?" debate imaginatively—boosting its foreign exchange in the process—by issuing ten different Elvis stamps.

Does Elvis Presley deserve a commemorative stamp? Can fifty million Elvis fans be wrong? Of course Elvis deserves a stamp! Not only are those fifty million fans right to admire the King, but not to be part of their ranks is to have let the past forty years of American pop culture pass you by. To dislike Elvis, to dismiss his music and his golden voice, is not to understand America itself and to miss the crucial point that Elvis was an American revolutionary.

It was the revolutionary Elvis that I wanted my students to meet at Graceland. Even though most of the students knew the rough outlines of the Elvis saga, I provided a brief rundown. He started life near the bottom, growing up poor, first in Tupelo, Mississippi, and then in Memphis. Even though he couldn't read a note of music, he fell in love with what was then called "race records," the rockin' blues sound of the black radio stations that played B. B. King and Howlin' Wolf. In 1954 Elvis made his first recording for Sam Phillips's Memphis-based Sun Records, in a style that drew from diverse sources—black and white gospel, Perry Como crooners, rural and urban blues, and country—creating a dynamic new musical synthesis later labeled "rockabilly." His earliest national recognition came in 1956 with the success of his first RCA Victor release, "Heartbreak Hotel." (This song's iconic power nearly two-score years later is evidenced in its use by Bill Clinton to galvanize his then-sagging presidential campaign in his late-night Arsenio Hall television debut. Clinton clearly knew how to woo the Elvis bloc.)

In 1956 this twenty-one-year-old ex–truck driver followed up his TV debut on "The Milton Berle Show" with an appearance on "The Ed Sullivan Show," gaining instant notoriety because CBS network censors would not permit the cameras to rove below his belt. Neither music nor adolescence was ever the same again. His growing legion of fans—to the young rocker's dismay—called him Elvis the Pelvis, while clergymen all over the country denounced him as a tool of Satan. His lifelong manager, Colonel Tom Parker, a hustler who once painted sparrows yellow to sell as canaries, wanted to expand Presley's market niche beyond hormone-driven teens, so he steered him into sappy patriotic ballads and to Hollywood, where he made some thirty eminently forgettable B movies. After years of mediocre movies and songs, Elvis came back strong to record some of his finest songs ("Suspicious Minds," "Burning Love," and "In the Ghetto") and to perform spectacularly on the December 3, 1968, Elvis TV special. By the early seventies he had become most at home in sequined jumpsuits, performing for the Las Vegas dinner crowd, surrounded by a mob of bodyguards known as the Memphis Mafia. He became depressed, developed an eating disorder, and ballooned to well over two hundred pounds, and he died on August 16, 1977, in a haze of prescription drugs. But this bare-bones outline of the vicissitudes of Presley's life scarcely does justice to his achievement as an American pop icon.

———

Walt Whitman said of himself: "Do I contradict myself? / Very well then, I contradict myself / I am large, I contain multitudes." Presley, like America itself, is large and contains multitudes. He was insolent yet courteous, narcissistic yet humble, a "greaser" yet a good army boy, Pentecostal pious yet hellcat hedonistic, multi-millionaire yet forever the poor boy. If Faulkner carried the albatross of the Old South around his neck, Elvis Presley's life and music carried with them the many tensions and contradictions of an evolving Southern and, more importantly, national culture. As rock critic Greil Marcus has written in his brilliant book *Mystery Train*: "Presley's career almost has the scope to take America in. . . . [He] has emerged as a great *artist*, a great *rocker*, a great *purveyor of shock*, a great *heart throb*, a great *bore*, a great *symbol of potency*, a great *ham*, a great *nice person*, and, yes, a great American" (emphasis Marcus's).

It is a concept of Elvis Presley as a great American that is hard to explain to his critics, and to most academics, primarily because the great historic Elvis has been lost to the gaudy histrionic Elvis. Listening to David Letterman Elvis jokes, reading that Elvis has been discovered alive at a Baskin-Robbins in Kalamazoo by some enterprising reporter for the *National Enquirer*, one can hardly blame those who still remember a sanctimonious Elvis standing alongside Richard Nixon, launching a war against drugs (at least the nonprescription variety). But the revolutionary Elvis has also been marketed to death, his face on virtually everything from toilet tissue to nail clippers, his name invoked by Democrats and Republicans alike, for their own ends.

I was hoping against hope to find the revolutionary Elvis at Graceland, the white man who by singing "race music" helped smash Jim Crow laws and segregation just as surely as the 1954 Supreme Court decision in *Brown* v. *Board of Education of Topeka* and the Civil Rights Act of 1965. This is a large claim, but I believe Elvis was not only a vessel expressing society's currents, just as William Faulkner was, but a shaper as well, even though Presley himself was unaware of his role. By acting instinctively, absorbing black music and culture because it moved his soul, singing whatever he wished without regard for arbitrary rules governing the proper songs white people were supposed to sing, using his body in a sexy manner because he felt like it, Elvis helped liberate the country from the strictures of its puritanical heritage while blurring the nation's black-white cultural boundaries, making black music popular with white teenagers. His "frontality" was an invitation to America's women to liberate themselves by expressing their own sexuality directly. Although an earlier generation of women may have swooned at Frank Sinatra, their reaction to Elvis was stripped of any euphemisms by his famed pelvis, freeing them up to behave like men—to express sexual longing and desire frankly.

The Dionysian Elvis liberated us in other, more profound ways. Before Elvis, particularly in the South, Monday through Friday was a time of sunrise-to-sunset toil; Baptist Sunday in the South was for repentance, salvation, churchgoing, and family prayers. But Saturday night was a time for excess, mayhem, drunken fights, midnight dances, and howling at the moon. Saturday night was the time to vent frustrations and blow off steam. Elvis's message to a whole generation of young Americans was that they weren't bound by this rigid cycle—Tuesday could be a Saturday night, Wednesday could be a Saturday night, every day could be a Saturday night. He pronounced rock and roll not merely a musical style but a life-style. One was not predestined to a life of work, drudgery, and more work—in a prosperous, postwar America people had choices. You could dance the decade away if you liked: Follow your heart, and you'll find happiness. It was this rock-and-roll attitude that triggered the social experiments of the sixties, which were a rejection by the baby-boomers of their parents' social values. In Eastern Europe and elsewhere in the world during the Cold War, the stakes were higher. Rock and roll took on political coloration: It stood for rebellion against totalitarian tyrants and for putting your head on the dissident block, where it might be chopped off. If one accepts this chain of reasoning, it becomes clear that Elvis Presley was more potent than all the armies of the world combined, mightier than any politician of the postwar era. But until Peter Guralnick, author of such American classics as *Feel Like Going Home* and *Lost Highway*, finishes his definitive biography of Elvis, this revolutionary side of the King will remain buried under the entrepreneurial spirit that has made Elvis a commodity.

When you see the sign for Elvis Presley Boulevard, you know you're approaching Graceland. The boulevard is lined with fast-food restaurants, strip shopping centers, and "unofficial" Elvis gift shops whose windows feature busts of the King and his painted likenesses on velveteen for sale. As we cruised down the Boulevard, we all teased Tom Tolan that he was the spitting image of the King, even making him slick his hair back to perfect his Elvis look. Later we made Tom pose next to pictures of the King in Graceland to prove our point. When we got them developed we howled with delight—he really did look just like Elvis.

A visit to Graceland, which Elvis bought when he was twenty-two years old for one hundred thousand dollars, takes on the aura of a visit to an amusement park, not a home. One doesn't walk to the second-most-visited home (after the White House) in the United States, one takes a shuttle bus from the gift shop. Whatever archival history may have been attached to Graceland has been lost to the forces of kitsch and religiosity. Graceland is run by Elvis Presley Enterprises, and all profits are held in trust for his sole heir, daughter Lisa Marie, who will inherit the estate in 1993. Graceland employs up to 450 people, depending on the season, and admission is $7.50, a modest fee compared to the amount charged by the Biltmore Estate. Our students were just seventeen of six hundred thousand visitors who annually queue for a glimpse of where Elvis lived, died, and is buried.

Since the students had always heard Graceland described as a mansion, they were disappointed, for their expectations had been shaped by the mansions of Long Island's Gold Coast. The medium-size, white-pillared, suburban Southern home was felt to be lacking. But we were thrilled to learn that his Aunt Delta still lives on the top floor of Graceland, because it added a human dimension to this product of the Colonel Parkers of this world. The students also enjoyed touring the house, for its interior is a frozen tribute to seventies taste, that awkward decade when Richard Nixon, Gerald Ford, and Jimmy Carter occupied the White House, and polyester, black lights, bell-bottom trousers, lava lamps, and eight-track tapes were the rage. The interior was designed by Elvis and his wife, Priscilla, and some of the choicer spots include the Jungle Room, with its carpeted ceiling, leopardskin lampshades, zebraskin sofas, and unpleasant use of ceiling mirrors; and the navy-and-lemon TV Room, outfitted with three screens so Elvis could watch three football games at once, an arm's length from the well-stocked bar. The lengthy Hall of Gold, crammed with platinum, gold, and silver records, leads to the Trophy Room, containing Elvis's costumes, outfits from his films, and his extensive gun collection.

As Alan Mindel pointed out, at Graceland "you get the churchgoing Elvis, not the pharmaceutical Elvis," which is not exactly surprising, considering the commercial nature of the place. The visitor to Graceland learns that Elvis's records, like McDonald's hamburgers, are reckoned in the billions. It always seemed to me unfortunate that he died in 1977, a truly clumsy year. Had Elvis been able to make it into the eighties, I'm sure he would have gone to the Betty Ford Clinic, cleaned up his act, started wearing cotton, gotten Christian counseling from Billy Graham or Johnny and June Cash, and staged yet another comeback, this time thin as a rail, singing Elvis Costello and Nick Lowe songs—and perhaps sold trillions of records.

I was most moved by the mass outdoor cry-in at the Meditation Garden, where Elvis (January 8, 1935–August 16, 1977); his mother, Gladys; father, Vernon; and grandmother are buried by the swimming pool. A forty-something couple with matching red bowling Windbreakers placed a dozen sunflowers on his grave and crossed themselves again and again in anguish, saying, "He loved us, he died for us"; a young stoner in torn blue jeans tossed a watch on the grave as an offering; a woman in an ELVIS IS A CAPRICORN T-shirt leaned against a rail dizzy, immobilized by

145

the sight of his grave. I overheard a man tell his wife how fortunate the garden sparrows were because they got to spend "all their days" close to Elvis, his wife nodding in dreamy agreement. Despite the overlay of commercialism, there is still something special about Graceland that makes the place a wellspring of remembrance—something that makes so much of America from the fifties, sixties, and seventies flash past.

After bearing witness to the outpouring of love at his grave, we hopped back on the minibus and were taken to the "official" Elvis gift-shop complexes, and the magic was gone. The same folks you bowed heads with at the gravesite were now elbowing each other to be first in line for souvenirs, often acquired with the words, "This Elvis collectible [fill in name of collectible: key chain, statue, playing cards] ought to be worth something down the pike." And perhaps, too, it's this American sensibility that mixes the sacred and the profane, the spiritual with the chance to make a buck, that makes Presley still a living presence.

Stacey Shepard, formerly Graceland's marketing director, says that over 60 percent of the visitors buy something at the gift shop. Among the notable early official products Greil Marcus reported finding in Elvis Presley Boulevard trinket shops were "Always Elvis," a wine advertised as "the wine Elvis would have drunk if he drank wine"; and "Love Me Tender Chunks," a dog food (presumably the dog food Elvis would have eaten if he were a dog). Below the counter one can find "Elvis Sweat," a glass vial with a prayer card produced by Madison Jest, Inc. ("The IMPOSSIBLE has happened. Elvis *poured out* his soul for you, and now you can let his PERSPIRATION be an INSPIRATION.")

While students snapped one another's pictures next to Elvis's pink Cadillac and fully customized airplane, the *Lisa Marie,* ensconced in front of the gift shop, I ventured back across the street to the "Wall of Love" that surrounds Graceland and is festooned with tens of thousands of messages from fans. There, a teenage girl with a Magic Marker was busy inscribing something to the King. "What are you writing?" I asked. Without looking up, she continued scrawling intently. "I'm asking Elvis to help me find a job." For some reason, in some warped way, this response made sense to me. It was the cult of Saint Elvis, a powerful intercessor and bearer of deeply felt prayers to a God who wasn't dead. Graceland is truly a religious shrine, and Elvis is a religious movement. Long as the movement doesn't preach hate or injure anyone, what's the harm? As John Lennon sang, "Whatever Gets You Thru the Night". . .is all right.

Although the revolutionary Elvis gets lost in a sea of high-camp commercialism and false piety, we've still got authentic relics—his golden hits and obscure classics. By the time we got back to the Majic Bus we were all Elvis-ed out, so I stuck *Bob Dylan's Greatest Hits, Vol. II* in the tape deck and when "Tomorrow Is a Long Time"—the only Dylan song Elvis ever recorded—came on, I thought of the older Elvis: "I can't see my reflection in the waters / I can't speak the sounds that show no pain / I can't hear the echo of my footsteps / Or remember the sound of my own name." And then I thought of the young Elvis—the one we all wanted to see on the postage stamp. Suddenly I didn't want *any* Elvis stamp branded "U.S. Postal Service–approved." Enough already. Just give me the soulful music of Alex Chilton and two aspirin, and maybe tomorrow I'd be able to find the remnants of the revolutionary Elvis that our visit to Graceland had nearly effaced.

As an antidote to Graceland's overcommercialization I thought a short spin around Memphis and a drive by the Lorraine Motel might help. There, in 1968, outside Room 306, Martin Luther King, Jr., was slain by James Earl Ray. The motel is now a nine-million-dollar National Civil Rights Museum focused on the fifties and sixties. Across the street we noticed an African American woman sitting on a sofa, to whom we paid no special heed. We stopped for a bite at a Hardee's. A stern-faced old man in a disheveled suit eating a cheeseburger enquired about our group. We told him of American Odyssey, and our visit to Graceland, and our drive past the Lorraine Motel. His sternness melted as he spoke animatedly about the Lorraine. He asked whether we had heard of Jacqueline Smith. He was not referring to former "Charlie's Angels" actress Jaclyn Smith but to a well-known Memphis protester, in fact, the sofa-sitting woman we had just seen, who has fought in vain to have the sacred soil where King fell reflect his vision by using it as housing for the homeless, not another tourist trap.

Memphis's Jacqueline Smith is a thirty-nine-year-old former motel desk clerk who lived at the Lorraine from 1977 to 1988. She had to be forcibly evicted to make way for the construction of the National Civil Rights Museum. Refusing to leave the premises, she continued to protest by camping out in a tent in front of the motel for more than two years, from January 1988 until July 1990, when two sheriff's deputies with a court order physically removed her as a trespasser on private property. Undaunted, she put down stakes on the sidewalk across the street, and for the past two and a half years has resided there, a daily living protest of the museum. She vehemently opposed the city council's decision to use the motel to attract tourist dollars, decrying it as an exploitation of sacred ground; but her sense of the right thing to do failed to win converts among the powerful. On view in the museum are such pseudoattractions as a replica of a Montgomery, Alabama, city bus like the one Rosa Parks rode in 1955 when she refused to give up her seat, as if Memphis were bereft of its own authentic exemplars.

Like Rosa Parks before her, Jacqueline Smith still refuses to budge. Along with her tent she has set up a protest table, written and distributed a pamphlet about her eviction plight and Dr. King's life, and continues her one-woman vigil to this day. "She is an angel of mercy," our Hardee's friend said sadly, closing his tale of the triumph of dollars over dreams with an anti-Memphis diatribe: "The Chamber of Commerce thinks this rat's-ass town is going to be America's great new tourist mecca. Hell, the crazy fat cats have built a fifty-five-million-dollar, five-level giant pyramid where Wolf River Harbor meets the Mississippi, thinking it's going to be another Statue of Liberty or Eiffel Tower. Memphis is Elvis-drunk." Though it wasn't on the itinerary, we all decided we at least had to see the pyramid—and besides, it was on the way.

The Great American Pyramid is framed by the I-40 entrance ramps to the Hernando DeSoto Bridge to Arkansas, which was our planned route north out of Memphis. The brainchild of Sidney Shlenker, the multimillionaire who once owned the Denver Nuggets basketball team and the Astrodome in Houston, the thirty-two-story, stainless-steel-coated pyramid has a base that covers 6.8 acres. The structure houses a twenty-thousand-seat arena and will soon be the permanent home of the College Football Hall of Fame and major exhibit halls. Designed as an homage to the Egyptian pyramid built by Cheops, the pyramid is in actuality an eccentric New Age American monument. Sidney Shlenker also saw the pyramid as a monument to America's musical heritage, much of which has been shaped by the Memphis sound—from the Beale Street blues of W. C. Handy to the Stax Record soul of Otis Redding to the Sun Record rockabilly of Jerry Lee Lewis and Elvis Presley. It opened in November 1991 with the Judds' farewell concert, and shortly thereafter Stormin' Norman Schwarzkopf spoke to a sold-out crowd of pyramid patriots. But Shlenker couldn't come up with all the money he had pledged, and the city dismissed him as manager before construction was finished. Shlenker sued Memphis and lost. The pyramid project was taken over by a Texas conglomerate unctuously named Leisure Management. Sidney Shlenker, the man who dreamed up the Great American Pyramid, left Memphis scorned and vilified. And so Leisure Management now runs what they call The Pyramid, while Shlenker has been pushed out of the picture. But a hundred years from now it will be Sidney Shlenker who is honored in Memphis, not the bean counters, for the pyramid isn't going anywhere, and it dominates and will continue to dominate the Memphis skyline. Shlenker's dream has become the city's signature.

From the outset many of Memphis's 650,000 residents believed that Shlenker's Great American Pyramid was a pie-in-the-sky boondoggle, the misbegotten product of the uncanny successes of Elvis Presley Enterprises and Federal Express, both Memphis-based businesses. Pyramid critics say the city was taken in "hook, line, and Shlenker" by an out-of-town shyster and point to Memphis's shaky record with tourist attractions, including the sixty-three million dollars spent a few years ago to develop Mud Island, in the middle of the Mississippi River, into an amusement attraction. The highlight of the Mud Island development is a five-block-long scale model of the Mississippi River (a river within a river, where the Gulf of Mexico is a chlorinated swimming pool with a white sand beach!). A Huck Finn playground and a talking Mark Twain robot polish off its list of main drawing cards. Business, needless to say, has been bad.

Like Ted Turner and Donald Trump, Sidney Shlenker is an example of the great-American-wheeler-dealer-visionary-entrepreneur-risk-taker who is so much part of our American heritage—"the frontier ethos, refined and transplanted to an urban context," in Larry McMurtry's words. As we drove past the Great American Pyramid, which has triggered a Mississippi River—monument war with Saint Louis and its beloved Gateway Arch, I laughed out loud. There it was, Sidney Shlenker's dream, the third tallest pyramid in the world, perched on the banks of the Mississippi River. From its observation deck visitors will soon be able to view the semi-impoverished city of Memphis and the increasingly polluted Mississippi Valley, enjoying a vantage point therefore reserved to dead pharaohs in faraway Egypt. As the Majic Bus slowly rolled across America's "Nile" on the De Soto Bridge, I wondered what the great Spanish explorer would have thought of the pyramid's observation deck, a surveyor's dream: I recognized that with the Snopeses William Faulkner anticipated the arrival of the Shlenkers, back in the 1920s. I thought what a shame it was that Elvis Presley would never perform there or get to see his sweat-soaked towel hung in one of its exhibition cases. And finally I surmised that Robert Johnson would have viewed Shlenker's dream as the black-majic mojo of the devil. As we entered Arkansas I thought of Bill Clinton, jogging across the nation looking for votes in McDonald's, and I knew our president understood what the Great American Pyramid was all about— it was in his blood—and I thought of the late Sam Walton, the Arkansas entrepreneur and founder of Wal-Mart, ranked the richest person in the United States, and I knew he would have liked to have had the Great American Pyramid built at his Wal-Mart Visitors Center in Bentonville, Arkansas. I thought, too, of Mitch Bernstein, American Odyssey's Sam Walton wannabe, who was slightly miffed that we weren't visiting either the pyramid or Bentonville.

Then I thought of the defiant Jacqueline Smith, who still refuses to budge from her vigil outside the Lorraine Motel, trying in her own way to keep the spirit of Dr. King's vision alive. Smith had fought the booster mentality and lost, but she kept the faith, a time-honored American tradition. Shlenker was able to sell his dream scheme to the boosters, who bailed out when the going got rough, another time-honored American tradition.

That evening as we drove through Arkansas, Missouri, and Illinois to Chicago, up I-55, the superslab that has replaced the still used Highway 61 as the principle road to the promised land of urban employment, the thought of Jacqueline Smith stayed with me. As we passed through Jericho, Arkansas, it was her defiance that made me think of what Maya Angelou painfully wrote about her native state: "Old crimes like moss pend from poplar trees. / The sullen earth is much too red for comfort." As we drove in darkness through the Mark Twain National Forest in southern Missouri, it was her struggle, pitting the sacred against the profane, that made me sad. As we delivered Stefanie into the tender, loving care of her parents in Saint Louis, I thought of Smith's compassion for those without a home. It was her integrity that came to mind as we cruised past the Lincoln Motel and Land of Lincoln billboards in Springfield, Illinois; the thought of her four-year struggle kept me tossing and turning on the bus floor that night, with the incongruous image of her sitting on a sofa without a home.

When an exhausted Frank finally pulled off I-55 for a few hours' sleep at a truck stop in Pontiac, Illinois, I got out for a breath of 4:00 A.M. fresh air. Parked next to us was an eighteen-wheeler with a giant Pink Panther cartoon decal on its side and a small Confederate flag underneath. The driver, in his twenties, wearing blue jeans, boots, and a backward baseball cap, was jawing with a transvestite in high heels, negotiating a deal. Conway Twitty's lost-love hit single, "It's Only Make Believe," was blaring from the truck's tape deck. I returned to the Majic Bus, lay down on the floor, and fell asleep with the song burned into my brain. I dreamed Jacqueline Smith was in my class and I was lecturing her on American life: Don't you realize, Ms. Smith, that Conway Twitty is right, "It's only make-believe"? Don't you realize, Ms. Smith, that nothing is sacred in America—

151

the land where we have visions of the Virgin Mary in our hot tubs and Elvis's face is found on dog food? Sometimes, Ms. Smith, you have to swallow the pain and move on to something else just as Mr. Shlenker did, for nothing is sacred in America. But be careful, Ms. Smith: William Carlos Williams was right when he said, "the pure products of America go crazy," and you're pure. And Robert Johnson was pure. And William Faulkner was pure. And Elvis Presley was pure. And Martin Luther King, Jr., was pure. And yes, Sidney Shlenker was pure. Now they're all gone, and Elvis Presley Enterprises, the National Civil Rights Museum, and Leisure Management are here instead. For the pure, authentic American does march, as Thoreau well knew, to the sound of "a different drummer," ignoring the bland, conformist crowds. Robert Johnson and William Faulkner and Elvis Presley and Martin Luther King, Jr., and Jacqueline Smith and Sidney Shlenker have all heard their own drumbeats, and history will ensure that they, not their surrogates, will survive.

7

Chicago: Our Kind of Town

Chicago likes audacity and is always willing to have anybody try anything once; no matter who you are, where you come from, or what you set out to do, Chicago will give you a chance. The sporting spirit is the spirit of Chicago.

—LINCOLN STEFFENS

CHICAGO HAS INSPIRED MORE GREAT WRITERS — THEODORE Dreiser, Sherwood Anderson, Richard Wright, Saul Bellow, Nelson Algren, James Farrell, and Ring Lardner, to name just a few — and more great appellations than any other city in the United States, with "the Windy City" being the most frequent, A. J. Liebling's "Second City" coming in a close second, Carl Sandburg's "City of Big Shoulders" the obvious choice for third. Nelson Algren mordantly labeled it a "city on the make," one where "someone is always forgetting to touch second," and an "October sort of city even in spring." "Chicago," the one and only Studs Terkel has declared, "is America's dream, writ large." Fred Fisher's 1922 hit song called Chicago "That Toddling Town," while Christopher Morley dubbed

153

it "Old Loopy" in 1935. Which Chicago our American Odyssey would find was anybody's guess.

After a hard week on the road and a particularly long drive heading north from Memphis (just as jazz and the blues had in the 1940s and 1950s), all we wanted from Chicago was a chance to enter the city gates and sleep, but we found ourselves stuck in morning-rush-hour gridlock, which began at Joliet, sixty miles south. The first week had taken its toll on the students, and because we had fallen behind schedule, we missed a free night's lodging at Chicago's Best Western Inn, spending it instead at a truck stop on I-55. Needless to say, we were all anxious to claim our second night's free accommodations.

Eventually Frank made his way down the Adlai E. Stevenson Expressway—the intercity leg of I-55—until we ran smack into shoreside Burnham Park, with blue, boundless, and choppy Lake Michigan as its backdrop. It was cold and windy, a few snow flurries volleying back and forth, people walking briskly with collars turned up to protect against the bitter sting of the frigid air. We were in the north again. Frank sped us down gusty Lake Shore Drive past the ugly concrete and pillars of Soldier Field, which in most other cities would long ago have been bulldozed to make room for an air-conditioned McDome—but not in Chicago, which admires cold stone, steel, and well-managed muscle. Students made mental notes of the Field Museum of Natural History, the Shedd Aquarium, the Adler Planetarium, and the Chicago Art Institute as we drove past. They would visit all of them Saturday afternoon.

The entire bus exploded with cheers when we pulled in front of the Best Western Inn of Chicago, and I came out five minutes later with a handful of room keys. For the most part it was two to a room, divided on a gender basis, with hot baths and naps first on everyone's Chicago to-do list. The students were free to explore the city by themselves but were again required to record in their journals what they learned and saw. We would meet at 9:00 A.M. the next day in the lobby to visit the "Robert Rauschenberg: The Early 1950s" exhibit at the Museum of Contemporary Art. Then, as a group, we would head over to the convention of the Organization of American Historians being held at the

Palmer House Hilton Hotel. While I participated in a panel discussion on "The United States and European Integration, 1947–1955," the students would be required to take detailed notes on any two of twenty conference sessions, such as "The Second Urban Crisis in Contemporary America," "The Politics of William James," and "Women, Family, and Immigration." That was the Chicago game plan. What we actually did was another matter.

For two days I had been looking forward to having that Chicago hotel room to myself so I could indulge in some diary writing, reading, and resting. But with Chicago at my fingertips, I decided I would write, read, and rest some other time. I took a quick shower, threw on a jacket and tie, grabbed two quick slices of anchovy pizza, and set out for the historians' convention to listen to papers on "The Use and Abuse of Discourse Theory in American History." It was here that the Chicago game plan began to unravel.

Conferences were invented to preserve the sanity of scholars. Without conferences at which to share research, information, and gossip, academicians would go crazy. Spending months in an archival repository looking at dead documents is a form of sensory deprivation, of solitary confinement. The academic conference is where we can show the world what we've been up to in the bowels of the library. This time, having absorbed the real America with such vivid clarity for the past week, I found the conference dry, juiceless, and joyless. "Meetings are indispensable when you don't want to do anything," John Kenneth Galbraith once quipped. I was in a mood for "doing." My enthusiasm for American history had been stoked again on the road, and I was much too restless to sit through any more papers. So as the session on discourse theory began, I quietly slipped out into the fresh air and looked up at Chicago's living architectural museum, happy to be playing hooky and out of the overheated hotel.

155

Chicago skyscrapers—courtesy of Louis Sullivan, Frank Lloyd Wright, Ludwig Mies van der Rohe, and many other architectural luminaries— are sturdy. They make the twin towers of New York's World Trade Center look like a plastic tuning fork. Three of the world's six tallest buildings are in Chicago: the Sears Tower, the world's highest at 1,454 feet; the Amoco Building, the fourth tallest at 1,136 feet; and the John Hancock, fifth at 1,127 feet. The mere sight of the skyscrapers was restorative; I was galvanized—but to do what? I was thinking of going to the top of the Sears Tower to see whether I could see the Illinois prairie, the Hub City's spaghetti bowl of train tracks, and the refineries of Gary, Indiana, when a truly inspired idea flashed into my head—go to Oak Park to see the studio home of Frank Lloyd Wright and the birthplace of Ernest Hemingway. But just as I flagged down a taxi I remembered that Hemingway once described Oak Park as a town of "broad lawns and narrow minds." By that time, however, my mind was working like a well-oiled machine, and a third, more exciting prospect appeared—a visit to the two-story terracotta-and-brick Chess Records Studio, where blues music was first recorded in Chicago.

In the 1940s and 1950s scores of black musicians with nothing but their empty-pocket dreams, harmonicas, and highway thumbs left the Mississippi Delta and Memphis to work the nightclubs and street corners of Chicago's South Side. Leonard and Phillip Chess, Polish Jewish immigrant brothers who owned several clubs on the South Side, decided to record the bluesmen they booked, seeking to capture the thunder-in-your-bones live nightclub sound. Over the next twenty years they recorded blues legends, including the likes of Muddy Waters, Howlin' Wolf, and Willie Dixon, as well as rock-and-roll pioneers Bo Diddley and Chuck Berry, who recorded his "Johnny B. Goode" at the Chesses' 2120 South Michigan Avenue address. The building, now designated a historic landmark, is being restored as a modern, working studio.

The taxi dropped me in front of the studio—a nondescript building, circa 1911—and I gazed at it remembering how, as an Ohio teenager, I used to get off on the Rolling Stones album *12 × 5*, recorded here, particularly the instrumental cut "2120 South Michigan Avenue." In fact, some say Mick Jagger and Keith Richards first met in a London record store while searching for Chess records. The Chess brothers sold the company and the building in the late 1960s, and MCA Records now controls the label and the records it produced. The studio is owned and operated by Gerald Sims, a former Chess studio musician who has converted it into a "living music museum where artists can record, where the public can hear lectures on the blues, and where tourists can visit."

As I peered into the grimy front windows hoping for a glimpse of anything—a broken glass, a cigarette butt, a bar stool—I was startled to feel a trembling hand on my shoulder, which made me jump. "Easy now, white bread," a man said. "Johnny B. Goode don't live here anymore." He introduced himself as Sudden Sam Lockwood, a blues harmonica player born and raised on Chicago's South Side. "What's a peasant like you doing in a high-class neighborhood like this?" he joked as he straightened my tie. The aptly named Sudden Sam was a sixty-something fellow who gave Big Joe Turner and Solomon Burke a run for the money when it came to belly tonnage, his cheeks as puffy as the late Dizzy Gillespie's, a cigarette behind each ear sticking out like a little horn, his salt-and-pepper Afro somehow refusing to embrace gray. Once I recovered from the Georgetown flashback and the fear that I would be robbed, we started conversing about Chicago's blues heritage and Chess records. Any blues artist I mentioned—say, Sonny Boy Williamson—elicited a stock response: "Sonny Boy, he was a good friend of mine, still owes me twenty dollars and I plan on getting it from him in heaven or hell, can't tell which just yet." When Sonny Terry's name came up, Sudden Sam pulled a harmonica out of his moth-eaten sharkskin suit, saying: "This is the way Sonny Terry plays it." Then, changing his style for the next number: "Sugar Blue taught me how to make this number cry," and off he went, blasting out another tune. I gave him five dollars for his spontaneous harmonica blues medley, which encouraged an offer of a "blues tour" of Chicago for that twenty bucks Sonny Boy Williamson owed him. I handed over a trusting twenty and said, "Let's do it."

For the next three hours he took me from one blues and R&B haunt to another, saying with an encouraging gesture to follow, "Come on, peasant," particularly when I seemed a little leery of where we were going. We stopped at the Cabrini-Green, a sprawling, graffiti-covered, combat zone of a public housing project where even the law of the jungle has given way to random violence. When we heard a loud boom, Sudden Sam laughed heartily: "It's killing time at the Cabrini-Green." He offered to take me into one of the bullet-pocked project buildings through a back-door fire exit to show me where R&B greats Jerry Butler and Curtis Mayfield once lived, but I declined, causing him to howl with laughter, to call me "white bread" again, and to start singing and harping Willie Dixon's "Back Door Man."

He showed me where Buddy Guy shoots pool, where B. B. King holds court, and where Sam's friend the Golden Goose Man was shot dead by a stray bullet. He pointed out Wax Trax Records Company, and he surprised me by being knowledgeable about such important new bands as Ministry and Black 47. We walked along Lake Michigan for about four miles, checking out fishermen's buckets (empty), watching the sparrows as they pecked the pavement looking for late-winter crumbs, and saying hello to the sturdy citizens flushed with cold who passed us.

At Lincoln Park, the site of the aborted "Youth International Party Festival of Life" assembled by Jerry Rubin, Abbie Hoffman, and Ed Sanders of the Fugs to coincide with the 1968 Democratic national convention, we stared blankly at the polar bears in the free zoo, who were clearly bored in their pseudoarctic setting, our hands buried in our pockets. Sudden Sam told me how he'd been in the park to hear MC5 perform when " 'Mare' Daley's [Richard Daley, mayor of Chicago from 1955 to 1975] Thugs began bustin' on the Fugs," perceiving the event as a Jets-versus-Sharks gang war rather than an example of police brutality. It was impossible to tell fact from fiction with Sudden Sam, but that didn't really matter: He was a master storyteller, a practitioner of the greatest of all art forms. We laughed empathetically at the businessmen clutching their briefcases, each with a copy of the *Chicago Tribune* clamped under one arm, the other arm permanently affixed to his head to keep his hat from taking flight. Then we hiked up Maxwell Street, where the blues stories continued, and sat at the delicatessen counter and had grilled cheese sandwiches and fries at Nate's, where Aretha Franklin sang "Think" in *The Blues Brothers* (starring John Belushi and Dan Aykroyd).

When Sudden Sam met up with an old friend at Nate's, I used it as an opportunity to tell my blues guide good-bye. "Be careful of trouble, white bread," he advised me as we parted, "and don't let your yo-yo string break and your gator wobble." As I left Sam, alley dogs were barking, a bum was scanning the sidewalk for a cigarette butt, parades of after-school kids were screaming out of tune, and a woman was staring out of her open window in solemn search of something lost. I thought of going back to Nate's and asking Sam to play harmonica for my students but decided simply to return to my hotel room. My mind drifted back to the stuffy convention center and all the papers being delivered bedizened with footnotes, and I eyed all the frenzied commuters anxious to get to homes in "safe" suburbs like Lake Forest, Norwood Park, and Palatine, and I was grateful for having met Sudden Sam Lockwood. Though I never got inside the Chess Records Studio, I received a real blues history education, my yo-yo string stronger than ever and my gator steady.

Just as my Chicago blues adventure was ending, Dan, Jay, Christine, and Janine's was beginning. Jay had read in *New City*, Chicago's free weekly alternative newspaper, that the legendary Son Seals—in my estimate, the greatest electric blues guitar player alive—was performing at the two-room, barrel-table blues bar known as the Wise Fools Pub, its walls lined with autographed photos of such greats as KoKo Taylor and John Lee Hooker, the music room dominated by a huge Mobil Oil Pegasus sign. Wise Fools occupies an 1878 building in Lincoln Park and is the oldest blues bar on Chicago's North Side. It was an evening the Hofstra students will never forget. As Jay said, "Hitting the blues clubs in NYC is cool, but the blues just don't seem at home there; the blues fit Chicago like a glove." Shooting pool in the smoke-filled bar while the sizzling, too-hot-to-touch guitar of Son Seals stung them with "Frigidaire Woman" and "I Can't Lose the Blues," they knew they were in Chicago. At the pub the nightly show starts at 9:30 P.M., and the musician plays from the floor, not on a stage, sweating on the dancers, casually ordering a beer as the fast, brusque notes bend and shriek and keep on screaming on. Dan and Jay, who had been ecstatic about the New Orleans music scene, were even more ecstatic about hearing the one and only Son Seals—christened by both the *New York Times* and *Rolling Stone* "one of the most important blues guitarists of his generation." Seals, who grew up in an Osceola, Arkansas, juke joint called the Dipsy Doodle, is known for his rugged style and intensity of play. When he launched into "Woman in Black," firing off notes in a machine-gun frenzy, all the students broke loose to dance up a blues storm. The original Hofstra quartet was joined by Tom, Kevin, Darlene, and Alison, and all of them lost their inhibitions in a haze of blue-collar smoke and grit as Son Seals's mean, guttural six-string notes cut through them like a railroad spike sledgehammering right through a steel rail, sparks and spit and sweat and sorrows flying with reckless extravagance. The students learned that to understand Chicago, it wasn't necessary to read Mike Royko's witty columns or listen to George Will praise the Cubs or Frank Sinatra sing "My kind of town, Chicago is," or even to have Studs Terkel lecture you on "working people." All you had to do was get a cold beer at the Wise Fools Pub and hear Son Seals talk you through "My Life," and you understood Richard Wright's Chicago, "an indescribable city, huge, roaring, dirty, noisy, raw, stark, brutal."

While students were enjoying Son Seals, Beth and I had dinner in the Greenhouse restaurant of the Ritz Carlton Hotel. We were looking out the window at horse-drawn carriages taking folks for romantic spring rides when three limousines and two police cars pulled in front. Just as we began guessing who it could be, in walked former British Prime Minister Margaret Thatcher, who was in Chicago to give a lecture. Seeing her appear out of the blue in the lobby in an electric cerulean suit had the unexpected, surrealistic quality of a painting by René Magritte and made our dinner an event. Afterward we strolled down the Magnificent Mile on Michigan Avenue and stopped to listen to a street choir singing in front of the Water Tower, a survivor of the Great Fire of 1871.

The next morning we all met in the lobby to begin our busy Saturday in Chicago. Originally I had planned for us all to visit the Museum of Contemporary Art and then head over to the Organization of American Historians conference, but Jared, Tom, and Alan began pleading with me to let them go to Wrigley Field to watch an afternoon Cubs-Brewers exhibition game. It seemed that on Friday, while I was following Sudden Sam around, the baseball-loving student trio had found their way by the El train to see Wrigley Field's famed ivy-covered walls. They were able to persuade a security guard to let them into the empty stadium, where they shouted, "Play ball!" just to hear the echo. When they found out from the guard that there would be an exhibition game in the park, they were overjoyed. Jared said he had always wanted to eat Cracker Jack and listen to Harry Caray sing "Take Me Out to the Ball Game" during the seventh-inning stretch. The only thing standing in the way of wish fulfillment was the historical conference. I relented to the baseball contingent, who were dressed especially for plea bargaining in newly purchased blue Cubs caps, to demonstrate their sincerity. This naturally led to further special pleading. Shari chimed in, saying how much she wanted to visit the redbrick, turn-of-the-century Hull House, now part of the University of Illinois in Chicago, where Jane Addams wrought social-work miracles. Other students, who wanted to visit the Field Museum of Natural History, the Shedd Aquarium, and the Art Institute, argued they wouldn't get to see them properly if they had to attend the conference as well. Truth to tell, even though I had to participate in a panel, there seemed to me no compelling reason to risk their eager exploratory mood for a convention they would probably find dull. A deal was struck: We would all go to the Museum of Contemporary Art to see the Rauschenberg exhibit, and then Frank would take everyone except the Chicago Cub trio to the Field Museum of Natural History, where we would all meet—even the Cubbies— at 5:00 P.M. for a Chicago deep-dish pizza dinner. Then we would all see David Cronenberg's film adaptation of William S. Burroughs's *Naked Lunch* at the Biograph Theater before departing the Windy City for Springfield, Illinois, around midnight. With everyone in agreement that this was a fine plan, we set out for the art museum.

Robert Rauschenberg, who studied with German artist Josef Albers at Black Mountain College in North Carolina, is a painter of undisputable innovation and brilliance. When I first saw his silkscreen *Axle* (1964)—in which photos of President John F. Kennedy appear as a leitmotiv—at the Museum of Modern Art in New York when I was twenty, it floored me. There, in this single silkscreen, lay the entire decade of the 1960s ripped open and exposed—its promises, its successes, and its ultimate failures—all contained in a single extraordinary work.

Rauschenberg's *Axle* said it all, and to my untutored eye it was a work of a real native genius. Excited by my discovery, I invested $49.95 in a Robert Rauschenberg art book. At that time in my life the price seemed like a fortune, but it was a worthwhile investment to own a book about an artist I intuited was a kindred spirit. It didn't take me long to learn that he was one of the most influential artists of the twentieth century. In fact Rauschenberg's semiabstract canvas *Curfew* (1958), in which he had cut a hole and inserted four Coca-Cola bottles, represents the birth of pop art, predating Andy Warhol's 1962 piece, *Green Coca-Cola Bottles*. Andy Warhol may have grabbed all the media attention and headlines, but it is Robert Rauschenberg who was our country's great postwar art innovator. Not only is he, along with Jasper Johns, considered the founder of pop art, but Rauschenberg also anticipated minimalism and conceptualism. Anyone seeking to understand American life and American consumer culture since World War II could find no better place to start than Rauschenberg's gigantic multimedia construction, *¼ Mile or 2 Furlong Piece*, begun in 1981 and still in progress. Though currently off exhibit, the piece has been displayed in several venues, including New York City's Metropolitan Museum of Art. In this 388-foot-long, still-growing retrospective of an artist and his era, Robert Rauschenberg—born Milton Rauschenberg in Port Arthur, Texas, on October 22, 1925—has given us (and continues to give us) a visual mélange of automotive, disposable, and recyclable America in a sequential but never-ending fashion.

Rauschenberg's one-work retrospective is pure future, and therein lies his electricity and relevance. It's his never-say-die zest for now, spurred on by the open spaces of tomorrow, that makes him not just an artist but a true American innovator: "He still comes off as a kind of Wunderkind who might be up to something very new next week," *New York Times* art critic Grace Glueck wrote several years ago. In *Quarter Mile* Rauschenberg includes three-dimensional urban and industrial pieces, such as highway construction signs, cardboard boxes, discarded public library books, and other selected symbols of our era, trying to cram as much America as possible into his work. Throughout are distinctive collages of silk-screened fragments of photographs and the printed word, reverberating with allusions to events of our time. "Painting relates to both art and life," Rauschenberg is fond of saying. "Neither can be made. I try to act in the gap between the two." And Rauschenberg makes sure he never paints himself into the painter's corner—embracing printmaking, photography, and many other art forms—including theater and dance—as both a performer and a designer. In 1964 he toured Europe and Asia with the Merce Cunningham Dance Company, and in the 1990s he is collaborating with rock artist David Byrne on a number of multimedia projects. Rauschenberg works at a driven, Picassoesque pace and believes, like Emerson, "Nothing great was ever achieved without enthusiasm."

Unfortunately, that was how most of the students responded to the exhibition—without much enthusiasm. Spanning the years 1949 through 1954, it showcased one hundred works—abstract expressionist paintings, imagist collages, assemblages of found objects, and early conceptual works—from the first phase of Rauschenberg's career. The only work that interested them was *Automobile Tire Print* (1953), in which Rauschenberg had directed composer John Cage to drive a Model A Ford down the length of a twenty-two-foot strip of paper after Rauschenberg applied ink to one of the automobile's tires. The students understood that in his art, Rauschenberg tries to maintain an open and unresolved dialogue between the sense of art and everyday consumer experience, but they remained

163

unconvinced that he has real artistic talent in the traditional sense and thought his *White Paintings* (all-white canvases) the handiwork of a con man. Alan Mindel said: "Rauschenberg is too self-conscious; he wants me to see something in his junk, but to me it's just junk. He throws every object imaginable, including dirt, pieces of fabric, insects, and stones, into such works as *Untitled* (1952). He dumps everything into this piece; I don't think there is an object Rauschenberg doesn't like." It was impossible to change Alan's assessment, though I got him to concede that the Texan's art was consistent with his well-known avowal: "I'm for 'yes.' 'No' excludes. I'm for inclusion." By including everyday objects rejected by our consumer culture, Rauschenberg's art got the students thinking about America's gluttonous habits—a nation with only 6 percent of the global population that gobbles 35 percent of the world's natural resources. None of them were touched by it as I was, but all learned to consider the question "What is art?" from a fresh new perspective.

After viewing the exhibit, the students checked out of their rooms while I participated in my panel on the European Community—an experience best summed up by Sinclair Lewis when he received the 1930 Nobel Prize for Literature: "Our American professors like their literature clear and cold and pure and very dead." But I caught up with a few friends, had a hearty lunch, bought a couple of those half-price books, and took a walk along Lake Michigan eavesdropping on park-bench conversations straight out of David Mamet's plays. While Jared, Tom, and Alan were shivering at Wrigley with double-fisted hot chocolates keeping them warm, fascinated by the people watching the game from apartments behind the left-field wall, the rest of the students were getting lost in the Field Museum, where they sat in a reconstructed Pawnee village and visited an Egyptian mastaba tomb complex that houses Unis-ankh, the son of a fifth-dynasty pharoah. But, in Kevin's view, "Seeing Cherokees and the Memphis Pyramid was tons cooler." They were more impressed by the Shedd Aquarium, which sits across from the Field Museum, jutting out into Lake Michigan. There they saw Beluga whales and dolphins in the two-million-gallon Oceanarium, the centerpiece of a Pacific Northwest Coastal recreation, complete with driftwood and beach pebbles. About a third of the students also visited the show at the Art Institute of Chicago, bypassing Monet, Renoir, Degas, and Van Gogh and heading straight for Grant Wood's celebrated 1930 *American Gothic*.

When 5:00 P.M. came around we all met in front of the Field Museum, threw a Frisbee around in the parking lot, and talked about how anxious we all were for a deep-dish pizza at Gino's East, rated the number one pizzeria in the United States by *People* magazine. Before we took off, we compared notes on what we had found unique about Chicago. The response was unanimous: Chicago was a sports-crazed town ruled by Iron Mike Ditka, now former head coach of the Chicago Bears, and Air Mike Jordan, the greatest NBA player of all time. But if it came to a battle of the Mikes for Chicago's heart, Jordan would win with a hands-down, take-no-prisoners slam-dunk.

When sports commentator Marv Albert asked Mike-or-Michael Jordan which name he preferred, the NBA icon who grows more beloved by America's youth with each passing day answered that it depended on whether they were talking about Gatorade or McDonald's. Add to that list of corporate sponsors Nike Air Jordans, Pepsi, and Wheaties, appearances hosting "Saturday Night Live," his own TV special, and a Saturday-morning cartoon: His image is an inescapable feature of Chicago and the nation's landscape.

Mike or Michael or Air Jordan has become a black Elvis with wings, his likeness everywhere: his face on the blood red double-decker Bulls buses chugging around town; his statue in Nike Town next to the Jordan-autographed Olympic shoes; his posters in every bar and restaurant; Jordan window mannequins are even used to sell clothing. But what was truly amazing was how many young Jordan imitators we spotted—thousands of teenagers, black and white, wearing crimson Chicago Bulls jerseys and black sneakers, their tongues hanging out of their mouths as if they had all been trained to pant like puppies at the same obedience school or as if they were trying to catch snowflakes even though it wasn't snowing or as if they were eating an invisible ice-cream cone or auditioning to be walking Rolling Stones logos. All these kids are sticking their tongues out because

165

they want to "be like Mike." Now don't get me wrong. I like Mike or Michael as much as the next guy and recognize that he is not just an NBA great but a supreme master of his craft whose airborne wizardry defies gravity as he reinvents basketball every time his Nikes hit the court. But if you're going to sign on to hundred-million-dollar corporate deals in a campaign aimed at convincing kids they want to "be like Mike," then the King of Jordan has got to learn to keep his tongue in his mouth or else Chicago will drown in a flood of teenage saliva.

During the entire ride to Gino's East, Jared—who had already sampled deep-dish pizza the night before at Pizzeria Uno, where it originated— lobbied mightily for Harry Caray's, a "celebrity" steak/chop/Italian restaurant chock full of baseball and Michael Jordan memorabilia. As the Majic Bus pulled in front of Gino's, I almost wished we had taken Jared's advice: There was a line two blocks long trailing out the door, helmeted policemen with walkie-talkies and billy clubs in charge of crowd control. The word was that it was an hour's wait. After debating whether to go elsewhere, we decided to brave the line—and boy, were we glad we did! Eating deep-dish pizza at Gino's East isn't just a meal, it's a real Chicago experience, at which you mix it up with the pepperoni-and-beer breath of locals and tourists alike in an intimate pub atmosphere. Gino's has long wooden tables carved with such sayings as DITKA FOR PRESIDENT, JORDAN RULES, and the ultimate Chicago hybrid JORDKA REIGNS SUPREME. Televisions blast ESPN sports nonstop, and sports chat about the Bears, Bulls, Black Hawks, Cubs, and White Sox echoes off the walls of the packed pizzeria as brick-oven-baked, black-pan pizzas steam in everyone's face. As for the pizza itself, Kenny summed it up best when he took the second bite of his first slice and said, "Damn, this is good."

After dinner, we stumbled out of Gino's in high-caloric stupor and set out for the Biograph Theater, where we were to see the movie of William S. Burroughs's *Naked Lunch* to prime us for our visit in Lawrence, Kansas, with the notorious author of the outlaw novel. Talk turned to Chicago and gangsters. A student had picked up a brochure for Untouchable Tours

("Chicago's Original Gangster Tour of the City Capone Made Famous"), a two-hour guided-bus venture of Prohibition-era gangster hot spots and hit spots given by Dixie Don Fielding and Southside Craig Alton. At Gino's one of the locals had told us about the city's generation gap. Chicago's old-time residents are Scarface Capone fans who nurture a deep respect and understanding of bootleggers and gangsters, while newcomers, particularly the young, tend to identify with John Dillinger, although in recent years Babyface Nelson has been gaining ground with the yuppies.

Though we never took the Al Capone tour, we heard all about it. One tour stop, Al Capone's modest redbrick, two-flat house at 7244 South Prairie Avenue on the city's far South Side, was the focus of a citywide hubbub a few years ago. Should the house be designated on the National Register of Historic Places with a plaque marking it as the onetime home of one of America's most notorious gangsters? Angry opposition came largely from Italian American organizations and the *Chicago Sun-Times,* which suggested an alternative: "Turn his victims' homes into landmarks." The Sons of Italy argued that such a designation "would assist in the stereotyping and defamation of all Italian Americans." Timothy Samuelson, the man who originally nominated the Capone house for landmark status, called the gangster "Chicago's most famous citizen" in a twenty-page report for the Commission on Chicago Landmarks, even though Louis Sullivan, Jane Addams, and Carl Sandburg might be more worthy of increased historic recognition. Samuelson lost his battle, but just because civic leaders officially stamped Capone persona non grata does not mean that his fame as a folk hero of demonic proportions has been disposed of.

Chicago's gangland mythology is having a pop-culture renaissance through movies, music, cartoons, and books. Thus it came as no surprise to me that many students were elated to learn that the Biograph Theater was where, in 1934, Public Enemy Number One, John Dillinger—betrayed by Anna Sage, the "Woman in Red"—was shot dead by an FBI team led by Melvin Pervis as he left after watching the movie *Manhattan Melodrama.* I was startled to discover how many students knew all about Dillinger's life of crime—a notorious bank robber, resourceful jailbreaker, elusive fugitive, and smart aleck who liked asking cops to take snapshots of him with girlfriends at the Chicago Century of Progress World's Fair at a time when he was the subject of the country's greatest manhunt.

The myths and lore that continue to surround Dillinger's death are certainly astonishing—that his penis was of such remarkable magnitude that it was preserved for posterity in a case at the Smithsonian Institution and that his brain was removed at the time of autopsy and taken to Northwestern University for study. Matt and Kevin had heard variants of the Dillinger brain myth, and Kevin built on it by saying that he had read "somewhere" that when the Dillinger family threatened to sue the brain had to be hidden, and was forgotten until the physiology department was renovated after World War II. At that time it was supposedly swiped by a Northwestern professor and given to a doctor friend in Kearney, Nebraska, where it was displayed in a local restaurant like the Egg in Sherwood Anderson's short story, a great conversation piece. Dillinger's brain was then purportedly sold to a Chicago doctor named—appropriately—Dr. Brayne. Matt's version was much less rococo. He had heard that Dillinger's brain had been sold to Jimmy Hoffa in 1962 and is now in the possession of the late Teamster boss's favorite aunt.

When I returned to New York from the American Odyssey journey I called the leading Dillinger scholar, Bill Helmer, author of *The Gun That Made the Twenties Roar* (1969) and longtime member of the John Dillinger Died for You Society. The society is founded on the notion of Dillinger as a "prominent economic reformer of the 1930s whose unorthodox banking methods enabled the U.S. Justice Department to overcome states' rights opposition to Federal Anti-Crime Laws." Its charter goes on to note that "Dillinger gave his life so a little-known division of the U.S. Justice Department might be transformed into today's awesome FBI." According to Helmer, the proud owner of several mustache hairs from Dillinger's death mask, Dillinger's brain was removed entirely at the Cook County Hospital morgue. When the body arrived for burial in Indiana, the undertaker alerted the Dillinger family to the fact that the brain was missing. A lawsuit against the FBI was averted when the family was assured the brain would be used only for scientific studies. But then the brain disappeared, as

Kevin had claimed, and there are many versions floating around as to the brain's current location. As to the whereabouts of Dillinger's penis, according to Helmer, there is no hard evidence, but the origins of the myth are quite understandable.

The night Dillinger was shot, a photographer for the *Chicago Daily News* had taken two photos of his corpse lying in the morgue, his arm protruding upward under the sheet, resembling a huge erection. Before it went into print, the photo was retouched, but enough people had seen the original for a rumor to run rampant that more than Dillinger's brain had been removed for scientific study, and that his penis had been sent to the Smithsonian, where it was preserved in formaldehyde. The Smithsonian and the National Medical Museum in Bethesda, two victims of the Dillinger penis rumor, receive so many inquiries that they have had to create form letters of denial. When I called the Smithsonian, introducing myself as a historian doing research on Chicago crime, the woman on the other end confirmed that they receive hundreds of inquiries and suggested I contact the FBI, which is "ultimately responsible for his brain and his member." I made a mental note to file the whole subject as a potential thesis topic for some hapless graduate student.

Back in the world of American Odyssey, Frank parked the Majic Bus in an alley across from the Biograph Theater, and we all dashed to the box office for tickets. With an hour to spare before show time, Matt came up with a brilliant idea: We would reenact the Dillinger shooting in front of the theater, and he would film our historical re-creation. We quickly read up on the FBI operation in a guidebook and assigned roles. Jared was to play Dillinger; Alison, the Woman in Red, the brothel owner who cooperated with federal agents to avoid deportation. Justin and Kenny played the G-men, using a broom, a boot, and a tennis racket as their submachine guns. While Matt choreographed the performance, a crowd gathered. Then, with the camera rolling, Jared and Alison walked out of the theater arm in arm. Kenny "G-man" Young fired three .38 bullets into Jared "Dillinger" Goldman, who stumbled fifty or sixty feet and fell dead in the alley to the thunderous applause of the spectators. In 1934, when Dillinger was actually shot, throngs of people dipped their handkerchiefs in the pool of blood for a souvenir. A local businessman poured water on the spot to dilute the blood and give more folks a chance to absorb some of Dillinger. Studs Terkel is right: "Chicago is not the most corrupt American city, it's the most theatrically corrupt."

After the reenactment we entered the Biograph to see *Naked Lunch*, a movie that took us into the underworld of William S. Burroughs. In Chicago's Siskel and Ebert terms, the students were divided—half thumbs-up and half thumbs-down. But we were not in the mood to really critique the film. It had been a long, eventful day in Chicago, and by the time we left the theater we were all ready for bed. It was midnight, and as Frank made his way to the interstate, Springfield, Illinois, bound, we listened to Son Seals's *Midnight Son* cassette, laughed one last time about Michael Jordan and Mike Ditka and John Dillinger, and said good-bye to Chicago— the biggest, baddest, boldest, brawniest, bluesiest, and best town on the make in the whole wide world. And as Frank got onto I-55, the last thing I remember him saying before I fell asleep was, "Boy, it's really windy out." That it was.

8

From Lincoln's Springfield to Truman's Independence

We must have many Lincoln-hearted men.
A city is not builded in a day.
And they must do their work, and come and go,
While countless generations pass away.

—VACHEL LINDSAY

IT IS DIFFICULT TO IMAGINE SPRINGFIELD, ILLINOIS, without Abraham Lincoln. His likeness is everywhere: on savings-and-loan signs and fast-food billboards, on dinner menus and flea-market posters, on taxicabs and bowling-alley walls. If you glance at the Springfield Yellow Pages you will find Lincolnland Baptist Church and Lincoln Rent-a-Car, Lincoln Land Pest Control and Lincoln Land Plumbing, a Lincoln Dialysis Center and a Lincoln Chiropractic Clinic. If a Martian anthropologist landed in Springfield, it would assume Lincoln was the supreme deity of the realm, his image as ubiquitous as Lenin's or Stalin's in Cold War Moscow. Although Lincoln, born in Kentucky and raised in Indiana, didn't come to Springfield until 1837, that he once said of the Illinois

171

capital, "Here I have lived," was enough to make our nation's sixteenth president the biggest industry in town (besides state bureaucrats).

Much like Lincoln himself, there is something mournful about Springfield and its bond with the great president, as if generations of citizens remain in a state of perpetual sorrow over his assassination. Springfield exudes the dead President Lincoln, not the vigorous Lincoln of New Salem rail-splitting fame. It is as if the people of the city of Springfield were participants in an ongoing 127-year-long wake, the downtown a ghostly mausoleum honoring the martyr, his marketing by local merchants a depressing by-product like the postcard and rosary-bead merchants in front of the great cathedrals of Europe, who are, in their own way, devout entrepreneurial Christians, evangelists of capitalism. In Springfield one senses not the country lawyer Lincoln with brooding eyes, big hands, and a book under each arm but the embalmed Lincoln lying in his velvet-lined, open White House coffin, arms folded, face powdered, a small patch of dried blood visible in his hair—a body robbed of spirit, mere decaying flesh laid out in his black Sunday best.

Perhaps our gloomy mood was intensified because we had arrived early on Sunday morning. The only activity in town besides the traffic lights were a minister in clerical garb and sneakers walking briskly down the street and a black cat who glared at our bus with green laser eyes, daring us to cross its path. Like so many state capitals that are small- or medium-size cities, Springfield shuts down over the weekend, becomes a ghost town, except for the afternoon tourists on pilgrimages who come from all over the world to stroll the Lincoln Heritage Trail. We of the Majic Bus joined their ranks.

Our first Springfield stop was the Illinois State Capitol for a photo opportunity with the towering bronze Lincoln statue. From there, we drove a few blocks to park the bus at the Lincoln Home National Historic Site, breakfasted at a nearby hotel, and took a guided walking tour through the home, which stands on a four-block site that includes seventeen other historic structures. Although there are more than three thousand Lincoln historic markers in America, Springfield is the only town in the country where "Old Abe's" ghost truly seems in residence.

The Lincoln home is the only one the Illinois lawyer-turned-Republican-president ever owned. He purchased it in 1842 after marrying Mary Todd, and it is where three of their four sons were born and one died. During Lincoln's 1860 presidential campaign, the home was a Springfield focal point for visiting delegations, parades, and strategy sessions. Lincoln's son Robert deeded the home to the state of Illinois in 1887, and it was immediately opened to tourists, who for a hundred years flooded in the millions to the president's green-shuttered brown house. The modest wood home was never meant for that kind of wear and tear, and the structure began to deteriorate. From 1987 to 1988 a $1.7 million restoration added structural reinforcement and climate control, and replaced weathered building materials. The house was stripped down to its foundation before it reopened in June 1988, and in the process many new artifacts were unearthed: old letters discovered between the walls; shards of expensive pottery; pieces of bottles that once contained medicine, such as bitters; one of the Lincoln boys' discarded shoes; and, most interesting of all, an unknown brick walkway leading to the south door. Although there were no earth-shattering historical finds, the Lincoln home serves as a model of historical preservation, and Shari, who is now working on her master's degree in public history, was more interested in how the home was rebuilt than in Lincoln's life as a Springfield lawyer and politician. The National Park Service also maintains a visitor's center near the house, with interpretive displays and films about the Lincolns. The students queried extensively during the tour, and when they were finished I gave my own short lecture on Lincoln. Like so many Americans the students were bewildered by the tabloid rumors they had heard—Lincoln was a manic-depressive, a wife beater, a racist, and so on. We discussed some of these charges, and I tried to inoculate them against sleaze history by warning them not to believe everything they read or hear. Their confusion was understandable, for the past five years' Lincoln revisionism has stirred up a feeding frenzy.

173

So many Lincoln anecdotes exist and so many differing historical interpretations of his life abound that it has grown difficult to distinguish fact from fiction, truth from gross historical distortion. More volumes have been published on Lincoln than on any other American figure, including Washington, and our nation's obsession with the Great Emancipator shows no sign of diminishing in the 1990s. Merely lifting my pen to write the name *Lincoln* and daring to publish a few pages on our sixteenth president will lead to dozens of letters pro and con, pointing out where I did Mr. Lincoln right and where I did him wrong. Our nation has so many Lincoln scholars that we should combine our six Lincoln colleges into one giant university, perhaps in Nebraska, where fifty thousand self-proclaimed Lincoln experts could teach the five million Americans who would love nothing better than to immerse themselves in Lincoln, take exams on Lincoln, and receive a diploma in Lincoln studies at Lincoln State in Lincoln, Nebraska. A natural for the university's president is Rutgers Professor Daniel Bassuk, founder of the Society of Lincoln Presenters, whose membership comprises eighty-four Lincoln impersonators in various parts of the country—men who put on stovepipe hats, Silly Putty their noses, create facial moles, and grow (or paste on) the all-important whiskers to perform on the banquet or classroom circuits and in Civil War reenactments and Lincoln's Birthday sales, many earning their living doing so. Bassuk's organization also boasts a ladies' auxiliary with eleven active Mary Lincolns. While Lincoln impersonators date back to 1880, it is no longer all fun and games being "Abraham Lincoln" in 1992. Frederick Klein, a six-foot-three-inch Lincoln, who runs the Lincoln Institute for Education in Springfield, Illinois, complains, "There are negatives in being an itinerant Lincoln. People sometimes try to knock your hat off. Others shout, 'Have you got Elvis with you?' I don't think that Lincoln should be subjected to that."

Frederick Klein has a point. We should not treat a man of Lincoln's stature, or even a Lincoln impersonator, with anything but respect. A mere six months after I had warned students to beware the historical distortions that abound about Lincoln, a flagrant example occurred. Toppling a stovepipe hat is child's play measured against the academic revisionism of Garry Wills. Regarded in some quarters as an academic heavyweight, Mr. Wills earned himself a *Time* cover story on October 5, 1992, complete with a large photograph of our sixteenth president. His piece of Lincoln revisionism, written to promote his newest book, *Lincoln at Gettysburg: The Words That Remade America,* ran under the headline "DISHONEST ABE" in bold block letters the size of a *National Enquirer* lead. The subhead reads, "America's most revered politician dissembled, waffled, told racist stories and consorted with corrupt politicians—all in his noble effort to free the slaves and save the Union." Wills's "Dishonest Abe" is a strained, two-page character assassination, a thesis built around a couple of chicken-bone facts, painting Lincoln as a foul-mouthed scoundrel, sex pervert, and racist—although, Wills concedes, an effective politician both despite and because of these alleged character defects. Nowhere in the article does Wills demonstrate that Lincoln did anything to deserve the moniker Dishonest Abe. That *Time* would publish such a condemnation of Lincoln is a sad commentary on the need to sell "news" magazines, on our times, and on the state of the historians' profession. Wills's contrived thesis offers the country and our young people such distorted insinuations as, "Given his record of double-dealing why do Americans admire Lincoln? He is not admirable because he was 'Honest Abe' but *because* he was devious." It is any historian's prerogative to demythologize Lincoln, to try to demonstrate why we shouldn't refer to a politician with Lincoln's immense political skills in "hesitating, obfuscating, and compromising" as honest. But to turn the argument on end and call him "Dishonest Abe" in a conveniently timed article published at the height of a presidential campaign in which Bill Clinton was being attacked as a compromiser and a "waffler," perhaps says more about a normally sober and reflective scholar who has confused notoriety with greatness and who equates character assassination with original thought.

Garry Wills wasn't the only one trying to capitalize on Lincoln in 1992. In his speech to the Republican National Convention in August, former President Ronald Reagan misquoted Lincoln to serve his oratorical needs, later claiming he wasn't to blame, because he had found the remarks in Herbert Prochnow's *Toastmaster's Treasure Chest.* Sotheby's in New York auctioned off a mere handwritten draft paragraph of Lincoln's famous 1858 "House Divided" (delivered in Springfield at the Old State Capitol Historic Site which we visited), for a half million dollars. And now, a group of scientists wants to bring Abraham Lincoln back to "life"—and I don't mean the talking robot that greets visitors in Disneyland's Main Street attraction, "Great Moments with Mr. Lincoln." Scientists want to study dried specimens of Mr. Lincoln's blood, 180 strands of hair, and seven bone chips to recover a tiny sample of his DNA. They will "chemically Xerox" the sample to produce enough DNA to test for the genetic defect that causes Marfan's syndrome, a rare condition (one in ten thousand people is affected by it) that they assert may account for Lincoln's lanky physique and giant hands. And why should we disturb the bones (or the DNA, for that matter) of our sixteenth president? The researchers answer: to make people with the potentially deadly disease feel better, because our greatest president shared their suffering: "If we can show that Abe Lincoln had Marfan's Syndrome, that will make a lot of people with the disease feel proud," said Dr. Brendan Lee, a leading Marfan's specialist. While in their own way all three of these 1992 stories honor Abraham Lincoln, when you're in Springfield you wish that Ronald Reagan had quoted him correctly, that the "House Divided" paragraph would be placed on display in a public museum, where it belongs, and you hope that the well-intentioned scientists don't pull a Zachary Taylor (whom they recently exhumed to see if our twelfth president was poisoned) and allow Mr. Lincoln to rest in peace.

From Lincoln's home we walked a few short blocks to 603 South Fifth Street, a house once owned by Lincoln's sister-in-law, which later became the lifelong residence of Vachel Lindsay, one of America's great twentieth-century poets. Lindsay was born November 10, 1879, in the house and committed suicide there in 1931 by drinking Lysol, his parting shot: "I got them before they got me—they can just try to explain this if they can!" In the fifty-two years of his life Lindsay wrote hundreds of memorable poems, especially about the Midwest of the teens and twenties. "I rate [his poems] among the supremely great American poems" Carl Sandburg wrote. Sinclair Lewis called him "One of our few great poets, a power and a glory in the land." Louis Untermeyer called Lindsay the greatest lyric poet since Edgar Allan Poe, and Harriet Monroe—who first published Lindsay's "General William Booth Enters into Heaven" in her influential journal *Poetry,* launching his career—compared him to Whitman.

But it is not wise to compare Lindsay to anyone, for he was our first modern poet and a multifaceted American original: our great Prairie Troubadour, the voice of frontier democracy, a believer in evangelical small-town Midwestern virtues, and preacher of the Gospel of Beauty. He tramped twenty-eight hundred miles on foot across America with a bandanna as his baggage, trading his poems for food and shelter, singing in the wheat fields of Kansas and the arroyos of New Mexico, propelled by manic locomotion to find the heart of our nation. Lindsay spent his life scribbling poems in his notebooks, reciting his hymn-tune rhythms at YMCAs in every city and town and hamlet across America. Flamboyance, Lindsay once said, was his "protest against the drab, square-toed, dull, unimaginative America which is gaining on all of us. America simply needs the flamboyant to save her soul."

Lindsay has sadly been omitted from many modern American poetry anthologies and was recently flayed by Elizabeth Hardwick in the *New York Review of Books*. She mocked the prairie poet for his bad verse and "unanchored enthusiasm." Spinach! It is time to get Lindsay back in print, to start appreciating his enormous contribution to the "New Poetry" movement of the early twentieth century and to spoken-word poetry, and his visionary teachings.

I lit my own small match to spark a long-overdue Lindsay renaissance by lecturing about him on his front porch in Springfield. He is the perfect vehicle for a discussion of agrarianism and populism and folklore in an American Studies class. Such poems or chants as "A Gospel of Beauty," "Johnny Appleseed's Hymn to the Sun," and "The Fairy from the Apple-Seed" are programmatic calls for Americans to make their own hometowns beautiful, to plant trees and flowers and crops and gardens, to beat back the smokestack ugliness of urban industrialism with community-sponsored beautification programs.

I read to the students part of "Bryan, Bryan, Bryan, Bryan," the poem celebrating the Nebraska Free Silver populist in his 1896 losing campaign against William McKinley, in which Bryan is called "the prairie avenger . . . smashing Plymouth Rock with his boulders from the West." Eviscerated by Bryan's defeat, Lindsay called it the "victory of Plymouth Rock and all those inbred landlord stocks."

But it was Lindsay's love of Lincoln, his hometown hero, of which I spoke most to the students that day in Springfield. For the Garry Willses and the Lincoln impersonators will come and go, but Vachel Lindsay's Lincoln prevails, for in verse he captured the essence of the sacred Lincoln, something revisionism, footnotes, and imitation can never hope to do. The ominous poem "Abraham Lincoln Walks at Midnight" (1914) empathizes with the heavy-hearted Lincoln, the Lincoln rocking in the rain over his son's grave, the Lincoln alone at midnight in the White House begging God to help him end the Civil War. The students were moved by the poem, three verses of which are reprinted here:

Abraham Lincoln Walks at Midnight
(In Springfield, Illinois)

It is portentous, and a thing of state
That here at midnight, in our little town
A mourning figure walks, and will not rest,
Near the old court-house pacing up and down,

Or by his homestead, or in shadowed yards
He lingers where his children used to play,
Or through the market, on the well-worn stones
He stalks until the dawn-stars burn away . . .

It breaks his heart that kings must murder still,
That all his hours of travail here for men

Seem yet in vain. And who will bring white peace
That he may sleep upon this hill again?

From Lindsay's front porch we drove to Lincoln's white granite tomb
and obelisk, which towers over Oak Ridge Cemetery on the outskirts of
town—also the resting place of Lindsay. It had shaped up to be a lovely
April afternoon, and the cemetery seemed more a place for the living than
the dead. The tomb of Lincoln, his wife, Mary Todd, and three of their
four sons is dominated by a bust of the beardless prairie lawyer Lincoln.
It is said that rubbing its nose brings good luck, but after millions of
visitors, there's not much nose left. Inside the tomb, important Lincoln
speeches in bronze grace the walls, with a life-size statue of the young
lawyer Lincoln labeled GREAT EMANCIPATOR, which I was happy to see
hadn't been rubbed away by some sandpaper revisionist. The actual grave
is marked by a marble monument with the words of Lincoln's Secretary of
War Edwin Stanton above: NOW HE BELONGS TO THE AGES. I thought of
Carl Sandburg's poem, "When Abraham Lincoln was shoveled into the
tombs, he forgot the copperheads and the assassin . . . in the dust, in
the cool tombs."

We all filed out of the cool tomb and sat in front of the monument in
the warm sun. Something about visiting Lincoln's tomb was redemptive,
as though we had all worshiped together, prayed together, and been jointly
relieved of our earthly burdens. Jared summed up our group feeling best
in his journal: "All around me is free air, free sight. Abraham Lincoln
sought the freedom of all people. It is fitting for this site to give such a
sense of freedom that I want to sing 'America the Beautiful'—O beautiful
for spacious skies. I am here. This is America and more than just a place
for the dead to lie. It is peace and freedom."

Our afternoon of Lincoln was still unfinished. From the cemetery we
went to Lincoln's New Salem State Historic Site, a reconstructed Western
settlement on the banks of the Sangamon River—one of the 275 rivers
that flow in Illinois—where Lincoln's father brought his family to live in

1831 and where they stayed until 1837. In New Salem we found the young, ambitious Lincoln who worked as shopkeeper, postmaster, surveyor, and finally lawyer and state legislator. Of all the Lincoln sites in the United States, New Salem—the largest reconstructed log-built town in the nation—is the best place to introduce the family to Lincoln; kids love it. Since 1932 Illinois has worked to reconstruct the village as it was in Lincoln's day, and what has resulted is a place that is less gentrified and more historically authentic than Williamsburg. Oxen pull covered wagons along the dirt street, blacksmiths and glassblowers and pharmacists demonstrate their crafts from the 1830s, and visitors can ride on the *Talisman,* a replica of the steamboat that traveled the Sangamon River in Lincoln's day. Everywhere in New Salem guides dressed in period outfits talk about what life on the Sangamon was like in the 1830s. Since it was early April and the streets were muddy, New Salem had few visitors besides ourselves. After walking around the village the students spent two hours in a park, recording their day with Lincoln in their journals and playing football.

We grabbed a late lunch at a nearby Dairy Queen in Petersburg, where we visited the home of Edgar Lee Masters, a contemporary of Sandburg and Lindsay whose famous book of free-verse poetry, *The Spoon River Anthology,* gave voice to the dead of provincial Lewistown, who speak of the spiritual impoverishment, hypocrisy, and—yes—decadence of life in a small town. After lunch we returned to Springfield to head south, determined to make Stefanie's parents' house in Saint Louis in time for dinner. As we drove by the Illinois State Capitol one last time I read what Carl Sandburg once said of Springfield: "When the present Springfield is gone and another Springfield comes in its place, Vachel Lindsay will be there through his lines of verse, alive and singing." And it will be Vachel Lindsay's Lincoln—the Great Emancipator haunting the streets of Springfield in search of peace—who will belong to the ages.

The drive from Springfield to Saint Louis down I-55 is an easy one, due both to the smooth, potholeless highway and the expansive flatness of the cornstalked land. Many of the students were amazed at the size of the barns, silos, grain elevators, farms, cows, and John Deere tractors they saw, but for the most part they turned their eyes inward, using these predinner hours to read or write in their journals. At a truck stop in Mount Olive, near the Mary Harris ("Mother") Jones Memorial—a tribute to the fiery early-twentieth-century labor agitator for the union rights of coal miners—a handful of the students got into a lengthy conversation with Tracy, a woman truck driver wearing a mechanic's jump suit and a warm smile. Matt filmed the episode as Christine, Janine, and Aíne toured her truck's sleeping quarters and studied her customized dashboard, complete with fuzzy white dice hanging from the ceiling and a signed picture of k. d. lang taped to the driver's door along with a panel Tracy called "the Hunk Hall of Fame," a magazine collage of her dream man: Garth Brooks's eyes, Clint Black's butt, Billy Ray Cyrus's legs, Elvis Presley's hair, and Dwight Yoakam's nose. Christine invited Tracy to tour the Majic Bus, and she was impressed, saying what by now was a commonplace: "You kids are lucky. If I'd a' been taught history on the road like this, I may've stayed in school." The women adored Tracy's trucker lingo, especially the way she referred to God as the Great Dispatcher in the Sky. During a radio interview in California, Aíne went on at great length about how impressed she was by encountering a woman with a spit-in-the-eye disposition who had the courage to earn a living at what most considered a man's job. Tracy had become a symbolic "road model" for her.

Back on the interstate, Shari and I engaged in a long talk about Abraham Lincoln and the need for more U.S. funding in historical preservation, her chosen field. In Springfield she had picked up an application at the Lincoln Home National Historic Site for possible summer employment there as a guide. (She already had graduate school applications out for a master's degree in public history and on returning to New York was greeted with the news that she had been accepted by most of the programs to which she had applied. Her visit to Chicago had convinced her that the Windy City was where she wanted to live, so she chose Loyola.) As we drove through the farmlands of Illinois, we discussed the perils the National Park Service faced in maintaining American heritage sites. According to a Lincoln site ranger, years of neglect have rendered unsatisfactory the repair, protection, and preservation of park resources and infrastructures all across the nation. From roads to trails, sewage systems to riverbanks, fire suppression systems to the roof that covers the house where Thomas Jefferson penned the Declaration of Independence—the backlog of deferred maintenance is going to cost more than two billion dollars. Shari, a Philadelphian, told me that the sprinkler system in Independence Hall is so antiquated that preservation experts believe a fire could level the building in less than thirty minutes. During the summer of 1991, when she worked in the city, leaky pipes flooded the basement of Independence Hall three times in three weeks. In fact, the fifty National Park structures that cover one square mile in Philadelphia need an estimated seventy million dollars' worth of renovation.

We arrived at the Pearlmans' more than an hour late for dinner. Stefanie Pearlman's ankle had been mending at her parents' Saint Louis home since her New Orleans street-dancing accident and she greeted us in jest at the door with a wagging, reprimanding finger for being late, crutches under her arms but ultimately all hugs. She had missed her Majic Bus compatriots and was anxious to get back on the road with us now that the ankle's swelling had subsided. It was great to be invited into a home to pig out, and the Pearlmans provided us with enough food, prepared by Grandma, to feed Coxey's Army: a giant mixed salad, garlic bread, spaghetti with meatballs (and without, for the vegetarians), mounds of baked goods, and plenty of milk and sodas. The Pearlmans were tremendous hosts, and over mouthfuls of pasta we told them of our recent Chicago adventures, including our John Dillinger reenactment at the Biograph Theater. To top off their hospitality, they had paid for four rooms at the nearby Marriott Hotel for the men to stay at while the women slept overnight at their home in what turned out to be a giant parody of a slumber party. While the women applied facial clay masks, made popcorn, and gossiped, the guys lived it up like Elvis at the Marriott, floating in the indoor pool and pouring down cans of beverages while sweating in the Jacuzzi. Before bedtime we watched CNN, blasted up the air-conditioning to achieve an arctic temperature, and discussed the next day's Saint Louis itinerary.

Kenny, who loved talking politics and history, brought up Saint Louis–native Charles Lindbergh's famed 1927 solo flight across the Atlantic and asked whether his acceptance of a Nazi decoration in 1938, combined with his isolationist "America First" policy at the time World War II broke out, did not mean that "Lucky Lindy" was anti-Semitic. After we had discussed this delicate issue at some length, Kevin jumped in and shifted gears, launching a lobbying campaign to visit the Mississippi River city of East Saint Louis (in Illinois) the next day to see if he could find the boyhood home of jazz great Miles Davis and the Street Hotel, where Chuck Berry wrote "School Days."

A huge fan of both musicians, I wanted to accommodate this off-beat request but quickly decided against it. Known as the Bangladesh of America, East Saint Louis is one of the most dangerous, crime-ridden, decaying urban centers in the nation, a place without any infrastructure that, by comparison, makes the South Bronx seem like a charming urban enclave for the rich. Block after city block of East Saint Louis is boarded up or burned out; it is not a community but a charred skeleton of one. Many buildings have been reduced to rubble as thieves cart away everything of value: bricks, aluminum siding, copper wire, even heavy cast-iron manhole covers from the potholed streets to be sold for scrap.

Unconvinced by my disastrous description, Kevin called the front desk and asked the night clerk whether East Saint Louis was as bad as I was making it sound. He delivered the perfect one-liner: "Well, the crime rate is finally starting to decline—you see, there isn't much left to steal." He went on to tell Kevin that selling crack had become East Saint Louis's most lucrative business, and that it's so widespread that peddlers often try to flag him down on nearby I-70 to hawk crack vials at twenty dollars a pop on his way to work. East Saint Louis traffic backups, he matter-of-factly told Kevin, often turn out to be caused by buyers lined up at drive-

183

through crack houses. Kevin got off the phone truly disillusioned. How could this be? East Saint Louis was the home of TV's June Cleaver, a point driven home on nearly every episode of *Leave It to Beaver*.

I explained to Kevin that there was a time in the early 1950s, when Chuck Berry was perfecting his duck walk and running guitar riffs at local nightclubs and barbecue jazz joints, when East Saint Louis was a model community, ranking second only to Chicago as a national rail and stockyard center. But almost all its industry has left, driven out by high crime rates and property taxes. Thousands of jobs have gone with the factories, leaving the city a pocket of nearly hopeless poverty in the generally economically well-off Saint Louis metropolitan area, a stark national symbol of the United States in disrepair. When it rains in Saint Louis, the sewers back up in East Saint Louis, and in winter these sewage ponds freeze, with a stench of raw waste so potent that it is inescapable. No, it was best for the Majic Bus not to tour East Saint Louis. I was in no mood to be like Chevy Chase in *National Lampoon's Vacation,* romanticizing life in a slum, asking directions to Miles Davis's old stomping grounds while our bus luggage got stolen, having to shout "Roll 'em up" when we heard the first gunshot, seeing the underfunded and underfueled police car run out of gas in a high-speed chase, and having to make constant detours because the garbage was piled so deep that entire streets were rendered impassable. As New York rappers Naughty by Nature sing: "If you're not from the ghetto, stay the fuck out of the ghetto." We would take this sound advice and stay on the Missouri side of the Mississippi.

The next morning the Missouri Marriott men all dived into the pool for refreshing wake-up swims, followed by pots of coffee and a box of glazed jelly doughnuts. Frank, who had slept on the bus, rose in a foul mood, yelling at Jared to turn his ear-splitting music down so he could think straight, chewing aspirins practically all morning long. We stopped at a record store to purchase two Neville Brothers tapes, picked up our other half at the Pearlmans', got the kinks out playing a short game of Nerf football in a field by their home, and headed straight for downtown Saint Louis and the Gateway Arch. Even on crutches Stefanie was anxious to show us her beautiful hometown, a crossroads city where South comes

North and East molds into West, filled with friendly people and unexpected architectural gems.

The Gateway Arch, which rises from the banks of the mighty Mississippi to form a colossal catenary 630 feet above the ground—a tribute to Thomas Jefferson and his Louisiana Purchase—is by far the most conspicuous landmark on the Saint Louis horizon, and it was where we parked the Majic Bus for our day of exploration. We walked down to the levee, where the arch's stainless-steel legs rise amid the trees and reflecting pools of a wide and well-maintained greensward, all of us in search of the best angle to capture this truly magnificent structure. Matt, videocam in hand, shot footage giving the illusion that the arch is in motion, soaring into the sky and curving back to earth. Alison needed no technological chicanery to breathe life into the arch, which she mentally perceived as more like a living being than an inanimate steel construction—a structure that changed moods from moment to moment. The arch was designed by the celebrated Finnish American architect Eero Saarinen as a tribute to the enlightened mind of Thomas Jefferson; it is the centerpiece of the park service's Jefferson National Expansion Memorial.

At our next destination, the subterranean Museum of Western Expansion beneath the arch, a life-size bronze statue of a pensive Jefferson dominates the entrance. With memories of Steve Ambrose's Lewis and Clark lecture still fresh, the students were primed with a rich understanding of the exhibits of the Native Americans and buffalo hunters, fur trappers, and sodbusters who played a part in America's Manifest Destiny. Had Jefferson not acquired this large track of land from Napoleon in 1803 with the Louisiana Purchase, we might well have needed our passports to explore western America. It cost the young nation fifteen million dollars— about five cents an acre—to double its size, and the students stood in awe of Jefferson's legerdemain in the deal. They had now seen the Jefferson Memorial in Washington, Monticello in Charlottesville, and now the Jefferson National Expansion Memorial museum in Saint Louis. The multifaceted accomplishments of our nation's third president had been

185

brought home to the students: Jefferson was no longer merely a slave-owning face on the nickel. Despite his moral failure, he could be judged a great American hero. Later that evening, as we drove through North Saint Louis, past the drug dealers and garbage heaps on Jefferson Avenue, the frightening alleyways and boarded-up homes, storefronts pockmarked with random bullet holes, and road chuckholes full of dark, greasy water, we all knew America was far from the paradise of Jefferson's dreams. But, as Bill Clinton rightly stressed in his inauguration speech, it's the responsibility of this new generation, of which the American Odyssey students are a part, to keep the Jeffersonian vision alive for all Americans.

Before visiting the arch we sat by the Mississippi, called the "strong brown god" by T. S. Eliot, who was born and raised in, and an expatriate from, Saint Louis. While we discussed *The Adventures of Huckleberry Finn*, the great Mark Twain's most significant contribution to American literature and required reading for the course, a chain of tugs pushing barges carrying fertilizers and oil up North floated down the muddy current, a scene straight out of the pages of Twain's *Life on the Mississippi*. Although some students had read *Huckleberry Finn* (or Cliff's Notes thereof) in high school, only now were they experienced enough to appreciate the humor of Twain's backwoods vernacular, his indictment of pre–Civil War attitudes toward slavery, and his general state of despair at the human condition. To contemplate *Huckleberry Finn* beside the Mississippi River—the source of Mark Twain's strength—was education and learning at its best.

Following my brief lecture on Twain's literary career, many of us took the four-minute train along a track up and down the legs of the arch. From the windows of the observation deck atop America's tallest monument—seventy-five feet higher than the Washington Monument and over twice as tall as the Statue of Liberty—there was a fantastic bird's-eye view of Missouri, Illinois, and the Mississippi River. And what a panorama we saw: The crowds pouring into Busch Stadium for the Cardinals' opening day like red ants returning to the anthill; the abandoned stockyards of East Saint Louis overgrown with weeds; railroad tracks disappearing in every direction over the horizon (though you knew they would somehow or another eventually lead to Chicago); the gridded squares and rectangles of the agricultural abundance of Illinois prairie, all made possible by John Deere's 1837 "plow that scours"; the great Mississippi, at this tremendous height reduced to a dirty little canal of gondolas transporting cargo we could scoop up like Lincoln Logs; the Saint Louis skyline, looking flimsy and fragile, as if a summer tornado could blow it all the way south into the Gulf of Mexico to become yet another Atlantis; and of course, the vast virgin woodlands to the west, Jefferson's bargain of bargains, so never ending that it seemed as if the land went on forever.

After returning safely to earth, some of us walked just west of the Jefferson National Expansion Memorial to the Old Courthouse. Part of the National Memorial, the 1839 building features exhibits of the history of Saint Louis, dioramas, movies on the Old West, a restored mid-nineteenth-century courtroom, and an exhibit on Dred Scott, a black man who sued here for his freedom in 1847. In a landmark case the U.S. Supreme Court decided against him. Scott nonetheless died a free man in Saint Louis, having been released by his owner two months after the decision. Below the Old Courthouse steps, a plaque commemorates the site where, at a public auction in 1878, Joseph Pulitzer purchased the *Saint Louis Dispatch*, forerunner of the *Post-Dispatch*, a paper still controlled by the Pulitzer family.

While the bulk of students were learning about Saint Louis history, the KDR boys and Aíne were learning about history of another sort—brewing. From the moment the students learned the Majic Bus would stop in Saint Louis, those four bombarded me with pleas to tour the Budweiser factory, home of the world's most popular—and their favorite—beer. For them Bud was not merely the King of Beers but a holy sacrament. To their way of thinking, to watch Bud being brewed, followed by what they assumed would be unlimited free frosty schooners of it, was about as good as life got in the United States.

As most of us started strolling toward the Old Courthouse the thirsty

187

four started jogging south on Broadway, away from the arch and downtown, past the large red-and-white checkerboard sign marking the home office of the Ralston Purina Corporation. On they jogged like never before, past the venerable Soulard Market, established about 1779 and now the oldest public market west of the Mississippi, its open-sided display areas brimming with fresh fruits and vegetables sold at old wooden stands, some operated by families who have rented stalls there for three generations. Their pace picked up as the smell of hops filled their nostrils, and they sprinted past solid old redbrick row houses; past the smell of garlic at Mike and Min's bistro; past McGurk's Bar, where "Danny Boy" was being sung even in midafternoon; until the smell of hops mingled with and was finally overtaken by the pungent odor of Clydesdale dung, and then they knew they had reached their New Jerusalem.

Out of breath and thirstier than ever before, they gazed with reverence on Anheuser-Busch's headquarters plant, which rose in front of them like an industrial Oz, a fortresslike factory left over from the last century. Before drinking, however, they were obliged to take a guided historical tour of the facilities.

In the mid-nineteenth century, a number of German breweries operated in South Saint Louis. Now only Anheuser-Busch survives. The brewing complex sprawls over seventy city blocks, not far from the Mississippi, whose waters the facility taps to make the thirteen million barrels of brew produced there annually. Before modern refrigeration, winter ice harvested from the river was kept in caves under the Soulard District, used as storage areas to keep beer cool in summer. In 1855 soap manufacturer Eberhard Anheuser lent money to a firm that acquired a small, failing beer maker the investors named Bavarian Brewery. When Bavarian went under two years later, Anheuser took over, hired his son-in-law, Adolphus Busch, as overseer, and in 1880 renamed the brewery Anheuser-Busch Brewing Association. The rest is history, and it's a history the KDR boys and Aíne understood well—ice-cold Budweiser.

They were now standing in a Busch theme park, Spuds Central, where more than five million bottles and nine million cans of beer a day are packaged and shipped worldwide.

188

. . . Shipped to Big Top Beer Distributors in Philly, where Kenny bought his first Bud six-pack when he turned sixteen; he immediately parked his father's 1979 brown Buick Regal by the frozen Delaware River and chugged his first can while pondering what the 76ers would do once Julius Erving retired and wishing the NBA would adopt the old red, white, and blue basketballs Doctor J used when he played with the old New York Nets of the ABA . . . Shipped to Arkansas, where an underage Justin, living with his mother on a commune, would occasionally sneak a Bud from the refrigerator and down it in solitude, sitting with his back against an Ozark pine tree behind the compound, wondering why his life was so screwed up and how he could escape it . . . Shipped in kegs to JFK Stadium in Philly, where Matt and his buddies emptied one in the parking lot before Live Aid in 1985, when they finally got a chance to see Led Zeppelin play.

Budweiser was a part of their lives, a part of growing up in America, and they were in Saint Louis, and they were going to pay their respects in the temple of hops—in Suds Central. At the visitors' center, displays traced the history of the brewing giant. A tour took the students to the 1891 Victorian Gothic brew house and bottling plant, where they were shown how beer is produced. In their debriefing all four agreed that the architectural high point is the brewery's fabulous stables. When the tour finished, it was bottoms-up with two complimentary glasses of Bud—not the all-you-can-drink bash they had hoped for.

In the meantime a solitary Kevin wended his way to the Loop—the neighborhood favored by Washington University students and the progressively correct of Saint Louis—and Blueberry Hill, a sixties-style bar that showcases Chuck Berry memorabilia. Ignoring the wall of Berry's 45s, the glass showcase displaying his many album covers, photos of Berry with such rockers as Keith Richards and Eric Clapton, and a Japanese translation of his autobiography, Kevin made a beeline straight to his American altar—"the Guitar that Shook the World"—Chuck Berry's Gibson ES-350T, introduced in mid-1957. Berry obtained one instrument, equipped with the renowned patent-applied-for humbuckers, shortly after the new model's debut. Kevin gazed in awe at the maple-necked guitar, with its

189

laminated maple top, rosewood fingerboard, lovely loop-style tailpiece, stereo wiring, and gold-plated hardware, given to Blueberry Hill owner Joe Edwards for barroom display a few years back by Berry, who lives just outside Saint Louis in Wentzville.

Young rockers like Kevin flock to Blueberry Hill to pay homage to this inspiring relic of American popular music, the electric guitar Berry used to record his late 1950 hits: "Johnny B. Goode," "Sweet Little Sixteen," "Carol," "Memphis," "Back in the USA," and many more. The Smithsonian could keep its Tin Pan Alley songbooks and Aaron Copland's "Appalachian Spring Suite" and "Fanfare for the Common Man" composition sheets, Kevin mused—here was the instrument used by his favorite rock-and-roll Founding Father, a Saint Louis poet as significant as T. S. Eliot who infused lyrics with relevant ideas about the direction of American culture. Eliot may have been a master of Oxford English and lofty universalist notions, but it was Berry who had the talent to transform everyday mundane American realities—automobiles, hot dogs, going to work, Coca-Cola, and adolescent love—into tunes and lyrics that mirrored and bespoke the problems and frustrations of America's first generation of baby-boomers at a time when the Cold War, lingering McCarthyism, and the threat of atomic destruction played havoc with the national psyche. In the end it was Chuck Berry's music that provided reassurance for traditional American values, something that buttoned-down crowd seemed unable to understand. Following a homesick Australian tour, Berry expressed his joy at returning to American hamburgers and crowded freeways with "Back in the USA," a sentiment shared by many American college students after their first summer excursion to Europe. In "Johnny B. Goode," which recounts the struggle of trying to break the chains of parental parochialism in the 1950s and 1960s, Berry was attuned to the national zeitgeist. So, on the measure of expressing how the nation views itself—the traditional role of the lyric poet—there is no doubt that Berry ranked with the best of them. "Roll over, Beethoven, and tell Tchaikovsky the news," Berry's 1956 composition, says it all. When NASA launched the famed *Voyager 1*, now some four billion miles out in space, its time capsule cradled copies of our Constitution, the

Declaration of Independence, and a Chuck Berry tape. To Kevin that made perfect sense.

Ordering himself a Rock 'n' Roll Beer at the bar, Kevin moseyed over to the Wurlitzer (officially declared by *Cash Box* magazine to be the best jukebox in America, and one of eleven at the bar), put in two dollars' worth of quarters, and punched in every Chuck Berry tune on the fret. He was impressed with the amazing collection of American pop-culture icons that adorned the walls of Blueberry Hill or were preserved under glass and key: Big Time Wrestling Dolls, made like G.I. Joes, including such great childhood heroes as Hulk Hogan, Captain Lou Albano, and Special Delivery Jones; pictures and clippings of Hopalong Cassidy; Howdy Doody memorabilia of all kinds, from puppets to clocks, shoe polish to lunch boxes, to children's puzzles of Buffalo Bob Smith, Phineas T. Bluster, Clarabell, and Flub-A-Dub in a display emblazoned HOWDY DOODY: THE FIRST HIPPIE; gargantuan Cardinal baseball cards of Lou Brock and Stan ("The Man") Musial; and framed copies of vintage "Archie" and "Superman" comic-book covers—in Kevin's view an underrated art. He flashed on a vicious rumor a New Jersey friend had passed: In November DC Comics would kill Superman off to boost sales. The possibility of such malicious corporate opportunism irritated him no end. He could only hope that the DC Comics executives' bottom-line mentality would be trumped by a stronger sense of patriotism before they did away with the Man of Steel, the superhero who fights for "truth, justice, and the American way," merely to lift sluggish sales faster than a speeding bullet. He stopped in the dart room, his head bobbing to the Smiths' "How Soon Is Now," as he watched serious players toss colorful darts at one of the seven official dart boards, the walls surrounding them filled with photos of past champions. Glancing at his watch, Kevin realized he was already five minutes late for his rendezvous with the Majic Bus, so he quickly downed his beer, bowed his head reverentially to "the Guitar that Shook the World," and headed for the door.

On Delmar Boulevard Kevin noticed that Saint Louis had its own version of the famous Hollywood Walk of Fame. The sidewalk slabs were embedded with stars and inscriptions memorializing the city's many celebrities, from Charles Lindbergh, whom he had discussed with his professor and friends the night before; to William S. Burroughs, whom he would get to meet personally the next afternoon in Lawrence, Kansas; to Josephine Baker, who he knew from watching a recent television documentary had been an international sex symbol in the 1920s and 1930s, predating Madonna by a half century, and the recipient of more than forty thousand love letters and some two thousand marriage proposals before her twenty-first birthday. He had to step on the stars of Howard Nemerov, the nation's 1988 poet laureate, and Maya Angelou, a poet and novelist of great distinction soon to be chosen to write an inaugural poem for Bill Clinton—two artists unknown to him and of little interest—as he searched for Chuck Berry's star. There it was, metaphorically shining as bright as Berry's greased-down Dippity-Do hair, only it was stained with pigeon droppings. With no time to spare, Kevin ran back into the bar, grabbed some paper napkins, and got on his hands and knees to spit-shine his hero's star; then he hurriedly flagged down a taxi, no small task in Saint Louis. Luck was on his side. A taxi magically appeared only a block away and off he zoomed into the flow of opening-day baseball traffic.

Only Frank was at the Majic Bus when Kevin arrived, the rest of us having walked down to inspect the dubious riverboat re-creations moored to the city landing, including two that never leave the dock—estimated to have cost a million dollars each—bearing the ubiquitous logos of McDonald's and Burger King. While we ate Quarter Pounders and Chicken McNuggets, Kevin dug into his duffel bag and found his *Chuck Berry Live at the Fillmore Auditorium* cassette, asked Frank to put it on, got comfortable on his bunk, glanced out his window where he could see half the arch and a stretch of the Mississippi, and opened to the bookmarked Chapter Nineteen of *The Adventures of Huckleberry Finn*. The chapter begins: "Two or three days and nights went by; I reckon I might say they swum by, they slid along so quiet and smooth and lovely. Here is the way we put in time. It was a monstrous big river down there—sometimes a mile and a half wide; we run nights, and laid up and hid daytimes; soon as night was most gone we stopped navigating and tied up—nearly always in the dead water under a towhead."

He laughed out loud, for it had just dawned on him that he was Huck and the Majic Bus was his raft, his vehicle for escaping the banality of his suburban existence. The major difference was that Huck never had it so easy, nor, for that matter, did the young Chuck Berry, fighting racial segregation wherever he went, having his original compositions ripped off and fleeced by whites like Pat Boone and the Beatles. At least John Lennon had the decency to say, "If you tried to give Rock 'n' Roll another name, you might call it 'Chuck Berry.' " He thought about how Chuck Berry employed car imagery to express and mirror important trends in American popular culture, even using the sounds of wheels and revving engines as background effects for such classics as "Maybelline" and "No Particular Place to Go." Listening to the Berry live tape, Kevin understood for the first time why his rock idol used the Greyhound bus in songs such as "Johnny B. Goode," "Bye Bye Johnny," and "The Promised Land." And who knew more about cars and their centrality to U.S. culture than Chuck Berry? After all, he had served a three-year prison sentence for auto theft when he was eighteen. Through his allusions to cars and the Greyhound bus, Chuck Berry created a cruisin' commentary on American life, its fluidity, its mobility, and the restlessness that lay beneath its surface, just as Whitman and Twain and Steinbeck and Kerouac did. Kevin proceeded to privately salute Thomas Jefferson for purchasing the Louisiana Territory, thereby letting all this movement happen. Kevin's thoughts caromed to an essay in which Mark Twain called his book *Tom Sawyer* "simply a hymn put into prose form to give it a worldly air." And now the whole idea of Whitman's "Song of Myself" made a lot more sense to him and the entire raw-river-rocking-guitar-hymn-catalog of Chuck Berry seemed an even greater accomplishment of national expression than he had supposed. Finally he castigated himself for being such a worrywart about punctuality and not lingering in Blueberry Hill awhile longer, at least until he had heard "Back in the U.S.A." blast from the Wurlitzer with one eye on Berry's famous guitar and the other on one of the dartsmen, hoping he would hit the bull's-eye.

Kevin's reverie came to an end as we all congregated back at the Majic Bus and swapped Saint Louis stories. Dan, Jay, and Janine had wandered around Laclede's Landing, a few blocks north of the arch, a covey of redbrick, cast-iron-faced Victorian warehouses cut by cobblestone lanes. They found the trendified bars, shops, and restaurants there nightmarish. From Laclede's Landing the spirit of Saint Louis appeared vulgar and common, at least on this opening day of the baseball season. Hordes of Cardinal fans milled around in bright red jackets, buying pennants, peanuts, and plastic helmets, screaming, "Saint Louie, Saint Louie!" and, "The New York Mets Suck!" as they chugged plastic cups brimming with Bud and Busch, listening to an awful country-rock band's version of Creedence Clearwater Revival's "Proud Mary," the lead singer repeating "Rollin', rollin', rollin' down the river," ad nauseum. These students felt a kinship with the patrician poet T. S. Eliot, who grew up not far from Washington University, learned how to read and write, and then wisely beat it out of this wasteland of a town. Jay, using the New Orleans French Quarter and Chicago's Wise Fools Pub as his unfair benchmarks, considered Saint Louis a huge disappointment. The City of Gabriels he had read about—home at one time or another to W. C. Handy, Josephine Baker, Chuck Berry, Ike and Tina Turner, Miles Davis, and ragtime's leading composer, Scott Joplin—had become, he said, the City of Gobblers. Everywhere he looked obese Cardinal fans were gorging on hamburgers, soupy chili, pizza, ice-cream cones, and hot dogs, washed down with the native brew. I sought to convince him that it was unfair to judge Saint Louis by an opening-day baseball crowd.

I sketched for Jay an avant-garde Saint Louis at the turn of the century. It was at the 1904 Saint Louis World's Fair, also known as the Louisiana Purchase Exposition, that the hot dogs and ice-cream cones Jay now scorned were both first introduced to the world. Electricity, then a novelty, lit up the fair's pavilions, causing a wave of Saint Louis excitement across America. The most popular song of that summer went: "Meet me in Saint Louis, Louis / Meet me at the fair. / Don't tell me the lights are shining / Anyplace but Here."

Out of courtesy to Stefanie, however, the three Saint Louis–bashers kept their harsh judgment to themselves and their journals, but I now felt a responsibility to enlarge their vision by seeing a little more of the city before dark. Off we went, our first stop Louis Sullivan's 1891 Wainright Building, one of the most human examples of that American invention, the steel-frame skyscraper.

We drove past the National Bowling Hall of Fame, with two kids in front spraying each other with Silly String; stopped for a few moments at Union Station, now a flashy new Hyatt Regency; and headed into Forest Park, a thirteen-hundred-acre tract adjacent to the West End residential section—site of the 1904 World's Fair and home to the History Museum; the superb Saint Louis Art Museum, with its incredible collection of Western art (especially rich in the work of famed local painter Charles M. Russell); the Saint Louis Science Center; and the Zoological Park, home base of TV's "Wild Kingdom" host, Marlin Perkins.

Jared wanted to explore South Saint Louis for the Italian neighborhood known as the Hill, where his baseball hero Yogi ("It ain't over till it's over") Berra had grown up. Janine wanted to find the large house at 3317 Morgan Street, where a widow named Kate Chopin wrote the novel *The Awakening* (1899), an honest portrayal of a married woman's sexual restlessness that has only recently been acknowledged as a great masterpiece of American literature. A great fan of both, I wished we could have, but we were short on time. It was now 6:00 P.M., and at 6:50 we were scheduled to attend a lecture by Professor John Gillingham of the University of Missouri—Saint Louis, on Europe 1992, the end of the Cold War, and the implications for American corporations like McDonnell-Douglas and General Dynamics, both headquartered in Saint Louis.

I had known John Gillingham, a forty-eight-year-old father of three (children and books) for four years and had come to respect his ability to understand contemporary events from a historian's perspective. He is, among other things, an astute observer of what's "going down" in Saint Louis, besides maintaining the healthy attitude that no student can ask a stupid question.

We arrived right on time. My class mixed with Professor Gillingham's, whose students were, for the most part, daytime-working adults, including

195

a police officer, a taxi driver, and a woman who sold flowers on street corners and in bars. Following the lecture on the New Europe, the class became an open forum. After Mitch asked a series of concerned questions about the potential military threat of a unified Germany, Kevin stuck his hand in the air and asked: "Is East Saint Louis as bad as they say?" To illustrate the depths of urban horror, Professor Gillingham told of fifty-five-year-old Walter DeBow, an African American who suffered permanent brain damage after being beaten into a coma by a fellow prisoner at the city jail in 1984. In a court settlement he and his family were awarded $3.4 million, which, with interest, had grown to $4 million by 1990. When debt-ridden, bankrupt East Saint Louis was unable to pay more than $1 million of it, a judge awarded the East Saint Louis Municipal Building and 220 acres of city-owned property to the DeBows. Walter DeBow and his family fought city hall in East Saint Louis, and they *won it*. Professor Gillingham said that East Saint Louis—a city that is more than $55 million in debt—couldn't even afford garbage collection, or radios for its few police cars. In driving his point home he told us of Curtis Fair, an irate East Saint Louis Little League coach who pulled a gun and took several shots at a teenage umpire when he disagreed with his calls. Curtis Fair was convicted of attempted murder and aggravated assault. At last Kevin Willey was convinced and he no longer wanted to visit East Saint Louis.

After class we all went to the Wedge, a local bar complete with pool table, jukebox, and the typical appetizers of nachos, potato skins, buffalo wings, and, most important, pitchers of Budweiser. The bar was packed, most eyes glued to one of the two televisions on which Duke was beating Michigan in the NCAA finals. It was great fun watching the game and talking with Professor Gillingham's students, who left us with an important piece of local information: a recent story about a drunken motorist who pulled into a police station drive-in window and began ordering a Big Mac and fries. The hapless fellow, referred to as a Hoosier by the narrator, was immediately arrested for driving while intoxicated. (In local parlance "Hoosier" does not mean an Indianan but is a generic and often derisive term for rural white migrants, from any state, judged to be "poor white trash.") For the remainder of the trip I heard the McDonald's story retold a dozen times, and "you Hoosier" became the Majic Bus epithet of choice to express disappointment or irritation.

At midnight we said good-bye to our new Saint Louis friends and Professor Gillingham. Frank had caught a few hours' rest while we were blowing off steam in the Wedge, and with his coffee thermos full, an Italian sub in his belly, and the Who's "Magic Bus" blaring from his Majic Bus for all to hear, he cattle-prodded us out of the bar, in a hurry to start his night drive to Independence, where we were to tour the Harry S. Truman Library at 9:00 A.M.

Frank had an easy, straight drive that night west on I-70, which bisects the "Show-Me State," listening to the songwriting genius of John Haitt, Steve Earle, Joe Ely, and Townes Van Zant. (The sobriquet "Show Me" is usually attributed to Congressman Willard Duncan Vandiver of southeast Missouri, who said in 1899, "I come from a country that raises corn and cockleburs and Democrats, and frothy eloquence neither convinces nor satisfies me. I'm from Missouri. You've got to show me.") On the "show-me" scale, Frank was right up there with the staunchest Missourian. That night he was in an especially "show-me" mood. When we passed Wentzville, Frank wanted to show Kevin Chuck Berry's home, but he decided it was better to let Kevin sleep. When we approached Fulton, he wanted to wake Tom to show him the impressive Winston Churchill Memorial on the site where the British prime minister made his world-famous "iron curtain" speech in 1946, but he decided it was better to let Tom sleep. When he drove past the Confederate Memorial State Historic Park, he wanted to show it to Shari, but in his heart he knew it was better to let her sleep. And when we arrived in Independence at 5:30 A.M., he wanted to show me that we had arrived in Harry Truman's hometown (also the birthplace of Neal Cassady), but he knew I would discover that on my own soon enough. Frank had learned to temper his "show-me" instincts and to balance our interests and needs: We were no longer paid passengers but family. Pulling off into a Howard Johnson's Motel parking lot, he

197

cut the engine, not interested in getting real sleep—just enough rest to get the sting out of his sore, road-red eyes.

After a heartburn breakfast, at Jim's Family Restaurant, of burnt eggs even ketchup couldn't cure, we entered the Truman Library and Museum when it opened, greeted in the foyer by a giant Thomas Hart Benton mural Truman commissioned from his fellow Missourian, called *Independence and the Opening of the West.* The mural was done in Benton's characteristic sculptural style, replete with iconic Americans—often with great, anatomically incorrect muscles. Truman himself painted a few strokes of the mural. The museum, which is devoted to the career of President Truman and to U.S. history from 1945 to 1953, includes a copy of the Japanese surrender document, a menorah presented to him by Abba Eban, and a working model of the battleship *Missouri.* Before the students were left to roam around on their own, I lectured on the early years of this most remarkable man—how he was refused entrance to West Point because of poor eyesight but went on to distinguish himself in World War I as a captain in the field artillery; how he married his high school sweetheart, Bess Wallace, in 1919 and opened a men's store in Kansas City, only to go bankrupt, spending the next ten years paying off his debts; and how he became a county judge even though he never attended college. Harry Truman was a great American, a personal hero of mine, and the type of individual whose character can inspire young people to become public servants.

With this warm-up on his Missouri years, the students scattered through the museum to learn more about senatorial, vice presidential, and presidential accomplishments of "Give-'em-Hell Harry." When we reconvened we had a lively discussion about such Truman "the buck stops here" decisions as his dropping atomic bombs on Hiroshima and Nagasaki, firing Douglas MacArthur, desegregating the military by executive order, blockading Berlin, dispatching American troops to fight in Korea, and supporting the creation of Israel. Only Truman's decision to use atomic weapons against Japan elicited any student disapproval—the group equally divided pro and con.

Although all the students found the Truman Library and Museum a fascinating American Odyssey stop-off, for Tom Tolan—an avid reader of U.S. political history—it was the trip's highlight. Truman is his favorite president, and Robert Donovan's two-volume biography of Truman is one of his favorite books. It was professional fun watching Tom reverentially study the exhibits, particularly intrigued by a replica of Truman's White House office and the table on which the United Nations Charter was signed. As he walked out to the courtyard by himself to pay his respects at President Truman's grave, I watched him bow his head, cross himself, and say a prayer—it was a touching moment for me. After leaving the library we toured Truman's home, which is preserved as though he were living there still: His drab green 1972 Chrysler Newport is still in the garage, his hat and coats still hang under the stairs, and his canes still lean in the corner of his study.

As a biographer of Truman's secretary of state, Dean Acheson, and secretary of defense, James Forrestal, I had visited the library many times before to pursue research, often staying at a nearby neighborhood bed-and-breakfast. After eight hours of research I would say good-bye to the dedicated archivists who assiduously provided me with boxes of well-organized documents from the Truman era (which I churned into citations and notes in my biographies) and usually walked to downtown Independence for dinner at the New China Restaurant. With a stomach full of egg rolls and sweet-and-sour pork, I'd walk five blocks down Maple Street to the Harry S. Truman National Historic Site, the Victorian house in which President and Mrs. Truman, when not in Washington, DC, lived from their marriage in 1919 until their deaths, and where Dean Acheson informed him of the North Korean invasion of South Korea on June 24, 1950. There I'd peer in the windows and walk around the house, wishing that President Truman were still alive to guide me on a walk around his Independence—that he could tell me about the origins of his town as the springboard for western expansion to the Santa Fe Trail in 1821 and to the Oregon and California trails in the 1840s; about the Civil War–era jail that had held such notorious characters as Frank James, William Quantrill, and the Youngers; and about nearby Fort Osage, the first U.S. outpost of the Louisiana Purchase. I wanted to hear his uninflected

Missouri voice tell me about his own Independence history, for example, the Union Pacific Station at Grand and Pacific streets, which played such an important role during his 1948 whistle-stop presidential campaign.

I am convinced that one of Truman's great strengths as president was his detailed understanding of American history. The air of Independence is composed of nitrogen, oxygen, and history. When you walk the streets of Independence, the ghost of Harry Truman is your companion. You see him as an old man ambling down the sidewalk at dusk, his open-road-style Stetson atop his head and his cane in hand, saying neighborly hellos; cocking his head to every train whistle; thinking back to when Missouri was part of the virgin West and to when the debate over whether his state would enter the Union a slave or a free state was settled by the Missouri Compromise; and to when steamboats serving the fur trade began chugging up and down the Mississippi and Missouri rivers in the early 1800s, soon to be supplanted by the railroads as the main avenues of commerce. He would recall the Battle of Wilson's Creek—one of the bloodiest in the Civil War—and how throughout all this Missouri turmoil good bourbon always kept spirits alive. Returning from his walk, he'd take off his hat and coat, pour himself a tumbler of Old Grandad, hold the glass up in swirling homage to America's rail-splitting past and aerospace future, and down the hatch it would go. Turning on his night lamp, he would pull out a history book—perhaps the *Diaries of James K. Polk* or Marquis James's *Andrew Jackson*—and he would read by the bay window in a big over-stuffed chair for hours, stopping only to kiss Bess good-night, until he heard the lonesome whistle of the midnight train, the signal it was time for bed. Tiptoeing up the creaky stairs so as not to wake his wife, he would climb into bed and fall straight to sleep, his conscience clear, as it had been all his life.

Having spent longer than we planned in Independence, we tried to make the most of the brief two hours we had left for lunch in Kansas City if we were to be on time for our meeting with William S. Burroughs in Lawrence.

During the 1920s and 1930s, the barbecue joints and jazz clubs of Kansas City, a town that can be sophisticated on the one hand and about as unpretentious as it gets on the other, birthed some of America's great musicians—Count Basie, Big Joe Turner, Benny Goodman, Lester Young, and Charlie ("Bird") Parker. Today Kansas City closes early, its showcase clubs are refined, not raw, and the innovation is gone, only the rehash surviving. Built on a levee overlooking a bend in the Missouri River, Kansas City has been said to have "more boulevard miles than Paris and more fountains than any city outside of Rome." The students, who had expected Kansas City to be a gridiron of livestock pens, grain silos, hayseed farmers in overalls, and restaurants with ketchup bottles on every table, were surprised to find the boulevards gently outlining the many hills of the city, exuding a modern, almost cosmopolitan flair. Punctuating the skyline are terracotta tile roofs and clock towers, rising like castles above Country Club Plaza, the country's oldest shopping center. The castles made me think of Walt Disney, who started painting in a Kansas City garage and left town in 1925, not long before the plaza was electrified.

Unable to find parking for the bus, we headed toward Crown Center, a redevelopment project south of downtown financed by Hallmark Cards, and got directions to Arthur Bryant's, a hot-and-spicy barbecue restaurant. There we had a quick feast of chicken and ribs to the music of Little Willie John. Jay mentioned how important Ernest Hemingway's brief stint as a reporter for the *Kansas City Star* had been to his career as a creative writer. We discussed at length why Missouri seemed to nurture native artists, settling on a version of the great-rivers explanation. Then it was off across the Missouri River on I-70, with the indomitable Iggy Pop singing "Homeboy" from his *Brick by Brick* LP, through Kansas City, Kansas, and on to Lawrence, home of the University of Kansas Jayhawks and William S. Burroughs.

9

William S. Burroughs and the Sunflower State

America is not a young land; it is old and dirty and evil before the settlers, before the Indians. The evil is there waiting.
—WILLIAM S. BURROUGHS

LAWRENCE AND ITS SURROUNDINGS WERE, THE STUDENTS DIS-covered much to their surprise, green and hilly, not at all the flat tornado land twenty years watching *The Wizard of Oz* and "Little House on the Prairie" had engraved in their minds. We parked in the Old West Law-rence Historic District, adjacent to downtown, a neighborhood of more than forty Victorian and Italian-style residences. It didn't take long to discover that Lawrence is a main-street town, a picture-postcard place of nickel candy stores, tobacco shops, and dollar movies that still prods the American psyche as the proper place to bring up children. It was Chris-tine's favorite town of the entire trip. Having read at least parts of *Naked Lunch* in preparation for the trip and seen the movie in Chicago, most students were puzzled as to why a writer as "far out" as William S. Burroughs

202

would live in such a pleasant but mundane "Main Street" community. As Peter O. Whitmer asked in *Aquarius Revisited,* his fine history of the 1960s counterculture: How could someone settle for the monotony of Kansas "after the rich crush of excitement that comes from living in places such as the French Quarter of New Orleans; the Amazon jungle before the Trans-Amazon Highway; Tangiers, when it was still a wide-open international zone; Paris before Pompidou and London with the Beatles and the Rolling Stones?" We spilled out of the Majic Bus onto the soft green lawn of the Lawrence Center for the Arts, where I lectured for a half hour on the Beat Generation, emphasizing the literary achievements of Burroughs's oeuvre and its influence on a significant swath of important American writers, his cutout method of writing, and his "algebra of need" philosophy based on the metaphor of control.

Many readers may be wondering why, out of all the important fiction writers in America, I chose to bring my students to visit with William S. Burroughs, a literary figure who, for the past fifty years, has tended to elicit an outraged and disapproving response from much of the cultural establishment. When *Naked Lunch,* first published in Paris, reached the United States, *Newsweek* deemed the novel a "masterpiece" and reported that it "carried a heavier burden of literary laudations than any piece of fiction since *Ulysses.*" Despite early acclaim for *Naked Lunch* from such cultural mandarins as Norman Mailer, Kenneth Allsop, Alfred Kazin, Mary McCarthy, and John Ciardi — an evaluation that has stood the test of time from a whole new generation of our best writers and by a substantial body of serious academic criticism — the recognition of Burroughs from the chattering classes has more often than not been grudging. His experimental novels — especially *Naked Lunch, The Ticket That Exploded,* and *Nova Express* — are regarded by some as a threat to the well-mannered, conventionally crafted, middle-brow novel, and rightly so.

Naked Lunch, a recommended but not assigned course text, deals with the control of consciousness and behavior through addiction — to sex, power, money, drugs, even to control itself. To Burroughs, a congenital outsider, control is the central concern of human experience. Bourgeois gentility and a bruised sense of decorum fuel many of his critics, appalled at the drug addiction, rough sex, and criminality of Burroughs's universe—which, he insists, is part of ours. But Burroughs is most incendiary because he elides the boundary between personal and political control. His brutal, fierce, and exact satire violates novelistic conventions as it trumpets an unacceptable conclusion—not only does the emperor have no clothes on, but the exalted ruler is smashed out of his gourd, has a boyfriend or two on the side, and, worst of all, the courtiers conspire not to see any of it. When themes of this nature lie at the heart of a writer's work, appreciation is often checked by the timidity of those who prefer not to think about them. Because *Naked Lunch* has no consistent narrative, no consistent point of view—in fact, is not a novel in the traditional sense—the reader must rely on clues Burroughs scatters in order to orient him or herself to its nightmare world. In the "Atrophied Preface," located, of course, at the end of the book, Burroughs says: "So instead of yelling, 'Where Am I?' cool it and look around and you will find out approximately. . . . You were not there for *The Beginning*. You will not be there for *The End*. . . . Your knowledge of what is going on can only be superficial and relative." The most useful clue to the technique of *Naked Lunch* lies in the title—coined by Jack Kerouac—which signifies "a frozen moment when everyone sees what is on the end of every fork." Appropriately *Naked Lunch* is a series of such moments, frozen like Eliot's in *The Waste Land*, linked by theme into a full-course naked meal.

What do young readers find appealing about a book like *Naked Lunch*? The inherent rebelliousness and unconformity of Burroughs—a grandson of the inventor of the Burroughs adding machine (the patent to which is now owned by UNISYS, a multibillion-dollar corporation), whose family was listed in the Saint Louis Social Register—is certainly a large part of the appeal. As Burroughs tests every boundary, every convention of bourgeois society, young readers can vicariously—and safely—enjoy thinking the unthinkable. After a walk on the wild side, they can consciously and perhaps gratefully choose, this time with informed consent, to remain within the dull, workaday world. Burroughs is a writer of Grimm's fairy tales for adults, speaking to our nightmare fears and, worst of all, perhaps our nightmare longings. His exploration of the horrific world of which grownups refuse to speak provides breathing space for young people.

Young readers, like the rest of the human race, are obsessed by sex. For the Yo generation, coming of age in the plague years of AIDS—in which an unlucky sexual encounter could spell death but for whom "Just say no" seems untenable—Burroughs's encounters with homosexuality, S&M, even "sex by hanging" and autoerotic asphyxia, is not all that shocking. To some students Burroughs seemed almost prophetic. When he wrote of "stomach tucks," the students thought of liposuction; when he described a fatal viral epidemic, they pointed to AIDS. When Burroughs wrote *Junkie* and *Naked Lunch* in the 1940s and 1950s drugs were not an overriding concern of the population at large. Now they are destroying our society, the cause of urban crime, and the focus of a governmental war. Young people find him uncanny in this respect—that his novels identified problems that recur and magnify over time. "Junk is the ideal product," Burroughs wrote in *Naked Lunch,* "the ultimate merchandise. No sales talk necessary. The client will crawl through a sewer and beg to buy . . . The junk merchant does not sell his product to the consumer, he sells the consumer to his product. He does not improve and simplify his merchandise. He degrades and simplifies the client. He pays his staff in junk." Of course bluestocking censors, confusing cause and effect, would say the publication of his books played a central role in breaching these heretofore unbreachable taboos. They fail to understand the essential role of art in society.

The Yo generation is also primed for Burroughs by popular music, especially the punk, heavy metal, and grunge movements that naturally embraced his gallows humor, nihilism, and rejection of humanism. When Sid Vicious of the *Sex Pistols* sang the Frank Sinatra hit "My Way," it was pure William Burroughs. When Patti Smith sneered, "Jesus died for somebody's sins but not mine," it was again pure William Burroughs. Rock bands such as the Insect Trust, Steely Dan, Hüsker Du, and Throbbing Gristle have named themselves out of *Naked Lunch*. The raucous MTV video "Just One Fix" by Ministry uses Burroughs as its centerpiece, as the now-ancient guru of the hard-core underground.

Burroughs also seems timely to our youth because of his conspiratorial view of government. Although such a take on government did not begin with Burroughs, he was the first major American novelist to make justifiable paranoia a significant literary theme. The idea of sinister forces controlling the world of appearances is commonplace in post-Watergate, post-Iran-contra, post–Oliver Stone *JFK*, post–J. Edgar Hoover-in-drag America, but it was regarded as science fiction when Burroughs invented the Nova Mob, a sinister consortium of CIA-bureaucrat-gangsters, drug runners, and greedy government power brokers. Burroughs's alternative world of Mugwumps, the Green Boys, and the Nova Mob, and such archetypal characters as Bradley the Buyer, Hamburger Mary, and Dr. Benway are imaginative and pointed stereotypes of certain types of individuals and groups in the modern United States.

Besides his role as elder statesman of the Beat Generation and the granddaddy of punk, Burroughs is often associated with British pop art, Francis Bacon, Andy Warhol, the Velvet Underground, minimalism, the black humorists—he is the first truly postmodern writer. Quite simply, when it comes to cultural impact and innovative style I agree with Norman Mailer's assessment that Burroughs is "the only American novelist living today who may conceivably be possessed by genius." Thus our pilgrimage to Lawrence.

Jim McCrary, an exceptional poet and Burroughs's assistant, stopped by to advise us that the venue for meeting with the great writer had been changed. We were to walk to the downtown gallery Artists En Masse (next door to the Casbah, a local vegetarian café), where Burroughs would soon meet us. What a gallery it was! Janet Hughes, a graduate art student at the University of Kansas, had created an astounding collection of multimedia abstract paintings, sculptures, and videos in a show she called "You Took the Words Out of My Mouth." The students were shocked that such a gallery show could exist in this ostensibly Norman Rockwell town. Dan and Jay led a last-minute mad dash across the street to the Raven Bookstore to load up on paperbacks of Burroughs's novels—*Naked Lunch*, *The Wild Boys*, *Exterminator!*, *The Place of Dead Roads*, and *Cities of the*

Red Night. As huge Burroughs fans, they wanted to have autographed copies of all his books. And then, as we all nervously studied the art pieces, William S. Burroughs ascended the stairs, with a small entourage, including the poet John Giorno, following. He shook hands with some of the students and then, using a cane for balance, pulled up a chair and sat down. We congregated in front of him, legs crossed, like on the first day of kindergarten or as if Uncle Remus were about to tell us his Br'er Rabbit stories.

His thin hair and his suit and Fedora were gray; his translucent skin was flushed but gray beneath. He asked how our trip was in a soft voice, nasal but deep, grandfatherly but remote and monochromatic. Each word started high and wound down low, descending the octave from high to middle C. For the next hour he fielded questions and sculpted responses on every topic under the sun, all the while staring at the wooden floor or at the tip of his cane, not making eye contact. His answers were succinct and pointed; he was part William F. Buckley, Jr., and part, as Kerouac saw him, "a Kansas Minister with exotic, phenomenal fire and mysteries." William S. Burroughs does not speak gibberish. Rather than ask Burroughs about his friendships with Jack Kerouac and Allen Ginsberg or about his experience with drugs, the students were more interested in his views of contemporary America and the human condition. Asked whether he planned to vote for president, he answered, "Yes, I'll vote Libertarian," making clear, however, his dislike of all politicians; he was only voting Libertarian because the party stood for near-abolition of government. The Internal Revenue Service, he stated, was an "abomination to basic rights of privacy," and he wished its liquidation. But what particularly moved Burroughs to vote Libertarian was its advocacy of personal freedoms—guns, drugs, abortions, and the like. "Government is necessary only to protect against force and fraud," he continued. "Three-fourths of the people in jail don't belong there." If police worried about pursuing murderers and rapists instead of "prostitutes, drug users, and car speeders like Rodney King," he went on, "then there would be much less real crime." Burroughs opposes foreign aid, government subsidies of business, censorship, and laws restricting private sexual conduct between consent-

207

ing adults or the recreational use of drugs. Like André Marrou, the Libertarian candidate for president, Burroughs believes government should be about a tenth its present size. When pressed by Stefanie to explain how he would stop juveniles from buying hard drugs such as cocaine or heroin if they were made legal, Burroughs delivered a solemn one-line answer: "Drugs are an inevitable part of life."

The most dynamic part of the conversation occurred when Justin, who loves guns, asked Burroughs about his collection. For the first and only time in our session, Burroughs seemed genuinely animated, proud to talk about his big Smith & Wesson .45 and his beloved Colt .45 with a fellow enthusiast. Norman Mailer's description of Burroughs — "a hermit, a mad prospector up in the mountains who'll shoot you if you come to his cabin at the wrong time" — seemed apt. Burroughs also spoke quite fondly of Lawrence, adding that the town had been home to Langston Hughes from 1909 to 1915 (the poet lived there with his grandmother until he was thirteen) and to Frank Harris, author of many novels, most notably *My Life and Loves.* When Alan asked what Burroughs thought of David Cronenberg's Kafkaesque film *Naked Lunch,* based on his novel, he replied that he "liked it a lot . . . Many had wanted to do it; I didn't think it could be done. David deserves great credit for his skill and daring." He spoke of enjoying his role as a defrocked junkie priest in Gus Van Sant's *Drugstore Cowboy* and said he was looking forward next to playing an insurance salesman, if only someone would offer him a part.

Asked about writers he admired, "T. S. Eliot," was his immediate response, and he pointed out that the great poet was a Saint Louis native like himself. He also mentioned Céline, Kafka, and "the hard-boiled detective writers" Raymond Chandler and Dashiell Hammett. Some answers were downright surreal. Alison, for example, asked, "What would you come back as if you could live your life all over again?" He forced a smile, the first we saw, and responded, "Well, if there's anything we don't need, it's more cows." He thought for a few seconds, and then said he'd return as a lemur. We all began laughing, but he insisted he was serious, and he spoke for the next few minutes with great authority on these chiefly nocturnal mammals, formerly widespread but now confined largely to

Madagascar. "Lemurs are a distinct superfamily," Burroughs informed us, describing their foxlike muzzles, large eyes, very soft, woolly fur, and long tails. From lemurs the discussion took a short evolutionary leap to cats, which, along with guns and lemurs, turned out to be a favorite topic of his. Toads were another creature he rated highly, and he told us that as a boy growing up in Saint Louis, he had "mastered the long-lost art of toad calling." He spoke of a book he was writing, to be titled *The Cat Inside,* about the personalities of his three cats—Ruski, Fletch, and Muty—and how they had taken over his house and become psychic guides for him. "My cats," he told us, "have saved me from a deadly, pervasive ignorance . . . Just touching one of my cats can make me weep." Kevin said *Naked Lunch* reminded him of a mix of pop artist Roy Lichtenstein and action painter Jackson Pollock, and Burroughs received the observation with genuine pleasure, saying, "Fiction is at least fifty years behind painting." He went on to recommend meditation as one good way for young people to get material for writing. "You [also] have to do a lot of good reading and thinking before you can do any bad writing," he added. When Alan asked whether he thought his novels had influenced the young people in Eastern Europe who tore down the Berlin Wall, Burroughs brusquely replied, "Why don't you ask the young people in Eastern Europe?" adding, "Now that America has lost the Russians as an enemy, I don't know what we'll do. Without enemies, nations can't exist."

The session closed with an explanation of the "cut-up-and-fold-in" method of writing: Take a printed or written page, cut it up, and rearrange the pieces to create unusual semantic juxtapositions. For Burroughs it is crucial to confound conventional language and the false reality he believes it produces. His parting words were a paternal charge to be careful on the rest of our odyssey, which produced a certain amount of tittering in the group, coming as it did from a man who has spent the greater part of his life on a quest for knowledge and experience, heedless of the price he or others might pay. Finally, he advised us to always, always remember that "good and bad things come in streaks . . . Learn that and you'll be all right."

Burroughs stood up slowly, leaned on his cane, posed for photos, and began signing books. He was not at all the outlaw they had thought they would meet, the students told me later. I wondered to myself what they had expected from the near-octogenarian—perhaps shooting out the light bulbs with a pistol. It was hard for the students to hold Burroughs's paradoxical life in their heads: hard for them to reconcile the haut−Saint Louis upbringing and Harvard education with the lifelong exploration of the forbidden. The aged writer, they thought, was the type of fellow they all wanted for an uncle but not a father. For the rest of the trip the students spoke enthusiastically about meeting William S. Burroughs, and Aíne, Justin, Dan, Jay, and Janine hungrily devoured his novels. They had met a true American original, a literary genius, and they would never forget it.

Frank had reluctantly missed Burroughs because he had arranged to rendezvous with his Oklahoma buddy, Joe McDougall, in Lawrence so they could at last build our bunk beds. When we returned to the Majic Bus it looked like a carpenters' convention. Plywood, saws, drills, and wood shavings were everywhere. Frank said they needed a few more "hammer-in-nail hours," so we decided to explore Lawrence. Kenny and Beth found the tracks of the Atchison, Topeka & Santa Fe and walked them, playing hobo for a few hours. Others went shopping in the downtown mom-and-pop stores. Five of the guys and I suited up for basketball and for the next few hours played full-court pick-up ball. It felt great, sweating all those road miles and carbohydrates out of our systems, not to mention all that Saint Louis Bud.

The return to the Majic Bus brought a pleasant surprise: The bunks made a huge difference and we now had a lot more stretching room. William S. Burroughs was still the hot topic as we pulled out of town, the discussion centering on how amazing it was that anyone who had led the life he had had managed to reach old age, an observation Burroughs himself has made. Frank had purchased a wooden University of Kansas Jayhawk weather vane, which Kevin attached to our side mirror: We had acquired a Majic Bus mascot. Those who had played basketball were in dire need of a shower, so Frank turned into a KOA campground just outside Lawrence, where for one dollar we could wash to our hearts' content. We all, nonbasketballers included, took advantage of the facilities and felt refreshed and renewed. There was a beautiful, subtle sunset, and everyone was in a state of unanticipated love for Kansas, the state Eisenhower called "first in freedom, first in wheat." Historian Carl Becker once wrote: "Kansas is no mere geographical expression, but a 'state of mind,' a religion, and a philosophy in one," and we had become ardent converts to the Beckerian view. Our collective state of mind was now one of utter happiness and contentment. We stopped at a Big Boy restaurant in Topeka for a salad-, soup-, and dessert-bar pig-out, and with bellies full we fell asleep on the bouncing highway of life on the road.

Energized by his fully appointed Majic Bus and the Rockies only a day's drive away, Frank night-owled it through Kansas, the Center of America, until the wee hours of the morning, listening to rock and roll, drinking black coffee, and savoring the solitude, the calm, and the silent camaraderie of his sleeping passengers. I had dozed off shortly after our salad-bar supper on the understanding that Frank would catch some shut-eye just outside Abilene. The plan was to visit the Dwight D. Eisenhower Presidential Library and Museum, lunch in Old Abilene, a re-creation of a street during the town's cattle heyday when Wild Bill Hickok was mayor, and then head for Boulder, for a party that evening at Naropa Institute, the only accredited four-year Buddhist college in America. But Frank had fallen into autopilot mode and had inadvertently daydreamed right past Abilene, realizing his mistake ninety miles too late. Relying on the motto he used to define himself—"Never turn back"—Frank put in a few more hours at the wheel, finally shutting off the motor on the empty gravel parking lot of Prairie Dog Town, a roadside tourist attraction just off I-70 in Oakley, Kansas.

Beth and I, the first up, stumbled out to greet the morning. We were accosted by a giant, looming ceramic prairie dog, advertising itself as "the world's largest," a phrase that signifies Tourist Trap to the cognoscenti. Our particular TT boasted a living five-legged cow and six-legged steer. By now we had developed a daily routine: Off the bus, stretch, brush teeth inside the nearest truck stop or restaurant, read the local newspaper or *USA Today*, inhale pots of coffee with cream, and wait for the others to follow. As the entire crew staggered into the home-style eatery with pictures of Christ adorning the walls, panic struck the hung-over short-order chef, and he frantically began cracking open dozens of eggs, tossing fatty strips of bacon on the griddle, and warming homemade sourdough biscuits to accommodate the unexpected caravan of grub seekers.

When Frank came in, I immediately confronted him about why he had bypassed Abilene. The Carter and Truman libraries had scored big educational dividends as the students discussed the Panama Canal treaties; the Camp David accords; the Iran—hostage crisis; the creation of Israel; NATO, the Marshall Plan, and the Truman Doctrine; and Walter Mondale and Henry Wallace for days after our visits. After Atlanta the bone of contention was whether Carter should have canceled American participation in the Olympics when the Soviets invaded Afghanistan. After Independence the burning question was whether Truman had been justified in dropping the atomic bombs on Japan. Historical debates sometimes raged on for hours, often dovetailing with exchanges on current political issues. For students to learn more about Dwight Eisenhower, Supreme Allied Commander in World War II and thirty-fourth president of the United States, was an essential part of the American Odyssey course, and now Frank "Midnight Rider" Perugi had negligently deleted Ike from the itinerary. With miles of experiences still ahead of us, I didn't want to magnify the incident out of proportion, but I made it clear to Frank that historical stop-offs were the bread and butter of the American Odyssey course. Frank apologized, and together we studied the road atlas to plan the day.

Sitting in a booth, staring blankly at the invaders from Long Island, was a shaggy, unwashed, blistered, and middle-aged Low Plains drifter with a long, tangled beard; snaggled, coffee-stained teeth; cracked, sun-weathered skin; and bloodshot eyes and pupils that rolled counterclockwise whenever he coughed, which was often. He was so dirty that at first glance he appeared to sport a tremendous tan. In the romantic road novels of Jack London, Jack Kerouac, and John Dos Passos, and in the folk songs of Johnny Cash, Bob Dylan, and Arlo Guthrie, the drifter would have been idealized—a free-spirited, unencumbered hobo. To the jaded eyes of New York commuters, he was the archetypcal half-mad homeless person who drags his life of alcoholic woes around in torn plastic bags and calls his bedbug-ridden blanket home. Perhaps the truth lay in between.

At my urging Jared assumed the role of interviewer and went over to ask our free-soiled breakfast partner about the vagabond life in western Kansas. The wanderer told Jared his name was John Brown and that his great-grandfather was the legendary "Old Man of Osawatomie"—John Brown of pre–Civl War "Bleeding Kansas" and Harpers Ferry reknown, more than likely a deluded tall tale—but the mere fact that he wanted to be a descendant of John Brown was in itself interesting enough for us to pay homage to him. Matt brought out the videocam and began filming the conversation. Brown said he was a homeless Vietnam veteran who wandered the Great Plains looking for Jesus Christ. "They loved the baby but they killed the man," he muttered intermittently, a bewildering punctuation to many of his thoughts. Jared asked what he thought of George Bush and Dan Quayle, and his reflexive patriotism exploded like a package of Black Cat firecrackers on the Fourth of July. He loved Bush and Quayle and wished he had been in Desert Storm so he could have "kicked some Ir-rackets' butts." The proudest day of his life, he said, was when Republican Senator Bob Dole of Kansas—himself a wounded veteran of World War II—saluted him at a Topeka veterans' rally in the late 1970s. Jared was clearly taken with our unsightly tumbleweed traveler and tried to befriend him. Later, on the bus, Jared told me more about John Brown's fifteen years of post-Vietnam vagrancy, how he slept in roadside ditches, cooked hot dogs and beans out of soup cans heated over gasoline-can fires, and ice-fished on the Arkansas River near Dodge City in the bitter cold, for winter carp dinners. What shocked Jared most was John Brown's vehement claim that he would kill himself rather than give up living under the stars or be forced into a shelter. He was homeless by choice and didn't appreciate self-pity from "indoor folk." One could almost have admired his fierce independence, had he not been so sickly and deranged.

In the meantime some of the students were wandering around Prairie Dog Town, watching the furry brown critters dash in and out of their burrows. As Frank and I were paying our breakfast bill, we noticed a rotating metal rack with postcards of unusual and beautiful rock formations. We were told by our Scripture-spouting waitress that these natural wonders, an Indian and pioneer landmark known as Monument Rocks (or the Chalk Pyramids), were located a difficult twenty dirt-road miles south of Oakley. Local legend had it that, in 1541, the explorer Coronado stood atop one of the wind-carved and water-eroded chalk pinnacles, which rise some seventy feet above the plain, and carved his initials with his sword. The detour decision was made; we were off to Monument Rocks.

As we headed south on U.S. 83, we saw cow after cow dotting the flatland prairies, and we now fully appreciated William S. Burroughs's remark about "too many cows." With a cloudless, electric blue sky above us and a brazen spring sun metaphorically radiating, "Welcome to Kansas: The Sunflower State," our spirits soared. Alison had brought her "Best of Peter, Paul and Mary" tape to the front, and the trio's melodious harmonies captured the essence of the moment. Six students crowded into the porch to sing along to such all-time campfire classics as "Puff, the Magic Dragon," "Blowin' in the Wind," "Five Thousand Miles," and "When the Day Is Done." Before long, Frank, who was crooning loudly, spotted the unmarked dirt road to Monument Rocks and hung a sharp left. The Majic Bus bounced gloriously along at forty miles per hour, over potholes and ditches of varying sizes, leaving a trail of dust and exhaust thick enough to choke a horse. As the bus approached Monument Rocks, the students sensed immediately that they had entered that other planet known as the American West.

It is difficult, even impossible, to describe in words the prairies, deserts, mountains, red rock gorges, and canyons of the American West. Even the photographs by Ansel Adams and Robert Glenn Ketchum and the high-tech hotshots of *American Photography Magazine* can't do the subject poetic justice. Breathtaking, awesome, desolate, forbidding, spiritually uplifting, and soul-melting are at best desperate adjectives called into service as convenient shorthand in a feeble attempt to describe the wholly indescribable. True, a handful of writers and explorer-diarists have had their inspired moments, capturing in words a glimpse of the unearthly beauty of the Great Plains, the Rockies, the Pacific Coast, and the Mojave Desert. Edward Abbey, Willa Cather, Meriwether Lewis, Mari Sandoz, John C. Frémont, Francis Parkman, Theodore Roosevelt, and Wallace Stegner come to mind. But even their most lapidary prose falls far short in descriptive accuracy and poetic power, an Icarian enterprise doomed from its inception. Even the great cowboy-and-Indian painters, Charles M. Russell, Karl Bodner, George Catlin, and Frederic Remington, are only technically competent at depicting the human and animal aspects of the West: pioneer spirit, mountain-man loneliness, the native hunter-gatherers of the High Plains, bison herds and golden eagles, Indian wars and cavalry charges, bear hunts and totem poles, and the general violence and raw brutality that characterizes the "winning of the West." Look carefully at any one of their self-styled "realist" landscapes, and you will cringe at their European purple sunsets, white chalk cliffs, green rushing water, and maroon rocks. No, you cannot paint the Painted Desert or sketch the Black Hills, nor should you try.

Monument Rocks was clearly off the beaten tourist path. Without a soul in sight, we unloaded from the bus, ignoring a weathered wooden sign that read, DANGEROUS: ROCK CLIMBING FORBIDDEN, and promptly began doing just that. A few students, reluctant to climb the High Plains escarpments, wandered around the base of the Chalk Pyramids, snapping photos, marveling at the badland barrenness, and basking in the serenity of the moment. We were standing in what 130 million years ago was one of the last inland oceans—the Cretaceous Sea. It was mind-boggling to think that this arid land known as western Kansas was once a sea, filled with exotic fauna and teeming with fifteen-foot-long carnivorous fish, and four-ton dinosaurs wading in its shallows. What caused the disappearance of the Cretaceous Sea—shifting of the continental plates and extensive volcanic activity—is also what caused the uplifting of the modern Rocky Mountains. One hundred million years ago, Monument Rocks was under water, and where muddy rivers flowed over marshy plains, Triceratops and

Tyrannosaurus stomped freely, and only six million years ago, in neighboring Wallace and Logan counties, saber-toothed cats, primitive badgers and ferrets, immense rhinoceroses, giant camels, prongbucks, peccaries, and llamas had free reign over the blond grasses, gangly cottonwoods, willow thickets, and marshes on the verdant savannah. Now all of it is an endless floor of dead bones. It was a relevation for the students to realize that America is not a New World, ready to be molded by the busy hands of eager immigrants, but an ancient and powerful, ever-changing energy force whose recalcitrance becomes palpable in the American West, where desolation will survive even the dark hour of the human apocalypse. As D. H. Lawrence once wrote: "[America] is full of grinning, unappeased aboriginal demons, ghosts too. . . . America is tense with latent violence and resistance."

After a mildly harrowing ten-minute, pebble-sliding climb, Kevin, Justin, Tom, and I reached the top of the largest rock pyramid and waved the others up. The view was spectacular, and as we gazed out at the distant horizon, which was empty of skyscrapers, telephone wires, billboards, and paved roads, we envied the pair of brown hawks that glided and swooped overhead with ease. Soon all but a few joined us on top, and a collective group giddiness, known as pure happiness, filled our lungs. From this bird's-eye vantage point, the Majic Bus resembled a Matchbox car. Like Gulliver, we might have reached out, simply picked it up, and rolled it down the dirt road all the way back to New York. The sun was beating down, and we sprawled out on the flat rocks, disregarding the surgeon general's guidelines—as is youth's wont—to take tanning advantage of our enhanced proximity to Apollo's rays. Justin, on an isolated corner of a windswept rock edge, began doing pushups with his shirt off, to the mock-encouraging *ooh*s and *aah*s of his female colleagues. Kevin was profoundly frustrated. Although he hadn't found Coronado's initials, he did find about five hundred other carved messages, from GOD LOVES WICHITA STATE UNIVERSITY to EAT ME. When he went to make his own addition, he discovered he had left his pocketknife back on the bus and had to scramble down the rock pyramids to fetch it.

The rest of us sunbathed all the while, until Frank lay on the horn.

Like a pack of mountain goats we sure-footedly made our way down just as Kevin was coming back. By the time we reached the bottom, our butts were caked with white chalk from sliding part of the way down. Now alone on top and standing on a ledge, Kevin cupped his hands and yodeled forth so loudly he was probably heard back in Prairie Dog Town. After thoroughly dusting each other off, we piled back on the bus, its engine already started, and patiently waited for Kevin ("Jim Bowie") Willey to finish his carving. Twenty minutes later, as Kevin sprinted the last few breathless yards back to the bus, he proudly exclaimed that he had chiseled AMERICAN ODYSSEY 1992 on top of Monument Rocks, seventy feet in the air, "somewhere around where that Coronado fella did it."

The unexpected blast of open space and prairie freedom had unified and electrified the group as never before, and we were now revved for the Rockies. "The health of the eye seems to demand a horizon," Ralph Waldo Emerson once wrote. "We are never tired, so long as we can see far enough." The experience reminded me of the moment in James Michener's novel *Centennial* when his heroine, Elly Zendy, first views the geologically similar Pawnee Buttes of northeastern Colorado: "They stood like signal towers or the ramparts of a castle, and they created such a strong sense of home that all of us halted on the hill to appreciate the noble place to which God had brought us." Exhilarated more than ever about what lay ahead, we were now only a brief two-hour, back-road drive from the Colorado border, and then it was on to Denver, Boulder, Rocky Mountain National Park, Telluride, Mesa Verde, New Mexico, and Arizona and Nevada, until we drove right smack into the Pacific Ocean.

While I was sunning atop Monument Rocks, it had become apparent to me that an hour in the company of the literary outlaw William S. Burroughs had not resulted in a meltdown of my conditioned Catholic guilt. My sense of virtue had begun tugging at me on two accounts: climbing the forbidden Chalk Pyramids and allowing Kevin to carve something in the rock. Searching for a rationalization on which to hang my troubled conscience, I free-associated to Woody Guthrie and the Dust Bowl, to all those people fleeing the "black dust" and the economic bankruptcy of their lives in Texas and Oklahoma. Woody's old guitar, on which was written THIS MACHINE KILLS FASCISTS, came to mind, and all the hungry depression children with hollow eyes for whom he sang lullabies, and the workers' songs he sang by campfire to weary fruit-picking migrants, and all the hard travelin' he did down the dirt highways and back alleys from the tobacco roads to the skid rows of America. I then remembered the so-called Communist verse of Woody's inspired American anthem, "This Land Is Your Land," diabolically censored from school songbooks at about the time Joe McCarthy was seeing Reds under everyone's bed. Now, sitting barefoot on the bus, the Great Plains rolling past, I borrowed Jay's guitar and started singing and strumming the vanished verse of America's finest populist folk song:

> As I went walking, I saw a sign there,
> And on the sign it said NO TRESPASSING.
> But on the other side it didn't say nothing
> That side was made for you and me.

Alison screamed, "I'm so happy," and Frank, Beth, Jared, Alan, and I whooped it up as I sang and played Dylan's "Desolation Row" and "Man in the Long Black Coat," Bob Marley's "Redemption Song," the Beatles' "Let It Be," Woody Guthrie's "Oklahoma Hills," Jerry Jeff Walker's "Mr. Bojangles," and a potpourri of old country-and-western standards. As a matter of logic, "This Land Is Your Land" was a feeble justification for my transgressions, but I felt redeemed nonetheless.

Outside, an endless ocean of prairie shortgrass swayed in gentle harmony from horizon to horizon, and an occasional yellow-breasted meadowlark dive-bombed across the road. We had all conceived of the prairie as a barren combination of drab brown and dun, accented by an occasional splash of green. But to our surprise the springtime landscape was a vast rainbow of colors, a palette made up of yellow and purple, pink and vermilion, one color shading into another. We all agreed with Walt Whitman's assessment of the prairie in *Specimen Days:* "As to scenery (giving my own thought and feeling), while I know the standard claim is that Yosemite, Niagara Falls, the Upper Yellowstone, and the like afford the greatest natural shows, I am not so sure but the prairies and plains, while less stunning at first sight, last longer, fill the esthetic sense fuller, precede all the rest, and make North America's characteristic landscape. Even [the prairie's] simplest statistics are sublime." Due to loss of topsoil, overfarming, and insecticides, Walt Whitman's great prairie is dying. But don't give up hope, for as I write plant geneticist Wes Jackson and his Land Institute of Salinas, Kansas, are working overtime in an effort to phase out conventional chemical farming by arranging a marriage between ecology and agriculture.

We stopped for a quick lunch and a diesel fill at Stephen's Restaurant in Sharon Springs and had barbecued beef sandwiches, bacon cheeseburgers, chili dogs, and fries washed down with cherry lemonade, the beverage of choice. The jukebox was half Hank Williams, Jr., and half bad seventies rock — Boston, Kansas, and Foreigner — and so we stuck to Mr. Monday Night Football himself. While Frank washed the bus, I used the time to highlight Kansas history for the students: covered wagons, called prairie schooners, following the Oregon Trail and leaving countless graves in their wake; such early explorers as Zebulon Pike and Major Stephen Long, who, during his 1819 scientific journey, wrongly labeled the Great Plains "the Great American Desert" on his survey maps; the Homestead Act of 1862, which drew millions of settlers to the plains; the Missouri Compromise and the Kansas-Nebraska Act; the notorious guerrilla William Quantrill and his Confederate raiders, who in August 1863 killed more than 150 Lawrence citizens and burned the city to the ground; journalist William Allen White and his nationally prominent and powerful *Emporia Gazette*; and the terrible murders of a family in the nearby town of Holcomb chronicled with such chilling aplomb by Truman Capote in his book *In Cold Blood*. Mitch had picked up a brochure in the restaurant for Liberal, Kansas, "Gateway to the Land of Oz," that touted a replica of Dorothy's house and the yellow-brick road, topped off by an Oz minimuseum with a pair of ruby slippers under glass. He importuned a visit until an onslaught of peer ridicule silenced him.

Back on the road we were listening to a Nina Simone live cassette in which she sings "Just Like a Woman" and chatting about what actually happened to Kansas aviator Amelia Earhart, when we saw the friendly WELCOME TO COLORADO sign. Frank was saying that we would make Denver in time for dinner and arrive in Boulder fashionably late for the poetry slam, when—*kaboom!*—we blew a tire. Frank sheepishly admitted that he had no spare and that we might have to spend the night on the side of the road as he went to look for a "new tread" in Denver. Momentarily panic swept over us; we were in the middle of nowhere. We spotted an oversize tractor coming slowly down Highway 40, and I flagged down the driver for help. Sixtyish and dressed in a blue-and-white-checked cotton shirt and pressed new blue jeans, he peered suspiciously at us through his black horn-rimmed Barry Goldwater glasses with a look on his face that said, "What in the name of God is a Majic Bus?" I introduced myself as a history teacher and pointed to our flat left rear tire. He shook and scratched his head and said, "Either ya'll been grinding over flint rock or somebody nailed ya on purpose." But he bore good news: Down the road a couple of miles, in Cheyenne Wells, was a truck-and-bus repair shop and maybe, just maybe, they might have the tire we needed.

Off we went, a bus full of nervous New Yorkers sitting with our fingers crossed, three wheel-thumping down the highway until we arrived at East Side Service. Frank explained the situation to a round-faced, baby-fat, grease-monkey teenager named Kurt, who wore a black Ozzy Osbourne T-shirt that said BITE THE BAT on the back, and had a silver biker chain connected to his belt loop—a prop to give himself a tough-guy edge. We were in luck; they had the tire we needed and could put it on in an hour. Relieved, I grabbed the basketball, recruited five bodies, and headed off for a bucket I had spotted on our way into Cheyenne Wells. As we clumped through a wheat field, an old Indian woman stared at us blankly from a turquoise mobile home with white chickens running around. The basket was connected to a small gray barn, and I knocked on the adjacent screen door to make sure it was okay to shoot hoops on the property. A kindly woman in a soft cotton flowered dress answered and said, "Why, that sounds fine by me," to my request. We went at it, three on three, for a sweaty, elbowing hour, and then we quit and returned to the repair shop. There we guzzled down cans of Lipton Iced Tea and Countrytime Old-Fashioned Lemonade and haphazardly threw around the Nerf football to kill the remaining time.

It turned out that the tractor man was right: The tire was a casualty of sharp Kansas flint rock—a penalty we had to pay for our detour to Monument Rocks. But that was behind us now: We were back on the road, aiming straight for the Rocky Mountains of our dreams.

10

The New Age, Buddhism, and Boulder

Till the gossamer thread you fling catch somewhere, O my soul.
—WALT WHITMAN

CROSSING THE COLORADO BORDER FROM KANSAS WAS A BIG letdown for most of the students. No two states sharing a common border conjure up such contrasting geographic images. Colorado is, after all, "the Rocky Mountain State," and the students were anticipating snow-covered, saw-toothed peaks and buttes; clear, fast-flowing rivers and creeks; white-tailed deer and black bear, and endless blue spruces and ponderosa pines. Instead they got more Kansas shortgrass prairie and cattle grazing on the flat, monotonous range. Their visions unrequited, they scanned the horizon, looking for mountains. The states were not like Disneyland, they learned, where crossing a boundary means that you suddenly enter an entirely new kingdom. They consoled themselves that the mighty Rockies must begin around Denver, known to the world as the "Mile-High City."

222

With two hours of driving ahead, we listened to the radio, stared at the rusted horse trailers, crooked corrals and outhouses, stagecoach-crossing landmarks, mobile homes, and small aluminum houses that dot the countryside. As traffic thickened and highways converged, the impressive modern glass-and-steel-towered Denver skyline rose up—but no Rocky Mountains, only a hint of rolling foothills on the horizon.

It was in Cheyenne Wells, still two hours from Denver, that I first heard muted student mutterings doubting the existence of the Rockies. This was Colorado? The unchanging scenery plus the basketball had zapped some of the students of their energy. Others quietly read Willa Cather's *O Pioneers!* or Jack Kerouac's *Dharma Bums*. I asked Kevin why he wasn't reading. He gave me a Groucho Marx sneer and said, "Outside of a dog a book is man's best friend. Inside of a dog it's too dark to read." I interpreted his cryptic response as meaning he didn't have enough light. By the time the Denver skyline was upon us, it was raining steadily and most of the students were asleep. Kevin, Shari, Beth, Stefanie, and I huddled on the porch, and I told them about a crazy week I had once spent in Denver. They seemed bored and tired, anxious for dinner, a hot shower, and a good night's sleep in a Boulder motel. I ignored their indifference and talked of the Denver I love.

If you are a history buff or a thrill seeker looking for the free and easy, wide-open, outlaw Denver that was home at the turn of the century to the card shuffler extraordinaire Jefferson Randolph ("Soapy") Smith or in mid-century to Neal Cassady and Jack Kerouac—for the great American pool-hall-blinking-Beat-neon-burlesque Denver night—then come quick, for it is still to be found but on the way to extinction. Larimer Street, the heart of the lower downtown district, escaped the Great Fire of 1863 but not the urban renewal project of 1970s. It was razed by the bulldozers and wrecking balls to make way for today's Denver's skyline. The stately Windsor Hotel—where Bat Masterson played blackjack, Buffalo Bill ate buffalo, Calamity Jane guzzled beer and chewed tobacco, Ulysses S. Grant swigged bourbon from the bottle, John L. Sullivan broke a Cornish fur trapper's jaw in a fight, and a suite boasted a bathroom especially redecorated with frescoes of cupids and Venuses for a visit by Oscar Wilde—has been demolished, sacrificed for an ugly, cold, cinder-block apartment building that has the gall to call itself the Windsor. One nineteenth-century survivor, the Brown Palace Hotel near the State Capitol, still flourishes, its place in history assured when one of its suites served as the summer White House during the Eisenhower administration, chosen in part because Mamie was from Denver.

Block by block a vibrant skid row has succumbed to New Age espresso bars and microbreweries, cafés and croissanteries where overfertilized ferns hang in your face, and pseudo–Southwest Indian art galleries, and branches of East Coast clothing shops like Brooks Brothers and Ann Taylor. More of skid row will soon be demolished to make room for Coors Field, the slick new home of the Colorado Rockies, a major-league baseball expansion team. And how will Denver recycle the miles of abandoned redbrick warehouses and hobo shantytowns that line the South Platte River and railyards? The Elitch Gardens amusement park and several condo complexes have come to town, pushing soup-kitchen bums and the urban poor farther down Larimer Street in a civic-minded attempt to protect the moneyed visitor from the psychological shock of seeing authentic poor people.

But a visitor to the corner of 15th Street and Larimer may still be lucky enough to catch Denver-based tramp poet David Barnet playing guitar and singing the traditional plains ballad "Home on the Range" or the Leonard Cohen gem "Sisters of Mercy," or to spot the Reverend Father Martin Philips, in clerical collar and black frock. The old Holy Roller has wandered the streets of Denver for a quarter of a century, with a giant silver crucifix dangling around his neck and a cardboard American flag stapled to his lapel. He aggressively pushes a collection bucket for the downtrodden in your face, putting your conscience to a test, telling you how he gave the Bicentennial prayer at the U.S. House of Representatives on November 13, 1975. Express disbelief and he'll tell you look it up in the *Congressional Record*, volume 121, offer you God's blessing, and walk away looking for another donor. If it's a presidential election year, Robert Edward Haines, a Stetson-hat-clad, God-fearing America Firster may be out campaigning under the slogan "Haines Holds the Reins." (His main motivation for running in 1992 was to shut the recently opened gambling casinos in Central City, Black Hawk, and Cripple Creek.)

On the corner of 23rd and Blake, the visitor may still find 75¢ mugs of Miller's Genuine Draft; get panhandled for a quarter every fifteen steps by the derelict of his or her choice; talk to a doddering old silver miner who remembers when Aspen was practically a ghost town; hear blind Tony Rodriguez tell of seeing the Virgin Mary in 1939 while praying for redemption at the Sacred Heart Church just down the block, sell any conceivable personal possession for a quick buck at Pasternack's Pawn Shop, where they've been hustling for cash since 1923 (you can even rent a room there for $140 monthly or buy a loaded pistol for $50); or listen to the midnight-Latin-jazz melodies of saxophonist Manuel Perez, the co-composer of "Tequila," whose rhythm and blues and swinging Spanish beat have kept three generations of Denverites dancing in the streets till dawn.

Hungry and lonely? Start walking to the northwest edge of downtown to 20th and Market, past the Denver Rescue Mission, which advertises fifty years of community service with its giant black-and-white neon flashing JESUS SAVES. In front the wheelchaired alcoholic denizens brag of the things they would do if they could walk or their "tools" weren't limp. Go past El Bronco Bar, where the jukebox never quits and tongues have been sliced off and thrown into the Platte River over the conduct of pool games or deprecating social assessments of one's female companion. Enter the rickety wooden door with the sign that reads EL CHAPULTEPEC—HOT BURRITOS AND COOL JAZZ NIGHTLY. Buy a heartburning bean burrito for $1.75 or a mound of spicy cheese nachos for $2.75, and strike up a conversation with owner Jerry Krantz. He'll tell you how Neal Cassady used to sleep in his car in the next-door parking lot and used his bathroom to clean up every morning. At night Cassady would be back drinking Johnny Walker Red, a Camel dangling from his mouth, to the finger-snapping rhythms of the bebop beat.

If you can hear over the distinguished house band jamming nonstop, ask Jerry to tell you about the famous musicians who have played El

225

Chapultepec and eaten his refried beans: all three Marsalis brothers—Wynton, Branford, and Delfeayo—the entire Count Basie Orchestra, the Midnighters' Hank Ballard, David ("Cleanhead") Vincent, Artie Shaw, Eddie ("Lockjaw") Davis, Buddy DeFranco, Sweets Edison, Buster Powell, and Clarence ("Gatemouth") Brown, just for starters. He'll tell you that El Chapultepec is more than a jazz joint, it is a microcosm of America—"a cultural and economic melting pot where people of all races, young and old, male and female, high and mighty, and just ordinary folks blend harmoniously." Ever since the repeal of Prohibition in 1933, El Chapultepec has served tequila shots with a lime twist, a salt lick, and an unknown extra liquor kick. When you feel like howling at the moon, it's time to leave. Denver makes ghosts out of people and neighborhoods quicker than any city I know.

As we left Denver, Jared's sports-talk button—which could be activated by even the mildest of stimuli—was set off by our slow drive past Mile-High Stadium. We discussed John Elway's rubber arm and the Denver Broncos' misfortune at losing four Super Bowls. We went on to speculate about why Colorado has been home to so many great boxers, including world heavyweight champion Jack Dempsey, and then the conversation sputtered to a temporary halt. Road construction mixed with rain slowed us as we worked our way past Stapleton International Airport and Colorado Petroleum facilities, the Salvation Army Rehabilitation Center, and the gaudy Grizzly Rose Saloon and Dancing Emporium. We suddenly realized we had missed the turnoff for Boulder. Transforming our mistake into a spontaneous adventure, Frank took exit 256 off I-70 to Buffalo Bill's Grave and Memorial Museum. Ever since the *New York Times* profile of our trip, in which I was quoted as saying that Frank resembled William F. Cody, Frank had become acutely interested in the Wild West showman, buckskinned scout, Pony Express rider, and buffalo hunter. Winding up Lookout Mountain Road, we reached the summit to find the museum (understandably) closed for the night and the granite grave protected by a cement-and-steel vault to keep vandals and thieves from Cody,

Wyoming, and North Platte and Omaha, Nebraska, from claiming Buffalo Bill's bones as their own.

Buffalo Bill died in 1917 at the home of his sister, Mary Cody Decker, in Denver. She hurriedly buried her seventy-year-old brother in "the biggest funeral west of the Mississippi," atop Lookout Mountain, causing a fusillade of angry proprietary protest from Nebraska and Wyoming, both of which claimed the international showman as a native son and wanted him buried in their soil. We saw no out-of-state grave robbers, however, only a half dozen cars with Colorado plates, cocooning teenagers using the spectacular twinkling light show of greater Denver to jump-start their burgeoning adolescent hormones. But, from what I know of Bill—a man who kept score of the 4,280 bison he rifled down during the seventeen-month period when he worked for a railroad "catering" firm called Goddard Brothers—I'd bet he is spinning in his vault because none of these nocturnal trespassers had to pay an admission fee to party at his sacred shrine.

Most of the students were asleep when Frank got back on the highway, and with a little map-reading help from me, he found I-36, which would take the Majic Bus to Boulder, Colorado—"the New Age Athens," "the Berkeley of Colorado," "the Chamonix of the Rockies," "the People's Republic of Boulder"—"ninety square miles surrounded by reality." Although revealing, these distorting catchphrases fail to capture Boulder, a distinctive and variegated city. Rated again and again by various national surveys as one of the most livable places in America, this Rocky Mountain university town of fewer than one hundred thousand residents is a pacesetter in urban planning and growth management, nurturing research-and-development firms, health care and community services, environmental awareness, and the *ne plus ultra* of the fitness life-style.

Baseball-player-turned-itinerant-evangelist Billy Sunday delivered a hellfire sermon in Boulder in 1909, denouncing the mining boom town as a "sinkhole of iniquity, crying for redemption." Boulder has found redemption. It has become the gem city of the Rocky Mountain States, a friendly place based on pragmatic idealism that welcomes transient remnants of 1960s hippiedom and nouveaux Beatniks, Asian immigrants and high-tech scientists, Buddhist monks and Catholic priests, hip capitalists and seasoned socialists with equally open arms. Boulder is unmarred by billboards; its businesses and services are community conscious and friendly; it is the kind of place where the company that collects garbage is named "Sunshine Trash Service." No resident is more than a ten-minute walk from jogging and hiking trails, a path along Boulder Creek, or open range. The town itself is the gateway to unsurpassed mountain recreation just beyond—the pristine beauties of the Roosevelt and Arapahoe national forests and Rocky Mountain National Park, with its spectacular Trail Ridge Road.

Although known as the home of the University of Colorado, Boulder also plays host to a number of alternative schools of higher education: the Boulder Peace Institute, the Hakomi Institute, Boulder College, the Rolf Institute, Boulder Graduate School, the Boulder School of Massage Therapy, and the Naropa Institute, which offers the only four-year accredited Buddhist study program in the Western world and is home to the Jack Kerouac School of Disembodied Poetics. After two weeks "on the road," we would make the Kerouac School our home for the next two days.

The Naropa Institute, a private, nonsectarian liberal arts college founded by Buddhist thinkers, offers undergraduate and graduate degrees in the arts, social sciences, and humanities. The institute occupies the old redbrick Lincoln Elementary School at 2130 Arapahoe Avenue, only a few blocks from the downtown Boulder pedestrian mall. The children's books and school desks from the building's prior incarnation have been replaced by a Japanese teahouse, Tibetan *thangka* paintings, monochromatic meditation rooms, and a ten-thousand-volume library largely devoted to Eastern philosophy. Instead of small children practicing their three Rs, 515 young adults practice "contemplative education"—an approach that balances academic and artistic disciplines through the cultivation of meditative awareness.

Naropa was founded in 1974 by the venerable Chögyam Trungpa, Rinpoche (a Tibetan title meaning "precious one"), a Tibetan-born scholar and meditation master trained in both the Kagyu and Nyingma schools of Tibetan Buddhism and known the world over by his many publications, of which the most notable is *Shambhala: The Sacred Path of the Warrior.* One of the foremost teachers of Buddhism in the West until his death in 1987, he envisioned Naropa as a college combining contemplative studies with traditional Western scholastic and artistic disciplines and modeled it on Nolanda University, which flourished in India at the height of Mahayana Buddhism, from the fifth to the twelfth century. Naropa's faculty is selected on the basis not of graduate degrees earned but of mastery and accomplishment in a chosen craft or discipline. Although Naropa offers more than a hundred classes per semester in contemplative psychology, interdisciplinary and religious studies, and creative arts—with specialized programs in dance/movement, music, theater, traditional arts, and visual arts—it was the Jack Kerouac School of Disembodied Poetics that brought the Majic Bus to Boulder. I was eager to see my students' response to Naropa and the Kerouac School.

In 1974, poets Allen Ginsberg and Anne Waldman cofounded the Kerouac School, which has become, in my opinion, the most innovative, rigorous, and constructive creative-writing program in the United States and the most conspicuous crossroads for our nation's poets. The Kerouac School has adopted Ezra Pound's belief that aspiring writers should take criticism only from one who has written a notable work of literature. As poet Robert Creeley explains it, "The unique thing about Naropa, about the Jack Kerouac School of Disembodied Poetics, is that the whole determination of its teaching is determined by poets and writers. There's no deft hand of the academics shaping the program." That philosophy alone has been sufficient to endear the school to me forever, for I have had my fill of the pretentious scholastic stick-in-the-muds who teach courses on Shakespeare or Dante or Blake but have written not a line of publishable poetry or prose themselves.

For eighteen years, with little or no attention from the bicoastal media and academic establishments, the Kerouac School has attracted world-class poets and novelists to teach, hold poetry slams, jazz jams, public raps, and international forums, with one ear tuned to the voices of today's young and the other tilted to the poetic epics of the past. Where else can the student receive personal instruction on experimental novel writing from William S. Burroughs; take poetry workshops with Diane DiPrima, Robert Creeley, Lawrence Ferlinghetti, and Gregory Corso; learn about traditions of American poetry from Allen Ginsberg; study playwriting with Michael McClure and Amiri Baraka (formerly LeRoi Jones); and learn the ropes of performance poetry from the dynamic duo of Anne Waldman and Bobbie Louise Hawkins? Artists the world over make Naropa a way station when traveling in the United States; the prime minister of Sri Lanka even stopped by a few years ago to see how Buddhism is practiced in the West.

Because of its commitment to the feminist movement, Naropa always attracts significant and controversial women writers to spend a guest semester, most recently Susan Sontag and Maxine Hong Kingston. After teaching a course on Chaucer at Naropa, Kate Millett, best known for her 1970 book *Sexual Politics,* claimed that Naropa's writing department is more interesting "than any English program in the country." A steady stream of guest lecturers comes to Boulder at Ginsberg's request, usually obliging with serious, publishable lectures. A few years back Norman Mailer, in safari suit, spoke memorably on the "American Soul." To save that soul, he recommended *inter alia* forming "an action corps that would break into houses late at night and smash television sets." In treating the psyche, the British psychiatrist R. D. Laing, who lectured on treating schizophrenia, advocated following Gandhi's principle of harmlessness: "If you don't know what to do, at least don't do anything harmful." Sound, sound advice.

Music is always reverberating around Naropa—performances of pieces by contemporary composers such as the late John Cage or Philip Glass's collaboration with Allen Ginsberg, transforming the Beat bard's "Witcha Vortex Sutra" from poem to opera. Classes on music theory are always related in a practical way to actual performance and composition and include intensive pitch and rhythmic training, as well as melodic and harmonic studies in both Eastern and Western music, with an emphasis on contemporary jazz.

This interdisciplinary approach—like that of Hofstra University's New College—is what makes the Jack Kerouac School of Disembodied Poetics so noteworthy and compelling. Most current educational approaches to poetry focus almost exclusively on the written, thus tearing poetry asunder from its historical role as oral communication. I believe our secondary schools should adopt the practice of teaching poetry through pop music. In today's MTV world this is the best way to tap into the creative juices of easily distractable teenagers, to increase their appreciation of language, and to allow them to feel a part of the human continuum. If the oral tradition of performance poetry is related to rap or hip-hop, Homer and the *Iliad* and the *Odyssey* may seem less alien.

The versatile and erudite Ginsberg, who spends part of the year at Naropa, is also professor of English at Brooklyn College. He is a veritable archive on the past fifty years of the American underground and the leading proponent of the poetics of pop. When Ginsberg performed and guest-lectured for a class I sometimes teach at Hofstra called "The Beat Generation and Counterculture in America," he mesmerized the students with his sincerity and energy. He performed his classic poem "America" as a vaudeville routine; shouted a punk vendetta against the military-industrial complex, titled "Bird Brain"; played his harmonium and sang William Blake's *Songs of Innocence and Experience,* most notably "Tyger, Tyger"; accompanied himself with finger cymbals on the moving dirge "Father Death Blues"; and chanted calypso, jazz poems, and street raps. If Mailer wants to shoot out all the TVs in America, Ginsberg understands that it's already too late—virtual reality is here to stay. On the publication of Ginsberg's National Book Award–winning *Collected Poems 1947–1980,* Bob Dylan called his poet-friend "a lyrical genius, con-man extraordinaire and probably the single greatest influence on American poetical voice since Whitman." At age sixty-five, when most of his cohorts are rocking, comfortably numb, on the front porch, Ginsberg is rolling on the cutting edge, collaborating with Clash songwriter Joe Strummer on "Ghetto Defendant," a cut from the band's *Combat Rock* album, and recently jamming with a tight-knit band of veteran session musicians to record some poems/songs on a scintillating disc for Island Records called *The Lion For Real*.

231

Ginsberg is committed to bonding poetry and music, defying formal constraints and boundaries. His record *First Blues* he touts as a collection of "rags, ballads and harmonium songs, chanteys, come-all-ye's, aboriginal song sticks, gospel improvisations, Renaissance lyrics, Blake hymns, bluegrass hillbilly riffs, country and western, fifties R&B, dirty dozens, and New Wave."

If Ginsberg is the king of performance poetry, Anne Waldman is next in line to the throne. Winner of the Heavyweight Poetry Championship held a few years back in Taos, New Mexico—a competition in which poets jump into a ring and take turns trying to outperform each other while the audience cheers, guzzles beer, stomps its feet in approval, and bets on the winner—Waldman has written more than seventeen dazzling books of poetry and produced two videotapes, *Eyes in All Heads* and *Live at Naropa*. Her poetry performances are something to behold. Anne moves around the stage like a sleek panther, using body language and voice inflections to convey her intense passion, breathing energy into the lifeless forms of the printed page. When Anne Waldman says "cut," you feel the knife. She directed the Poetry Project at Manhattan's Saint Mark's Church in the Bowery for more than a decade before founding and directing Naropa's writing and poetics program.

Waldman believes that good poetry can and should be accessible, innovative, and easily communicated to students. Free-verser Walt Whitman articulated this principle explicitly, Langston Hughes knew it instinctively, Vachel Lindsay and Carl Sandburg made it their poetic lifeblood, and Bob Dylan put a match to the nation's young by writing jukebox poetry that spoke directly to his generation's concerns. Teachers should help students realize that Tom Waits and Hart Crane, Joni Mitchell and Emily Dickinson, Sister Souljah and Gwendolyn Brooks are all passionate, creative, original voices whether they shout slang in the angry, urgent idiom of the LA streets or write with pen and ink in a fine leatherbound book in Amherst. "Slang is a language that rolls up its sleeves, spits on its hands, and goes to work," Carl Sandburg maintained. Rap lyrics are part of an African American tradition dating back to slavery where the constantly evolving language is used to delineate insiders from outsiders. Literature professors must learn to be aware of and pay attention to what is turning on the generation of students they are teaching. If professors mock students for being ignorant of Emerson or Melville, students can't believe their supposedly enlightened literature teachers have never heard of Axl Rose or the Suburban Lawns or Public Enemy or the Dead Milkmen. The conclusion students draw from professional ignorance of pop culture is that the occupant of the ivory tower is clueless to what's going down in the real-world America. Perhaps they're correct.

Just thinking about Naropa while listening to George Clinton's guitar on "Maggot Brain," from his Funkedelic days, got me psyched for Boulder. The students were reading two books by Kerouac and were eager to visit the eponymous school. Before parking at the school, Frank drove a block farther down Arapahoe Avenue, to the simple, neat, but unpainted Arapahoe Lodge, to drop off students who elected a bed instead of a bus bunk for the next two evenings. The rest of us headed for the soft green grasses of Naropa's 3.7-acre campus. I phoned a buddy of mine, David Griffith, who studies art at the University of Colorado (or Ski University, as it is sometimes called), who had volunteered to act as a Boulder guide for our group. David's reaction to seeing the Majic Bus was, "*Wow*, this is *really* radical!" He and his girlfriend, Kat, led ten of us on a hike around Boulder that ended at J. J. McCabe's rock club, a popular hangout, to hear the local Grateful Dead cover band, Shakedown Street. We were amazed by the number and variety of bikes chained to the bike racks in front of the bar: Diamond Back and Bridgestone mountain bikes, Trek touring bikes, and Merlin, Concord, and Serotta racing bikes. We later learned that in bicycle-friendly Boulder, seven out of every ten townies own cycles and tend to tool around town fashionably and pragmatically attired in skin-tight Lycra and space-age helmets (some with mirrors).

Dan, Jay, and Janine, the students who were most enthusiastic about visiting Naropa because of their love of poetry and Kerouac, were instantly at one with New Age Boulder, soaking up the scene. To progressive young people, Boulder is the American Mecca, the citadel of alternative living and the youth culture capital of the West. The more traditional students in the American Odyssey class dismissed Boulder out of hand as being a New Age yuppie town populated by high-income hipsters (men with pony-tailed Bono hair and coke spoons instead of crosses or Stars of David around their necks, and women in long, tie-dyed prairie dresses) hanging out in trendy health-food restaurants and whining about environmental decay even though they cruise aimlessly about in Saab Turbos, BMWs, and Jeep Wagoneers gassed up on credit cards for routine mountain joy rides. But even the traditionalists were able to get past the retro-hipness of Boulder, seduced by the three dramatic slabs of sandstone outcroppings of the Western foothills known as the Flatirons, the clean air and streets, the fresh scent of pine, the dozens of nearby ski areas, and the massive iron buffalo at the south end of the University of Colorado's beautiful red-roofed campus. Perhaps there is a grain of truth to the cynical first impressions the traditionalists had of Boulder, but on the important issues of quality of life, the rest of America has a lot to learn from this community. And while most other cities in the country are struggling through a four-year recession, corporate R&D money keeps pouring into Boulder. They must be doing something right.

After a few hours of dancing at J. J. McCabe's we headed for pizza and pinball at Jalino's. Then, still exhausted from climbing Monument Rocks, dealing with the flat tire, and driving in the rain, we said good-night to David and Kat and quietly ambled through the unbroken misty darkness of the shadowy, tree-lined streets back to the Majic Bus. I myself was anticipating the luxury of an open bunk instead of the bus floor. The next morning had been left open, and we were all to meet at 2:00 P.M. at Naropa for a lecture on the main tenets of Buddhism, followed by a meditation session and a visit with writer Bobbie Louise Hawkins at her home-workshop.

The next morning I got up at the crack of dawn, spied on two rosy finches pecking hungrily at a berry bush, suited up, laced my Nikes, and went running (not jogging) in the dry, thin mountain air for six gorgeous miles down the East Boulder Trail, passing two startled deer and a fawn watering on Boulder Creek. After showering at the Arapahoe Lodge Sauna, I met Mike O'Keefe, our contact at Naropa, for hazelnut coffee and bran muffins at the institute's on-campus vegetarian café. As Mike and I planned the day's agenda, Naropa students stopped by to introduce themselves, eager to learn how our Majic Bus journey was proceeding.

I had planned to meet David and Kat at the Penny Lane Coffeehouse (next door to Abbey Road Books) for sixteen-ounce glasses of double café lattés at noon. They preferred the neo-Kerouac-boho crowd at Penny Lane, "the best bean house in Boulder," to the Euro-style Trident, where politically correct yuppies and yubbies (young urban Buddhists) congregate over fizzy-phosphate Italian sodas, gourmet coffees, and clove cigarettes to discuss nuclear fallout, Foucault, and organic carrot farming. Penny Lane hosts weekly amateur poetry readings under the daunting rubric "So You Think You're a Poet Productions." With two hours to traipse around Boulder on my own, I strolled up and down Pearl Street, popping in and out of shops, bumping into student upon student.

I walked to the civic and spiritual heart of Boulder, the Pearl Street Mall, which runs for four blocks through the middle of downtown. Before the sixties, Boulder was a sleepy college town, a place where underage students hung out at taverns downing pitchers of 3.2 beer, trying desperately to cop a buzz from the diluted homeopathic imitation of the real thing. Boy, have times changed. The mall, a collection of refurbished two-story, turn-of-the-century buildings surrounded by wooden benches, grassy plots, and legions of squirrels, is filled with street-carnival bustle and high-altitude air redolent of coffee beans. There, CU students, foreigners, scientists, artists, New Agers, Buddhists, Sufis, corporate types, political activists, employees of the National Center for Atmospheric Research and the National Oceanic and Atmospheric Administration, teenagers, Sikhs, skinheads, naturalists, Denver commuters, day laborers, and night workers harmoniously consume and consort in the many cafés, bookshops, and boutiques.

People watching is a popular spectator sport in Boulder, and I meandered through the groups clustered around and enjoying the sounds and antics of a menagerie of street entertainers, ranging from a troupe of Hare Krishna acrobats juggling skittles to classical violinists to a big brass band that swings to the forties golden trombone melodies of onetime CU student

Glenn Miller. The best spot for hearing musicians is the Zen rock garden–playground. There on this particular visit I was treated to the out-of-tune four-chord guitar strumming of Token Terry Templegone, a shaggy, torn-denimed, artillery-belted, and perpetually high (so he himself proclaims), reformed Bay Area heroin addict who says he tried to intentionally OD back in 1969 when he learned that Pig-Pen of the Grateful Dead had, as Tennyson might have put it, "crossed the bar." He now practices Yoga so he can master proper breathing, a life-insurance policy against hyperventilation on that inevitable day when Jerry Garcia dies—the day the music really stops. Now twenty-five years the wiser, Terry strums for change or cigarettes, morning, noon, and night, on the mall. His beat-up old Gibson guitar, a bluejay feather dangling from a fret, is adorned with colorful stickers and decals in homage to the sixties spirit: a chorus line of black Dead skeletons tipping their top hats; a Cap'n Crunch–box glow-in-the-dark pink-and-blue dinosaur "surprise"; a clenched fist silhouetted against a green marijuana leaf inscribed, BOYCOTT WHITE POWDERS—BRING BACK HEMP; a more calorific but less controversial Ben and Jerry's Natural Ice Cream ad in red and white; a rainbow-colored Harley Davidson insignia with the peace sign in midfield; a CALL 800 JERRY BROWN FOR PRESIDENT endorsement; and, in negation of all the foregoing, a simple white bumper sticker with bold black block letters that advises, JUST SAY NOTHING.

Token Terry's song selection varies, but his C, G, F, and D chords don't. Unlike so many of Boulder's retrofashion hippies, who have the "Hey, man!" and "Far out!" lingo down, Token Terry is the authentic article, living out of a ragged suitcase the ostensibly carefree life-style of the sixties myth. A veteran of Altamont whose profile can be glimpsed during a three-second crowd shot in the rock-concert documentary *Gimme Shelter*, Terry's repertoire is pure, undiluted psychedelic sixties, from Jefferson Airplane's "White Rabbit," to Buffalo Springfield's "For What It's Worth," to Buffy Saint-Marie's "Universal Soldier." To solicit tips he sets a gray felt pillbox hat on a soiled purple bandanna, a bandanna that, he says, was given him by Buddy Miles, drummer for the Jimi Hendrix Experience, in exchange for a bag of Mexican ragweed during his Haight days, years ago. Boulder is his new Jerusalem " 'cause the cops let you smoke hemp in peace"; it's where "the hip meet the trip." When he's not working as a street minstrel or loitering around town, he helps Jack Herer, self-proclaimed "world authority on the history and uses of the hemp plant," crusade and petition to legalize marijuana, "the world's premier natural renewable resource." Token Terry claims hemp is "God's great healing plant." Terry believes if hemp were legalized all across America, urban violence would cease, racism would recede, and in John Lennon's words, "the world will live as one." He puts his mouth where the money is, so to speak, as an unpaid volunteer for the Rocky Mountain Hemp Coalition. He graffitis every dollar bill he can get with the words "I grew hemp" ballooning from the mouth of George Washington. That the Father of Our Country grew hemp at his Mount Vernon estate is proof positive for the coalition that pot is as wholesome as apple pie and should be legalized.

Listening to street music is just one of Boulder's pleasures. For most of the students a source of endless amusement consisted of hanging around restaurants and cafés reading the New Age self-improvement advertisements and bills posted on kiosks: REGRESSION THERAPY AND TRAUMA RELEASE WITH ADVANCED CERTIFIED ROLFER HANNAH PIERCE, GET RICH THROUGH THE "SPIRITUAL TEACHINGS" OF GURUMAYI CHIDVILASANANDA, AROMATHERAPY CUSTOM-BLENDED OIL MASSAGE WITH DAWN SINGER-KREST, A DIALOGUE BETWEEN ELECTRO-ACUSOPE AND MYOPULSE COMPUTER-AIDED MICRO-CURRENT TECHNOLOGY AND YOUR "POLLUTED TISSUES," FREE I CHING TOSSING AT THE BOULDER PUBLIC LIBRARY, UNDERWATER MASSAGE WITH SUSAN MELCHING, INC., GAY CRYSTAL READING FOR "RECENT DISCOVERERS" WITH QUEEN WILMA, and FRIENDLY WITCHCRAFT HEALING WITH TONYA were just a few of the more colorful signs.

What amused and entertained my students has serious roots. New Age is a broad-based philosophy and religious and social movement with many modes and variations but a common set of principles. Adherents believe that they are God, that all is one, and that there is no right or wrong, no good or evil—that people consciously or unconsciously choose everything that happens to them. By looking inward, New Agers have to find a method

237

to permit them to live guilt and stress-free. The mystical roots of this growing phenomenon are antithetical to and distrustful of rational thought. New Age has nevertheless become the religion and ethos of a large portion of the young members of the professional middle class in search of deeper reserves of energy. That generation will soon assume responsibility for America. "What virtually all participants in the New Age movement have in common is the belief in a cosmic destiny for humankind, which individuals pursue mainly through mystical examination of the self, and in a 'new age' of existence that will be peopled by superior beings who have undergone a process of inner 'transformation,' " journalist Fergus M. Bordewich wrote in a 1987 *New York Times Magazine* article, "Colorado and the New Age." Boulder's conservative Christians, not surprisingly, view the New Age as the devil's work and, in an excess of religious zeal, have staged public book burnings of *The Modern Witch's Spellbook* by Sarah L. Morrison and *Out on a Limb* by Shirley MacLaine, among other titles, in hopes of excising the seeds of this perceived evil. A wide variety of camels poke their noses under the New Age tent: the Church of Scientology and the Unification Church; nominally secular self-improvement programs such as Lifespring and est; plus an odd assortment of teachers or gurus who blend psychotherapeutic techniques with Eastern mysticism, the occult, the teachings of Aleister Crowley, the purported healing power of pyramids and quartz crystals, Shirley MacLaine's reincarnation reality, pre-Christian paganism; witchcraft; and tarot cards. Boulder, the proud laboratory of the New Age, seems unaware or unconcerned that this whole scene may appear quite odd or even absurd to outsiders.

Holistic health also plays a large part in the New Age movement, and herbal teas, organically grown fruits and vegetables, and nitrate-free foods are deemed a necessity for purifying the body. Juicers are the newest rage, for both at-home use and in cafés, with carrot and wheat grass already considered passé, displaced by parsley, spinach, ginger, beets, and mixes of two or more fruits. The class vegetarians, Janine, Dan, and Alison, found Boulder simpatico, a community filled with health-conscious people who like themselves refuse to eat corpses of any kind. Alfalfa's, an organic New Age grocery store, is where the vegetarians shopped.

For eating out, this diet-conscious crowd congregated at the New Age Café and Health-Food Store where the menu featured spinach-sesame, three-bean, mock tuna (garbanzo beans shrewdly marketed as "dolphin-safe for real"), or awesome adzuki bean salads; hunza yogurt with dried fruit; ginger carrot-raisin and mock ham salad with a side cup of magnificent miso barley veggie soup. New Age magazines are sold amid drum-size bottles of zinc, vitamins, herbal diet powders, and dried nuts and fruits, and pale vegetarians comb *Shaman's Drum, Wildfire, Yoga International, Gnosis, Inward Path,* and *Planetary Citizen* for the latest self-improvement tips to scribble down in spiral notebooks unwilling to pay $4.50 for a single issue.

I stopped for a snack at the New Age Café. As I sat down with a bottle of rainbow fruit juice and a copy of the *Daily Camera* newspaper, a tiny, moonstoned, and daydreamy granola woman sat next to me, reading Rick Field's *Chop Wood, Carry Water.* Putting her book down, she sipped her Lemon Zinger tea, one of the best-selling products of Boulder's own Celestial Seasonings Tea Company, and out of nowhere asked whether I was a vegetarian. When I naively informed her of my personal progress—I rarely ate beef or pork but indulged in poultry—she reprimanded me sternly: "A person of spiritual intensity does not eat flesh," clearly considering me an unreconstructed cannibal. Others had overheard and began evil-eyeing me—an infidel in their New Age tofu temple. I let a few uncomfortable moments pass, pretending to read my newspaper in order to save face, then wiped my mouth with a biodegradable napkin, gently placed my empty juice bottle in the recycling bin as a sign to all that I had redemptive potential, and headed for the door. To my right I saw row upon row of well-organized shelves stocked with over-the-counter homeopathic remedies, pills, and "vibrational liquids," which purport to inoculate and protect against the ravages of poison, disease, bacteria, and virus, and just about any conceivable negative mental state or accident under the sun.

The café, it seemed, was the Wal-Mart of homeopathy. There, in the guise of medicine, were homeopathic remedies—highly diluted doses of natural substances—that in massive quantities could, in many cases, cause the very symptoms that afflicted the buyer. The range of conditions covered by the homeopathic pharmacopoeia is alarming: rabies, dog bites, hepatitis, shock, rattlesnake bites, warts, whipworm, scorpion stings, sickle-cell anemia, black widow and brown spider bites, grief, flu, asbestos sickness, salmonella, radioactive fallout, allergies, cysts, canine distemper, mumps, liver, lung and intestinal flukes, and on, ad infinitum. Each remedy is individually packaged in cardboard containers and costs between five and ten dollars.

Astounded by the breadth of the homeopathic merchandise, I decided to ignore the social opprobrium to which I had been subjected and people-watch instead. What kind of desperate soul would purchase these nostrums? A middle-aged, curly-haired, and bespectacled man, a Kurt Vonnegut look-alike, grabbed a bottle of Oxo, the remedy for herpes, from the shelf and headed toward the cashier, knowing he was about to limit his prospects with the comely young woman in the granny gown who would take his money.

Watching one person turned out to be enough for me, so I did some research on homeopathic remedies. Here's one example: Say you fear being bitten by Fang, your neighbor's menacing Doberman pinscher. Buy a bottle of Dog Bite 3–2x and pop the tiny white marshmallow-shaped pellets daily until the supply is exhausted. Use two bottles for a lifetime guarantee against predations by Fang—or any other dog, for that matter. You are now vibrationally protected from canine attack. I wondered whether the U.S. Postal Service knew about Dog Bite 3–2x, an ostensible lifesaver for their dedicated minions.

For New Agers in Boulder, homeopathy has moved beyond vogue to become a rage, and it's spreading across United States to the tune of more than $100 million a year. Many of the Boulderites I spoke with said they frequently consult homeopathic physicians, who—unlike AMA healers who deal only in specific illnesses—carefully chart the whole patient's health status and then devise a unique, personalized cure based in part on blood chemistry readings. To homeopathic believers disease and misfortune are primarily spiritual matters: The key to a healthy body is bringing the body's natural immune system back into balance. More heterodox homeopathic believers merely say, "If antibiotics don't work, why not try homeopathics?" Though homeopathic medicine may seem to defy common sense, logic, and medical science, one should never underestimate the possible benefits of these remedies, be they placebos or not. That the Food and Drug Administration seems wholly unconcerned with the truth in labeling of a remedy that protects one from dog bite is a symptom of deregulation run amok. But you have to take all of these New Age fads with a grain of salt and an understanding smile, for, as Robert Frost once said: "Education is the ability to listen to almost anything without losing your temper or your self-confidence."

Next I headed to the heart of the CU campus, the Student Union. New Age Boulder has not, by any means, engulfed cowtown Boulder. Meat of all kinds is still exceedingly popular, as epitomized by the life and legend of that ultimate carnivore, Alferd Packer. Packer is remembered fondly at CU, where the student cafeteria bears his name and his bust greets prospective diners. In 1874 this son of the Centennial State, a silver-and-gold prospector, and five of his companions were snowed in, trapped high in the San Juan Mountains with no food or provisions. Apparently they lived for a while off pine gum, rosebuds, and their own roasted moccasins. When the spring thaw finally arrived sixty-five days later, Alferd Packer was the only survivor of the harsh winter. He showed up at the Los Piños Indian Agency, alone, long haired and bearded, telling conflicting versions of how he had managed to stay alive in below-zero weather while the others had not. Some locals began to raise suspicious eyebrows, particularly because he appeared to have gained a great deal of weight during his ordeal. Some Ute Indians reported finding strips of human flesh along the trail Packer had taken, triggering an official investigation. Packer was accused of killing all his prospecting buddies, driving an ax through the skulls of four while they slept and shooting the fifth as he attempted to escape. He lived off human steaks all winter long. Arrested, Packer managed to escape the wooden jail in Saguache and fled to Wyoming, where he lived under the name John Schwartz. Discovered nine years later, he

241

was convicted on five counts of murder and sentenced to forty-five years of hard labor at the Canyon City Penitentiary. He served only five before being paroled by Governor Charles Thomas. In his last years Packer served in another capacity—as a security guard—a promotional gimmick for the *Denver Post*, which had run front-page campaigns supporting Packer's pardon, in the process augmenting its circulation substantially. Packer died in 1907 a folk hero, signing autographed pictures of himself to the moment of his final breath.

In our more politically sensitive times, Colorado has now, at long last, provided a historical plaque listing the names of the victims. The state has officially designated the site of Packer's "handiwork," near Lake City, the Alferd Packer Massacre Site. Motorists can't possibly miss it: A gigantic billboard with a cartoon portrait of a hungry Packer directs them to the precise spot. In downtown Lake City, the Hinsdale County Museum displays, with pride, replicas of the skull fragments, complete with hatchet marks, plus the actual buttons from the clothes of the five men Packer dined on—or off. Grant Houston, Lake City's town historian, is quick to brag about their competitive advantage over the Donner Party Museum in Truckee, California, for those starving pioneers ate only those who had already died. In 1989 the mass gravesite was dug up and the butchered bodies exhumed to try to determine whether Packer had actually axed his companions or eaten them, as he claimed, after they had died. The concrete scientific conclusion, reported by James Starrs, professor of law and forensic science at George Washington University, was that "Packer clearly cannibalized the five gold prospectors"—nothing more. The dig itself led to an Alferd Packer revival in Lake City and initiated an annual summer reenactment of the event.

The Last Trial of Alferd Packer, produced by the students at nearby Western State College in Gunnison, is Lake City's idea of summer stock. Every September, Lake City holds the Alferd Packer Jeep Tour and Barbeque on "Cannibal Plateau." Meanwhile, Packer's simple military tombstone—on which his name is misspelled "Alfred"—is swiped every spring from Littleton Cemetery by CU fraternities to serve as the centerpiece for their Alferd Packer Raw Meat Eating Festival. As if that were not enough, ever since the University of Colorado officially named its cafeteria in the Student Union the Alferd Packer Memorial Grill, this "exemplary" Coloradan has become a campus mascot. Recently Colorado governor Roy Romer unveiled the small marble bust of Packer that sits on a pedestal at the hub of the grill. At the end of each school year students celebrate with a barbecued-rib bash and a raw-hamburger-eating contest, all in honor of this most unlikely of "heroes."

From campus I moved on to one of the town's many state-of-the-art outdoor-sporting-goods stores, which cater to the elite athletic eccentrics who move to Colorado because of its obsession with physical culture and its enthusiastic acceptance of extreme sports: mountain marathon running, ice climbing (frozen waterfalls are a favorite), skydiving, hang gliding, Bungee jumping, downhill skateboarding, hot-air ballooning, whitewater kayaking, power canoeing, snowboarding (surfing downhill), dogsledding, bareback mountain climbing, llama trekking, alpine sliding, snowmobiling, rappeling, and soaring, for starters.

Ever since the gold strike of 1859, when pickax miners flocked to Boulder in search of the new El Dorado, it has been home to those interested in rigorous alpine recreation; the surrounding Colorado Rocky Mountains contain more than a thousand peaks over two miles high. Hard-core Colorado "body Nazis" work at night jobs, arising at dawn to go ballistic up, down, and around the Rockies. Elsewhere in the United States, if you ask someone what they do, they'll tell you about their job. Not in Boulder. There the reply will be some variant of, "I'm a summer skydiver and a winter snowshoe runner, but I'm starting to indoor wall climb year round." Pick a garage at random in Boulder and you're likely to find alpine skis, a snowboard, rollerblades, a skateboard, mountain bikes, climbing equipment, and boxes full of hiking boots, ropes, down jackets, and expensive skintight ski suits.

My next destination was Narayan's Nepal Restaurant, home to hard-core mountain athletes. There they devour *thukpa* (Tibetan-style noodles) or *tarkari* (spicy vegetable curry) and swap alpine experiences with coreligionists over beer or tea. For Boulder's outdoor-minded snowheads,

Nepal is the ultimate travel destination. Mount Everest and the Himalayas are the holy of holies. In fact, with this crowd, if you haven't climbed Everest, you're dismissed as being another run-of-the-mill Colorado amateur recreationist. In Boulder the traditional mountain climber's rationale, "because it was there," has been replaced by "because I haven't done it yet."

The restaurant's Nepalese owner, Narayan Shrestha, a businessman-philanthropist, gives much of his time and money to nonprofit organizations such as Helping Hands and the Sann Research Institute, which provide sanitation and medical and educational services to villages in his native country. He is equally zealous about promoting and popularizing the Himalayas in Boulder. Ever since 1986, when he opened Old Tibet—a store selling books, trinkets, authentic clothing, and thangka paintings from Tibet and Nepal—the forty-one-year-old Buddhist businessman has served as a self-designated goodwill ambassador between the United States and Nepal.

The success of Old Tibet led to Narayan's Gateway to Nepal, a travel agency that organizes trips and treks to Katmandu and the mountainous region beyond for the growing number of moneyed adventurers. He opened the restaurant in 1990, and business boomed. In 1991 he added autographed photos of bearded men acting like mountain goats and stunning pictures of snow-capped peaks, dedicated a downstairs wall to retired pitons and oxygen masks, and christened the place Club Makalu: Narayan's Climber's Bar. Narayan even landed the high priest of mountain climbing—Sir Edmund Hillary, who with his Sherpa guide, Tenzing Norkay, was the first to reach the summit of Mount Everest, in 1953, to speak at the grand opening. More than a thousand people showed up to meet Sir Edmund. According to a local newspaper, the British mountaineer was astonished to discover that a quarter of the yummies (young urban mountain men) he encountered had duplicated his feat. Always one to look for a new gimmick, Narayan named his house drink "the Hillary"—ginger ale and scotch on the rocks—the legendary explorer's spirit of choice. The entrepreneurial Nepalese has now opened three new businesses in nearby Fort Collins—a restaurant, an Asian grocery–spice store, and an-

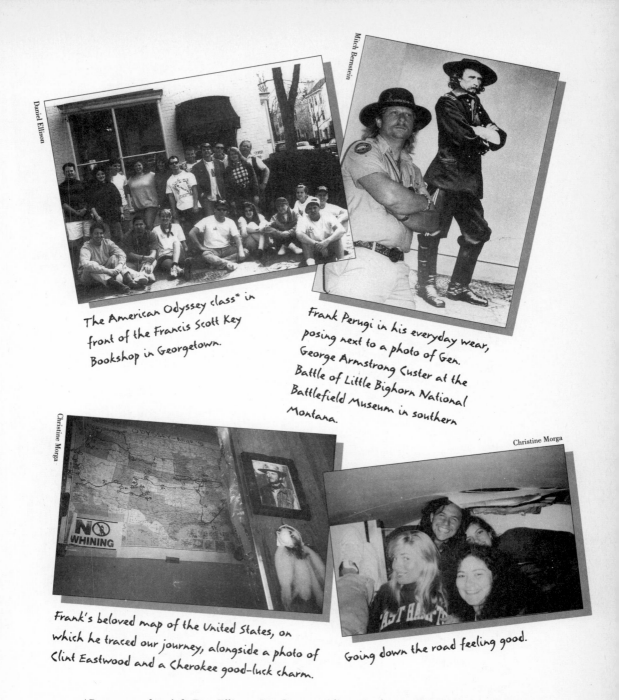

Daniel Ellison

Mitch Bernstein

Christine Morga

Christine Morga

The American Odyssey class* in front of the Francis Scott Key Bookshop in Georgetown.

Frank Perugi in his everyday wear, posing next to a photo of Gen. George Armstrong Custer at the Battle of Little Bighorn National Battlefield Museum in southern Montana.

Frank's beloved map of the United States, on which he traced our journey, alongside a photo of Clint Eastwood and a Cherokee good-luck charm.

Going down the road feeling good.

*Bottom row from left: Dan Ellison, Jay Caputo, Alison Andrews, Kenny Young, Janine Hayes, Aine Graham, Darlene Dudash, Justin Buis, Matt Price. *Top row from left:* Tom Tolan, Shari Berkowitz, Alan Mindel, Stefanie Perlman, Christine Morga, Mitch Bernstein, Jared Goldman, Doug Brinkley, Kevin Willey, Beth Neville, and driver Frank Perugi.

Jay, Mitch, and Beth at the Biltmore Estate in Asheville, North Carolina.

Janine ("Dark Star") Hayes in front of a piece of the Berlin Wall at the Jimmy Carter Library in Atlanta, Georgia.

Street entertainer Little Sparrow, singing "Abraham, Martin, and John" behind Ebenezer Baptist Church in Atlanta.

In Biloxi, Mississippi: The Gulf of Mexico and dead seagulls.

Café Vieux Restaurant in New Orleans.

Kevin Willey and Alison Andrews dancing to jazz on Bourbon Street in New Orleans.

Visiting William Faulkner's home, Rowan Oak, in Oxford, Mississippi.

We encountered the homeless and destitute in every city.

Tom Tolan, who strikingly resembles Elvis Presley, posing in
front of a painting of the King at
Graceland in Memphis.

Paying our respects at Elvis Presley's
grave in Graceland.

NO
WHINING

Aine, Beth, and Janine aboard
the Majic Bus.

Mitch Bernstein against a backdrop of
Lake Michigan and Chicago.

Chicago Bulls mania was evident all over the Windy City.

Blues-guitar wizard Son Seals, talking to some of the students after a blistering set at Wise Fool's Pub in Chicago.

A trucker near the Mother Jones monument off I-55 in Illinois.

Waiting for a guided tour of the Abraham Lincoln House in the historic district of Springfield, Illinois.

The Gateway Arch in Saint Louis.

American culture at its finest—the McDonald's riverboat on the Mississippi River in Saint Louis.

Poet Jim McCrary and Doug Brinkley waiting to meet William S. Burroughs in front of the Full Moon Café in Lawrence, Kansas.

William S. Burroughs talking about his life in literature at Artists en Masse Gallery in Lawrence, Kansas.

Shari Berkowitz

Daniel Ellison

Shari Berkowitz on top of Monument Rocks in western Kansas.

Dieseling up in Kansas at one of the many truck stops we frequented.

Daniel Ellison

Daniel Ellison

Jay Caputo (third from left) playing drums with friends he met at Naropa Institute in Boulder, Colorado, the only fully accredited Buddhist college in the Western world.

Author and teacher Bobbie Louise Hawkins, reading to us at her home in Boulder, where we learned the French poetry game "Exquisite Corpse."

Daniel Ellison

On our way to Estes Park, Colorado, gateway to the Rocky Mountains.

Mitch Bernstein

The Majic Bus was stopped dead in its tracks by snow high in the Rockies. We took advantage of the situation and went hiking.

Beth Neville

Frank being harassed by policemen in Telluride, Colorado, for driving too slowly.

Mitch Bernstein

Camping in Mesa Verde National Park.

Stefanie Pearlman

Kevin Willey admiring the cave dwellings of Mesa Verde National Park.

other Tibetan speciality shop. Because of his civic-spirited approach to business, he was recently elected vice president of the Boulder Lion's Club and has started a chapter of the club in his hometown of Khandbari. The American myth—the immigrant who makes it big in America—lives on.

I met with the students at Naropa as scheduled, and they all had unique Boulder experiences to report: Some students who had missed the staples of home refueled on corned-beef sandwiches, bagels, and lox at the New York Delicatessen. Others chose the retrosixties scene, sipping cappuccino at Café Bohemia and leafing through *Beat!*, Boulder's original music magazine, and *ICON*, the alternative arts paper. Others bought red-hots and jawbreakers at an old-fashioned candy shop in the renovated Boulderado Hotel, visited earlier in the century by Helen Keller, Theodore Roosevelt, Clarence Darrow, Ethel Barrymore, and Robert Frost and currently rumored to be haunted. Some wandered off to the Hill for coffee at the CU hangout Espresso Roma, at 13th and College, attracted by a large, dark-sunglassed portrait of Roy Orbison painted on the white-brick side.

Mike O'Keefe, the institute's public relations administrator, began our guided tour by explaining the *thangka* painting of Buddhist Saint Naropa drinking blood out of a skull cup that confronts visitors at the front door of the main building. The painting represents the transformation of confusion into wisdom. The energetic and razor-witted assistant director of the writing program, Andrew Schelling, spoke to us for thirty minutes on Kerouac's spontaneous poetics, Pound's *Cantos*, and William Carlos Williams's "no ideas but in things." Dan asked what impact *Mexico City Blues*—Kerouac's jazz poems of 242 choruses, and required reading for the American Odyssey course—had on contemporary poets, and a lively discussion ensued on the differences between Joyce's stream of consciousness and Kerouac's spontaneous prose. The conversation turned to censorship in the arts and how attempts to censor Ginsberg's signal poem

245

Howl were overcome shortly after its publication in 1956, and how it is now one of the most widely read poems ever written, translated into more than twenty-two languages. Jay, who was writing his senior thesis on J. D. Salinger, offered some insights into the difficulties the publicity-shy author encountered from attempts to ban his classic novel about youth alienation, *The Catcher in the Rye.*

After this go-round about literary outlaws, we decamped to a long, shedlike building that houses the Dharma wheel—five windowless, cell-like chambers, each painted a different color and each representing the five basic energies of tantric Buddhist practice: red, blue, green, yellow, and white. The purpose of the rooms is to get individuals in touch with certain emotions and to help cleanse the soul of anger and frustration through color meditation. For example, in the blue room everything— carpet, walls, low ceilings—is blue, illuminated by blue ceiling and floor lights. We split into groups of four and sat motionless for ten minutes, meditating to the color vibration of our respective rooms. Then we traded rooms. Disagreements erupted over whether the red room brought out passionate or violent anger. We were instructed that there is no such thing as a "right" emotion—one feels what one feels. Darlene, who practices tai chi and yoga and attends Indian "sweats" in New Jersey and Long Island, was primed to enjoy this exercise in meditation and self-discovery.

Next we were taken to Meditation Hall, a small auditorium with blue cushions lined up in neat rows on the floor instead of seats. With shoes off, we sat lotus-style, the heavy scent of joss sticks filling our nostrils as we listened to John Morecock, a Buddhist teacher, outline the history, tenets, and principles of Buddhist thought. He stressed that for Buddhists the cardinal problem is not sin but ignorance or false awareness. In fact, he said the word *awareness* so often that in the student journals it became synonymous with Buddhism itself. With the exception of Darlene, the students had no prior knowledge of Buddhism and were shocked to learn that over two hundred fifty million people were practitioners or adherents of some variant of the faith.

After the lecture we meditated with great earnestness for fifteen minutes, trying to free our minds from the frenzy of the New York mind-set.

The students took the meditation exercise seriously and mocked neither the practice nor its teacher.

By the time we exited Meditation Hall, our host had a couple of pickup trucks revved and waiting to take us to Bobbie Louise Hawkins's small Victorian house on Bluff Avenue, which a hundred years ago was a gold miner's cabin. Amiable and all smiles, the radiant middle-aged author, who was raised in western Texas and New Mexico, invited us into her multipurpose art room. That room, which she calls the Bijou, is known around Boulder as the site of writing workshops and readings, one-act plays, and folk-music hootenannies. Hawkins is one of the best teachers of prose, for she has such an instinctive way with young people that talking with her about the weather can be a riveting experience. First making sure we were all comfortably seated, she rolled up her sleeves like a labor negotiator ready to cut a deal and began asking the students questions about themselves. Within minutes she had ignited a candid, wide-ranging free-for-all between them—from abortion rights to condoms, from the poetry of her ex-husband Robert Creeley to her eight years globetrotting with pop-jazz-folk musicians Rosalie Sorrels and Terry Garthwaite in a three-woman storytelling, music-making, and performance poetry show. She spoke at length about her admiration and affection for D. H. Lawrence, inspiring Aíne to buy *Lady Chatterley's Lover* and *The Rainbow* at a Boulder bookshop the next morning. Captivated by her vitality, generosity, and stunning sense of spoken language, the students were impressed that a woman so obviously avant-gardist could also be such a warm, down-home human being. "If more writers were writing like Bobbie Louise Hawkins—economically and truly about the only human things that interest us in prose— the past, the family, love, hate, duty, forgiveness," novelist Reynolds Price has written, "then maybe a few more thousand Americans would be reading narrative fiction and nourishing themselves on the oldest of all, safe and enduring pleasures: news and fun and consolation." Hawkins read from her latest book, *My Own Alphabet*, a collection of Ambrose Bierce–like short pieces that target the need for self-liberation in a world of relentless constraints, using her sharply honed wit, not rage, as the weapon. Aíne, Janine and Stefanie were so taken by the comic feminist perspective of *My Own Alphabet* and by Bobbie Louise Hawkins herself that they bought copies of just about her entire oeuvre: *One Small Saga, Almost Everything, Back to Texas, Frenchy,* and *Cuban Peter.* For the rest of the trip they traded copies and read out loud hilarious passages and listened to her Flying Fish recording, *Live at the Great American Music Hall,* picked up by one of the students in Boulder.

After this indoor session we sat in her lovely English garden of roses, lilies, and lilacs, enjoying the crisp Colorado air and the late-afternoon sun. We took off our shoes and sat in a circle, wiggling our toes in the cool grass. We were eager to play a French Dadaist poetry game Hawkins had imported, called Exquisite Corpse. The game begins when one person writes a line of poetry on a piece of paper. Content is unimportant—it's "first thought, best thought" that counts. The paper is passed to the person on the right, who adds a line, folds the paper over to cover the first line, and passes it to the person on the right. The third person contributes a line, folds the paper over the previous two lines, and passes it to the right, and so on, until everyone in the circle has contributed a line of poetry. The last person reads the collective poem out loud. It was great fun, and the students could count themselves novice poets. Hawkins then led an exercise in democracy on the issue of pizza toppings and ordered five large pizzas for delivery. We continued playing Exquisite Corpse until the pizzas arrived. On first whiff, we attacked the pies like a family of famished rabbits in a cabbage patch. The pizza disappeared in a matter of minutes, but we lingered a bit, conversing about Boulder, Buddhism, and anything else that came to mind. We said good-bye to our gracious hostess and headed back either to the Majic Bus or to the Arapahoe Lodge. The students agreed it had been an exhilarating day; now they were free for a night on the town.

That evening David, Beth, and I drove up Flagstaff Mountain for a panoramic view of Boulder at dusk. On the ascent we passed cyclists and lean runners on the Flagstaff road, and mountain cragsmen in shorts carrying lengths of line over their shoulders, heading downhill after an arduous day climbing the dramatic Flatirons. My stomach flip-flopped in recognition as we passed the Flagstaff House Restaurant, where, I told my fellow passengers, I had tasted rattlesnake for the first and last time. David said he often went to the top of Flagstaff Mountain to transform his worried mind into a calm one. A few breaths of air in that perched, privileged position and all his worries evaporated into the thin mountain air. He felt light and unburdened, he said, as if he'd lost five pounds with every inhalation.

We stayed until sunset, and as we descended, David told of how he loved to downhill-skateboard ("hellcat" was his term for it) Flagstaff Mountain. The treacherous mountain road twisted and curved and was difficult even to motor down. The thought of skateboarding seemed reckless in the extreme but also intoxicating. Prompted by Beth and me, David agreed to demonstrate his derring-do. David pulled the car to the side of the road, jumped out, popped open his trunk, and grabbed his beloved Santa Cruz skateboard—an old seventies Kryptonics made in Boulder, which he had acquired for free from the dumpster behind the factory—and off he went.

Beth took the wheel and with headlights shining and hearts in mouths, we followed David down the mountain as he literally leaned and rolled like a surf rider down the limb of the highway. It was awesome to watch him maneuver as if the board and his feet were one, brazenly courting disaster. When we reached bottom, Beth and I saluted his skill and bravery.

We picked up his girlfriend, Kat, and the four of us drove around Boulder, sticking our heads out of the window, enjoying the crisp night air and the star-filled sky. We stopped for a good, cheap spaghetti dinner and ended the evening at a funky basement coffeehouse, listening to and laughing with a local folk band that perform satirical originals—a cross between Jonathan Richman and Tom Paxton. Boulder had been a great educational stop, a diverse world unto itself high in the Rocky Mountains. We knew that the next day we would finally get to hike in those snow-capped mountains. What we didn't know was that we would get stuck in them.

11

The Rocky Mountains and Mesa Verde National Park

We simply need that wild country available to us, even if we never do more than drive to its edge and look in. For it can be a means of reassuring ourselves of our sanity as creatures, a part of the geography of hope.

—WALLACE STEGNER

THE MOST DIFFICULT PART OF AMERICAN ODYSSEY WAS keeping everyone punctual, myself included. On the one day when all the students were packed and ready to roll on schedule, Frank was not. If he didn't show soon, our hiking time in Rocky Mountain National Park would be cut short. Just as my anxiety was turning to panic, Frank bounced out of a taxi, apologized for being fifty minutes late, and muttered on apologetically about his unanticipated trials and tribulations trying to track down an old trucking buddy who lived "somewhere" on Colfax Avenue (which just happens to be the longest continuous street in the United States!). Frank hunkered down to avoid further scrutiny and shouted, "Load 'em up!" Several reporters from KGNU-FM Public Radio Boulder accompanied us as far as Lyons to conduct on-the-road interviews with students, aiming to capture the spirit and sounds of America's youth cruising down a Colorado highway toward the tallest peaks in the Rockies.

When Frank turned the ignition, everyone was aboard except Dan, Jay, Alison, and Janine, who had lingered to the last moment in drawn-out good-byes to Naropa friends they had made. Boulder's ambience and the spirit of Naropa—in Dan's words, how "cool" it all was—had captured their souls. Dan, a senior, had decided to begin his postgraduate education by attending Naropa's summer writing program with Allen Ginsberg, Amiri Baraka, and Anne Waldman. Janine, who writes with great confidence and authority, also vowed to return. Inwardly I wondered whether they had the gumption to make it happen. I understood and identified with Dan and Janine's enthusiasm for Boulder and Naropa—I had shared their passion a decade earlier—but could they escape the force of inertia once they returned home? (I am proud to report that both returned to Naropa in July, where they practiced Exquisite Corpse, breathing exercises, and free-verse writing underneath Boulder's cobalt blue skies. And what a time they had! Dan said he "learned more about art, literature, writing, and myself in a month at Naropa than I had in four years of university.")

Not all the students were taken with Boulder or Naropa. Some, like Alan, thought the institute's curriculum hopelessly idealistic and considered the student body a flock of lost Buddhist sheep, with yogurt for brains and alfalfa sprouts for hair, who wouldn't know a good hamburger if it came up and bit them. These same students condemned Boulder as a "honky heaven" for stoned Dead Heads and New Age misfits, although they showed a certain amount of envy of the material aspects of the Boulder life-style: cruising around in stylish Jeeps, skiing and cycling the year away in the latest fashions. Alan Mindel revealed this ambivalence most clearly in a telling line that crept into his journal jeremiad against Boulder's alternative life-style: "God, they're cool, a fringe society basking in the Rocky Mountains. They've all escaped and I could be one of them."

It wasn't until I heard students reading for KGNU from their course books and journals that I realized that what I believed in theory had happened in fact: The American Odyssey was turning out to be a profound

251

experience. Janine's rendering of Kerouac's "64th Chorus" and articulate explanation of why its lizard images had moved her was heartfelt and profound. Aíne, who had been taken with Bobbie Louise Hawkins, read one of her funny short pieces with extraordinary timing, grace, and self-assurance. Kevin read from *The Adventures of Huckleberry Finn* in the style and voice of a riverboat storyteller. Dan read Beat poetry and a few journal jottings of his own, while Jared recounted some of the more prosaic vicissitudes of life on the road in a crowded bus "chock full of smelly feet." And Alan's stream-of-consciousness monologue on Boulder pretentiousness was so witty that Spalding Gray may soon have to look over his shoulders. As we headed out of Boulder, the students were speaking into a microphone as the guitar strains of a new John Lee Hooker blues song drifted softly over us all. I felt complete and utter contentment. I knew now that the entire educational adventure was a bona fide success. As for Frank, he was on his best behavior in the media eye, proud that his Majic Bus was the literal and metaphorical vehicle of all this learning— and the object of all this free publicity.

Working our way through Boulder's edge city, down I-36 to Estes Park, we found ourselves on one of the most scenic and spectacular drives in the United States. To the east, the wide-open land pays homage to the breadbasket farmlands of Kansas and Nebraska; to the west, broken rocks, mixed forests of scattered ponderosa and lodgepole pines, aspen, and jagged rock formations signal the front range of the Rockies. This discontinuity is simultaneously soothing and eye-opening. Pickups and Jeeps whizzed past, as did clutches of bandannaed motorcyclists taking full springtime advantage of Colorado's libertarian no-helmet law. We passed young girls in riding breeches jumping fences at equestrian centers in preparation for summer competitions, in all likelihood dreaming of blue ribbons to hang on their bedroom walls next to posters of a clean-shaven Garth Brooks and the "achy-breaky" heartthrob, Billy Ray Cyrus. Countless poor relations of the sleek show horses at the equestrian centers— tired, old workhorses—dotted the landscape on one stretch of U.S. 36; so many, in fact, that I concluded there must be a dog food factory somewhere along Denver's South Platte River warehouse row.

We stopped at Hygiene, a town founded by a buffalo-robe-trader-turned-German-Baptist-minister. There a utopian sect, known as Dunkards, for their rite of total immersion in water, had built out of stone the Church of the Brethren and the Hygiene Home and Sanitarium, which have been demolished. The site is now surrounded by ranches and solar-bubbled second homes. Shortly after we crossed the Saint Vrain River, we stopped at the Cider Chalet (which has expanded its line to include cement bird feeders) for cups of ice-cold forty-five-cent all-natural cherry, apple, blackberry, boysenberry, black raspberry, and grape slushes. As we waited our turn in line, we studied two gangly teenage boys constructing the kiddie-kart racetrack for the upcoming season of motorhead thrills for the station-wagon set.

Colorful wildflowers—sky pilot, avens, and forget-me-nots—had popped up on both sides of the highway, originally a stagecoach path, that cuts directly to Estes Park. As we turned a particularly crooked bend leading to a small settlement, we spotted a sign welcoming us to LYONS'S DOUBLE GATEWAY TO THE ROCKIES, the trip winner for "gateway" braggadocio. At the quaint, tourist-oriented, main-street-type town, the students stopped for sandwiches and ice-cream cones at Lyons's Soda Fountain while I concluded the radio interview on the steps of the old, redbrick Western United Methodist Church. Asked for a one-line definition of America, I quoted Gertrude Stein: "Conceive a space that is filled with moving." Then Beth, Christine, and I dashed into the Saint Vrain Supermarket, bought four Colorado Instant Lottery tickets, scratched off the boxes with a coin, and became "instant" losers. We consoled ourselves with an eclectic and decadent assortment of edibles, perhaps some sort of allergic reaction to too much tofu and alfalfa sprouts: barbecue chips, giant dill pickles, strips of smoked beef jerky, and Sweet Tarts. As the Majic Bus left Lyons to begin our dramatic ascent to Estes Park, Johnny Cash bellowed, "San Quentin, you've been living hell to me," on the tape deck. Listening to the man in black while driving deep into the Rockies is about as Americana as it gets in America.

253

Paralleling a high, fast-moving stream, spilling and falling over smooth stones, we drove past the rustic Inn at Rock'n River—a rainbow-trout-fishing farm and bed-and-breakfast that advertises recent catches as long as twenty-six inches. Log cabins were spied through the brush, half hidden by aromatic blue spruces, aspens, and pines, and occasionally also by three-ton boulders. Smoke spiraling from their stone chimneys hinted that frosty times might still be ahead. The bright, deceptive sun of Lyons left us unprepared for the heavy snow flurries we encountered on entering Roosevelt National Forest.

Our appetite for around-the-bend adventure was whetted. On the other side of the road, a truck pulling three snowmobiles zoomed downhill. This and the sight of two small—and unexpected—glaciers suggested to us that what we'd planned as a casual hike might be more like an arctic trek. In the Rockies snow is a year-round natural phenomenon. There was little traffic, but every business we passed had a few cars parked out front, including a gallery of Slavic art—which might have been picked up by an errant tornado in Slovakia and set down, incongruously, in the Rockies—and a general store with a produce stand displaying Florida tangerines and California grapefruit in the Colorado snow. Billboards are prohibited on this scenic byway, but it was nevertheless littered with state-sanctioned ADOPT A HIGHWAY signs—an irony that grated on me. The Majic Bus was wheezing up the steadily increasing incline. We were managing twenty miles per hour in a thirty-five-mile-per-hour zone, as we lumbered upward in "I think I can, I think I can" fashion. Impatient and angry vehicles tailgated us in an intimidation attempt to force us to pull off and let them pass. After five minutes of headlight flashing, we obliged by exiting at the Lion Gulch Trail scenic overview. For our capitulation we earned a panoramic calendar shot of the grand, snow-blanketed Rocky Mountain Front Range and the town of Estes Park nestled below; we were also dusted by our first Colorado snowflakes.

Estes Park is a squeaky-clean imitation Swiss village of five thousand year-round and fifty thousand summer residents. The eastern sentinel of Rocky Mountain National Park, the tenth oldest and one of the busiest in the park system, with more than three million visitors annually, Estes Park is a tamer, less commercial version of Gatlinburg or Jackson Hole. The town is nevertheless disfigured by such tourist eyesores as a large blue-water tube slide ("the blue intestine"), miniature golf courses, Gran-Prix Go Karts, Krazy Bumper Kars, Double Bumper Boats, Lake Estes Executive Golf Course, and the like. These human-made blemishes do shrink, however, in the face of the unsurpassable Long's Peak (14,255 feet), which dominates the Front Range skyline, looming over Estes Park in its snowcapped glory, dwarfing the entire town into a series of barely anchored gingerbread dollhouses that could blow away momentarily at the mountain's behest. The main shopping thoroughfare, Elkhorn Avenue, was a frenzied beehive of activity, creating the illusion that Christmas was only a few days away. A bronze bighorn sheep, the state animal, greeted us in the center of town, evidence that these crag climbers call the surrounding Colorado high country home. The cultural climate was also markedly different from Boulder's. Estes Park was a real mountain town, where the Jeep tires were bigger, male hair ran shorter, ROSS PEROT [not Jerry Brown] FOR PRESIDENT signs were everywhere, and hiking and cowboy boots had replaced the sandals, Day-Glo Keds hightops, and Birkenstocks on men and women alike.

The town's landmark, the Stanley Hotel, best known as the setting for the Jack Nicholson movie *The Shining*, was built by Massachusetts industrialist F. O. Stanley, inventor of the Stanley Steamer, in 1909. Stanley had come to Estes Park to recuperate from tuberculosis. He was so taken by the beauty of Long's Peak and the curative powers of the dry mountain air that he decided to build an elegant resort hotel there. He instituted a Lyons – to – Estes Park jitney, Stanley Steamers replacing horsedrawn stagecoaches, to shuttle tourists to his hotel, and business has been booming ever since.

Eager to push on to the park itself, we briskly browsed around town— I purchased a July 1950 issue of Max Brand's *Western Magazine* for five dollars at an antique shop—and then drove the mile or so to the entrance to Rocky Mountain National Park. The park, which straddles the

Continental Divide, boasts an incredible seventy-eight peaks that are more than twelve thousand feet high. Our plan was to drive the narrow, winding fifty-mile Trail Ridge Road (U.S. 34)—the highest continuous automobile road in America—connecting Estes Park and Grand Lake, stopping off for a few miles of trail hiking along the way. No sooner had we entered the desolate park than Alison shouted, "Look to your right!" A magnificent herd of bighorn sheep had descended from the high meadows and craggy peaks and were clinging vertically to the side of a rugged cliff no more than thirty yards away, their gray-brown hair camouflaging them so completely against the rocks that only flashes of their prominent white rumps blew their cover. Frank stopped in the middle of the road and turned off the ignition to avoid spooking the magnificent and rarely seen rams and ewes. Tiptoeing off the Majic Bus, we snapped photos or just gazed in awe at these magnificent creatures.

Unlike deer or elk, bighorn sheep do not shed their massive curling horns. The horns are found on both sexes, although the ewes' are more spiked than curled. Since we were there in April, not November, which is the beginning of their breeding season, we did not witness their dramatic horn-clashing square-offs, which are said to echo as far as fifty miles. But we did witness their legendary surefootedness as they skillfully clambered up the steep terrain to escape our cameras and stares. The seldom-seen male bighorns weigh as much as 350 pounds and are the largest mountain sheep in North America. In the early 1800s nearly 2 million bighorn sheep called the Rocky Mountains home; today, because of human encroachment, there are only about 20,000 left, a third of which live in Colorado.

With snow still flurrying, we continued through the park toward the Trail Ridge Road. We came upon a herd of fifty elk grazing in a green alpine meadow below Deer Mountain (10,859 feet), cold air steaming around their large muzzles. What a sight! Some of the elk eyed us and, deciding we weren't a threat, went back to feeding on Parry's clover, marsh marigolds, and other grasses and sedges. With their deep brown manes, distinctive off-white rump patches, caramel brown backs and sides, and the huge antler racks on the bulls, these immense Rocky Mountain monarchs stand four to five feet tall at the shoulder and weigh anywhere from 400 to 900 pounds. Once the most common hoofed animal in North America, they were nearly extinguished in the name of human progress and today can be found only in the West. By 1910 Colorado's elk population had dwindled to only 700. Today, because of reintroduction and recovery programs, there are nearly 175,000 in the state. In fact, the elk have become somewhat of a nuisance in Estes Park, meandering (fittingly, perhaps) down Elkhorn Avenue or gnawing, power-mower fashion, on the fairways of the city's two golf courses.

Matt, eager to video-tape the herd, was the first off the bus; the rest of our herd followed. We trod gingerly across the high meadow, as though it were a mine field, trying to get as close as possible to these majestic animals—but not too close. Except for the windsong and the crackle of our footsteps, the land was silent. Cognizant of our herd watching theirs, the elk appeared unconcerned and uninterested. They had evidently seen droves of *Homo touristiens* before and found our antics boring. We all felt an indescribable exhilaration observing these animals at close range. Suddenly one of the bulls bugled an unforgettable foghorn alarm to his harem of cows and to the rest of the herd, and they high-hoofed it out of there, stampeding fifty yards away, into the thinly veiled forest cover. Greedy from their two unexpected wildlife encounters, the students now demanded nothing less than to see a mother black bear nursing her cubs. I said I'd look into it.

Here, isolated high in the "Roof of the World," surrounded by brilliant, snow-covered peaks and mountainsides dotted with stands of conifers, Douglas firs, limber pines, and aspen groves, flurries melting on our flushed faces as we spied on elk and bighorns at close range, our spirits were elevated. We were soaring with the eagles, and our only wish was that this moment could be frozen in time.

But reality impinged as we left the elk meadow. Frank was nervous about the "snowplowed" winding, treacherous roads with neck-breaking drops ahead—worried that the Majic Bus could hit a hidden ice patch or

257

be met head-on by a powerful gust of wind and slide off an exposed ridge. So we cautiously began our ascent into the fragile high-alpine tundra, a step below the sky, within kissable reach, only the snow buttercups defiantly pushing up around the edges of bleached white snowbanks giving proof that spring had already arrived and we were not likely to be trapped in a blizzard.

At ten thousand feet we ran smack into a sign reading, ROAD CLOSED. Behind it were about three feet of fresh, unplowed snow stretching as far as we could see. Stunned, we got out to help Frank turn the bus around. After this gear-shifting feat was accomplished, Frank shut the engine off, stuck in a Billie Holiday tape, and despite the most spectacular high-alpine view imaginable, went to sleep, letting us loose to tackle the snow. We were, as naturalist John Burroughs once wrote, "rooted to the air through our lungs and to the soil through our stomachs. . . . Walking trees and floating plants."

The students dug out boots and parkas from their duffel bags and off we went, using the snow-packed Trail Ridge Road as our hiking path. At some points students were waist-deep in the scuddled snow. Kenny scampered up the side of a hill and then couldn't find a way down. A handful of us waged major-league snowball battles, Justin beaning everyone with his Nolan Ryan iceball specials. We snapped photo after photo as we hiked up the closed road, playing such games as "Albino Man," which in common parlance is known as tackling. But soon all was not fun and games: Jared had begun gasping for breath, his nose bleeding, and he became nauseated by the cold, thin high-altitude air and the loss of oxygen. Known as acute mountain sickness (AMS), the condition usually strikes people at an altitude of around eight thousand feet, where oxygen levels are about half those at sea level. I also began feeling dizzy, my temples throbbing, so we cut our hike short. Still, it was an exuberant moment in the trip.

A wide-awake Frank was ready to go, and we began to brake our way back to Estes Park, determined to find a route that avoided backtracking. We learned at a gas station that U.S. 7 was open and would take us to Ferncliff. There we could latch on to U.S. 72, the high-mountain route to

Central City. We were chilled and comfortably numb, happy, and mountain giddy as I played the uproarious "Lost in the Ozone Again" by Commander Cody and his Lost Planet Airmen in honor of Jared, our martyr to AMS. Flurries had turned to misty gray rain as the bus rattled with urgent chatter, the pressing student question being where to celebrate Matt's birthday. We stopped at the Baldpate Inn to make sure our directions were correct and U.S. 7 was not snowed in. Repository of a world-famous key collection (twelve hundred of them) started by Clarence Darrow, the inn is guardian to such certifiable relics as the keys to Hitler's desk and air raid shelter, Mozart's wine cellar, General Washington's Valley Forge headquarters, the front door of the Southern Bank of Kentucky, the first bank robbed by Frank and Jesse James, George M. Cohan's key to the city of Chicago, and the key to the alarm box that reported the Great Chicago Fire of 1871.

We stopped next at the Long's Peak Inn Conference Center, built at the turn of the century and operated for many years as a training site for nature guides by the father of Rocky Mountain National Park and arguably one of America's greatest naturalists, Enos Mills. Here we got a breathtaking view of the east face of Long's Peak, where climbers test their skills on the "Diamond Route," and some of us marveled at a pair of stunning mountain bluebirds scouring for insects. The cabin where Mills wrote more than twenty nature books is tucked away in a pine grove across U.S. 7 from the famous conference center, now used as a Salvation Army retreat. The Mills cabin is open to the public by advance reservations with his daughter Edna Mills Kiley, a well-known grass-roots naturalist working in her father's tradition. Kiley's philosophy is grounded in reaching out to as many people as possible to expose them to the life-enhancing beauty of the great American outdoors, and she takes visitors on guided nature-trail walks while explaining her father's views on conservation.

Enos A. Mills (1870–1922) was one of the most beloved naturalists this country ever produced. In my opinion he had a more consequential impact on environmental awareness than did his friends John Muir and John Burroughs, for he founded the profession of nature interpretation.

259

Like Muir's in the Sierras and Burroughs's in the Catskills, Mills's walks up and around Long's Peak were central to his life's work. He lectured all across the United States—from the White House to one-room schoolhouses—a crusader for the importance of conservation and the necessity of stopping commercial interests from despoiling the American wilderness. His vivid writing style made for riveting reading, and his articles appeared in such periodicals as *Colliers*, the *Saturday Evening Post*, the *Atlantic Monthly*, and *Harper's*. In lectures or print he always ended with an appeal for people to start forest preserves. On learning of Mills's death, English novelist and poet Thomas Hardy wrote: "It is as if a mountain peak had sunk below the horizon."

Mills's writings were the *National Geographic* TV specials of his day. In his book *The Grizzlies*, he sits like the proverbial bump on a log, pad and pencil in hand, enjoying a grizzly splashing in a pond or sliding down a snowbank. The fearless Mills taught a whole generation of Americans to look at these animals through something other than the sights of a shotgun barrel. There are no longer any grizzlies in Colorado, and should a black bear be spotted in the vicinity of Rocky Mountain National Park, it is tranquilized and relocated to some faraway spot. Against any form of killing for sport, Mills would have been mortified to learn that as recently as 1992 the Colorado Wildlife Commission (CWC) permitted spring hunting of black bears, which is in practice genocidal because the killing of lactating females orphans their nursing cubs through starvation, predation, and accident. Mills's spirit lives on in the concerned citizens who lobby across the United States to end bear hunting as a sport in all states and seasons.

Fundamental to Mills's teachings is nature's interconnectedness—each acre of forest or prairie is an essential piece in the larger planetary puzzle. He believed that one became a true naturalist or outdoor enthusiast only by learning about nature in one's own backyard, from the movements of ants to the habits of squirrels to the falling of leaves to the shifting of wind.

Mills knew better than anyone that saving trees—producers of the oxygen necessary for humans to breathe, to exist—was the single most important environmental measure. He tried to educate Americans to the fact that even so-called nuisance animals, for example, the woodpecker, had an irreplaceable role to play in nature's interconnected system. As his daughter once told me on a hike to her father's cabin, "The trees are the front line. If we lose them, we're done for." According to the Washington-based World Watch Institute, planet Earth has lost two hundred million hectares (five hundred million acres) of trees since 1972, an area roughly one-third the size of the continental United States.

From Long's Peak and the Mills Homestead, we continued on Highway 7 at an elevation of about 9,000 feet, past Mount Meeker and Wild Basin and Meadow Mountain, past gravel turnoffs with primitive signs announcing hidden ranch properties with names like H-Bar-H Ranch or Antler Crest. The elevation dropped to 8,500 feet as we reached the village of Allenspark and ordered coffee to go at the Hummingbird Café from an attractive woman with jet black hair adorned with hummingbird jewelry. Hammered to the outside café entrance was a rusted can of Dinty Moore Beef Stew—we didn't ask why. The flurries returned, and gray-shadowed dusk was upon us. We all still felt a little dizzy from the high altitude and hungered for some hot food. Frank leaned on the horn hard as he wove the bus into the other lane to avoid an old man on a bike pulling a cart behind him, who had mysteriously made it this high in the Rockies with his homemade four-wheel contraption. A Jim Croce tape played, bringing back to me long-buried memories of junior-high-school crushes and adolescent awkwardness that were not in the least bit nostalgic, only painful.

We were now on U.S. 72—the Peak to Peak Highway—and Frank was a little concerned about the icy road conditions. The narrow two-lane road was worse than the Trail Ridge Road, with the added negative that it was now nighttime. The students were hungry, and antsy to find a place to celebrate Matt's birthday. There were no taverns, no cafés, no nothing to be found on this desolate, high-altitude, blacktop cliff-hanger of a road. We headed straight up U.S. 72, skimming the sky, for more than twenty minutes, and not a single vehicle came from the opposite direction. Then, just barely visible in the dark sleet, a neon MILLER'S PREMIUM DRAFT BEER sign glowed invitingly from the window of a log cabin. Was it a mirage? Frank slowly braked to a halt and pulled in front. Barely visible in the neon glare was a sign that said, MILLSITE INN. By the look of the half dozen pickup trucks and couple of cars, this was where the action was. No doubt about it, this was where we would have Matt's birthday bash. We all dashed in under the wooden porch and pushed open the doors, invaders from another planet, beamed up from the starship *Enterprise*. It was noisy and smoky inside, and though we did get a few strange looks, for the most part everyone kept talking just as if the invasion of twenty people was a common occurrence.

Kenny and Justin went straight to the bar to treat their frat "bro" to a birthday beer while the rest of us glanced at the amazingly variety of dinner possibilities. It was sooty but cozy and down-home inside, with wonderful photographs and paintings on the log walls. We had our choice of twelve different submarine sandwiches, pizza, appetizers, soups, chili, grilled food, salads, and a selection of entrees that included New York strip, eggplant Garibaldi, and fettucine Alfredo. We were astounded by the scope of the menu. Our waitress told us it was the closest we "wayfarers" would get to Mom's home cooking at an elevation of 9,345 feet— that they used "only the freshest ingredients" and even made their own hamburger buns.

Once we ordered, I took in the scene. The majority of the crowd of about thirty were broad-hatted ranchers. There was also a group of Bohemian artists and thrill seekers who spent their days skiing unbroken powder down spine-tingling chutes and their nights mingling at the bar. A mountain dweller with the spirit of Saint Anthony the Hermit and the disposition of Foster Brooks spent the entire evening throwing back shot after shot of Wild Turkey and putting his arm around any shoulder that came within reach. As the rest of us ate, Justin and Kenny struck up a lively conversation with Greg the bartender, who was also the mayor of Ward, Colorado, the town of fifty we were in. Carol Jenkin, a painter, initiated a conversation with Darlene and Stefanie, and so we were all mixed together, singing birthday toasts to Matt and listening to ranchers complain about everything from the Feds to Toyota trucks to gambling in Central City. Greg, the boisterous owner-politician, was wearing a chartreuse Cayman Islands T-shirt with an open flannel shirt over it, giving him the look of a mountain Jimmy Buffett. Candy, a Jane Fonda clone who was friends with the owner, was so excited by the concept of the Majic Bus that she demanded an instant tour. These were good people, and this was a good place, and we were having a good time. After three hours of our hobnobbing and fraternizing with the locals, the entire bar emptied out to offer good-bye handshakes and tour the bus. The parting request from the ranchers was to carry their message back East: BLM (the Bureau of Land Management) was siphoning off their lifeblood by telling them how to ranch. With the show-off sounds of Ray Charles blasting from the tape box, off we went into the ghoulish night, laughing, screaming, and singing while Frank tried to concentrate on the road. After an hour of struggling through the inky blackness, Frank pulled over to the side of the road, tilted his hat over his eyes, and called it a day, snoring instantly as the rest of us shivered in our sleeping bags, listening to the somber drizzle and the blasting, cradle-rocking wind. A few hours later the hard pink light of dawn streamed through the windshield, waking Frank. He snapped to and in robotic fashion drove the twenty remaining mountainous miles to Black Hawk – Central City for a thermos of hot wake-up coffee and a one-two slap of ice water on his face.

In 1859 these historic twin towns were known as "the richest square mile on earth." Gold strikes along Gregory Gulch amounted to more than sixty-nine million dollars, fueling the first big rush to Colorado (then part of the Kansas Territory). For years thereafter the town and surrounding mining camps captured the nation's imagination as the brawlingest and bawdiest of boom towns, prompting droves of fortune-seeking settlers to head west. In 1878 Central City opened its Victorian jewel of an opera house — reputedly the most beautiful between Chicago and San Francisco — and trainloads of Denverites flocked to see Sarah Bernhardt, Otis Skinner, Edwin Booth, Oscar Wilde, and Buffalo Bill. Forced to close when the gold and silver booms leveled out, the opera house reopened, completely restored, in 1932 with Lillian Gish in *Camille*, playing to standing-room-only crowds. After World War II, the twin towns fell into a ghostly state of decline, with only an occasional trickle of tourists interested in tacky T-shirt shops and abandoned mines. But what Bruce Springsteen sang about Atlantic City when casino gambling transformed the dying Jersey boardwalk town from bust- to boomville—"Everything dies, baby, that's a fact/but everything that dies someday comes back"— applies to Central City and Black Hawk today. In October 1991 Colorado voted to allow limited-stakes casino gambling in the forms of slot machines, blackjack, and poker. The transformation of these towns by the introduction of gambling astounded Frank and me as we rolled past casino after casino, with names like Glory Hole, Golden Coin, Silver Hawk, Calamity Jo's, Red Dolly, Bullwhackers, and the Nitro Club—all spruced up with offers of breakfast buffets and "heritage gambling" in the morning sun. In other words the saloons and gambling parlors are back, and so are the crowds, pulling slot machines or pushing the spin buttons, hoping to win the fast fortune, the big-buck bonanza. Never in our wildest dreams did we imagine getting stuck in bumper-to-bumper traffic at 6:30 A.M. in Black Hawk– Central City. With the designation of these towns as a historic district, the casinos are required to maintain the original building facades and unique historic flavor of the free-and-easy boomtowns of the 1870s. Anachronisms such as neon lights and canopy awnings are eschewed by the sensitive casino developers.

Beth blared out The Band's "Up on Cripple Creek" country-rock classic as we headed into Black Hawk, the old-mining-town-turned-slot-arcade, and parked for breakfast. When Kevin asked an old-timer—in a green Cripple Creek Rotary Club jacket emblazoned with a SUPPORT AMERICAN TROOPS insignia—if anybody still mined for silver and gold outside town, the native ridiculed Kevin's naïveté and said, "Boy, don't believe your eyes, for your eyes are just telling lies. This casino stuff is horseshit. This is still a pick-and-pan town." He then shouted "Hey, John!" to another old-time local who came over and introduced himself as "Mountain John,"

264

a seventy-one-year-old hard-rock miner in the process of starting to dig at the Mollie Kathleen mine just outside town. Mountain John was the living embodiment of the mythic miner, complete with a silver beard Santa Claus might kill for. His take on the scene still rings in my ears: "The coin clink will dry up here in town once the casino novelty wears off, but my pick will be echoing in these hills for another two hundred years, at least. Hell, it might never stop."

From Black Hawk Frank got on US-6 and entered I-70 West, just east of Idaho Springs, the scenic 274-mile interstate run from Denver to Utah. No sooner had we gotten on I-70 than we took Exit 240 to Idaho Springs for the express purpose of seeing the towering forty-foot statue of Steve Canyon, charmed aviator of Sunday comics fame, erected in 1949 as a tribute to the servicemen and -women of World War II. The huge, grotesque comic-book statue is America's surreal half-pint response to the Colossus of Rhodes. The commemorative plaque reads: THE UNITED STATES TREASURY SALUTES STEVE CANYON AND THROUGH HIM, ALL AMERICAN CARTOON CHARACTERS WHO SERVE THE NATION.

Back aboard the bus we were having an animated conversation about the Silver State. Tom, a good Catholic, was surprised to find a Cabrini Shrine in Colorado just off I-70. The site, I explained, had been chosen by Mother Frances Xavier Cabrini—founder of the Missionary Sisters of the Sacred Heart and the first U.S. citizen to be canonized by the Roman Catholic church—as a retreat for her nuns. Legend has it that when Mother Cabrini was confronted with the realization that the location she had chosen had no water source, she tapped her cane at a hillside spot and instructed all the men present to dig there. They discovered a spring that has flowed year-round ever since. She was canonized in 1946, three years before Washington paid homage to Steve Canyon. The state of Colorado has designated the holy spring a secular historical landmark.

Shari, our resident Civil War authority, asked whether the town of Breckenridge, Colorado, was named after President James Buchanan's vice president and Confederate President Jefferson Davis's secretary of war,

John C. Breckinridge of Kentucky. I parried the question with an author-itative, professional *no* because the spellings were different. The Colorado ski town's name had only one *i* in it. (Five months later, in the process of writing this book, I happened on a Colorado guidebook that said that, yes, the town was indeed named after the Kentucky politician. But in 1861, bothered by Breckinridge's role in the Civil War, the pro-Unionist town residents no longer wished to honor "Confederate scum." Colorado was still a part of Kansas Territory at the time, so they had to petition Congress to change the name. Washington's legislators obliged by chang-ing the first *i* to an *e*—Breckenridge.)

Kevin, who was doing his senior thesis on the multifaceted career of Arthur Schlesinger, Jr., had just finished the historian's latest book, *The Disuniting of America*, and was full of questions. A half dozen of us, including Tom, who had also read the book, had a heated discussion about multiculturalism, a debate that is roiling academe. Tom and I con-tended that Schlesinger is correct: Arguments against ethnocentrism are being taken too far by people like CUNY professor Leonard Jeffries, who teaches that all whites ("ice people" in his nomenclature, which eschews the pseudotaxonomy of other racist theorists) are evil and are hell-bent on the genocide of the African American community. Kevin, under the sway of the rap group Public Enemy, counterpunched that the African Ameri-can community needed to create a grand, mythic history and claim an-cient Egypt as a black African nation to achieve psychological parity in the self-esteem game. Isn't this what happened in the United States, Kevin continued, with John Winthrop's "City on the Hill," or Manifest Destiny, or fighting every war with the smug assumption that "God is on our side"? This was difficult to refute, so I took the conventional historian's way out and offered a not-too-convincing "two wrongs don't make a right."

The conversation veered to a lingering and desultory discussion of whether America was in a state of decline that finally broke off when we caught a glimpse of the giant hillside shopping mall skiers affectionately called Vail—a glittering, giant condo complex in the middle of the pristine White River National Forest. The town has what John Updike derided in *Rabbit*

Run as "the lakelike depth of a supermarket parking lot crammed with shimmering fins." Eyeballing Vail, the America-in-decline debate ringing in my ears, with an insistent bass rumbling of Kevin and Alan reciting Gerald Ford jokes gleaned from Chevy Chase on "Saturday Night Live" reruns, made me think of a T. S. Eliot poem about England between the wars: "And the wind shall say: 'Here were decent godless people: Their only monument the asphalt road / And a thousand lost golf balls.' "

The conversation had spun itself out. Students returned to their compartments to write in their journals or to read Cather or Kerouac. We decided to stop at a Denny's-ish twenty-four-hour eatery in Glenwood Springs, a town at the confluence of the Colorado and Roaring Fork rivers, for quickie sandwiches. The KDR boys asked to "take the waters" at the world's largest outdoor mineral hot-springs pool, but there was no time. We had to make Mesa Verde National Park by nightfall. When their request continued in whine mode, I said, with as much menace as I could muster, that I would take them to another historical graveyard: Linwood Cemetery, on the eastern promontory of town, where we would see the final resting places of the notorious gambler and shootist of OK Corral fame, Doc Holliday, and the noted bank robber and one-time member of Butch Cassidy's legendary Hole-in-the-Wall Gang, Kid Curry. They quickly clammed up.

With most everyone quietly reading, Frank, Beth, and I soaked in the passing view of the flat, fertile irrigated green of the Grand Valley of western Colorado. It felt good to be in the dry desert sun, out of all that snow and high-altitude dizziness. This part of the state, known as the Land of Dinosaurs, is where the remains of the first-known Brachiosaurus were discovered in 1990. Back around Rifle we had left the Rockies temporarily, and we were now looking at the red-walled canyons and rosy spires of the great Uncompahgre Plateau. Right outside Grand Junction we stopped at the Colorado National Monument and peered down the two-thousand-foot-deep, burnt-orange-and-red rock canyons, at the solitary sandstone monoliths, arched windows, and balanced rocks, that rise from the canyon floors. The students marveled at this colorful desert scenery and at the Colorado River, which slices right through the Grand Valley like a snake in the sand.

Despite its proximity to the Colorado National Monument and Grand Mesa—the world's largest flat-topped mountain, described by guidebooks as "a ten-thousand-foot-high Island in the Sky"—Grand Junction has never caught on as a tourist mecca. Driving through downtown to find the connection for U.S. 50, we gained some sense of why. With Neil Young's "Too Far Gone" as background, we peered out at the gritty working-class sights: the Victory Chapel, "Where Jesus Christ Is Saving Lives"; Carpet Times; trailer park after trailer park; the Brinkley (no relation) Electric Company; block upon block of concrete pipes; G. J. Truck Car Wash, with a large American flag painted on the side; Killer Bee Motorcycles and Western Slope Motorcycle Salvage, protected from incursions by barbed wire; and oil-grimed, coal-stained tanks, trucks, and trailers motionless in a rusted railyard. The nearby uranium mines that spelled boom for Grand Junction in the 1950s are, for the most part, closed. (One travel writer of the period, ignorant of the dangers of exposure to nuclear radiation, actually recommended touring a Grand Junction uranium mine as the "radioactive icing" on a family's "vacation cake.") Real estate is still cheap throughout Grand Junction (called by some the Three-Mile Island of the West because many hundreds of its homes are built on or out of uranium tailings, which emit low-level radiation).

As we headed east on U.S. 50, we were in flat cattle country, even passing a miniature-horse farm. Crossing the Gunnison River, we entered Delta, an "All-American 1992" town of indigenous optimism that strikes Wallace Stegner's recommended balance between mobility and stability, complete with a Dairy King, sweet-corn stands, downtown murals of idyllic Rocky Mountain scenes, and the Thunderbird Lounge West, where local Ute Indians drink ice-cold Coors in dark, air-conditioned solitude.

Driving south on U.S. 550 out of Delta headed toward Montrose, site of the Black Canyon, we played a haunting tape of the great Ute wind-flute player R. Carlos Nakai, letting "the smell of distance" excite us, in Stegner's words. If we were surprised to see local farmers selling sweet cherries as well as onions, peaches, pears, plums, grapes, and apricots at roadside produce stands, we were downright astonished to pass first the Hast Llamas Ranch, followed in swift succession by the Helgenberger Llamas Ranch, the Dolores Creek Llamas and Ostriches Ranch, and the Log Hill Llamas and Alpacas Ranch. The herds of Peruvian transplants range in size from twenty-five to one hundred and the animals are sold for breeding, packing, and wool production, and—due to their gentleness—as therapeutic companions. In clearing a trail from Denver to Durango, the National Forest Service recently used llamas instead of horses or mules for hauling, because the soft-footed llama causes less environmental damage than do its hoofed competitors. Ranch kids all over western Colorado, as well as in parts of Northern California, Oregon, and Washington, are now getting their first riding lessons on the backs of these gentle members of the camel family. In fact, once a year the town of Mancos, Colorado, holds a Llamathon.

Just outside of Montrose, with the San Juan Mountain Range approaching in the distance, we stopped briefly at the Ute Indian Museum, a storehouse of relics dedicated to Ouray, chief of the Southern Utes, and his wife, Chipeta. Then we were on our way past the Willie Wonka—like facilities of a large Russell Stover Candy factory and into a stretch of great lush pastureland, the Uncompahgre River meandering with us.

Soon hitting Ridgway, the ranching town where the memorable Hollywood Westerns *True Grit* and *How the West Was Won* were filmed, we left U.S. 550 and headed west on State Highway 62, part of the 236-mile-loop drive known as the San Juan Skyway. Just out of town, the road begins climbing up the 8,970-foot Dallas Divide. At the top the view south is spectacular, with 14,150-foot Mount Sneffels puncturing the bright blue southwestern Colorado sky in a way New Yorkers might relate to that of a Manhattan skyscraper on a brilliantly clear day. With split-rail picket fences, sweeping vistas, and low-growing mats of grasses on both sides of the road, we turned onto State Highway 145 to Telluride—named, depending on your source, either for tellurium, a gold-bearing ore, or, "To hell you ride," in homage to the boisterousness of the 1880s mining town—where we were to have dinner.

269

Telluride has grown into a mountain playground of global repute: It is America's "Pristine Paradise," according to *USA Today*. *Rolling Stone* has sanctified Telluride as "A Safe Haven for Utopia Seekers," which may say more about the mellowing of the magazine's readership than it does about the town. The most well-rounded "in" ski-resort town in the United States, Telluride is also known as the "Festival Capital of the Rockies": June is bluegrass, July is jazz, August is chamber music and mushroom gathering, and come September, the acclaimed film festival and hang-gliding competitions. As we entered the old Victorian mining town of thirteen hundred full-time residents, we passed an old Phillips 66 station (at the top of the endangered-stations list) and an easy-to assemble prefab "Lincoln Log" community. The swift San Miguel River rushed by on our right and a rickety Smokey the Bear stood on our left, saying, ONLY YOU CAN PREVENT FOREST FIRES, evidence of the incendiary potential of the thick Engelmann spruces and aspens in the surrounding San Juan and Uncompahgre national forests. As we read the sign, we noticed smoke billowing from a distant slope. Later we learned that what we had seen was a Forest Service "prescribed burn"—an attempt to get rid of gambel oaks and other thick undergrowth that hinder forage production for deer and elk. The succulent new regrowth provides a more nutritious and abundant food source for wildlife.

A few miles outside of Telluride, Justin shouted an alarm from the back of the bus: A Colorado police car was following us. Frank instantly grew irritable. Even though he was logging the trip and all his paperwork was in order, Frank, both a fatalist and a realist, often reiterated that "if a cop wants to make a bust they can always find something." After the car had trailed us for five minutes or so, the red siren flashed and we were pulled over, just as we entered the main street of Telluride. Two police officers straight out of Hollywood casting approached the open front door and asked Frank to get out. They began inspecting the bus and kept asking over and over, "Why were you driving so slow?" Frank's invariable reply: "Because we were going up hill and this bus is old." Alison and Dan were snapping photographs of the cops, which made them very uncomfortable and perhaps scared them off our scent. "Next time drive faster," Frank was instructed in a Joe Friday monotone, as they headed back to their patrol car. Justin and Kenny sided with the police. Frank, they teased, was driving like a "road pansy." Because of his brother's auto death via an off-duty policeman, he had no sense of humor when it came to cops, and they always "messed up his karma." I asked the guys to knock it off.

Squeezed into a box canyon along the San Miguel River, with the snow-capped Uncompahgre Range surrounding the downtown National Historic District, Telluride, the site of Butch Cassidy's first unauthorized bank withdrawal, is an old 1880 gold-silver-zinc-copper-lead-mining town that has transformed itself in recent years into one of Colorado's most successful ski towns, known for its brightly colored, perfectly maintained half-million-dollar storybook homes. We split into small groups to stroll around, thrilled to learn that the nearest traffic light was sixty-eight miles away. A Big Rock Candy Mountain dream town if there ever was one, an Aspen without the glitz, Telluride is nonetheless part-time home to an increasing number of celebrities and entrepreneurs: Oprah Winfrey, Sting, Jackson Browne, Oliver Stone, and Ralph Lauren. Alan said Telluride was the incarnation of his imagined vision of Dr. Seuss's Whoville. Some of us stopped at the Steaming Bean Coffee Company for a cappuccino among skis, used books, and Mark Knopfler's distinctive guitar from his recently released *On Every Street* album. I had Beth take a photo of me on the platform in front of the New Sheridan Hotel and Opera House, where William Jennings Bryan delivered his famous "Cross of Gold" speech in 1903.

Ten of us had a pizza dinner at Eddie's while others ate at the Lost Dollar Saloon or the Athenian Senate, where boxer Jack Dempsey once washed dishes. Without doubt Telluride was the most authentic and beautiful hideaway resort we had ever been to, but everyone felt the people were rude. We had apparently arrived the day after the ski season ended, and the locals must have run out of the psychic fuel that cranks up their professional welcoming smiles and they were taking a short break just

271

being themselves. They were in no mood to cater to tourists; in fact, we had disturbed their one week off before the summer tourists flocked into town.

On our way out of town we motored by the Telluride Ski Resort and Mountain Village, a billion-dollar self-contained condominium complex. The sight of the slopes ignited ski lust in many of us, though the virgin winter powder had melted into a packed platinum with stretch marks and springtime brown mud. Alison was so taken by the scene of sunset and abandoned mines that she demanded that Frank pull over so she could take a photo; after a few minutes of haggling he capitulated. Tracy Chapman was singing "Fast Car" as we drove past the white clapboard houses of Rico, Telluride's economically poor neighbor. We were now on Highway 145 to Dolores and then Cortez, where we would get on Highway 160 for a few short miles to Mesa Verde National Park, our campsite for the evening. We were in the part of the United States known as Four Corners, the only place where four states—Colorado, New Mexico, Arizona, and Utah—converge at one spot. In other words, you can put a foot in four states at one time.

The southwesternmost portion of Colorado is marked by a distinctive juxtaposition of terrain as the snow-covered peaks of the San Juans give up their hold to the desert canyons and high, flat mesas of the Colorado Plateau. Once home to thousands of Anasazi (a Navajo word meaning "ancient ones"), this beautiful area has become famous for the Anasazi cliff-dwelling ruins at Mesa Verde. Constructed with mortar under protective cliffs, these generally well-preserved living quarters are fascinating to see. Mesa Verde, the only national park dedicated to human handiwork, attracts six hundred thousand visitors every year. Its many cliff dwellings set in great open rock alcoves create a feeling of fantasy and romance and seem more the invention of a Hollywood set designer than the remnants of seven hundred-year-old Indian villages.

Much of what archaeologists surmise about the early Anasazi—who around A.D. 1300 simply abandoned their southwest Colorado home—is speculative because they kept no written records. Both the origins and the demise of Anasazi culture are shrouded in mystery. The generally accepted theory is that around the time of Christ, nomadic Indians wandered into southwest Colorado, settling in the mesa lands. While living in shallow alcoves, the early residents began making baskets, earning the name "Basket Makers." By A.D. 550 they had advanced to making simple pottery from the area's rich, reddish soil and to living in pit houses. Over the next two hundred years, a pueblo culture emerged, as the Indians learned to build dwellings of stone. The zenith of Anasazi culture occurred in about 1200. By this time many of their settlements, including Mesa Verde, had been built beneath overhanging cliffs. The site was probably chosen because of the proximity to a water source, and in fact some of the walled compounds dating to this period enclose natural springs. By 1300, however, these impressive cliff dwellings had been completely abandoned. Various theories speculate on the gradual and unexplained departure, the most popular being that the Anasazi left because of a prolonged drought. Wallace Stegner, contemplating the sprawling desert metropolises of Los Angeles, Las Vegas, and Phoenix, all without their own water supplies, has warned that "every Western city hell-bent for expansion might ponder the history of Mesa Verde."

Although known to Utes for years, the ruins were "officially" discovered by Richard Weatherill and Charlie Mason while they were out looking for stray cattle in 1888. The impressive finding rocked the scientific world, and overtime looters soon stripped the area of some of its artifacts. The protagonist of Willa Cather's *Professor's House* captures the sensation on first seeing the Mesa Verde cliff dwellings: "I had come upon the city of some extinct civilization hidden away in this inaccessible mesa for centuries, preserved in the dry air and almost perpetual sunlight like a fly in amber, guarded by the cliffs and the river and the desert." In 1906, to protect the pre-Columbian ruins, after an intense lobbying effort by the Colorado Women's Club, the park was finally established by President Theodore Roosevelt.

It was nighttime when we wove out of the San Juans and into the lurking town of Cortez. Originally an agricultural center, it has become a tourist stopover, for visitors not only to Mesa Verde but to many lesser-known prehistoric sites and museums as well—Hovenweep National Monument, Cortez Center, Crow Canyon Archaeological Center, Ute Mountain Tribal Park, and the Anasazi Heritage Center. Sleeping Ute Mountain, rising to the southwest of Cortez, is aptly named—its shape is an easily identifiable profile of a sleeping Indian with arms folded across his chest. Some Indians believe the legendary Ute will awaken one day and lead them to overcome their enemies. From Cortez, Mesa Verde is just ten miles east on Highway 160.

Because of budget cuts there was no one at the information/fee booth as we entered the park and began our five-mile ascent to the Morefield Campground. This was to be our first night camping out. Even though there were stubborn snow patches refusing to melt all over the park, it was still perfect for sleeping out under the stars—provided you had thermal underwear, a down jacket, two blankets, and a sleeping bag.

We had nearly the entire campground to ourselves. Our only neighbors were two college students from Stuttgart, Germany, garbed in identical Batman sweatshirts, slept inside their VW van; they were trekking across the United States for three months, living out their Wim Wenders fantasies. When told about the Majic Bus by one of our students, they said we had stolen the idea from "The Partridge Family." Germans apparently know more about American TV sitcoms than we do. The difference is, we regard them as entertainment, and they see them as material for serious analysis.

Flashlights were a necessity as we fumbled around in the dark, pulling six tents out of the luggage berth. Alison, the appointed tent czar, took the leadership initiative, barking orders, surveying tent sites, and hammering stakes. Kenny and Justin got a fire started, and soon they had a roaring blaze going. Jared brought out his CD box and put on Tom Petty's *Full Moon Fever* to complete our Western camp setup. We sat around the fire, told jokes, and laughed about our Colorado experiences. A coyote howled in the distance, silencing everyone. The sky was a field of stars, and every few minutes someone would spot a shooting star and shout,

"See it!" We felt as if we were fifteen again, sleeping out in the backyard, munching on pretzels and chips and shining our flashlights on trees in search of intruders.

Conversation turned to the mysterious Anasazis. We speculated as to whether disease or external enemies, in addition to drought, caused them to abandon their homes. We also tried to come to terms with the fact that Native Americans have been living in the Southwest for at least ten thousand years, leaving behind thousands of traces of their existence, and that we were the "new kids on the block," or worse. The conversation turned to the depredations on those traces through pot hunting, and to the looting of America's ancient heritage for big bucks on the international art market. Jared put on R.E.M.'s "Losing My Religion," which, along with Robbie Robertson's "Broken Arrow," Roger McGuinn's "I'm So Restless," Van Morrison's "In the Garden," Sam Cooke's "Wonderful World," Ricky Nelson's "Travelin' Man," and the entire Bob Dylan Bootleg Box Set, had become American Odyssey anthems. A lone coyote howled back at R.E.M., leading Frank to lecture us about not leaving any food out overnight. Stefanie had donned her flannel pajamas and said good-night, starting a chain reaction. Soon everyone but Matt, Kenny, Jared, and Justin was asleep, for the most part comfortable in their down bags. It was the soundest night's rest I had the entire trip.

The next morning Frank arose first and made pots of black cowboy coffee. I was grateful, for it got the chill out. There was a shower facility at the campground, and the students staggered toward it, self-programmed always to take advantage of hot water whenever it presented itself. All was calm as we purposefully readied ourselves to explore the cliff dwellings and ruins.

We planned to start our day at the visitors' center on Chapin Mesa, to learn which ruins were open and when guided tours were offered. Kevin, in a spirited mood, insisted we play his Benny Goodman swing tape on our ride down the Ruins Road to our destination. At the visitors' center a guided tour of Spruce Tree House, an outstanding cliff below the museum, was arranged. Stimulated by our night outdoors, most of us first chowed down a healthy cereal-and-grapefruit breakfast in the cafeteria and then studied the artifacts in the archaeological museum that tracks the history of the Anasazi.

The huge amount of space the students devoted to writing about Spruce House is an indication of how fascinating these cliff dwellings are. The park ranger allowed us to climb down into an excavated kiva—a round ceremonial structure—with a reconstructed roof to help us envision the Anasazi's religious rites. We explored away the afternoon, marveling at the Anasazi's gift for masonry, while red-tail hawks swooped through the blue skies, proudly showing off for visitors. A half mile north of the museum, we turned off on the two six-mile loops of Ruins Road Drive that took the Majic Bus, Benny Goodman still swinging away, past mesa-top ruins and overlooks to cliff dwellings in the canyons below. On one loop we visited Cliff Palace, the largest cliff dwelling in the world. Not only did the students write more about Mesa Verde National Park, they took more photos there than anywhere else on the class tour. Mesa Verde country, full of red canyons, wildlife, and traces of the Anasazi, offered enough mystery and adventure to last a lifetime.

John F. Kennedy once said, "The United States has to move very fast to even stand still." This sentiment was doubly true for the Majic Bus. We couldn't spend another evening in Mesa Verde, for Santa Fe was calling us. For the next three hours students read Larry McMurtry's *Last Picture Show* while listening to Matt's bootlegged Grateful Dead tapes, with their twenty-minute extended version of "Keep on Truckin'." The song had now taken on a new meaning for us all; it expressed a sentiment we could all relate to. Colorado was behind us.

12

Billy the Kid, D. H. Lawrence, and the Land of Enchantment

New Mexico was the greatest experience from the outside world that I ever had. It certainly changed me forever. Curious as it might sound, it was New Mexico that liberated me from the present era of civilization, the great era of material and mechanical development.

—D. H. LAWRENCE

FOR LOTS OF FOLKS NEW MEXICO IS A LAND OF ENCHANT-ment filled with piñon pine—clad mountains, sere brown deserts, Santa Fe cuisine, Georgia O'Keeffe colorscapes, ancient adobe villages, and robust, ever-changing light. But for me New Mexico will always be first and foremost the land of Billy the Kid. It was my first unparented trip to the state, in 1982, that reconnected me to my favorite childhood hero, Billy the Kid, a mythical American figure, the baddest and boldest boy of them all.

Like all great outlaw heroes, from Jesus Christ and the Buddha to Robin Hood and Jesse James, the New York Bowery—born Henry McCarty (alias William H. Bonney and Billy the Kid) never really died, even if his black granite tombstone in Fort Sumner, New Mexico, has JULY 14, 1881 chiseled on it. Billy has risen from the dead as the great American Lazarus, the living, breathing cultural icon of the untamed West, an all-purpose symbol for young rebels, a protean figure who defies accurate classification by the *Encyclopædia Britannica* by taking on new historical dimensions as the context demands. From the dime novels of the 1880s to the 1990 movie *Young Guns II*, complete with Emilio Estevez as the Boy Bandit and a Jon Bon Jovi soundtrack, the legend of Billy the Kid has been reinvented to meet audience needs and the compelling generational issues of the times.

In today's America, Billy has been transformed from a legendary-outlaw folk figure into a full-fledged mass-culture hero, primarily through the magic of Hollywood. Although I don't recall studying him in school or seeing any of the forty-five movies devoted to some aspect of the life of the young gunslinger, who has been breathed into existence by such actors as Roy Rogers, Robert Taylor, Paul Newman, Marlon Brando, Audie Murphy, and Kris Kristofferson, my friends and I knew all about the notorious baby-faced outlaw as if by osmosis. First there were the heated arguments over who got to be Billy in our monumental cap-gun showdowns, theatrically rolling over and playing dead in the grass when mortally wounded by a well-aimed pop. That Billy had purportedly killed twenty-one people in cold blood, one a year for the twenty-one years of his life, was of no import to us. What did matter was that he had broken the laws of the land, every one of them, done as he damn well pleased, and stood up to authority in the person of Sheriff Pat Garrett, the surrogate for our own in-house sheriff—Dad. It was the Kid's defiant, Dionysian swagger that helped us define ourselves and assert our independence in a voiceless struggle against authority. That Billy was shot dead by Pat Garrett only enhanced his allure. When one of us kids was caught smoking cigarettes or staying out past curfew and had to face the long, reprimanding walk with Dad to the metaphoric woodshed for punishment without benefit of trial, the code of the Kid prescribed how we were to behave: Grit your teeth and pretend that it doesn't hurt. In our teens Billy the Kid, the literal outlaw, was replaced by cultural outlaws, long-haired rock-and-roll rebels. The more our parents hated the "noise" and screamed,

"Turn it down!" the more special the band became. During high school the Kid would have been forgotten had it not been for Bob Dylan in his movie soundtrack album *Pat Garrett and Billy the Kid*, singing "Knockin' on Heaven's Door," and Billy Joel in his single "The Ballad of Billy the Kid," reminding us of the psychological debt we owed the legendary gunman.

By the time I entered college, Billy the Kid had faded from my consciousness, lurking in my toy chest of memories. It was not until after I graduated from Ohio State University in 1982 that I unexpectedly reconnected with the Kid.

My then-girlfriend and I were on our way to summer jobs in Phoenix when our old white rust-bucket Chrysler Le Baron broke down outside Santa Rosa, New Mexico. We were stranded for two days in an air-conditioned roach motel while a new and expensive transmission was installed. On its face this might sound romantic, but it was not. The innkeeper, whose cooking was on a par with his motel management, had permitted the unmistakable odor of curry to seep into the walls of every room in the motel, causing the flowered wallpaper to peel. There was no relief—three Marlboros and spritzing insect repellent made no dent. Desperate to escape, I hit upon the idea of making an expedition to the grave of Billy the Kid, two hours due south in the dry eastern New Mexico plains town of Fort Sumner. We hitched a ride outside Santa Rosa with a burly trucker named Liz, who promptly labeled us "stray poodles." She showed us her cab, stuck in a Charlie Pride tape, and drawled, "Charlie's my road company so it looks like you poodles get each other and the breath of the Almighty," and thumbed us to the back of her flatbed sixteen-wheeler for a scenic ride to Fort Sumner. What could be more hip, except perhaps drinking wine on James Dean's grave in Fairmount, Indiana, or camping out on Jim Morrison's in Paris?

Initially our spirits soared as the stiff, powerful wind whipped in our vacuumed ears and chafed our faces. But after ten minutes the novelty and skin began wearing off when Liz picked up speed. Panic swept over us as our eyes began to burn and tear. Could we hang on for two terrifying hours? Unable to communicate to Liz how sore our arms were or that sand was filling our every orifice, we resigned ourselves to a rendezvous with

279

death—alas, just as we were learning to live. I said an Our Father and a Hail Mary and thought about how especially upset my mother would be when she found out that I had died as a result of hitchhiking.

Somehow we survived the ordeal. Two hours later we were still alive. Liz stopped a couple of miles south of Fort Sumner, and we breathed a deep sigh of relief. All we could think of was escaping this heartless Calamity Jane, hugging each other, and finding an air-conditioned purveyor of giant-size paper-cup servings of Coca-Cola that also had mint-fresh rest rooms. She pulled off the highway, dismounted from her cab, and helped us jump down. "How was your ride?" she asked matter-of-factly, tilting her head toward the grave of Billy the Kid, only a hundred yards away.

"Terrible," I replied. "We could have been killed."

"But you weren't, honey," she laughed. "And now you've got a real Wild West war story to bring back east with ya. You'll thank me when you're old—and gray." Suddenly, feeling slightly chagrined by our whiney ingratitude for deprecating the value of a near-death experience, I offered her some gas money, which she stoutly refused.

"Honey, I want you to have this," she said as she plopped a silver medallion into my hand and rubbed my head maternally. "You've got the spunk of Billy the Kid and the gypsy blood of Saint Christopher." It was a religious medal, the kind found in Catholic gift shops. On one side was a 3-D picture of Saint Christopher, the patron saint of travelers until his passport was unceremoniously revoked by the Vatican after nearly two thousand years of service; on the other, an engraved picture of Billy the Kid. Both sides were engraved: LET IT BE FREE.

"My daddy gave it to me," Liz continued. "He was a member of the Billy the Kid Outlaw Gang Club, the Catholic Church, and Triple-A. I'd have given it to my son, but he was killed in a motorcycle accident in Mexico three years ago." Before I could say another word she had climbed back in her truck, shouted, "Say a prayer to Billy for me!" and ground off toward Las Cruces. A moment later she had disappeared from sight. We were silent and sad, looking at the medal as we slowly walked past a baseball diamond with collapsible bleachers and a boarded-up concession stand, heading into the old fort's graveyard to see the iron-shackled tombstone of Billy the Kid. As with Buffalo Bill's grave in Colorado, this site had been fenced to prevent thievery by daring necrophiles in search of a one-of-a-kind collectible—a precaution taken for good reason. The Kid's tombstone was stolen in 1950 and not recovered until a Granbury, Texas, police officer found it in 1976. It was swiped again in February 1981 and discovered several months later in Huntington Beach, California. The inscription on the tombstone reads: THE BOY BANDIT KING—HE DIED AS HE HAD LIVED. Twenty-one notches are marked across the top, framed by the additional murderous scorecard, 21 MEN. As Liz requested, I said a prayer to the Kid and asked God to forgive all of us Americans for our bloody, violent sins.

As for the medal, though I didn't know what to do with it, I felt I had to do something. A strange sense of responsibility swept over me. I did not want the medal, but it seemed wrong to get rid of it. The unlikely duo of Billy the Kid and Saint Christopher had become my burden. Was it a good-luck charm or did it mean bad luck? Did it mean anything at all, or was it merely a token of kindness from a mourning mother? For some reason I couldn't let the medal go, and so, ever the optimist, I cast it as a good-luck charm—my rabbit's foot and four-leaf clover all in one. I would guard it, keep it safe, and perhaps carry it to my grave.

Now, almost ten years later, I was sitting on the floor of the Majic Bus, heading to Santa Fe, retelling the story to a few fascinated students, and showing off the relic from my earlier visit. When we stopped at the Dairy Queen in Farmington for shakes and sundaes, I lectured on the historical Billy the Kid as distinct from his mythical *Doppelgänger*, sorting out, where possible, facts from fiction. The subject turned to why Billy the Kid had become such a cultural icon. Why had America adopted a murderer with no apparent redeeming social value as a folk hero? We could arrive at no clear definitive answer. Kevin perhaps summed it up best: "Violence is at the core of the American Dream because for poor people it's what gets you ahead." As we idled away over ice cream, the radio announced that John Wayne Gacy, the Chicago "crawl-space killer" convicted of murdering thirty-three young men and boys between 1972 and 1978, might soon be up for parole from Illinois's Menard Corrections Center. Just the news as usual in America.

The discussion of our country's obsession with violence continued as we cruised down Highway 44, and it dawned on me that what a decade ago I had chosen to treat as a good-luck charm had now lost its allure. When we stopped two hours later to diesel up in Los Alamos, I walked to the back of the station, and like Muhammad Ali (then still Cassius Clay), who—after being refused service at a Louisville restaurant in 1960 and then chased by racist bikers—ripped his Olympic gold medal off and heaved it into the darkness of the Ohio River, I threw my Billy the Kid–Saint Christopher Medal into a canyon, toward the Sangre de Cristo (Blood of Christ) Mountains, washing my hands of any further responsibility—I hoped.

The last hour of the drive to Santa Fe, Janine and I listened to Robert Hunter's acoustic *Box of Rain* cassette, which she had brought along. Hunter—lyricist for the Grateful Dead—whispered his renditions of "Rum Runners," "Reuben and Cerise," and "Scarlet Begonias," all alone with his haunting six-string, as we left Los Alamos—birthplace of the atomic bomb, trapped between the ancient Jemez Mountains on one side and the rugged Sangre de Cristos on the other, a grayish ghost moon overhead. It might have been 1945 again, with the gunslingers of Los Alamos, J. Robert Oppenheimer, Enrico Fermi, Edward Teller, and the other bleary-eyed and coffee-fatigued elite members of the New Mexico physics club feverishly at work in their underground laboratory, convinced that the Iron Age would be over if they could just unlock a few more of Mother Nature's secrets. Then a thundercloud broke, rain exploded on the windshield, and soon thereafter the lights of Santa Fe were upon us.

Santa Fe, the capital of New Mexico and the fine arts capital of the Southwest, is a picturesque city of only fifty-five thousand. It is easy to get lost in its maze of adobe walls, narrow, winding streets, and one-way alleys built for burros, not buses. Will Rogers summed up Santa Fe's geography succinctly on his first visit: "Whoever designed this town did so while riding on a jackass, backwards and drunk." For an unwieldy two-ton bus, it's almost impossible to negotiate. But fortunately it was a quiet Sunday evening at 9:00 P.M. and the streets were nearly empty, allowing Frank to make the tortuous turns and twists with relative ease. The students were eager to locate the first halfway decent watering hole to celebrate Tom's twenty-first birthday. Jared jumped off and asked an old, black-shawled Indian woman pushing a baby carriage for directions to the Plaza and before we knew it we were on W. San Francisco Avenue, three blocks away from the spectacularly lighted Palace of the Governors (1610–1612), reputedly the oldest public building in the United States, built ten years before the Pilgrims landed at Plymouth Rock. In the 1880s it was the residence of Governor Lew Wallace, who wrote *Ben Hur* there. On our right we saw a crazed neon sign flickering, EVANGELO'S COCKTAIL LOUNGE. It appeared to be a perfect incarnation of a dingy, rowdy New Mexico bar—a memorable venue for a birthday bash. And better yet—a sign from providence—there was a giant parking spot, tailor-made for the Majic Bus, in front of a Navajo rug shop only a few storefronts away.

A group of well-lubricated Harley road warriors were lounging out in front of the bar, shooting the bull, as we disembarked. One wolf-whistled at the female students, and another—a gnarly-looking tattooed and bearded fellow—gestured toward the blue wooden doors and said, "Come on in, ladies." To our surprise the interior was not Southwestern but wacky French Polynesian in flavor, complete with bamboo, wooden wind chimes, starfish, hanging stuffed parrots, and cut-paper tropical fish mobiles. What happened next I'm not quite sure. All I know is that in a matter of minutes a giant party for the entire bar was under way. When I asked the bartender for a beer, he said in a thick Hispanic accent and impatient tone, "Come on, man! We have over three hundred beers. What's your brand?" I went with Dos Equis, but soon everybody was buying Corona, Moosehead, Dixie, and St. Pauli Girl, to name but a few of the three hundred. Bottles were clinked and cheers were shouted. "This round is on me," reverberated through the bar in rare gestures of generosity. The jukebox selection was one of the best I'd ever seen: Entire LP song lists were displayed for the choosing on the new ROWE compact disc player. You got twenty-three plays for five dollars, unshackling listeners from the tyranny of greatest hits. You could also play your most obscure personal favorites and forgotten pop classics. Not until we entered Evangelo's had we encountered a jukebox on which you could hear entire albums of Charlie Parker, Elvis, Buddy Holly, Aretha Franklin, R.E.M., U-2, the Beatles, the Byrds, Bob Marley, Sam Cooke, Buckwheat Zydeco, John Mellencamp, Janis Joplin, Henry Mancini, the Supremes, the Grateful Dead, the Rolling Stones, Elvis Costello, the Cowboy Junkies, the Who, Santana, and Patsy Cline, just for starters. Everyone began to mingle and mix, and twenty animated conversations roared over Bob Seger's "Turn the Page." Christine and Janine struck up a conversation with three ponytailed Pueblo hipsters, one wearing dark Ray•Bans and a faded velveteen Navajo shirt, another's lack of teeth giving him the sad, jowled appearance of Geronimo in his last years. The third and oldest wore a beat-up Billy Jack hat and boasted of owning a used-car dealership in nearby Española—and, oddly enough, of fasting every Monday and Tuesday. He was pouring down Elephants, an imported beer from India; for when the clock struck midnight he would, he asserted, go cold turkey for two days. He seemed friendly enough, but when "A Whiter Shade of Pale" came on, he started singing and swaying and mumbling the words in such a loud, obnoxious manner that I thought we were in for trouble—but nothing came of it.

Behind the bar was a framed black-and-white photograph of Ernie Pyle, the distinguished war correspondent who won a Pulitzer Prize in 1944 and made Albuquerque his home base. I talked with Nick Klonis, the Greek American owner who bought the place from his father, a friend of Pyle's. Nick had followed his father's tradition of catering to the locals, not credit card tourists. While Nick went to open another round of beers, two polo-shirted real estate hustlers, who preferred to call themselves "builders," bragged to me about how "rich idiots" from California and New York were flocking to northern New Mexico and writing out four-hundred-thousand-dollar checks for one acre and a poorly constructed pseudo-adobe house with a true market value of fifty thousand dollars.

"They're buying into the 'Land of the Howling Coyote' myth," the more boisterous one crowed. "A few years back shops started hanging wooden signs with howling coyotes and Georgia O'Keeffe cattle skulls, and presto!—the snooties had a new playground, and I have more money than I know what to do with." Twitching and biting straws as if late for an appointment or wired on cocaine, they broke off the conversation and fled the bar when a dark green Mercedes pulled in front and honked. Though I was left with the uneasy feeling that Santa Fe–the–community had turned into Santa Fe–the–commodity, I shrugged off this observation. It was too late in the evening, and I was having too much fun to assume the role of urban sociologist of the Southwest.

The students were having a grand old time talking to the locals. One old-timer began telling stories about working at the Norman Petty Recording Studios in Clovis, New Mexico, during the 1950s, when Waylon Jennings and the Fireballs of Ratón made their first recordings. Student eyes popped out when he gossiped about the day Buddy Holly drove in from Lubbock, Texas, to start making magical hit after magical hit; the guy even bragged that he had mopped up Holly's sweat after he cut "Peggy Sue." As Nick shouted "Last call!" it was bottoms-up and handshake good-byes. We all lingered awhile outside. The bikers told Dan and Jay about a good campground fifteen miles out of town. Frank awoke from his catnap and, smelling a street party, blasted out a Muddy Waters blues tape, turning the Majic Bus into a monster jukebox. Languidly everybody loaded onto the bus—everybody, that is, except the KDR boys, who had mysteriously disappeared. Frank, tired and ready to set up camp somewhere outside town, insisted we abandon them; they needed to be taught a lesson. This, of course, was impossible, so Kevin and I formed a search party. We found them blocks away, flirting with some women from UCLA in front of the Santa Fe Hilton. We rounded them up, warning that Frank was verging on a coronary and they should apologize promptly. This finger-in-the-dike advice was useless: Their pseudorepentant faces were red flags to Frank, who came charging down the street like a Pamplona bull, snorting every four-letter word yet invented. He reminded them in no uncertain terms that wandering aimlessly around town and making others wait for them was intolerable and he could kick them off his bus at any time. The trio made not a peep, but for the next few days Matt brooded and moped about this dressing-down: "Nobody talks to me that way. Frank's going to get his." But notions of revenge baked out under the New Mexico sun, and in a few days they were buddies again.

With a full crew on board, we headed toward Taos on Route 285-68. We had been told to look for Camel Rock—the landmark for the Tesuque Pueblo Reservation, an unusual, wind-eroded sandstone formation that resembles the head and humps of a camel—then turn right and set up camp. Latecomers like ourselves could register with the reservation in the morning; it would cost us only a flat fifteen dollars. We found an isolated spot and built a fire. It was a cool desert night, so we huddled close to the flickering flames, trying to stay warm. One by one the students dropped off, until only five of the guys remained awake, feeding and stoking the fire, talking into the wee morning hours about nothing memorable. Kevin and I, guided by a fickle fluorescent moon that appeared and disappeared behind shifting cloud formations, took a hike down the terracotta lunar landscape of dirt-clod gullies, stepping around sagebrush and yuccas, bumping into miniature forests of gnarled piñon pines and huge red-rock boulders. As the titanic moon vanished for another day and the purple-pink sun rose in the east, it was a signal to us night walkers (and talkers) to yield to nature's cycle and grab a few hours' shuteye.

The day got off to a lazy start; the students awakened slowly, hung over. Rejuvenated by aspirin and showers, they tossed a Nerf football around, went swinging in the playground, made credit-card calls home to Mom and Dad, wrote in their journals, skirted Camel Rock, raided the under-stocked shelves of the reservation's convenience market, and wandered around Tesuque Pueblo, where residents sell handcrafted silver-and-turquoise jewelry and rugs and pottery from their adobe homes. I chatted with Ramas Romero, the campground manager—who spoke of the insatiable popularity of parlor Bingo and of gaming in general on the reservation—and a sixteen-year-old youth from nearby Pojoaque Pueblo, wearing a Pittsburgh Pirates baseball cap and bragging about obtaining permission from his tribe's medicine man to shoot "a real mean mother" of a red-tailed hawk for feathers for a religious ceremony. The conversation turned to scorpions, and the boy recounted how his friend Micki had been bitten by "one of those little bastards" and he himself had recently killed "a fat sandy brown one" in his house while he was lying on the sofa watching Saturday-morning cartoon television.

By lunchtime we were packed and ready to return to Santa Fe—"the City Different"—for the afternoon and then move onto Taos for dinner and a good night's regenerative sleep, to shape us up for our upcoming white-water-rafting expedition down the Rio Grande. In Santa Fe we split into small special-interest groups, for which I had prepared a list of recommendations. At the top was a visit to the Museum of Fine Arts—Santa Fe's first Pueblo Revival–style structure, built in 1917, and the progenitor of a regional architecture that continues to this day. The museum has a fine collection of paintings by such American artists as Marsden Hartley and Georgia O'Keeffe and Taos masters Ernest Blumenschein, Bert Geer Philips, Joseph Henry Sharp, and Eanger Irving Course. I told them to be sure to have a look at Gerald Cassidy's *Cui Bono?* (c. 1911), a transcendent life-size realist portrait of an old Pueblo Indian with a white blanket wrapped around his head. He looks to me mysterious and Moroccan, although he is in Taos. With a sad, resigned gaze, he peers out of the disappearing world he tried to protect for himself and his people, his eyes engaging the viewer from the engulfing white culture. He is asking, *Cui Bono?* ("Who benefits from this?")—a question I was asking myself by day's end. My other recommendations were that they visit the Cathedral of Saint Francis, founded by Santa Fe's first archbishop, Jean-Baptiste Lamy, who is credited with resuscitating the Catholic faith in New Mexico and immortalized in Willa Cather's novel *Death Comes to the Archbishop* and Paul Horgan's Pulitzer Prize–winning biography, *Lamy of Santa Fe;* and the impressive collections at the Wheelwright Museum of the American Indian and the Museum of Indian Arts and Culture.

The students scattered, and I led a group of five to San Miguel Chapel. The self-proclaimed oldest church in the United States, built in 1610 by Tlaxcala Indian slaves from Mexico under the direction of Franciscan padres, it is more accurately the oldest church in continuous use in the United States. The exterior is stark adobe with a simple faded white wood cross on top. Against a blazing azure blue sky, San Miguel's austerity captures the power, pain, and glory of Christ at Calvary. But as we moved inside, this powerful feeling was rudely shattered. Although the Christian Brothers, who have owned and operated the mission since 1859, should be commended for taking care of this unique American landmark, they must also be held accountable for transforming its dignity and spirituality into a vulgar, money-focused, faux-Disneyland operation. No attempt is made to help the endless tourists who traipse throughout the chapel to connect, even momentarily, with something deeper. Flashbulbs flash and crowds babble disrespectfully to overcome the disquieting male baritone voice booming out the church's history over an intrusive sound system. The students believed that one of the redeeming values of churches and cathedrals is that they serve as islands of tranquility where people can meditate, pray, or collect their thoughts, safe and secure beyond reach of the hustle and bustle of outside hassles and intrusions. The Christian Brothers should remove the loudspeakers and replace them with some less-intrusive method, the students all agreed. To make matters worse, the tacky San Miguel Gift Shop ("the oldest house in America") is visible directly to your right as you enter the chapel. "It is a disgrace [to] God!" Beth exclaimed, right in front of the cashier.

Here, attached to "the oldest church in America," you can buy such Christian souvenirs as the *Chile Lovers' Cookbook* and coffee cups emblazoned with your zodiac sign. Is nothing sacred? Still, the wooden altar screen, nearby hanging *ristras*, and eighteenth-century religious art—including carvings, oil paintings, and a *retablo*—are beautiful, and a few of us crossed ourselves with holy water and knelt before the crucifix and prayed.

We walked across the Old Santa Fe Trail, opened in 1821 and one of America's most famous travel routes, to have lunch at the barrio's best-known restaurant, the Pink Adobe. With overpriced, mediocre food served by haughty help, the famed Pink Adobe ("Santa Fe's oldest restaurant") is all windup and no delivery. We should have intuited that we were in for a fleecing right away, for on entering, the first things you see are framed pictures of the owner, Rosalea Murphy, an Ethel Merman look-alike, with a Panama-hat-clad J. R. Ewing (Larry Hagman) and a spaced-out George Bush. We were seated in the hokey Dragon Room Bar, its name an apt metaphor because the dragon-lady owner has prominently posted the rules: PROPER ATTIRE REQUIRED, NO TANK TOPS, NO CUT-OFFS, like some latter-day WANTED: DEAD OR ALIVE posters.

With our shirts tucked in, our hair brushed, and our manners in place, we ordered their world-famous New Mexican specialties—Tamale Plate, Enchilada Plate, and Green Chili Stew—and regretted not having gone to the Taco Bell on Cerrillos Road. The management became discombobulated because the five of us wanted to sit at a table set for four. Our waiter, born and raised in New England, rolled his eyes in disgust when we asked for more tortillas. The topper of this exercise in culinary mediocrity was the waiter's query as to whether we would like to purchase an autographed copy of Rosalea's *The Pink Adobe Cookbook.* I asked the waiter if I could have a word with this Southwestern Zsa-Zsa, to tell her personally what I thought of her restaurant. She was "unavailable," he said, and besides, she only discussed "culinary issues" by appointment. We left disappointed and disgusted. Still hungry after this high-priced fiasco, we stopped at the trusty Woolworth lunch counter on the Plaza and spoon-shoveled delicious bowls of their famous Frito Pie—a mixture of Fritos, chili, and cheese—for $2.35 a serving.

Our group of five then split up for the afternoon. Beth and I roamed the art galleries on highly commercialized Canyon Road, touted as the third-largest art market in America. We were moved by the distinctive work of Native American artists Ronald Begay, Fritz Scholder, and Kevin Red Star, and sculptor Allen Houser, which stood out among the flood of posters, paintings, lithographs, ceramics, and etched glass of the overexposed

R. C. Gorman, whose work can be found in poster shops and "artists' colonies" from Laguna Beach to Gatlinburg to Provincetown—or wherever saltwater taffy is sold. The ubiquitous Gormans got on our nerves, and we were forced to conclude that not since Peter Max and Leroy Neiman has an artist gone so far with so little. We wandered into the Fenn Gallery on Paseo de Peralta, where Gerald Ford and Cher acquired their R. C. Gormans, and strolled in their lovely sculpture garden, which is complete with a goldfish pond, ducks, a macaw, and a potbellied pig. The merchandise inside was far less impressive: sentimental paintings and sculptures of cowboys and Indians astronomically priced for the Palm Springs set—the idolaters of Bob Hope, Frank Sinatra, and Nancy Reagan. Prices ranged from $5,000 for a modest Maynard Dixon to $575,000 for Georgia O'Keeffe's *Early Spring Tree*.

As Beth and I crisscrossed Canyon Road, we were amazed at how many Georgia O'Keeffe look-alikes we passed—fifty-something women with tan, leathery, sunspotted skin who are earthy enough to have eschewed a facelift, unlike their New York and LA friends. Wearing a Southwestern sunbonnet just as Georgia O'Keeffe did (and Taos's Greer Garson does) and a pair of loose-fitting bright orange, purple, or yellow balloon pants a painter wouldn't have been caught wearing, the O'Keeffe poseur makes no pretense of possessing artistic talent or sensibility although she whiles away her afternoons hobnobbing with gallery owners about the next art opening she's been invited to or where she last spotted Gene Hackman or Dennis Hopper.

We were almost flattened by the Coyote Express shuttle bus, which whizzes tourists from place to place. At the Zaplin-Lampert Gallery, we stared sadly at Albert Bierstadt's incredible but depressing photograph *The Last Buffalo* and studied a couple of T. C. Cannons, whose painting *Mama and Papa Got the Going Home to Shiprock Blues* blew a few holes in the way most of us look at American Indian art. (Cannon died when he was thirty-two in a car crash in Santa Fe.) We recrossed Canyon Road for coffee at the Canyon Café and contemplated our next goal. Deciding to get haircuts, we pursued the holy grail of an appointment, going from shop to shop begging to be squeezed into any appointment book, but to no avail. As five o'clock approached (the designated time to meet back at the bus), Beth finally finagled an opening at the Loretto Hair Salon. Beth had turned her four prior failures into a learning experience. She told Loretto's she was Rosalea's New York niece and *had* to get a cut before the six o'clock opening at the Allene Lapides Gallery. Honored at having near royalty in her humble shop, *voilà!* a hairdresser found that an immediate spot opened up for Beth, while I continued on.

My mood was glum. Thoughts of Cassidy's painting *Cui Bono?* and the excesses of tourism, imported California culture, and rampant commercialism that had overrun Santa Fe annoyed me no end. Fortunately I stumbled upon the most rejuvenating and uplifting sight of the day: Santa Fe Dave's Outlaw Furniture. Real estate hustlers and opportunist developers had not taken over completely. The spirit of Santa Fe was thriving in an old, abandoned gas station on Cerrillos Road.

David Hall, better known as Santa Fe Dave to customers of his "It's-not-on-the-Plaza Outlaw Furniture Store" and to avid readers of his caustic advertisements and satirical articles, is a modern-day Mark Twain taking potshots at Santa Fe's anything-for-a-buck establishment: the real estate sharks; oleaginous Plaza-area business owners; cutthroat California art dealers; Mayor Sam Pick; the Catellus Development Corporation, which wants to erect a hideous building surmounted by a sixty-foot glass tower on the thirty-seven-acre railroad property off Guadalupe Street; *New Mexico* magazine, which moved its subscription address to Escondido, California; the Abruzzo family, which wants to scar and carve up a nearby mountain to build a ski resort; and just about any "jackass" (Dave's all-purpose epithet) who wants to turn Santa Fe into a playground for the rich. Dave conducts this campaign from his two-thousand-square-foot gasoline-station-turned-furniture-shop on Cerrillos Road. The fifty-year-old Santa Fe native, normally attired in cowboy hat and bandanna, comes with his own Establishment credentials: A Princeton University graduate (1965) and former teacher and principal of Bruno Bettelheim's Orthogenic School at the University of Chicago who returned to his hometown because he "grew tired of eastern clouds." What he found, Dave says, was that the Santa Fe of his childhood had been taken over by greedy out-of-state

developers and wealthy California art-market manipulators who had transformed his town into one giant T-shirt shop. "In the nineteen-fifties we
didn't like Texans very much," Santa Fe Dave explained. "They were
always comin' here with lots more money than we'd ever dreamed. And
they were a mite louder than we were used to. To tell the truth, we liked
'em better than we like Califurnians now. Texans respected our culture
and our way of life. They didn't want to make everything a spittin' image
of where they came from. They'd never dream o' puttin a house on top of
a hill." In 1990 he began selling cowboy memorabilia at Outlaw Furniture, "the kind of store Santa Fe used to have when it used to be the way
it used to be before the locals who used to be downtown sold their stores
to the guys and gals who came in on the train." One of Santa Fe Dave's
early newspaper advertisements for Outlaw Furniture read: "It's Not California: No pre-fab individuality, No LA gear, No palm-tree pretentiousness, No status cars, No perfect form and pretty faces, No New Age crystals,
No past-life regressions, No 'wannabe' Indians, No California clichés, No
houses on top of hills, No name-dropping, No cutesy cartoon gates in the
historical section. Tough stuff only."

It's the "wannabe Indians" that most annoy Santa Fe Dave. "In the last
few years I have met a lot of people claiming to be Indians who don't
know their *si pa pu* from a hole in the ground." What repels Dave is the
prevalence of what he calls tourist art and pseudo Indians, propagated
and proliferated by the Plaza merchants and their California and New
York cousins. "[Their] goals are unity, harmony, resemblance, and sameness. If you give customers too many choices, too much variation, all you
end up with is a bunch of confused tourists and no sales. All tourist art
is supposed to resemble all other tourists art." In Santa Fe that means no
escape from howling coyotes, saguaro cacti (which aren't found in New
Mexico), cheap jewelry, iridescent paintings of idealized landscapes, and
postage-stamp Indians. Tourist art demands marketable color schemes. "If
it is the wrong color it won't sell." Dave elucidated the formula: "The best
colors today are coral, cyan, mauve, cerulean blue, fuchsia, magenta,
chartreuse, adobe, and Navajo white. Put those colors in your paintings,
combine them with the right forms, place them in the right gallery at the

right price, and you've got an endless series of 'repeatable,' 'mineable variation' winners." Not so at Outlaw Furniture. There you can find just about any type of New Mexican folk art you can imagine and a few you couldn't. For example, Dave has a section in which every object sports a picture of Our Lady of Guadalupe. According to tradition, her first reported appearance was to a Mexican Indian. She affirmed that Indians were just as capable of being saved through Christianity as were Spaniards. Thus she is associated with the native people of Mexico: Objects with her picture include yellow-and-blue gearshift knobs, trash cans, altars, cabinets, key rings, Levi's jackets, and playing cards. Santa Fe Dave's "Jesse Helms section" includes Robert Mapplethorpe photography books and framed reproductions of his infamous sadomasochistic self-portraits, antique wooden sex dolls (Billy the Boy and Girl), and an authentic mule deer's ass purchased by Bob Wade, a local artist, with an NEA grant. Outside the store the shopper can contemplate his chrome bumper sculpture garden, the cowgirl practice seat (it's worse than you think), and a forty-foot-tall windmill called Catellus Tower in honor of the San Francisco-based developer bent on building high-rises downtown.

Santa Fe Dave doesn't work by himself. His partner in the quest to degentrify Santa Fe is the Skull Man, one of the Southwest's leading collectors of and dealers in animal skeletons and skulls. During the fat, free-spending Reagan years, the Skull Man was R. L. Beseda, a leading Houston real estate developer and owner of a savings-and-loan. But when the S&L went belly-up so did R. L. Beseda; he lost millions. Bankrupt, he retired to Santa Fe and began combing the continent for skulls and bones. He let his gray beard flow in the style of a Sierra Mountain gold prospector or a Missouri muleskinner and began selling his ossified finds in front of Outlaw Furniture. And what a collection of bones he has accumulated: skunk, elk, coyote, moose, deer, buffalo, alligator, and Texas Longhorn skulls, and rattlesnake skins and heads. Along the way the Skull Man expanded his inventory with peace pipes, knives, and arrowheads, grizzly-bear teeth, and other outdoor collectibles. So efficient is the Skull Man that once a week a group of Pueblos drives seventy miles on a clandestine entrepreneurial buy to stock up in bulk on his arrow-

293

heads and longhorn skulls. They in turn multiply the Skull Man's prices by five and retail them to unsuspecting tourists who come to gawk at the indigenous people of our nation as if they were alien Others in a Smithsonian diorama.

Another Santa Fe Dave associate has also developed the capitalist spirit. Jerry Austin, the live-in guard of Outlaw Furniture, was recently hired by Perrier to peddle their imported mineral water. Austin was a homeless, handlebar-mustachioed whittler of cowboy statues when Santa Fe Dave put a roof over his head and gave him a job. One afternoon an ad agency executive browsing through Dave's eclectic merchandise spotted Jerry. Taken with Jerry as the incarnation of a John Wayne Western desert rat, the ad man hired him to model for Perrier. Now the image of Jerry Austin inhabits the double-fold-out Perrier ads in *GQ, Esquire, Forbes,* and *Cosmopolitan.* When not modeling, Jerry lives in Outlaw Furniture's garage, guarding the premises from would-be memorabilia rustlers.

That Santa Fe Dave has to guard his emporium is testimony to the fact that he doesn't sell junk. Dave's client list for his Old and New West folk art would make the Plaza merchants green with envy: Dennis Weaver and Tab Hunter are regulars; country singer Randy Travis is the satisfied owner of a recently purchased horse's ass from Santa Fe Dave's annual "Backside Art Show," in which, in this age of specialization, the objet d'art consists of the hindquarters of equine species—horses, burros, mules, and deer. Dave organized and advertised the show as a tribute to the Plaza merchants and Canyon Road charlatans who hawk cutesy carved-in-Taiwan coyotes bedraped in a kerchief for one thousand dollars as an artifact of the great state of New Mexico.

Santa Fe Dave has two pieces of advice to visitors to his beloved city: (1) To save hard-earned dollars before buying downtown, check out Santa Fe's weekend flea markets, where everything is cheaper and one can haggle; (2) to save the heart and soul of Santa Fe, boycott T-shirts, food, paintings, and anything with a coyote on it, for "the coyote conspiracy is run by a syndicate of foreign businessmen hell-bent on bilking innocent visitors who think the coyote is a local symbol."

Together Santa Fe Dave, the Skull Man, and Jerry Austin are a trio of self-styled outlaw agitators, with the sisyphean task of keeping the city, state, and region they love from becoming an imitation Los Angeles—an air-conditioned nightmare of high-rises and congestion and fake coyotes. They do it with humor and Western panache. In their own small way they are the caretakers of a Santa Fe that was and a Santa Fe that will, perhaps, be again, for they are the harbingers of a new America, one in which, as D. H. Lawrence said, "The skyscraper will scatter on the winds like thistledown, and the genuine America, the America of New Mexico, will start on its course again."

A good jaw session with Santa Fe Dave had lifted my spirits and I sprinted the quarter mile to the bus, embarrassed at being more than a half hour late. My students let me have it, needling me on the importance of punctuality—one of the Ten Commandments of our collective journey, as I had preached on any number of occasions. Everyone had enjoyed Santa Fe, and the only task left before heading to Taos was to buy tickets for rafting on the Rio Grande. Frank pulled in front of the El Dorado Hotel, and we ran into Santa Fe Rafting Company and Outfitters, signed liability waivers, listened to safety information, and received directions on where to meet our guides the next morning. It cost twenty-five dollars for the half-day excursion, and all the students except one signed on. Hearing how high the river was and how wet they were going to get, several students dashed to Woolworth's for cheap, throwaway sneakers and slickers. (This added precautionary measure paid off; the rafting company supplied us with appropriate rain gear, but the reality was that we got soaked despite the protective garb.)

Rafting tickets in hand, we headed out of Santa Fe on U.S. 84-285 past Camel Rock, turning northeast at the Pojoaque Pueblo to drive along the High Road to Taos, known for its surreal landscapes, grand vistas, and picturesque villages founded by early Spanish settlers and missionaries. The relative isolation of the entire area has enabled these villages to retain some semblance of their Spanish colonial heritage in spite of their "annexation" by the United States many generations ago.

In the village of Chimayó we stopped at the chapel Santuario de Chimayó, the Lourdes of the United States. The village, which has incorporated much that is typically American, is home to the only shrine in the United States that carries the Vatican imprimatur of the miraculous. Tradition has it that on Good Friday night in 1810, a friar saw a mysterious light emanating from the earth. Villagers digging at the spot found a large wooden crucifix. The mud found in the vicinity of the El Posito well near the altar is believed by the faithful to possess miraculous curative properties, as the pile of discarded crutches, neck braces, vials of blood samples, and eye patches left at the altar starkly testify. During Holy Week fifty thousand pilgrims pray at this sacred Catholic shrine, many hoping to be healed.

Darkness was rapidly encroaching on the day; the outline of the snow-covered, crimson-bathed Truchas peaks was barely visible as we wound around the rim of a deep canyon and into Truchas itself, the village where Robert Redford's *Milagro Beanfield War* was filmed. As we drove on, the heavens opened and a steady tattoo of rain beat down on the roof. The bister walls of the adobe farmhouses were now enveloped in ancient shadows of blue-black, like mourning veils. As we descended into the outskirts of Taos, we stopped briefly in Ranchos de Taos to pay tribute to the San Francisco de Asís Church, immortalized in pigment by Georgia O'Keeffe's brush and on film by Ansel Adams's camera.

Taos and its surroundings possess an immobility and a fixity that speak of the first days of Creation. Most visitors come to this remote part of northern New Mexico for the art galleries and museums or to check off Taos Pueblo and Kit Carson's home from their to-do lists, or to ski Angel Fire or to four-wheel-drive around the enchanted circle. But it is the stillness of the land under the constantly shifting hundred-mile sky that causes some individuals to inhale this region not just as part of their life but as their entire reason for struggling, laughing, and dying. To those who stay, Taos is chosen not by the mind but the soul. One cannot move to Taos; one's soul comes to settle there.

We drove down Paseo de Pueblo Norte, past Taos Plaza, a two-block stretch of art galleries, adobe T-shirt shops, and fine eating establishments, parking the bus behind the sprawling, rustic Taos Inn. The inn's large, flickering blue neon eagle sign is the town beacon for travelers driving through what the Indians call a misty, she-rain night. Rain gear and umbrellas were unfurled as we dashed for safety—the more affluent in the group to Doc Martin's restaurant at the Taos Inn, and those on a tighter budget to McDonald's or La Cocina de Taos. After eating, Beth and I strolled in the rain through the Kit Carson Memorial State Park and Cemetery, but we were spooked by seeing the crooked tombstones at night. We hastened back to Paseo de Pueblo del Norte and sat under a storefront awning, evaluating the summer fashions worn by J. C. Penney window mannequins across the street, and talked for an hour of growing up in America.

D. H. Lawrence had been on my mind, and I spoke of spending the summer of 1984 at Edinburgh University studying modern British literature and in the process becoming a passionate devotee of the audacious English writer. I was intoxicated by the immediacy of Lawrence's words, by his refusal to isolate reason from passion. Ironically it was this outlander Lawrence who taught me how to see Americans, understand them sympathetically, and search beyond any surface grotesqueness. Jack Kerouac, Thomas Wolfe, Jack London, Emily Dickinson, and Sherwood Anderson were all part of my development, but it was Lawrence's insights and vision of the new American "consciousness" in *Studies in Classic American Literature* that shaped the way I view my country. Lawrence made me proud to be part of a nation that produced such homegrown revolutionary authors as Walt Whitman, Nathaniel Hawthorne, Edgar Allan Poe, and Herman Melville, and to really understand how they had liberated the American mind and soul from the repressive and spiritually bankrupt European order. No sentimentalist, Lawrence taught me also that "the essential American soul is hard, isolated, stoic, and a killer. It has never melted."

I went on to tell Beth how a transformative reading of Keith Sagar's masterful biography *The Life of D. H. Lawrence* made a pilgrimage to visit

Lawrence's beloved 160-acre Kiowa Ranch essential. There, fifteen miles north of Taos, his cremated remains lie in a mausoleum high up in the Sangre de Cristo Mountains, and his spirit resides. For it was there, in northern New Mexico, that Lawrence found spiritual solace after years of wandering. And that, I discovered, was what I had been desperately seeking in my midtwenties. In his essay "New Mexico," Lawrence wrote: "In the magnificent fierce morning of New Mexico one sprang awake, a new part of the soul woke up suddenly, and the old world gave way to the new."

I wanted to experience Lawrence's "magnificent fierce morning of New Mexico," to connect with my own country — a connection I was unable to make within the confines of the lounges, libraries, and lecture halls of academe. So I loaded up a brown Oldsmobile LTD for my second journey to New Mexico. I had moved beyond postcards of Billy the Kid. I spent weeks in Taos, lodging at the cheap adobe-faced Abominable Snow Mansion Skiers' Hostel. For ten dollars a night a guest obtained a dorm-style bunk, clean sheets, a view of Taos mountains, and his own personal key. Nearly every day for a month straight I drove down Route 150, past the blinking yellow crossroad light, to the village of Hondo Arroyo, which is situated near the entrance of Kit Carson National Forest, and parked my car in the gravel lot of a dilapidated grocery store. And nearly every day I would look at the snoring storekeeper slumped in an oak rocker, a *Field and Stream* magazine spread over his lap and his boots perched on the counter while katydids frolicked on his white muscle shirt. I'd hike the mile to the dirt-road entrance of the Kiowa Ranch and then climb five miles uphill. My only companions were the passing quail, elk, deer, wild turkeys, jackrabbits, and armies of flying ants. NO PIÑON PICKING signs dotted the trail. Finally, the wooden A-frame ranch house appeared, protected by a ramshackle white picket fence and a flock of waddling ducks quacking an alarm to the ranch's caretaker at the approach of an interloper.

Lawrence and his wife, Frieda, had lived at the ranch — a gift from the writer-collector Mabel Dodge Luhan — for twenty-two months during a three-year period between 1922 and 1925. From the house, I'd follow the serpentine trail up to the small white shedlike stucco mausoleum in which lies Lawrence's silver-plastered crypt surmounted by an eagle statue, the initials DHL carved on its front, the walls painted with sunflowers and elm leaves. Lawrence's ashes were mixed with the plaster, so the visitor is surrounded, so to speak, by the author. After paying homage to Lawrence, I'd sit outside and contemplate one of the most spectacular mesa views in the United States, the sweet smell of juniper filling my nostrils. Lawrence said of the spot: "It had a splendid silent terror, and a vast far-and-wide magnificence which made it way beyond mere aesthetic appreciation. Never is the light more pure and overwhelming than there, arching with a royalty almost cruel over a hollow, uptilted world. . . . Those that have spent morning after morning alone there pitched among the pines above the great proud world of desert will know, almost unbearably, how beautiful it is, how clear and unquestioned is the might of the day."

Now, recalling the earnestness and passion of my earlier journey, I became melancholy. At that sacred place high in the Sangre de Cristo Mountains eight years ago, I had put my life in order, deciding to forgo law school for the life of a historian, and to break up with my girlfriend and go it alone for a while. And now, as if that visit had occurred only yesterday, I was sitting in a chilly Taos rain, a history professor guiding my students back to the land that changed my life. I realized that as their lives were changing, they would need to choose their own directions. My students would have to find their own sacred moments and places. The scheduled sunrise visit to the Lawrence ranch was called off.

Slowly everyone staggered back to the bus, ready to call it an evening. We stopped three miles north of town at Taos Pueblo, home of the Taos-Tiwa Indians. The pueblo's distinguishing feature is its multistory apartment-like adobe architecture. We took a short walk around the village, which has existed in one form or another since 3000 B.C. and is closed to outsiders at night. Two scrawny light brown "old yeller" dogs accounted for the only activity. We examined the outdoor stepladders and admired the *horno* ovens, used for centuries to bake traditional loaves of bread. Had Columbus explored the "new" world in 1492, he would have found in Taos a complex, sophisticated culture. The traditional pueblo way of life has survived the centuries with only limited intrusions from modernity.

There is no electricity or plumbing, telephones are forbidden, and residents still collect water by bucket from the sacred Rio Pueblo, which flows from Blue Lake, a spiritual center for the tribe.

It was too wet for camping, so we headed down I-68 to find a cheap motel. This was one evening I needed the solitude, privacy, and comfort of my own room: Sleeping on the bus was not an option. We pulled into the Koshari Inn, a moderately priced run-of-the-mill motel now remodeled to resemble an old Western town. Half the students bunked on the bus while the others checked in, two to a room. I fell into my room and was asleep almost instantly.

My wake-up call came from the front desk at 6:30 A.M., and I had a hard time shaking the sleep out. Lori Beecher and Ellen Schaffer of "Good Morning America" were still determined to do a story on us, and my first project of the day was to find out the details. They had picked sunrise at the Grand Canyon, two days away, but wanted Matt (our in-house student video chronicler) and me to edit our three hours of already existing tape down to ten minutes at their Albuquerque ABC affiliate. A 4:00 P.M. appointment was arranged for that day, immediately following our rafting adventure. Looking forward to our fifteen minutes of fame, the students rushed to call home to tell parents and friends.

We boarded the bus and drove south on I-68, past greedy crows scavenging for a breakfast of mice and dead lizards. We found the Pilar Café, where three raft guides, trained in emergency medicine and river rescue, were to meet us. The rain had stopped and the weather forecast was for clear skies; it seemed like the perfect day for a river outing. We connected with the guides and followed their three frill-free Dodge vans, each pulling a trailer with a state-of-the-art blue-gray inflatable rubber raft strapped to the back, down a hidden road that led directly into Rio Grande State Park and Wild Recreation Area. We parked, and the guides' rain gear, orange life jackets, and oars were distributed. Even those of us who had rafted before hosted butterflies in our guts. Russell Dobson, the lead guide and owner of the company, with more than ten years of rafting experience, lectured us on safety. The precautions boiled down to the two fundamental rules of rafting: 1) Stay in your raft, and 2) if you fall, fall into the raft. Steering your raft through white water and around rocks was highly desirable but not necessary for safe passage; each vessel had a human guide in the rear, with double oars in stern-mount configuration, so little paddle maneuvering by us would be needed.

The river was high. Springtime temperatures had melted the mountain snows, and recent rains had contributed to the swell, but we were going to give the world-class Pilar Race Course a go anyway. Through the course the Rio Grande, occasionally no more than a muddy trickle, drops 425 vertical feet, alternating long stretches of quiet water (punctuated by foamy turbulence that would have us hanging on to the raft) with all the might the instinct for survival could muster. White water is rated on a scale of 1 to 6, 1 being calm and 6 being unrunnable. Pilar is graded 4—the venture was bound to get wet and wild.

Each student was given a raft assignment, and with a push from shore, off we went. Calm prevailed as the three rafts pirouetted the river, our guides barking instructions, trying to get us trained before we hit the heavy waters. Kenny and I chatted away about the beauty of the cottonwoods and other deciduous trees that punctuate the gaily patterned basalt and pumice cliffs and bluffs (which are being gutted as the jean companies mine the pumice to make stone-washed denim). Our guide pointed out two eagles mating and a handful of sandpipers strutting their stuff on the sandy bank, and he explained the prehistoric geography as we floated down the mythic American river. A large monarch butterfly landed on the prow, a living hood ornament. The group's jitters evaporated and, Zen-like, we felt at one with the river. We glided through the tall, rugged cliffs of Pilar Canyon and pulled next to a polished rock shallow to stretch out for a few minutes and pick wild grapes. Then the rapids came in quick, choppy, consecutive fashion, ten minutes of calm between each whitewater shoot. The farther downriver we went, the rougher the water. Albert Falls was our get-wet initiation as the ice-cold Rio splashed us out of Zen mode. After we survived that bit of rapids, the rest was easy. We threaded through the slit of the Eye-of-the-Needle and rode the Narrows and Big Rock with rodeo aplomb. Between shoots we engaged in oar wars, the objective to drench enemy rafters into a state of supreme wetness. Hours evaporated in what seemed to be minutes as we laughed and played on the Rio Grande, in awe of the massive rock pillars that towered over us. And then Godzilla was upon us, the mother of Rio rapids. My raft was the last to encounter Godzilla, so we had the unenviable opportunity to watch the others bob and weave, tossed like helpless corks in the maelstrom. As we neared the falls I had a sensation not unlike the one you get when the chain pulls the roller coaster uphill. Suddenly we were flying down Godzilla as huge waves slapped us again and again, nearly knocking two of us out of the raft. Just as suddenly, we were out of the turbulence, sopping and numb, but safe in a pool of river calm.

Frank had driven the Majic Bus downriver and was parked along the river, videocam in hand, to record the end of our epic journey—if not for posterity, at least for parents. We shored the rafts next to a picnic table spread with sodas, fruit, baked goods, and bagged snacks provided by the rafting company. There were primitive locker rooms for changing at the site, so we could snack in warm, dry clothes. While we munched, Frank pulled me aside. When he had retrieved his 800-number phone messages, he interpreted a disjointed call from Alan's mother as an emergency (Alan had told Frank his father was ill and that he might have to fly home at a moment's notice)—wrongly, as it would turn out. But it was up to me to relay to Alan that his father had taken a turn for the worse. Alan decided he would catch the next plane out of Albuquerque to New York, to be with his dad.

Outwardly dry, chilled to the bone from the river and now from our compatriot's crisis, we headed somberly to Albuquerque. Alison, Janine, Beth, and I sat on the porch, trying to comfort Alan. We promised to scream "Get well!" to his father on "Good Morning America," and to stay in touch from the road. I had unthinkingly chosen a melancholy Kate Wolf cassette to play and we all sat morosely and mournfully staring out the window, brooding about Alan's family crisis. When Wolf sang a chilling, sorrowful ode about "never knowing her father" until he died, Janine grew miffed at my insensitivity and accused me of taking mood music a step too far. As soon as we got back on a main road, Frank pulled off at a gas station so Alan could call home. From the minimarket where Jay and I were buying a bag of chips we heard a loud, happy yelp. Alan's father was on the phone, reprimanding his son for failing to call home for three days. Mr. Mindel was worried about whether Alan had made plane reservations to come back to New York for the Passover holiday. Alan was giggling uncontrollably, thrilled and relieved to find an angry, overprotective father on the other end of the receiver. Alan got off the phone a changed young man, nonjudgmental, and thankful that his father was alive. (Sadly, Alan's father was to die that August.)

Embarrassed by the consequences of the misunderstood message, Frank apologized profusely, and all was forgiven. We now were traveling through the Cerrillos Hills, where, centuries before the Spaniards, Indians had mined for turquoise, as they still do today. The scenic Turquoise Trail goes through dilapidated ghost towns with wooden barns and rickety corrals, and through village after village of tin-roofed and painted adobe houses, always clustered around a miniplaza and church. In Golden, site of the first gold rush west of the Mississippi (1825), we realized we were way behind schedule, so we cut over to I-25 in an attempt to make up some time. In a state of perpetual disrepair, I-25 was lined with traffic, and Frank did his best to thread through the road construction obstacles. When we finally hit Albuquerque, Matt, Frank, Jared, and I were an hour late for our appointment to edit American Odyssey highlights for "Good Morning America." The rest of the group were free to discover Albuquerque on their own.

Straddling the Rio Grande and cradled in the west by the ten-thousand-foot-high Sandia (Spanish for "watermelon") Mountains, half-Anglo, half-Hispanic, Albuquerque is a city of firm, handshaking hospitality and a perfect year-round climate. Albuquerque's downtown has been spruced up a bit in recent years but not overgentrified and homogenized like that of Santa Fe. A trip down Central Avenue, the local alias for a chunk of the famed Route 66—"the Mother Road," as John Steinbeck called the highway running from Chicago to Los Angeles—reveals that one can still get one's kicks, a newly pressed shirt, rosary beads, a potted cactus, and enough food to fill the belly for two days, all for five bucks.

303

The first sign that Albuquerque might be a poor man's paradise starts with Central Avenue, where the parking meters have been ripped out and only the rusting gray poles and relentless sidewalk-dwelling weeds remain. I interpret this as a sign of rejuvenation, not decline, evidence that Albuquerque has abandoned trying to fill its coffers coin by coin, by taxing parking. Besides, free parking helps downtown merchants compete with the edge-city shopping malls and discount stores. And indeed, small, privately owned businesses are standing tall, unflinchingly determined and proud, in Albuquerque, confident they will survive the recession by selling products for a fair price.

Take, for example, Simon's Uniform and Western Wear Store on Central Avenue, where since 1932 they have been outfitting the Albuquerque, Santa Fe, Zuni, and Navajo police, not to mention the State Highway Patrol, among various other law enforcement agencies. Find out for yourself the eternal truth of Justice Oliver Wendell Holmes's observation: "You know you are getting old when the policemen start to look like children." Wander into Simon's store on an afternoon when a fresh batch of peach-fuzz police academy graduates is groping through the merchandise, buying up the various components that make up cop haute couture. They select their shiny black seventy-five-dollar Justin Roper boots with the same boyish awe that comes from being outfitted with your first Little League uniform. John Montoya, the jolly and unassuming owner for more than twenty-five years, has seen the law-enforcement customers come and go. Astute state businessman that he is, John wants them all to return, so he prominently displays the book *The Tactical Edge: Surviving High-Risk Patrol*, in hopes of keeping his clientele alive. He runs an operation strictly for professionals and refuses to serve the soldier-of-fortune crowd that buys paramilitary equipment and hunting gear to be properly attired for blowing away backyard squirrels with bazookas.

Those folks have to walk a block down Central to the Gismo Store, where khaki fatigues, Vietnam ammo supply boxes, and hundreds of army surplus products are sold to armchair soldiers and has-been rent-a-cops. From Gismo's ceiling hangs a large black flag bearing a grinning white skull wearing a green army field hat, atop two ominous M-16 semiautomatic assault rifles substituting for the traditional crossbones. The flag's motto reads: U.S. MARINES: MESS WITH THE BEST, DIE LIKE THE REST. If visitors feel the need for an antidote to this flood of testosterone, they can simply cross the street to Garson and Sons—whose sign features a blue cross, chalice, and host—to find air-conditioned serenity. They've been selling religious articles to largely Catholic Albuquerque since Pope John Paul II was just a baby in Warsaw. Crucifixes come in any model and size, from one inch to six feet, from fifty cents for a portable aluminum version for the poor man's pocket to a thousand-dollar hand-carved marble rendition. The hot items of 1992 were the crucifix bird feeders, the twenty-five-dollar framed picture of the pope, and the Nintendo-compatible "Bible Adventures," advertised as "the first video game to revolutionize Bible Study for the Next Generation." Because of an expansion of the Christmas section, the departing visitor is exhorted by a sign reading: PEACE IS NOT A SEASON . . . IT IS A WAY OF LIFE. In other words, buy tree ornaments year-round.

If you're short on time and able to visit only one downtown institution, the choice is easy: the Man's Hat Shop. Since 1946 they've been hatters to real ranchers, wranglers, rodeo stars, and just plain folks—that is, to a clientele that knows cows from cattle. The store stocks more than four thousand hats, priced from ninety to five hundred dollars. The major Western hat brands include Resistol Hat Company of Garland, Texas, which took over the world-renowned-but-bankrupt Stetson Hat Company a few years back. These companies' "combined cowboy punch" dominates the Western hat market, relegating the American Hat Company and Bailey, Inc., to a distant second and third. The problem is finding the hat that fits both your head and personality. Want the Dwight Yoakam look? Then go for the Resistol "Quarter Horse," made a beaver buckskin with a horsehair band. If Charlie Daniels is your druthers, then the black Resistol 5X beaver "Bullrider" should be your topper. Are you more conservative? Then order the Stetson 4X Beaver "Open Road," which has been seen atop influential heads from the Alamo to the White House, or the Stetson 4X Beaver "Rancher," advertised as "fine headgear for the western gentleman." If you're still uncertain, ask owner Stuart Dunlap, who personally designed, fit, and creased the Resistol 5X Beaver "Cattleman" hats for all eight Marlboro Men, achieving for them all a consistent lean-mean-but-honest John Wayne look. More recently, he designed the "Old Buckaroo" Tom Mix—style hat Arlo Guthrie sports on his fine new *Ropin' the Wind* album. Arlo, you see, has a serious hat fetish and buys his toppers only from the Man's Hat Shop—at least that's what Arlo scribbled on the autographed picture that hangs behind the counter.

Has all this shopping gotten you hungry? On Central Avenue the Chili Tree offers a humongous *carne* chimichanga and a side bowl of red-and-green chili that will burn your belly but not your wallet. Or upscale it a notch, and try the famed red chili sauce that tops the enchiladas and burritos at the forty-eight-seat Duran Central Pharmacy, where "the pilli meets chili." Or head on over to Second Street and burn your brains out on the free "killer salsa" at M&J's Sanitary Tortilla Factory, or go farther down the road and get take-out tamales, carnitas, or stuffed sopaipillas at El Modelo Mexican Foods and eat them in the shade of Crossroads Park next to a snappy wall painting of hanging red peppers that reads: NUEVA MEXICO—SÍ. Or sit in the sun by the giant, slightly tarnished, brown-yellow-purple-and-red Alexander Calder—ish sculpture. Chile peppers, you see, are New Mexico's drug of choice. They turn an ordinary, bland meal into an event; they are rich in vitamin C and have more carotene than carrots; and, most important, they are brimful of capsaicin, a natural chemical that ignites the tongue and triggers the brain to release a nice little stream of endorphins—the body's natural painkiller—a runner's high without the torn ligaments.

Is your mouth on fire? Have a cold *cerveza* at Jasie's El Amigo, where the gasping air conditioner and strings of dancing white tree lights contribute to alleviating a dusty throat and a burning tongue. Or mosey on down to the El Rey, where those with marinated livers swirl cheap bourbon and listen to George Jones and Hank Williams howl away their lonesome sorrows on an old-time country jukebox that plays for quarters or a swift kick.

306

If specialty coffees and baked goods are your thing, then drive east on Central, past all the remnants of the old Route 66 auto-repair shops; past the Sunshine Musical Hall, where the Desert Chorale performs; past the beautifully landscaped University of New Mexico and the all-night Frontier Restaurant, a *huevos rancheros* meeting place for students and ordinary folk alike; past the American Wildlife Taxidermy Shop and the Comic Book Warehouse; and past the old Lobo Theater and a dozen or so ranch-style motels with names like the Sand and Sage, Tewa Lodge, the Aztec, and the Motor Highway House, all advertising cut rates and the comfort of sleeping in an "American-owned" bed with a well-worn Gideon's Bible in the desk drawer. And then at last you'll find yourself in Nob Hill, home of great bookstores and the Double Rainbow Coffee House. Get an espresso jolt of the local roasted piñon coffee, with its distinctive nutty flavor and long-term side effects, and realize it's a hell of a thing.

Now, you may be saying at this point, "Sure, Albuquerque has delicious, reasonably priced food and drinks, but does it have the artistic flair of Santa Fe?" The answer is a resounding yes! Forget about the Santa Fe Opera. (What kind of fool wants to see *Don Giovanni* or *Der Rosenkavalier* in the desert?) Albuquerque offers the KiMo Theatre, Central Avenue's art deco pueblo picture palace—a true architectural and entertainment landmark—built in 1927 by Oreste Bacheci, a successful dry-goods merchant who left Italy for Albuquerque in 1885 with his architect friend Carl Boller. Their dream motion-picture theater eschewed then-fashionable Moorish and Chinese motifs for a building that is distinctively Southwestern.

Boller combed the pueblos of Acoma, Isleta, Cibola, and the Navajo Nation in search of ideas, symbols, and artifacts for the interior. The plaster ceiling beams are textured to look like logs and painted with dance and hunt scenes, and the air vents are disguised as Navajo rugs. The crowning achievement was the inspired commissioning of Carl von Hassler, a Russian-born artist from New York's Ash Can School, to paint seven murals depicting the cobalt blue sky and peaceful pueblos of New Mexico. Standing in the empty 725-seat auditorium and taking in von Hassler's murals, which have survived both fire and boiler explosions, one can imagine the Albuquerque of sixty years ago, when the KiMo first opened. Movies were ten cents, Calvin Coolidge was president, townspeople used horses for transportation, and the bandit legend of New Mexico's archenemy Pancho Villa was still fresh and growing. The imaginative visitor may be able to hear Frances Farney on the metallic-pitched, footstomping Wurlitzer organ. For years Farney held her audiences spellbound before, during, and after the main features, from *Painting the Town Red* to the first musical, *Melody of Broadway*. She loved to pound away for visiting Hollywood royalty like Gloria Swanson, Tom Mix, and Ginger Rogers when they visited the KiMo. The KiMo doesn't show movies anymore, and Frances Farney is long dead, but her legacy still lives on, for Farney was a kindly woman who once offered the motherly advice, "You can be anything you want to be, honey," to an eager young usher named Vivian Vance. Taking these words to heart, the ambitious high-schooler left New Mexico to audition for acting jobs on Hollywood's back lots. Frances Farney never lived to hear the laughter Vivian Vance inspired as Lucille Ball's sidekick in "I Love Lucy," the universally loved television sitcom. Vance is now dead too—but her electronic ghost lives on in black-and-white particles in your television set today. No one can predict accurately when it will appear, but if you flip through fifty-seven cable channels long enough, I promise that Vance's hallowed ghost will come to you, right there in your own home, hotel, or office. And through her protégée, the sound of Frances Farney and her Wurlitzer echo through time.

We walked into the KOAT Action 7 newsroom in Albuquerque and were greeted by flickering televisions tuned to the Geraldo Rivera show. The Channel 7 producer welcomed us by saying they were too busy preparing the six o'clock news to be of any assistance, but he had reserved an editing room in which we could work. The prospect of no help made me anxious, but without reason, for Matt knew how to operate all the equipment. We started transferring selected highlights onto a videocassette. The process was more time consuming than we had expected. At 6:30 P.M. an engineer warned us that Federal Express closed at 7:00, and it took a good fifteen minutes to get to the office. He called us a taxi while we hurried through the remaining tape to make sure we had included some Rio Grande rafting. At 6:50 Jared and I sprinted to the waiting taxi. When we explained our desperate plight to the driver and how we *had* to get our film to "Good Morning America," he put the pedal to the metal and shot off like a crazed car thief with the police in hot pursuit, running every red light and stop sign we passed. Our driver relished the challenge of this renegade ride. Clutching the car doors so we wouldn't be slammed around, Jared and I exchanged frightened "this-guy's-nuts" looks and in an expression of mutual terror that might have been choreographed, we cried in unison, "Holy shit!" This spontaneous explosion of unanimity provoked hysterical laughter from the driver as he simultaneously flipped the finger to some law-abiding brave soul who dared to honk as we flew over a dip in the road. We arrived at Federal Express in one piece and with three minutes to spare. I rushed to the office, filled out the airbill, and then dropped the pen in victorious relief. The driver, who had waited outside, now calmly transported us to the Hotel La Posada de Albuquerque, Conrad Hilton's first hotel in his native state and our group's designated meeting spot.

Parched from our mad dash, Jared and I sat in the hotel bar and drank Pepsi after Pepsi, recounting the episode in hair-raising detail to the others as they trailed in. After an hour we were able to laugh off our harrowing taxi ride and anticipate, excitedly, the Grand Canyon trip and "Good Morning America" taping, which would take place in two days.

To obtain directions to I-40, I dashed into the 66 Diner, a former transmission shop turned into a 1950s-style burger-shake hangout, complete on this particular evening with a parking lot full of desert low riders — customized vintage classics such as eight-cylinder Buicks, Ford LTDs, and Chevy Impalas refitted with plush interiors and hydraulic suspension systems. I asked a car owner attired in a Peyton Hot Dog bowling shirt for help. My targeted helper, it turned out, was a former pitcher for the Albuquerque Dukes, the city's Triple-A farm team of the Los Angeles Dodgers. My request prompted unsolicited accounts of what good buddies he was with Orel Hershiser. It took five minutes of Orel-and-me this and Orel-and-me that, but I finally got directions and dashed out.

We found I-40 and were on our way to Gallup, where we would veer south to the Zuni Indian Reservation. There were thunder and lightning in the distance as we passed the uranium mines of Grants. The smells of a new summer and a day's end mingled in the air as giant raindrops splashed down from the tearing western sky. This lava-rock area is the New Mexican badlands, or *malpais* (Spanish for "bad country"), and wherever one looks, high bluffs rise up in the distance. By the time we crossed over the Continental Divide near Thoreau, the rain had stopped. Most of the students were weary from our day of white-water rafting, and sporadic chatter floated over the silence of exhaustion.

Miles Davis's "Sketches from Spain" filled the bus with a contemplative, soothing rhythm, and we achieved a collective meditative moment as Miles's trumpet slowly summoned us off to sleep. By the time we reached Gallup—called "the Indian Capital of the United States" because the town is surrounded by the Navajo Reservation, the largest in the United States—only Frank, Beth, and I were still awake. We had stopped at a Dunkin' Donuts to fill Frank's thermos, and Beth had gone along to buy a few bran muffins. I stayed on the porch reading, by flashlight, *The Dark Wind*, a mystery novel by Albuquerque-based author Tony Hillerman. Suddenly two of Gallup's men in blue had boarded the bus and were reconnoitering with their high-powered searchlights.

"What are you doing?" asked one as he raked the aisle, looking for I-don't-know-what.

"Reading a book and waiting for the driver to come back from getting coffee," I responded in what I hoped was a respectful tone.

"Why are you in Gallup?" the other asked, his beam now blinding me.

"So the driver can fill his thermos with coffee," I replied, squinting.

"Oh, I see," he said. As he shut off his flashlight I could see his face for the first time; he was a simulacrum of Freddie Prinze—the star of the TV sitcom "Chico and the Man."

"So you like Tony Hillerman?" Freddie's look-alike queried.

"Sure, I guess," I equivocated, not wishing to venture what might be a controversial opinion.

"His daughter used to date my son," he said.

"Is that so?" I replied with studied neutrality.

"Yeah, he's a good guy. Where are you coming from?"

"Albuquerque."

"What did you do there?"

"Went to Channel Seven to send a film of our bus trip across the United States to 'Good Morning America' in New York."

" 'Good Morning America'!" he repeated, astounded. I saw from his face that I had gone in an instant from potential drug runner to television celebrity. "I watch that every morning. Joan Lunden is my favorite."

"Well, we'll be on this Friday, live from the Grand Canyon."

"Oh, wow! I won't miss it!" he burbled, adding in his official chamber-of-commerce voice, "Now y'all drive safe and enjoy the rest of your stay here in New Mexico, and tell Joan that the Gallup police love her." We shook hands, and they returned to their patrol car.

Then, to cement my celebrity, I shouted at the retreating figures, "Hey, do you guys know John Montoya of Simon's Uniform and Western Wear Shop on Central Avenue?"

"John Montoya! You know John Montoya? This uniform—the one I'm wearing—I bought it from John Montoya," he gushed.

"Sure. He's a good friend of mine," I puffed (taking a cue from Orel Hershiser's good buddy).

"Hey, sorry we hassled you earlier. No hard feelings?"

"No hard feelings," I assured him with magnanimity.

Gallup was still safe from the unsavory.

When Frank and Beth returned I told them of the encounter, but they seemed more interested in their muffins than my story. Disappointed that nobody cared, I punched my foam pillow into the corner by the icebox, cracked my dirty toes and sore ankles, slid into my down sleeping bag, and fell into a restless sleep, closing yet another chapter in the American Odyssey.

13

Fifteen Minutes of Fame, Route 66, and the Grand Canyon

66 is the path of a people in flight, refugees from dust and shrinking land, from the thunder of tractors and shrinking ownership, from the desert's slow northward invasion, from the twisting winds that howl up out of Texas, from the floods that bring no richness to the land and steal what little richness is there. From all of these the people are in flight, and they come into 66 from the tributary side roads, from the wagon tracks and the rutted country roads. 66 is the mother road, the road of flight.

—JOHN STEINBECK

GALLUP, NEW MEXICO, BELONGS ON MOTHER TERESA'S TOP-ten list of godforsaken places of the world, right up there with Calcutta, Frank told me as we were pulling out of town—which looked to me like just another motel row. A "drunk city," Frank continued, a real dangerous downer because early on any given morning you could see the crowds of desperate alcoholics waiting for the bars to open, working themselves up to drinking away the day and the long desert night. At 2:00 A.M., when the bars went dark for a few brief hours, they made the "dreary march" home to snatch a few hours' sleep, to be refreshed, so to speak, for to-morrow's oblivion. Whenever Frank was in Gallup—which during his trucking days had been quite often—he was overcome with gratitude at how lucky he himself had been in avoiding a similar fate. As he drained

312

the coffee from his thermos and contemplated his good fortune, the students asleep peacefully in the back, Frank also thanked his lucky stars for the blessing of a wife who understood his wanderlust and tolerated his peripatetic livelihood showing people the United States, thumbing his nose at the false idol of security. It was in this mood of supreme gratitude that Frank prevailed on me to forgo our planned route, Highway 53 through the Zuni Reservation and its turquoise jewelry and silversmith shops, and roadrunner it across I-40—formerly a leg of the now-nonexistent Route 66—all night to surprise our charges with the glory of sunrise at the south rim of Grand Canyon.

Frank had motored the Gallup-to-Flagstaff superslab during both its Route 66 and now I-40 days many times before, in his trucker incarnation, and never tired of the harsh, timeless quality of the northern Arizona landscape. This was Zane Grey country, the land of the romantic Western, in which the hero, always triumphant, rides through purple sage into a scarlet sunset, his tough-but-tender sweetheart perched on the back of his saddle. Frank was one of 150 million readers who have purchased and absorbed Grey's Western vision of cowboy life and culture where men have dignity and are self-reliant and justice always prevails. Driving his herd of students through the night, properly attired for the part in Stetson hat and leather cowboy boots, Frank saw himself as the embodiment of a Zane Grey hero, pushing through the flattened high-desert landscape, his mind bursting at the seams with memories, and memories of memories, of his own life, of fistfights, lost fortunes, love gone bad, and death, always death. He was unafraid of dying; it was from rusting away in suburbia that he wanted to escape, preferring to go up in flames like Casey Jones, with one hand on the brake, the other on the whistle. He said he liked driving this stretch of highway at night, when most of his fellow travelers were escape artists like himself—escaping the sun, if nothing else.

At this late hour our uprooted travel buddies seemed like kindred spirits of the midnight moon and the highway line—long-haired guys with sleeping bags Bungee-corded to the backs of their bikes; the brand-new green Chevy Blazer with California tags and a BRING HOME THE POW'S AND MIA'S bumper sticker; the orange-and-silver U-Haul trucks that promise

MORE FOR YOUR MONEY; the big, gas-guzzling Cadillac with chrome tail fins headed for a swap meet in Barstow, California; the DRINK DR. PEPPER truck on a mission to deliver refrigerated soda to soothe the raw throats of opening-day gamblers at the Hollywood racetrack; a pregnant-looking cement truck from Phoenix on its way to pave yet another piece of poor, carved-up Arizona; the pickup trucks pulling trailers of terrified almond-eyed horses, hoofing on the floorboards for freedom and dreaming of the fields of wild oats they left behind in Iowa or Nebraska; the recession-rate Greyhound Bus passengers, most asleep now, but the tips of a few cigarettes glowing like red beacons in the back; the two teenagers escaping the isolation, lassitude, and entrapment of their provincial hometown for a mad, sweaty dash to a cheap tourist motel in the Painted Desert for a moment of passion; the earnest Midwestern station wagons of Grand Canyon—bound moms and dads, grateful the backseat kids were finally asleep, and confident that by sneaking through the desert during the wee morning hours the radiator wouldn't overheat; and with the continual procession, the never-ending procession, of eighteen-wheel semis anxious to dump their loads in Riverside or San Bernardino or Los Angeles, inhale a tenderized T-bone at a Sizzler, and grab $24.95 worth of air-conditioned motel sleep before heading back in the other direction on I-40, to reconnect with their Oklahoma or Missouri wives and put another Band-Aid on their bruised, tired marriages. The romance of the old Route 66 always had a westward vector toward California's orange blossoms; traveling west to east held no allure. Indeed, architect Frank Lloyd Wright viewed Route 66 as "a giant chute down which everything loose in the country is sliding into southern California."

As we crossed the New Mexico—Arizona border, Frank's Route 66 memory bank opened as we passed the fifty-foot tepee of the Tomahawk Indian Store and its FREE ICE FOR YOUR JUGS sign. Frank reminisced about the old days when I-40 was Route 66. Time and again he would fall for those LAST CHANCE FOR GAS signs when three other filling stations sat just down the highway, or be suckered by the billboards puffing 50 PERCENT OFF AT WINSLOW'S STORE FOR MEN, where he inevitably purchased a new bolero tie and cheap white tube socks. These roadside merchants knew how to capitalize on the uncertainty of the desert. Over the years Frank had also amassed a collection of Route 66 trinkets—rubber tomahawks and pottery ashtrays and petrified-wood key chains—at tourist traps, now relocated to I-40, like Geronimo's Apache Trading Post and the Jack Rabbit Store, involuntarily drawn by their billboard come-ons: PET A LIVE BUFFALO, TOUCH A TWO-HEADED RATTLESNAKE, SEE 250-MILLION-YEAR-OLD DINOSAUR SKULL. It was a source of solace to Frank and me, as we sped through northern Arizona on this particularly cool evening, that some aspects of the old Route 66 survive—beyond mere consumerism—in the desert hucksters who prey on uncertainty and curiosity and wanderlust simultaneously. Frank had left a part of himself behind with each tongue-in-cheek postcard and peace pipe purchased during his fifteen years of travel. Geronimo's Apache Trading Post and the Wig-Wam Teepee Lodge were his friends, survivors like himself. Women had come and gone, tomorrow was never what it was supposed to be, but it was all worth the effort as long as Frank could connect once or twice a year with these desert trading posts. He tapped into these embracing symbols of wanderlust that energized his own need to keep on truckin' to his own diesel beat. They had the same restorative effect as listening to Otis Redding on a rainy Chicago night.

Frank shifted the Majic Bus into fourth gear and accelerated down the dark, straight night road. With student interruptions momentarily quelled, he could now make a little time. Driving on a night like this, we could feel the vastness of America—this continent under our wheels—and smell the asphalt of the open road we lived for, literally and spiritually. Our mood was temporarily broken when Frank was forced to slow down at the Arizona Agricultural Inspection Station, just as the Joad family and their fellow Okies in *The Grapes of Wrath* had to. We solemnly assured the authorities that the Majic Bus was transporting no produce, plants, or perishables—in other words, no fruit flies. In an error of judgment he has never since repeated, Frank once joked to an inspector that the only "perishable" on his truck was the water bottle labeled APACHE TEARS he had purchased in Gallup, and he was made to pull over while they searched his entire rig.

315

To pass the time Frank hummed to himself, mainly Woody Guthrie ballads and Pete Seeger folksongs, and crooned the words to Little Feat's "Willing." As he warmed to his vocalizing, he ratcheted up to outright singing, still to himself, and his repertoire expanded to Bobby Troup's bluesy "Get Your Kicks on Route 66." Over the years Frank had accumulated various renditions of the 1946 pop hit, rescued from Long Island garage sales and thrift shops, and he liked to play them—snaps, crackles, pops, and all—on his portable plastic phonograph. Frank had also acquired the "root sixty-six" rendering of the Rolling Stones and Chuck Berry, but it was Nat ("King") Cole's version that gave him goose bumps. Cole's ice-smooth voice somehow put his life in focus. Unable to leave well enough alone, Frank began digging through the cassette box for an old Asleep at the Wheel tape, with their own personalized Texas swing version, but then he abandoned the impulse—we didn't need studio music; our mood was too sober. Every so often we would pass a forlorn Western windmill, and Frank commented that he wished the rusted hulk could blow all his unpaid bills and debts away into the clear, stardust sky. He mused about pulling off in Holbrook to buy a flamboyant Hopi kachina doll or a Zuni necklace with semiprecious stones for his daughter, but the Grand Canyon at sunrise took precedent. He would get her a Donald Duck souvenior from Southern California. As he sliced through the lunar beauty of the Painted Desert's windswept plains, mesas, isolated buttes, and barren valleys, he thought about exiting and parking for the evening so the students could see this one-of-a-kind stone forest, officially known as the Petrified Forest National Park, in the morning. But Frank was goal oriented, and he knew he had to press on.

A Sante Fe Railroad freight train paralleling I-40 was chugging neck and neck with the Majic Bus, and Frank began an imaginary race with the engineer. For five miles it was an even heat. Every time the train whistle moaned in the cool desert night, Frank responded note for note, the New York nasal horn in comic harmony with that of his brother-in-arms. Frank's roadrunner duet awoke some of the students, who cursed sleepily at Frank's idea of musicality. The tracks eventually tilted southward, and Frank watched the train disappear over the horizon, an iron horse acting out the Charlie Chaplin fantasy of receding down the darkening road of the great American night.

Just west of Holbrook, the twin cement stacks and blinking red lights of the Cholla Power Plant towered above the interstate, part of Arizona Public Service's answer to keeping the juice flowing into the large desert cities of Phoenix and Tucson. That some kid could plug his Fender guitar into a basement amp in Tempe or Mesa for a jolt of rock-and-roll juice from this intrusive eyesore bothered Frank. Wouldn't it be great if windmills—or wind turbines, as their builders now call them—could relegate the Cholla to the dustbin of industrial irrelevance, perhaps to be converted into a giant group den in which coyotes could nurse their pups. If wind turbines became a reality, Frank pondered, then a twenty-first-century Zane Grey imitator, penning pulp Westerns, would have his space-suited cowboy hero shooting at the new computerized machines, longing for the good old Cholla Power Plant days. The times forever change, but nothing is forever extinguished.

The longer Frank stared down I-40, the more he realized that nearly all the roadside attractions of fifteen years ago were now dust in the wind, dried-up tumbleweed landmarks of a period in his life when time stood still: an abandoned white stucco building, the headlights just catching the words SINCLAIR GAS: 60¢ A GALLON on top of a smashed green neon dinosaur logo; a boarded-up Arizona Indian Popsicle stand overrun by barrel cactus and smoke trees; the Mormon town of Joseph City, no longer offering conversion hospitality to motorists but highway-patrol speeding tickets; the waterless Manilla and Cottonwood washes poised in anticipation of flash floods that no longer come; and the Little Colorado River, the trickle of whose usual springtime torrent might may soon cause it to be redesignated a creek. As he approached Winslow, Frank once again began singing to himself as I tried to sleep, this time the celebrated Eagles song "Take It Easy," which immortalizes this old Route 66 town in one of its verses. Frank could relate to the phrase about having "seven women on his mind," but found "it's a girl, my lord, in a flatbed Ford, slowing down to take a look at me" preposterous. Men were everywhere; women didn't need to pick them up on the road.

Bypassing Winslow, Frank decided he would stretch twenty miles down the road to Astronaut Park, dedicated to Americans who have died in the exploration of space. Besides clean rest rooms, the park had the additional fringe benefit of overlooking a meteor crater 570 feet deep and three miles in circumference. Advertised as "this planet's most penetrating natural attraction," the crater was created twenty-two thousand years ago by a wayward nickel-iron meteor. We got out, walked to the crater edge, and listened to the stillness. Back by the bus were metal picnic tables, some scrub trees and cacti, and a framed stainless-steel plaque quoting Ronald Reagan: THE FUTURE DOESN'T BELONG TO THE FAINTHEARTED, IT BELONGS TO THE BRAVE! Frank liked this "Death Valley Days" lingo and copied it into his log book for possible inclusion in a Majic Bus promotional calendar he was working on. It was now 3:30 A.M. He would have to step on it if he was to deliver his human cargo to the Grand Canyon for the 5:30 sunrise.

For a time Frank sort of tuned out, just as local television broadcasts do around this time of night, when the emergency test comes on, and I caught a brief stretch of sleep. It wasn't until he entered the piny woods of Coconino National Forest and Winona, the town nearest Flagstaff, that he snapped to, singing "Get your kicks on Route 66" once again and laughing out loud at the throwaway line, "Don't forget Winona." As he passed the rows of modest, shingleless, sun-warped aluminum ranch houses, broken-down Pontiacs and Buicks decorating the front lawns, Frank tried to imagine life in Winona, but all his sleepless mind could conjure up was crackling radios, snowy TVs, piles of old *National Geographic*s, and all sorts of accumulated junk. Stacking this rather bleak version of Winona against his New York life, Frank thought the scenario not so bad and toyed briefly with maybe someday retiring in Winona. Then he thought of the 110-degree heat and the fast-approaching "Great Drought" and switched his mental retirement channel to a log cabin in the Smoky Mountains of Tennessee.

Soon the San Francisco peaks rose out of the flat landscape in front of us, barely visible in the morning darkness. Banks of frozen snow covered both sides of the road as we followed a parade of dense pine trees into Flagstaff, the seat of Coconino County, whose area is twice that of Massachusetts. A brochure we had picked up in Gallup claimed Flagstaff as the "home of planet Pluto," because astronomers at the local Lowell Observatory discovered it with their telescopes in 1930. Frank had impossible hopes of finding Pluto with his own small telescope in the crystalline, starry sky, but—remembering he was in a race with the sun—drove on.

From Flagstaff, Frank took U.S. 180 north through the Kaibab National Forest and the blue-tinted, snow-capped San Francisco mountains, one of which is the highest point in Arizona. There was little traffic, and Frank was now confident we would make sunrise. After that we would camp for two nights and enjoy Grand Canyon National Park. I used the last leg of our night dash fumbling through some guidebooks, refreshing my knowledge of America's most renowned natural treasure.

The Grand Canyon is a chasm cutting deeply into a mountainous region called the Kaibab Plateau. Its first fully documented exploration did not occur until 1869, when an energetic and determined one-armed Civil War veteran, John Wesley Powell, led nine men with four boats in a daring expedition. Starting in Wyoming on the Green River, Powell's party made its way down to the Colorado River, then downriver to Glen Canyon and the Grand Canyon. Undeterred by losing three men and one boat, Powell's party covered more than a thousand miles of river in just ninety-eight days. Powell took a second journey in 1871 and published an account of this trip, *The Exploration of the Colorado River of the West*, which encouraged many travelers to explore for themselves the world's most spectacular example of the power of erosion.

Grand Canyon tourism began to boom in 1901 with the completion of the Santa Fe Railroad. The three-hour train trip from Williams, Arizona, was a major improvement over the bumpy eleven-hour stagecoach ride from Flagstaff. Grand Canyon Village was developed shortly thereafter, led by the Fred Harvey Company, which opened El Tovar Hotel in 1905.

In 1908, under the authority of a statute for the preservation of American antiquities, Theodore Roosevelt declared the Grand Canyon a national monument. A supportive visitor, Roosevelt urged leaving the Grand Canyon "as it is. You cannot improve upon it. The ages have been at work upon it, and man can only mar it." The sentiment to conserve was ratified in 1919 by legislation creating Grand Canyon National Park, signed by President Woodrow Wilson. In 1979 it was named a World Heritage Site, joining Victoria Falls in Zimbabwe, the Great Barrier Reef (off the coast of Australia), and other distinguished natural and cultural sites considered invaluable to all humanity. I was anxious with jangled excitement at the prospects of the student response and was grateful for Frank's heroic race with the sun.

As the Majic Bus entered the south entrance of the park through a forest of yellow pine and ponderosa, it was still dark. Four mule deer were faintly visible as they feasted on shrubs and grasses. We parked in front of Bright Angel Lodge, a log-and-native-stone structure designed by architect Mary Jane Colter. Opened in 1935, the lodge, with its environmentally sensitive, pioneer-style construction, has been called Colter's "ultimate Grand Canyon achievement."

With the engine off, the only sounds piercing the silence were the raucous caws of what must have been at least fifty shiny black ravens swooping overhead, hunting for abandoned french fries or small rodents. Matt shouted everyone awake. It was 5:30 A.M., and we were at the Grand Canyon in time for sunrise. Slowly the realization that Frank had driven all night long to get us here on time rippled through the yawning passengers. There was a real nip in what was still the night air, and we scrambled to find jackets, sweaters, and sweatshirts. Darlene, Kenny, and Matt were the first out, dashing into the lodge perched at the edge of the canyon to use the rest rooms and purchase cans of Fanta orange soda from a machine, to kill their morning breath. Then we all trailed out the lodge's back door to walk the fifty yards to Lookout Studio. The sun was just barely peeking out, and beholding the Grand Canyon brought "Oh, my

God!" to everyone's lips, with Dan winning the prize for saying it the most. Everyone jockeyed for position for the most dazzling panorama, as the sun began painting the hues of the canyon walls. Guidebook hype had prepared none of the students for the canyon's beauty and its kaleidoscope of colors. They were literally speechless. It was their first indication of the power of wind, water, and time. Now they understood for themselves how John L. Stoddard felt nearly a century ago: "To stand upon the edge of this stupendous gorge, as it receives its earliest greeting from the god of day, is to enjoy in a moment compensation for long years of ordinary uneventful life."

After a full hour of gasping at the canyon, the students staggered into the Bright Angel dining room for a hearty breakfast of steak and eggs, hash browns, mixed fruit, and waffles. The male students had developed various amounts of facial stubble, for razors hadn't been used since Boulder. Their hair pushed in a thousand directions, their clothes rumpled, the men yawned and stretched, making guttural noises not of discomfort but of confirmation that they were alive and well. The women regarded these male morning displays with studied indifference; they, too, had discarded old notions of presentability early in our venture. Group harmony had been achieved.

Breakfast over, we drove to the Mather Campground, which—although it had no water and electric hookups—was an ideal piny setting for us to create a pup-tent city. The campground was full, and since we hadn't made reservations we were almost shut out, but we eventually finagled a spot. We were all excited at the prospect of having two days to explore the Grand Canyon by horse, helicopter, or foot, but our adrenaline was also flowing in anticipation of being live on "Good Morning America." Kevin, our resident artist, had been recruited by Frank to paint a giant American flag on the side of the Majic Bus, with the words *American Odyssey* underneath and all our first names stenciled in white under the windows where we slept. Still unaware of precisely what "Good Morning America" wanted us to do, we hoped we could all stand in front of the Majic Bus and shout, "Good morning, America!" in unison, then sing Steve Goodman's "City of New Orleans" while Jay played it on the guitar.

For Frank, the opportunity to promote his bus on national television was his American dream come true. As the tents were set up, Kevin got out his brushes and went to work.

I left the students for my own room at nearby Yavapai Lodge, tucked away in a juniper forest, where a hot bath and some sleep were priorities and doing laundry was a necessity. I also needed a day in my own room to make phone calls. Hofstra's public relations office, New College administrators, and my answering machine were going berserk with calls from all over the country asking me to do radio and television interviews or to visit some specific town. The *New York Times* article had snowballed the Majic Bus into its fifteen minutes of fame. CNN wanted to film us on the road; Bill Moyers wanted me to talk on his show; reporters from *The Oregonian* and the *Los Angeles Times* wanted to talk with us live on the Majic Bus; National Public Radio wanted to do a special "Politics and Culture" program, with students reading passages from their course texts, as we had done in Boulder. We were offered free hot-air-balloon rides in Long Beach, a free week at a Lake Tahoe resort, and an all-the-crabs-you-can-eat dinner in Boston. Local historians from six different states called to offer red-carpet treatment should we visit their historical communities. The outpouring was simply incredible. The American Odyssey course had clearly touched a national nerve. People were tired of hearing only the bad news about America—the news of doomsday and national decline. They felt, as Sinclair Lewis had, that "the trouble with this country is that there are too many people going about saying 'the trouble with this country is . . .' " It was now up to me to sort all this enthusiasm out before our television appearance turned things upside down.

A room of my own also gave me a chance to finish reading John Updike's recent classic American downer *Rabbit at Rest,* an anti—*On the Road.* When I read Updike, I ask, as Emerson did in another context: "Can we never extract the tapeworm of Europe from the brain of our country man"? Updike fancies he has put his finger on our national pulse in his Rabbit quartet. Our problem, he says, is that Americans don't know the word *enough*, which is probably true, but to my mind this disregard of limits is the core of our national genius. Updike wants Americans to contract, to tie the covered wagon to the fence post, to stop longing, to settle down, to quit running in search of God-knows-what and turn inward instead. I felt like telling him to do as John Steinbeck did in *Travels with Charley*: Take a spin around the real America in a camper. He might just enjoy a piña colada Slurpee at a 7-Eleven and meet some interesting people and hear some good tales in the Wonder Bread rowhouses and Whopper warehouses. As Charles Kuralt wrote in his book *American Way*, "I don't think it does any harm just once in a while to acknowledge that the whole country isn't in flames."

That evening, over rubbery chicken and mushy rice, with flags of the world hanging from the cafeteria ceiling, we all reconvened, and the students told me of their adventures. Alison had led a band of students down the Bright Angel Trail, reaching the halfway point at Phantom Ranch (a unique resort at the bottom of the canyon) before retracing their steps in the hard uphill, foot-blistering climb back to the rim. Throughout dinner we heard much about sore feet. Other students had been less ambitious and took shorter hikes along the rim. As we ate we noticed that ours was the only group of Americans in the cafeteria. There were more Japanese and German visitors at the Grand Canyon than Americans. I later learned that all the lodges had self-imposed a ceiling of 50 percent foreigners in order to reserve beds for native sons and daughters.

In fact, the real danger to the Grand Canyon is not foreign invasion but the thick haze that can turn it from a breathtaking natural wonder into a sad tableau of spreading industrial pollution and government inaction. On many days, particularly in winter, the haze is so thick that visitors on one rim can barely see the other side. The main culprit is a giant coal-burning plant in northern Arizona that for environmentalists has become a symbol of industrial irresponsibility—the Navajo Generating Station, a 2,250-megawatt power plant fueled by 24,000 tons of coal a day. A towering, brownish-yellow plume of soot and smoke pours from its three 775-foot smokestacks across the fragile desert landscape. The plant has become the new outlaw of the American West. "The Grand Canyon is to the United States what the grand cathedrals are to Europe," said William K. Reilly, former head of the Environmental Protection Agency. "It's part of our heritage." The EPA has now forced the plant to implement a series of expensive measures to control air pollution and to reduce sulfur dioxide emissions by 90 percent.

After dinner I had arranged for a Mormon church leader who was a friend of Beth's to lecture briefly about Joseph Smith, founder of the Church of Jesus Christ of Latter-Day Saints. The students were fascinated to learn that an angel had told Smith where to unearth a book written on golden plates, and how, with miraculous help, he translated it into English as the Book of Mormon (1830). Following Smith's revelation that polygamy was lawful, the Mormons were deemed undesirables and were chased from state to state, from New York to Ohio to Missouri to Illinois, where Smith and his brother were killed by a mob in 1849. Most of Smith's followers went with Brigham Young to Utah. The students were surprised that today 75 percent of Utah and 25 percent of Arizona and Idaho are Mormon. Not a single student had ever studied the Mormon experience or knew about the Book of Mormon. The question-and-answer session that followed was lively, and I was pleased to discover later that the students had retained what they heard, for they all passed an exam question on the history of Mormonism with flying colors.

The next morning Christine, Aíne, Dan, Janine, Beth, Alison, and I rose at the crack of dawn to go horseback riding along the east rim, through famous Long Jim Canyon. We taxied to the Moqui Lodge and Restaurant, where we purchased our tickets for the four-hour ride. Our guide, Buck Schrader, was in authentic cowboy garb, from boot spurs to black Stetson, but proved to be a gentleman, not a roughneck. Originally from a farm in north-central Ohio, Buck said he had been riding horses since he was old enough to walk. Now, with twenty years of Grand Canyon trail riding under his belt, he is a park institution, his longish brown hair, handlebar mustache, and cheerful smile enduring symbols of the old Fred Harvey brand of wholesome hospitality. When Christine told Buck he looked like the Marlboro Man, he shrugged off the intended compliment by saying he only smoked generic menthols.

Buck assigned the horses based on our previous riding experience. We were allotted seven very different horses: two mixed breeds, a quarterhorse, an Appaloosa, a roan, a sorrel, and a paint. When we had saddled up, Buck led us out of the corral, past a water-treatment area, and into the thick pine forest. For the next four hours we had an incredible experience talking with Buck about his encounters with porcupines and bobcats, hailstorms and lightning strikes, Gene Autry and Chuck Connors. He talked to us about prescribed burns and horse psychology. He was impassioned about such Western writers as Louis L'Amour and Will James. To be on a horse looking out over the Grand Canyon's sensuous physical beauty is as close as one can get to living the romantic American West of Currier and Ives. Being on horseback created an atavistic illusion of being lords and masters of all we surveyed, mixed with downright awe at witnessing two billion years of our earth's evolution. It was a perfect morning.

While our group was seeing the Grand Canyon in the old-fashioned equestrian way, Matt, Kevin, Kenny, and Justin were the modernists, taking an AirStar helicopter ride. The four spent an hour hovering over the massive, sheer canyon walls, following the path of the sun-kissed Colorado River as it snaked through the mile-deep gorges. Matt videotaped the ride, capturing some spectacular footage of such rock formations as the Zoroaster and Buddha Temples, Wotan's Throne, and Tonto Plateau. The audio portion of his tape consists of the deafening propeller and the four repeating, "It's incredible," again and again. The skies are always crowded over the Grand Canyon, handling up to fourteen hundred flights a day—more than twice as many Washington, DC's National Airport! Yet the park has only a single runway, no radar, and a poorly placed control tower. Kenny said the sky had so many planes in it that "it seemed like the Grand Canyon was Grand National Airport."

At dusk we all assembled at the campground and admired Kevin's perfectly painted American flag. I lectured about the Chiricahua Apache warrior Geronimo, one of the most famous Indian leaders in the Southwest,

325

who for fifteen years had led campaigns against the Mexicans because in 1858 they had killed his entire family. The students were saddened to learn that Geronimo spent his desperate last years in military confinement at Fort Sill, Oklahoma, reduced to performing as a Bad Injun in Buffalo Bill's Wild West Show. We also discussed the Mexican-American War of 1846 and debated whether President James K. Polk's militant expansionism could be justified if considered in light of the time; most students thought it could be but also believed Thoreau was right to refuse to pay taxes he considered unjust.

The group's enthusiasm about being on "Good Morning America" was momentarily dampened when I broke the news that the producers wanted only one student and me to speak. Kenny Young was my choice. Kenny had been in four of my other classes, and I was confident he wouldn't be camera-shy. Currently in law school, Kenny is blessed with the gift of gab. The students had no complaint with my selection, for they knew Kenny was the perfect group representative. In any case, all of the students would get on the air, since the show would be using some of the footage we had Federal Express-ed them from Albuquerque. Briefing over, many of the students rambled over to the cafeteria for dinner. It was Darlene's birthday (our third), and they were going to celebrate by shooting pool. As always, Darlene was in good spirits.

I was dying to get some exercise and found there were lighted hoops behind the park's employee recreation center. Jared, Matt, Justin, and I took a taxi to the outdoor basketball court. To our dismay the court lights weren't working. Still, the recreation center's floodlights cast just enough illumination to make two on two possible. The canteen connected with the center was brimming with off-duty employees enjoying a beer and listening to American rock. We decided to play half-court and went at it in the near darkness, Justin and I versus Matt and Jared. Passes would hit us in the head and shooting was blindly instinctual, the ultimate object of the game being not to run into the pole. Still, we were working up a healthy sweat. As Matt and I fought for a rebound, he twisted his ankle and fell. I ran to the canteen for ice. By the time I got back, his foot had swelled considerably and was already black and blue. The game was over. We helped Matt hobble back to the Majic Bus. For the rest of the trip his ankle bothered him, but Matt was a stoic, saying that in life one "had to endure pain." Near the end of our trip, in Missoula, Montana, he was well enough to play again.

I had difficulty sleeping that night, apprehensive that my alarm clock wouldn't go off and I would oversleep. We were to meet at Yaki Point, where the Kaibab Trail begins, at 5:00 A.M. sharp, to rendezvous with the crew from "Good Morning America." After the live shot, the Majic Bus would be off to Las Vegas. The Best Western rooms I had reserved there had been abruptly canceled. The arrangement I had made hinged on availability, and because it was Easter weekend, Vegas's six Best Westerns were sold out, leaving us homeless. Indeed, amazing as it sounds, *all* of Las Vegas's seventy-five thousand motel and hotel rooms were occupied. When I called the Mirage begging for accommodations they said my best bet would be the Excalibur, which had the most rooms in town— one thousand more than they did—and was touted as the world's largest hotel. This is saying a lot, when one considers that Vegas is home to nine of the ten largest hotels in the world. I spoke to the head of public relations at the Excalibur about my American Odyssey course and our Easter weekend predicament. He seemed willing to help. I had Hofstra fax him a copy of the *New York Times* article, the course itinerary, and the syllabus, for added legitimacy. A deal was struck. If I mentioned the Excalibur on "Good Morning America," free rooms, dinner coupons, and Excalibur T-shirts were all ours. If I didn't, I was told to "drive right on past, and not even think of stopping in." The folks who ran the blackjack tables sure knew how to strong-arm a desperate professor and his charges.

That morning at 4:30 A.M. I told the students of our lodging problem. Excited at the possibility of staying at one of Vegas's premier casino hotels, they pleaded with me to go along with the dubious proposition. I promised to try.

Using flashlights, we packed up the tents. The Majic Bus was in ship-shape, as Frank had scrubbed it inside and out, just in case the "Good

Morning America" crew wanted a tour. Frank had changed the bus marquee to read LAS VEGAS instead of BIG BAD WOLF, to give us a sense of high purpose. The students squawked, but Frank paid them no mind. For appearances' sake, the "Big Bad Wolf" had to go, but it would reappear a minute after taping finished.

We started for Yaki Point with the stars still shining but in rapid retreat. I was reading Alan's journal, which he had left me when he returned to New York for Passover. It was all neatly typed, for he had brought a laptop computer with him and found printers along the way. I was struck by one of his responses to the Grand Canyon: "It is as if God took the earth, whipped out a stencil, and began to make cuts." Alan had added to the very full job description of the Old Testament God of Creation another task: tectonic architect.

Because of the Pacific–Eastern time difference, our Grand Canyon sunrise at 5:40 meant we would be live in the East at 8:40. As we approached the Yaki Point overview, a coyote crossed our path, which meant either good or bad luck, I couldn't remember which. The parking area was deserted, except for two television trucks with thick tentaclelike cables protruding octopus fashion from the rear door, powering an elaborate lighting system only ten yards from the canyon rim. The producer directed a cowboy-hat-clad Kenny and me to stand with our backs to the canyon, a few short feet from the edge. If we fell over, it meant instant death and the end of our great experiment in education. With a juniper on each side to brace us should the wind suddenly gust, they connected us into the electronic grid with microphones and earphones and said Charlie Gibson would be asking us questions live from New York. A chill spring breeze was blowing over the canyon, and Kenny and I began to fear we would be unable to stop our teeth from chattering when we tried to speak. Alison came to my aid with her down vest to put over my sweatshirt, which helped considerably. The stars had now faded and a moody blue glow illuminated the air. The crickets were making music ever so lightly, at a dying tempo, as though they had been rubbing their legs together all night long and had finally grown weary and were about to peter out from sheer exhaustion. The students all gathered in front of us, bubbling with anticipation and giving Kenny and me thumbs-up encouragement. During a commercial break Charlie Gibson asked how we were doing and said we would be on right after Joan Lunden finished her interview with Wynonna Judd. And then, as if on cue, an orange fireball of a sun began rising behind us, shooting out rays of pink, purple, and red.

Charlie Gibson began by asking whether American Odyssey was a serious academic endeavor, and I gave him a serious, deep-voiced yes with a few minutes of explanation. Kenny answered several questions, and before we knew it, our fifteen minutes of fame were about to end without my having mentioned the Excalibur. The students were jumping up and down, crossing their arms to make giant Xs. Then Charlie asked me one last question: "What kind of response have you gotten from the American people?" I talked of the supportive letters and invitations we had received from all over the nation, adding, "People have offered us free meals at their homes, and the Excalibur Hotel and Casino in Las Vegas is going to give us free rooms tonight." It came out in such a matter-of-fact fashion that it hardly seemed like a plug; I had slid down the slippery slope with ease. And then the interview was over, the sun blazing at our backs. We would have to wait three hours, over breakfast in Williams, to see how we aired, but the mood was celebratory. If the Excalibur didn't renege and the ABC censors didn't delete the plug, these weary student travelers were about to bask in the lap of Las Vegas luxury.

Less than sixty miles from the Grand Canyon's south rise, Williams—named after Bill Williams, the Baptist circuit rider from Missouri credited with being the first white American to explore the region, in the 1830s—secured its fame as "Gateway to the Grand Canyon," and, by the early 1980s, as the only town possessing a main street that was still part of Route 66. Then, on October 13, 1984, the inevitable happened. The nearby six-mile stretch of I-40 was officially opened. Williams now had the distinction of being the last Route 66 town to be bypassed. It had taken almost two decades, but the interstate had finally managed to replace the old highway linking Chicago to Santa Monica. Actually, it took not one but five different interstates to replace the great diagonal highway. I-55, a north-south highway from Chicago to the Gulf Coast, replaced 66 in Illinois. I-44 from Saint Louis to Wichita Falls, Texas, took over the bend of 66 from Saint Louis to Oklahoma City, and I-40, the major east-west route from North Carolina to California, usurped Route 66 traffic from Oklahoma City all the way to Barstow. The final few miles of Route 66 in Southern California were replaced by I-15 and I-10. Route 66, which since 1926 had been the Mother Road in millions of trips, vacations, adventures, relocations, escapes, and songs, was gone—destroyed forever.

A short time after Williams was bypassed, a gathering of officials from the American Association of State Highways and Transportation voted to decertify U.S. Route 66—an unconscionable insult to the Mother Road. No Route 66 signs are posted; no Route 66 appears on the map. Bureaucrats may think they can simply legislate Route 66 out of existence, turn a national symbol into a concrete superhighway, and erase history and collective memory. What they fail to appreciate is that Route 66 wasn't just a highway, it was a destination in itself. "The road is like Elvis Presley," one Williams citizen noted. "It just won't die." And it hasn't. In the late 1980s the historic Route 66 Association of Arizona began hanging up memorial signs in honor of the old road, which had become the "Main Street of America," and now Williams was abuzz with Route 66 hoopla and civic pride.

No sooner had we parked the Majic Bus in Williams than a young boy with Good Friday off from school waited for us to disembark so he could sell a chunk of the Mother Road. For five dollars you could possess your own Route 66 relic in a clear plastic bag. It reminded me of the German kids who sold pieces of the Berlin Wall to tourists. I bought a chunk of highway on our way to an old Route 66 motel in which we would be able to watch "Good Morning America" from the lobby TV set. The students took breakfast in shifts, filling themselves with pancakes, eggs, and hash browns at various cafés around town. Alison purchased what she came to regard as her most cherished American Odyssey souvenir—a Route 66 T-shirt. Kevin bought a Route 66 "road of flight" poster lettered in large print with Steinbeck's words from *The Grapes of Wrath*. At last, the moment we were waiting for arrived. Our "Good Morning America" segment was on, and my experiment in product placement had not been excised. The prospect of being homeless in Las Vegas—"the City without Clocks"— dissipated. We were on our way to a destination that attracts twenty million visitors yearly, tourists who leave behind ten billion dollars in the pursuit of pleasure.

Frank had pulled the Majic Bus onto Main Street, known as Bill Williams Avenue, and parked illegally next to a HISTORIC ROUTE 66 sign. The students had lost the opportunity to travel down the great golden road but for consolation they would at least have a photograph of themselves in front of a Route 66 sign. It was the only time on the entire trip that Frank behaved like General Patton, barking orders to squat or shift or stand next to the sacred sign, the Majic Bus as a backdrop. And then cameras clicked, and we all scurried back onto the bus before a police officer could write us a traffic ticket.

Frank and I lingered by the sign a moment longer in silence. We were both gripped by the same sense of nostalgic regret, of time lost, of anger that Route 66 would never be again. And then, tipping his Stetson toward the sign, he bowed and said a rueful "Thanks." As we jumped on board, he abruptly turned around and shouted, "Frank Perugi will be back!" at the Route 66 marker, adding, "And now I got I-40." Then he shifted into gear, heading determinedly to Kingman and beyond that to the dry, beautiful, but desolate Mojave Desert, an unnerving terrain of collared lizards, Joshua trees, and scorched skeletons—skeletons with the flesh long gone, bleached by the sun, nothing more now than abandoned bone.

14

Slot Machines and Neon Nights in the Mojave Desert

Las Vegas is the most extreme and allegorical of American settlements, bizarre and beautiful in its venality and in its devotion to immediate gratification, a place the tone of which is set by mobsters and call girls and ladies' room attendants with amyl nitrite poppers in their uniform pockets.

—JOAN DIDION

IT'S 102 SCORCHING MILES FROM THE SUN-BAKED STRIP TOWN of Kingman across the creviced arroyos of the Mojave Desert on I-93, most of it only two lanes, to Las Vegas, the most flamboyant oasis in the world. The harsh drive is hot and dusty, through a largely uninhabited, parched brown mountainous terrain appearing almost totally devoid of vegetation. An occasional one-blink town interrupts the barbed-wire fences, highway markers, and life-giving arteries of telephone and electrical wires. Sand is everywhere, and it blows in relentless sheets across the highway even when wind velocity is low. Tumbleweed loses its luster as a romantic icon of the Old West and becomes an annoying obstacle every five minutes to anxious, cool-Pacific-bound motorists. In summer cyclonic storms are accompanied by cloudbursts that can drop an inch of rain in an hour,

332

making flash floods a common occurrence. This long, arid, merciless, but exquisite stretch of desert looks and feels lethal, particularly once the fearsome, humanoid Joshua trees start twisting up. When the wind blows at a saguaro cactus you hear a brittle sound, the tuning of the needles. But when the wind blows against a Joshua the tree doesn't budge or make even the slightest noise; they are at one with the desert. Christine felt the Mojave was dying of starvation; Janine called it "lizardland." Whenever we passed a sign of human habitation, we wondered who would choose to claw out a life here.

Bob Dylan's *Blood on the Tracks* LP was playing. His cabaret poker song "Lily, Rosemary and the Jack of Hearts" got me psyched for the comforts and corruptions of Vegas. Jared and Tom could barely contain their desire to play the sports book. Tom was convinced a ten-dollar bet on the Minnesota Timberwolves plus 17-1/2 over the Utah Jazz wasn't gambling but stealing. Jared's plan was to parlay five-dollar bets on several NBA games plus, after a studious perusal of the *Racing Form*, a no-lose bet on Caesar's Jackpot, running at the Meadowlands. The KDR boys were focused on Friday-night carousing, not gambling, and Stefanie and Shari were ecstatic about the prospect of sleeping and reading in the air-conditioned comfort of the Excalibur. For the students who had liked Boulder's megaglitz, Las Vegas conjured up a neon inferno, a slot-machine purgatory of lounges filled with female impersonators singing Judy Garland songs and leisure-suited Wayne Newtons saying, "You've been a very special audience."

As we pushed through the desert, students sat in their berths reading Hunter S. Thompson's *Fear and Loathing in Las Vegas,* the famous (or infamous, depending on your outlook on life and literature) account of a journalist's foray into the wilds of Las Vegas to cover the Mint 400 Desert Race for a sports magazine, his Samoan attorney at his side in a red convertible, carrying enough illegal drugs with them to throw all of Nevada into an altered state of consciousness, if not outright psychosis. Thompson has a well-deserved reputation as a literary bull in the china shop of western civilization for his oeuvre of classic, off-the-wall books—*Fear and Loathing in Las Vegas, Fear and Loathing on the Campaign Trail '72, The*

Great Shark Hunt, The Curse of Lono, and *Generation of Swine*—burnished by his incarnation as Uncle Raoul Duke in Gary Trudeau's "Doonesbury" cartoons. Some students, Justin and Jay in particular, both thought *Fear and Loathing* the most hilarious writing they had ever encountered. When they got back to New York they were thrilled to learn that the Prince of Gonzo had just written a soon-to-be-published account of the 1992 presidential election process: *Better Than Sex: Confessions of a Campaign Junkie*. Others were offended by Thompson's hallucinogenic, trippy prose, known the world over as gonzo journalism. But, by the time the Majic Bus pulled out of Las Vegas thirty-six hours later, everyone agreed that the zany book, which opens with "We were somewhere around Barstow on the edge of the desert when the drugs began to take hold," punctured the heart of Sin City in all its Sodom-and-Gomorrah decadent excess and delight.

Even though Frank was doing sixty miles per hour, car upon car of fast-lane hedonists whizzed around us, hurrying to get out of the furnace-like heat and hit the ultimate arcade—a combat pleasure-zone known as the Strip. I-93 north to Las Vegas is the road of dreams. Entertainment-craving motorists zoom past, drawn by million-dollar jackpots, ninety-nine-cent shrimp cocktails, and sequin-nippled showgirls. I-93 south from Las Vegas is the aftermath, a funeral procession of fractured fantasies, hung-over and empty-pocketed drivers needing, at the minimum, an aspirin fix and escape from the ardent yellow sun.

About an hour out of Kingman, Hoover Dam was upon us. The building of Hoover Dam was a mind-boggling feat of engineering, greater even than the construction of the Panama Canal. The students gazed with endless fascination on this triumph of American enterprise. In 1930, the nearest civilized outpost to the dam site was the languid railroad juncture of Las Vegas forty miles away. In order to build the dam and divert the Colorado River, two hundred miles of poles and cables had to be run from a power plant in San Bernardino, California. Just to prepare for actual construction, railroad tracks had to be laid to transport heavy equipment, and an entire town had to be built to house the more than five thousand workers who would toil day and night to complete the project, braving extreme conditions, including one-hundred-degree heat. These men excavated nine million tons of rock, roughly enough to build the Great Wall of China, and poured nearly seven million tons of concrete, enough to pave a two-lane road from Miami to Los Angeles. The world looked on in awe as the diversion tunnels were closed and Lake Mead began to fill up. Averaging fifty injuries per day, with ninety-four resultant deaths during the forty-six months of construction, Hoover Dam was completed in February, 1935, two years ahead of schedule. A short while later the first turbine turned, and electricity began flowing as the canyon-gouging Colorado River was finally tamed by American engineering ingenuity and construction might. Today Hoover Dam supplies four billion kilowatt-hours of electricity annually and lights the countless bulbs of the Vegas Strip, and a half million Vegas homes.

We crossed over Hoover Dam and entered Boulder City, the only municipality in Nevada that prohibits gambling. Though the puritanical descendants of engineers and builders may have forbidden gambling itself, they apparently had fewer qualms about appearing frivolous or wasting energy in the process. Long ago some zoning board composed of leading citizens approved the town's brightly lighted hotels, flaccid knockoffs of the Stardust and Flamingo, in secret, perhaps subconscious, competition with their glittering Vegas cousins. And so, even before you reach Sin City, there is an inconsequential tease for the explosion of garish neon hotels, all-you-can-eat restaurants, and blowsy casinos that make Las Vegas the capital of resource waste in the United States—a category in which our nation has no global peer.

In Las Vegas, using water means using it up. Because of severe water shortages, the city and county have banned further filling of luxury lakes from the valley's water supply. Newcomers to Las Vegas usually come from lustier climates and insist on trying to reproduce green grass lawns, flower gardens, and golf courses in the middle of the desert. Oasis suburban communities and subdivisions with names like Montego Bay and Crystal Cove have drawn so much water from the Colorado River that they have almost exhausted the supply; a water crisis is at hand. Now the Las

Vegas Valley Water District has announced it will run through available water reserves by 1995. The question that confronts the community is how to supply water to a population expected to double by 2030. The only possible solution is to pump water from as far as three hundred miles away, which will outrage ranchers. One thing is certain; Las Vegas must confront this crisis at once.

Coming back to Las Vegas, I was immediately struck by how much the town has grown in recent years, while the students were shocked at the town's sprawl. As the rest of the United States is trapped in recession, Las Vegas leads the nation in number of jobs created the fourth year in a row. Only 23 percent of Nevadans were born in Nevada, the lowest ratio in the nation. The 1990 Census credits Las Vegas as the fastest-growing city in America, luring newcomers with the prospect of good jobs in a variety of industries, cheap housing, low taxes, safe streets, and endless sun. Tourists may be losing money at the gambling tables, but the town's newest residents are getting rich quick the old-fashioned way—full employment. During the 1980s Clark County's population grew from 460,000 to 740,000—an almost unprecedented growth increase of 61 percent. An astounding 6,000 people a month move to this twentieth-century desert town. To accommodate this mass migration, the Las Vegas construction industry has become the boom of the nation, as construction workers from the LA Basin pour into Nevada to build houses, industrial parks, hotels, and strip malls, all of which seem to mushroom overnight. Road maps are useless for driving the outskirts of Vegas; they're all out of date. Buildings are hammered together and occupied months before the streets they're on are paved and cement sidewalks poured.

And all this says nothing about the millions of people who continue to flock to Vegas for games of chance. More might be on the way, for ground has been broken for a super-high-speed train to cover the three hundred miles between Las Vegas and Los Angeles, although the project is temporarily on hold. Anyone who thought the legalization of gambling in Atlantic City; Deadwood, South Dakota; and the Colorado mining towns; or on Indian reservations and Mississippi riverboats—not to mention the thirty-two states that have turned themselves into bookmakers by sponsoring lotteries—would cut into Las Vegas's business has to think again. Las Vegas hotel and casino business has never been better, and the city's McCarran International Airport has become the fastest growing in the nation. What is Vegas's secret? The town has transformed its image from "Sin City" to "Family Values Vacation Village." That's right—with every passing day Las Vegas looks more and more like a Disney theme park, complete with water slides, Velcro wall jumping, circus attractions, exotic zoo animals, dolphin and shark tanks, video game arcades, and miniature golf courses, all topped off by a fifty-four-foot volcano that erupts every twenty minutes, shooting flames and steam high into the desert sky. And the newest and biggest feature of Las Vegas's mega-family-resort-hotel-casino-amusement center is where we would be staying—the four-thousand-room Excalibur, which opened in 1990.

The Excalibur, a medieval-looking monster of a hotel on the corner of Tropicana Avenue and the Strip and owned by Circus Circus Enterprises, is listed in *The Guinness Book of Records* as the world's largest hotel. A facade of turrets and spires and a 265-foot-tall bell tower front four one-thousand-room tower walls, giving the Excalibur its kitschy Camelot motif. Two dinner shows "knightly" in the "arena" feature banquets at which diners eat roast meat with their hands while watching a jousting match. The King Arthur theme includes music, dance, magic, even fire eating. In the Renaissance Village (the Excalibur shamelessly avoids any fine historical distinctions, and besides, a medieval village doesn't sound too inviting) employees dress in medieval costume or as court jesters, talking to young children just as their cartoon-costumed counterparts do at Disneyland. In the "dungeon" families find not racks, thumbscrews, and iron maidens but the Excalibur's Dynamic Motion Simulator, an ultra-high-tech film simulation of a roller coaster in which hydraulically activated seats are synchronized with on-screen action. White-water rafts, bobsleds, racing cars, and runaway trains are shot in seventy millimeter at sixty frames per second (twice the normal speed) for the (simulated) thrill of a lifetime. While the parents gamble away their children's college educations in the upstairs casino, the kids are sugar-loading on free cotton candy at King Arthur's Round Table. Hunter S. Thompson's *Fear and*

337

Loathing observation about Circus Circus applies: "This madness goes on and on, but nobody seems to notice."

It was late afternoon when we arrived at the hotel. Jared couldn't contain his eagerness to gamble and rushed in to lay some cash on Caesar's Jackpot. I asked the rest of the students to wait outside on a grassy knoll while I negotiated for the free rooms with the public relations department. Walking into the casino from the familial intimacy of the Majic Bus was a surreal sensation worthy of Hunter S. Thompson. *Gaming and Wagering* magazine estimates that one hundred million Americans gamble, nearly 45 percent of the population. It seemed to my road-weary eyes that every one of them was pulling slots or playing the gaming tables in the Excalibur. As I walked past the sword-decorated Jester's Lounge, where keno (a game brought to America by the Chinese who worked in the silver mines and helped build our railroads) was being played, a small combo band broke into "La Bamba" while two couples danced the twist. I asked a pit boss dressed like a knight for directions to the administrative offices. He gave me a hasty, unchivalrous glare and said, "Little John will help you," pointing to the information booth.

The place was like a national convention of Overeaters Anonymous. Carbohydrate junkies from around the nation were carrying plastic buckets full of change and eating popcorn as they frantically waddled down the long rows of one-armed bandits to drop countless coins into seductive machines. They looked up only to accept a watered-down drink from a Snow White–cleavaged cocktail waitress, their fingers crossed that three sevens would pop up. A glance around the floor revealed that tourists had followed Bugsy Siegel's advice in his first advertisement for his Fabulous Flamingo in 1946: "Come as you are." The apparel ranged from tux to tank top. Polyester was the fabric of choice among the septuagenarians. The baby-boomers wore cotton T-shirts with obscure or slightly berserk personal messages such as KISS ME I'M A BUTT-KICKING COWBOY, or I'M TOO SEXY FOR MY WIFE. Multicolored Hawaiian shirts also dotted the floor, draping deluded, flabby, out-of-shape men aspiring for a week to dress

338

like either the hairy-chested Magnum, P.I., or the lovable Hawkeye Pierce. Hordes of California undergraduates, baseball caps on backward and high-top Reeboks unlaced, cluttered the casino, turning Camelot into a spring break rave. The sports book was filled with degenerate, overweight lugs from Chicago penciling the odds sheet as they took huge drags on cigarettes and complained that CBS was wrong to can Jimmy the Greek for making racial slurs. I worked my way through this air-conditioned beehive of "One pull can change your life" dreamers and took the elevator to the third floor.

To my surprise, on entering the public relations office I was greeted by an ecstatic chorus: "Professor Brinkley!" The Excalibur's management had watched our "Good Morning America" performance and was pleased. With a round of handshakes and congratulatory pats on the back, they happily sent me off to the front desk for keys, bestowing on me quantities of T-shirts, visors, posters, stickers, dinner-and-drink coupons, and other free-bies. The students had grown impatient in my absence, but the sight of me returning with all the Excalibur loot produced wide grins. Mitch, always concerned with the Madison Avenue side of life, was glad to be staying at a hotel with a public relations staff so clever that they could turn the American Odyssey students into walking Excalibur billboards. I passed out keys and left the students with two parting instructions: to meet at my room the next day at 4:00 P.M. for their midterm exam, and not to lose too much money. Everyone followed the first instruction, and all but Kevin followed the second.

Alone in my large air-conditioned room I stared out the window at the mish-mash of minimarket gas stations, garish casinos, cheap motels, twenty-four-hour restaurants and generalized all-purpose glitz, the glow of neon illuminating the Strip as though the sun's efforts were too feeble for Vegas denizens—it was still light out, the sun just beginning its descent behind the islandlike pastel mountain ranges. I felt as insular and alone as Howard Hughes must have felt every evening, hiding in self-imposed exile on the ninth floor of the Desert Inn, always avoiding cameras, sneaking out the hotel back door during the wee morning hours, wearing rubber gloves, clutching tissues in one hand and a bottle of rubbing alcohol in the other, a drove of Mormon advisers always twenty yards in front and in back of the billionaire master financier.

Labeling Howard Hughes a paranoid eccentric or a recluse short-circuits deeper reflection on him and his place in the American saga. His entire life is a symbol of American individuality and enterprise gone haywire. Born in 1904, the same year as Bugsy Siegel and Las Vegas itself, Hughes inherited, from his father, the multi-million-dollar Hughes Tool Company when he turned twenty-one. Too imaginative for the grunt-grind monotony of the tool business, Hughes moved to Hollywood, where he launched his career as a film producer, airplane designer, pioneer pilot, and airline mogul. In 1966 Hughes sold TWA for a half billion dollars cash and—ever the maverick—immediately looked into how much the entire state of Nevada might cost. Although he never bought the state, Hughes moved his cash in a big way, embarking on the most robust buying spree in Nevada history. When the dust settled, Hughes owned the Desert Inn, the Sands, Castaways, and the Frontier. But he never realized his master plan of building a space-age airport to accommodate the giant supersonic (SST) jets of the future, which would have turned Las Vegas into the aerogateway to the West. In all he dropped $300 million into the venture. In fact, Hughes is remembered for grand schemes that never became reality, like his failed flying hotel—the *Spruce Goose*, with a 320-foot wingspan, the largest wooden aircraft ever built (which, incidentally, has been sold by the city of Long Beach, California, to McMinnville, Oregon).

When I lectured to the students on Hughes, they thought he sounded a lot like Ross Perot. Although Hughes ultimately contributed nothing to the Las Vegas skyline or industrial sector, his persona alone added a facade of legitimacy to the city's Sin City image—although, ironically, sin was a major element of Nevada's charms in the Hughesean ledger. Besides the dry climate, casinos, and aerospace dreams, it was retail sex that brought him to Nevada, for, according to *The Intimate Sex Lives of Important People*, "Probably no other person in history invested as much money in his sex life as did Howard Hughes."

It didn't take the students long to figure out that retail sex is an integral part of Las Vegas's appeal. In fact, retail sex is nearly as prevalent an illegal business in Las Vegas as gambling is a legal one. Bugsy Siegel, an incurable ladies' man, is credited with establishing Vegas's two-pronged sexual heritage—hotels designed with separate modular wings for easy access by call girls without having to pass through the main lobby entrance, and casinos adorned with young, pretty, suggestively attired long-legged girls. Today Siegel's dual sexual legacies flourish, largely because of Hughes's institutionalized Whore Invasion of the 1970s. As an aide to Robert Maheu, Hughes's chief of staff, once wrote: "When you get into the hotel business, you back into the whore business. Every man who enters the business must decide how he feels about pandering or, at least, supplying the furniture of love." Dan, Jay, and most of the female students found the Vegas commoditization of women degrading; a few students, on the other hand, thought we should lighten up and see it as fun and alluring.

Over the past fifty years the state of Nevada has passed statute after statute aimed at either controlling or eliminating legal prostitution. Through the passage of Statute 244-345(8) in 1971, Nevada made prostitution illegal in counties with a population of more than 250,000, and the formerly legal brothels of Las Vegas's Clark County were shut down. But closing the brothels did not reduce prostitution, and a decade later, in the early 1980s, John Moran was elected Clark County sheriff on a platform of promising to rid the county of its highly visible prostitution problem. In 1982 police arrested thirteen thousand professional prostitutes; in 1984, roughly six thousand, and in 1985, about five thousand. Streetwalking prostitution was almost eliminated. In 1986, 90 percent of all prostitution-related arrests were made inside the hotels, as undercover detectives arrested the working girls in lounges. Trying to relieve itself of its unsavory image, Las Vegas was about to be reborn as a family vacation town. By 1990 both images were flourishing side by side. Other systems were invented to ensure that the world's oldest profession could thrive well out of harm's way. The visitor who is so inclined merely lets his fingers do the

341

shopping through the yellow pages. Ordering up an "entertainer" from the phone book is as easy as ordering breakfast from room service—except the former may be delivered much faster.

In 1971, when prostitution was made illegal, the first phone book sex ads appeared, under the euphemism of "Escort Services"—two small display ads with girls in discreet two-piece bathing suits. Three full pages appeared in 1975, with enterprises such as Delivery Girls, Concubines Incorporated, and Suzy Wong's Matchmaking competing for clients. The ordering-sex-by-phone business began to boom, and by 1977 "Escort Services" and "Massage Parlors" filled five pages each. In 1981 "Dating Services" was added, with one full page, plus a half page of "Adult Maid and Butler Services" to tantalize the shopper. In 1982, as part of Sheriff Moran's new crackdown, these listings were mostly eliminated. Instead, a new, consolidated listing emerged—"Entertainers"—thirty pages' worth in 1992, with such come-ons as "You're Not Trained Until You've Been *Dominated* by Mistress Victoria Cat" and "She-Male—You Won't Believe the Secret We Keep Tucked Away." So, after Vegas's two-decades-long battle against prostitution, the phone company appears to have been the primary beneficiary.

While the students had seen similar ads in papers like the *Village Voice* back in New York, they were stunned to find vending box after vending box of anonymously published, garage-printed, free "Playmate" rags lining the Strip from the Tropicana to the Sahara. Filled with provocative photos of women in blatantly erotic poses, listing local phone numbers, these Las Vegas directories promise to deliver an alluring selection of "Centerfolds, Models, Dancers, Housewives, and College Students," direct to your hotel room. These guides reach beyond Clark County, with ads that say: "Sex is for sale in Nevada's legal brothels . . . just forty miles north of Las Vegas in scenic Nye County, the world's oldest profession is booming."

Because brothels are now illegal in Clark County, there has been a brothel-developing boom in neighboring sparsely populated Nye County. With names such as the Cherry Patch and Mabel's Whorehouse, brothels are thriving despite the AIDS epidemic. Nye County advertises that its prostitutes are inspected weekly for genital diseases by a physician and that venereal diseases are "virtually nonexistent"—like Ivory Soap, 99.44 percent pure—except that HIV carriers can't be detected by physical examination. In the process Nye County has become the Amsterdam of America, with a flood of hungry male customers shopping at its sex supermarkets. In the AIDS era, however, the advertisements have been modified: "A prerequisite of sex with the girls is that they make their own inspection of each customer's sexual organs, and they are well-trained in this area. If any disease is spotted, the customer is, of course, respectfully refused service. The chances are *amazingly slim* that a customer will pick up any sort of disease whatsoever at a house of prostitution in Amargosa Valley, Nevada." AIDS equals death, and these brothels offer *"amazingly slim"* reassurance!

That night I walked up and down the Strip by myself, visiting its highlights: Hirohito's limousine, a 1935 Packard, in the Imperial Palace Auto Collection; the world's largest gold nugget, weighing in at sixty-three pounds and valued at a million dollars, discovered in Australia and now residing behind plate glass in the Golden Nugget lobby; the International Hotel, where Elvis Presley made his great Las Vegas comeback during its opening month; the Sands Casino, headquarters in the 1960s to the Rat Pack—Frank Sinatra, Sammy Davis, Jr., Dean Martin, Peter Lawford, and Joey Bishop—where they made the quintessential Las Vegas movie, *Ocean's Eleven;* the three-thousand-pound Wheel of Fortune at Las Vegas World, twenty-six feet in diameter rotating on a four-and-a-half-inch steel shaft, larger than all the other Las Vegas wheels combined; Bonanza, "the world's largest gift shop," where the gag sign TO HELL WITH HOUSEWORK, I'M GOING TO VEGAS is the big seller; and the glass-caged white tigers at the Mirage. In front of Caesar's Palace, I stared at the large, garishly lit water fountain and pondered Allen Ginsberg's poetic observation of Vegas: "Does Engelbert know the name of the mountains he sings in? When gas and water dry up, will wild mustangs inhabit the Hilton Arcade?" Inside I bet on greyhound racing, a sport popular in Great Britain but actually

343

invented in the United States, and won $20. With twenty bucks extra in my pocket, I stopped at the Stardust Hotel and gorged on their $7.95 steak-and-lobster special, complete with "all-you-can-eat warehouse buffet" and then returned "home" to the clashing purples and reds of the Excalibur's medieval slot fantasyland, where I lost the twenty on the "Win 4,700 on Any Royal Flush with 5 Coins Bet Draw Poker." I decided to call it a day.

The next morning I met up with a bunch of the students cashing in their complimentary coupons at the Round Table Breakfast Buffet. Most had shied away from the gambling tables, satisfying any gambling impulse by pulling the handles of slot machines at a smorgasboard of casinos. Slots, a Vegas speciality because they require no a priori knowledge of games or their rules, were invented in San Francisco by a young American mechanic named Charlie Feay in the mid-1890s. Had he been able to keep the patent on all the hotel and casino and grind-joint slots in Vegas, he would easily have died the richest man in the world. Although it is true that large payoffs are regularly made to lucky slot players, the fact is that the payoff is calibrated mathematically to the casino's gross revenues. There is no gamble on the part of the casino, for the slots are set to provide a predetermined profit, calculated on a purely mechanical basis.

Though most of the students more or less broke even, Kevin ("High Roller") Willey lost $250, the rest of his trip spending money, in a more imaginative and exotic fashion, on roulette—an Egyptian game first made popular in Europe by the French. He might have lost more had it not been for a recalcitrant ATM that denied his supplication for more cash. Kevin's only response as he inhaled his blueberry pancakes floating in syrup was to curse those "damn green zeros." He tried to cadge $10 so he could recoup his losses, but everyone told him to get lost. Depressed by his bad luck and the revelation of a hitherto hidden compulsion to gamble, Kevin was learning an important life lesson, courtesy of the American Odyssey educational venture: Stay away from "Lost Wages," Nevada. I told him to study for the afternoon midterm and offered to front him a couple of hundred dollars when the Majic Bus was out of Nevada and in the casino-free zone of California.

Students spent the afternoon studying either in their air-conditioned rooms or by the pool. I escaped the Excalibur for a long-overdue haircut at a butchery near the Liberace Museum down Tropicana Avenue. There an eighteen-year-old electric razor artist named Cher gave me what she called the "Michael J. Fox look." In reality it was closer to Moe in the Three Stooges. Then I sneaked into the big blue swimming pool at the Island of Vegas at the Tropicana, basked in the ninety-degree sun, and sipped a banana daiquiri in delicious privacy. I returned to the Excalibur in time to administer the midterm, twenty short-answer questions like, "Do you consider William Faulkner a realist writer?" or, "Explain the history of the Biltmore Estate," and two essay questions, one on *Fear and Loathing in Las Vegas*, and the other on *Leaves of Grass*. I graded the exams a few days later in San Francisco, and all the students did well. With the test ordeal behind them, we headed for a buffet supper.

Although Tom, Jared, and Stefanie wanted to spend another night at the Excalibur since we had free rooms, I decided most of us had had our fill of Vegas. We'd pull out of town after we cruised the Strip downtown to soak up all the neon craziness for one last time and then head through the Mojave to wake up by the redemptive Pacific Ocean as an Easter Sunday gift. This get-out-of-Vegas plan elicited profuse thanks from Dan and Janine, who repeatedly resorted to "megacheesy" to describe every aspect of Vegas. Dan expressed his contempt for the whole medieval Excalibur motif ironically, by purchasing a multicolored felt court jester's hat, complete with little bells, at the hotel gift shop. Our group dinner ended in a brief reprise of the food-fight scene in *Animal House*, when Stefanie dumped an ice cream sundae over Kevin's head in retaliation for some food stain he had inflicted in Kansas. Fortunately the eruption did not escalate. Justin and Kenny squeezed in a few hands of low-stakes blackjack at the five-dollar table before we headed out to the Majic Bus at 9:00 P.M., where a well-rested Frank—who had slept the day away in his room—was ready to take us screaming down the Strip. The mood was festive, everyone sporting new tans, ready to raise a little hell.

Our goal on this Saturday Night Strip cruise was Fremont Street, the Times Square of the West. Off we went, out of the world's largest hotel parking lot and into the heavy flow of horn-blowing, bumper-to-bumper chaos known as Las Vegas Boulevard, the Excalibur looming to our left and the Tropicana on our right twinkling to the whoosh of silver dollars and poker chips gliding through the dextrous fingers of dealers at the green Polynesian gaming tables. Before us glittering signs, which in 1964 Tom Wolfe described as "Boomerang Modern, Palette Curvilinear, Flash Gordon Ming-Alert Sprial, McDonald's Hamburger Parabola, Mint Casino Elliptical, Miami Beach Kidney," hawked everything from penny slots to sky's-the-limit dice games. As we passed the Desert Rose Motel, which gave Larry McMurtry the title of his affectionate and poignant novel about an aging showgirl and her ties to Las Vegas, a group of about fifteen teenagers in the street started shouting, "The Majic Bus, the Majic Bus!" in youthful jubilation. Mel (the Velvet Fog) Tormé was blasting from the bus speakers as Alison, Dan, Jay, Alan and Christine popped their heads out of the ostrich chute, then climbed on top to wave to passersby. Our own contribution, the BIG BAD WOLF on our marquee, glowing warm red, became a shooting star—an added attraction in the galaxy that was Vegas.

With students waving from the top, the Majic Bus was an oddity on the boulevard of oddities. As we cruised past the twenty-four-hour Denny's (complete with a U.S. Post Office) and the Metz Nightclub, with the words HOT! HOT! HOT! flashing, a giant, giddy street party was under way. Kevin, Tom, and Jared were leaning out the front door at every red light, to shake people's hands and invite them on board. Asphyxiated by the Velvet Fog, I popped in a Little Richard–Jimi Hendrix tape for a breath of fresh air and turned the volume full blast. The Majic Bus had achieved an uncontrollable energy, best described as Saturday night fever. We weren't just driving the Strip, we were part of the action, the best float in the parade. All the infamous neon signs seemed to be sparkling especially for us. The Aladdin Hotel's golden genie's lamp glowed invitingly through the night, inviting a magic rub to make our easy-money dreams come true. The Dunes Hotel, easily recognized by its eighteen-story minaret-topped sign scheduled for lavish demolition in 1933, diffused the classic simplicity of its message by positioning a new van in front with a sign reading, WIN THIS CAR, also offering a chance to participate in a Revlon "Looking Good Makeover Show," seemingly mundane bait on the street of dreams. Bally's neon boast was a fifty-thousand-square-foot casino—large enough to house the Super Bowl. The Barbary Coast announced DOUBLE DECKS AND DOUBLE ODDS. At Caesar's Palace, with its fountains and lighted Miami-aqua building, there was a romanesque statue of Julius Caesar lording it up in front.

Frank pulled over by the Mirage, where we talked to people who were flocking into the showroom to see the magic of Siegfried and Roy and their big cats. Outside, among palm trees and cascading waterfalls in an artificial tropical paradise, we waited for the Mirage's giant volcano to explode. Matt was recording all the Vegas lunacy on film while the rest of us, cameras poised, waited for the volcano to blow, as if we were on a whale watch. When the flames shot up in the air everybody howled and applauded. Jared had begun giving curious sightseers spontaneous tours of the Majic Bus; Frank handed out his business cards; and Matt taped man-on-the-street interviews with random passersby. As Little Richard sang "Good Golly, Miss Molly," Darlene and Kevin began dancing with strangers in the streets.

The craziest moment of our entire trip dissolved and we were off again, past the prosaic Fashion Show Mall and the Emporium Gift Shop to the Frontier Hotel, the last remnant of the beginnings of the Las Vegas Strip. In front two dozen workers were picketing with a litany of grievances: lowered workers' pensions, lowered wages for most job classifications, lost workers' health insurance, and destroyed workers' job seniority and job security. Lonnie Wilkes, the three-hundred-pound union representative, in khaki shorts, a yellow golf shirt, white socks, and a Dodgers cap, said all 558 striking employees were on the picket line thirty hours a week. They claimed to have halved the Frontier's business. Hearing only Wilkes's version, without knowing the nitty-gritty details of the dispute, we enthusiastically showed our solidarity with the workers by shouting, "The Frontier is a bad bet!" and laying on the horn until it pierced every ear on the block.

And then we were crawling down the Strip in standstill traffic again, causing an even greater ruckus. In front of the Riviera's Mardi Gras Food Court, Jared asked a man if he wanted to "come in and see the beds." Unfortunately our visitor turned out to be a peep-show pervert who had misinterpreted Jared's invitation as a proposition, and Matt had to bounce him off the bus. Undaunted, we pushed on, past a statue of a giant white ape in front of Circus Circus, enticing his evolutionary betters/bettors to come in and to lose their money and enjoy the all-you-can-eat prime rib buffet—the order of these endeavors apparently the customer's option. We pressed on past the Sahara and the Wet 'n Wild Swim Park, whose clock tower reported that it was eighty-five degrees out; past Big Dog's Draft house, with its HOLY COW! sign; and past Vegas World, where FRENCH TOAST 99¢ indicated we were heading into the low-rent end—subterranean sawdust joints, adult books, tattoo parlors, seedy pawnshops, crystal-ball readings, Valentino's Zoot Suit Collection, all-night Odyssey Records, and Reliable Bail Bonds from Joe Ez's Hock Shop.

Here quickie marriage chapels abound—The Little White Chapel, where Joan Collins once celebrated the sacrament of marriage, and Graceland Chapel, where Jon Bon Jovi tied the knot. In this part of Las Vegas nearly seventy-five thousand nuptials are performed annually, some two hundred every day of the year. Just as the NRA wants no obstacles between the impulse to own a gun and its purchase, Nevada's method for promoting family values has been to deregulate marriage: no waiting period, no blood test, and a minimum age of eighteen (but with a notarized parental affidavit of consent, the age is sixteen). Appointments aren't necessary. All they need to do is show up, at any hour of the day or night, and in seconds a couple will hear, "I now pronounce you . . . ," and the deed is done.

Past these twenty-four-hour chapels, listening to U2's "In the Name of Love," we turned left on Fremont Street and entered Vegas's incendiary around-the-clock glittering gulch of neon. Students hopped out to pull a couple of last-chance slots at the Pioneer Club and to snap shots of Vegas Vic, a giant neon cowboy, flicking his Bic. And then it was over. We were exhausted, and it was time to head out of town and back into the pitch-black Mojave Desert, the land of the lonely Joshua trees, then on to California.

Before departing the Sin City—sorry, I mean Family Values Vacation Village—we purchased a case of soda at a Union 76 station offering "free aspirin and tender sympathy," and then off we sped, west on I-15, for the five-hour drive to Los Angeles. Jared insisted we listen to Steely Dan, especially a verse that went, "Then you swear and kick and beg us that you're not a gambling man/But you find you're back in Vegas with a handle in your hand." Jay assured Jared he would never come back if he could help it and grew proportionally happier with our increasing distance from neon. Jay played his blues guitar with a fresh, invigorated Stevie Ray Vaughan abandon.

Tom sat on the porch and asked about the atomic weapons the U.S. government had exploded over the years at Jackass Flats, outside Las Vegas. It was a good question, because more than 120 atomic bombs were exploded above ground between 1951 and 1962 at the Nevada Test Site Range, so close to Las Vegas that mushroom-cloud watching became a spectator sport. Although some on board the Majic Bus would not have been sorrowful had the glow of Las Vegas emanated from radioactivity instead of neon, then–President Kennedy, British Prime Minister Harold Macmillan, and Soviet Premier Nikita Khrushchev had been more far-sighted. In 1963 they signed the Nuclear Test Ban Treaty, which banned the testing of atomic weapons in the atmosphere and underwater, saving the citizens of Nevada, as well as its livestock, from needless exposure to radiation. Nevertheless, since the treaty did not ban underground testing, five hundred explosions have been set off at the Nuclear Testing Site near Las Vegas. In the wake of the Cold War's end and the ecological disasters at Rocky Flats, Savannah River, and other nuclear facilities, one would consider it high time to rethink our underground testing policy, in order to preserve our citizens' health and the fragile ecology of the Mojave Desert—its pure air and its unique flora and fauna, which have adapted to every harsh and brutal environmental test but the recklessness of humankind.

349

The Mojave Desert forms a rough triangle across the eastern part of southern California, from fifteen miles north of Palm Springs to Death Valley, from the southern tip of Nevada to the Tehachapi Mountains fifty miles north of Los Angeles. Even though the Mojave is home to the lowest point in the Western Hemisphere—Death Valley's Badwater, 282 feet below sea level—Californians call it the "high desert" because most of the Mojave lies above 2,000 feet. In some part of this harsh land, summer air temperatures routinely approach 120 degrees Fahrenheit, with ground-surface readings near 190 degrees. Water is an obsession, for the average yearly rainfall is only about four inches.

In the Mojave about 80 percent of the land belongs to the federal government, which grants leases to individuals and corporations. In theory this arrangement is supposed to protect the desert from exploitation while making it economically productive. In practice the system is destroying the Mojave's ecological integrity. For more than a century, ranchers and miners had depended on the government to support their way of life; typically, Mojave ranchers own less than 1 percent of the land they use. No environmentalist has so uncompromisingly articulated the case for ending government-subsidized human intrusion in the delicate desert ecosystem than Edward Abbey. A crusader for the desert wilderness, Abbey took on the ranchers a few years before his death in 1989 in "Free Speech: The Cowboy and His Cow." He wrote: "Western cattlemen [were] nothing more than welfare parasites," who had overgrazed the public lands of the West to the point at which they were "cowburnt." "They've been getting a free ride on the public lands for over a century, and I think it's time we phased it out. I'm in favor of putting the public lands livestock grazers out of business. First of all, we don't need the public lands beef industry. . . . Only about two percent of our beef, our red meat, comes from public lands of eleven western states." Abbey concluded that "if all our 31,000 western public land ranchers quit tomorrow, we'd never even notice. . . . They've had their free ride. It's time they learned to support themselves."

A big part of the battle now focuses on protecting the desert tortoise, a prehistoric and marvelously adapted reptile that's become to the Mojave what the spotted owl is to the forests of the Northwest—a living symbol of the struggle between two competing American values: reverence for nature and commitment to unfettered economic development. With a life-span matching that of humans, these lumbering creatures with patterned shells spend 85 percent of their lives in underground burrows, hibernating in winter and estivating (estivation is a moisture-conserving process) in summer. In spring they emerge to gorge on their favorite food, desert wildflowers. In August 1989 the desert tortoise was placed on the endangered species list, its numbers in the western Mojave having fallen by more than 50 percent in four years. A respiratory disease in domesticated tortoises released in the wild by disenchanted pet owners appeared to be the primary culprit. Blame also landed on cattle, motorcycles, and off-road vehicles that tear across the open desert, crushing the tortoises in their camouflaged burrows. The owners of off-road vehicles, weekend road warriors from the LA area, believe they have a God-given right to tear up the entire desert. Ravens, which prey on the tortoises, were also blamed for the decline. As towns, dumps, landfills, sewage sites, roads, road-kills, snakes, and birds have become more prevalent across the Mojave, so has the population of opportunistic, intelligent ravens. These flying scavengers have increased 1,528 percent in the last twenty years, according to the *Los Angeles Times*. Soon after the tortoise was placed on the endangered species list, forty ravens were found poisoned to death near Victor Valley, California, perhaps as a warning to the owners of off-road vehicles.

A partial, less violent solution is at hand—the California Desert Protection Bill, originally sponsored in 1986 by two California Democrats, Senator Alan Cranston and Congressman Mel Levine, and reintroduced in both the Senate and the Congress by California's newly elected Democratic senators Dianne Feinstein and Barbara Boxer and Congressman Rick Lehman (D–Calif.). The bill would redraw the map of southeastern California. The Death Valley and Joshua Tree national monuments would be enlarged and converted into national parks. The 1.5-million-acre East Mojave National Scenic Area, located between Death Valley and Joshua Tree and presently administered by the Bureau of Land Management (BLM), would become Mojave National Park. And an additional

4.4 million acres of BLM land would be congressionally designated as wilderness to be administered under the Wilderness Act. In all, the bill would create three national parks and seventy-nine wilderness areas totaling 8.8 million acres, an area nearly twice the size of New Jersey. Off-road-vehicle use would be curtailed in some areas, current mining would generally continue, and livestock grazing and ranching would continue in the BLM wilderness areas but be phased out in the new national parks. Needless to say, the California Desert Protection Bill is unpopular with the ranchers and mining companies that live, work and speculate in what is known as the Lonesome Triangle—one of the least-populated pieces of California.

I was talking with some of the students about the California Desert Protection Bill as we approached the California–Nevada line. While Frank stopped at the gigantic border casino-hotel called Whiskey Pete's to diesel up, some of the students went inside to see the well-advertised "authentic death car" of the charismatic 1930s bank robbers Bonnie and Clyde, romanticized in the Warren Beatty–Faye Dunaway film in 1967. In the course of a conversation with two tired, drunk Clark Mountain rare-earth miners from nearby Baker, California, Justin asked what they thought of the California Desert Protection Bill. The miners flew off the handle in an angry tirade of name calling—Sierra Club members were "garden pansies," Senator Alan Cranston "a queer Communist who wishes he was Mexican," the bill itself "un-American horseshit." Alarmed by the intensity of their rage, I carefully probed the reasons behind their charge against Cranston, expecting a Rush Limbaugh–style attack on him as welfare liberal—despite the fact that the miners' paychecks were heavily subsidized by U.S. taxpayers through government land agencies. Instead I heard the astounding and confusing argument that Cranston was a Communist because "he helped those good-for-nothing wetbacks in the Mexican Revolution of 1935." I said I was unclear as to what the two were talking about, so for support, the more ornery of the two grabbed a John Birch–like pamphlet from their truck's glove box: *Alan Cranston: The Shadow in the Senate.* He proceeded to read selected passages on Cranston's fifty-year record of extreme-left-wing radicalism, culminating in his sponsorship of the California Desert Protection Bill, from which came the inescapable conclusion as to Cranston's treason. One of the unreconstructed Patrick Buchananites then pulled me aside to probe, ominously, why I had "allowed" Jay and Dan to have "hippie hair." Increasingly nervous that one of these zealots would assume that his National Rifle Association membership card carried with it the privilege to fire on anyone with whom he disagreed, I began herding the students back on the bus. We chalked up the incident to evidence of how acrimonious the battle in the West between environmentalists and land users had become. It was a conflict we encountered again and again, a volatile issue not fully appreciated on the East Coast.

Shortly after crossing into California, we all fell asleep while Frank listened obsessively to both sides of Elton John's *Madman Across the Water* twice through. At one point, he later told me, he rewound the tape four times in a row to melt his soul into the cut "Indian Sunset." His brain thoroughly Eltonized, Frank got drowsy and pulled into the parking lot of the Roy Rogers Museum in the small town of Victorville for a two-hour catnap. Thus we awoke next to a giant twenty-four-foot statue of the famous film horse Trigger rearing on his hind legs that welcomes visitors at the entrance. Inside the stuffed and mounted carcass of the real Trigger is on display.

At 6:00 A.M.—sunrise on Easter Sunday—Frank awoke and steered us onto the LA freeway, I-10 to I-101, past Pasadena, Glendale, and Thousand Oaks, his mission to get the Majic Bus around Los Angeles and to the beautiful blue Pacific Ocean at Ventura by 8:00.

For those of us unlucky enough to be awake, the view of greater Los Angeles from the Majic Bus was depressing in the extreme. To East Coast eyes accustomed to the glories of maples, oaks, and evergreens, the naked, semidesert vista seemed inhospitable to such dense human habitation. The occasional tall, spindly palm that periodically punctuated the

353

skyline was not embraced in the Eastern definition of trees. The monochromatic dusty brown sameness was intensified by the low-lying stucco
rectangles that hung one another as far as the eye could see, the classic
clarity of the simple form lost in their infinite numbers, the geometric
solidity and stability of their shape undermined by the specter of the San
Andreas Fault. "A big hard-boiled city with no more personality than a
paper cup," the prolific detective novelist Raymond Chandler once called
LA. But what was really depressing was the assault on our olfactories.
Smog, sometimes thick and yellow, sometimes poisonously invisible,
began to seep through the crevices of the Majic Bus, causing eyes to burn
and lungs to constrict. We could smell the noxious mixture, concocted
from our own emissions—from factories, cars, and every form of human
endeavor, trapped in the inversion layer of the LA Basin and baked to
perfection under California's beneficent sun. Ozone, the most dangerous
pollutant, must be cut in half to simply meet the minimum federal and
state clean-air laws. The nearby mountains, now masked by the brownish,
brackish air, are no longer accessible to the human eye. But what was
ultimately depressing was not what you could see, but what you should see
and could not—mountains. They have been relegated to John C. Frémont–
Bear Republic memory, a recollection refreshed perhaps once or twice a
year—Paradise lost. Don't get me wrong, there is a lot I like about the
Greater Los Angeles area: the glorious Pacific sunsets, blue-whale watches,
the Capitol Records Building, midnight at the Anti Club, Olvera Street,
Malibu Lagoon State Park, McCabe's Guitar Shop—the list could go on
and on. But given our limited amount of time, the LA area seemed to me a
congested tangle to be avoided at all costs. The students would get a taste
of the Southern California lifestyle at its best in Santa Barbara.

Staring out the window as we entered and abruptly left one population-
100,000 suburb after another, all searching for a metropolis, all dovetailing into one another with no sensible geographic demarcation lines except
as parts of a Med-fly quarantine circle, I felt a certain amount of guilt for
hurrying by the Hollywood Boulevard exit without showing the students
the homeless Vietnam vets leaning on wooden crutches, and AIDS-
afflicted poor people begging for "spare change" in front of the Dog House,

salivating over its unbeatable breakfast specials, or begging in front of the wig and costume stores and wax museums up and down the famed Walk of Stars as red vans cruised by advertising "Hollywood fantasy tours." But no, the students would miss the underbelly reality of Hollywood Boulevard, and I would forgo the opportunity of finding Nathanael West's broken typewriter in one of the thrift stores on Vine. It was Easter Sunday, and we were seeking redemption and forgetfulness basking in the sun on a beautiful Santa Barbara beach.

15

Santa Barbara and Carmel (Or, Looking for Clint Eastwood in Steinbeck Country)

Californians are a race of people; they are not merely inhabitants of a state.

—O. HENRY

THE STUDENTS AWOKE IN A EUPHORIC MOOD, GREETED BY A view of the blue-green Pacific Ocean, palm trees, and sandy beaches. Years of California dreamin' were now an Easter Sunday reality. It was a gorgeous, balmy, cloudless day, the kind of afternoon that has caused countless millions to pack their belongings and head west to the promised land by the Hollywood Sea. Darlene was on the porch, oscillating between the ecstasy of being in California and self-reproach for neglecting to purchase chocolate bunnies and marshmallow chicks in Las Vegas to distribute for the holiday. For the first and only time on the trip, Justin Buis was the first awake, sneak-smoking half a pack of cigarettes in the bus bathroom in anticipation of being with his father, who lived in Santa Barbara. The game plan was to drop Justin, along with Matt, off at his

356

father's house so the three of them could spend the holiday together sailing. The rest of the gang would enjoy the day swimming in the Pacific and soaking up some rays after a nice Easter Sunday brunch together. The next morning Justin's father would drop the boys off at the campground where we were staying, then off we'd go, clinging to the famed California coastal highway, Route 1, from San Luis Obispo to Big Sur to Carmel.

As we approached the sun-drenched Santa Barbara hillsides, with Donovan singing "Hurdy Gurdy" and "To Susan on the West Coast Waiting," I suggested a brief detour off 101 through the exclusive village of Montecito, home of such celluloid celebrities as Robert Mitchum, Jane Seymour, Steve Martin, Sigourney Weaver, and Michael Douglas. A slim two miles wide, Montecito is a series of hedge-lined estates terracing up from the Pacific to the rugged Santa Ynez Mountains. Magnificent—and wondrously eclectic—homes and gardens flourish in great profusion in this lush, eucalyptus-grove enclave of Santa Barbara. The floral chaparral landscape of Montecito and Santa Barbara, only ninety miles from Los Angeles (or "Loz Anja-Sleaze," as it is known to some of the haughty locals), has been dubbed "America's Mediterranean Arcadia." Julia Child lives in Montecito, which also happens to boast some of the country's best restaurants. We stopped to ask directions to the San Ysidro Ranch Hotel from a young, smartly dressed, patrician, dog-walking couple, with two children in tow, who took the initiative by asking whether we were looking for "Girlie" Bryce's glitterati Easter egg hunt. I almost said yes, intuiting a free brunch, but decided against crashing because we weren't properly dressed. They pointed toward forty-five Hansel-and-Gretel cottages dotting a hillside of the Santa Ynez Mountains and said, "There's your spot." When I tried to make a little weather chitchat about what a hot Easter we were going to have, the woman snapped, "Hot! You call this hot?! It was 133 degrees on June 17, 1959, in Montecito! *That's* hot!" and strutted off to "Girlie's" party.

The hotel, which borders the Los Padres National Forest, has more than five hundred acres of its own land. I had hoped we could brunch at the Stonehouse Restaurant, a converted nineteenth-century citrus-packing warehouse, but as it turned out, reservations were needed. The ranch is more than an attractive lodging with a good restaurant; it's a place with a very special "beautiful people" history worthy of at least two segments on Robin Leach's "Lifestyles of the Rich and Famous." Here John and Jacqueline Kennedy honeymooned, John Galsworthy rhapsodized about the beauties of the mornings, and Laurence Olivier married Vivien Leigh in a secret midnight ceremony attended by Katharine Hepburn and Spencer Tracy. The maitre d' suggested that if we were interested in local history we should visit the old Montecito Inn, once owned by Charlie Chaplin and Fatty Arbuckle and immortalized by Richard Rodgers and Lorenz Hart in "There's a Small Hotel," from the 1936 musical *On Your Toes*. But we decided instead to park the Majic Bus in downtown Santa Barbara and try our brunch luck on Stern Wharf.

Nature has both blessed and cursed Santa Barbara, a city aptly described as the northernmost point in Southern California and the southernmost point in Northern California. It has a marvelous Mediterranean climate, breathtaking scenery, glorious fauna, and wide, palm-fringed beaches. But a price is exacted for living in this terrestrial paradise of white or earth-toned houses perched on hillsides with incredible views of the Pacific: earthquakes, mud slides, and drought. After a 1925 earthquake flattened the city, residents rebuilt it in Spanish colonial style. They forbade any new buildings exceeding four stories, and the commission they established to review design proposals still exerts an iron grip over the cityscape. But the biggest recurring problems are the devastating semiannual brush fires in the surrounding mountains, making this part of California the "most flammable place on earth." The Painted Cave blaze of 1990 still has locals talking about the wall of flames that burned through brush and clusters of oaks, eventually gutting houses. "Brush fires come cheap," a local merchant told Alan. "It's putting them out that comes high."

Although we escaped such evidence of Mother Nature's wrath, in downtown Santa Barbara no one was safe from the possibility of being picked off by a whizzing teenage roller-blader decked out in electric pink and blue-black O'Neill water sportswear, racing around State Street and Cabrillo Boulevard. In most American towns kids can't wait to get a ten-speed bike; in Santa Barbara puberty apparently begins with the first pair of Brauer precision in-line skates and a Flyer or Attack II Boogie Board, an absolute must for riding the glassy surf 365 days a year.

In Santa Barbara, as elsewhere, the Beach Boys are irrelevant rock relics; to the teenage wharf rats, their music seems as ancient as that of the Andrews Sisters. It's reggae and other Third World beats—epitomized by Ziggy Marley and Shabba Ranks, who together symbolize the hip, laid-back Jamaican vibes essential for digging the beach—the majority bops to now. Other kids—those with shaved heads and pierced noses—view the whole rasta-dreadlock-good-vibes attitude as a bunch of stoned nonsense, slamming down instead to the fast, melodic, punk-power pop metal of Bad Religion, Pennywise, and Big Drill Car. Henry Rollins is their idea of poetry, and when he screams, "Life is Meaningless," they all instinctively agree.

If the roller-bladers, skateboarders, and loud bass rap and reggae blasting from the boom boxes don't knock you flat, the reckless and ubiquitous Limousine Surreys, rented at Surf 'N Wears Beach House by lazy European tourists, probably will. (The long-running television soap opera "Santa Barbara" has been playing prime time in Europe for years, and Europeans arrive in town looking for the glitz of the Capwell and Lockridge families.) And if you're a "respectable" teenager and not wearing Bill A Bong Clothing from Australia, Stussy or Gotcha beachwear, or O'Neill sportswear, you're derided as an "out-of-tuner" or a "landlocker." "In" bathing suits this year either glow in the dark or bear psychedelic prints. The unbreakable law of bikini shopping is: The less coverage, the more cost. And, as a final warning to the consumer, the so-called art of Santa Barbara (and other coastal towns such as La Jolla, Newport Beach, and Laguna Beach) has been swamped by aqua-drenched Wyland prints of whales and dolphins. They are as ubiquitous in Southern California as felt paintings of dogs shooting pool are in Dollytown, Tennessee.

It was extremely crowded along the oceanfront, so we parked the Majic Bus at Eladio's Restaurant at the corner of State Street and Cabrillo

Boulevard. We walked to a stone bridge at the main intersection in town and found a large, attractively designed environmental sign that read: MISSION CREEK ESTUARY IS A VALUABLE RESTING AND FEEDING SITE FOR MIGRATORY WATERFOWL, AS WELL AS A FEEDING HABITAT FOR NUMEROUS SPECIES OF SHOREBIRDS AND WADING, DIVING AND AERIAL FISHES. Below that, the interested citizen or visitor could garner details about the estuary's aquatic and wetland plants and birds: the red-throated loon, belted kingfisher, great blue heron, great egret, brown pelican, and five different types of gulls. The beauty of their names alone gave me a frisson of pleasure. As I read to the bottom of the sign, my eye fell on the object of all this environmental concern, the Mission Creek Estuary. In actuality it was a filthy, polluted trash heap. I thought of Magritte's famous painting of a pipe with the words *This Is Not a Pipe* scripted below it. Wake up, Santa Barbara! An environmentally correct sign about an estuary is not an environmentally correct estuary. If this wealthy town, reputed to be full of environmentally concerned citizens, can permit the Mission Creek Estuary to become a polluted eyesore, it bodes ill for the environmental movement in the rest of the nation. Perhaps if all the folks heading to "Girlie" Bryce's had spent the afternoon picking up litter from the estuary instead, an authentic sense of civic pride, not its mere representation, could have been achieved. How can Santa Barbarians walk over the estuary and not want to clean it up—if not for themselves and the animals who live there now, at least for those young roller-bladers and other creatures who'll soon inherit this country. At a minimum, if the town chooses to treat the estuary as a cesspool, it shouldn't add hypocrisy to its sins by erecting signs that pretend it cares.

Hungry for a good breakfast, we crossed Cabrillo Boulevard, passed a fountain with three steel dolphins leaping out of the gurgling water, and headed down Sterns Wharf, where the smells of hot tar, saltwater, and dead fish weigh the air. Built in 1872, and owned from 1945 to 1955 by Jimmy Cagney and his brothers, the wharf stands strong today as the oldest working wooden wharf in California and the premier visitor attraction in Santa Barbara. As we began our half-mile stroll along the Pacific Ocean, a sign clued us in to wharf rules: NO BARE FEET, NO FISHING, NO HIGH HEELS, NO BICYCLES. (Apparently, however, one can toss litter wherever one wishes, with impunity.) Urged on by a large, undulating California bear on a flag flapping in unison with the Stars and Stripes, and our stomachs growling, we decided on the Harbor Restaurant for brunch. A hostess led us upstairs so we could sit on the deck and watch the kelp float in the green Pacific, now dotted with colorful sailboats and a bobbing fleet of fishing boats, as well as a drab oil-drilling platform that spilled ecological devastation in 1969, and the wildlife sanctuaries of the nearby Channel Islands.

The restaurant, puffing its seafood specials and a choice of eighty-six California wines, seems to have begun life as a yacht club facsimile, but over time surfer motifs have negated any clubby aspirations. The clientele has changed from rich blue-blazers to Jimmy Buffett "parrot heads"— that is, from those who yacht to those who like to drink margaritas and daiquiris and wouldn't think of getting themselves wet or seasick. With surfboards hanging from the ceiling, plaster statues of men catching waves that swell right out of the walls, and tropical fish tanks of colorful clown fish and darting leopard sharks, the Harbor Restaurant was an ideal Sunday brunch spot for us, so we put down stakes on the outdoor porch, ready to eat.

Our waiter was an enormous blond, blue-eyed brick house of a man in his early forties almost bursting out of a Reyn Spooner Hawaiian shirt, an apron tied around his waist, a Long Beach State football helmet watch on his wrist. Most of us decided to start off with Virgin Marys or freshly squeezed orange juice, followed by eggs Benedict and fresh fruit. It was obvious our waiter had to have played football, so I asked whether he had been on a team in college. "Sure did, Michigan State University," he replied. With further probing I discovered that our waiter had not only played college football, but he was a five-time NFL all-pro linebacker. Our waiter was the great Brad van Pelt.

When Jared realized that Brad van Pelt was pouring our coffee, he went bonkers. For Jared, van Pelt was a boyhood hero, and he knew every minute, trivial detail about van Pelt's football career and personal life. He fell into a trance combining incredulity and nirvana. Here was Jared

361

sitting in the California sun drinking OJ, the Pacific Ocean under his feet, with a boyhood idol serving *him* breakfast, pouring *him* water. California was indeed a magical land, Jared concluded—for a fantasy like this, let alone the reality, could never have come true in New Jersey.

As he watched van Pelt bus a table he remembered how he used to scream, "Sack 'em!" with gusto each autumn Sunday for twelve years straight as Number 10 made quarterbacks like Joe Theisman and Ron Jaworski scramble for their lives. Now, on this particular Sunday, Jared was ordering his all-pro tackling hero to scramble him up some eggs on the double, and the role reversal was disquieting. He thought of the line in Bob Dylan's "Times They Are a-Changin' " about how the first one now will later be last, and he felt a premature stab of pity for Brad van Pelt. For fifteen minutes Jared drilled our waiter on life as an All-American under the legendary coach Duffy Dougherty at Michigan State, winning the Maxwell Trophy and the Chevrolet Defensive Player of the Year title in 1972; on what it was like being a member of the famed Giants Crunch Bunch, along with Lawrence Taylor and Brian Kelly; on how it felt to be traded to the LA Raiders and to spend his last year with the then-hopeless Cleveland Browns. Finally Jared asked the clincher: What in the name of glory was van Pelt doing waiting on tables in Santa Barbara? He comfortably fielded Jared's question, saying he was learning the restaurant business from the bottom up, and that he would soon be managing Duffy Dougherty's Gridiron Grill on State Street, a new family sports restaurant about to open.

Jared listened excitedly as van Pelt described this utopian sports bar complete with four satellite dishes; twenty TVs, of which three would have giant screens; and sports memorabilia adorning every wall and foyer. To their ESPN-besotted minds there was no such thing as too much sports. Jared got van Pelt to sign a cocktail napkin while Beth snapped a few photos of them together. But as the ex-footballer went about his new duties, Jared grew somewhat depressed. The initial excitement of meeting his hero had worn off, and now Jared was left with a longing in his gut, a feeling of loss he couldn't quite articulate. For a moment, just for a moment, he wished the glaring California sun would fade and it would rain on him real hard—the cold New Jersey November rain of his junior high days, when he would cut across the muddy practice field, drenched, the sounds of the marching band rehearsing floating out of the music room, getting ready for the coming Friday game. And he would reach into the pocket of his Minnesota Vikings jacket and pull out some slightly petrified Halloween candy corn covered with lint, wipe them clean, pop a few in his mouth, and watch his breath rise like smoke from his mouth. Perhaps he was realizing that back then was as good as life got.

After brunch we strolled around Santa Barbara, providing an opportunity for Easter prayers at the Santa Barbara Mission, the crown jewel of the chain of twenty-one mostly eighteenth-century missions dotting coastal California from San Diego to San Francisco. Although the mission charges a one-dollar entrance fee, it has happily resisted vulgarity and overcommercialization, unlike its Santa Fe counterpart. Other downtown destinations included Red Lion Resort—owned by Fess Parker, a screen actor who played Davy Crockett and Daniel Boone—for a "cuppajava" (as the locals say), or just sitting under the huge Morton Bay fig tree enjoying the subtropical climate. The mammoth tree is said to provide shade for ten thousand people, which goes to prove that Texas isn't the only place where they like to tell tall tales. On this particular Sunday, the tree was the resting spot for a dozen homeless men hungrily ripping into little Easter baskets provided by a local church. Two disheveled gamesmen in an alcohol haze were shooting marbles with the malted-milk eggs they had been given, occasionally retiring one from active play to pop into their mouths. This abject poverty is now a scrim to the chic shops that are turning State Street and its shaded *paseos* into a Mediterranean-style Rodeo Drive, where boutiques, galleries, and gourmet shops boast of their showy clientele of expatriate Beverly Hillers and elite *rancheros visitadores*, from Ronald ("the Gipper") Reagan to Michael ("the Gloved One") Jackson. Nothing is simple in Santa Barbara, a town where even the pizzas are designer and the antiques on Brinkerhoff Avenue are "guaranteed to be genuine."

On our way out of town we dropped off Matt and Justin, got back on Route 101 going north, listening to L. L. Cool J.'s "Going Back to Cali"

363

and some new hip-hop group's retool of James Brown. As we whizzed up the coast, we passed Goleta Beach, site of the first (and only) attack on continental U.S. soil since the War of 1812: A Japanese S-17 submarine lobbed sixteen shells at the Ellwood Beach oil field on February 23, 1942. We drove past the Earl Warren Showgrounds, a tribute to the great liberal chief justice of the U.S. Supreme Court (and former California governor), and then past huge hillside ranches and miles and miles of orange groves. Smelling the sweet scent of orange blossoms mingling with the salty ocean breeze made me long for a California Johnny Appleseed out there somewhere, planting seeds so orange trees could reclaim the endless urban concrete.

There is a string of beautifully maintained, sparkling, sandy state beaches between Santa Barbara and San Luis Obispo, and I had chosen Refugio State Beach as our campground because the thirty-nine-acre park has more than a mile of ocean frontage and palm trees line the shore near the mouth of Refugio Creek, creating a picturesque, tropical atmosphere. Ideal for basking on a sandy beach, lying under palm trees on the greensward, building a nighttime beachfront fire, studying the interesting tide pools, and hiking along the two-and-a-half-mile-long path that connects with El Capitan, Refugio had the added attraction of a basketball court. Working on our tans was important; exercising was essential.

By the time we arrived at the park entrance it was 2:00 P.M. Most of the students were already in their bathing suits, raring to take their first Pacific plunge. Frank maneuvered the bus into the campsite, next to a wooden picnic table, chasing away a clan of scavenging seagulls fighting over low-stakes debris. Frank barely had the engine off before we poured out of the bus and sped past the giant palm trees and camp convenience store to splash. For the next four hours we took restorative ocean swims and dips; roasted in the sun; tossed the Frisbee around; read aloud some Charles Bukowski cantankerous, booze-fueled poems (whose publisher, Black Sparrow Press, founded in 1966, is headquartered in Santa Barbara); discussed the odds of getting skin cancer; and let our nostrils fill with the smell of barbecue, hoping the delicious aroma emanated from Frank cooking us supper.

Sprawled for hours on the sand like sea lions, our bodies turned brown just like theirs. Shortly after high tide, surf fishermen began casting off in hopes of catching walleye or rubberlip or other surf perches that follow the tide in to feed on sand crabs and shellfish. Somewhat dehydrated but refreshed, we watched a fishing boat skim homeward with its catch in the late-afternoon sun, trailing hordes of hungry gulls. After a heated but brief debate over who was the most sunburned, we returned to the Majic Bus, expecting to find an Easter feast spread out on the red-and-white-checkered tablecloth. Instead we got Chef Perugi snoring in a hammock he had tied to two salt cedar trees, his Stetson pulled over his eyes and an empty bottle of the newly invented Jack Daniel's Lynchburg Lemonade cocktail in his hands. Frank had taken Easter off.

While the women students showered and put on clean clothes, the guys played a few intense games of basketball, working up not only a sweat but an appetite. A Mexican family at least fifty strong had taken over the volleyball net and horseshoe pit, and the sand was flying to the beat of Flaco Jiménez. As we lay exhausted on the grass, catching our postgame breath, we watched a queue of blindfolded youngsters taking turns with a broomstick, swinging with all their might at a donkey *piñata* hanging from a strangely contorted tamarisk tree. Finally, a girl no more than ten, wearing a Teenage Mutant Ninja Turtles T-shirt, broke the donkey open with some help from Dad—to the shrills and shrieks of her brothers, sisters, and cousins. Packages of assorted LifeSavers tumbled to the ground, and like human vacuum cleaners, twenty little hands sucked up the candy in an instant, leaving the *piñata* breaker in tears: By savoring her triumph a moment too long, she didn't get any candy.

After showers we recruited three heavy-armed, twelve-year-old Bart Simpsons to sneak-attack Stefanie with their giant Super 100s water guns, and they proceeded to drench her. Stefanie was out for our blood for the remainder of the trip. It was dark out now, and none of us had eaten dinner. The convenience market was closed, and we had no food except a few bags of Chee·tos. Frank was awake now but refused to leave the hammock to take us Easter-night grocery shopping. The nearest open store was twenty miles away, and we needed wheels. Christine had an idea.

That afternoon she and Aíne had met Kevin and Shannon, the surfer-dude sons of Ted Parr, the Refugio Beach ranger. The Parrs lived on a cliff overlooking the ocean, in a small gray saltbox house with broken lawn furniture scattered around the yard. Perhaps if we knocked on their door and asked, one of the sons might take us shopping. Beth, Jared, Dan, and I decided to give it a try. Kevin Parr said he'd be glad to. The five of us piled into his sardine-can white Honda Civic with a grungy white fuzz-covered interior. He sped out of the campground, blasting KTYD Rock 99.9 from the stereo. It was a no-brainer to realize that Kevin was wild on wheels. He began honking at road signs, saying, "Look, there's a friend!" (Ha-ha!) *Honk! Honk!* "Look, there's another friend!" Kevin had taken the hellcat Jeff Spicoli from *Fast Times at Ridgemont High* as a role model. We arrived at the grocery, purchased bags of hot dogs, hamburgers, chicken, and fish, not to mention a variety of snacks, ringing up a three-hundred-dollar bill. Although Beth, Jared, and I snickered about our chauffeur's penchant for the horn, we were grateful that he had gone out of his way for us.

No sooner had we squeezed back into his car than Kevin started laying on the horn again and barking out the window at the stars, or "awesome glowers," in Kevin's lexicon. As he accelerated to ninety miles per hour our gratitude evaporated, and we became frightened. Then Kevin upped the ante, in an attempt to scare us even more, by shutting off the headlights. "Now the cops can't see us," he chortled as we raced down Route 101 in the pitch black. After twenty long seconds of passenger panic, he switched the headlights back on, shrieking hysterically and calling us scaredy-cats. We bit our tongues and said nothing. This was the second crazy ride Jared and I had experienced that week—the first being the mad dash to the Federal Express office in Albuquerque—and we feared it might be our last. We returned to the park all in one piece, however, heroes not for surviving this trial by automobile but for arriving with bags of food. My zest for living honed by the little spin with Kevin, I found the rest of the evening perfect. After feasting on grilled burgers and potato salad, we blissfully walked to the ocean to watch the breaking foam white-wash the beach, and the offshore waves glow and glitter mysteriously while their miniature star showers cascaded through the surf, courtesy of the phosphorescent plankton *Noctiluca*, named for its night light.

The ranger's son had said the grunion—small, silvery fish—would be running that evening, the females anchoring themselves in the sand to lay as many as three thousand eggs at a time. Thousands would arrive late at night with the highest tides, following a full or new moon. A few of the students elected to wait up for the usually predictable grunion run while enjoying the full moon on the Pacific. When the grunion came, they would, they said, try to catch them with their bare hands. The moon came and went but no grunion. At sunrise they returned to the Majic Bus to call it quits.

Later that morning Mr. Buis delivered Justin and Matt on time, more burned than bronzed. They had enjoyed their Easter sailing the Pacific together and bragged unmercifully for an hour about what the rest of us had missed. Most of the students went for swims and showers while Frank brewed pots of his worst cowboy coffee yet, the kind with a mouthful of grounds in every sip, causing many students to spit-spray out their first taste. Frank just laughed. He was in a jovial mood, for he was convinced his longtime fantasy of meeting Clint Eastwood was going to come true. For weeks Frank had dropped broad hints about visiting Clint Eastwood's restaurant, the Hog's Breath Inn, in Carmel on our way to San Francisco; somewhere in New Mexico I had added it to our agenda. From that moment on Frank had a hunch, a premonition, that Eastwood, the former mayor and still a resident of Carmel, would be in his inn the night of our arrival. And tonight was the night. In anticipation of the encounter, Frank shaved, put on his best Western outfit, and took down his framed photo of a sneering Clint Eastwood from *The Good, the Bad and the Ugly* and polished it spotless with Windex. When Matt came stomping into the bus with sandy shoes, Frank threw a fit; he wanted the Majic Bus kept immaculate, "in case Mr. Eastwood decides he wants to inspect our quarters." All day long we teased Frank that he had become a hybrid of Felix Unger and an expectant mother. His knowing response? "You'll eat your words."

By 11:00 A.M. we had packed our tents and camping accessories and were ready to head north up the beautiful Central Coast, the shoreline between the state's two megalopolises, which embodies all that is uniquely Californian—rolling surf crashing into wide beaches, gnarled cypresses, and dramatic cliffs and mountains. Californian chauvinists claim there's nothing to equal it on the face of the earth, and by the time the Majic Bus made it to Big Sur we tended to agree. Beth, who had sworn nothing could rival the Hamptons, abandoned her stance and admitted, after watching the afternoon sun shimmer on the Pacific, that she was ready to drop everything and move to the Golden State.

Twenty miles from Santa Barbara, I had Frank exit at the landmark Anderson's Pea Soup restaurant in Solvang for cups of gourmet coffee, and heavenly vanilla and strawberry meringues. We moved on to consume other pastries at Olsen's Danish Village Bakery and Coffee Shop, a Danish-style village complete with cobblestone walks, gaslights, stained-glass windows, and a population predominantly of Danish descent. Introduced to Olsen's bakery by my parents a few years ago, I leave William S. Burroughs to his particular obsessions; my fantasies are of Olsen's pastries. Students who wanted something other than sweets headed to Paoli's Italian Country Kitchen for pasta.

The entire town of Solvang looks like the product of Walt Disney's imagination, but it is an authentic Danish town transplanted by emigrants in 1911, with a Hans Christian Andersen museum honoring Denmark's most famous storyteller (author of such universally beloved fairy tales as "The Ugly Duckling," "The Emperor's New Clothes," and "The Princess and the Pea"). Steep-pitched copper roofs with high dormers create an Old World atmosphere, as do the Scandinavian architecture, windmills, and a facsimile of the Little Mermaid statue that graces the Copenhagen harbor. A few students phoned home from the Chimney Sweeps Inn while others bought postcards, toiletries, or *æbleskiver*, a tasty Danish pastry. It was an absolutely gorgeous day, clear except for an occasional high cirrus cloud, the countryside surrounding Solvang a rainbow dazzle of thousands of acres of flowers. We took a short detour to the Santa Ynez Valley town of Ballard, where we bought ten dollars' worth of sweet corn from a stand (six for a dollar), a couple of bags of peaches and persimmons, and whisked by the Presbyterian church Ronald Reagan attends. Not wanting to kill too much time, we headed back to 101 with our heads popped out of the roof, enjoying the fine weather, oaks of every kind, fields of flowers, and horse-breeding ranches.

At Lampoc, the former prison home of Ivan ("Greed is Good") Boesky and the other crème de la crème American male white-collar criminals, we got on Route 1, which we would follow all the way to Carmel. Highway 1, as it's usually called, was the first in the country to be declared a scenic highway, in 1966. Unless the fog gets too thick, the coast is almost always in view from the road. At times the emerald waves break on rocks 1,120 feet below, while only a few miles later the highway is just 20 feet above the surf. The two-lane road is in perfect condition and the scenery is the finest in America, but the abrupt twists and steep climbs are unnerving. The students found it hard to believe nature could be so majestic—we were speechless most of the afternoon, particularly when we stopped for a few moments at the delightfully gaudy Madonna Inn, where we went from the sublime to the ridiculous.

The Madonna Inn, a pinkish castle set on a hillside off the highway, has no connection to the pop star except for a love of the garish. Pink is everywhere—trash cans, pay phones, and soda machines are all pink. Guest rooms have their own color schemes and their own names painted on the doors. The Safari Room, for example, has jungle green walls and carpet, and upholstery made of zebra, leopard, and tiger prints. The Pony Room recalls a barn, and the popular Caveman Room sports a stained-glass window of a Neanderthal in a cavelike stone grotto. It connects, via a secret crawlspace tunnel, to the Daisy Mae Room. There is liberal use of exposed rock as a decorative material. Think as I might, I could come up with nothing remotely historical or academic to justify our visit to the Madonna Inn except that it is an example of California's outrageousness and love of fantasy. The students were impressed not so much by the inn's decor as by the fact that its ridiculous gimmick actually works—the inn, we learned, was booked solid for the next three months. "Innovation always pays," Stefanie told me solemnly as we headed back to the highway.

As Route 1 angles north and west from San Luis Obispo toward the ocean, the landscape is broken by a procession of nine volcanic rocks. Last in this geologic parade is a 576-foot dome called Morro Rock, standing like a miniature Gibraltar but connected to the mainland by a sand isthmus. Years ago, before conservationists and common sense prevailed, Morro Rock was a quarry. Today it's a nesting area for peregrine falcons; the region as a whole serves as a bird sanctuary. Morro Rock is the first signpost indicating you have left Southern California and are entering Northern California, and regionalism is so strong that some people argue that North and South should become two different states.

Just outside Morro Bay we passed a sign for Paso Robles, the city nearest the spot where the great James Dean wiped out at the Y intersection of Highways 46 and 41, smashing his Porsche into the side of a 1950 Ford Custom Deluxe Coupe that had pulled out in front of him. Dean, estimated by troopers investigating the accident to have been traveling in excess of 85 miles per hour, had received a speeding ticket for going 110 in a 35-miles-per-hour zone just two hours earlier, in Bakersfield. A small marker was erected on the site in 1987 by a Japanese businessman, who now wants to put up a giant memorial monolith. Dean's death was on my mind that afternoon, not only because of the Paso Robles sign but also because we were heading into John Steinbeck country, and *East of Eden* is both my favorite Steinbeck novel and my favorite Dean movie.

It has always seemed to me that "9/30/55," the day the twenty-four-year-old antihero James Dean died, marks the end of the American innocence, the day when raw road glamor and hipsterism lost its soulful allure and became representative of self-inflicted Hollywood youth tragedy. I dug out Mark Dinning's classic car-crash tearjerker "Teen Angel" and played it in a Majic Bus tribute to James Dean. The 1959 song is not about Dean but about a train barreling down the line toward the narrator's car, stalled on the railroad tracks. He gets his girl out of the car in time (apparently, in 1959, females had not yet learned how to open car doors by themselves), but she runs back inside to search for the high school ring he had given her. He tries to stop her but fails. The narrator laments his foolish if devoted sweetheart; "I'll never kiss your lips again, they buried you today." After "Teen Angel," I needed something more upbeat: the Bob Dylan–Sam Shepard composition "Brownsville Girl." Cheered because it's about the living road spirit of James Dean, a spirit that will never die, I turned the volume way up.

North of Morro Bay, Route 1 passes villages such as Harmony (population eighteen) and Cambria, a whaling-center-turned-artists'-colony with ridgetop homes, sandy beaches, and rock coves around every bend. The sense of the sea and its power was never very far away. We came to San Simeon, site of the much-touristed Hearst Castle built by newspaper magnate William Randolph Hearst, millionaire master of yellow journalism and the inspiration for Orson Welles's film *Citizen Kane*. The entire complex, which receives more than a million visitors a year, took twenty-seven years to build. In the 1930s and 1940s, when Hearst was in residence, hosting film stars such as Charlie Chaplin, Mary Pickford, and Cary Grant, the grounds contained the largest private zoo in the world. Ninety species of wild animals, including lions and tigers, roamed about. Today it's much more dangerous, because busloads of Japanese and German tourists have been known to trample over an innocent to snap a photo of where Clark Gable once micturated. Why expose my students to this sort of risk, especially since American Odyssey's focus was on America, not on what one immensely wealthy American bought on his European shopping expeditions? The Majic Bus drove right on past San Simeon.

Route 1 winds north past tide pools, big sea-washed rocks, pocket beaches, state parks, and jade coves. To leeward the hills give way to mountains as the highway ascends toward the dramatic Big Sur coastline. Big Sur is one of America's most magnificent natural areas. Only fifteen hundred residents live in this rugged region of scraggy cliffs and flower-choked canyons through which Route 1 weaves, the distant roar of the surf always present. Each turnout affords a glimpse into raw, wild nature as the Santa Lucia Mountains drop down to the Pacific with dizzying grandeur, and redwood trees serve as a natural fortress against intruder winds. With Van Morrison singing "She Gives Me Religion" and wisps of fog intermittently interrupting our view, we all sat with our noses to the window, hungering to get out of the bus for a hike or, at the very least, a view unimpeded by glass.

We pulled over at Nepenthe, a favorite hangout with tourists and locals, its deck an excellent place to sit, drink, and gape. Silly arguments sprang up over which was more spectacular—Big Sur or the Grand Canyon. Jay and Dan were ecstatic, having read so much about this rugged coastline in Jack Kerouac's books *The Dharma Bums* and *Big Sur*. Now they were staring out eight hundred feet above the water, seeing the beauty for themselves. Alison said she wanted "to melt her life away there," as she stuck her face in the crisp breeze, which was still carrying hints of recent winter. Most of the students hiked a trail that brought them within mere feet of the ocean, the sounds of waves crashing along the rugged cliffs and beaches, the sea lions barking out a native symphony. Tide pools swirled, alive with small ocean creatures—sea anemones, urchins, starfish. Green and red algae stuck to huge rocks. Looking far out over the ocean we thought we saw sea otters, serenely floating on their backs, their chocolate brown fur glinting like satin; they could have been kelp, without binoculars we couldn't be sure. Swimming was now out of the question; the water looked frigid and the tide treacherous.

When we got back to the restaurant we momentarily thought we were back in Boulder, as a flood of hippies had taken over. One awfully nice fellow we met—with waist-length hair, a tie-dyed shirt, and John Lennon glasses—identified himself as a game-show script writer and told me that Orson Welles and Rita Hayworth had spent their honeymoon at Nepenthe. He was disappointed to learn that I wasn't having the students read Richard Brautigan's *Trout Fishing in America*, which, he said, "tells it all like a primitive, like Thoreau." An admirer of Brautigan's work myself, I told him I'd consider the book for a future American Odyssey course.

Dusk was encroaching as we continued our journey north on Route 1 to the community of Big Sur, which stretches the length of the six-mile-long Big Sur River Valley. Lacking a business or civic center, the town consists of houses and stores dotted haphazardly along the Big Sur River. The place received its name from early Spanish settlers who called the

Daniel Ellison

Daniel Ellison

Driving under the ever-changing sky of northern New Mexico.

A Pueblo jewelry saleswoman taking an afternoon siesta in Santa Fe.

Beth Neville

Dan, Alan, and Janine eating ice cream at a Dairy Queen in New Mexico after hearing about Billy the Kid.

Floating down the Rio Grande in New Mexico, heading for rough white water.

Darlene Dudash in Santa Fe.

Alison Andrews pays homage to Route 66—the Mother Road—in Williams, Arizona.

Kenny Young and Doug Brinkley at Yaki Point in the Grand Canyon, shortly before "Good Morning America" began filming.

The Majic Bus goes screaming down the strip in Las Vegas, blasting out Little Richard and Jimi Hendrix.

The students were amazed by how slot-machine playing in Las Vegas is almost a religious obsession.

Jared Goldman with five-time NFL all-pro-defensive-end-turned-Santa-Barbara-waiter, Brad van Pelt, on Stern's Wharf.

The Majic Bus finally makes the Golden Gate Bridge.

On Jack Kerouac Street in front of the famous Beat hangout City Lights Bookstore in San Francisco, where the students were given a guided tour.

The stone remnants of Wolf House at Jack London's Beauty Ranch in Glen Ellen, California.

Stefanie Pearlman on the northern California coast.

Douglas Brinkley in Big Foot country, California.

Paul Bunyan's ox at Trees of Mystery on scenic Redwood Highway U.S. 101 in Klamath, California.

The Majic Bus in Humboldt–Redwood State Park. We stopped to move a huge tree branch that was blocking our path following the Ferndale earthquake.

The rubble of downtown Ferndale an hour after the quake hit northern California, leaving us in a state of shock.

Daniel Ellison

Dressed in Day-Glo jumpsuits at Ken Kesey's farm in Pleasant Hill, Oregon, ready to take a ride on the famed bus "Further".

Beth Neville

Daniel Ellison

The Majic Bus meets up with Further.

Ken Kesey brought the students to meet his former Merry Prankster buddy Ken Babbs and his family.

Praying with a Crow medicine
man on his reservation in
southeastern Montana.

Tourist shop Indians at the Battle of
Little Bighorn National Battlefield in
Montana.

Buffalo herds at Theodore Roosevelt National Park
in North Dakota.

Celebrating Alan's birthday at the Rough Rider Hotel in
Medora, North Dakota.

Kevin Willey branding cattle at a
South Dakota ranch on May Day.

Mount Rushmore was an obligatory stop.

wilderness south of Carmel *el país grande del sur,* "the big country to the south." Later it became a rural retreat and artists' colony. Henry Miller, who assiduously wished to avoid what he called the air-conditioned nightmare of America, lived in this out-of-the-way retreat from 1947 until 1964. During his residency he wrote *Big Sur and the Oranges of Hieronymus Bosch, Plexus,* and *Nexus.* We stopped by the Henry Miller Memorial Library, hoping to tour the small frame house and museum that contain volumes from the novelist's library as well as his own provocative works, but it was closing, disappointing Jay, Dan, Janine, and Alison, all fans of *Tropic of Cancer.* They settled for the consolation of a walk around the premises.

Alison was even more disappointed when we had to bypass the Point Lobos State Reserve, a 1,225-acre peninsula and underwater preserve containing more than 300 species of plants and more than 250 species of animals and birds. I, too, wanted to visit the reserve, because it is the park Robert Louis Stevenson used as his model for Spyglass Hill in *Treasure Island,* perhaps my favorite childhood novel. But it was now dark, and we had spent the entire day along the coast. Frank was itching for his fated rendezvous with Dirty Harry, so it was on to the Hog's Breath Inn in Carmel.

Wealthy Californians migrate to Carmel to live out their comfortable fantasies of rural life. The town possesses one of Northern California's most beautiful beaches; cliffs with lonely, wind-sculpted cypresses; a gloriously restored Spanish mission; and a main street lined with jewelry stores, kitsch-for-the-rich art galleries, boutiques featuring the latest in conservative fashion, and hokey gift emporiums. Window shopping is a favored pastime, and locals are recognized by their cashmeres and their Burberry raincoats. Carmel's the place Californians come to wear their winter clothes in summertime.

But paradise has a price, for both outsiders and residents. Local ordinances forbid parking meters (police chalk tires to keep careful track of how long cars have parked), customary-size street signs, address numbers, billboards and, as we were about to find out, buses. The five thousand residents, who think they are special somebodies because they are fortunate enough to have the means to live in this quaint toy town, have no postal deliveries. Everyone has a box in the post office and religiously collects mail from there, where they can complain about tourists and Clint gawkers.

Ironically, the Reagan-Bush tirade against government regulation fell on deaf ears in this wealthy enclave. Carmel has more blue laws and phony freedom-infringing regulations than Reagan has liver pills. It is illegal to wear high heels. If you trip and fall on a faulty sidewalk while in heels and try to sue the city, think again. You'll be slapped with a violation and a fat fine. Fun of any kind is strictly limited in Carmel: Singing and dancing are illegal not only on the streets but in bars, cafés, restaurants. A town that bans singing?! How can people be denied their basic civil liberties in the United States? And we don't even know where Carmel stands on humming! Until Clint Eastwood's tenure as mayor, even the outdoor eating of ice-cream cones was prohibited. Worse yet, this bastion of military retirees, old-money shipping magnates, agribusiness giants, and hokey Hollywood hustlers legislates what is and is not art. If you want to put up a poster in your store window, *any* poster, it must pass muster by the Artistic Review Board of the City Council, whose views on art can be readily inferred. Big Brother is everywhere in Carmel, hellbent on legislating taste. The problem is not just that he has bad taste, which he does—Carmel's idea of chic is an anemic pseudo–French Impressionist seascape with barking seals, or a portrait of clown Emmett Kelly—but that he is imposing his standards on everyone else.

Although now a town for the superaffluent, who regard local resident Merv Griffin as an artiste because he produces "Wheel of Fortune" and discovered Pat Sajak, Carmel was once the adopted home of several *real* San Francisco intellectuals. Poet George Sterling came in 1905, followed by novelist Mary Austin. Eventually such literary luminaries as Upton Sinclair, Lincoln Steffens, and Sinclair Lewis settled, for varying periods. Jack London, Joaquin Miller, and Ambrose Bierce visited often. Finally, photographers Ansel Adams and Edward Weston located here. But the figure most closely associated with this "seacoast of Bohemia" was Robinson Jeffers, a poet who came seeking solitude in 1914. Gleaning rock from the shoreline, he built Tor House and Hawk Tower, where he lived and wrote haunting epic poems about the coast. Today the artists' garrets are gone, replaced by the equivalent of a shopping mall for tourists and foolish well-to-do.

Don't even consider thinking a Bohemian thought in Carmel, the picturesque police state on the Pacific.

We parked the Majic Bus by Robinson Jeffers's Tor House and Hawk Tower and walked to the foot of Ocean Avenue to see Carmel Beach, cypress trees casting shadows, the dazzling sand dunes bright white even though it was nighttime. Frank was antsy to get to the Hog's Breath Inn, and in just a matter of minutes we found the outrageously named bistro, which gave us hope, albeit short-lived, that Carmel might still be redeemed. The inn was not some small neighborhood restaurant but a full-fledged tourist attraction. After Frank poked his head into every nook and cranny, searching in vain for Clint Eastwood, we were seated at a large table in an open-air courtyard with a flagstone patio, complete with benches, heavy wooden tables, comfortable director's chairs, and overhead heaters. A boar's head, tusks and all, adorned one wall of the English-style pub, and the menu was full of pricey meat and seafood dishes.

The waitress gave us a classic Clint Eastwood dirty look and took her time officially acknowledging our presence. After all, what could be more subversive than seventeen college students and their professor? When she finally deigned to take our drink orders, Frank got right to the point: "Is Clint Eastwood due in tonight?" We all squirmed with embarrassment as he popped the question, but when Little Miss Haughty retorted, "What do I look like, an appointment book? How am I supposed to know?" we quickly came over to his side. Frank was temporarily crushed by this gratuitous put-down, and Alison took the waitress to task for being so rude. Jay, Dan, and Janine led a "Let's get out of this overpriced, snobby, tourist trap" revolt. They had spotted a warm, friendly-looking restaurant called Jack London's on the way and asked if they could go there instead. Though bruised, Frank was still convinced that Clint Eastwood would show, so half of us stayed with him while the other half left for Jack London's. Undeterred by the waitress's snippy response, Frank began asking other workers when they had last spotted Eastwood. The bartender told Frank the famous actor had shown up for a half hour earlier in the evening. This encouraged Frank, but as two hours ticked by he came to realize his fantasy would remain unfulfilled.

Our experience at the Hog's Breath had begun to take a toll on Frank's hero worship. He kept asking out loud how Dirty Harry, the tough guy who said, "Read my lips," could be responsible for a bar filled with pretentious, buttoned-down yuppies and Euro-trash. He had imagined the Hog's Breath Inn as a place working people, farmers, and ranchers would come for a beer. Instead it welcomed the idle rich for champagne and brie. He expected the clientele to be dressed in American clothes—Levi's jeans, cowboy boots, and Nikes; instead it was full of Italian-designer wearers and cologned guys named Biff wearing Top-Siders without socks. He had thought the food would be hearty American fare; instead it was meager portions of indifferent meat and seafood. All Frank got for his exertions was a glimpse of Clint Eastwood posters and endless attitude from self-actualizing New Agers who listened to Kenny G, wore wristwatches that beeped, and discussed the growing interest accumulating in their trust funds.

As we got up to go, Frank was still hanging on to the myth by his fingernails: "Mr. Eastwood has been so busy filming *The Unforgiven* he probably doesn't realize his place has been overrun by prepsters," he rationalized uneasily. Despite his disillusioning evening, Frank wanted to believe in Clint Eastwood as a high-plains drifter, a no-nonsense-or-frills kind of guy. But most of the American Odyssey students could not forgive Eastwood for owning such a pretentious, unfriendly place. To Eastwood's credit, during his two years as mayor of Carmel he fought some of the blue laws, mainly so he could expand the Hog's Breath Inn and make more money off of the other local schemes. Nevertheless, it took courage to take on the City Council; I guess that counts for something.

Jack London's was hopping by the time we arrived. The students had eaten "Call of the Wild" burgers and "Sea Wolf" selections like Monterey Fish and Chips and Calamari Maison. They had just begun reading London's Alaska stories, including *The Call of the Wild* and *White Fang*, and it was fun to be in a café that celebrated his writings. In a few days they would be visiting the Jack London State Historic Park, the great writer's ranch, in Glen Ellen, California. Two college women from Santa Cruz, volunteers for the Humane Farming Association, were lecturing some of the students on the dangers of eating veal. They asserted that the USDA acknowledged that sulfamethazine (a known carcinogen) and drugs such as penicillin, streptomycin, and neomycin have all been found in veal. The catch, they claimed, is that some of the drugs and chemicals found in veal have not been approved by the FDA or any government agency for human consumption. They went on at great length about how "milk-fed" veal calves are, in fact, not fed mother's milk or allowed solid food. Instead they are fed a liquid mixture laced with antibiotics. "Their entire life is spent chained in a crate," one of them exclaimed, verging on tears. "They can't even turn around!" All who heard her plea quickly signed her Toxic Veal Task Force petition—if for no other reason than to allow her to move on.

Frank had struck up a conversation with a gray-bearded German psychoanalyst named Werner who had lived right on the ocean in Carmel for forty years. Werner invited us to park the Majic Bus in his driveway for the night and take showers at his house in the morning, and he promised that his wife would make us homemade sourdough biscuits with pots of coffee to complement a Pacific sunrise from their back patio. We accepted the kind offer. Jay and Dan had met a former guitarist with the Marshall Tucker Band who said he was in Carmel to visit his friend Michael Nesmith, formerly of the Monkees. He was going to come with us to Werner's and sing folksongs for the American Odyssey students. We had a mini-party under way.

As we left Jack London's our two guests joined the Majic Bus gang. Jay had broken out his guitar and was singing Johnny Winter's "Mean Town Blues" with abandon, his long curly hair hanging in his face like Slash of

Guns N' Roses. But in his insurrectionary act of singing, Jay had recklessly violated one of Carmel's Ten Thousand Commandments. The Carmel police, their antennae finely tuned, could sense an illegal song in a second. After we had driven about three blocks, two police cars, sirens screeching, came at us from different directions. Jay stopped singing. The police came aboard and began yelling at Frank for driving his tour bus through Carmel, calling him an idiot. I attempted to intervene and explain that we would be going barely a quarter of a mile, to park the Majic Bus in Werner's driveway for the evening. "No, you're not!" the cop bellowed. "You have a choice: You can either get out of town or spend the night in jail!" At this, Werner blew a gasket and began shouting that we were all friends from New York that he had invited to his home, and that the Carmel police force was acting like the Gestapo. Werner was in a state of complete and utter rage. Not wanting the conflict to escalate, I told the officers we would leave town immediately, and so while one policeman took Werner and Michael Nesmith's alleged buddy away in a patrol car, their fate unknown, the other officer instructed us to follow him. He would give us an escorted bum's rush out of town. Ten miles later he pulled into a grocery store parking lot in Monterey. "I want you to stay put here for the evening," he ordered. "If you leave before sunrise, I'll have you arrested." When I asked why we were being treated like criminals when all we did was have dinner in town, he told me to shut up.

Frank wanted to leave as soon as the police officer disappeared. I convinced him it wouldn't be wise, and so we all slept in the parking lot. I had trouble dropping off as the word *Gestapo* Ping-Ponged in my brain. I wondered whether Carmel, in its open and wanton abuse of police power, might not be in the vanguard of wealthy American towns, which, as the U.S. population in general grows poorer, may go to any extreme to wall off and wall out "the other." I shuddered, because American Odyssey was clearly pegged as alien by the paid enforcers of the Carmel establishment. I thought about the French Revolution and the many exquisite châteaus of the Loire Valley, today bereft of any contents because they were looted by furious French citizens some two hundred years ago. Could it happen here? Probably not, I concluded, because ordinary American folks would take one look at those paintings of Emmett Kelly or the barking seals, say, "The hell with it," and leave. On that cheerful note I fell asleep, with Leonard Cohen singing on my Walkman: "Like a bird on a wire/Like a drunk in a midnight choir/I have tried in my way to be free."

When the sun started to rise, Frank turned on the engine and headed to the waterfront for coffee. California's first capital, Monterey has a long Spanish history; the landmark buildings tell the story. More recently, in the raffish boom times John Steinbeck captured in *Cannery Row*, Monterey was home to a fishing fleet that hauled in 240,000 tons of sardines a year. When the sardines suddenly disappeared after World War II, the fishing industry collapsed. In the last few years, fantasies of making it big once more have found form in the redevelopment of Cannery Row and Fisherman's Wharf, now the sites of thriving restaurants and spiffy new hotels. Frank and some of the students grabbed egg sandwiches and coffees to go by the wharf, and then we were off to Salinas to visit John Steinbeck's home. We were on a tight schedule because we were expected at 1:00 P.M. in downtown San Francisco at Channel 7 KGO-TV, where my sister, Leslie Brinkley, works as a reporter. We were to conduct a special PBS radio interview for thirty minutes, live from the News 7 studio, with the students reading favorite passages from course texts. At 2:00 P.M. we would meet the great poet and owner of City Lights Books, Lawrence Ferlinghetti, for a tour of his store. Then we would check into the Americania Best Western Hotel, and the students would have two nights to discover San Francisco for themselves.

Minutes out of Monterey on Highway 68 to Salinas, a police siren sounded behind us, forcing us to pull off the road. Without even inspecting the Majic Bus or asking Frank for his license, an officer ordered us to follow him to the Salinas Motor Vehicle Department. Ten minutes later, four police officers were strip-searching the bus, while the students sat on the parking lot curb, reading Steinbeck's *Wayward Bus* and taking turns bringing back bags of fast food. For three hours the cops detained us, writing tickets for every regulatory lapse they could, from failing to display a tour

379

bus decal to having a crack in the rearview mirror. I tried to explain to the officers that we were a student group discovering America for university course credit, waving the *New York Times* article in front of them like the Shroud of Turin, hoping to produce a miracle of compassion. But the *New York Times* had no miraculous powers on the West Coast. Then I told them we would miss our PBS radio appointment in San Francisco if they continued looking for reasons to bust the Majic Bus. PBS had no magical powers with these guys either. They simply refused to acknowledge my existence, playing deaf. A few students, sensing a long delay, got directions to 132 Central Avenue. Near the center of town, at this address stands a Victorian house with gingerbread gables, carved brackets, and a graceful Queen Anne tower, which is John Steinbeck's birthplace. They took a quick tour of the house, which has been restored to its turn-of-the-century appearance, and bought paperbacks of *The Pastures of Heaven* and *Of Mice and Men* in the cellar gift shop. They were back in time to take in my lecture on "John Steinbeck's California," delivered in the Salinas police station parking lot. Meanwhile, a red-faced, anguished Frank was pulling his hair out in disbelief at the two thousand dollars' worth of tickets they had slapped him with.

Steinbeck was born in 1902 in Salinas, county seat of Monterey County and marketing center for an incredibly fertile agricultural region often called the "Salad Bowl" of the nation. There he passed his childhood years and attended school, working during the summers in a local sugar refinery. In the early 1920s Steinbeck traveled north to the San Francisco Bay Area to attend Stanford University. He left Stanford without a degree, living briefly in New York and Los Angeles before returning at the beginning of the Great Depression to the Monterey Peninsula, where his family owned a summer cottage. Here his writing skills gelled, eventually winning him the Pulitzer Prize in 1940 and a Nobel Prize in 1962, six years before he passed away in New York City.

Sitting in our classroom without walls, so to speak, lecturing on this

great American writer, I was compelled to comment on how dramatically

Steinbeck country has changed since the writer left in the 1940s. The once-quiet town of Salinas now bustles with more than one hundred thousand souls and look-alike agglomerations of strip malls and parking lots. Steinbeck would no doubt decry all the commercialization, although he might enjoy the irony in the fact that he himself was responsible for most of the fuss. Had he not written so memorably of the hills, valleys, and towns of the central California coast, had he not created characters who arrested the imagination and stirred the heart as powerfully as Doc of *Cannery Row*, Cal and Aron Trask of *East of Eden*, Ma and Pa Joad of *The Grapes of Wrath*, and George and Lennie of *Of Mice and Men*, California might be a little less crowded than it is. Steinbeck's stunning literary accomplishment is truly a national treasure, and without him the landscape of American literature would be a much less fertile place.

Frank was furious over the profusion of tickets he had received, and he felt that had Matt not been filming the white-glove inspection, the police would probably have impounded the vehicle. When I pleaded with one officer to let us go, he said, "I know they let things go to hell back in New York, but we don't here in Monterey County." We were being punished for trying to have a little fun in Carmel. When we finally pulled out of the station, a dispirited and depressed Frank solemnly took down his picture of Clint Eastwood and shoved it under his seat, never to be seen again.

We got on I-101 heading north to San Francisco. It was now 12:30 P.M. and there was no way we would make the Channel 7 newsroom in time to do the PBS radio program. This was a real disappointment because Alison had prepared to read and discuss William Least Heat Moon's beautiful *Blue Highways*, Jay was psyched to read from Hunter S. Thompson's *Fear and Loathing in Las Vegas*, Dan was going to read from *The Dharma Bums*, Janine from Bobbie Louise Hawkins's *My Own Alphabet*, and Kevin from his journal. Shortly after the police detained us I had called PBS to let them know our predicament and was told that if it looked as if we couldn't make the San Francisco newsroom, we should find a conference-

381

call telephone at 12:50 and call a number they gave me. We began frantically searching for a conference phone. Jared spotted a sign that said: LOVE CONNECTION: DATING SERVICE. They were bound to have telephone facilities, we assumed. Frank left the freeway, and all the would-be on-air performers and I rushed in the front door. I explained our plight to the receptionist and told her that the PBS time clock was ticking. She sought out her manager, who pronounced sentence upon us: "Our phones are only for clients. You're not clients, so 'bye." Frantic, we ran across the street into a modern glass building and entered a local San Jose developer's office. When the receptionist heard our tale of woe she immediately agreed to help. Without any further questions she ushered us into a posh boardroom with a beautiful oak conference table. Enthroned in the middle of the table was a telephone designed for conference calls. I called PBS Radio at 12:58, and the program, "Politics and Culture in America," went on as scheduled.

The students rose to the occasion, particularly Alison, who articulated why learning on the road was better than sitting in a classroom. While we were talking, many of the office workers came in to listen, and the receptionist brought us doughnuts and pots of coffee. This unexpected hospitality salved the wounds we had received during the past eighteen hours, although the kindness of strangers does not absolve the police state of its iniquities. The radio show was a glorious success, lifting sagging morale. I called the City Lights Bookshop to tell them we had been delayed. They said we could stop by for a tour whenever we wanted but they wouldn't be able to guarantee Lawrence Ferlinghetti would be around. We offered our good Samaritans profound gratitude and thanks and darted back to the Majic Bus, ready for San Francisco, the city of romance.

During the next hour we drove through miles of industrial centers and community parks, the sun smiling all the while, listening to the Grateful Dead and Jefferson Airplane, in homage to the Haight-Ashbury days and San Francisco's famous Summer of Love. Carmel poet George Sterling once called San Francisco the "cool, gray city of love" and after being scorned in Carmel, Monterey, and Salinas we were badly in need of some loving kindness. And then, as the Dead were singing "Eyes of the World," San Francisco was upon us—the "gold and white acropolis rising wave on wave against the Pacific sky," in John Steinbeck's words. We were ready for its Golden Gates to open up for us with expansive hospitality, and they did.

16

San Francisco: The Gold and White Acropolis

Don't loaf and invite inspiration.
Light out after it with a club.

—JACK LONDON

THE SKY WAS A VIOLET BLUE, WITH SCATTERED LUMINOUS
cloud fragments drifting about in little clusters, as we entered San Francisco. Sunlight fell over the rooftops and down the steep, crooked streets.
San Francisco's spectacular Mediterranean-style cityscape spills over seven
major hills, rising in crescentlike waves above the always-numbing bay
waters. Students immediately decided, as we hit the traffic of Union Street,
that on top of one of those hills—whether Nob, Russian, or Telegraph—
was the place to be, an aerie from which to savor an unimpeded panorama.

San Francisco, poised on the edge of the continent, had resonated in
student psyches for years, and it was interesting to hear the breadth of

personalities, films, and events they associated with the area: Clint Eastwood's original *Dirty Harry*, Sam Spade, Alcatraz escapes, Harvey Milk's
murder, Patty Hearst and the Symbionese Liberation Army, the Grateful
Dead, Willie Mays, Joe Montana, gay parades, Lynette "Squeaky"
Fromne's assassination attempt on Gerald Ford, Bill Graham, rock concerts—and, of course, earthquakes. As we passed Union Square, with its
unexpected palm trees and eager flower merchants, the Majic Bus was
bursting with excitement and Frank battled the one-way streets, clanging
cable cars, and happy Spandex-clad pedestrians and joggers who rushed
across the street in clusters—like fog, beyond rules—moving in every and
any direction. Plagued in recent years by serious urban problems, San
Francisco no longer evokes the unalloyed vision of the alluring and
sensuous life it once enjoyed. To images of cable cars, sourdough bread
with rich butter, and the Golden Gate Bridge, the city—in common with
many others in the United States—is plagued with AIDS, Chinatown gang
wars, unaffordable housing, and pervading homelessness—and more earthquakes.

But if you consider San Francisco in terms of its neighborhoods, then
the magic remains and San Francisco is still "the liveliest, heartiest
community on our continent," as Mark Twain described it about a hundred
years ago. In North Beach's Tosca Cafe you encounter middle-aged, beret-
wearing idlers with foamy white mustaches, still reading *Rolling Stone*,
perhaps recalling its mythic past, when Bob Dylan and Allen Ginsberg
were evicted for unruly behavior, or pehaps making poetic connections
between fog and cats, as T. S. Eliot did in "The Love Song of J. Alfred
Prufrock." In the Tenderloin district, the aptly named sexual marketplace,
downtown businessmen emerge from the twenty-four-hour peep shows and
porn movie houses, shirttails in disarray, to the whoosh of mops and the
odor of ammonia emanating from the private viewing stalls, while the
curbside alcoholics chortle at their temporary reprieve from reality on the
wild side. In Chinatown—the largest Chinese community outside Asia—
Sony battles the Buddha for the heartstrings of merchants (and their sons,
daughters, and grandchildren) who overcame the Chinese Exclusion Act of

1882 and its infamous extensions. Those merchants are still drinking ancient herbal teas to cure all ills and clinging to their assigned zodiac animals in the Chinese lunar calendar.

At Fisherman's Wharf—where they devour crab cocktails from plastic bowls—tourists watch hairy-armed, white-aproned Saint Peters execute torrents of ocean-fresh fish, while all around them street mimes in gold chains juggle fire sticks to a tambourine beat, garnering engaging smiles and endless pennies in return.

In Haight-Ashbury, Day-Glo has faded and freedom is now equated with conga-line roller-skating across "Hippie Hill," in Golden Gate Park. There the flowers are now rooted in soil, not in the barrel of a gun; the site of the Great Human Be-In of 1967 has been converted to a polo field. On Castro Street traumatized people spend grief-filled days working on the Names Project—a gigantic, ever-growing quilt of ten thousand hand-sewn panels pieced together as a memorial for those who have died of AIDS—and rainbow flags, symbols of the gay liberation movement, flutter from windows and flagpoles. On fabled Nob Hill the prestigious Pacific Union Club perches high over the city—immune, members believe, from the prevailing urban ills, a sophisticated retreat where tee times at Pebble Beach and the quality of wild game served at the Huntington Hotel dominate conversations over brandy and cigars. In the Mission District, the lilting Spanish of Salvadoreans, Bolivians, Colombians, Mexicans, and Guatemalans floats over the rows of Dolores Street palm trees, and salty, almost tropical air blows the smell of corn tortillas and the sound of salsa down Balmy Alley, where color explodes on the Diego Rivera–style murals that entreat for peace in Central America. And, of course, there is Japantown, with its massive five-acre Japan Center Complex, where memories of World War II "relocation" camps still linger among the elders, and sushi, sake, and the Kabuki Hot Springs leave visitors ready to move to Kyoto or a remote buddhist retreat near Mt. Fuji.

Until now, the students had experienced San Francisco secondhand, in the words and images of others. Now they were anxious to create San Francisco for themselves. They felt as Maya Angelou had as a young girl—"intoxicated by the physical fact of San Francisco." We would be staying two complimentary nights at the Americania Best Western Hotel, and students were free to roam, provided they recorded their insights and experiences in their journals. Tom Waits was singing "Blind Love" as we pulled in front of the Channel 7 KGO-TV newsroom on Front Street to meet my sister, Leslie, a reporter for the station. She was scheduled to talk to us about her life as a roving journalist—and about earthquakes.

For four-score years one date in San Francisco's history dominated all others: Wednesday, April 18, 1906. On that fateful day a devastating earthquake destroyed much of the city, followed by a fire that engulfed most of what was left. With the passage of time and the townspeople's concerted effort to refer to the disaster as the Great Fire, the Great Earthquake faded from memory. It even lent its name to an amusement ride at Fisherman's Wharf. All this changed, however, on October 17, 1989, when the Loma Prieta earthquake shook the Bay Area to its very foundations. Although the fatalities were intensely localized—nearly all the one hundred deaths that occurred took place in the mile-long collapsed section of the Nimitz Freeway—the quake disrupted life in the Bay Area, not merely because of damage to buildings but because elements of the transportation system were severely disrupted. A week after the quake hit, some ten thousand residents were still unable to reach their homes because landslides had blocked key roads, including Highway 17, the link between San Jose and Santa Cruz. The Bay Bridge, connecting San Francisco with Oakland, was shut down for a month because a section of the upper half had collapsed onto the lower. The Embarcadero Freeway in San Francisco and Interstate 880 in Oakland had to be demolished; permanent replacements are years away, forcing traffic onto surface roads.

My sister was with a news crew in a van crossing the Bay Bridge when the earthquake hit. Their vehicle bounced violently, like an involuntary member of a trampoline act. Once off the bridge, they looked back and saw it had snapped in two and that cars had slid from the upper deck to the lower, motorists emerging from their cars in shock. An instinctive reporter, heedless of likely aftershocks, Leslie accompanied a California

387

Department of Transportation truck to where the bridge had collapsed, becoming the first on the scene. She saw a couple trapped in a car dangling from the upper deck; they were soon rescued. Leslie began filming the damage as helicopters arrived to ferry away injured motorists and dead bodies were pulled from the wreckage. Cars were pancaked to one-foot heights, squashed with people still inside. For the next few days Leslie covered the quake aftermath for Channel 7 at the Nimitz Freeway.

Now, as she welcomed the students to the newsroom, Leslie spoke of the many gruesome sights she had witnessed and of how the earthquake had affected the psyche of the community. After hearing her stories, many students felt relatively lucky to live in New York, where—for all the city's urban ills—the threat of earthquakes is relatively slim. The ever-sports-minded Jared wanted to know how the earthquake had affected the "Baysball" World Series between the Giants and the Oakland A's, for he somehow couldn't process the TV image of sixty-two thousand fans in Candlestick Park awaiting the start of the World Series, rocking in the big quake, and then calmly sitting back and awaiting the first pitch (an exaggeration, my sister told Jared). Still, one nonchalant Giants fan did hold up a quickly made sign: THAT WAS NOTHING—WAIT TILL THE GIANTS BAT.

Leslie also talked of behind-the-scenes life at the station, a discussion that was of particular interest to Christine and Matt, both contemplating careers in video production. Leslie closed by quoting San Francisco's then-mayor (now a U.S. senator) Dianne Feinstein: "California seemed undaunted, [though] we'll never be a match for Mother Nature. But the principal thing that seems to arise from the ash and rubble of a quake is the strong resolve to rebuild and get on with life."

While Leslie briefed the students on the history of North Beach, our next destination, I called City Lights to let them know we would soon arrive for their presentation on the store's role in the San Francisco poetry renaissance of the fifties and sixties. After I brought the students to North Beach and City Lights and checked them into the Best Western, Leslie would pick me up for dinner in Walnut Creek, where her ten-month-old baby, Alexa, my beautiful niece, would be the main attraction.

So, with the Majic Bus parked in front of the studio, off we walked through the streets of San Francisco to the seedy Tenderloin District and then on to North Beach, where City Lights is located. Suicides occur an average of one every ten days in the Tenderloin—the last flopping place on the continent for lost souls. In 1989, citizens in the twenty-block neighborhood banded together to force cheap, fortified, one-dollar-a-pint wines off the grocery shelves. They hoped to reduce the number of street winos who panhandle, urinate, and fight among the five thousand children who share public spaces with them. Nonetheless, we passed a half dozen forlorn derelicts with bottles of Thunderbird and Night Train Express. Unable to depart from the tradition of drinking in the Tenderloin simply because some residents found them offensive, they had merely taken their meager business elsewhere. After walking about ten blocks, we saw the words CITY LIGHTS BOOKSELLERS AND PUBLISHERS painted across the top of the building at the corner of Columbus and Broadway; it was a literary landmark worth journeying across the United States to see.

It was difficult for students to comprehend that when poet Lawrence Ferlinghetti opened City Lights in 1953, it was the first all-paperback store in the United States—and paperbacks weren't considered "real" books back then. Soon Ferlinghetti—whose *Coney Island of the Mind* is an American classic—moved into publishing many Bay Area poets and novelists, inaugurating what columnist Herb Caen called San Francisco's Beatnik era. Asked why North Beach was a beacon for so many Eisenhower-era Bohemians, Ferlinghetti purportedly replied that it was the "only place in the country you could get decent cheap wine." Ferlinghetti also credited North Beach's rich mix of ethnic restaurants and coffeehouses. The Beatnik era blossomed into the psychedelic sixties of Allen Ginsberg's Flower Power and Ken Kesey's acid-head rock before it spun itself out. Because of our own encounter with the Salinas police, the students missed Ferlinghetti (who now spends more time on painting than poetry), but we were treated to a tour of City Lights by press editor Bob Sharrard.

The first sign that the times they've been a-changing at City Lights is

389

that a bookshop that made its reputation printing and selling "Pocket Poetry"—six-inch-square paperbacks of poetry for working people—now guards its doors with an antishoplifting device. Abbie Hoffman's notorious book entitled *Steal This Book* would clearly be unwelcome in the sober-minded nineties. Ferlinghetti's fine abstract canvases adorn the walls, his painting *Books Are Trees Made Immortal* the most eye-catching. In the Poetry Room, Sharrard spoke of City Lights and the Beat poets who launched San Francisco's renaissance, the either-or-ness of the times symbolized in the black-and-white checkerboard floor, black-and-white photographs of Ginsberg, Joyce, Pound, Bukowski, Rimbaud, Corso, Whitman, Creeley, Cassady, and Kerouac on the walls, and racks of black-and-white post-cards of poets, painters, jazz musicians, and novelists available for the picking. Following a question-and-answer session, Sharrard led us down a book-lined wooden staircase past Indian resistance movement FREE LEONARD PELTIER posters and T-shirts and a community bulletin board bearing homemade flyers—LEARN FOLK DRUM RHYTHMS FROM INDIA, and LOOKING FOR GARRET IN NORTH BEACH—and advertisements for basement productions of Sartre's *No Exit* and Shepard's *Sad Lament of Pecos Bill on the Eve of Killing His Wife.*

The basement was filled with books color coded by subject. (The green section, naturally, contained a broad inventory on the environment.) City Lights resembles a coffeehouse or gathering place more than it does a bookstore, and chairs are scattered throughout; people sit on them and read as if they were in a library, free from commercial imperatives. Many students found the names and number of progressive newspapers for sale astounding: *Women and Revolution, The Catholic Worker, Resistance News, Socialist Worker, Spartacist,* and *Vietnam Today* among them. I told them they should have expected such plenitude in the city where *Mother Jones* is published. The United States, they were discovering, is a nation of subcultures, with a newspaper (or computer bulletin board) for every cause, cult, and interest group imaginable. Most students purchased at least one book at City Lights, and Dan picked up the complete works of Jack Kerouac. Then we crossed Jack Kerouac Alley so students could take photos of City Lights and its mural depicting French symbolist poet Charles

Baudelaire, with his heart on fire, accompanied by a sign that reads, PRINTERS' INK IS THE GREATEST EXPLOSIVE. Then we dropped by Vesuvio's Bar, a surviving Beat hangout.

Many iconic Beat hangouts are no more: the Coexistence Bagel is now a video store and the hungry i (which hosted Lenny Bruce's and Barbra Streisand's first West Coast appearances) a topless bar. But Vesuvio's— "a Rendezvous for the Creative People of Bohemia by the Bay since 1948"—has endured, its interior unchanged since the days when Dylan Thomas and Jack Kerouac tried to drink away their sorrows there. The bar's motto is still intact: W. C. Fields's " 'Twas a woman who drove me to drink . . . and I never had the decency to write and thank her." As we traveled across the United States, I noticed that the traditional claim to fame of the hospitality industry, "George Washington slept here," had been replaced by "Dylan Thomas and/or Jack Kerouac drank here"—the White Horse Tavern in New York and Vesuvio's in San Francisco the apparent originators of the phenomenon. It seems that these two writers hoisted a few in every bar in the country, but Vesuvio's offers Beat gawkers an added attraction: a Jack Kerouac cocktail (rum and tequila mixed with orange and cranberry juice). Vesuvio's looks like a Left Bank bistro—people play chess and read books under Tiffany-style lamps. They drink heartily under the watchful eye of Virginia Woolf, whose image looms over customers from behind the bar. Aíne and Dan were reading *The Dharma Bums* in Vesuvio's for their upcoming San Francisco examination, and it felt terrific watching them. Kevin stood in the John Wilkes Memorial Booth, on the second-floor balcony, and read aloud from the same book. Then we listened to a blind Chinese violinist, unshaven and wearing black slippers, play "The Spring Comes to the Field" and "Moonlight on the Imperial Palace." Our journey back to the Eisenhower era was over, and we walked back to the Majic Bus in a rueful mood.

That evening, and the next day and night, the students explored San Francisco on their own. Their journals reveal that San Francisco was their favorite cityscape of the journey, a town they found conservative yet burgeoning with personal freedoms and liberties. Kevin, Darlene, and Tom had a wonderful evening on Pier 39, stuffing themselves with seafood washed down with good California wine, watching the impromptu street entertainers and spending a late evening listening to the Brian Melvin Trio at the Pier 23 Jazz Club. Alan and Alison spent an afternoon at the Exploratorium, which they described as an "alive" science museum with a mind-boggling variety of interactive exhibits to delight visitors of all ages. Beth, Shari, and Stefanie attacked Chinatown with gusto, enjoying not only the obligatory pressed duck, won ton soup, and egg rolls at the Mandarin but taking a window-shopping tour down Grant Avenue, impressed by the goldfish and porcelain dolls and free offerings of ginseng. As might have been predicted, Mitch, our Sam Walton enthusiast, enjoyed just strolling around the financial district, where he marveled at the 853-foot TransAmerica pyramid and appreciated the massive black granite sculpture by the Japanese artist Masayuki, *Banker's Heart,* which struck a chord with him. Tom joined Jared at Alameda County Stadium to see the Oakland A's (Mark McGuire hit two homers). Dan and Jay spent a memorable evening at the Warfield, listening to Van Morrison belt songs from his double CD *Hymns to the Silence,* along with back-catalog classics. When Van the Man launched into "Crazy Love," Dan wrote, "It was like hearing God for the first time." (Although I thoroughly enjoyed playing with my niece, I really regretted not joining Dan and Jay; music doesn't get any better than Van Morrison.)

But of all the students, the KDR men—Kenny, Justin, and Matt—had the most unusual and educational experience. After checking into their hotel rooms, the three went to the nearby Casa de Brazil restaurant and feasted on *feijoada,* the delicious mélange of meats and beans that is Brazil's national dish. In front of the restaurant stood a homeless Vietnam vet, a man who survived on disability augmented by begging. He was on crutches because his leg had been blown off at Hue in 1967, and he was wearing a green army jacket decorated with buttons with such sayings as SHAZAM, PEACE IS PATRIOTIC, and WATER IS TOXIC. The KDR men struck up a conversation with Bill, a goateed refugee from the sixties. Most students had wanted to do San Francisco on foot, climbing the steep hills with a scenic Coit Tower bench as a reward, but the KDR men, led by Justin, wanted to see the entire Bay Area, including Marin County, Oakland, and Berkeley, by car. Bill, who claimed to have been "born and raised in the San Francisco shade," offered to guide them the next day for the modest fee of lunch. They agreed and made an appointment to meet him in front of the restaurant. That evening, as they hung out at John's Grill—a great, gritty pub featured in *The Maltese Falcon* and something of a shrine to Dashiell Hammett, the detective writer Raymond Chandler credited with "taking murder out of the parlor and throwing it into the alley where it belongs"—the KDR men debated whether they should blow off Vietnam Bill. Anyone with a WATER IS TOXIC button, they thought—apparently unaware of the enormous battles between urban and agricultural interests over water quality in the Bay Area—couldn't be playing with a full deck.

Leaving the issue unresolved, with Justin behind the wheel of a rented Chrysler LeBaron, they pulled in front of Casa de Brazil the next morning, saw Vietnam Bill in front, and shouted, "Come on in." It was a decision they wouldn't regret. That afternoon and into the evening they went everywhere with Vietnam Bill, who proved to be an armchair historian of the 1960s Bay Area. They visited the wind-scoured Coit Tower, impressed not only by the panoramic view but by the engineering integrity of the Golden Gate and Bay bridges. Justin steered them down Lombard Street (the "crookedest street in America") while Bill told them of midnight bicycle races he participated in as a teenager in which skinned elbows and mild concussions were commonplace. Bill directed Justin to Mission Dolores, the sixth of the twenty-one adobe missions founded by Father Junípero Serra, and he pointed out several new cracks in the wall, a result of the 1989 earthquake, and the mission cemetery, where more than five thousand Indians are buried.

They laughed when Vietnam Bill called people with neckties "imperialists," cable cars "matchboxes," and the entire city of San Francisco "Beulah Land." He had a lingo all his own, partially formed, as they privately diagnosed, by taking one too many tabs of Orange Sunshine acid. They spent much of the afternoon in Haight-Ashbury, Vietnam Bill pointing out such sites as Janis Joplin's old house on Lyon Street; the famed Psychedelic Shop, now a pizzeria; the laundromat where he once washed his clothes with the band Moby Grape; and 710 Ashbury, onetime Victorian home of the Grateful Dead. When Kenny casually inquired about Jerry Garcia's current residence, Bill said, "I'll show you all," and before they realized what was happening, Justin found himself driving over the burnt orange Golden Gate Bridge, eventually exiting I-101 and weaving around back roads until they found themselves in front of Jerry's Marin County ranch. For a Dead Head that's as cool as it gets.

On the way back into San Francisco, Vietnam Bill told them the best time to visit the Bay Area is October, when the Mesoamerican holiday The Day of the Dead is celebrated in the Mission District: "If you're in the right frame of mind, you can hear the bone mariachis play." It's also when brown eagles glide horizontally, on their ninety-inch wingspans, over Hawk Hill at Marin Headlands in Golden Gate National Recreation Area. When Kenny asked about the Vietnam War, Bill always avoided direct responses, talking instead about the more than six hundred thousand Vietnamese refugees who have settled in the United States, including forty thousand in the San Francisco Bay Area. These "boat people" were special to him, Vietnam Bill confessed, for whenever he saw one of them he was haunted by "how he might have murdered one of their family members." Kenny stopped asking questions.

Bill said black-and-white relations weren't very good in the Bay Area, and he sensed a riot in the air. When pressed for the source of his premonitions, Bill laughed and began singing a Dead verse from the song "Money Money": "Knockin' off my neighborhood savings and loan/To keep my sweet chiquita in eau de cologne." On this point Vietnam Bill was prescient, even if he was off as to cause, for a few weeks later, on April 30, an unruly mob of seven hundred people rampaged through the streets of downtown San Francisco, breaking windows, looting department stores, and setting trash fires, all the while chanting "Rodney, Rodney, Rodney!" outraged that the Los Angeles police who beat Rodney King—a beating frozen for posterity in a bystander's videotape, stunning the nation—had not themselves been deemed criminals by a Simi Valley jury.

It was dark out when they dropped Vietnam Bill off at Union Square. They were grateful he had spent the afternoon showing them around but were now more than ready to say good-bye. They scraped up thirty dollars among them for Bill, and as he gave them a thumbs-up farewell, he shouted a Deadism at them and anyone who cared to listen: "Give me five/I'm still alive/Ain't no luck/I learned to duck." And as Justin pulled away they saw Bill cadging for a "help a vet" handout from a pedestrian who looked through him as if he were invisible. Whatever else one can say about Vietnam Bill, he is a tenacious survivor.

While the KDR trio drove around the Bay Area with Vietnam Bill, I was settling myself in Berkeley (or "Berzerkeley," as it's sometimes called by local wiseacres), a university town of unparalleled ethnic and cultural diversity, inextricably linked in the national psyche with the tumultuous 1960s and 1970s—free-speech protests, antiwar sit-ins, and draft card burnings—and, of course, drugs. Though nostalgia for that eventful time still lingers, today's Berkeley is a mecca of high-tech and computer businesses that is also home to an astonishing total of fifty-five small-press publishers. If most American cities brag about their local sports heroes, Berkeley boasts about its intellectual and scientific ones. In 1988 UC Berkeley had fifteen Nobel Prize winners on the faculty, the same number claimed by the entire former Soviet Union that year.

More than 160 books have been written about Berkeley, but I wanted to take a reprieve from other people's words and hang out in the cafés, write in my journal, and watch the ongoing street theater. Nevertheless, my day took a fascinating turn, thanks to a chance-encounter-turned-conversation with Qyv, a twenty-two-year-old Berkeley Gutter Punk (BGP) with a five-year-old Florida king snake wrapped around his neck, a green Mohawk, a SID VICIOUS: BANNED FROM BASEBALL T-shirt, and a face pierced apparently everywhere by silver rings: twelve in each ear, plus three in the lips, five in the eyebrows, and eight in the nose. Qyv's utter rejection of conventional bourgeois values (of which his wearing of a snake was emblematic) was beyond late-adolescent rebellion, beyond fashion. It was something I had never seen even on the streets of New York, and it was reflected in his attitudes. This is what Qyv told me about himself and his fellow Gutter Punks:

The BGPs are a group of violence-prone street anarchists whose hobbies are throwing bottles and clobbering one another with nail-embedded sticks. Ecstasy is their "rave drug," with psychedelic mushrooms a close second. BGPs despise Dead Heads, hippies, and "granolas," who are all "spaced out and unrealistic." They parody granola notions such as the belief that right thinking will save Brazil's rain forests. The alienated BGPs believe the rain forests are beyond redemption, the apocalypse just around the bend, and the world ruled through violence.

The Gutter Punks—the bored, middle-class, nihilistic spiritual children of William S. Burroughs—read science fiction trash and gather at the Twilight Zone, a death-rock club where the gloom-and-doom crowd hangs out. They hate rap and listen only to hard-core indie record labels, and they dine at Trinity Church every day for the "quarter meal," where twenty-five cents gets you a five-course spread. The BGPs sneer at anything smacking of sixties Berkeley, be it People's Park, which has become known as "Crackhead Park"; the Free Box for homeless people, from which most of the donated hand-me-downs are stolen by young hoods; the racks of made-in-China tie-dyed shirts for sale in front of Bank of America on Telegraph Avenue; or the dreadlock rasta con men from Oakland who, Qyv asserts, preach Bob Marley and spin lies about living in the Staggerlee ghetto for wide-eyed, white-skinned, knapsack-carrying graduate-school social workers in order to hustle a sympathetic sandwich or mooch a joint. But it is the ever-so-serious UC Berkeley students and faculty for whom Qyv and his cohorts reserve their real vitriol as they deconstruct their fellow players in life's vanity fair.

Like his attitudes, Qyv's caustic, Johnny Rotten–style commentary revealed an existential rage. Nothing matters; life itself is one big lie. Although I talked with others in Berkeley that afternoon—at Rasputin Records, Cody's Books, and the Ecology Center—it was Qyv and his snake who showed me just how threatening the search for self-identity and self-definition could be to those who have thrown in the towel altogether.

After my overdose of Gutter Punk cynicism, I felt the need for some spiritual refreshment, so I headed back to San Francisco to pay a visit to Bishop Franzo King of Saint John's Cathedral African Orthodox Church, a man of compassion whose ministry is predicated on helping those in despair. Founded by Bishop King in 1971, Saint John's has taken the lead in caring for the Bay Area's poor and homeless—feeding and counseling those in need and providing hope and shelter to the hopeless. The church differs from other African Orthodox congregations in two ways: The congregation is racially and ethnically integrated, and it is not gospel music that resonates during its religious services but the tenor sax sounds of John Coltrane.

The teachings of Jesus Christ run deep in the bishop's blood, for both his parents were ordained Pentecostal ministers. As a young man, King, a jazz enthusiast since the cradle, heard the tenor and soprano sax genius John Coltrane not only play but also deliver his message of love. While the soon-to-be bishop was familiar with Coltrane's music, he was unprepared, even astounded, to encounter the artist's "powerful presence" and "astonishing humility." He found Coltrane to be a spiritual healer, a man communing with God. "My goal is to live a truly religious life and express it in my own music," John Coltrane once said. "If you live it, when you play there's no problem because the music is part of the whole thing. My music is the spiritual expression of what I am: my faith, my knowledge, my being." So, when Bishop King founded Saint John's Cathedral Orthodox Church, he made John Coltrane its patron saint, and now two "Holy John" icons, in the traditional Byzantine style, grace the walls of his church. During services local musicians play Coltrane's music, and when the Sisters of Compassion serve their free five-course vegetarian meals to the Bay Area hungry, it is Coltrane's "Humble Offering to God (A Love Supreme)" that adds the spiritual nourishment, the baptism of sound.

Coltrane read Krishnamurti and the Cabala, but he remained a devout Christian, though he considered the playing of his saxophone a meditation or inner prayer for all humanity, regardless of race or religion. "I know that there are bad forces, forces put here that bring suffering to others and misery to the world, but I want to be the force which is truly for good," Colrane told a reporter in 1966, less than a year before his death. Bishop King has seized on the spirituality of Coltrane's music, using his church as a living memorial to the great tenor man, and in so doing has attracted hundreds of worshipers. I did not find Bishop King in church that April afternoon, only seven people on their knees in meditation. The icon of John Coltrane, sax in hand, was looking down on them while someone from somewhere behind the altar was playing the tenor man's theme to "Resolution." As long as the notes lasted all of us knew that God was in Saint John's Cathedral.

That evening I walked all over San Francisco by myself, wrote an exam for the students to take the next morning, and finished grading the ones they had written in Las Vegas. In many ways I found giving exams the most unsatisfying part of American Odyssey. None of the students had been able to keep up with the assigned reading, but what they were reading, they loved—Kerouac's *Dharma Bums* and McMurtry's *Last Picture Show* particularly. Reading had become almost secondary, for what the students were really learning about America couldn't have been taught in New York, or from a book—or in any stationary university, for that matter. Our constant movement, like rock-and-roll gypsies or wandering minstrels or gunnysack troubadours or transcontinental truckers, blowing into town for twenty-four hours and then moving on to the next city: That was their education. We were seeing America without intermediaries, not through television tubes or newspapers or magazines, but with our own eyes.

As I watched the students, fortified by wake-up coffee and Danish, hunched over the tables in the closed Americania Best Western bar, taking their early-morning essay exam, I decided that the next time the class was taught I would try to deemphasize exams and instead use the Majic Bus as a "vehicle" to focus attention on certain social and environmental problems. T. H. Watkins, the biographer of FDR's secretary of the interior Harold Ickes, had written a wonderful book on California's desert called *Time's Island,* and as I read it that morning, I promised myself to make American Odyssey II not only educational but a public relations venture to help the Sierra Club—headquartered in San Francisco—lobby for passage of the California Desert Protection Bill in 1993.

Checkout from the Best Western took some time, for students had incurred incidental costs such as phone calls and breakfasts, leading to haggling over who owed how much. Frank had spent the night at his cousins' in Sausalito and was rejuvenated from his day off, ready to push up into the Pacific Northwest. Finally loaded, we put on Barry McGuire's apocalyptic sixties anthem "Eve of Destruction" and plopped the Majic Bus into midmorning traffic. We drove down Embarcadero Drive and pulled off for one last glimpse of the seals, who have abandoned Seal Rock in favor of Pier 39, where they have grown fat and lazy on tourist handouts. Then we climbed straight up Bay Avenue, peering behind ourselves at San Francisco Bay and Alcatraz Island. Although none of the students had made a visit to the former prison of *Birdman* movie fame, it was a topic of idle chatter. Said Mitch: "I could have escaped from Alcatraz, no problem." Replied Stefanie: "You *belong* in Alcatraz." Chimed in Kevin: "No, Mitch is right, it's swimmable." You get the picture, but the point is that Alcatraz has become symbolic of the individual overcoming immense obstacles to achieve freedom.

We drove through the Presidio's eucalyptus groves and Monterey cypress and pine. In this post – Cold War era, Fort Mason has been transferred from the U.S. Army to the National Park Service, and, *voilà!* swords are being beaten into plowshares and barracks turned into museums, art galleries, and boating shops. We caught our first close-up view of the Golden Gate Bridge, its unmistakable rust color more beautiful than gold would have been. To Bay Area residents, crossing the bridge is a chore that means paying an annoying toll and often facing a traffic jam. But for us less jaded Easterners, the Golden Gate Bridge was a destination in itself; just crossing it was exhilarating. No sooner had we navigated its length than we exited Highway 101 for lunch in Sausalito.

Sausalito is a stroller's town, the best spot in the Bay Area for watching the clouds float over Alcatraz and the San Francisco skyline and seeing the terns and gulls comb wharf restaurants for scraps to bring back for a feast on their seaweedy rocks, leaving behind a trail of molted tail feathers as compensation. The hills of Sausalito are cluttered with small "view homes," made of unfinished, splintery wood to give them a weathered look, all showcasing dramatic porches and cliff-hanging decks. While some students went to Houlihan's for lunch, a few of us walked down a short minipier, spotting some rock-clinging starfish and a phalanx of tiny sand crabs who went charging up a concrete embankment only to be sloshed back down by wavelets just as they reached the top. It was relaxing just to walk up and down Bridgeway, Sausalito's main thoroughfare, watching the sailboats circle around Angel Island State Park, and weigh anchor in the towns of Belvedere and Tiburon. During Prohibition, before the Golden Gate Bridge was built, Sausalito was the bootlegging center of the Bay Area, and the contempt for booze laws is clearly still alive: We saw a youngster no more than fourteen sitting on a pier with his feet perched on the CONSUMPTION OF ALCOHOLIC BEVERAGES PROHIBITED ON FISHING PIER sign, defiantly swigging from a bottle of cheap California wine—the kind they've banned from the Tenderloin. After ninety minutes of Sausalito we all congregated at the fourteen-foot-tall elephant statues in the Plaza Viña del Mar, tossed a Frisbee until the stragglers showed up, and then took off for the Sonoma Valley, to the home of Jack London.

It has been said that if the Napa Valley belongs to Robert Louis Stevenson, then the adjacent Sonoma Valley belongs to Jack London. Both areas produce some of the finest wines in the world. As we headed up Highway 101 north to Highway 37, we began seeing grapes growing everywhere, wooden sticks aiding and abetting them in their skyward embrace of the warm California sun. Every half mile or so we passed vineyards with wine-tasting lures, as well as signs offering GRAPES $.59/LB.

The students had just finished reading two Jack London novels: *The Call of the Wild* and *White Fang*, and an intense discussion broke out over the Darwinian themes in these works. Then, as we entered the tree-lined town of Glen Ellen and saw the Jack London Village Shopping Center, we knew we were drawing near the writer's famed Beauty Ranch, now Jack London Historic State Park.

Besides being a writer and adventurer, Jack London (1876–1916) was an enthusiast of scientific farming, soil conservation, and animal husbandry. Today his eight-hundred-acre ranch includes terraced vineyards as well as forested mountainsides interspersed with open glades and clearings. "If we redeem the land, it will redeem us!" was a Jack London motto. And Beauty Ranch, located in California's exquisite Valley of the Moon, is a lasting memorial to London's redemptive agrarian dream. The park contains a picnic area, London's cottage, stables, stone barns, silos, and the writer's pride and joy—his pig palace. "I have just completed a pig pen that will make anyone in the United States who is interested in the manufacture of pork sit up and take notice," London wrote in 1915. "There is nothing like it in the way of piggeries ever built." London loved the Sonoma Valley, where, he said, "the air is wine," and his ashes are buried on his ranch, under a large unmarked red-lava rock on the footpath to Wolf House, the ruins of London's huge stone-and-redwood dream home, which was destroyed by a spontaneous-combustion fire in 1913, just weeks before completion. Never one to quit, London started plans to rebuild: "I am the sailor on horseback! Watch my dust! Oh, I shall make mistakes a-many; but watch my dream come true. . . . Try to dream with me my dreams of fruitful acres. Do not be a slave to an old conception. Try to realize what I am after."

As we disembarked from the Majic Bus, I lectured the students on the life of Jack London. It was a life of physical and financial extremes: newspaper boy at ten; cannery worker at fourteen; oyster pirate at sixteen; tramp, gold prospector, and "work beast" all before twenty. I spoke of his early intellectual mentors Charles Darwin and Herbert Spencer and how

401

he later come to admire Karl Marx and Friedrich Nietzsche. It was the complex philosophies of these four men, along with the writings of Mark Twain and Rudyard Kipling, that captured the brilliant but untutored mind of Jack London and permeate his writings. For his entire life as a writer, London was torn between the apparently contradictory impulses of Social Darwinism and social justice, between individualism and socialism.

After discussing how these differing impulses played out in *The Call of the Wild* and *White Fang*, both dog stories born of his gold rush experiences in Alaska and the Klondike, we entered the House of Happy Walls, the home of his second wife, Charmian, which was built in 1922 and which she occupied until her death in 1955. Of all the exhibits, the students most enjoyed the Jack London World Travels display, which tracks his globetrotting from 1894, when he was nineteen and joined Kelly's Industrial Army in its march on Washington, to his 1902 trip to Europe to cover the Boer War, to his 1904 stint as *San Francisco Examiner* correspondent during the Russo-Japanese War, when he visited Yokohama, Seoul, Kunsan, Chemulpo (now Inchon), and Manchuria, to his extensive tour of the South Pacific Islands and Australia on the *Snark* from 1907 to 1909. Some students, Justin especially, were so turned on by London that they bought gift-shop copies of such lesser-known London classics as *The Star Rover* (the first California reincarnation novel) and *The Game* (about boxing), and the two superb autobiographical novels *Martin Eden* and *John Barleycorn: Alcoholic Memories* (a temperance book still used today by Alcoholics Anonymous to help people maintain sobriety). From the museum we took the footpath, enjoying the valley's silence, which was broken only by the hum of insects and the distant cackle of two crows fighting over the carcass of a small animal. Tiny white butterflies were everywhere, and—though the tall, dry waves of grass and the twig- and moss-filled creek ravines spelled drought and imminent brushfire if rain did not arrive soon—it was a perfect day. As the students basked in the beauty of London's ranch their esteem for him grew.

One issue that came up in my lecture was whether London committed suicide on November 22, 1916, two months before his forty-first birthday. According to thoughtful scientific analysis, the answer is an unequivocal no. Ever since Irving Stone falsely claimed, in his error-filled *Sailor on Horseback*, that London took his own life by swallowing morphine sleeping pills, every subsequent London biographer has uncritically repeated and even embellished the story. If Stone's book overflowed with historical errors, even worse is the biography *Jack*, by British writer Andrew Sinclair, which even presumes to dramatize the suicide that never was, piling error after error on Stone's foundation of untruths. But perhaps most painful to the true London scholar was the repetition of suicide allegations in the November 1991 *Amerian Heritage*, usually the epitome of historical accuracy. Because London lived such a colorful life, his biographers tend to get pumped up themselves, paying little heed to factuality in an effort to heighten the drama. The scientific argument against suicide is that it is impossible for London to have swallowed two vials (or even one) of morphine tablets, as the theorists claim, because that amount of morphine kills very quickly—in a few hours at most. London died twelve hours after he was found, leading all the medical experts who have considered the case to conclude that he died from uremic poisoning, not morphine. A serious biography of London to be published shortly by Dr. Earle Labor, of the Centenary College of Louisiana, should set the record straight.

Another annoying aspect of American Jack London scholarship is the dismissiveness shown by many writers who portray him as merely a mischievous literary vagabond. Today London, translated into eighty languages, is the most widely read American writer in the world, with an incredible following in Japan, Russia, and Poland. Most of his fifty-nine books are out of print in the United States, although in Japan, for example, twenty-four titles are available. If it weren't for Star Rover House in Oakland, which publishes some of his books in paperback, only a few of his novels would be available. This is to say nothing of his more than five hundred nonfiction articles and two hundred short stories, all written by the time he was forty. The American "academy" wants to pigeonhole London as a minor writer with a few very good books, more interesting as a case study of a failed novelist than as a literary genius. They say London burned out, but in truth he became a better writer as he aged—just read the classic story "The Water Baby," written in 1915. If you measure Jack

403

London on a worldwide yardstick of shelf life—books that still bring a sense of adventure and struggle that transcend national boundaries—then he is a writer of the greatest distinction.

We left Beauty Ranch in high spirits and headed out of Glen Ellen on Route 12—the Sonoma Highway—through the beautiful, sun-drenched wine country. A helicopter was flying over a spiraling wisp of pine-forest smoke as we drove past—would you believe?—the Smothers Brothers' Vineyard. Once back on Highway 101, we followed Russian River to Cloverdale and connected with Highway 128 to Boonville, passing miles of recently planted Douglas firs, barns decorated with strange Amish-like hex signs, and indecisive deer torn between indulging in one last bite of grass or disappearing behind the tree cover as the Majic Bus came rolling by. In Boonville we stopped for snacks at the Redwood Drive Inn Coffee Shop, where we saw a group of dirty, shirtless children looking old beyond their age, their innocence gone, like Sally Mann's kids in the haunting photos she took of them in Virginia. Something didn't quite seem right in Boonville—a community where, we later learned, unicorn spottings are reported, elves are known to appear at every full moon, and Bigfoot has put in an appearance. Later that evening in Mendocino we were told about Boontling, a local dialect spoken by two hundred residents of Boonville who "harp" (speak) this odd jargon dating back to 1880. Boonville is, or was, the home of the Boonville Hermit, who, until his recent disappearance, called the stump of a fallen redwood tree home. Darkness was approaching as we finally ran into the ocean at Albion, the fog as thick and creamy as vanilla pudding. It rose from the ground as though we were in a production of *Peter and the Wolf* and the ice machine backstage were in overdrive. After a few miles of this we arrived in Mendocino anxious for dinner.

In the February 1993 issue of *Sunset* magazine Mendocino would be crowned the most picturesque town in the West. It didn't take us long to see why. Poised comfortably on the tip of a spectacular coastal peninsula, where foaming waves from Asia smash against the fissured bluffs, Mendocino, a New England–like village in the middle of California redwood country, is both quaint and touristy, a bed-and-breakfast community with a never-say-die history. Many of San Francisco's hippies migrated to this part of California, made famous in song by the Sir Douglas Quintet, and we encountered more than a few barefoot flower children in front of Mendosa's Market as we parked the Majic Bus to walk around the town's wooden sidewalks. Gray-whale watching and abalone diving are common Mendocino pastimes. A few of the students immediately recognized Mendocino as the setting for Angela Lansbury's "Murder She Wrote" home. But food, not exploration, was the imperative of the moment. Many students were now on very tight budgets, having had too much fun in Las Vegas and San Francisco, so they were looking for a good, cheap meal. We were told to head up Highway 1 for five miles to Caspar, where for four dollars we could get a bellyful of Mexican food at Cathy's Corner Café in the Caspar Inn.

The fog, which still clung to us as we entered the ocean village of Caspar and parked next to the Lighthouse Church, lent the evening an air of mystery in which silence was sound and the music and voices emanating from the Caspar Inn simply echoes. As we approached the inn and its adjoining Mexican café, we felt like invaders. But in spite of our momentary alienation, it turned out to be a memorable evening, for the place was filled with good music and friendly people. The Caspar Inn, despite its far remove, is a legendary music spot, a place where Charlie Parker's wife once worked and where musicians such as Mose Allison and B. B. King have been known to play for free. Bonnie Raitt, who lives nearby, occasionally comes over just to hang out and sing along to whatever is playing on the jukebox. That evening the pool table had been shoved aside, and a local band that reminded me of the Flying Burrito Brothers rocked out country-tinged tunes all night long. We ate tacos and nachos, and danced and talked with the locals, who enjoyed hearing about the Majic Bus; then some residents of a nearby redwood grove offered to let us park on their property for the evening, so we could take hot showers in the morning, an offer we gladly accepted. That evening as we all got ready for bed, dropping off in shifts as if biological clocks had become synchronized, we were glad to be back on the road—for as nice as our accommodations in San Francisco had been, the Majic Bus had become our home. Tomorrow we would get to discover California's redwood trees, the world's tallest, largest living things, but for now we just drifted off to sleep, enveloped by fog.

17

Redwood Battles, Bigfoot, Paul Bunyan, and Earthquakes

I believe we have to be warriors. And whether it's writers or actors or rock-and-roll players or teachers or politicians, warriors are what interest me and what I aspire to. Talent is not as important as being a warrior, working to fight your battle.

—KEN KESEY

MOST OF US WERE UP AT THE CRACK OF DAWN, CRAVING hot showers and the warm morning sun. All traces of last night's fog had evaporated, and we were greeted by cloudless blue skies and a colony of Douglas squirrels chattering on tree limbs as they munched on pine cones and suspiciously watched us yawn and stretch. We were parked in a lovely pine forest, the only other noise the haggling of two Steller's jays over ownership of a stale hamburger bun that had been tossed to them. This was a day scheduled for pure, unadulterated leisure, a day to enjoy the redwood empire and the Pacific Coast of Northern California. While half of us showered at the house of our Caspar Inn friends, the other half snored away. Frank wrote a thank-you note to our hosts, who let us use the house while they bolted to work, entrusting us with their keys.

For the next two hours we crawled up Highway 1, listening to Kris Kristofferson and singing along with his "Me and Bobby McGee." The windshield wipers were on fast though it wasn't raining; we were merely conducting an experiment to determine whether they slapped in time with the music. Once again we gaped in awe at the shifting seascapes, coastal pines, crashing waves, expansive ocean views, hulking fortress rocks, dizzying cliffs, swooping red-tailed hawks, and grass-covered headlands exploding with purple and yellow wildflowers. A little north of Fort Bragg, we stopped to take in the fresh salt air at windswept MacKerricher State Beach and stared silently at the near-motionless harbor seals from Laguna Point.

Student bellyaching over missing breakfast and demands for an early lunch were reaching almost mutinous proportions. The next town of any size was still tiny: Leggett, the "Southern Gateway to Redwood Country." Leggett takes its gateway boosterism seriously, directing visitors to the Chandelier Drive-Thru Tree, distinguished by a hand-hewn opening through its twenty-one-foot-diameter base large enough for vans but not buses. Not only did the students get to see their first giant redwoods, but over breakfast they were initiated into the ferocious square-off between lumber interests and environmentalists over the future of these ancient, awesome trees—the tallest and oldest in the world. In Mendocino and Humboldt counties everyone loves redwoods; the problem is some love them horizontal and others love them vertical. At the Redwood Diner the owner of the nearby Leggett Inn told us that the redwood giants were simply a cash crop waiting for harvest. As for the spotted owls, placed on the Endangered Species List in 1989, he volunteered to "shoot every last one of them screeching hooters." A few of us ventured into his inn to see his dogs, and what should greet us but a large portrait of John Wayne. We certainly weren't in the Bay Area anymore. As Mitch saw it, "California is the land of unbelievable extremes, both in geography and people. Nobody seems to be centrist. They're either extreme left or extreme right."

We had all picked up bits and pieces about the spotted owl and redwood controversies back in New York, but we had underestimated just how vitriolic the battle has become. As we educated ourselves on the issue, we were to learn that merely uttering the words *spotted owl* is enough to get you shot at in parts of Northern California, and organizing proenvironment demonstrations invites car bombs.

Mendocino and Humboldt counties have a split economic personality: Hippies grow grade-A marijuana (the region is the sinsemilla capital of the world), and loggers cut down trees. The transplanted hippie newcomers are becoming exceedingly rich, while the fifth-generation loggers are being laid off, causing understandable tensions between these two very different subcultures. Our innkeeper despised hippies and was suspicious of the Majic Bus. Though his parting words to us—"Just remember all those books you read are made from trees" were true enough, the atmosphere was too explosive to respond to his faulty logic. There was no way to tell him that it does not follow that lumber companies should therefore destroy virgin forest by cutting down two-thousand-year-old redwoods. Why not harvest young pines, spruces, firs, oaks, and maples? I admire the sturdy qualities of these hardworking lumberjacks, but I wonder why they fail to understand that the redwoods are in a different category: They belong to the American people; they are our great cathedrals, "the most unthinkably glorious body of timber to be seen anywhere," as Jack London wrote.

John Steinbeck called *Sequoia sempervirens*, the Pacific Coast redwoods, "ambassadors from another time." Today, thirty years and a billion buzz saws after Steinbeck wrote those words, the old-growth redwoods that remain are endangered relics—for the truth about our ancient forest is that there isn't very much of it left. Massive redwood forests have been preserved in Northern California, Oregon, and Washington national parks and wilderness areas. They are utterly magnificent, dwarfing any possible comparison. But, standing among them, one can't help but rue any destruction that occurs in the name of misguided notions of progress. For the sad fact is that 130 years of logging have eliminated 95 percent of California's giant coastal redwoods. There are so few of the two-thousand-year-old redwoods left that some park rangers in the Pacific Northwest know the survivors by individual names—the Sleeping Giant, Flatiron, Sneaky Pete. So few old-growth redwoods remain in Mendocino County today that environmental action groups are saving them tree by tree, not grove by grove. Were it not for conservationist warriors at the turn of the century—the Save-the-Redwoods League—none would be in existence today. Beginning in 1902, the league lobbied federal and local governments to create state and national parks, managing to protect 75,000 acres of old-growth redwood forest. With the help of various other conservationist groups, such as the Sierra Club and the Wilderness Society, they have also protected thousands of acres of second-growth redwoods—younger trees that will someday themselves be ancient sentinels to inspire future generations. So today, out of 95,000 total remaining acres of virgin redwood forest, 75,000 are protected, but 20,000 remain unprotected in private ownership, mainly scattered on timber company lands. Most of the unprotected old-growth acreage is in Humboldt and Mendocino counties, property of the Big Three: Louisiana Pacific, Georgia Pacific, and Pacific Lumber Company (PALCO), which last is a subsidiary of Texas junk-bond king Charles Hurwitz's Maxxam Corporation. Redwood is a prize luxury wood because it doesn't rot. In the seven short years since 1985, PALCO has speed-logged nearly 2,000 acres of old-growth trees—20 percent of the unprotected acreage—turning previously pristine ancient forest into barren, scorched-earth patches, blighting the landscape for miles.

To cut down our ambassadors to the past—which were alive when Julius Caesar crossed the Rubicon, when Jesus delivered the Sermon on the Mount, when Constantine moved the capital of the Roman Empire from Rome to Byzantium, when Mohammed recaptured Mecca, and when the Buddha wandered and meditated—to build hot tubs, porches, and decks reveals the spiritual emptiness of those who counsel that the marketplace is the best arbiter of right and wrong. Even *Fortune* has denounced Charles Hurwitz as a redwood raider.

Provoked by Hurwitz's rapid depredations, a group of activists in Northern California formed the Environmental Protection Information Center (EPIC) to stop his plunder—with only sporadic success. While EPIC works to save the redwoods through legislation, a band of grass-roots environmental activists have founded Earth First!, which uses guerrilla tactics to stop the "harvesting" of two-thousand-year-old trees, and to force national attention onto the plight of our ancient forests. Distrusting the political system, Earth First! resorts to "direct action." Copies of *Ecodefense: A Field Guide to Monkeywrenching* in hand, these modern redwood warriors disable bulldozers by slashing hydraulic hoses or pouring dirt into crankcases, pulling up road survey stakes, spiking trees with sixty-penny nails that damage saws, barricading roads so trucks can't get to logging sites, climbing trees about to be logged and refusing to get down, staging sit-ins in front of bulldozers, or hugging trees and refusing to let go. The spirit of Earth First! is naturally maligned in the national press, for the movement involves commandos with flashlights destroying machines as much as it does daytime organizers who have fun bringing national attention to the redwoods and have perfected the art of guerrilla street theater. Most environmental groups, such as the Sierra Club, frown on monkeywrenching sabotage because of its unlawful methods and its risk of harm to loggers. In 1989 then–Earth First! spokesman Dave Foreman saw his group's incursions as the first shot to save Planet Earth. "We're in a war," he claimed, "the war of industrial civilization against the natural world. If you look at what the leading scientists are telling us, we could lose one-third of all species in the next forty years. We're being told that by the end of the century the only large mammals left will be those we choose to allow to continue to exist. We're in one of the great extinction episodes in three and a half billion years of evolution." Foreman is no longer associated with Earth First!, and although the loosely knit organization continues its outrageous actions, they no longer spike trees, obeying an agreement they reached with loggers.

Led by Judi Bari, EPIC and Earth First! staged "Redwood Summer 1990," in which three thousand environmentalist radicals marched from timber town to timber town, protesting against the clear-cutting of old-growth redwoods. Thanks to the demonstration, PALCO was forced to halt its destruction of the Headwaters Forest, a three-thousand-acre old-growth redwood grove, and Bari was nearly assassinated by a car bomb. Her pelvis was shattered, leaving her to raise her children partially paralyzed. She blames the FBI and is suing them. A hundred years from now environmental radicals like Judi Bari will be seen as martyrs, national heroes who paid a heavy price for trying to save our ancient forests. Bari has been able to broaden her political base and has actually resurrected the old Industrial Workers of the World (IWW) union, forming Local Number One, and creating a tentative but blossoming alliance of loggers with Earth First! activists. Some loggers at PALCO are now meeting with EPIC and Earth First! in hopes of sending Charles Hurwitz back to Houston, where he belongs; these loggers are convinced now that they have more in common with the hippies, whose kids go to the same schools as the local children, than with the out-of-town corporate types. They have begun to realize that PALCO's speed-logging will leave them jobless in a few years. As amazing as it sounds, redneck loggers and longhair hippies are beginning to work side by side, despite corporate attempts to divide and conquer. PALCO has hired a PR firm to wage an ad campaign to spruce up its image. Even the prologging citizens of Mendocino and Humboldt counties are angry about what happened to Bari. They feel guilty when they see her crippled for life and are now turning that very real anger on their employers.

Over a two-day period the American Odyssey students learned a great deal about these timber wars, and they learned to love the giant Pacific Coast redwoods like nothing else they saw on the trip. Alison best expressed our group sentiment: "Being among the Giants is a spiritual experience undreamed of back East. They are holy breathing entities, the stillness of a grove the perfect spot for meditation."

From Leggett we continued north on Route 101, past souvenir shops featuring "Redwood Carvings for Christ" and Helen's Beer Garden. A convoy of lumber trucks rumbled by us as we pulled off to look at the World Famous Tree House, a four-thousand-year-old tree that contains a room twenty-one feet by twenty-seven, with a fifty-foot ceiling. Since all the roadside attractions in this part of California rely on disfiguring the giant redwoods to draw tourists, at least they won't chop them down. As we entered Richardson Grove State Park, the scenic Eel River flowing on our right, the students were bubbling with excitement at the grandeur of the redwoods. From the sublime we suddenly—and inexplicably—fell prey to a tourist trap we couldn't resist. Called "Legend of Bigfoot," it lured us in with a giant redwood statue of the North American sasquatch. Bigfoot is an American fascination, especially for young people, and in the Pacific Northwest it's an obsession of sorts.

Without a doubt one of the most compelling of the world's mysterious animals—right up there on a par with the Loch Ness monster—is the elusive Bigfoot (alias Sasquatch, Hairy Ghost, Woolybooger, Injun Devil, Skookums, *Seah-tik*, Braxton Monster, Wild Swamp Ape, Wild Man, *Oh-Mah*, Snallygaster, and *Dwayyo*). The foul-smelling, hairy, apelike beast is purported to stand about eight feet high, weigh as much as eight hundred pounds, and sport dark hair two inches long all over its heavyset, broadshouldered body. Legends about the creature predate European settlement of North America. The Huppa tribe, originally located near the Legend of Bigfoot attraction, is a repository of hundreds of stories about encounters with these nocturnal, solitary carnivores who roamed the Klamath Mountains. Northwest Indians say their ancestors shared fishing sites with the sasquatch—the Indian word means "wild man of the woods." Thousands of sasquatch sightings occurred in the nineteenth century; even Theodore Roosevelt wrote of an encounter in *Wilderness Hunter* (1892). The name Bigfoot entered the national vocabulary in 1958 when members of a road crew reported that an animal kept leaving sixteen-inch, five-toed footprints on a newly graded California road. The AP wire picked up the story, and Bigfoot became a permanent part of American folklore. Since 1958 thousands of Bigfoot sightings have been reported and footprints found. The most compelling evidence of Bigfoot's existence came in 1966, when Robert Patterson made a sixteen-millimeter film of an eight-foot, hairy humanlike creature walking across a sandbar. Some scientists insist the film is a fake perpetrated by an attention-seeking charlatan; other experts disagree. Even the most skeptical scientists must admit, however, that dismissing the hundreds of different five-toed footprints preserved in plaster over the years requires the assumption of a three-decade-long hoax of gigantic proportions.

Bigfoot sightings are a part of growing up in the Pacific Northwest (and in the United States), and I hope they never end. It is reassuring to find that our imaginations have not been entirely wiped out by too much rationality. (Let's also make sure that we always maintain enough wilderness all over North America to keep the mystery of Bigfoot alive.) In case the reader has developed a case of regional envy, believing that the Pacific Northwest holds a Bigfoot monopoly, be of good cheer: Bigfoot has most recently been spotted near Cleveland, Ohio. In fact, so many spottings have occurred that an 800 Bigfoot hot line has been set up in the Buckeye State. Bigfoot was recently sighted walking in the middle of the Cuyahoga River, a river so polluted that it once caught fire. The return of Bigfoot says much about the effectiveness of the clean-up effort that followed the June 22, 1969 blaze. One never knows where one of North America's estimated 2,500 Bigfoots will surface; so far they have been spotted in every state but Rhode Island and Hawaii. Somehow I think Bigfoot will show up there eventually, too.

After poking through the Legend of Bigfoot gift shop, where redwood coffee tables sell for eighty dollars and unfinished sofas for up to twelve hundred, we continued north on 101 through Garberville, EPIC's headquarters, and Phillipsville, where we hopped onto the world-famous two-lane Avenue of the Giants, the thirty-three-mile alternative redwood tour that winds around the south fork of the Eel River. This is my favorite drive in the United States: It is surrounded by the most magnificent trees in the world, which form a green canopy that allows only an occasional shaft of sunlight to filter through its cool, dark density. Driving the Avenue of the Giants is a form of time travel. In an odd way you feel as though you are tunneling through primeval forest for the first time, clearing a path where no other has been, hoping to catch a glimpse not of deer or bear but of Bigfoot or a unicorn. Here the secrets of the gods are tucked away under mossy rocks and among the ancient redwood roots that have linked up to form one of the last great natural fortresses against techno-civilization.

Once through the dense grove, we saw a large sign for Hobbiton, U.S.A., a nature walk that passes concrete recreations of scenes from J. R. R. Tolkien's fantasy novel *The Hobbit* and his *Lord of the Rings* trilogy. Bearing the San Francisco Hobbit Club seal of approval, the attraction features excerpts from the books. A tape-recorded Hobbit enthusiast with a phantasmagoric voice tells visitors about Hobbit Bilbo Baggins, who lives in a cozy hole in the side of a hill; Gandalf the wizard; hordes of dwarfs; and Smaug, the fierce dragon. You're also likely to meet stoned-out San Francisco hippies. After bypassing the Hobbits, we stopped at Chimney Tree. Topped by a storm and hollowed out by fire, this giant became a natural shelter for hunters and travelers at the turn of the century. Not far from Hobbiton, just over Ohman Creek, is the Log Chapel Inn, a place for loggers to pray. A sign in front reads, THIS IS NOT A SANCTUARY, proud the chinked logs that make up its walls were not environmentally protected.

We had planned to drive farther up the coast to camp in Redwood National Park, but we were so taken with the magnificent giants in Humboldt Redwood State Park that we decided to spend the night right there. We pulled into the utterly desolate Williams Grove Campground, unloaded the bus, and began some late-afternoon exploration of redwood groves and tranquil glens. Many of us returned to the Eel River, where we skipped rocks, admired the tanbark oaks, big-leaf maples, and cottonwoods along the riverbank, and watched two youngsters with a golden retriever fish for juvenile steelhead trout and squawfish, catching only suckers. We waded in the rumbling water and crossed a log bridge that brought us to the other bank, where the students percolated almost simultaneously with a single thought: This was the most glorious college credit they ever earned. Matt found a perfect walking stick, which he later used to ward off comrades-turned-bandits who were trying to swipe hot dogs and hamburgers off his grill. At dusk a friendly ranger showed up at our camp and told us about such local fauna as the gray fox and the common king snake. When Alan asked whether the campground was always so deserted, the ranger laughed and replied, "No, sir, in the summer it's busier here than a one-legged man in an ass-kicking contest." The ranger also explained to us the difference between the coast redwoods, under which we were camping, and the giant sequoias, which climb the Sierra Nevada slopes inland. Conversation died down as he pointed out that an American kestrel, North America's smallest falcon, had lighted on a branch, apparently conducting reconnaissance for a late dinner.

That evening we had the best feast of the trip. We built a roaring fire and told campfire stories, thought we heard a spotted owl hoot, and tried to convince ourselves that the other night sounds we heard were bats, not Bigfoot. We camped by the Eel River, sleeping soundly to its cool, repetitive rush, under so many shooting stars that we stopped bothering to point them out.

Frank got everyone up early the next morning, making us scrambled eggs and cowboy coffee while the students took turns taking sponge baths in the sinks of the nearby restrooms. We cleaned up our campsite and packed and loaded ourselves and our belongings on the bus for another day of redwood exploration.

Suddenly we felt as though the bus was bobbing on water. Branches began to come down from nearby redwoods, and we watched in shock as the solid cement of the paved parking lot bent as though it were returning to its original thick, liquid state, more like gum than concrete. For ten seconds none of us could process what was happening. Jared thought perhaps a bear was shaking the bus. Then, in near unison, we all realized it was an earthquake, and we intuitively sensed it was more than a run-of-the-mill tremor that Californians would take in stride. Thrushes' songs turned into human-sounding shrieks as we dashed from the bus to a nearby clearing, to stand in the open, our eyes warily fixed on the giants surrounding us. Now we were at least positioned to try to dodge any that threatened to come down on us. In a strange way it was exhilarating, a moment of instantaneous mental clarity, snapping any lethargy we might have been harboring. We had just begun to calm down when an aftershock followed. Alan likened the tremors to "standing on one of those Magic Finger vibrating beds, except it was the earth." We had been standing in the clearing for ten minutes or so when the ranger reappeared to see whether we were all right. He confirmed what we already knew—this was a major earthquake. We weren't too far from the town of Fortuna, so we decided to get out of the park as quickly as possible.

It gave us an ineffable and unforgettable sensation to drive down the two-lane Avenue of the Giants—the sunlight now vanquished because of the all-encompassing redwood shadows—our fingers clutching the sturdiest objects near us as if they were teddy bears, convinced another aftershock was imminent. Every quarter mile or so we had to get out of the bus to clear branches from the road, fearful that just around the bend a fallen two-thousand-year-old giant would thwart us. Once out of the Avenue of the Giants, we breathed a bit easier, anxious to find out the quake's magnitude—as if Professor Richter's scale could somehow help us calibrate the magnitude of our own internal tremors—and learn whether California was now an island. As we arrived in Fortuna, the self-described "Dead Redwood Capital of America," with stacks of cut logs piled everywhere, another quake hit. For twenty seconds it felt as if Frank were driving over a field of speed bumps. Not certain where to go, we parked at a strip mall and dashed inside Round Table Pizza. People were glued to the big screen in back, watching CNN, as the Atlanta-based anchor talked by phone to a woman in Fortuna, California. Fortuna!—that was where we were! Camaraderie was instantly established with the locals because we had all shared the quake experience. The first quake had struck at 11:20 A.M.; the second, minutes before we entered Fortuna.

Wolfing down pizza, we headed over to Main Street, now a boulevard of shattered glass, Bank of America's now-storefrontless building looking particularly vulnerable to looting. Damon Gym at Fortuna Union High School and the Veterans Memorial building were piles of rubble. Matt walked up and down Main Street with his videocam, taping the destruction, while Jared interviewed stunned shopkeepers about the extent of the damage. Jared caught Juana and Luis Mendoza sweeping up shards of plate glass from their Imperial Furniture Store, and he asked for their

417

thoughts on the quake: "We pray to God nobody was hurt," they answered, with tears in their eyes. They had just expressed everyone's hope. A fireman told us the epicenter had been the nearby town of Ferndale and that most emergency vehicles were headed over there; despite a certain amount of nervous student protest, I told Frank to drive to Ferndale to see if we could be of any help. I also thought we might film the destruction. As we left Fortuna an eerie calm enveloped the town, the only sounds the monotonous sweeping of brooms and the tires of emergency vehicles, seemingly in unspoken agreement to avoid panic by keeping their sirens silent.

Frank took Route 15 south to Ferndale for two miles but police barricades halted our progress. We told the officer we wanted to see if we could help. After a moment's hesitation he waved us through. We crossed the Eel River again, the only vehicle on the road, and eventually reached the picturesque Victorian village of Ferndale, designated a historic landmark by the state of California because of its history and architecture. All of Ferndale's turreted and gabled Victorian gingerbread homes, with their woodwork tracery, are colorfully painted and surrounded by white picket fences. The earthquake, we learned later, had leveled thirty-nine of the beamless structures and rendered sixty-four others uninhabitable. We parked in front of the Shaw House Inn and immediately began investigating the damage.

Main Street had been hit the hardest, with bricks and glass everywhere. A Nissan Sentra had been crushed to scrap metal by a wall of tumbling bricks. The Hobart Gallery and the Village Florist looked as though someone had tossed a stick of dynamite through their front windows, and there was nothing left of Valley Grocery. Everywhere we looked homes had collapsed, many cut right in half, literally moved to the right or left by as much as ten feet. One woman, anxious that we film her damage for insurance purposes, took us inside to inspect her kitchen floor, on which the refrigerator had toppled, splattering ketchup, mustard, milk, and pudding everywhere. Asked what she was going to do, her reply was, "What else? Start cleaning." Her stoicism was representative of the entire town. Ron Richardson, the UPS-delivery-man-turned-mayor, had called a town meeting on Main Street shortly after the quake hit. The community calmly voted on a number of issues by yeas and nays, including the decision to allow the press in to film the damage, and a strategy for dealing with the crisis. The Victorian-style celery-colored office building at the Humboldt County Fair Grounds became earthquake relief headquarters, while the Ferndale Volunteer Fire Department organized to provide free food and coffee.

Matt and I passed as press representatives, getting around the police barricade by wearing the ABC "Good Morning America" hats that a cameraman had given us at the Grand Canyon. We were the first "national" correspondents on the scene. In fact, Matt was the first person to tape all the damage, including emotional interviews with survivors. I telephoned my sister, Leslie, at KGO-ABC in San Francisco, and she was shocked to learn that the Majic Bus was in Ferndale. She put me on hold, and before I knew what was happening, an ABC News correspondent was interviewing me live on the air about the extent of the damage. When the station learned that Matt was busy videotaping Main Street, they pleaded for the tape, promising him a stringer's fee. An agreement was reached. The Majic Bus would meet with a Channel 7 helicopter at the Humboldt County Fairgrounds to hand off the tape. That evening Matt's video images entered the nation's living rooms via ABC.

No one had been killed in Ferndale, and only minor-to-moderate injuries were reported. The people of Ferndale had demonstrated grace under pressure, the power of community organization, and it was a display I'll never forget. Although damage costs totaled in the millions, two days later local merchants threw a Main Street barbecue. Citizens donated what they could to make it a unified bash. A local meat company provided free food, farmers brought vegetables, bakeries made special treats, and beer and soda flowed freely. In the midst of disaster, the citizens of Ferndale stuck together, neighbor helping neighbor without complaint, just planning how to rebuild their historic town brick by brick, board by board, to its former Victorian glory.

When we returned from our journey, a copy of the *Humboldt Beacon* sent by a Ferndale citizen would be waiting in my Long Island mailbox, with a note saying, "Tell your students thanks for trying to help when we were hit." President Bush had declared Humboldt County a disaster area, and the vice president's wife, Marilyn Quayle, had been dispatched to Ferndale. She'd made the front page, above the fold, discussing government aid to the citizens. But on page nine was a picture of the American Odyssey crew in front of the Majic Bus, with a story about the class under the headline "Earthquake Shakes New York Students." True, we were shaken, but we were also deeply moved by how the community of Ferndale pulled together in the midst of crisis. When we got back on U.S. 101 North to Eureka, we had a clearer understanding of how democracy works, and we were proud of our form of government as never before.

In April 1992, Eureka, the largest city in Humboldt County, was in the middle of a painful recession. Many laid-off loggers and jobless fisherman could be found swapping war stories in the best bar on the Pacific Coast: Jimmy Dunn's Cosmopolitan Pub (since 1885), on the corner of D Street and Second, where the sign reads: AN IRISHMAN IS NEVER DRUNK AS LONG AS HE CAN HOLD ONTO ONE BLADE OF GRASS AND NOT FALL OFF THE FACE OF THE EARTH. In 1928, at the height of Prohibition, Jimmy Dunn was found guilty of selling homemade hooch and holding marathon poker games in his bar, and he was sentenced to a year in a Contra Costa prison. In his final decision on the U.S. Supreme Court, Justice Oliver Wendell Holmes sealed Dunn's fate and put him away. On release Dunn returned to his Irish bar. He died in 1947, unrepentant. Today his picture holds a place of honor behind the bar, next to a collection of four-leaf clovers, elk antlers, and mounted deer heads. In the very back of the dark, cozy bar, lifelong customers retire their electric power saws on the wall, just as football players hang up their cleats after their last game. For old loggers and fishermen, retiring in Eureka doesn't mean the Senior Citizens' Center or the Old Folks' Home but a bar stool at Jimmy Dunn's, swirling drinks, jawing about the white-lightning years when drinking illegally was fun, environmental activists hadn't been born, and so many salmon ran the rivers you could drop a net while smoking a cigarette and pull up a thousand. They don't forget the past at Jimmy Dunn's, as they take turns shuffling over to the country-and-western jukebox, dropping in their last quarters, pushing selections 110 and 210 again and again to hear Bob Willis sing "Faded Love" and "San Antonio Rose" yet another time—always one last time.

We stopped at Jimmy Dunn's for postearthquake beers and sodas, took a drive past the Carson mansion, a beautiful gingerbread Victorian home that is now a private club, and then headed north through Redwood National Park, with its twenty-eight thousand acres of secluded beaches, coastal redwoods, and the world's tallest tree. On the way we spotted an elk herd standing motionless across from a salmon cannery with a sign advertising SALMON JERKY $9.18/LB. We tried hard to imagine the taste of salmon jerky and surmised the elk knew something we didn't. In the middle of the park, in a lodging village called Klamath known for its Golden Bear statues, which guard Klamath Bridge, we decided to visit the Trees of Mystery, just as dusk was blanketing the redwood forest with a foggy mist.

Among America's roadside attractions, Trees of Mystery is one of my favorites. In addition to seeing redwoods wind-contorted into a variety of shapes from ferocious bears to bearded biblical figures, the visitor can pray at Cathedral Tree while Nelson Eddy sings Joyce Kilmer's overappreciated poem "Trees" from hidden loudspeakers. Trees of Mystery also boasts giant statues of the legendary ax-wielding lumberjack Paul Bunyan and his boon companion, Babe the Blue Ox. Paul Bunyan, the great folk hero of American logging and lumber camps, was a man of superhuman strength and skill, fearless and invincible. All the students rushed from the Majic Bus for a photo op with Paul Bunyan and Babe.

Although Paul Bunyan tales had been around since the 1840s, it is former lumberjack W. B. Laughead's superhero axman, as presented in his 1922 pamphlet *The Marvelous Exploits of Paul Bunyan*, commissioned by the Red River Lumber Company, who popularized the larger-than-life legend. Today, in this part of California, by using clear-cutting techniques and machinery to replace lumberjacks, lumber companies have made real-life Paul Bunyans obsolete, victims of automation. The Paul Bunyans of the world are no longer found in wilderness areas or logging camps feasting on stacks of pancakes; they are boozing it up in Jimmy Dunn's or standing in line in downtown Eureka, waiting patiently for a monthly welfare check.

From Trees of Mystery I called Ken Kesey at his farm in Pleasant Hill, Oregon. We talked of the earthquake, the redwoods, and of course, how the Majic Bus was doing; Kesey loves talking about buses. He gave me detailed directions to the farm and guessed that 1:00 P.M. would be our likely arrival time, adding that he'd "take care of us" once we made it to Pleasant Hill. The students were ecstatic to hear that Kesey had agreed to meet us.

We decided to spend the night camping in Jedediah Smith Redwoods State Park, named after the first American to travel overland from the Mississippi River to California, in 1826. From Klamath we drove to Crescent City, where we provisioned at the twenty-four-hour Safeway, most notably with salmon steaks, and had a bizarre encounter with a born-again Christian couple who boarded our bus uninvited, good manners apparently taking second place to evangelical zeal. They treated Tom as the professor, blessed us, and handed out free copies of a book called *Cosmic Conflict: Good and Evil Wage War on Planet Earth*. They told us they thought the Majic Bus was a divine messenger from God—the Elijah Express, they called us—spreading goodwill to the earthquake-plagued area.

It was pitch black out as Frank veered away from the coast to cut inland to U.S. 199 toward Oregon. Soon we entered the state park, and before we knew what was happening Frank slammed on the brakes, for he had seen a sign for picnicking. The road to the picnic site was not meant for buses or large RVs, but with food defrosting we had no obvious options, short of turning back to Crescent City, which was unthinkable for Frank. He steered us down the road—"footpath" might have been a more accurate description—barely clearing the hanging branches and narrowly avoiding redwood roots. At the terminus sat four or so splintery, forlorn picnic tables in an old-growth redwood grove about fifty yards from the Smith River, the last major river in California without a dam. Frank broke out his newest acquisition, a Coleman gas lantern, and like on the first day of Creation, there was light. Too lazy to set up tents on the damp forest floor, everyone elected to sleep in the bus, particularly since we would be taking off at the crack of dawn. Coolers and bags of food were broken out, and with a giant group dinner under way I took a solitary walk to the Smith River, where I sat and played on my marine band harmonica such songs as "Shenandoah" and "Green, Green Grass of Home," and got pumped up at the prospect of spending the next afternoon with Prankster extraordinaire Ken Kesey. The cold and damp invaded the Majic Bus, and moisture seeped into our bones, causing stiff necks and stuffed noses. We let the fire die out early that cold and eerie night. By midnight everyone had fallen asleep to the music of Patsy Cline, all of us silent and listening, snug in our sleeping bags, feeling the presence of ghosts all around us though we were seemingly alone in the grove of redwoods.

Frank grabbed only a few hours' sleep, the wheel serving as his pillow, and by 4:00 A.M. he had cranked up the motor, anxious to cross into Oregon with enough time to wash the Majic Bus so it would shine for Ken Kesey. For the first time on the trip I felt really uncomfortable on the bus floor, and I got up with Frank, listening to Hoyt Axton's "Pusher" and "No No Song." We talked about Kesey and the Merry Pranksters and how Earth First! activists are really second-generation Pranksters, environmental warriors with a redwood-size sense of humor that the FBI just doesn't understand. Frank knew every detail about Kesey's Furthur bus history but had never read his novels, *One Flew Over the Cuckoo's Nest* and *Sometimes a Great Notion*. I dug out my copy of *Sometimes a Great Notion* and with the aid of a flashlight read Frank a pungent Oregon passage: "Always get the skin rash up here. And athlete's foot all the way to the ankle. The moisture. It's certainly no wonder that this area has two or three natives a month take that one-way dip—it's either drown your blasted self or rot." Our damp night in Oregon was confirming Kesey's astringent assessment.

Talk turned to Bob Dylan. For weeks I had been trying to get free tickets for the students to see Dylan perform in Seattle, but we still had no word from his manager. If we could see Kesey in Oregon and Dylan in Washington, American Odyssey would have outdone itself—our transcontinental journey would have been more than a mere success: an event, a happening.

We were still in the Siskiyou Mountains as we entered Oregon, Frank and I chatting all the way to Cave Junction, home of Noah's Ark Petting Farm and Oregon Caves National Monument's prehistoric marble-and-limestone caverns. By the time Frank made it to Grants Pass for diesel and a pigs-in-a-blanket breakfast-to-go from Elmer's Pancake House, I was fast asleep. The next thing I knew we were on the side of I-5, broken down at the Sexton Mountain Pass. It seemed quite serious—a blown engine, perhaps. Frank thought it would take us at least two days and five thousand dollars to get a new one delivered and installed. Beth and I stuck out our thumbs and flagged down a compassionate eighteen-wheel Mayflower Moving semi that took us to Fat Harvey's Truck Stop in Canyonville. In short order we phoned Hofstra, arranged for a garage to send a mechanic to diagnose the Majic Bus, and made reservations for the Iron Horse Stage Line Company to take us first to Kesey's farm and then to Portland. When I informed Kesey we had broken down and would be late, he said not to sweat it, adding out of his long years of bus experience, "The bus always breaks down just when you've got to be somewhere." Meanwhile, back at the Majic Bus, Frank was organizing a roadside scrambled-egg breakfast as students nervously wondered how they were going to get home.

An Iron Horse Bus arrived at Fat Harvey's in an hour, and we headed over to rescue the students at Sexton Mountain Pass—only to find a resurrected Majic Bus, passengers all aboard and ready to go. It turned out the breakdown had been due only to a loose bolt or two. Delighted, I paid Mr. Iron Horse fifty dollars for his services, and we got back on track to

Kesey's, the students relieved and happy to be in motion, competing for spots through which they could poke their heads out of the roof holes and they could feel the wind in their faces, wave to hitchhikers, point out such sights as berry patches with signs announcing PICKERS WANTED, a "Memorial Garden" with a gigantic white plaster Jesus and a flock of white plaster sheep, tree farms and sawmills and rusted-car graveyards. This was green, damp Oregon, and we were searching for a big white star inside a blue circle painted on Ken Kesey's red barn, Bob Dylan's "Jokerman" was blasting through the Majic Bus, and we were all ready to encounter the high priest of the sixties, now a Pleasant Hill dairy farmer.

18

Further with Ken Kesey and Bob Dylan in the Grunge Belt

He not busy being born is busy dying.
—BOB DYLAN

KEN KESEY'S WILLAMETTE VALLEY FARM IS OUT OF THE way, address-free, and not particularly easy to find. But as Ralph Waldo Emerson wrote, "If a man can write a better book, preach a better sermon, or make a better mouse trap than his neighbor, though he build his house in the woods, the world will beat a path to his door." And American Odyssey was following the beaten path to Ken Kesey's door. Kesey is many things to many people: novelist of unusual force, accomplished magician, fireside storyteller, creative-writing instructor at the University of Oregon, inventor of tie-dye clothing, popularizer of Day-Glo colors, ringleader of the psychedelic sixties, college wrestler-turned-wrestling coach, dairy farmer, carnival showman, outlaw legend. He is the man who threw

426

a party in San Francisco and saw half of America show up. The Kesey persona that had drawn us to his Pleasant Hill doorstep was that of Kesey the catalyst, the last wagon master, the innovative unsettler who with his band of Merry Pranksters helped trigger a revolution of consciousness in the 1960s with his notorious 1939 International Harvester bus Furthur. He is still fighting the good fight today, though at a less frenetic pace, with his successor bus, Further (or Further II).

The students had read Tom Wolfe's best-selling *Electric Kool-Aid Acid Test*, an account of the maiden transcontinental journey of Kesey and thirteen of the Merry Pranksters. In 1964 the giddy band traversed America from California to New York in a psychedelic painted bus promoting LSD. Behind the wheel was none other than counterculture folk hero Neal Cassady, the greatest roadie ever, the model for Dean Moriarty in Jack Kerouac's *On the Road*. Wolfe chronicled the wanderings of "the Hieronymus Bosch bus . . . with the destination sign in front reading 'Furthur' and a sign in back saying 'Caution: Weird Load.' " But as journalist Paul Perry and Prankster Ken Babbs pointed out in their book *On the Bus*, this most infamous and riotous transcontinental bus trek ever was an event of immense historical and cultural importance, for "the torch had been passed from the Beat to the Psychedelic, with Cassady as the driver, the tour guide, the swing man, foot in both eras, the flame passing from Kerouac to Kesey."

The psychedelic sixties can apparently now be viewed with that certain historical detachment that time eventually accords to all eras, no matter how tumultuous. In 1990 the Smithsonian's National Museum of American History sought to purchase the original Furthur from Kesey. "It is not a typical bus," said a museum public-affairs officer. "Its historical context is important for what it meant to the literary world of a certain generation." The only trouble was that Furthur was defunct, rusting and rotting away on Kesey's Oregon farm, covered with moss and spiderwebs, in a state of complete moldering disrepair, impossible to rebuild. Instead of informing the Smithsonian of Furthur's demise, Kesey, his Pranksterism having survived the eighties intact, bought a similar 1949 version of the bus. With his son Zane and several Prankster friends, among others, he went to work refurbishing and repainting this successor, bringing it to a high sheen of Day-Glo glory.

The prank was to palm off the simulation as the original for the unsuspecting Smithsonian to display. Besides the thick layers of Day-Glo paint and psychedelic doves, clouds, shooting stars, and squiggles that cover Further II, Kesey added some fresh interior touches: Dada collages and photo clippings of personalities ranging from Marilyn Monroe to Joseph Stalin on the sides, and at the wheel a large drawing of Neal Cassady, the psychedelic Saint Christopher of the American highway. Kesey transferred Cassady's driver's seat, an authentic relic from the original bus, into Further II, to maintain continuity with the Beat days past. A small bronze statue of a court jester, a jokerman, became the hood ornament. Beanbag chairs and sofa cushions were scattered about the floor, making the interior an unlikely misalliance between a bourgeois living room and a traveling opium den. Beyond listing such details, the only way to describe Further II is as a kaleidoscope of explosive colors, a Day-Glo fireworks display on wheels, a rainbow-sherbet swirl of every color under the sun, and then some. The Grateful Dead donated a high-powered stereo system for the bus and Kesey traded in his reel-to-reels for CDs. He enlisted an adventurous crew largely comprised of former Pranksters and younger soulmates, inviting them to cross the continent. In Washington, DC, they would help pass off Further II as the real McCoy at a Smithsonian ceremony—where, who knew, maybe the fruit punch might get laced.

In November of 1990, Kesey and company took to the road, stopping at shopping malls and roadside restaurants, bringing smiles to the lips of the locals. They hit San Francisco for a dose of nostalgia, cruising past Longshoremen's Hall, site of the infamous Trips Festival of January 1966, where the Pranksters and others inaugurated what became the first strobe-light and acid-rock-sound show. They passed Golden Gate Park and the meadow where the Summer of Love Be-ins were held, and headed to (you guessed it) the Haight-Ashbury district. All the while, the Dead's new sound system was blasting Bob Dylan's "Positively 42nd Street" and "Mr. Tambourine Man" and the Grateful Dead's "Mexicali Blues" and "Run for the Roses," causing necks to crane, cyberpunks to give the thumbs-up, and college-age Deadheads to beg for a spin.

Kesey wanted to show a new generation of Americans that despite death and divorce and personal disasters, the Prankster spirit survives—that, in his words, they've "made good on a promise." "We have to reestablish the whole idea of trust in this nation," Kesey declared at a Further II rally in Berkeley. "The war is not on drugs, it's on consciousness. If Jesse Helms wants to lock horns with God, I can take him up there and introduce him in twenty minutes. But it won't be the Southern Baptist God with the big voice and the white beard; it'll be the God of the stars and the lights and the planets and the colors."

A few days after the rally, Kesey's bus was shanghaied in Stockton, California, stolen by Zane and some of the younger crew, and driven back to Oregon. On the pavement where the bus had stood, Kesey found a chalked outline of Further and a simple inscription of the Prankster motto: "Nothing lasts." Kesey had been outpranked by his son. Zane's message was that Further II was alive and running and didn't belong in a museum. *Don't you know, Dad, rust never sleeps.* Ken Kesey returned home, and he ensconced the new bus in his barn, to be called into service on special occasions or when the spirit moved.

As Frank left I-5 and headed down Highway 58 to the small town of Pleasant Hill, all eyes were peeled for a Dairy Queen, the landmark at which Kesey had instructed us to turn left. Speculation was rampant as to whether Kesey would take us for a spin in the new Further. I volunteered that I thought it was unlikely. Besides our being hours late, the skies were gray, indicating rain was imminent. I surmised we would sit around and talk about *One Flew Over the Cuckoo's Nest* and Neal Cassady, eat some potato chips and pretzels, and leave.

O ye of little faith. I should have known better, for one of the greatest things about Ken Kesey is that he never does the expected, the predictable; in fact, unpredictability is his hallmark.

Finally we spotted the Dairy Queen, turned left, and followed a curvy country road past brown, moon-eyed cows and ranch-style homes with lawns sprouting a thousand varieties of green vegetation—until we saw a white star painted in a bright blue circle on the side of a red barn: We recognized Kesey's homestead. Our excitement mounted at the sight of a yellow road sign with a black silhouette of a kangaroo on it—a warning that we were entering the uncharted kingdom of Keseyland.

As we cleared some low-hanging tree branches and turned up the dirt driveway, the students caught their first glimmering of Kesey's predilection for bright colors: a family of peacocks showboating and strutting about the place, their piercing cries announcing our arrival. Anticipation was running high. My students could scarcely believe they were about to meet the cultural warrior of the sixties whose legendary Merry Prankster antics they had heard about for years, from aging hippies at Dead concerts or from "weird, trippy" uncles who had taken Scott MacKenzie's musical advice and headed to San Francisco.

When we got out of the bus, there was Ken Kesey with his son Zane (who runs Key-Z Productions), all smiles and hearty handshakes, keenly interested in whether his directions had been sufficient. Wearing a darkish blue jumpsuit over a tie-dyed shirt, a hay straw in his mouth and a navy blue sailor's cap—the kind Jack London used to wear—on his head, Kesey looked forty, not fifty-six, being possessed of both the silveriness of Paul Newman and the beefy demeanor of Gene Hackman. "Come on inside," he offered, "we've got some hot dogs and beans ready for you all." Kesey knew how to win over young people's hearts—free food. With no lunch in their stomachs, save a roadside breakfast snack, they dug in with a vengeance. We were chowing down in a psychedelic version of Pee Wee's Playhouse—posters of Wavy Gravy, the Dead, and Neal Cassady hung on the rustic walls, and a giant ball of hemp twine lay stationary on the floor. Day-Glo paint covered everything, from Kesey's suitcase to his dog's tail.

It was amazing to watch his famed charisma at work. Within minutes he had captivated the students with charming stories and an irresistible smile. Everyone would have "sailed to the farthest galaxy with him if he just gave the word," as Jay later said. "Hurry up and eat," Kesey prompted,

430

"we've got pretty good weather and enough daylight hours to take Further out for a spin." We all gulped in disbelief. Had he said we were taking Further for a spin? Kesey opened a closet and began pulling out Day-Glo jumpsuits for us to wear, as well as crazy hats—including one with fuzzy brown bear ears, which Stefanie donned. It was really happening. We were going to drive around the Oregon countryside with Ken Kesey's foot on the accelerator.

Suitably attired, we followed Kesey and Zane out to the bus barn. Sure enough, there was Further II, a rebellion in color, an affirmation of life. While Kesey got the bus road-ready, some of us walked back past a murky pond filled with springtime bullfrogs to a mossy grove of trees where an old wooden fishing boat called "Deeper" was rotting away, decomposing, becoming one with nature once more. With trees drooling moss and a chorus of croaking frogs, it felt more like the Louisiana bayou than like Oregon. Near the boat lay the original Furthur, like a fallen warrior, still recognizable as a bus, with a cardboard skeleton sitting approximately where Neal Cassady once sat. The paint job was more Picassoesque and less Pollackian than I had imagined. The famed roof bubble still gave the bus a futuristic aura, though the glass was now opaque from twenty-five years of soot. As we jogged back to the barn, not wanting to be left behind while the others went on the ride of a lifetime, we noticed that almost every yard object had been transfigured with a bit of Day-Glo—an electric pink hose or chain, a blue ax or a yellow hammer—the colors arrested the eye, altering our perceptions of the commonplace.

Kesey and Zane were all smiles as we boarded Further II in our Day-Glo jumpsuits and silly hats. Half of us climbed to the roof, where it was bound to get wild and windy; the other half plopped down in the beanbag den—which had the distinct advantage of being surrounded by speakers so the passengers could groove to manic music and Kesey's Neal Cassady–inspired speed-rap monologues. Kesey had hijacked American Odyssey and we were loving every minute of it. Frank was in a schizoid state of bus envy and bliss; the Furthur legend was a part of his fantasy life like nothing else, and now he was playing the role of Kesey copilot in Further II. Captain Kesey, concerned about keeping his crew in sync, had rigged up a microphone system so that two people on the top deck with headphones could report on traffic flows, crowd reactions, police sightings, and other such external factors. Beth and Zane were our top-deck communication links with the subterranean downstairs. Our positions assumed, Further II rolled off into the damp Oregon countryside, with no clear direction, going nowhere slowly, in a blaze of Day-Glo glory.

Kesey began speed-rapping into the overhead microphone, telling us about the history of the Willamette Valley—his equivalent of Faulkner's Yokapatawpha County. Kesey was born and reared in this part of Oregon; his brother still runs a creamery in nearby Springfield. Kesey had a yarn to spin about every barn and creek and cow pasture we passed.

But his tone became somber when he told us of Mount Pisgah, a sacred Indian burial spot, where he prays every Easter Sunday for his son Jed, who died in a freak accident a few years ago. A van carrying the University of Oregon wrestling team, of whom Jed was a member, had hit an ice patch and slid off a cliff. Kesey was at Jed's hospital bedside when he died. Quoting Faulkner, Kesey once told a reporter: " 'Every so often the dog has to battle the bear just so he can call himself a dog again.' I felt the bite of the bear when Jed died. I didn't feel it was God's will that he be up there in a van without seatbelts, without a CB to call ahead to a hospital. I felt there was stuff that had happened that was unfair and that could be changed." Wanting to avoid other wrongful deaths, he sued the state of Oregon, the university, and the National Collegiate Athletic Association, won the case, and then turned around and bought the Oregon wrestling team a forty-thousand-dollar van with safety belts and emergency radios. Jed is buried at Kesey's farm next to a chicken coop, not too far away from where the original Furthur rests in peace.

Suddenly, Kesey shifted gears and began talking animatedly about tree farmers and loggers and bears and eagles, free-associating to images he saw in the clouds, just as a light drizzle began to fall. As Further II cruised through the small town of Lowell, we waved to a group of kids on bicycles who howled with laughter on seeing this far-out crew in far-out clothes in the most far-out bus their young minds could imagine. Something about being in this outrageous bus unshackled the mind and soul, and we all screamed with ecstatic delight. Suddenly everything was electrifying, almost holy, in the old Ginsberg-Kerouac way. Holy rock. Holy hill. Holy herd of deer in the holy meadow chewing on the holy grass.

Kesey turned disk jockey, introducing Neil Young's "Sugar Mountain" as "a song that will tell you all you want to know about what it was like in the sixties." Next came Bob Marley's "Redemption Song" and the Grateful Dead's "Truckin'," followed by an old peyote chant by Native American Jim Pepper called "Witchi Tai To." But it was Sam the Sham and the Pharaohs' "Wooly Bully" that really got us going. When I got on the headphones to ask him how the students below were doing, Kesey responded that he had given them "their thee-sis" and "they had all passed with flying colors." As the speakers pounded out loud music, Kesey drove us all over his beloved green corner of Oregon, waving and screaming at every car and person we passed, and finally stopping in front of a rambling farmhouse by a creek, where he parked and ushered us out of the bus.

It was the home of Prankster Ken Babbs, clown prince, instinctive raconteur, idea man, vaudevillian, and longtime Kesey friend. He introduced us to his family and gave us a tour of his home, which included a basketball hoop in the living room and a studio where he mixes audiotapes and acts as archivist of the hundreds of videotapes from various 1960s happenings, including the Merry Pranksters' 1964 bus tour. Babbs led us down to the creek, where we played with his dogs, skipped a few stones, and meandered about. Then it was back on the bus for more outlandish liberation, including a stop in front of a bar where a scene from National Lampoon's *Animal House* was filmed. We returned to the farm—our faces flushed, as happy as pigs in mud—where Kesey put us to work loading hay onto a trailer hitched to the back of a tractor. He took us for a ride to feed his cows, the students tossing the bales off the back to a chorus of hungry moos.

Kesey was truly an incredible host, kind and generous. Back at the house he offered the students beer and soda while pouring himself a stiff bourbon. We then sat around while he played videotapes of the Pranksters with the Grateful Dead (then the Warlocks), Jerry Garcia beardless and innocent looking, a youth rather than a guitar legend. Kesey answered all sorts of questions about the sixties and his life as a writer and warrior.

The students were astounded to learn that he had never seen the movie version of *One Flew Over the Cuckoo's Nest*. He had sold his film rights for only twenty thousand dollars and never received royalties from the movie, but what really galled him was that Jack Nicholson, whom he dislikes intensely as an actor, was miscast in the role of R. P. McMurphy. We talked for a while about his *Sometimes a Great Notion*, the story of a family that defies a labor union—and thus their entire community—by continuing to log their forest. The students responded by updating Kesey on what they had learned about the timber wars in Humboldt and Mendocino counties.

Kesey told the students about his third novel, *Sailor's Song*, which he had just finished; it's an apocalyptic story that takes place in the early twenty-first century in a little Alaskan fishing village called Kuinak. The lead character, Ike Sallas, is an Earth First!–type eco-radical. (I returned to Oregon that August for Kesey's book party, camping in his backyard for a staged promotional event officially called "The Third Decadenal Field Trip." Over a three-day period a thousand people showed up in Kesey's backyard to participate in his Giant Talent Contest, featuring Anne Waldman and bands like the Mud Farmers, the Greyhound Daddies, and the Swan and Boogie Patrol Express, all of whom primarily played folk rock. Shoshone poet Ed Edmo performed "Through Coyotes' Eyes," and Dead lyricist Robert Hunter read some new poems. Ramblin' Jack Elliot was also there, singing train songs, the blues, and pretty much the whole American songbook. As for *Sailor's Song* itself, the novel moved me so much that I decided to bring my students to Alaska for American Odyssey II, for as Kesey wrote: "Alaska is the end, the finale, the Last Ditch of the Pioneer Dream. From Alaska there's no place left to go. . . . So it came down to Alaska, the Final Frontier as far as this sick old ballgame goes. Top of the ninth . . .")

Kesey spoke to the students about comic books and superheroes, with special emphasis on Paul Bunyan, the Lone Ranger, and Captain Marvel.

He tossed the I-Ching while making frequent references to the Bible, described his 1975 trip to Egypt in search of the occult Hidden Pyramid, and spoke with great respect and fondness about Arthur Miller, Norman Mailer, and Thomas Pynchon. His kindest literary words were directed toward Faulkner and Sherwood Anderson, and he positively lit up when he heard we had visited Jack London's Beauty Ranch. While the students watched another video, Kesey showed me the study where he wrote, and we discussed the state of contemporary literature.

At 9:00 P.M. it was time for the Majic Bus to hit the road. We had spent seven unforgettable hours with Ken Kesey. Before parting, Kesey thrilled the students with magic tricks—coins disappearing in one ear and out the other, playing cards floating in the air—proving himself a magician through and through. He also handed out calendars of Further II, autographed them, and came outside to tour the Majic Bus. He disapproved of the way the interior was compartmentalized, preferring the open-spaced beanbag living area of Further. He was right, but there wasn't much we could do about our structural arrangements. With handshakes, we said good-bye to our host, moved by his incredible generosity, humor, and humanity. Ken Kesey is a great teacher because he cares, because he inspires. We would never forget whipping around Oregon with him in Further II.

The afterglow of our visit kept the Majic Bus abuzz for an hour. The energy had propelled Frank into overdrive and every five minutes he announced some new scheme as to how we could radicalize his now unacceptably conservative—nay, reactionary—Majic Bus. Before long, though, the students began to drop off to sleep, until only Tom remained awake, reading a biography of John J. McCloy by flashlight. Eventually even the supercharged Frank began to tire. He pulled off in Salem and parked across from the State Capitol, at Willamette University, founded by Methodist missionaries in 1842 and billed as "the oldest university of the West." That evening the bus yawned to the rhythm of Frank's loud, throaty snore.

For the first time during the entire American Odyssey journey, I awoke before Frank. I took a solitary walk around the State Capitol, pausing to admire the rooftop statue of the quintessential *Oregon Pioneer*, as a mother scolded her son for spilling orange juice on his Barney the Dinosaur T-shirt—only to find her stridency parried with vociferous howls and tears of outrage.

When I got back, the Majic Bus motor was running, Frank wide awake but in need of coffee. He was ready to ferry us to Portland, where we would be staying that evening in the Theatre Ballroom of country singer and hair-product entrepreneur Geoff Thompson. Thompson, a thirty-five-year-old Arista recording artist, had seen us on the "Good Morning America" show at the Grand Canyon. Intrigued by the notion of education on the road and wishing he had had the opportunity to learn in such a "ramblin' way," he had called New College at Hofstra University with an offer of free accommodations in his hometown of Portland: We could camp on the carpeted floor of his refurbished ballroom, which also had backstage showers. It was an offer we gladly accepted.

Sprouting from the banks of the Willamette River, Portland is poised between the beaches of the Pacific Ocean and the year-round ski slopes of Mount Hood. But as we searched for Geoff Thompson's office it was the Portland Building—with *Portlandia*, the largest hammered-copper sculpture since the Statue of Liberty—that caught our immediate attention. It didn't take us long to realize that Portland doesn't like cars—one-way streets and NO PARKING signs confronted us everywhere, communally announcing to us: "You should have used mass transit." Portlanders demand that rides on buses and light-rail transit be free throughout the three-hundred-block downtown area, convinced that fewer cars mean less congestion and air pollution. Our first impression of Portland registered how squeaky clean the city was—to be expected, I guess, from the state that pioneered the environmentalist revolution. Oregon was the first state to introduce a "bottle bill" mandating refundable deposits on cans and bottles, the first to secure public access to every mile of its ocean beaches.

If Dartmouth environmentalist Noel Perrin ever gets his way and our country converts to electrical cars, Oregon will be in the forefront and Portland, flanked by ancient pine and evergreen forests, will clearly make the transition with ease.

Eventually Frank found paid parking in a lot adjacent to the Theatre Ballroom. Lugging our bedrolls and bags, we took the elevator to the fifth floor and entered the world of Geoff Thompson Hair Products, their New Wave corporate office space resembling an Upper East Side New York Beautiful People hair salon where the minimalist interior is a pricey product of interior decoration and not a concession to cutting corners. Geoff was there to greet us, handing out copies of his new cassette, *Geoff Thompson*, with one hand and complimentary bottles of his hair-care products with the other. Besides hosting us in Portland, he offered to act as "guide" to those of us who wanted a walking tour of the city. He also alerted us that Madonna was in town to film *Body of Evidence*, in which she plays a blonde temptress charged with murder. The entire community was on a "Madonna Watch," the *Oregonian* reporting her every move.

He led us into his ballroom, a wonderful space with four chandeliers, new red-and-gold carpeting, a dance-worn stage, and a high ceiling with wooden beams. This palatial hall was home to the Knights of Pythias in the 1920s, next housed an underage nightclub, and then was recycled by Thompson as a showroom for his MEN product line. Everybody grabbed a carpeted spot to call bed. Geoff had devised a "key system" so the students could stay out as late as they wished. He pointed us toward the shower facilities, left us alone, and went back to his business. We were free to discover Portland on our own.

Most students rated Portland the most livable city in America, a small city/big town that has everything from great bookstores to clubs, coffeehouses, theaters, restaurants, and shopping plazas. Most important to Jared and Tom, it has the Trail Blazers basketball team. Unlike most American cities, Portland citizens are actually *fighting* to live in the downtown area. Everybody, it seems, wants to be part of an urban environment that works. The people with money are moving back in; nobody wants to live in the suburbs anymore, for the inner city offers enchanting neighborhoods of

437

varying architectural styles, from the stately old mansions of King's Hill to the historic bungalows of Ladd's Addition, in southeast Portland. This metropolis, which abhors edge-city sprawl, could serve as an urban model for the rest of America. Art-conscious Oregonians have secured a fund for public art through a one-percent tax on new building construction. The result is some of the finest outdoor sculpture in the world. As an indication of how important public art is to Portlanders, back in the 1970s a local pub owner named Bud Clark posed for a popular poster captioned EXPOSE YOURSELF TO ART, featuring a man in a trenchcoat flashing a public sculpture. Bud's poster brought him citywide attention and shortly thereafter he was elected mayor.

Portland is also an outdoorsy, sports-minded, "deep ecology" community where nature reigns supreme over snack shops and smokestacks. Everyone in Portland dresses as if they're about to go hiking; every third person you see is dressed by the likes of L. L. Bean, Moonstone, or Patagonia.

Mitch was overjoyed to discover Nike Town, the retail showcase store for Phil Knight's Portland-based shoe empire, which is like a combination of F. A. O. Schwartz and Disneyland. Ever since our visit to the Biltmore Estate, Mitch had been sensitized to how much money there was in souvenirs. As the Majic Bus traipsed across America, he took note of regional souvenirs such as tomahawks in Cherokee, voodoo trinkets in New Orleans, Elvis everything in Memphis, gangster wear in Chicago, New Age products in Boulder, turquoise jewelry and kachina dolls in the Grand Canyon, coyote anything in Sante Fe, Wyland whales in Santa Barbara, Emmett the Clown in Carmel, Bigfoot dolls and redwood furniture in Northern California, Day-Glo in Keseyland. Now in Portland, standing in Nike Town, it came to him: He had a vision of how to make his first million. What America needed was a national Americana catalog that capitalized on cultural regionalism and diversity, just like that polo-shirt genius Ralph Lauren had done with his most recent ad campaign. As Mitch stared at the display of broken John McEnroe tennis rackets exhibited under clear Plexiglas floor tiles in Nike Town, he realized that to launch this catalog company properly he would have to move to the West Coast, perhaps even to Portland, to get more "in tune" with Americana

438

products. He would start his business with Indian artifacts and redwood trinkets. Although Mitch was a New Yorker through and through, Nike Town brought home to him that business innovation is a West Coast phenomenon, concentrated particularly in Orange County, the Silicon Valley, and Oregon. He would follow Horace Greeley's advice to "Go west, young man"; or as Willy Loman said in *Death of a Salesman,* "You got to go where the diamonds are."

While Kevin, Frank, and I spent some time drinking coffee in the sun at Captain Bean's Espresso House—followed by even more at Starbuck's Coffee at the Pioneer Courthouse Square fountain, listening to a folk duo called Guilty of Everything sing the Leadbelly ball-and-chain repertoire for the lunchtime brown-baggers and mah-jonggers—Janine took Dan to a doctor. A Rocky Mountain wood tick had decided to call Dan's right arm home when we were camping in redwood country, burrowing in so deep that it was impossible to tweeze it out. Ticks cannot be ignored in a world that harbors Lyme disease, a debilitating ailment. So even though the Portland doctor removed the invader, Dan worried that the disease had already lodged in his bloodstream. Bucked up by his peers' reassurances that he would be all right, Dan took the danger in stride, getting off on his Gus Van Sant–style photorealism shoot of the North and Northeast districts where *Drugstore Cowboy* was filmed, his eye on the many homeless and strung-out souls who inhabit even the most prosperous of cities.

That evening we all brought our individual Portland experiences back to the Theatre Ballroom to share. Many students had been handed free copies of *The Next Step: 50 More Things You Can Do to Save the Earth,* with tips on recycling, advice on joining the Green PTA or becoming an organic farmer, and a discussion of the importance of holding garage sales— that "uniquely American sport," in the words of the manual. They had learned that in 1989 the Portland City Council banned polystyrene foam, meaning no nonbiogradable waste like McDonald's Big Mac "clamshell" food containers or Dunkin' Donuts coffee cups would choke local landfills. But what impressed the group most about Portland was how the two spectacular peaks of the Cascade Mountains—Mount Hood and Mount Saint Helens—were almost always in view, arresting the students' attention as they casually strolled about the clean, beautifully landscaped city. With the Columbia and Willamette rivers cradling downtown, the Pacific Ocean only seventy miles away, and the evergreen and Douglas fir and mountain peaks just waiting to be explored, everyone agreed that Portland was perfection. They would soon learn that its nightlife was equally inviting.

American Odyssey went as a group for a soirée at Powell's Bookstore, which in an earlier incarnation was a car showroom. Now, instead of chrome and sparkplugs, the space boasts more than a half million different new and used titles. What the Strand is to New York City, Powell's is for the entire Pacific Northwest. Powell's also features wonderful author readings in their third-floor Purple Room. We had stayed overnight in Portland so we could spend an evening with South Carolina novelist Josephine Humphreys, to hear her read from her newest book, *The Fireman's Fair.*

If you haven't read Josephine Humphreys, you should—starting with *Dreams of Sleep* and *Rich in Love*, novels that are exceptional in their exploration of themes of marriage and the disintegration of American family life. As we traveled America we were hearing a lot about the "decline of family values," that phrase chanted like a mantra by the Bush-Quayle coterie, with little serious exploration of what it meant. The family has changed in America because America has changed. Josephine Humphreys writes about the real pressures on the American family in a contemporary, relevant social context, a sophisticated "Roseanne" for the reading population. With a gift for creating detailed, compassionate, and believable characters, Humphreys, the forty-eight-year-old mother of two, dissects the changing American family in her fiction and superimposes it on the changing socio-economic realities of our time, on the loss of our agricultural and urban national identities displaced by the communal emptiness of suburban expansion. What makes Humphreys so exciting to read is her sense of individual and collective renewal, the sense that you can always start over again, you can build a new life out of the wreckage of the old.

In a nation with a divorce rate approaching 40 percent, Humphreys's message to the members of splintering families is that life goes on: Don't despair; pick up the shattered pieces and rebuild. This was the message we heard at Powell's when she read from *The Fireman's Fair*, a novel about a community rebuilding and working together in the wake of a devastating hurricane that has leveled a coastal South Carolina town. Her prose observations on the South Carolina hurricane matched what we witnessed and felt in Ferndale after the earthquake.

Aíne was particularly impressed to learn that after years of teaching English at the Baptist College in Charleston and raising a family, Humphreys decided at the age of thirty-nine to quit teaching and do what her heart had always told her to do—write fiction. She had burned out as an overworked academic, unhappy and stressed out, tired of all the bureaucratic pettiness. So, like Sherwood Anderson walked away from his Elyria, Ohio, paint factory, she upped and quit, resurfacing a few years later as a novelist of intense power. Her first book, *Dreams of Sleep*, won the PEN American Center's Ernest Hemingway Prize for the best first novel of 1985.

During a question-and-answer session, Aíne asked Humphreys whether she saw an advantage to starting her career so late. "I think that I worked harder as a result of waiting that long," Humphreys answered with a smooth, rich Southern accent. "It was now or never. Once you decide to grab the bull by the horns you have to bring him down. As a young woman I never felt that kind of pressure to dig my heels in." Alison told Humphreys about how her hurricane imagery had exactly captured our feelings about being in the earthquake, and a lively discussion ensued about how crises unite the people who endure them together. When a middle-aged man from the folding-chair crowd of about forty people observed that this "crisis together" idea was "exactly" what Ross Perot was trying to get across in *United We Stand*, the Texas billionaire's best-selling blueprint for rebuilding America, Humphreys's dry response was, "If you want to think that, sir, it's you own prerogative, but try not to." Afterward many of the students bought paperback copies of *The Fireman's Fair* for Humphreys to autograph; it had been a well-spent two hours. On our way out the manager gave the students free Powell's T-shirts and sweatshirts, as well as a discount on books purchased.

From Powell's everybody set off in different directions, pursuing various interests. One group headed over to the Bridgeport Brewery and Brew Pub, the oldest of Portland's more than twenty-five microbreweries and restaurants that make their own beer. In fact, according to the National Association of Brewers, Portland has more brewing activity for its size than any other metropolitan area in the nation. "The City of Roses" has become "the City of Suds." Other students, pleased that Portland offered many New York–style pizzerias, went to Café Coexistence for slices to eat while reading alternative newspapers. They also met a "captive-bred-bird" activist named Meg, who made a case for leaving wild parrots, cockatiels, and parakeets in their native habitats. By buying an exotic bird born and raised in the USA, she said, you help save the lives of thousands of other intelligent, beautiful, and often endangered birds in the wild— many of whom die en route, drugged and stuffed into boxes or mattresses by "dealers" smuggling them into America. Though the students, too polite to blow her off, expressed no interest in birds, she elaborated on her obsession for what seemed like hours. When she left, her parting words were: "The next time you buy a bird, demand documentation that it is American-bred," and finally fluttered away.

Another group, of which I was part, met Geoff Thompson and friends at the River Place Marina for dinner by the Willamette River. To our surprise, there was Mitch, eating seafood and talking business with executives of MEN, testing his Americana catalog idea out on them. After dinner we went to Portland's Chinatown, which is considerably smaller than San Francisco's but boasts the magnificent China Gate spanning Fourth Avenue at Southwest Burnside, commemorating the 135-year contribution of Chinese culture to the area. Unable to find a Chinese restaurant in Chinatown still open for a drink, we settled on a Thai place. One thing is abundantly clear about Portland: It has become an eastern outpost of the Pacific Rim, a town where businesspeople from all over America come to work for NEC, Matsushita, and Fujitsu, and end up eating sushi for lunch while reading Benjamin Hoff's *Te of Piglet*.

That evening, as I lay on the ballroom floor in my sleeping bag, it dawned on me that American Odyssey was coming to an end. It is important to finish with a bang, and I vowed to make sure the students lived each remaining moment fully. Tomorrow we'd make a stellar start, driving to Seattle ("the Emerald City") to see Bob Dylan perform at the Paramount Theater. I could hardly wait.

The next morning I awoke as if still dreaming, with the faint but unmistakable strains of Dylan singing "Absolutely Sweet Marie" from *Blonde on Blonde* infiltrating my consciousness from afar. Aíne was already up, phoning home. Together we looked out the window to discover the source of the music. Lo and behold! It was our own Frank Perugi maintenancing his bus while listening to Dylan in the now-empty lot where we had parked. From our vantage point the Majic Bus looked isolated and forlorn, like a lone shopping cart in a grocery store lot after closing.

It was only 6:00 A.M. but Frank was anxious to get a jump on the day. When I heard Dylan sing "To live outside of the law you've got to be honest," I knew it was going to be a day to remember, so I shouted everyone up with a call of "We're leaving"—in actuality giving them an hour to shower and pack their bags. We were ready for Seattle, but on our way we would visit Mount Saint Helens National Monument, not far over the border, in Washington.

Once the gem of the Cascades, today Mount Saint Helens resembles those parts of Northern California clear-cut by corporate technopredators with power saws. But Gaia herself caused this environmental catalysm, a giant volcanic eruption spewing forth on May 18, 1980—the worst natural disaster in recorded American history. Black ash shot up from the crater and blotted out the sky for hundreds of miles. The black stuff blanketed both countryside and city, with Yakima, eighty miles away, catching a layer an inch thick.

We stopped first at the visitors' center, to watch a film featuring graphic shots of Mount Saint Helens blowing its top and heaving debris into Spirit Lake and the flooding Toutle River, which then rushes with black ash, toppling and soiling homes, trees, and everything else in its way. As we hiked the trail toward the mountain itself, a ranger approached and told us that the area surrounding the volcano is coming back to life: Saplings are pushing their way through the soil, butterflies fluttering about, berries returning to some bushes. And as we stood looking at a fog-shrouded Mount Saint Helens, trying to imagine what it must have been like on May 18, 1980, the park ranger exclaimed, "Look there!" and pointed to a rabbit, with evident delight. There was once a time, before the eruption, when rabbits were ubiquitous throughout the park. Today they're an unusual sight but are becoming more common. "You see," the ranger told us, "that little rabbit is a sign that nature's power of destruction is no match for its power of regeneration."

The rest of the afternoon was spent driving up I-5, all the while listening to Dylan, taking a short break to tour the State Capitol in Olympia. Students were still needling me about my Dylan obsession, but I had actually converted some into true believers by encouraging them to listen more carefully to his music. The converts had learned to value him as I did, not only as a poet but as one of the most significant American songwriters of this century—right up there with the Gershwins, Irving Berlin, Cole Porter, and Hank Williams—as well as a vocalist of extreme power. All those "Dylan can't sing" critics have closed minds, like the yahoos who look at a Jackson Pollack canvas and say, "You call that painting?" Without equal for integrity, longevity, and historical contribution, he is the poet laureate of rock and proof of Henry Miller's dictum that "to sing . . . it is not necessary to have an accordian, or a guitar. The essential thing is to want to sing." And by wanting to sing in the early 1960s, Dylan singlehandedly destroyed Tin Pan Alley.

As we approached Seattle, I gave the students a quick rundown of the city. Over the past few years, Seattle has gained a well-deserved national reputation as one of America's most attractive and livable cities, offering clean air, spectacular scenery, first-class restaurants, and national sports attractions, entertainment, and recreation. But as we crawled bumper to bumper past Tacoma and Seatac and entered Seattle via an overused stretch of I-5 (the entire length of which runs from San Diego to Vancouver), we realized that this port town is afflicted with a horrendous highway congestion problem.

Seattle, like Minneapolis, Atlanta, and Portland, is an American city for the 1990s. But its fine reputation is a two-edged sword. Considered the ideal cityscape, Seattle is growing by leaps and bounds and as the population increases so do poverty, crime, and homelessness. In recent years, other American cities have dealt with their homeless problems by buying the dispossessed one-way bus tickets to Seattle, knowing they would be taken care of by its vast network of generous mission programs catering to the poor. Meanwhile, as rents have skyrocketed upward many low-income families have been forced onto the streets. There are an estimated seventeen thousand homeless children (less than sixteen years old) in the Emerald City, and teenage alcohol and drug addiction and prostitution are rampant. Seattlites now have to stay and deal with their urban problems, for there is no escape except the banality of the suburbs, to which some might flee under the delusion that the blight won't follow.

Suddenly, as if the Paramount were a giant magnet exerting an irresistible pull, the Majic Bus stopped in front of the famous theater. The marquee promised BOB DYLAN, LOU REED, and DAVID BYRNE, all playing different dates. Many students photographed this incredible all-star roster of lyrical geniuses. With the afternoon light fading, people were already gathering in front of the theater, selling concessions, drinking beer and cups of Starbuck's coffee, and just hanging. Frank parked right next to the Paramount, in an outdoor lot, and soon all sorts of curious onlookers came to gawk at the Majic Bus. Frank gave guided tours and was delighted to receive the highest accolade possible from an American youth: "Wow! This is really cool, man!"

The show was sold out but Dylan's office had come through with a handful of free tickets. There was a problem, though: I had requested eighteen tickets but was only given eight. Fortunately, it turned out that I had won only half my students over to Dylanophilia; the other half happily opted to wander about Seattle while we attended the performance. We were all to meet back at the bus at 2:00 A.M.

As the non-Dylanites took off—most of them would have dinner atop the landmark Space Needle—the pavement in front of the Paramount turned into a three-ring circus, with vendors hawking Dylan T-shirts and buskers singing the blues and Neil Young, all made poignant by a solitary

445

woman with a homemade cardboard sign, HELP ME, I'M DYING OF AIDS, pleading for survival money. A motorcycle gang from Walla Walla, Washington, wearing Dylan's incendiary words "You don't need a weatherman to know which way the wind blows" emblazoned on their jacket backs, were just standing around, stroking their ZZ Top beards. Three University of Washington sorority women dressed for a night out on the town were being chatted up by two young policemen trying to muster the courage to ask for phone numbers. A cluster of typical high-schoolers were skirmishing in the battle of the sexes. The male skirmishers' uniforms featured stone-washed jeans and Nike hightop sneakers, temporary tattoos (which fade away in five days), a small silver earring, and a puberty mustache. This is the "in" look to impress their female counterparts, whose flirtatious uniforms consisted of bright candy-apple lipstick and skintight, bosom-popping tank dresses; their role required them to feign indifference as they competed fiercely with one another for the guy deemed coolest.

A ventriloquist with a real tattoo of a half-moon on his performing hand manipulated a handmade Dylan marionette to strum "The Times They Are A-Changin'," winning an occasional handclap but no money. Serious-minded, tweedy fifty-year-old men rubbed their beards nervously as they realized that what they'd thought would be a Peter, Paul and Mary–esque journey down memory lane was turning out to be an unanticipated exposure to the Seattle grunge rock scene. Two Sinéad O'Connor look-alikes caressed each other in front of the ticket booth, free of inhibition but not self-regard, making sure the onlookers knew they were French-kissing. The inevitable splash of tie-dyed Deadheads were analyzing Jerry's most recent hemorrhoid and going over Dylan's song list from his last two concerts, with "Just Like Tom Thumb's Blues" penciled in as "When You're Lost in the Rain in Juarez." Two thirty-something couples in expensive evening wear, recipients of comps from Boeing, were standing around looking polished and fast-forwarding into middle age as they talked about leaving before the encore to escape the post-concert stampede, and how these undisciplined kids better stay in their assigned seats—no repeats of the recent Tracy Chapman concert when the kids swarmed to the front during "Revolution," obstructing the thirty-somethings' precious fifth-row view. A nondescript balding man in khaki pants and a pro-Clinton (I believe) T-shirt, that read, STOP THE MASS MURDERER! VOTE FOR THE SLIME BAG! made a purchase from a sinister, stoned, and sly-smiling drug pusher selling his goods in the open by yelling, "Get your med from Panama Red." But mainly there were lots and lots of nice backpacky, bright-eyed Bellevue and Bremerton youths with rosy cheeks and an outdoorsy, rain-forest glow, looking as if they just stepped off the pages of an L. L. Bean catalog; perhaps they learned of Dylan through *The Traveling Wilburys*, volumes I and III.

Once we had tickets in hand we had two free hours to run around Seattle and get some dinner. Kevin and I lingered in front of the Paramount for a while longer, talking to three grungers from an aspiring garage band from Renton, Washington, who tried to impress us by bragging that they had played on a bill with Alice in Chains and Coffin Break. Although I'm a big fan of such Seattle grunge garage bands as The Melvins, the Screaming Trees, Soundgarden, and Nirvana, and though I play the Mudhoneys' LP *Every Good Boy Deserves Fudge* with mind-blowing regularity, I was clearly not *au courant* on the Grunge City underground scene. When I asked whether Sub Pop, the city's leading independent rock label, was responsible for coining the term *grunge rock*, they quickly and rightly counterpunched and pointed out that *grunge* is just a media label and anyway it wasn't created, it just happened, and I was two years too late. They did credit fellow Washingtonian Jimi Hendrix as the John the Baptist of grunge because he poured lighter fluid on his guitar and turned the amp up from 10 to 11. These rebellious acts made Hendrix a genuine hero of the disenfranchised and disaffected suburban youth raised in the featureless subdivision of the Puget Sound area, the kids weaned on two-for-one deals at Arby's. And the grungers immediately offered exciting anecdotes of midnight rendezvous in Renton's Greenwood Cemetery, where they communed with Jimi's bones. The only good thing they had to say about Renton was that Hendrix is buried there, one rocker adding that Jimi was not a god, but his guitar riffs were a message from God. Basically none of them cared for Dylan, particularly since he made Christian rock LPs. They had come to the show out of respect for Jimi, for he loved

447

Dylan's music and recorded "All Along the Watchtower," "Like a Rolling Stone," and "The Drifters Escape." Their attitude toward seeing Dylan, the middle-aged nasal sensation from the sixties, paralleled the Seattle-based band Nirvana's lyrical interpretation of life on their generational anthem "Smells Like Teen Spirit": "I feel stupid and contagious/Here we are now, entertain us." When I asked if there was a message behind the so-called grunge movement besides the joys of wearing plaid flannel shirts and sporting goatees, they (to my surprise) chewed on the question, as if they had never really thought about it before. "Well," the drummer finally replied, "It's all about fighting your fight, risking your life in your own way."

Fighting it out has been a Seattle tradition ever since the first logs were slid down "skid road" and fortune seekers came to make a lumber or fishing dollar. In recent years the showdown has centered on whether to destroy the Pike Place Market, a city landmark built on the waterfront in 1907 and known as a hub for selling fresh produce, seafood, and farm products. History- and civic-minded citizens formed preservation groups and development councils and have not only succeeded in saving the Pike Place Market from the wrecking ball, but managed to turn it into Seattle's greatest tourist attraction. The good news is that they did not sponge-scrub away the authenticity and laminate the life out of the place like so many other ill-conceived urban renewal projects, but struck a balance between the charm of the past and the needs of the present.

Although many of the market vendors sell status products and tourist toys, others—like the City Fish Company, the oldest fish market on the Pacific coast—is a no-nonsense operation, bringing in fresh Puget Sound catches daily. What a selection of fresh seafood, the fins on the sleek iced salmon still moving, still heaving their gills! From the great green waters of Puget Sound come salmon in great profusion: silver, king, coho, chum, pink, and sockeye. Too bad nine out of ten major salmon species are at dangerous risk of extinction in the Pacific Northwest, with no plan for saving them in the works. An old Asian woman, physically unable to crack a smile, pointed with her crooked forefinger at each trough of halibut, wanting two of each: ling, black, true, rock, and snapper. Ron Akrish, a polite young worker who knew his seafood, patiently catered to her fish-wrapping idiosyncrasies while we meekly waited to be served. The Guey duck clam, indigenous to the Puget Sound, was immense, and if I had seen it as a kid, nightmares of being devoured by it surely would have followed. Kevin and I discussed what to get, for salmon was out of the question since we wouldn't be able to cook it for a day. We went with some oysters: a dozen little olympians, perfect for shooting; a dozen quilicenes, small but extremely tasty; and a dozen pacifics, large and filling. Next, we went for a mixture of Dungeness, king, and snow crab legs. We carted out our purchases and cracked them open in the nearby Market Place Park, next to a giant totem pole, and we gazed out over Elliot Bay at the steady stream of barges and fishing boats coming into port from Singapore and Alaska Bay.

To top our seafood feast Kevin and I walked around the Pike Place Market and paused to listen to a brightly attired Peruvian folk group playing near Left Bank Books. In the store's window was a poster of Joe Hill, the famed union organizer, labor agitator, cartoonist and songwriter who composed "Workers of the World Unite!" and sang from his IWW red book along the Seattle wharf to angry longshoremen and failed prospectors. His "Workers of the World" lost out to the downtown real estate brokers, whose offices are found on every block preaching "Location, location, location" as the new religious credo to the influx of "in-the-market East Coasters and LA exiles" anxious for a piece of the Emerald City, where the skyrocketing prices are still below San Francisco's.

With showtime approaching, we dashed into the Virginia Inn for a postprandial bottle of Thomas Kemper's Pure Draft Root Beer, brewed in Poulsbo, Washington. Theresa Litourneau, the bartender, is known around Seattle for her skill in matching one of their seven micro-beers with a customer's personality and mood. The crowd was eclectic, a *New York Times* lay on a table, and Lloyd Cole was on the CD player. When Theresa let us sample a fruity unfiltered Widmer Hefeweizer brewed in Puget Sound we didn't want to leave—but Bob Dylan would soon be appearing on stage, and not wanting to miss a chord, we bolted.

449

Dylan was tremendous that evening at the Paramount Theater, clad in black, aging not like a glitter-rock star à la David Bowie, Rod Stewart, or Mick Jagger but like an ornery old bluesman traveling the highways and byways of the world to his dying days. This Seattle show was part of Dylan's "The One Sad Cry of Pity Tour." Instead of publicly announcing a promotional record tour, Dylan just hits the road with a band or by himself whenever he damn well feels like it. One can never tell where Dylan's singular voice will surface: at West Point singing "Blowin' in the Wind" to cadets; on the Grammies during the Persian Gulf War, dressed like Ché Gueverra in a beret singing "Masters of War"; at Bill Clinton's presidential inauguration, dressed like a cowboy, singing "Chimes of Freedom" in front of the Lincoln Memorial; at Bally's Casino Hotel in Atlantic City and Las Vegas, singing "It's Alright Ma (I'm Only Bleeding)," sneering when he spits out the line "Money doesn't talk, it swears"; with his son-in-law, folksinger Peter Himmelman, singing "Hava Nagilah" on a Lubavitch telethon in LA; or at a sold-out Columbia Records Celebrates the Music of Bob Dylan (or "Bobfest," as Neil Young called it during the show), where an audience of 18,200 people, not to mention those watching the telecast in sixty-eight countries, or on pay-per-view cable outlets in the United States, witnessed an extraordinary event where such artists as Stevie Wonder, Lou Reed, George Harrison, Tom Petty, Neil Young, Eddie Vedder, Johnny and June Cash, Willie Nelson, Kris Kristofferson, Eric Clapton, Chrissie Hynde, John Mellencamp, and many others each sang a Bob Dylan song or two, in tribute to the great rock poet's thirty years of making albums. Dylan ended the concert as a lone folkie, picking his guitar and blowing the harmonica on the holder around his neck. He sang "Song to Woody," a cut from the first of his forty albums. After fifty-one years, the Dylan myth of the kid who came to New York City from the country's heartland with nothing but his guitar and went on to recast popular music is more alive than ever.

This leg of "The One Sad Cry of Pity Tour" was one on which Dylan played in small, attractive venues in Australia and the Pacific Northwest; the Seattle show in an intimate theater turned out to be a masterful performance. Backed by a new line-up—including John Jackson; former

Asleep at the Wheel bassist Tony Garnier; Bucky Baxter on pedal steel, dobro, and mandolin; and Ian Wallace and Charlie Quintara on drums—Dylan was in great spirits as he launched into a bluesy version of "Rainy Day Women #12 & 35" followed by a rollicking rendition of "Cat's in the Well," to launch the evening. Beth, Kevin, and I were sitting in the very front, Dylan only a few feet from us. From the first minute onward, Dylan was in control, and when the band eventually left the stage midway through the set he played amplified acoustic guitar by himself and sang "Gates of Eden." We were all stunned. Over the years I had seen Dylan perform in over a dozen venues in Europe and North America, but to be able to share in his music with my students tonight beat all the other occasions hands down. By singing "Gates of Eden" Dylan was bringing all our Majic Bus visions back home with poetic images like these: "The cowboy angels ride," "The foreign sun it squints upon / A bed that is never mine," and "With a time-rusted compass blade / Aladdin and his lamp"—phrases that spoke to our American Odyssey experiences. After an hour and a half of fine music, his voice never sounding better, Dylan ended with a moving encore rendition of "Blowin' in the Wind." He walked offstage and disappeared to his own bus, ready to head down the highway to his next gig.

After the show, Beth, Dan, Jared, Janine, Kevin, and I walked in a misty rain up the Pike Street Hill in search of Café Paradiso—my favorite Seattle haunt—for specialty coffees. Seattle is the city that started the craze for specialty coffees across America, cutting into the vacuum-can business of Folgers and Maxwell House in the early eighties. Specialty coffees now account for 20 percent of all coffees sold for home use in America and are expected to reach 50 percent in the next ten years. We had big cups of sharp and aromatic Kenyan coffee at Café Paradiso, and reclined in a dark, subterranean corner, listening to Joan Armatrading sing, casually admiring the abstract art on the walls, conversing about Dylan and Kesey. It irritated all of us to no end that some people continue to view Dylan and Kesey as sixties icons, not as contemporary artists with their muses still intact, still doing pretty much what they did in the sixties, refusing to sell out. Kesey's latest novel, *Sailor's Song*, and Dylan's

451

newest album, *Good As I Been to You*, are testimonies that these two transcendental artists are still in top form, and as we sail into the nineties, they'll continue to pioneer. After all, it was Dylan who wrote "My Back Pages," which carries the refrain, "I was so much older then / I'm younger than that now."

19

The Badlands, Black Hills, and Cattle Branding

For better is it to dare mighty things, to win glorious triumphs even though checkered by failure, than to rank with those poor spirits who neither enjoy much nor suffer much, because they live in the gray twilight that knows not victory nor defeat. . . . Life is worth nothing without action.

—THEODORE ROOSEVELT

A LEADEN RAIN DRENCHED US AS WE LEFT CAFÉ PARADISO and sprinted and splashed our way to the Majic Bus, jackets flung over our heads, arriving out of breath and chilled to the bone but right on time for our 2:30 A.M. departure from Seattle. Frank was in an ebullient mood; the fact that Dylan was still at it, still singing the songs that make a difference, his harmonica sounding as skeletal as ever, gave Frank the strength to drive straight through the night across the entire state of Washington. He wanted to have us in Spokane in time for breakfast at Thadeus T. Thudpucker's Restaurant, "Home of the World's Largest Chicken-Fried Steak." Larry McMurtry has written that "only a rank degenerate would drive 1,500 miles across Texas without eating a chicken-fried steak," a sentiment Frank shared. While in Washington, he would never pass

Spokane without stopping at Thudpucker's to tackle one of their gargantuan steaks.

Everyone changed out of their wet clothes, putting them in plastic garbage bags for laundering that wouldn't get done until we returned to Long Island. No sooner had Frank gotten on I-90 than everyone but Matt and Kenny went to sleep. They had promised to keep Frank company as he battled the nail-driving mountain rain through the Snoqualmie and Wenatchee national forests, past the ponderous bulk of Mount Rainier, and then across the Yakima River, which runs into the Columbia—a river so powerful that even the Grand Coulee Dam hasn't been able to tame her.

It's experiences like these that Kenny and Matt will remember forever: those dark nights on the road in the rain when you're thankful for just having shelter from the storm, cognizant that if the headlights go out or the windshield wipers stop working you're as good as dead, your life extinguished as you plunge off a ridge, to be found in the morning at the bottom of some obscure mountain in some obscure county outside of some obscure village. On nights like this anything could happen and you have to drive alive, for you never know when a slinking coyote will appear, its fur matted but dry even though it's trotting through pouring rain. On nights like this, when the spirits are on the hunt, all you can do is be aware and take nothing for granted—you never know when a falling rock might tumble down or a shape-changing raven might suddenly appear.

The three guys talked about coyotes for a while, speculating that if the apocalypse comes and human life is wiped out it's the coyote who will reign supreme, with an army of ravens and roaches to serve him. Frank knew from years of experience that on evenings like this you drive slow and pray, and the long Mickey Hart drum solos on Matt's Dead bootleg frightened him. It wasn't right, Frank thought, to make a drum sound that haunting.

Suddenly Kenny shouted, "Look!" Standing on the shoulder of I-90 outside the town of Ritzville was a large, round-faced, baggageless man dressed in a T-shirt and jeans, thumb up for a ride. It was the phantom hitchhiker of American campfire lore. This thumbing wanderer reminded Kenny of the Haunted Mansion attraction at Disneyworld, where toward the end of the flesh-and-blood tourists' journey the translucent, glowing green image of a hitchhiking ghost joins them for a ride. Frank was tempted to stop, but his reflexes weren't fast enough and the roads were too wet for him to slam on the brakes. Trying to dissipate the ghosts by mood music, the boys popped Credence Clearwater Revival's "Who'll Stop the Rain" into the tape deck, staring blankly at what they could see of the highway line.

It was still pouring when Frank pulled into Spokane and I got up off the bus floor to see what was happening. Gangs of all-night drug dealers eyed our vehicle suspiciously from under the doorway of the curtainless Norman Hotel, and two rainy-night hookers with umbrellas hung out in front of the Dead End Tavern, its neon 7-Up sign still lit and helping to illuminate the Spokane Adult Erotic Boutique and Video Center. Every time these streetwalkers hear the air brakes of a Greyhound arriving in the depot across the street, they primp in a cracked doorway mirror and start promenading in their high heels and miniskirts, hoping for Grants but resigned to ending up with Jacksons.

Frank parked in the lot at Thadeus T. Thudpucker's to catch a few hours of rest, dreaming of an eight-pound chicken-fried steak smothered in thick, creamy gravy. But, unable to sleep because of the rain and unwilling to wait two hours for Thudpucker's to open, he cranked the engine back on and decided to forgo the manhole-size treat and the pictures of the Cartwright Family—Little Joe, Hoss, Ben, and the rest of the gang—that grace the restaurant's walls. Just as he pulled out of the lot, guess who he saw—the phantom hitchhiker whom he had bypassed two hours ago.

This time Frank opened the Majic Bus's door, feeling sorry for a solitary soul who'd been out in the rain all night. The traveler introduced himself as Vancouver Bob and said he was headed for Iowa. Frank told Bob he would give him a ride through the Idaho panhandle and into Montana but would have to drop him off once the students woke up. For the next five hours, the two of them talked, all the way to Missoula. Meanwhile I slept soundly; none of the rest of us stirred till 10:00 A.M.

Vancouver Bob was a Christian pilgrim who had had a divine revelation

455

compelling him to leave his wife and children in Canada and head to Ames, Iowa; an angel had told him he would meet Jesus in a cornfield there. Frank concluded that Vancouver Bob was a little touched in the head; nevertheless, Bob made for good conversation, and that was essential if Frank was to stay awake and get us to Missoula by lunchtime. Frank and Bob chatted on as they entered Idaho, where they were greeted by the Jacklin Seed Company building and greyhound dog racing facilities.

Just down the road stood a giant marquee sign that read: I CONSIDER EVERYTHING A LOSS EXCEPT THE JOY OF KNOWING JESUS. This was the part of Idaho that had been in the news as the new home of the Aryan Nation. The FBI had been aggressive in confiscating the white supremacists' stockpile of guns and other weapons, and a standoff between the FBI and an Aryan Nation leader had recently brought the area unwanted publicity. Just past Coeur d'Alene, Frank pulled over to stretch at the isolated and untouristed Old Mission State Park, where in 1852 the Coeur d'Alene Indians built a mission under Jesuit supervision. The stuccoed building might have seemed more at home in the California chapparal than among the Idaho cedars.

Then it was back on the road, entering Montana via the Lolo National Forest. Several students became very angry—downright furious—at Frank when they awoke to find he had picked up a "tramp," and they were very vociferous in holding me accountable. I promised that we would part company with Vancouver Bob in Missoula. As I reminded the students, Vancouver Bob may not have been in the trip's original script, but then neither was so much else that we'd found most meaningful.

If states were food, Montana would be the biggest and best T-bone steak you ever savored. Montana ranchers are the hard-handshake types, with fatherly smiles, leathery skin, and year-round tans (even though they hardly ever come in contact with direct sunlight). The Majic Bus had brought us into the Rocky Mountains of Montana, where snow still lingered on the peaks and pine scented the air. The rain had stopped and the sun was out. As we drove east on I-90 through the Rockies, it dawned on me that the real heroes of the West have to be its road builders and telephone workers, whose accomplishments with construction and maintenance are unthinkable to us — but maybe not to the likes of Kit Carson or Merriwether Lewis.

By the time the Majic Bus reached Missoula, it was 2:00 P.M. The students had spent the early part of the day reading *The Last Picture Show*, writing in their journals, talking to Vancouver Bob, and getting anxious to eat. After a quick cheesburger lunch Frank parked the bus on the street next to Bonner Park, where six of us played full-court basketball for three straight hours. Later the basketball players walked over to Miller Hall on the University of Montana campus (easily spotted by means of the big white *M* on the hillside) and sneaked in to take showers. Outside of Miller Hall there was another basketball court, and after we had all showered, Justin challenged me to a little one-on-one. He defeated me handily, three games to one, and for the rest of the evening we paid the price for our extra fun, remaining sticky with sweat.

Meanwhile the rest of the group was exploring Missoula on their own. All later agreed it would be another perfect place to live, the quality of life as good as in the other medium-sized college towns we had visited, like Boulder and Lawrence. And all this time, Frank and Bob slept under an oak tree, both in need of rest after the long and rainy night.

By 9:00 P.M., everybody was ready for dinner—we chose the Creekside Inn and then a drink at Charlie's (a bar with no sign, but the best beer joint in town)—and the Majic Bus hit the highway again. We planned to wake up in the morning near the Crow Indian Reservation, where we would visit the Little Bighorn Battlefield National Monument. The students who'd been irritated by our guest had softened, and Vancouver Bob was going to stay with us one more night. He told us he'd had a dream under the oak tree that God wanted him to present himself at the exact spot of Custer's last stand. Who was I to thwart God's plan? What was more, the students had grown fond of Vancouver Bob, and they wanted to help him accomplish his mission. That evening Frank made great time, passing Butte and Bozeman, the Yellowstone River, and Gallatin National Forest before finally pulling into a truck stop in Billings.

Today most of our nation's 4,400 truck stops have broadened their services to cater to the general public, as well as to eighteen-wheelers; Billings is one of those towns where locals come to the truck stops to eat and shop. The twenty-four-hour breakfasts and the signs like MY WIFE RAN AWAY WITH MY BEST FRIEND AND I STILL MISS HIM are still current at these truck stops, and you can still fill your tank with diesel—but that's about all that's left of the old days. Nowadays, most of them are multipurpose community centers where checks are cashed, money is transferred, and clothes are laundered. The modern truck stop comes complete with restaurants and telephone booths, a convenience market, a nondenominational chapel, video games, a post office, a thirty-foot-long salad bar, clothing for sale, and souvenirs galore . . . and on and on. In many cities hard hit by the recession, a truck stop has come to be the town center, for it's open every second of the year and prices are reasonable. At the truck stop in Billings, we took showers, watched MTV, and called home, announcing our scheduled arrival to parents and friends while eating the crepe special of the day.

Just east of Billings we got on I-90 South, passing the Livestock Connoisseur Company and its pens filled with cattle ready for slaughter. This is an impoverished part of Montana, and we noticed mobile-home park after mobile-home park, with kids running around barefoot while their moms hung wet clothes on the lines, cursing the cloth as well as their rootedness, knowing they would never be able to escape the daily grind of life on the Great Plains.

I was wearing a gift that Vancouver Bob had bought me back at the truck stop, a green T-shirt depicting a wolf. Bob had been intrigued by a lecture I'd given when I'd enthusiastically told the students about a handful of colonizing wolves who had migrated back into Montana from Canada. Wolves are extinct or endangered in all but two states: Alaska and Minnesota, which has one thousand. Over the years the animals have been systematically wiped out by poison or by bounty hunters: Ranchers pay good money for dead wolves. Recently Hollywood has turned the livestock-devouring lupus into a warm, doglike hero, and this image, combined with the efforts of environmentalists, has turned the tide of public opinion in favor of the wolves. Now ranchers can be arrested if they have anything to do with killing a wolf. We all kept our eyes and ears peeled for wolves, but they weren't showing themselves that night.

When we stopped at the Crow Agency, where we were to meet with a medicine man, Vancouver Bob got off and all of us wished him well on his mission to find salvation in Ames. The Crow medicine man, who asked that I not publish his name, greeted us in front of a little museum on the reservation. He brought us all to a couple of picnic tables in back, and for the next forty minutes he related the history of the Crows, mentioning they are the only tribe who has never fought with the U.S. government, and explaining how they are trying to save their sacred past while working for a prosperous future. Christine, who had been so disappointed in Cherokee, felt greatly relieved to hear him speak about preserving the earth and the importance of the sun dance, the peyote rituals, and tobacco societies.

At Crow Agency, isolated in southern Montana, the 7,800 native tribespeople have maintained their dignity, making money from dead-Custer tourism but nonetheless instilling their religion in the young. We all laughed when the medicine man said that thanks to *Dances with Wolves*, New Agers, and the revisionist disputes over whether to celebrate the Columbus quincentennial of 1992, he was proud to be able to call himself "new Native chic." Together we all meditated, and he offered a prayer that "the winds of change will finally bring truth." It was a moving moment. As for George Armstrong Custer, our medicine man called him "a glory hound," expressing a view that would come to be shared by many of us.

After our visit to Crow Agency, we drove sixteen miles down the road to the Little Bighorn Battlefield National Monument, which memorializes one of the Northern Plains Indians' last armed efforts to preserve their ancestral way of life. The grasslands here are awesome, rolling on and on for miles, but most visitors make their way to this remote part of the country for one reason: to see the valley of the Little Bighorn River, where on two days in June 1876, Colonel George Armstrong Custer and 260 of his soldiers met defeat and death at the hands of several thousand Sioux and Cheyenne warriors.

459

Although Frank likes to style himself "the Buffalo Bill of busing," I had been telling him for weeks that he looked much more like Custer. As we entered the visitors' center, we were greeted by a life-size photograph of the famed cavalryman, and in unison, three of the students shouted, "There's Frank!" Dan found the similarity so astounding that he positioned Frank in front of the photograph so he could snap one of his own. The Majic Bus now had a George Armstrong Custer clone to keep our Elvis clone, Tom Tolan company.

The battlefield tour, from the spot where the Seventh last camped, on June 24, 1876, to the location of Custer's last stand, was fascinating; the area is similar to Gettysburg in the number of monuments erected, except that here many small headstones are scattered all about the grassland and crows fly overhead. Only the site of little white boys in warbonnets, their parents holding their rubber tomahawks, tarnished our time spent at the Crow Reservation's Battle of Little Bighorn monument. It also saddened us that we would never be able to hear the cries of the buffalo and wolves that are long, long gone.

From the Crow Agency, we continued our journey through Montana, our destination now the Badlands town of Medora, North Dakota, where Theodore Roosevelt spent his Wild West days. Harold and Sheila Schafer, two of the most colorful and generous people I know, live and work there. I serve with them on the board of the Theodore Roosevelt Association, and when they heard about American Odyssey they insisted we pay them a visit and stay at their Badlands Motel for free. Harold would be called away to Bismarck on business, so it would be Sheila who entertained us.

Harold Schafer, a flamboyant eighty-year-old philanthropist whose son, Ed, has recently been elected governor, is a North Dakota legend, the youngest man ever to receive the Horatio Alger Award from American Schools and Colleges. In 1942, at age thirty, Schafer founded Gold Seal, originally a one-man cleaning-wax company. By the time he was thirty-six, he would be a self-made millionaire. Schafer traveled the state of North Dakota trying to convince storekeepers to carry his product. The more stores he visited, the more he noticed that women did most of the shopping, and for that matter, most of the window cleaning and silverware polishing. Schafer came up with the idea of calling his product Glass Wax, coloring the thick cream pink (which he believed would appeal to women), and retailing it for $0.59 a pint. In its first year, Glass Wax sales equaled $902.02; soon that product alone would be making $40 million a year.

Riding on the success of Glass Wax, Schafer, the traveling Dakota salesman, launched his next product line: Mr. Bubble. Schafer had noticed that bubble bath was always sold in the cosmetic sections of stores, at exorbitant rates. With daughters of his own, he recognized that what was needed on the market was a cheap, industrial-strength box of suds; for the more bubbles there were, the more the kids liked to take baths. Thus was born Mr. Bubble. An aggressive radio and television campaign made Mr. Bubble a national baby-boomer sensation; the smiling cartoon bubble face on the box was as lovable as a Hanna-Barbera character. Gold Seal gradually developed other top products, such as Snowy Bleach, but none would equal Mr. Bubble.

Instead of using the millions Gold Seal was earning just to make more money, Harold Schafer and his vivacious and talented actress/wife/business partner, Sheila, restored the Badlands town of Medora, most of which they now own, and set up a nonprofit public corporation: the Theodore Roosevelt Medora Foundation. "We all need heroes," Schafer has said. "Theodore Roosevelt was gutsy, and his is still a great name in world history. Medora is a great part of North Dakota history." Due to the Schafers' restoration efforts, Medora—and a sizable chunk of the North Dakota Badlands now protected as the Theodore Roosevelt National Park—is the single best family vacation spot for capturing the American West of cowboy-and-buffalo lore. Unlike other national park gateway towns like Gatlinburg, Jackson Hole, or Estes Park, Medora refuses to go neon; the foundation insists that the historic town stay rustic and authentic.

It was 9:00 P.M. when we finally crossed into North Dakota, seeing not another car on the highway as we passed Home on the Range, a "find yourself" retreat on the sweeping plain. It was a cool, clear, windy night and along the roadside we kept catching the red-eyed flash of unknown critters. We met Sheila at the Schafers' two-story Little Missouri Saloon, known as the final resting place for hundreds of cowboy and straw hats that permanently hang from the wooden ceiling beams. A few local ranchers and teenagers stared at the spectacle of the Majic Bus discharging its load of New Yorkers in the Badlands. Sheila greeted us in front of the Little Missouri with enthusiastic hugs, then led us inside to celebrate Alan's twentieth birthday with the biggest T-bone-steak-a-thon imaginable—not to mention mounds of baked potatoes, salad, and ice cream. What an evening! After dinner, at the instigation of a couple of locals, we began doing the limbo to Chet Atkins's guitar picking, shimmying under a large wooden stick. An old cowboy couple was doing the Texas two-step, rattling the jars of beef jerky and the two toy trains behind the bar. After a few hours of this madness Sheila left us to ourselves, but handed us keys for her Badlands Motel, where we would stay for two nights.

The next morning we all met Sheila at the covered wagon in the front yard of her home. Inside her historic log house she showed us such unlikely collectibles as a table once owned by John Quincy Adams and a spittoon used by Clark Gable. The giant fireplace in the living room is made from six-million-year-old lava, and the entire house brims with TR memorabilia.

After feeding us coffee, juice, and doughnuts, Sheila took us for a walking tour. Medora's roads have been paved and streetlights have been installed, but it's still the same wooden-planked Dakota town that Theodore Roosevelt fell in love with. Everywhere you walk in Medora, you bump into TR's past.

It was buffalo hunting that first brought Theodore Roosevelt to the rugged Badlands when he was twenty-four years old, an asthmatic with a flamboyant zest for buckskin clothes and the outdoors. In the Badlands, TR learned to be self-sufficient—playing the patrician was of little use there. Not long after the hunt, he went back to New York, but he couldn't get the Badlands out of his mind. When on Valentine's Day, 1884, tragedy struck Roosevelt—both his mother and wife died on the same day and in the same house—he headed back to the Badlands to escape the redoubled pain, thereby reigniting a spark in his somber spirit. Upon reaching Medora, TR rode along the cottonwood banks of the Little Missouri River, looking for the ideal spot in which to begin his new life. The result was his first Badlands home, the Maltese Cross cabin, which grew into a thriving cattle ranch. He soon started a second ranch, the Elkhorn, thirty-six miles away, and he hired a number of guides to run the day-to-day operations. In a matter of months the other ranchers accepted him as one of their own and elected him president of their stockmen's association. Meanwhile TR hunted almost daily and wrote American classics like *The Winning of the West* and *Ranch Life and the Hunting Trail.* His books gave an unknown artist/illustrator named Frederic Remington his start. The Badlands made TR sturdy and self-reliant; he considered his five years there fundamental to developing his character and confidence: "I heartily enjoy this life, with its perfect freedom, for I am very fond of hunting, and there are few sensations I prefer to that of galloping over these rolling, limitless prairies, rifle in hand, or winding my way among the barren, fantastic, and grimly picturesque deserts of the so-called Bad Lands." Shortly after World War II the North Dakota Badlands that TR loved so much were designated a national monument; in 1978 they became Theodore Roosevelt National Park.

TR once quipped that the Badlands "look just exactly as Poe's tales and poems sound"—for like so much of the West, their horizon and colors are hard to describe in words. Clearly the Badlands get their allure from the stark and barren buttes, the sculpted hills and ravines, the maze of odd and intricate canyons that are millions of years old and have stoically refused to relinquish their prehistoric status. But it's the unspoiled plains surrounding these canyons and the plenitude of animal life still abounding, that make being in this part of North Dakota so memorable. Sheila had ranch hands drive us all over the area, pointing out herds of buffalo and elk and deer and pronghorn antelope. We felt as if we were on an African safari. A highlight was getting to see a buffalo calf, its leery mother ready to charge our truck if we got too close.

Later that afternoon we met with Park Superintendent Pete Hart, who before coming to North Dakota had worked at the Grand Canyon, Yosemite, Cape Cod, and the Great Smoky Mountains. During the winter of 1971 to 1972, when he was superintendent at Mount Rainier, he entered the *Guinness Book of World Records* for measuring at a weather station the most amount of snow ever: ninety-two feet. Pete showed us a film about the park and spoke to the students about the wildlife we had already seen and some we might still encounter. Buffalo were the main topic of conversation, for Hart's park has been extremely successful in reintroducing them into the wild. TR was our nation's great conservationist, and due to his efforts as president the buffalo were saved from extinction and allowed to remain wild within the national park system. Today there are more buffalo in North Dakota than lived there in the 1880s, when TR was a rancher. Six hundred now roam the three units of Theodore Roosevelt National Park alone.

Hart told us about the problems national parks are facing from poaching; bears are particular targets, for their gall bladders are considered an aphrodisiac in Japan. The stealing of dried buffalo skulls is another menacing problem, and the drilling done by reckless local oil companies is destroying much of the grassland areas adjacent to the park. In their journals the students wrote many pages reporting what we learned from Pete Hart; one thing they all agreed upon was that these park supervisors and rangers across America are doing a tremendous job.

Stefanie found the museums in Medora and at the visitors' center particularly interesting because she was writing her senior thesis on TR. She could hardly believe her eyes when she saw the actual shirt, complete with bullet hole, that TR was wearing when he was shot during the Bull Moose campaign of 1912. In spite of the bullet he took that day, TR went on to give an hour-and-a-half-long speech. He would carry the lead ball to his grave.

Our drive through the park was so awe inspiring that it is next to impossible to write about: herds of massive buffalo lumbering across the road, black-tailed prairie dogs popping from burrow to burrow, elk ripping grass up by the roots, a fat badger waddling out of a hole, wild horses streaming across the grasslands, and cottontail rabbits bounding over hummocks. At one point, on a hundred-colored cliff near Medora, Dan saw a rattlesnake and panicked; he sprinted back to the safety of the Majic Bus, terrified by the lingering image of its coil and angry that he'd got buffalo chips imbedded in his shoe. Alan climbed up a hill and suddenly found himself caught in a cactus patch; his arm swelling, he cursed as he pulled out the needles. The wind there was the most forceful we had ever felt, and as we looked out over the Painted Canyon, we did all we could to prevent the whirling sand from blowing up our nostrils. None of us could understand how it could be so windy in the Badlands yet so silent. The Badlands are a state of mind, not a location—not merely a cemetery of wind-carved stone and mysterious crags, but an evocation of spiritual presence.

That evening Sheila gave us a chicken dinner at the Rough Rider Hotel, where TR once spoke to a crowd from the balcony bully pulpit. We celebrated Alan's birthday for a second night, and Sheila gave all the students Medora souvenirs and copies of Edmund Morris's Pulitzer Prize – winning book, *The Rise of Theodore Roosevelt*.

Then it was off to the Iron Horse Saloon, where Shari beat everyone in pool (again) under the hanging Bud light, and frosty schooners of delicious beer cost only a buck and pickled Ukrainian eggs are seventy-five cents each. Elk horns and rodeo pictures hang everywhere, and for some reason all the locals smoke Winstons as their cigarette of choice. Behind the bar glow two round red lights, giving the bar a sensual feel—until you look up and saw a dead prairie dog hanging from a beam. With Steve Earle singing "Copperhead Road," the locals as friendly as could be, the evening crystallized into one of those moments when everything is just right, when worries go flying out the window, when the people you're with are your true friends, when you don't give a damn about anything but Now and your only possible concern is that Now won't last forever. Soon our roads would diverge, leading us away from each other and from this place.

That evening we all stayed up together at the Badlands Motel, watching CNN coverage of the post–Rodney King LA riots. Just when we were feeling great about America, the Simi Valley jury's not-guilty verdict in

465

one of the most sensational police brutality cases in recent history reminded us of the racist flip side of America—which, for one extraordinary day in the Badlands, we had happily forgotten.

The sky was still star-filled and the moon aglow as we crammed our newly rearranged bags into the bus bay, getting ready to leave. The night clerk had made pots of coffee for us and everyone just stood around the Majic Bus, taking measured sips of the steaming brew, admiring the shadowy Badlands once again. Even though we'd had only a few hours' rest, nobody felt sleepy; we were all too keyed up by the prospect of what lay ahead—our scheduled return to Long Island and a stationary life. Reality was beginning to impinge on our collective illusion of adventure without end.

As we entered the highway darkness just outside town, two buffalo by the roadside bellowed, seeming to wish us well on the last leg of our journey. Down the road just a few miles, in the town of Belfield, we stopped in the Trappers Inn and Rendezvous Lounge for a breakfast of egg sandwiches to go. Stuffed birds and animals are everywhere in the room—a small grizzly bear, two coyotes, and a gigantic beaver (miscast as guardian of the homemade-pie refrigerator). Rusty old traps adorn the wall, and there are enough antler racks to be able to hang every John Deere hat from Billings to Bismarck. Across the road an American flag freeze-dried on a billboard announced: ONE NATION UNDER GOD WITH LIBERTY AND JUSTICE FOR ALL.

All over Belfield homes and businesses have been repossessed, from the First National Bank itself to the town's fire department, on which a sign is posted: THIS PROPERTY IS FOR SALE. Now that the oil boom is over, Belfield's only moneymaking activity is signaled by the auctioneer's gavel knocking down farm equipment and abandoned ranches, and the sound of dishes clattering at the Trappers Inn. The recession hit Belfield hard, and driving through town made me think of Jim Hightowers's quip "The only difference between a pigeon and the American farmer today is that a pigeon can still make a deposit on a John Deere."

When dawn broke, the Majic Bus was heading down the desolate two-lane Highway 85, which would take us through fertile countryside all the way to South Dakota. I marveled at the wide-open, uncrowded spaces and at the people in this part of the nation, who are still connected to the land. Theodore Roosevelt's observation "I would never have been President if it had not been for my experiences in North Dakota" made perfect sense as we drove into the Little Missouri National Grassland region, where TR used to ride for days at a time.

We crossed the Cannonball River and stopped at the County Store in Amidon. There, underneath a flapping American flag, four weathered old wheat farmers in blue jeans sat around a card table, stiffly sipping black coffee and gazing out across the grasslands at White Butte (the highest point in North Dakota). They were in no real hurry for Carolyn, the owner, to finish fixing the screen door and cook them up the reliable, no-frills, well-done quarter-pound breakfast burgers she had fed them for the last twenty years. Faded parchment-colored newspaper clippings of local boys who joined the armed forces to serve their country were pasted in patriotic display on the wall. Close by hung the only known painting of Lebanon Lutheran Church, tiny, white, and windswept, now boarded up and closed to all but the desperate winter-blue cattle who barge in every December to escape frostbite by huddling near the altar.

From Prairie Public Radio in Dickerson came the strains of Strauss's "Blue Danube" waltz—incongruous, I thought, here in North Dakota, where rural American values would seem to leave no space for nineteenth-century Viennese culture. And yet the waltz is not out of place in the home state of Lawrence Welk. As we purchased a few cartons of orange juice, one farmer warned us to watch out for the sheriff, who lurks in his patrol car in front of the dilapidated Slope County Senior Citizens Center, hoping to trap unsuspecting motorists who whizz through the one-block town at highway speed in violation of the twenty-five-mile-per-hour speed limit. It is the income from traffic tickets that keeps postponing the day Amidon will no longer be even a blip on the radar screen of existence.

467

———

All morning long we listened to the Highwaymen—Johnny Cash, Willie Nelson, Waylon Jennings, and Kris Kristofferson—and their rendition of Bob Seger's "Against the Wind," which seemed to sum up my innermost feelings so well that I thought it had been written for me. It is pop music, not television, airplanes, computers, or faxes, that ties America together and provides the creative heart and soul that make our regimented lives bearable. The prairie wind whistled through the bus, reminding us that this part of the country has yet to be conquered by oil wells or plows. Small branches whipped across the road; their presence seemed almost miraculous, because there were no trees in sight.

We crossed into South Dakota, where a sign read, WELCOME TO BEEF COUNTRY. But no cattle were in evidence; only the large hay rolls on which they feed were there to greet us. As we left the southern end of the solitary one-room-schoolhouse town of Buffalo, we saw scattered flocks of sheep sunning themselves and grazing in the short-grass ravines, surrounded by scattered rocks that didn't seem to belong among them. The placid sheep made patches of this landscape look strangely similar to the English countryside. We were at the geographical center of America, which moved to this unpopulated section of southwestern South Dakota in 1959 when Alaska and Hawaii became states (stripping Smith Center, Kansas, of the honor). So fierce is the wind in the slightly rolling hills of western Dakota that at the occasional rest centers and picnic areas, the heavy metal garbage cans have to be sunk into deep holes—even locks and chains can't hold them when heavy gales from the north unleash their wintertime force. Even on a sunny, blue-sky spring day, the wind is so strong here that the odds of a kite surviving are miniscule. On days like this, the scattered clouds leave giant dark shadows on the plains, creating the illusion that the soil is black. But it is not the warm, inviting blackness of fertility.

We entered Belle Fourche, which boasts that it is "the Center City of the Nation" and a "gold-country town." Although the first claim may be true, Christine pointed out that the second is clearly a fantasy, for Main Street was littered with blown-out tires and abandoned businesses. The harsh outline of the Black Hills was on the horizon, and under their rugged gaze we all felt that the string of here-today-gone-tomorrow businesses scarcely seemed to matter in the scheme of things.

Morning turned to afternoon, and we were geared up to get to the town of Spearfish—which may not sound promising, but when you've been on Route 85 from Belfield to Belle Fourche for hours on end, a Dairy Queen is a welcome sight. It was early May in the Black Hills, the time of year when the water-slide parks start to clean out their flues and sandpaper over rough spots to avoid post—Memorial Day scraped-back lawsuits. The Spearfish Dairy Queen was a real hub of activity, with RVs and pickups pulling in and out, coughing diesel over us as we sat with our burgers and sundaes at outdoor tables. In fact, the proliferation of RV trailers with GOOD SAM CLUB decals on the road was quite astonishing; they had all been hosed down and hitched up for short excursions, stiff trial runs in preparation for the big summer out-of-state adventure.

When you approach the Black Hills National Forest, where it is said one can still follow the hoofprints of General George A. Custer's 1874 expedition, every road sign hawks GOLD JEWELRY and BUFFALO SAUSAGE. We were on our way to Mount Rushmore and "George Custer slept here" country. The terrain is one of rocky cliffs with pines jutting straight out, leaving you to wonder how such towering trees can be born and sustained out of stone. As you approach the city of Deadwood, where casino gambling has been legalized, signs direct you to the site where *Dances with Wolves* was filmed. Kevin Costner was so taken with the Black Hills that he bought a home here, sinking his considerable Hollywood bankroll into casino ventures; Costner is so popular in South Dakota that he is being courted by the Democratic party to run for the U.S. Senate. Adding to its scenic dimensions, the area also has its share of manufactured roadside attractions, ranging from *The Black Hills Passion Play*, in which a cast of 250 dramatizes events of the final seven days of the life of Christ, to the

469

Flintstones' Bedrock City, a Stone Age—type town where the main draws are Brontoburgers and Dino Dogs.

Avoiding the false-fronted 1880s-style Deadwood casinos, we stopped outside town to visit Mount Moriah Cemetery, one of the Old West's original Boot Hills, where the likes of Wild Bill Hickok, Calamity Jane Canary, and Potato Creek Johnny are buried. The students went wild photographing the final resting places of these legendary figures, and we all gave our legs a much-needed stretch. From the cemetery, our tape deck blasting the Doors' "Riders on the Storm," we traveled down the Black Hills Parkway, past Trout Haven and Pactola Lake to Keystone, the town adjacent to Gutzon Borglum's "shrine of democracy"—the celebrated Mount Rushmore.

Mount Rushmore, the world's largest sculpture, receives two million visitors each year and is probably the most recognizable monument in America, along with the Statue of Liberty. At the end of every day for the last forty years it has appeared on television: The major networks sign off with Katherine Lee Bates's "America the Beautiful," flutter some flags, and focus on some wheat waving in the wind, then flash to Gutzon Borglum's gargantuan chiseled faces of Washington, Jefferson, Lincoln, and Theodore Roosevelt, just before the emergency broadcast signal officially announces the day has ended.

Borglum began carving the mountain in 1929, when he was sixty years old. He died twelve years later without completing the four faces as he envisioned them. His son, Lincoln, put the finishing touches on TR's face and the lapels of Washington's coat and declared Mount Rushmore complete on October 31, 1941. They opened the monument to the public, but just as a grand dedication was being planned, the Japanese bombed Pearl Harbor and government funding for the project ceased. The monument was not officially dedicated until July 4, 1991. It had taken fifty years of agitating by the Mount Rushmore National Memorial Society, with help from *USA Today* founder Al Neuharth, to arrange an official "patrioglitzorama" dedication. Bob Hope emceed, and famous Dakotans Mary Hart and Tom Brokaw took part. The dedication tactfully neglected to mention that Gutzon Borglum dreamed up the monument despite—or perhaps because of—being known to possess jingoist, racist, and anti-Semitic attitudes.

Borglum never saw an American he didn't like—except Jews, Catholics, Latinos, and African Americans. In no uncertain terms, Mount Rushmore as Borglum conceived it would celebrate white Protestant America. The original megalomaniacal plan was to carve all four presidents to the waist with inscriptions (undetermined in Borglum's lifetime) cut five inches deep into the rock and gilded; the letters would have been visible from three miles away. Borglum had also planned on tunneling a museum large enough to house a collection of twentieth-century inventions and a national archive—the Hall of Records, he called it—to showcase the glory of white America. An eight-hundred-foot staircase would take visitors to the Hall of Records entrance at the top of the mountain.

For all its remarkable achievement, the Mount Rushmore we were about to see was an unfinished work—created by the drilling might and imagination of a man who liked his Americans white. As the Majic Bus pulled into the parking area, the students were both curious and excited. But reactions to the sculpture itself varied. Tom judged it pretty impressive, a reminder of the debt our nation owes these four great leaders, whereas Dan viewed Mount Rushmore as "bad art" and called it "real cheesy." Mitch found it inspiring and thought it would be awesome to have a condo with a balcony looking onto those rock faces. Kevin felt the monument looked small, less impressive than the late-night TV images he had seen. Everybody realized that this was probably American Odyssey's last major touristic photo op, so we all went into a clicking frenzy.

Our fellow-viewers were a gumbo of Americans: a black-leather Harley club from Wisconsin who had come early to find a campsite for the August Black Hills Motorcycle Classic, when they and eighty thousand other bikers would be holding a bash; a Latino priest from San Antonio; an American Legion group from Clarion, Pennsylvania, who came by bus just to see the carved faces for themselves and to place wreaths on a number of graves at the Black Hills National Military Cemetery; a couple from

Baltimore who had recently retired to Rapid City; a guy with a raccoon on his shoulder that was getting as much attention as the carved presidents; and busloads of schoolchildren who had been looking forward to this field trip since the early March snow began to melt.

As I stood there looking at the chiseled faces on the mountainside, with this eclectic assortment of folks milling about, it became apparent to me that one of the main lessons we had learned from American Odyssey is that this country is big enough to include everybody. As the cliché goes, our diversity truly is our strength. There seemed to be an irony or connection between Borglum's desire to limit his America to white Anglo-Saxon Protestants and his failure to finish Mount Rushmore. Clearly we are better off because his particular dream was never realized. The Hall of Records is still an empty tunnel, and even the narrow-minded Borglum could not decide what mottoes should be chiseled in the granite.

Like Mount Rushmore, America is still an unfinished dream, its streets paved with misery and gold; our tongues speak with both malice and mercy. Just how we will end the dream remains unclear, for the challenges to achieving true national glory are many, and the winds of change sometimes blow at cross directions. Someday, if we can harness our inherent energy and optimism with even some tenuous sense of unity, "America the Beautiful" will be not an anthem to end the day but a hymn to start a new morning. Until that day comes, Mount Rushmore is best left unfinished, a call toward the promised land to come, not a boast of the historical promised land that never was.

To the Sioux, the carving on Mount Rushmore is sacrilegious. The Black Hills, in the heart of which lies Mount Rushmore, are holy land to them. And "not only did they desecrate our sacred land," wrote Tim Giago, founding editor of Rapid City's *Lakota Times*, but they also "memorialized four presidents who committed acts of atrocity against our people."

With a weekly readership of fifty thousand and subscribers in all fifty states, over the years the *Lakota Times* (the nation's largest Native American newspaper) has done a lot to further the cause of the Sioux; for example, its reporters have uncovered concrete proof that the U.S. government stole Mount Rushmore from the tribe. Giago, a former reporter for the *Rapid City Journal,* started the paper in 1980 with a four-thousand-dollar loan, naming it after the dominant Sioux language. The paper has earned a reputation as "the voice of the Plains Indians," confronting businesses that try to make a buck by dehumanizing Indians in racist advertisements. On the wall of Giago's office hangs a bright red pennant for the Cleveland Indians baseball team. Alongside it are flags for the "Pittsburgh Negroes," the "Kansas City Jews," and the "San Diego Caucasians." Beneath them hangs the statement NOW YOU KNOW HOW NATIVE AMERICANS FEEL. The paper remains supportive of the Crazy Horse Memorial and endorsed Costner's *Dances with Wolves,* but on the flip side of the coin, it is leading an attack against the Hornell Brewing Company.

In March 1992 Hornell introduced Crazy Horse Malt Liquor, packaged in a forty-ounce clear container shaped like a whiskey bottle, and labeled with the image of a Native American. Crazy Horse, an Oglala chief of the 1870s, is a hero to many Native Americans because he fought U.S. government ownership claims on the Black Hills, refusing to allow his tribe to be confined to a reservation. Crazy Horse's defeat of Lieutenant Colonel George Armstrong Custer at the Battle of Little Bighorn makes him especially popular with Native Americans today. As the *Lakota Times* sees the situation, 115 years after a federal soldier murdered Crazy Horse in a U.S. government jail, the government is setting out to further assassinate everything he stood for by permitting the sale of Hornell's product. Recently elected Colorado senator Ben Nighthorse Campbell calls the sale of Crazy Horse Malt Liquor part of an "absolute American tragedy;" the fight to prohibit its marketing is already being dubbed "the Second Battle of Little Bighorn."

Hornell brought out Crazy Horse as just one in a new series of Wild West–marketed drinks, including Jim Bowie Pilsner and Annie Oakley Lite. But there is a difference between naming a beer after a hard-drinking Caucasian and calling one by Crazy Horse's name. For one thing, the incidence of alcoholism among Native American teenagers is twice the national average, and the Fetal Alcohol Syndrome rate among Native

473

American infants outstrips the national average by twenty to one. Crazy Horse was a spirited and militant leader of the Sioux Nation; he witnessed alcohol's destruction of his people and adamantly opposed its consumption. Today substance-abuse counselors still use Crazy Horse's anti-alcohol teachings in their work with Native Americans. Moreover, even Hornell finally seems to have recognized the enormity of their misstep; they are bowing to pressure from the surgeon general and various members of Congress and have promised not to sell Crazy Horse Malt Liquor in the fourteen states with the largest populations of Native Americans. But this concession does not do enough. In South Dakota, one of those fourteen states, people are paying up to fourteen dollars—more than five times the standard retail price—for a bottle.

While Crazy Horse Malt Liquor continues to thrive, establishing a false association between the Sioux warrior and the substance he abhorred, a memorial to the great leader is slowly taking shape: Korczak Ziolkowski's three-dimensional, six-hundred-foot granite carving of Crazy Horse. After watching Borglum carve four white presidents on Mount Rushmore, Sioux chief Henry Standing Bear asked Ziolkowski to create the monument at Thunderhead Mountain. "My fellow chiefs and I would like the white man to know the red man had great heroes, too," Standing Bear wrote to the sculptor in 1947. That same year Ziolkowski, forty years old and with only $174 to his name, started work on the monument, planning to make it ten times larger than the Mount Rushmore sculpture. Ziolkowski died in 1982, but his progeny have taken up the cause. Eight of his ten children are blasting away at the Thunderhead Mountain project, using dynamite, bulldozers, picks, and shovels, in the quest to carve an epic monument for Crazy Horse. The Thunderhead project is financed strictly by visitors' fees and contributions from individuals; million-dollar federal and corporate grants are refused on principle, as the artists insist they will not take "blood money."

From Mount Rushmore, the Majic Bus headed past Horse Thief Lake to have a look at the Crazy Horse Memorial. Darlene had been particularly anxious to see it. Sympathetic to the plight of Native Americans, Darlene thought the Henry Standing Bear–Korczak Ziolkowski idea to memorialize Crazy Horse in stone was a good one. She was especially pleased that the dream included a university for Native Americans, as well as a museum and a medical training center.

We knew the Crazy Horse memorial was a work-in-progress, but we didn't quite realize how much work was left to be done. In the forty-five years since its beginning, precious little progress had been made on the sculpture itself. The projected completion date now stands in the mid-twenty-third century. Even Darlene was somewhat disappointed by the sight of the uncarved mountain, but she likened the memorial's construction to building a medieval cathedral, which could often take centuries. Though the pace continues to be slow because of the creators' high-minded principles about accepting tainted money, when the project is completed, it will be the largest sculpture in the world, outsizing even the Sphinx.

Those who labor on the Crazy Horse Memorial, just like the medieval artisans before them, may never live to see their lives' work finished. But to them that makes no difference in the scheme of things, not when compared to the generations of Native Americans who lived without hope, being systematically exterminated. In the meantime, Crazy Horse Malt Liquor keeps rolling off the assembly line.

When we left the Crazy Horse memorial, our plan was to make a straight shot home, punctuating the two-thousand-mile grind back to Long Island by only a short hike in the South Dakota Badlands National Park. But we weren't quite ready; something about the Crazy Horse monument had left us melancholy and introspective. After praying with the Crow medicine man in Montana, listening to his coyote stories, and feeling moved by his elucidation on the continuation of Crow traditions, we all felt cast down at seeing this American family trying to celebrate Native American achievements by chiseling the image of Crazy Horse in granite.

This was not the note I wanted for American Odyssey's finale; we had to finish with a full-fledged bang. Frank suggested a stop in Chicago for a farewell deep-dish pizza dinner at Gino's. Beth wanted a good-bye bash at some roadside juke joint. But the rest of us agreed that both plans smacked too much of premeditation for a venture that prided itself on its footloose spontaneity. Just as our collective blues began to fog the windows of the Majic Bus, an inspiration for one last unforgettable event came to us in the form of a most unlikely place—Wall Drug, in the center of the tiny town of Wall, South Dakota (population 760).

On our way to Badlands National Park, Mitch had asked whether we could visit Wall Drug, a forty-six-thousand-square-foot combination cowboy kitsch museum, discount store, Wild West tourist trap, saloon, and restaurant situated in the middle of the South Dakota prairie. Mitch had learned about the place in one of the business classes he had taken at Hofstra, and he tempted me with tales of the company's history, campaigning to add the unusual mercantile to our itinerary.

Ted and Dorothy Hustead, Wall Drug's founders, are high on Mitch's list of entrepreneurial heroes, their Horatio Alger story as fantastic as the Schafers'. During the Great Depression the Husteads purchased the small-town pharmacy for three thousand dollars, securing the promise of a local doctor to refer all of his patients to them. Despite the promise, business was bad—there simply weren't enough sick folks in Pennington County to support a pharmacy. The Husteads were verging on bankruptcy when Dorothy came up with a desperate scheme to save the failing business. Every night as she lay in bed she had heard the rumblings of passing traffic on the nearby highway. There must be some way, she thought, to draw all those travelers into the drugstore. "We got plenty of water and ice," she told her husband, "so why don't we put up a few signs on the highway offering free ice water?"

Ted recognized it was a long shot, but as the old adage goes, "Nothing ventured, nothing gained." He put up some billboards along what is now Interstate 90—and, barely minutes after the first signs were up, thirsty travelers began to beat a path to the store. More and more customers flocked in, and business boomed. The Husteads kept adding to their line of merchandise and free attractions: the world's largest "jackalope" (the mythical American hybrid, a giant jackrabbit with an antelope rack as well as the obligatory big ears); Johnny Rio, a life-size animated manne- quin who stands behind a set of saloon doors, ready to outdraw any visitor who can muster up a quarter to test himself against the mechanical mas- ter; the animated Singing Cowboy Orchestra, which renders Gene Autry's "Happy Trails" as if performed under pillows; the Chuck Wagon Quartet, which sings patriotic favorites; and a large-scale replica of Mount Rush- more bearing a PLEASE DON'T CLIMB ON FACES (small plastic models-of- the-model are offered for sale).

The Husteads went on to reason that these thirsty, souvenir-seeking motorists must also be hungry, so they started serving the tastiest buffalo burgers and the best nickel cup of coffee in the Badlands. Finally, they expanded their billboard advertising to all fifty states, with such knee- slappers as HAVE YOU DUG WALL DRUG? and WALL I'LL BE DRUGGED. With the most aggressive billboard campaign ever launched, one that put even Burma Shave to shame, the Husteads made a fortune.

Over the years, Wall Drug has lived by the motto "Something for every- one." Today, even a religious impulse can be satisfied with their Travel- ers' Chapel, a reproduction of a nineteenth-century Trappist monastery from Dubuque, Iowa. They love everybody at Wall Drug, except Lady Bird Johnson, whose Highway Beautification Act of 1965 forced the sec- ond generation of Husteads to dismantle billboards throughout much of the country.

The company survived this near-fatal blow by going global, as I later discovered. A few months ago, I was in Amsterdam crossing over a canal bridge and to my utter amazement there was a sign that read: 5,333 MILES TO WALL, S.D., DRUG. Do the citizens of Amsterdam, a city known for its many antinuclear demonstrations, not realize that by spending their guild- ers at Wall they are providing an indirect (though minute) subsidy to the missile makers? Wall Drug, located in the heart of missile silo country, is surrounded by over fifty Minuteman missiles, making it, in the words of *The New Roadside America*, "the best-defended tourist attraction in the world." It is Wall Drug's policy to supply missile crews with free coffee and doughnuts, so if the Dutch are ever accidentally nuked, it could well be a Wall Drug—induced caffeine-and-sugar high that leads the prairie bomb boys to press the button.

Given Wall Drug's rich and fascinating history, I decided to accede to Mich's request and pay the place a visit. There was much to keep the students amused as they roamed through Wall Drugs's sprawling attractions: Alan bought an expensive cowboy hat and poncho; Jay and Dan studied the prints of Gutzon Borglum's oil portraits of his parents, painted in Europe before he emigrated to America; Christine and Janine admired the jackalope; and Kevin searched for a phone so he could call his girlfriend back at Hofstra to report he would be home in forty-eight hours. Meanwhile Beth, Shari, Tom, and I went to play pool at the Cactus Saloon.

Beth was still glum over the prospect of returning to life in Long Island as she had known it. Traveling America had changed her way of thinking about herself and her life. The open road had freed her soul, and she dreaded returning to life at a desk. She could now imagine herself living high in the Rockies—in Ward, Colorado, perhaps, watching the seasons change—or maybe in San Francisco, where the people were friendlier than in New York. She could imagine herself in other places, too, perhaps as an Atlanta lawyer or a Seattle doctor, for at twenty-two she had unlimited options. But it was the Dakota Badlands that had marked her most deeply. Of all the experiences of our six weeks on the road, it was the whistling wind at Painted Canyon—a wind violent in force yet somehow liberating—to which she most wanted to return. As she lit a cigarette and stuffed a coin in the jukebox to play Robbie Robertson's "Broken Arrow," she vowed to herself to come back to the Badlands. In an attempt to dispel her blues, Beth told Shari to rack 'em up.

Shari, in contrast, was in a clearly different frame of mind, demonstrating her post-Medora sense of self-confidence, as she cleared the table of all the balls without missing a beat. Some of the other students came by, and we drank farewell toasts in back of the saloon, our melancholy slowly transforming to joy with each toast.

478   While the pool game was progressing, I eavesdropped on a boisterous

conversation among four local ranchers wearing identical blue jeans, cowboy boots, and perfectly pressed Western shirts, each one's Stetson tilted at precisely the same angle, each grinding a toothpick with his teeth. We may have been in Wall, but these were no drugstore cowboys. The conversation wasn't about livestock or the weather but about the LA riots, the consensus being that the police should have been more aggressive and cracked a few more skulls. Unable to let such simplistic nonsense pass, I walked over to them and interjected another viewpoint: "Excuse me, gentlemen," I said, and talk ceased, all eyes focusing on this rank stranger. "I'd like to propose a toast." As they raised their glasses high, I started off slowly: "To the great state of South Dakota." Their suspicions began to abate. Then, in a pronouncement that in some locales might have earned me an on-the-spot hiding, I added, "and to Senator George McGovern, Senator Ted Kennedy, and the Reverend Jessie Jackson—true patriots of this great nation."

For a fleeting moment I thought I had gone too far and that they might lynch me from the tree that grows through the roof of Wall Drug. Out of all the names in the gauntlet I had flung down, it was that of their former home-state senator, George McGovern, that really galled them. They circled me menacingly, chanting McGovern's name again and again, with epithets unprintable in the *New York Times*. If they were to be believed, the 1972 Democratic presidential nominee was the anti-Christ, the Satan upon whom they blamed the prohibition against shooting prairie dogs, the federally mandated reintroduction of the endangered black-footed ferret onto their ranch land, the cut in defense expenditures that could reduce the number of Minuteman missiles (traditionally a growth industry in the region during the Cold War), and the possibility of licensing and thereby restricting the God-given right to carry a gun. You name it, if these guys thought it was bad, McGovern and his liberal cronies in Washington were to blame.

Once the ranchers had vented their spleens and I saw that they weren't about to crush my larynx, I took up McGovern's defense, and an intense political brouhaha got under way. They felt the 1971 Vietnam War speech in which he said, "Every senator in this chamber is partly responsible for sending fifty thousand young Americans to an early grave," was a piece of unforgivable demagoguery. I had previously tried to avoid this sort of argument in the interest of American Odyssey, but since I was the instigator this time I would have to see it through. Before too long the students joined the fray, and as more students gradually came over to the bar, the ranchers realized they were outgunned. "We're not ferret farmers, by God, we're cow punchers—and the feds better get this through their heads," we were told time and again.

It turns out they were really decent, courteous, hardworking family men. The leader was Roger Barber, owner of the Bar-7-Bar ranch in Owanka, which is about twenty miles from Wall. I told Roger about American Odyssey and he liked the idea—even if he didn't much like my liberal politics. In a demonstration of Western hospitality, Roger refused to let any of us buy our own drinks, insisting that as long as we were visitors to his town, our wallets would stay in our back pockets and handbags. Meanwhile, Janine was arguing with one of the other ranchers about how immoral it was to kill prairie dogs, and he went ballistic. Ranchers from southern Saskatchewan to northern Mexico loathe these somewhat cuddly creatures, for they eat the same grasses—including some roots—upon which domestic animals graze. In addition, many a good horse has been known to break a leg by accidently stepping into one of their holes. "Don't say things like that around here, honey," he told Janine. "We like any color in Wall but *green*"—meaning environmentalists, of course, not money.

Roger, overhearing their conversation, decided to defuse this argument with "an offer we couldn't refuse." He would put us up for the evening in a Wall motel, and at 5:30 A.M. the next morning he would meet us at the Silver Dollar Café for a pancake breakfast on him, then lead the Majic Bus with his pickup truck to his Bar-7-Bar Ranch, a five-thousand-acre spread of prime grazing land where he raises Charolais cattle and has a stable full of horses. Tired of East Coast misperceptions of life on the range, he wanted to show these New York students what life in the Great Plains was all about. He would lecture to the students on land use and husbandry and heifers. Whoever wanted to could mount horses and ride the range, or feed the livestock, or go prairie-dog hunting with scoped rifles from his gun collection.

This offer had a little something for everyone, for while Dan, Janine, Christine, Stefanie, and Shari refused to pull a trigger, Matt, Kevin, and Justin could hardly wait to obliterate those grassland rodents with semiautomatic weapons when they stuck their furry, nonsensical heads out of a hole. The students who belonged to the "pro–prairie dog coalition" found the hunt idea brutal and barbaric, yet they were intoxicated by the notion of riding a horse around on the open range.

May Day ranching turned out to be a glorious experience. We rolled out of our motel beds and climbed onto the Majic Bus, then Frank followed Roger to his ranch and we began a day we would never forget. While some of the students rode horses—an exhilarating experience—others sat rifle in hand in the back of a pickup truck, firing ammo at every prairie dog that was foolish enough to stick its head out of a hole and bark. Turkey vultures were flying overhead, hoping to catch the scent of warm blood. All morning long we heard *bang*s—but the hunters hit nothing but dirt; the wily varmits always just managed to dodge death by a whisker. You couldn't help but think of those Elmer Fudd–Bugs Bunny cartoons, in which the animal is always more clever than the man. It became impossible not to like Roger Barber and envy him for living on such a dream spread.

Finally Roger offered us one last, very tempting adventure: Would we like to help him and his neighbors with the annual cattle branding that afternoon? Student response was immediate and enthusiastic. Under normal circumstances I would have said yes straight off, but it was late Saturday afternoon and we had to be back at Hofstra on Tuesday. I told Roger and the students that I was all for it, but the final decision was up to Frank. After all, he was the one who would have to do double-time on the highway.

Frank was out in the bus sleeping and when I woke him with enthusiasm for Roger's offer, he said, "No way, too many miles to do and not enough hours." He had promised his daughter that he was going to pick her up from school on Tuesday, and he wasn't going to miss that for a cattle branding. I went back inside the Cactus Saloon and told Roger that Frank couldn't do it; his Hofstra contract said he would deliver the students back on Tuesday afternoon and that was exactly what he planned to do.

Disappointed that he wouldn't be able to show the students a real Western branding, Roger said, "Tell Frank again, this time with a five-hundred-dollar cash offer attached to it." Upon hearing "five hundred dollars," Frank snapped to, realizing that this rancher was serious about hospitality. He put on his boots and Stetson and went to meet Roger, who then peeled off five crisp hundred-dollar bills and handed them to Frank. With cash in hand, the two hit it off famously. Frank agreed to spend the evening in Wall; we would leave for home by 2:00 A.M. By night-owling it for forty-eight straight hours, living on caffeine stamina and happy thoughts of reuniting with his family, he would be able to deliver us punctually.

After our four hours at the Bar-7-Bar Ranch, Roger led us to the Dean Shell Ranch in Wasta. The students were delighted to participate in the highly ritualistic May Day cattle branding. Here was an opportunity to learn firsthand about the unusual mores of cowboys, mythic figures they had thought were more a part of Hollywood's imagination than real workaday Americans. On this day the Dakota air is thick with burned flesh, and the testicles of the castrated steers—a delicacy known as mountain oysters—are cooked on a coal stove and eaten as a rite of passage. Janine and Christine were terrified by the whole spectacle; the almost human-sounding screams of pain that accompanied the castrations were unbearable to them. The cattle had HORROR written all over their faces; it was to her a nightmare of machoism, as fathers instructed their sons to eat the freshly cut and roasted testicles in a bid to increase fertility and manhood.

About seventy ranchers were participating in this yearly event, neighbor helping neighbor. One ranch hand showed Kevin how to tackle the cattle and bring them down to the ground. With a cowboy hat on his head and dirt on his jeans, Kevin looked like a real rancher. He and Kenny helped hold the cattle down as the Dean Shell Ranch insignia was blazed onto rump after rump. Most cattlemen name their ranches after their brands and revere the symbol as highly as a knight does his crest. Branding is hard, physical work, and for the class vegetarians, it induced nausea.

As we said good-bye to the ranchers, refusing a batch of mountain oysters to go, we all realized we had been transformed by the event, even those of us who had abhorred the violence. Like Theodore Roosevelt, we had felt this exposure to cowboy culture changed the way we viewed American society. This ritualistic neighborly cattle branding was done voluntarily, to meet a common goal together. It was this type of brotherhood and sisterhood of people in harmonious action, like that we had seen in Ferndale, that could conquer mountains or shut down a company. Main Street may not be what it used to be, but the spirit of Main Street, of community action, is as strong as ever in America.

As we got back on the interstate for our mad dash home to New York, it was reassuring to know that the American people were still fighting to preserve their heritage and uphold their dreams.

Afterword

College is always on the road to somewhere else.
—TOM ROBBINS

FROM THE DEAN SHELL RANCH IN SOUTH DAKOTA FRANK hammered and clutched the Majic Bus toward home, cruising at breakneck speed. We detoured off I-90 for the ninety-minute scenic drive through Badlands National Park—which Frank actually accomplished in forty minutes. Along the park drive, the purplish sunset had a strange side-effect on the rock formations, coloring them with a turquoise glow. As we drove through the adjacent Buffalo Gap National Grasslands we argued about the difference between the terms *buffalo* and *bison* (there isn't one) and barely missed killing three wild turkeys that suddenly fast-walked in front of us as if they were roadrunners. We discovered a small beige lizard had boarded the Majic Bus; when it saw us it swiftly darted under the rest room door.

484

We came to the border of the Pine Ridge Indian reservation, the second largest reservation in the nation; in 1890 the atrocious Wounded Knee Massacre took place here, the U.S. Army killing several hundred unarmed Sioux men, women, and children. The students found it odd that Black Elk, one of the most well known Native American history figures, was a devout Roman Catholic catechist. Nebraska poet John G. Neihardt's *Black Elk Speaks: Being the Life Story of a Holy Man of the Oglala Sioux* had been an assigned text, and a visit to Wounded Knee was on our itinerary, but time was working against us. Alison, who had also read Dee Brown's *I Buried My Heart at Wounded Knee*, pleaded to visit the collective gravesite and Crazy Horse's burial mound on the reservation, but we couldn't—our days of historical adventuring were over. "Tell the students we'll only make fast-food stops the rest of the way," Frank instructed. "We're highballing it back to Hempstead."

Philosopher Frank had transported himself back in time to become Trucker Frank again. When I went to the bathroom to hunt for the lizard he ejected Santee Sioux poet-activist John Trudell's *AKA Graffiti* cassette, which I had put on for mood music, and replace it with C. W. McCall's *"Convoy" and Other Trucker Favorites* followed by *The Best of Tex Ritter*. Frank was deadeye determined to unload his passenger cargo at Hofstra and then pick up his greatly missed daughter at school; from now on chitchat had no place. Instead of making normal conversation with the students he just spoke out loud, as if reporting information to other truckers on the CB, and for the remainder of the trip he spoke in a dieselman lingo foreign to our ears. When the Majic Bus was burning fuel in excess he cursed and said he was "working for Standard Oil"; when he saw a truck hauling a mobile home he referred to it as a "shanty shaker." When we spotted a chemical truck with a red FLAMMABLE warning sticker on the back Frank called it a "boom wagon" driven by a "suicide jockey." His usual disdain for Toyota pickups became even more vitriolic, and he started calling them "puddle jumpers" and "sushi wagons." Every day we were on the road Frank had asked Beth to fetch him his logbook—now, for the first time, he called it his "lie sheet."

When students complained they were hungry, Frank pulled off in a rundown truck stop he called a "choke and puke" and told us this would be our only stop until we hit Des Moines, so we'd have to "fill up our tanks with food" then and there. As we headed inside we all mumbled that Frank was taking this trucker stuff one step too far. No sooner had we cut through the blue-smoky and broken-fan dining area to find seats at the counter than Christine spotted two cockroaches feasting on a piece of half-eaten jelly-smeared toast lying on a plate. Dan, appalled at the sight, shouted, "Oh, my God!" In a straight line we marched right out of the "choke and puke," demanding that Frank find us a Dairy Queen.

Since we weren't far from Mitchell, South Dakota, I suggested that we exit the freeway, hunt for a DQ, and then drive by the Corn Palace for a quick look. The students seconded the proposal when they heard that the Corn Palace, a concert/entertainment venue built in 1892, resembles a Russian Orthodox church except that it's decorated inside and out with native corn, grain, and grasses of natural color. Frank reluctantly agreed, and sure enough, just before we hit downtown Mitchell we found a DQ, where we bought milkshakes and corn dogs to go. We parked across from the five-story Corn Palace and enjoyed the view while dining on the Majic Bus roof. Mitchell considers itself "the Corn Capital of the World," and that certainly appeared to be more than just a boast. We ate our corn dogs across from the Corn Palace while listening to KORN – AM radio and eyeing two high-schoolers with letter jackets vaunting The Fighting Kernels hop out of a Chevy pickup brimming with corn ears, to stalk across Corn Street sharing a bag of cheese popcorn.

After dinner we ran into more Fighting Kernels at the Mitchell 7-Eleven, where we'd gone to buy provisions for the long drive home. While the American Odyssey students were busy at the Big Gulp dispensers and nacho-cheese pumps I asked the cashier, who was reading *Circus* magazine, what the Corn Palace is used for today. Before he answered me, he bellowed, "Get out of here," to a grunge kid who had walked in with a boom box blaring Sonic Youth. Once the boom-box boy left, the cashier calmed down, composing himself to answer my question: "Well, the last show I saw at the Corn Palace was the University of Nebraska Cornhuskers marching band performing for Thanksgiving."

With bags of BBQ chips and Smart Food popcorn ready to keep us fortified for the next twenty hours, we got back on I-90 and cruised to Sioux Falls, then dropped down to Sioux City, Iowa, where I-29 starts to follow the silt-laden Missouri River all the way to Omaha. Christine was sitting on the porch, and at her request we listened to the Red Hot Chili Peppers' "Under the Bridge," a love song to the city of Los Angeles. We were all feeling ashamed about the Rodney King verdict of April 29, and wished the Majic Bus could make amends, but we didn't know how. Trying to postpone the final moments of American Odyssey, I suggested we drive to downtown Omaha and park in front of Malcolm X's birthplace on Pinkney Street, put flowers at the site, and blare out Arrested Development's "Fishin' 4 Religion"—but Frank nipped the idea in the bud: We were definitely on the homeward trail.

That evening American Odyssey felt like a family, everybody laughing, the harsh jokes and jabs of days past replaced by tenderness. Jay sat on the porch, strumming his six-string; he was not jamming his usual blues but finger-picking soft ballads like "The Streets of Laredo" and "The Streets of London." All the students were getting their journals ready for submission, and after glancing at the quality and length of student entries, I announced that the final exam was canceled. They would be graded solely on their two midterm exams and journals—and everybody would automatically pass, simply for surviving the journey.

By the time the Majic Bus made it to Des Moines, all the students were sound asleep. Frank and I talked for a while about Casey Jones, the greatest train engineer ever. We had both first learned about him in Boy Scout songbooks, progressing later to the more adult Mississippi John Hurt and Grateful Dead versions of the Missouri trainman's life. Of the three varying versions explaining why Casey Jones wrecked the Cannonball on that fateful evening in 1900, we both preferred the Boy Scout version, in which the wholesome hero dies on duty, exhausted from lack of sleep. Not wanting to leave Frank up by himself thinking about the wreck of the Cannonball, I put on Junior Walker and the All-Stars' upbeat "Roadrunner" and went to bed, thinking about the endless miles of concrete only four feet away from my rumbling stomach.

We awoke the next morning with fresh eyes, the sun blazing down on neatly planned cornfields that testified to the marvel of Breadbasket geometry. It was our last full day on the highway and it went by in a flash. From Rock Island, Illinois, to Cleveland, Ohio, the road was a blur of constant motion from which we culled a few unforgettable images: Jared begging to play his soundtrack from the movie *Hoosiers* when we were in Indiana; Alison banging her head repeatedly into the bus wall, chanting, "Please don't take me back to Long Island"; Christine asking when she could register for American Odyssey II; Tom ecstatic when we saw a sign in Eureka, Illinois, for Ronald Reagan's birthplace; Darlene anxious to preview the Ohio landscape, knowing she would soon be going to school in Dayton; Beth reading me a published entry from Ken Kesey's notebook: "Well, if the meek take over this show, they're gonna have to show some spunk doing it"; Janine sharing poetic passages from her personal trip notebook; and me bowing my head in respect when we drove past Clyde, the hometown of Sherwood Anderson, known in literature as *Winesburg, Ohio*.

It was midnight when we hit Cleveland. Frank pulled off the road for a three-hour nap at a truck stop that was more like a turnpike Taj Mahal than a gritty bastion of highway convenience. The students spent their time showering, playing pool, and devouring farewell-highway orders of buttermilk biscuits with gravy. Inside the Mack Cap Lounge, truckers with big guts, sore behinds, and bad kidneys were unwinding with Karaoke, a popular amusement imported from Japan that puts you onstage to sing the lyrics to a taped song. Kenny and Matt, with more nerve than

I could ever muster, dubbed themselves the Road Rebels and sang "Born to Be Wild" to jeers of "Get off the stage, yuppies!" The lounge reeked of diesel fumes and stale cigarettes; hungering for fresh air, I walked around the parking lot (which was the size of a moderate shopping mall) and discovered a mobile eighteen-wheel church. The chaplain who owns the rig, a card-carrying member of Transport of Christ, told me he travels all over America in his "Mobile Chapel," pulling into truck stops to teach the Bible to his fellow pilgrims on wheels. He established the missionary chapel right after the rig he was driving crashed down a hillside, smashing the cab but leaving him to emerge virtually unscathed, with nothing more than a sore neck—a true "road miracle."

When our three hours had elapsed, Jared woke Frank up with a full thermos of hundred-mile coffee and we blasted off down the Ohio Turnpike—no Bigfoot in sight—aiming straight for the Pennsylvania Tunnels, which (if Frank followed a horizontal line through the night) would burrow us straight through to Breezewood by breakfast time. We closed our eyes in sleep; never again would we see BIG BAD WOLF on the Majic Bus marquee lighting up the night.

Crossing into Pennsylvania signified our return to the East Coast, and I woke up east of Harrisburg to the smell of May in the air, thinking of New York City and realizing that American Odyssey was over. There were things about the Big Apple I had truly missed: the *New York Times* and *Village Voice* on newsstands; bagels and cream cheese; Vin Scelsa's Sunday-night radio show, "Idiot's Delight"; East Village pizza slices; ale at the White Horse Tavern; shortcuts through Central Park; Edward Hopper's *Early Sun Morning* at the Whitney Museum of American Art; bullfrogs in the Chinatown windows; curry dinners in Little India; the blue-gray Pan Am building; poetry readings at the 92nd Street Y; the small-press shelves at Saint Mark's Bookshop; stolen cassettes on sale for a dollar in front of Cooper Union; Wall Street brokers rushing past Alexander Hamilton's Trinity Church grave, too self-involved to notice it or care; Umberto's Clam House on Mulberry Street; spotting Arthur Miller

489

walking in SoHo; the Haughwout Building; basketball in Tompkins Square Park; Orchard Street rack shopping on Sunday afternoons; what Henry James called the "solid, honorable dwellings" across from Washington Square's Triumphal Arch; soca and reggae dancing at Kilimanjaro; raw oyster—shooting at Grand Central Station; the smell of incense in the Strawberry Field section of Central Park, where John Lennon's wake is still not over; coffee with whipped cream at the Hungarian Café on Amsterdam Avenue, where the Cathedral Church of Saint John the Divine rises out of tenement ash; Off-Off Broadway Sam Shepard plays; reading Chester Himes in Sylvia's Restaurant and daydreaming about what it was like when Langston Hughes could be seen walking down Lennox Avenue; and most of all, just sitting in the lobby of the Chelsea Hotel, where so many notables wrote their masterpieces (none as fine as Thomas Wolfe's *You Can't Go Home Again*; when I'm in New York not a day goes by that some image from that novel doesn't dance around in my mind). When all is said and done nothing compares to the bustle and brawn of New York. If cities were boxers New York would knock all challengers out in the first round without breaking a sweat. With images like these rushing to mind, calling American Odyssey a victory and sending the troops home didn't seem too traumatic; I always had New York City, which can never be fully explored.

Everybody was getting mentally prepared to return to their former lives. Over the past weeks on the road we had created enough memories to fill a lifetime photo album and we all knew things would never be quite the same again. The students were exchanging journals and penning in paragraphs of eternal friendship. Not knowing how to end the trip, how to express my gratitude and demonstrate my fondness for them, I took to composing poems in their journals, the only gift I thought worth giving. Already, a number of post—American Odyssey group activities were being planned. In a few days we would all polish our shoes and appear on "Good Morning America" together as a group, sharing our road experiences with the nation. With smoothness and grace, Aíne and Jay would answer questions Charlie Gibson asked. We would also lunch together at Hofstra's University Club, a welcome-home affair hosted by our university president. But I knew the bonds we had forged would be subject to the forces of old lives and new directions, and that soon, when we saw each other on campus and shouted out a hearty hello, it would feel almost counterfeit, like seeing an old grade-school chum for the first time in twenty years and not knowing how to act or what to say. But during the last hours on the bus, right up until we crossed the George Washington Bridge into New York City with Dylan rasping, "I'm going back to New York City, I do believe I had eno-o-o-ugh," we sat tightly glued together as a cohesive unit, viewing ourselves as one person, not twenty.

As I mused there on the Majic Bus, passing through the last great urban center of the trip, I thought about the young people who hadn't had the chance to make the journey. It is my hope that with financial support and organization from the private sector, urban high school students who perform well academically might be rewarded with a six-week bus journey across America. In an ideal world, an American Odyssey would be a part of every high school student's education. Such a journey gives meaning to what students read in books, and provides a psychological frontier in which they can explore themselves and imagine their place in our nation's future. In our less-than-ideal world, I recognize that to financially-pressed school districts, such a suggestion sounds utopian. Nevertheless, it is my hope that the private sector might step in to support and organize American Odysseys for deserving students. It would be an investment in human capital to educate active, oriented citizens who can pour their youthful energies into the betterment of their communities.

When we finally reached Long Island Frank treated us to pizza pies from Carmella's, picked up his daughter from St. Catherine's school, and introduced us to his wife. Everybody was now scurrying to make sure they had all of their belongings, not wanting to forget the inevitable missing sock. As we pulled into the Hofstra campus, parents and friends waited to greet us. Jared stuck Tom Petty's "Into the Great Wide Open" in the tape deck one last time, making an already emotional moment almost unbearable. As the students hugged the people they had missed, you could see their eyes darting about, hoping to connect momentarily with one of their American Odyssey mates, desperate for a fleeting nod of understanding. With all the bags unloaded, Frank proud that he had delivered his cargo all in one piece, he looked us over one last time, gave a thumbs-up and said, "Don't let the rapture pass you by." Then, with the single word HOME replacing BIG BAD WOLF on the marquee, the Majic Bus pulled out of Hofstra, leaving only a thin trail of exhaust.

Solemnly, I departed from the student-union lawn, with my duffel bag in one hand and student journals in the other. As soon as I unlocked my office, ready to tackle the stacks of mail and the never-returned phone calls that had come in during the trip, I put John Coltrane's *Love Supreme* in my tape deck and flipped through the journals once again, feeling sad yet victorious. Alan Mindel's laptop-typed journal was the first I looked over, for he had written extensively every day. Starting at the end, I read his final entry, which poignantly summed up our weeks spent on the road:

Tearing up Lincoln County, blue highway road warriors coasting through the North American plains, leaving all to chance, going full force to the extreme in a suicide mission to find the American Dream. From the palm trees to the evergreens. Out of the Big Apple into Seattle. Eating grits and avocados. Touching the good life and feeling good people's pain. Laughing at the fast lane, trying to stay insane. Three thousand miles away from home, trying to find a place of our own—the American Odyssey.

Postscript—American Odyssey 1993

Afoot and light-hearted I take to the open road,
Healthy, free, the world before me,
The long brown path before me leading wherever I choose.

Henceforth I ask not good-fortune, I myself am good-fortune,
Henceforth I whimper no more, postpone no more, feed nothing,
Done with indoor complaints, libraries, querulous criticisms,
Strong and content I travel the open road.

—FROM "SONG OF THE OPEN ROAD"
Leaves of Grass
Walt Whitman

ON MARCH 15, 1993, I EMBARKED ON MY SECOND AMERICAN Odyssey class tour, this time taking twenty-seven Hofstra students on *two* Majic Buses for nine weeks all the way to the frozen wilds of Alaska. Stretching across 586,000 square miles—a fifth of the area of the continental United States—this majestic wilderness borders two oceans and three seas, and we got to see a good portion of it. This time around was every bit as exciting as the maiden journey I wrote about in *The Majic Bus*, perhaps even more so, and as before, each student earned six semester hours toward graduation. Perhaps it is best simply to say that "American Odyssey II: Alaska Bound" was an unbelievable and at times surreal experience. What follows is a brief sketch of our educational expedition.

Ecstatically we ventured out of Hofstra University's expansive parking lot—formerly the airstrip from which Charles Lindbergh had embarked on his historic 1927 transatlantic solo flight—to our first destination: the Walt Whitman Birthplace in Huntington, New York, a national literary landmark. Surprisingly, it was in our own backyard, but none of the students had ever visited it before. Barbara Mazor Bart, executive director of the birthplace, was amazed. "They're from Long Island and they've never been here, one of the most historic homes in America," she told a *New York Times* correspondent. "But," she added, "if Walt Whitman were alive he'd be on the Majic Bus." The first floor of the Birthplace has been made into a small reading room, and we all crammed into it for an afternoon of oral poetry, alternating between *Leaves of Grass* and students' free verse. Whitman's "Song of the Open Road" was deemed *the* poem of our journey and was read aloud often at California camp fires and Alaska lodges. For the next nine weeks, poetry would be as much a staple in our lives as food and water and inexhaustible hospitality, accorded us wherever we went. "As we drove cross-country, virtual strangers opened their hearts, hotels, and even their restaurants for us," senior Joanna Lowenstein wrote in a magazine article after we returned to New York. "A barrage of kindness seemed to follow us wherever we went. People all across the country would hear about us and become very excited at the concept of such a course about America."

New York City gave us a big send-off party from the Nuyorican Poets Cafe, a happening venue. World-renowned poets and writers such as Anne Waldman and Amiri Baraka read their recent compositions along with many of the American Odyssey students. Miguel Algrinn, the Puerto Rican poet-owner of the Nuyorican, who has translated the Nobel Prize—winning poet Pablo Neruda into English, unleashed a celebratory bash we'd never forget. Over 750 people saw us off with a poetry-music extravaganza that lasted until the early morning thanks to the nonstop music provided by such brilliant African groups as Badou and his band Dahadadaoodahda.

We were now on the road, stopping first in H. L. Mencken's Baltimore, and then in Washington, D.C., where we held a bookstore seminar on politics with former senators George McGovern and Eugene McCarthy; toured abolitionist Frederick Douglass's house and historic Georgetown; and enjoyed a pizza dinner with former Louisville mayor and health-care expert

Harvey Sloane and his wife, Kathy. They prepared us for our visit to the Bluegrass State, the next stop on our itinerary.

In the course of a few days in Kentucky we visited the governor in Frankfort, hiked the Cumberland Gap, camped in a restored Shaker Village, saw Daniel Boone's grave (even though Missouri also claims to house his bones), toured Stephen Foster's "My Old Kentucky Home" in Bardstown, visited the Lexington homes of Henry Clay and Mary Todd Lincoln, and had a discussion on current events with the mayor of Louisville. One evening, after much effort, we even found the boyhood home of Muhammad Ali and staged a spontaneous historical protest of sorts. Why was there no historical marker on the unkempt Ali home, we asked, when everywhere we looked there was a marker for Civil War Confederate heroes such as Jefferson Davis? On our way out of town, after an amazing barbecue lunch, we crossed the George Rogers Clark Bridge (over the Ohio River) to Jeffersonville, Indiana, where we toured the Louisville Slugger baseball bat factory. Each student was presented with a miniature souvenir bat with the name of a baseball immortal such as Hank Aaron or Willie Mays engraved on the side. For the next weeks these bats served as everything from drum sticks to ice breakers to bug killers.

Vagabonding onward we arrived in St. Louis and did all the tourist things one would expect and were also treated to two very special events: a lecture by historian and activist Robert Tabscott on the abolitionist Elijah Lovejoy and an all-you-can-eat-and-drink rock-and-roll party at Blueberry Hill with Chuck Berry and his daughter, Ingrid Berry. The legendary blues piano great Johnnie (B. Goode) Johnson joined the Berrys on stage for a blistering set that included "Roll Over Beethoven." This was rock-and-roll history in the making and American studies at its best and the students went wild when one of the bus drivers, J. D. Williams, sat in with the band and played some steady, mean drums for a couple of numbers.

In Lawrence, Kansas, a community filled with hospitality, we not only once again met William S. Burroughs at The Full Moon Cafe but also hooked up with Dan Wildcat, chairman of natural and social sciences at Haskell Indian Junior College, who invited us to the school's medicine

495

wheel symbol, sculptured from prairie grasses. Wildcat explained to us that the circular symbol serves as a reminder that neither Earth nor its native peoples can suffer the continued environmental injustices of the previous five hundred years. After an essay exam administered in a Best Western motel—one of three the students took on the road—we left town driving through the open Kansas prairie with Ian Frazier's *Great Plains* as our guide. "The Great Plains have plenty of room for the past," Frazier writes. "Often as I drove around, I felt as if I were in an enormous time park."

There were other stops in Abilene and Denver and Boulder and Steamboat Springs until we made it to Woody Creek, Colorado, where the Majic Buses spent an uproarious evening with Dr. Hunter S. Thompson, who explained to us Gonzo Journalism and the art of controlling one's political environment. He also had us feed his rare, exotic peacocks and read aloud irreverent passages from his book on the 1992 presidential campaign, *Better Than Sex: Confessions of a Campaign Junkie*. Instead of autographing student copies of *Fear and Loathing in Las Vegas*, Hunter, always the indomitable showman, shot a hole through them with a shotgun.

After touring Aspen and Colorado National Monument, where we encountered a snowstorm, the Majic Buses headed into the canyon lands of Utah. Just as we approached Arches National Park, Majic Bus #2 blew its engine on a desolate highway, stranding us for many hours on the roadside until a tow truck finally came to the rescue. Craig Gordon, who came to Hofstra from Nassau Hebrew Academy on Long Island, saved the day by breaking out his Passover provisions. "It was the second day of Passover, and I'd brought enough matzo for eight days of the holiday, knowing you can't find kosher food on the road," said Gordon to a *Chicago Tribune* reporter. "When people got hungry I brought out my Passover provisions, and gentile kids who had never seen matzo before wolfed it down."

Eventually we all piled on one bus and headed in existential fatigue for Las Vegas to regroup and relax. Then it was onward to the Mojave Desert, where we connected with Elden Hughes, the Sierra Club member most responsible for trying to save this fragile California ecosystem. We spent two days hiking among the dazzling, springtime wildflowers and the lumbering desert tortoises, climbing sand dunes and resting against Joshua trees. Nighttime was spent camping on top of Lookout Mountain, roasting hot dogs, and listening to Elden play Pete Seeger and Burl Ives songs on guitar. Our wilderness experience made all of us even more determined to make sure that the California Desert Protection Bill gets passed by Congress and becomes an act, creating three new national parks. Throughout our journey we constantly lamented the industrial assaults on nature by everything from salt-borne fertilizers to acid rains from strip mining to hydroelectric dams.

We spent a few quiet days in California camping along the rugged coast, reading Bukowski, Miller, Steinbeck, and Kerouac, and eventually landed in San Francisco. Using City Lights Books as their base, students were free to discover the Bay Area on their own. One afternoon we discussed the Beat Generation with poet Diane di Prima and playwright Michael McClure, visited the John Coltrane Church of God, and met with gay-rights activists on Castro Street. Another evening we were the guests of filmmaker Gus Van Sant and actor River Phoenix (who died six months later) at the first screening ever of Mr. Van Sant's *Even Cowgirls Get the Blues*, based on Tom Robbins's novel, which was an assigned American Odyssey text.

Once again we visited Jack London's ranch, and a few days later, after camping out with members of Earth First! in Humboldt Redwoods State Park, we staged a "Save the Redwoods" protest at a meeting of the State Forestry Commission in Eureka. After a stop in Redwood National Park, where the silence of the woods and the sound of the water soothed souls, we headed in the rain for an Oregon highway gypsy retreat run by the Green Tortoise Bus Company, where Hofstra senior Gail Greenstein led the festive dancing in the environmentally aware "Tranquility Hut." All the while the music never stopped—drums and guitars were to the Majic Bus what coal is to a locomotive.

It was then back to Ken Kesey's farm, only this time we participated in an impromptu musical festival, with our host handing out a stunning array of unusual instruments. Within minutes the students were blowing into strange-shaped horns, ringing cowbells, scrubbing washboards, and dancing as Kesey shouted out lines of spontaneous rap into a microphone. After an hour of this musical mayhem, we toured Kesey's home and fed his Mexican

497

jumping rat while Kesey spoke with our group for quite a while about literature and his philosophy of being a "warrior."

From Kesey's we headed to Portland and then onward to Seattle, where we toured the wharf and met with the leading proponents of home schooling. After a good night's hotel rest we were off to La Conner, Washington, to spend an evening with Tom Robbins. It was truly amazing how many of the students were "Robbinsheads," and they had brought their well-worn copies of *Even Cowgirls Get the Blues*, *Another Roadside Attraction*, and *Jitterbug Perfume* to be autographed. Robbins was a gracious host and gave a wonderful lecture on anarchy and the art of writing. Then it was through customs and across the border into Vancouver, Canada.

Tammy Cimalore, my fiancée and chief organizer of the trip, had arranged with the Alaska Marine Highway for overnight ferry service from Prince Rupert, British Columbia, to Haines, Alaska, on the most incredible and visually arresting journey imaginable. Glaciers and bald eagles, horned puffins and blue whales, ten-thousand-foot glacier-crested peaks, and lushly forested islands were just part of this breathtaking experience through the pristine waterways of Alaska's panhandle, known as the Inside Passage. All students were required to read John McPhee's *Coming into the Country*, Joe McGinniss's *Going to Extremes*, Ken Kesey's *Sailor Song*, and the collected short works of Jack London to gain a better appreciation of our forty-ninth state, and so we approached the last frontier with a fairly good knowledge of what to expect. In the morning we made stops in Wrangell and Juneau to see the state capital. It is impossible to describe the recuperative beauty of Admiralty Island National Monument and Glacier Bay National Park and Preserve—the sight of such unspoiled wilderness really makes Yellowstone seem like a concrete theme park. Eventually we landed in Haines, where the locals treated us to a salmon bake and a tour of nearby gold rush areas. On the Chiklat River near Haines as many as thirty-five hundred bald eagles gather each year to feed on a run of late-returning salmon. By bus we headed into the white mountain peaks of the Yukon, grinding our way up Route 7 past roadside glaciers until we merged into the all-weather, two-lane Route 1 (the Alaska Highway) at Haines Junction. Many folks along the way said the two Majic Buses would never make it up the fabled fourteen-hundred-mile Alaska Highway, constructed in 1942 in an astonishing eight months, that if the potholes didn't kill us the steep inclines would. But with J.D. and Frank as our guides we successfully worked our way through the sudden and sheer vistas and stark springtime beauty of the North Country, the mountains of Kluane National Park and Wrangell–St. Elias National Park and Preserve always on our left. Towns like Kluane and Destruction Bay and Beaver Creek, with their racks of drying fish and satellite dishes, will forever be in our memories, and by the time we made it to Tok for a late-night steak supper, we were treated to the unforgettably transfixing galaxy display known as the aurora borealis, the northern lights. All the uncomfortable bus-bouncing and fast-food road calories were worth this heavenly sight. The air was getting thin, our heads light, and we collectively agreed that this expansive part of our nation must be preserved forever.

We spent over a week exploring the varied roads of Alaska, using Anchorage and Fairbanks as our main bases of operation. We visited a glacier by foot and helicopter; whitewater rafted down the scenic Kenai River; watched the Kodiak Indians perform folk dances and games; touched the Alaska Pipeline (the state's north slope region provides 10.5% of America's current oil needs); photographed Mt. McKinley at Denali National Park and Preserve; saw the famous Gold Rush site of Cripple Creek; toured the Large Animal Research Center, which contains several species of reindeer, caribou, and musk oxen; cursed Exxon for the Valdez oil spill; and met the folk who raise mush dogs for the yearly eleven-hundred-plus mile Iditarod Trail Sled Dog Race from Anchorage to Nome. Studying Native American art was high on our list of activities, and we also had the opportunity to meet a few of the Alaskans John McPhee profiles in *Coming into the Country*. It didn't take us long to realize that Alaska was unlike any other region of our nation. "Alaska is a foreign country significantly populated with Americans," McPhee wrote in his truly wonderful book. "Its language extends to English. Its nature is its own." By the time we made it to Fairbanks, we were encountering close to twenty hours of light each day. The concept of darkness had been left on Long Island.

Our journey out of Alaska was more grueling than the trip in. We made it to the North Pole—a kitschy Alaska town that gladly welcomes thousands of

"Dear Santa" letters each December—with ease, but as we entered the Yukon we were met with snow and sleet and fearless moose who refused to budge from the middle of the road. We were all quite relieved to make it to Whitehorse, the capital of the Yukon, where rest and cash machines were the order of the day. Our next major destination was Edmonton, Alberta. Even though our buses were broken into overnight there and a number of bags and boom boxes were stolen, we all rose to the occasion and spent a large part of the afternoon touring historic sites and playing kickball in a city park.

Leaving Edmonton we made our way to Calgary, where country music and Gordon Lightfoot reign, and clung to Route 1 through such flannel-shirt towns as Medicine Hat, Swift Current, and Moose Jaw until we arrived for a night's rest in Regina, the capital of Saskatchewan. Besides studying Canadian history, students developed a daunting visual perspective on how vast and unmarred most of Canada still is. Compared to such provinces as the Yukon Territory and Saskatchewan, states such as Nevada and Kansas suddenly seemed congested and overpopulated.

We all cheered patriotically as we reentered America at Fortuna, North Dakota. To celebrate, we picnic-lunched near Williston at Fort Union National Historic Site, situated on Lake Sakakawea. By nightfall we had made it through the treeless North Dakota plains of small towns and large farms and burgeoning badlands. American Odyssey students were hosted once again by Harold and Sheila Schafer in town, and we hiked and climbed and slid our way around Theodore Roosevelt National Park. As Beatrice Masey wrote of the North Dakota Badlands in her 1919 *It Could Have Been Worse* account of a transcontinental motor journey from New York to San Francisco, "You may read of them, see pictures of them, or see them from a train, but you have really never seen their wonder, their grotesquely beautiful grandeur until you stand in their midst as we did." Besides the molting buffalo and rutting elk and anxious antelope we encountered, the students were thrilled to meet author Larry Woiwode. After an evening of barbecue, Woiwode spoke to the students about life in his beloved North Dakota, and handed out signed copies of his books *What I'm Going to Do, I Think*, and *Beyond the Bedroom Wall*, and *Born Brothers*. All of us, including Woiwode and his family, spent the next glorious morning horseback riding through the navigable portions of the Badlands.

From Medora we bypassed Mt. Rushmore and instead visited Bismarck and Fargo, eventually regrouping in Saulk Centre, Minnesota, where the Majic Buses parked side by side on the original Main Street, made famous by Sinclair Lewis's celebrated novel. In the morning I lectured on Lewis's literary career over omelettes and English muffins at the Main Street Cafe. All the students had read *Main Street*, but few found Lewis's controversial exposé very riveting or relevant—after reading Kathy Acker, William S. Burroughs, and Charles Bukowski, Lewis seemed tame. We spent the afternoon on a guided tour of Lewis's home, strolling down Main Street and watching a movie of his life at the visitor's center. Then it was on to St. Paul–Minneapolis, where we hunted down F. Scott Fitzgerald's haunts, shopped at the World's Largest Shopping Mall, toured the state capital, and visited the Walker Art Museum, with its remarkable outdoor sculpture garden. The special traveling exhibit at the Walker was "Fluxus," an ultramodern, interactive art show that proved to be a highlight of the trip for many of the students.

Chicago was the last major stop of American Odyssey 1993, where the National History Museum and Jane Addams's Hull House were favorite stops. We had our end-of-class bash at Blues, a smoky North Chicago beer joint with Matt "Guitar" Murphy providing the music. Since our 1992 trip, the Wise Fool's Pub had closed down, unable to make it in a franchised America where Planet Hollywood and Hard Rock Cafe rule. To give the students a taste of Chicago's famed Southside we visited the impoverished neighborhood, known previously from Jim Croce's song "Bad Bad Leroy Brown" and witnessed a SWAT team of police, guns drawn, make a drug bust. As Ron Kiesleg said about Chicago's Southside, "The neighborhood crest seems to be a torn, windblown plastic garbage bag."

After our Chicago blues party we headed straight for Hempstead, stopping just long enough to grab cheap grub and take cold showers in an Ohio truck stop. At a truck plaza in Bloomsbury, New Jersey, we encountered Howard Jones, a full-time chaplain and highway theologian for Christ. His rig is a twenty-four-hour mobile chapel, healing the souls of the road-weary like some modern-day St. Christopher. As he approached our buses, we were leery, confident that he was going to panhandle for money and not believe we were all stone broke. Inside, he blessed the buses and proclaimed, "The Good Book exists only when a living mind re-creates it." Those of us who heard him couldn't help but relate what he said to our own learning adventures on the road, devouring fiction, history, poetry, and music and making it forever part of us. Aspects of America that previously seemed abstract and unimportant—such as the Mojave Desert or Alaska—were now deemed essential parts of our American mosaic. The art of reading had been reclaimed; from now on books would be of daily importance to the American Odyssey Class of 1993. "I can honestly say this trip has given me the inspiration to go out into the world with a feeling of excitement and a new zest for life that will remain with me always," senior Joanna Lowenstein wrote upon her return. "I think the most important lesson I learned from Professor Brinkley is that the only limitations in life are the ones we put on ourselves. The American Odyssey experience has surely been evidence of the boundless human spirit." Fellow Long Islander Walt Whitman would have applauded Joanna's classroom discovery of self and nation, for as he wrote in "Song of the Open Road":

From this hour I ordain myself loos'd of limits and imaginary lines,
Going where I list, my own master total and absolute,
Listening to others, considering well what they say,
Pausing, searching, receiving, contemplating,
Gently, but with undeniable will, divesting myself of the holds that would
*   hold on me.*

No matter how hard a teacher tries, freedom—to be one's own master, total and absolute—can not be taught in a classroom. And so we take to the open road.

THE HOWLIN' WOLF
January 1, 1994
New Orleans

Acknowledgments

THE MAJIC BUS: AN AMERICAN ODYSSEY WOULD HAVE BEEN impossible to write without the encouragement and enthusiasm of many people. Chief among them are the American Odyssey students themselves. Most of them were graduating seniors and went on to a postcollege life of bigger and better things: Kenny Young (University of Delaware), Darlene Dudash (University of Dayton), and Stefanie Pearlman (Washington University) are all in law school, and Shari Berkowitz (Loyola University, Chicago) is pursuing a master's degree in public history. Matt Price works with a Philadelphia real estate firm; Kevin Willey is an account executive for Nautica; Dan Ellison has been studying photography at Tel-Aviv University and showing his work in the New York area; Jay Caputo is a manager at a bookstore, preparing to study American literature in graduate school; Justin Buis is running his own automotive detailing service; Aíne Graham works for a clothing company in New York. Even though they weren't at Hofstra while I was writing this book, we stayed in touch and they were willing to comment on chapter drafts, point out textual errors, keep my morale up, and lend pictures for the book.

The students who remained at Hofstra had a more hands-on role in the making of *The Majic Bus*. Alan Mindel provided me with constant counsel. He has been in the difficult position of taking classes and managing his recently deceased father's Queens hotel, The Adria; it is somewhat ironic that he tried to keep my weary spirits up when he himself was under so much pressure. Jared Goldman stopped in my office almost daily to see if he could help me with the book, and I often asked him to look up some obscure fact. Tom Tolan wrote a special essay on Portland and Seattle that was quite useful in writing Chapter 18. Christine Morga and Janine Hayes likewise read over some chapter drafts, offered comments, and made me laugh about the almost impossible deadline I faced, always encouraging me to slow down and take it a little easier. Mitch Bernstein paid me the compliment of finding American Odyssey so enriching that he created his own innovative educational program and spent a month in Orange County gratis (courtesy of the Marriott Corporation), writing a research paper on the different styles of doing business in Southern California and New York. Last but not least of the students, Alison Andrews conducted library research, provided me with vitamins, and helped me think through some of the writing of the book.

Hofstra University, particularly New College, deserves a great deal of credit for supporting me in this innovative educational endeavor. Dean David Christman, whose role in the creation of American Odyssey is elucidated in the text, is a man of deep commitment to academic excellence and innovation. Elaine Mullen helped the students sort out various financial concerns and last-minute hitches, for which I am grateful. Kathe Sweeney couldn't have been more patient in dealing with students who pestered her daily with pleas to register for the course. President James Shuart, Provost Herman Berliner, and Vice President of Public Relations Mike DeLuise couldn't have been more supportive of American Odyssey, and I feel privileged to teach at the university they run like a fine-tuned wheel. Beth Neville of the admissions office, who also went on the trip, deserves much of the credit for offering constant support in writing the book and for sharing her Majic Bus experience with various high schools across America. Beth is a remarkable person and neither the trip nor the book could have been done without her. Many thanks are also due the Secretarial Services team at Hofstra, who helped me through all phases of this book.

In a special category is the faculty of New College who gave moral support to the writing of this book. Robert Sobel, Warren Mintz, and Linda Longmire read over various chapters and offered useful critiques and encouragement. Lew Kern, a first-rate historian and a good friend, took over one of my classes during the Fall 1992 academic session, thereby lightening my teaching load so I could focus my energy on the writing. Finally, Ignacio Götz and Linda DeMotta, professors with whom I team-taught a class during the Fall 1992 semester, picked up many of my classroom responsibilities and patiently tolerated my brain-dead behavior on the days after a night of writing. Over the years I've learned to respect Professor Götz as both a teacher and a philosopher; to be around him is to constantly learn new things. My friend John Allen Gable, executive director of the Theodore Roosevelt Association and well-known Deadhead, helped me in so many ways it is difficult to count them. He carefully read over, critiqued, and made editorial suggestions on more than half the manuscript. His encyclopedic knowledge of pop culture and American history were tapped regularly. I've learned to trust John's judgment because he is usually right.

Likewise, over the years it has been my great fortune to have Helaine Randerson as a friend and kindred spirit. She is outstanding as a source of ideas, an inspiration, a patient teacher of writing and editing, a critic, and a person I can always count on to help out in a pinch. Her commitment to innovative liberal education, the women's movement, and progressive politics is unqualified; and her prodigious efforts to help me through all aspects of writing this book were indispensable and will never be forgotten. Ambassador William J. vanden Heuvel, president of the Franklin and Eleanor Roosevelt Institute, constantly showed faith in me and this project, even sending me postcards with Winston Churchill quotes about "keeping one's chin up" when he sensed my stamina for writing was ebbing. As a teenage admirer of Thomas Wolfe and FDR and later an assistant to Robert Kennedy, Ambassador vanden Heuvel has developed an intuitive feel for the American people unsurpassed by anyone I know. Nancy Mattutat worked as my research assistant on this book and was tremendous. An elementary school teacher turned periodicals specialist, she was able to track down every newspaper and magazine article I just *had* to get my hands on. This would have been a much lesser book without her constant and uncomplaining research efforts:

Needless to say, Frank Perugi, owner and operator of the Majic Bus, Inc., based in Franklin Square, New York, deserves special mention. Frank and I have become great friends; he is the best trailblazer in America. Anyone interested in traveling America with Frank should call (800) 324-4920.

My agent, Lisa Bankoff, is one of the best in the business. Her wise counsel and enthusiasm for this project have been unqualified from the start. It was Lisa who told me that Harcourt Brace and Company would be the best publisher and Claire Wachtel the best editor for the book.

The godmother of this book is Claire Wachtel, senior editor at Harcourt Brace and Company. Without Claire's initial enthusiasm, *The Majic Bus: An American Odyssey* would not have been born. When the actual writing began, Claire saved me from myself time and again when I "got up on my soapbox." Her editorial comments were always right on the mark and her confidence in me as a writer kept me plugging away until I finally crossed the finish line. We've had a lot of fun working together, and I consider our friendship one of the longterm benefits of writing this book. Rachel, thanks for letting your mom stay in Binghamton during the hectic last week of production.

Besides Claire overseeing the endeavor, I wish to thank the rest of the editorial team: assistant editor Ruth Greenstein, whose contributions throughout the editorial and production processes were numerous and vital; copy editor Sue Llewellyn, who helped pull the manuscript together with a keen and authoritative sensibility to language; Susann Cokal, a walking thesaurus whose magic with words enchanced the book immensely; and Robin Hicks, who served as all-around research assistant during the frenetic last weeks. The entire staff in Maple-Vail Composition Services in Binghamton, New York—especially Brad Freeman, Dave Hogan, Bruce Hunter, Bob Kubisa, and Pat Woodruff—deserve thanks for putting up with this crew. They provided around-the-clock assistance that included Pat Stack's hot potato soup and infinite patience.

Others at Harcourt Brace and Company merit special mention: Rubin Pfeffer, president, who supported this project from its inception, deserves my thanks for running a publishing house with so many hard-working, bright, talented, and dedicated people. These include the phenomenal Leigh Haber, director of publicity and advertising, who helped me understand the promotional necessity of having this book coincide with my American Odyssey II departure for Alaska; Warren Wallerstein, director of production, who pulled out all the stops to produce this book in two months; art director Vaughn Andrews and book designer Trina Stahl, who worked tirelessly to produce a beautiful-looking book.

On a personal and professional note: Tammy Cimalore has done so many things to make this book a reality that whatever I wrote in appreciation would be an understatement. Besides offering me shelter from the storm so I could concentrate on writing this book, she edited chapters, provided me with constant encouragement, researched facts, and shared all aspects—the joys and the pains—of the project. *The Majic Bus* is as much her book as it is mine. As for my parents, Edward and Anne Brinkley, all I can say is, Thank you! You gave me the best childhood a kid could ask for. All my memories of growing up in Georgia and Ohio are fond ones, and our days together on the road remain my most cherished memories. As long as you like the book, I am happy. Finally, to America, the true hero of this book, I offer a quote from Sinclair Lewis: "Intellectually I know that America is no better than any other country; emotionally I know she is better than every other country."

As for the Anchor paperback edition of *The Majic Bus*, grateful thanks is due to Jon Furay and Charlie Conrad. Not only did they allow me to make last-minute textual changes, but they encouraged me to write a new Preface and a Postscript, anxious for the reading public to know that American Odyssey is an ongoing educational endeavor.

Selected Bibliography

THERE ARE SO MANY GUIDEBOOKS ABOUT THE UNITED STATES THAT the difficulty for travelers is deciding which to use. To my mind, all these works dim in comparison to the annual travel guides (tour books) published and distributed by the American Automobile Association (AAA). Whether you want a fast fact, a historical overview of a state, lodging and restaurant advice, important statistics, or points of interest not to miss in your travels, the AAA guides beat the rest hands down. For only fifty dollars a year, membership in the AAA entitles you to their legendary emergency automobile service anywhere in the United States, and you also receive maps and guidebooks, as well as trip tickets that offer detailed directions on the best, most convenient route to your destination, taking into account updates on construction and the like—all for no extra fee.

If for some reason you're allergic to the AAA and want some other American travel tips I recommend Fodor's over all the rest. These guidebooks contain wonderful essays about the state or region you plan to visit as well as the usual sightseeing descriptions and dining/lodging tips. In writing *The Majic Bus: An American Odyssey* I consulted AAA tour books and Fodor's 1991 and 1992 guides more frequently than I care to admit. In addition to these traditional guides, I stumbled on two offbeat travel books that are positively priceless for anyone interested in discovering unusual American roadside attractions: Mike Wilkins, Ken Smith, and Doug Kirby, *The New Roadside America* (New York, 1992), and Vince Staten, *Unauthorized America* (New York, 1990). More than any of the other travel guides, these two books led the Majic Bus to sites, as Staten says, "that the Chamber of Commerce won't tell you about" and helped me immensely in the writing of this book. Many roadside pamphlets not cited were also useful—and, of course, fun.

Before embarking on American Odyssey, I reacquainted myself with several seminal road books that got me in the right frame of mind for journeying through our beautiful nation: Jack Kerouac, *On the Road* (New York, 1957); John Steinbeck, *Travels with Charley* (New York, 1962); William Least Heat Moon, *Blue*

508

Highways (Boston, 1982); Charles Kuralt, *A Life on the Road* (New York, 1990); Henry Miller, *The Air-Conditioned Nightmare* (New York, 1945); Earl Pomery, *In Search of the Golden West: The Tourist in Western America* (New York, 1957); Allen Ginsberg, *The Fall of America* (San Francisco, 1972); Ian Frazier, *Great Plains* (New York, 1989); and Dayton Duncan, *Out West* (New York, 1987).

Another writer I should mention is Wallace Stegner, at last count author of sixteen works of fiction and twelve of nonfiction. His latest contribution is the memoir *Where the Bluebird Sings to the Lemonade Springs* (New York, 1992), which deals in part with the future of the West and should be mandatory reading for all Americans.

Finally, this book couldn't have been written without the help of the *New York Times* (hereafter *NYT*). The quality of its travel and feature articles about America is unparalleled; without them *The Majic Bus* couldn't have been written. Due to my extensive use of *NYT* articles, I cite only those from which I drew information directly.

CHAPTER 1

It gives me great pleasure to cite my parents' family-vacation tapes as a source and an inspiration for this chapter. For information about the history of roads and highways in the United States, see Phil Patton's truly indispensable *Open Road: A Celebration of the American Highway* (New York, 1986). To learn more about Harleys and the American psyche, I read Jack Smith, "Hog Heaven," *Town & Country*, October 1990; Mark Marvel, "The Certified Hog," *Esquire*, July 1989; and Peter C. Reid, *Well Made in America* (New York, 1989). Over the years I've read everything published by and about Jack Kerouac, but four books in particular helped me in writing this chapter: Ann Charters, *Kerouac: A Biography* (San Francisco, 1973); Tom Clark, *Jack Kerouac* (San Diego, 1984); Brad Parker, *Kerouac: An Introduction* (Lowell, Mass., 1989); and Gerald Nicosia, *Memory Babe: A Critical Biography of Jack Kerouac* (New York, 1983). My many conversations with Stanley Twardowicz have given me the unique advantage of personalized insights into Kerouac and I'll always treasure his wonderful, priceless stories. And if I hadn't read Tom Wolfe's *Electric Kool-Aid Acid Test* (New York, 1968), I would never have thought to create American Odyssey.

CHAPTER 2

I interviewed Frank Perugi three times (October 6, 23, and 27, 1992) to write this chapter. For a brief history of the Green Tortoise, see Bill Richards, "Trip on the Green Tortoise Can be Hair-Raising If You Aren't Hip," *Wall Street*

Journal, January 14, 1991. An important article on Greyhound is Jason Departe, "Some Take the High Road, Some Take the Bus," *NYT*, December 25, 1991. For information on Georgetown nightlife and Washington, DC, crime, I read Martha Sherrill, "Georgetown on My Mind," *Town & Country*, May 1992; Felicity Barringer, "Two Worlds of Washington: Turmoil and Growth," *NYT*, July 12, 1990; J. M. Fenster, "Inside Washington's Work Places," *NYT*, October 6, 1991; "Georgetown in a Battle over Its Image of Wealth," *NYT*, November 11, 1991; and Barbara Gamarekian, "The Capital Convenes after Dark," *NYT*, October 6, 1991. For articles pertaining to the history of the Francis Scott Key Bookshop, see Emily Durso, "Remembering Martha Johnson," *The Georgetowner*, October 21–November 3, 1988; Larry McMurtry, "Marty Johnson and Her Books," *Washington Post*, October 23, 1988; and Bert Barnes, "Martha C. Johnson, Owner of NW Bookshop, Dies at 85," *Washington Post*, October 19, 1988.

CHAPTER 3

For Georgetown and Washington, DC, information, see Fred J. Maroon, *Maroon on Georgetown* (Charlottseville, Va., 1985); Allen Drury, *Advise and Consent* (Garden City, 1959); Martha Sherill, "Georgetown on My Mind," *Town & Country*, May 1992; and Gini and Dan McKain, "Springtime on the Potomac," *Trailer Life*, March 1992. While there is as yet no good biography of Sam Shepard, a few monographs are valuable sources for understanding his career as a playwright; in particular, see Linda Hart, *Sam Shepard's Metaphorical Stages* (Westport, Conn., 1987); Ron Mottram, *Inner Landscapes: The Theater of Sam Shepard* (Columbia, Mo., 1984); Kinball King, *Sam Shepard: A Casebook* (New York, 1988). Shepard on violence is taken from Michiko Kakutani, "Myths, Dreams, Realities—Sam Shepard's America," *NYT*, January 19, 1984. For a good profile of Shepard, see Jennifer Allen, "The Man on the High Horse," *Esquire*, November 1988. For fairly up-to-date information on Charlottesville, see Joan K. Peters, "Walking in Jefferson Country," *NYT*, May 27, 1990; and B. Drummond Ayres, Jr., "College Town of Mr. Jefferson Offers Genteel Haven for Rich and Famous," *NYT*, August 21, 1991.

CHAPTER 4

For the story of the artistic happenings at Black Mountain, see Martin Duberman, *Black Mountain: An Exploration of the Community* (New York, 1972). The best biography of Wolfe is David Herbert Donald, *Look Homeward: A Life of Thomas Wolfe* (Boston, 1987), although for an understanding of his novels I prefer Richard S. Kennedy, *The Window of Memory: The Literary Career of Thomas*

Wolfe (Chapel Hill, N.C., 1962). Other interesting studies of Wolfe include Andrew Turnbull, *Thomas Wolfe: A Biography* (New York, 1967); Elizabeth Nowell, *Thomas Wolfe: A Biography* (Garden City, N.Y., 1960); and Floyd C. Watkins, *Thomas Wolfe's Characters* (Norman, Okla. 1957). In addition to Wolfe's own prose, his published letters are a must for all who are interested in his career. For more information on George Washington Vanderbilt and his Biltmore Estate, see Jerry E. Patterson, *The Vanderbilts* (New York, 1989).

On the rise in the value of Confederate currency, see John Shelton Reed, *Whistling Dixie: Dispatches from the South* (Columbia, 1990). Three books on the Great Smoky Mountains and the Cherokee Reservation were of great help: Michael Frome, *Strangers in High Places* (Garden City, N.Y., 1966); Harry Middleton, *On the Spine of Time: An Angler's Love of the Smokies* (New York, 1991); and Eliot Porter, *Appalachian Wilderness: The Great Smoky Mountains* (New York, 1970). Useful articles were Earnest B. Fergurson, "Atop the Great Smokies," *NYT*, May 21, 1989; Joseph L. Kreuzman, "Red Wolves Return to Great Smoky Mountains" *National Parks*, March/April 1991; and Lawrence S. Earley, "On the Rebound," *National Parks*, May/June 1992.

CHAPTER 5

For information about the Carter Center and the Atlanta Project, see Jimmy Carter, Appendix, in *Turning Point: A Candidate, a State, and a Nation Coming of Age* (New York, 1992); Ronald Smothers, "Carter's Civic Crusade Tries to Meld Two Atlantas," *NYT*, April 11, 1992; Kristine F. Anderson, "Aim of Atlanta Project to Aid Community," *Christian Science Monitor*, February 27, 1992; "Jimmy Carter's Courageous Cure," *Business Atlanta*, May 1992; Helene Cooper, "Atlanta Urban-Revival Program Draws High Expectations but Some Concerns" *Wall Street Journal*, August 3, 1992; and James Fallows, "Plains Talk," *Washington Monthly*, November 1992. Also of use was Edwin A. Peeples, "Atlanta's Gone With the Wind: 1939," *Town & Country*, December, 1989.

For information pertaining to the King Center and Coretta Scott King, see "The Woman Behind the King Anniversary," *Ebony*, January 1990; Peter Applebome, "Atlanta in Contrast: Civil Rights and Racial Hate," *NYT*, December 22, 1989; Renee D. Turner, "Birthplace of a National Hero," *Ebony*, January 1989; "What Martin Luther King Would Do Now About: Drugs, Poverty and Black-Jewish Relations," *Ebony*, January 1991. Of the many important articles written on Malcolm X in 1992, the most stimulating I encountered were Playbell Benjamin, "Malcolm X Remembered," *Spin*, December 1992; and Sheila Rule, "Malcolm X: The Facts, the Fictions, the Film," *NYT*, November 15, 1992. The thesis about European cities and roads was developed by Phil Patton in *Open Road* (New York, 1986).

New Orleans is such a fascinating, culturally diverse city that this chapter's brief sketch doesn't even begin to do it justice. In addition to guidebooks I found the following articles useful: Stephen Birnbaum, "New Orleans Has It All—And Then Some!" *Good Housekeeping*, May 1989; Donald Lee Keith, articles in *New Orleans* magazine, June, July, and November 1989; Ben Sandmel, "A Vibrant Legacy," *The Atlantic*, April 1989; and Ben Sandel, "Fat's City," *Mother Jones*, November 1989.

CHAPTER 6

For the Mississippi Delta and the blues, I used the following: Eudora Welty, *One Time, One Place* (New York, 1971); Hodding Carter, *Lower Mississippi* (New York, 1942); David L. Cohn, *Where I Was Born and Raised* (Boston, 1948); Robert Palmer, *Deep Blues* (New York, 1981); William Ferris, *Blues From the Delta* (New York, 1979); Jennifer Ackerman, "In the Delta, the Blues Play On," *NYT*, April 21, 1991; and, most important, Greil Marcus's revised-edition profile of Robert Johnson in *Mystery Train: Images of Rock n' Roll Music* (New York, 1990). For information pertaining to Oxford life, see Frederick R. Karl's magisterial biography, *William Faulkner: American Writer* (New York, 1989), and William Morris's *Faulkner's Mississippi* (Birmingham, Ala., 1991). I also consulted *NYT* reviews of these books.

The literature on Elvis Presley is expansive, but for the best understanding of the historical Elvis see Marcus's profile in *Mystery Train*. For a superb evaluation of the Elvis phenomenon, see Greil Marcus, *Dead Elvis* (New York, 1991). Other helpful texts include Jerry Hopkins, *Elvis: A Biography* (New York, 1971), and *Elvis: the Final Years* (New York, 1980); and also an article by Albert Goldman, "Down at the End of Lonely Street," *Life*, June 1990. For information on Graceland tourism, see Caroline Arthur, "Going to Graceland," *American Demographics*, May 1989. For information on Jacqueline Smith, see "Protester Is Removed from King Motel Site," *NYT*, July 17, 1990, and Ronald Smothers, "New Dream from an Old Nightmare," *NYT*, February 7, 1989. For information pertaining to Sidney Shenkler and his Great American Pyramid, see Jocelyn Craugh, "Memphis to Open Pyramid Entertainment Complex," *Travel*, November 26, 1990, and Peter Applebome, "Era of the Great Pyramid Is Dawning in Memphis," *NYT*, July 23, 1989. Great thanks are due Peter Guralnick and Sid Graves, director of the Delta Blues Museum, for reading this chapter and making helpful suggestions.

CHAPTER 7

The most useful guidebooks to the Windy City are Fodor's 1991 and 1992 *Chicago*, which I used extensively in writing this chapter, as well as Marilyn J. Appleberg's *I Love Chicago Guide*. Various *New York Times* articles were useful, including Isabel Wilkerson, "What's Doing in Chicago," July 12, 1992; William E. Schmidt, "What's Doing in Chicago," November 4, 1990; and Suzanne Wincklet, "Landmarks of the Loop," September 15, 1991. For information on Chess Records studio preservation, see Jane Holtz Kay, "Landmarks of the Common Folk" *NYT*, October 25, 1990, and "Chicago: Music Mecca for '89," *Ebony*, May 1989. For evaluations of Son Seals, see Karen Schoemer, "Putting a Sharper Edge on Traditional Blues," *NYT*, March 9, 1990; Dan Kening, "Rising Son," *Chicago Tribune*, June 10, 1991; and Peter Guralnick, *Lost Highway: Journeys & Arrivals of American Musicians* (Boston, 1979). For information on Robert Rauschenberg and the exhibit we saw of his early works, see profile in the 1987 *Current Biography*; Walter Hopps, *Robert Rauschenberg: The Early 1950s* (Houston, 1991); and Calvin Tomkins, *Off the Wall: Robert Rauschenberg and the Art World of Our Time* (New York, 1980). For information on Michael Jordan, see Jim Naughton, *Taking to the Air: The Rise of Michael Jordan* (New York, 1992); Robert Lipsyte, "Athletes Are Leashed But Their Tails Wag," *New York Times*, June 12, 1992; Richard Stengel, "Yo Michael! You're the Best!" *Time*, June 24, 1991; "Michael Jordan Explains Why He Sticks Out Tongue While Playing Basketball" *Jet*, March 5, 1990; and Mike Lupica, "I Want My Mike TV!" *Esquire*, December 1991. For information regarding Capone and Dillinger's loves and lore, I spoke with experts Sandy Jones of Fort Collins, Colorado, and William J. Helmer of Chicago, whose book *The Gun That Made the Twenties Roar* (New York, 1969) is a classic. The March 1990 issue of *Chicago* magazine, devoted to gangland mythology, was incredibly useful. For the debate over whether to preserve the Capone house, see William E. Schmidt, "Is Honor Due House That Was Home to Capone?" *NYT*, March 22, 1989, and "Capone House in Chicago Won't Get Historic Status," *NYT*, April 21, 1989. Studs Terkel and Mike Royko are great heroes of mine, and my comments in the text are not meant to be put-downs. For classic Royko, see Mike Royko, *Like I Was Sayin'* . . . (New York, 1984). Also, I take this opportunity to ask Chicago to preserve Nelson Algren's home, and to thank Robert Rauschenberg for his encouraging words.

CHAPTER 8

As I mentioned in the text, there are so many books on Lincoln one doesn't know where to begin. Two excellent fairly recent books deserve special mention: Stephen Oates, *With Malice Toward None* (New York, 1977), and James Mc-Pherson, *Abraham Lincoln and the Second American Revolution* (New York, 1990). My comments about Lincoln scholarship are meant to be satirical, and I don't mean to denigrate the fine works written on our sixteenth president. My information and quotes about Lincoln impersonators came from Harold Holzer, "Disarmingly Abe," *Americana*, February 1992. For information on Lincoln's Springfield, see Harold Holzer, "Lincoln's New Home," *Americana*, January – February 1989; William T. Anderson, "In the Footsteps of the Lincolns," *Saturday Evening Post*, July/August 1989; Beverly Bare Buehrer, "Lincoln's Springfield Home," *Early American Life*, February 1989; William T. Anderson, "Mr. Lincoln's Springfield," *American History Illustrated*, March 1989; Garry Wills, "Dishonest Abe," *Time*, October 5, 1992. For articles about cloning the genes of Abraham Lincoln to test for Marfan's Syndrome see Malcolm S. Forbes, Jr., "Shame on Them," *Forbes*, July 22, 1991; Natalie Angier, "Gene Is Isolated in Deadly Disease," *NYT*, July 15, 1991; and "Lincoln to Log Back In," *Science World*, February 7, 1992. On Ronald Reagan misquoting Lincoln, see Herbert Mitgang, "Reagan Put Words in Lincoln's Mouth," *NYT*, August 19, 1992. For Lincoln on the auction block, see Rita Reif, "Lincoln's 'House Divided' Draft to Be Sold," *NYT*, August 18, 1992. There is no good biography of Vachel Lindsay, but the following books, articles, and pamphlets are of interest: Mark Hannis, ed., *Selected Poems of Vachel Lindsay* (New York, 1963); Robert F. Sayre, Introduction, in Vachel Lindsay, *Adventures, Rhymes & Designs* (New York, 1935); Eleanor Ruggles, *The West-Going Heart: A Life of Vachel Lindsay* (New York, 1959); David Virgil Felts, *Trading Rhymes For Bread*, (Springfield, Ill., 1968); George S. Bonn, *We Need More Lindsay-Hearted Men* (Springfield, Ill., 1961). Particular thanks are due Mrs. Barbara J. Archer, executive director of the Vachel Lindsay Association, for the many kind courtesies she has shown me over the past years. Those interested in finding out more about Lindsay should write to the association at 603 South Fifth Street, Springfield, IL 62703. For a well-written but mean-spirited evaluation of Lindsay see Elizabeth Hardwick, "Wind from the Prairie," *New York Review of Books*, September 26, 1991.

For information on Saint Louis, Missouri, and Chuck Berry I relied on the following books and articles: George Lipsitz, *The Sidewalks of St. Louis: Places,*

People, and Politics in an American City, (Columbia, Mo., 1991); William Barnaby Faherty, S. J., *St. Louis: A Concise History* (St. Louis, 1989); Cathy Johnson and Patti Delano, *Missouri: Off the Beaten Path* (Chester, Conn., 1990); K. M. Kostyal, "St. Louis Spirit," *National Geographic Traveler*, September/October 1992; D. Ray Wilson, *Missouri: Historical Tour Guide* (Carpentersville, Mo., 1988); *Story of the Gateway Arch* (St. Louis, 1992); Howard A. Dewitt, *Chuck Berry: Rock 'N Roll Music* (Ann Arbor, 1985); Robert Christgau, "Chuck Berry," *The Rolling Stone Illustrated History of Rock and Roll* (rev. ed., New York, 1980); Tom Wheeler, "Chuck Berry in Outer Space, Johnny B. Goode Forever," *Guitar Player*, February 1981. For information on the plight of East Saint Louis, see Isabel Wilkerson, "Ravaged City on Mississippi: At Rock Bottom," *NYT*, April 4, 1991; Elizabeth Levitan-Spaid, "East St. Louis Mayor Fights Decline," *Christian Science Monitor*, July 25, 1991; and "Winner of City Hall Faces Big Tax on It," *NYT*, October 5, 1990.

CHAPTER 9

Thanks are due Jim McCrary of William S. Burroughs Communications for arranging for American Odyssey students to meet the great novelist. The following books on Burroughs were helpful in writing this chapter: Jennie Skerl, *William Burroughs* (Boston, 1985); John Tytell, *Naked Angels* (New York, 1988); and Ted Morgan, *Literary Outlaw: The Life and Times of William S. Burroughs* (New York, 1988). Peter O. Whitmer's profile of Burroughs in *Aquarius Revisited* (New York, 1987) was quite useful. I would also like to thank him for reading a draft of the chapter and making helpful suggestions. Gary Indiana's "Burroughs," in Ira Silverberg, *The Making of Naked Lunch* (New York, 1992) is a stunning and brilliant evaluation of Burroughs's influence on modern culture. For books on Kansas I used William Least Heat Moon, *Prairy Erth* (Boston, 1991), and the beautiful portrait of the prairie rendered by Ruth Carol Cushman and Stephen Jones in *The Shortgrass Prairie* (Boulder, 1988). Also used, to a lesser extent, were Robert T. Bakker, *The Dinosaur Heresies* (New York, 1986), and Lawrence T. Collins, ed., *Natural Kansas* (Lawrence, Kans., 1985). Willa Cather's *My Ántonia* (Boston, 1954) and James Michener's *Centennial* (New York, 1974) are wonderful novels about the prairie.

CHAPTER 10

Kurt Chandler, "Naropa's New Age," *Sunday Camera Magazine*, August 17, 1986, and Clifford D. May, "Town That Can't Sit Still," *New York Times Mag-*

azine, November 3, 1991, were my main sources for this chapter. Boulder's *Daily Camera* allowed me to go through its clipping files for Naropa Institute, skiing, and the New Age, and I'm extremely grateful. I used many of their articles. Thanks are in order to Anne Waldman, Bobbie Louise Hawkins, and Sue Seecoff at Naropa for helping me with this chapter. For information on Tibetan art I relied on Barbralu Fried, "Boulder Becoming Center for Tibetan Art Form," *Daily Camera*, August 25, 1974. A truly wonderful history of Buddhism in America is Rick Fields, *How the Swans Came to the Lake* (Boston, 1992). I picked up information on Alferd Packer from various guide books.

CHAPTER 11

A truly useful guidebook was Bruce Caughey and Dean Winstanley, *The Colorado Guide* (Boulder, 1991) as well as Stephen Trimble, *The Bright Edge: A Guide to the National Parks of the Colorado Plateau* (Flagstaff, Ariz., 1979). Much information in this chapter came from *The Colorado Quick Fact Book* (Topeka, Kans., 1992). The University of Nebraska Press has recently reissued a number of Enos Mills's nature books, including *Wild Life on the Rockies* (1909) and *The Spell of the Rockies* (1911). The best recent essay on Mills is Bill McKibben, "Hero of the Wilderness," *New York Review of Books*, November 9, 1989. For Telluride I relied heavily on Jon Bowermaster, "Telluride's Formula for Success," *NYT*, November 17, 1991. Information on the San Juan Mountains came from Scott S. Warren, *San Juan Skyway* (Durango, Colo., 1990). For Mesa Verde National Park, see David Grant Noble, *Ancient Ruins of the Southwest* (Flagstaff, Ariz., 1991).

CHAPTER 12

As a collector of books and articles on Billy the Kid, I can recommend to the general reader two essentials: Stephen Tatum, *Inventing Billy the Kid* (Albuquerque, 1982), and Robert M. Uttey, *Billy the Kid* (Lincoln, Nebr., 1989). For a collection of beautiful prose pieces about the Land of Enchantment, see Tony Hillerman, ed., *The Spell of New Mexico* (Albuquerque, 1976). My favorite guidebooks were Charles L. Cadieux, *The New Mexico Guide* (Golden, Colo., 1992), and Todd Staats, *New Mexico: Off the Beaten Path* (Chester, Conn., 1992). Santa Fe Dave provided me with copies of many of his satirical articles, which have been published in various alternative papers. D. H. Lawrence's essay "New Mexico" has been widely reprinted but may perhaps be most easily found in Edward D. McDonald, ed., *Phoenix: The Posthumous Papers of D. H. Lawrence* (New York, 1936). For information on Central Avenue, see Jill Schneider, *Route*

66 Across New Mexico (Albuquerque, 1991). Issues of *New Mexico* magazine (1991–92) were also useful.

CHAPTER 13

In recent years several excellent books have been published about Route 66, which I found most helpful: Michael Wallis, *Route 66: The Mother Road* (New York, 1990); Warren Anderson, *Vanishing Roadside America* (Tucson, 1981); Tom Snyder, *A Route 66 Traveler's Guide: A Roadside Companion* (New York, 1990); and Quinta Scott and Susan Croce Kelly, *Route 66: The Highway and Its People* (Norman, Okla., 1988). Useful articles on Route 66 include Dirk Johnson, "Now Only Ghosts Ride on Highway of Dreams," *NYT*, March 3, 1990, and Lauren Young, "Route 66," *National Parks*, March/April 1991. For historical information on the Grand Canyon, I relied on John F. Hoffman, *The Grand Canyon* (Casper, Wyo., 1977). Fodor's 1992 *Arizona* was also useful. Thanks to Ellen Shaffer and Lori Beecher of "Good Morning America" for helping out so much.

CHAPTER 14

The primary source for this chapter was Deke Castleman's *Las Vegas* (Oakland, Calif., 1991), a truly superb guidebook. Much of the information on Howard Hughes, sex, tourism, and wedding chapels came from this book. For a good profile of Bugsy Siegel, see Al Stump, "Mobster," *Los Angeles Magazine*, September 1991. For Las Vegas's attempts to become a family vacation center, I relied on three outstanding articles: Trip Gabriel, "From Vice to Nice," *NYT*, December 1, 1991; Robert Reinhold, "Las Vegas Transformation: From Sin City to Family City," *NYT*, May 30, 1989; and Doug Bradford and Mark Brazill, "Las Vegas . . . A Land with People of Vision," *Nation's Cities Weekly*, August 19, 1991. For a useful brief history of Nevada gambling, see Samuel Siffon, "Las Vegas: An Oasis," *American Heritage*, May/June 1990. Two additional guidebooks I found useful were Fodor's 1992 *Las Vegas* and Deke Castleman, *Nevada Handbook* (Chico, Calif., 1992). In recent years I've read three books that are a must for anyone who is Nevada bound. Hunter S. Thompson, *Fear and Loathing in Las Vegas* (New York, 1971); Larry McMurtry, *The Desert Rose* (New York, 1983), and John Gregory Dunne, *Vegas—Memoir of a Dark Season* (New York, 1974). Finally, even if you don't go to Las Vegas, be sure to read Tom Wolfe's brilliant essay about the City Without Clocks in *The Kandy Kolored Tangerine-Flake Steamline Baby* (1965).

The part of this chapter about the Mojave Desert couldn't have been written

517

without the help of Elden Hughes of Whittier, California, a longtime Sierra Club activist, who is one of the real driving forces behind the California Desert Protection Bill, and Adam Werback, a twenty-year-old sophomore at Brown University, who was one of the founders of the Sierrra Student Coalition (SSC) in 1991. The SSC is one of the most exciting things to happen to the environmental movement in a long time. Its members have become an "environmental strike force," able to react swiftly and powerfully to urgent-action needs. During 1992, in support of the California Desert Protection Bill, they collected twenty-five hundred signatures a week and staffed full-time phone banks on a day's notice. Both Elden and Adam have been listed among the Sierra Club's one hundred "Environmental Heroes." In recent years many articles have been written about the need to save the Mojave Desert from ecological destruction; I found the following ones particularly informative: Kim Heacox, "A Poet, a Painter, and the Lonesome Triangle," *Audubon*, May 1990; Alan Rich, "True West," *Travel Holiday*, March 1990; and David Darlington, "The Pastures of Class-L Heaven," *Sierra*, September/October 1989. *Time's Island: The California Desert* by T. H. Watkins (Utah, 1989), with its inspiring pictorial focus, also played an important role.

CHAPTER 15

For information on Montecito, see Diane Solway, "Magnificent Montecito," *Town & Country*, February 1989. For Santa Barbara see Ray Riegert, *Hidden Southern California* (Berkeley, 1992); Cheri Rae McKinney and John McKinney, *Walk Santa Barbara* (Santa Barbara, 1990); and Barney Brantigham, *Around Santa Barbara County with Barney* (Santa Barbara, 1992). Two American classics about Big Sur are Jack Kerouac, *Big Sur* (New York, 1962), and Henry Miller, *Big Sur and the Oranges of Hieronymus Bosch* (New York, 1957). An excellent book on the history of Carmel is Harold Gillian and Ann Gillian, *Creating Carmel* (Salt Lake City, 1992). In addition, the following articles about life in the Monterey Peninsula were useful: Nan Birmingham, "Pacific Paradise," *Town & Country*, January 1990; Robert Lindsey, "What's Doing Around Monterey," *NYT*, September 30, 1990; and Brian McGinty, "Steinbeck Country," *American History Illustrated*, September /October 1989. Throughout Chapters 15, 16, and 17, I used the California State Park Service's *Visitor's Guide to California State Parks* (Sacramento, 1990).

CHAPTER 16

Fodor's 1992 *San Francisco* was extremely helpful as I wrote this chapter. Other books include Lawrence Ferlinghetti and Nancy J. Peters, *Literary San*

Francisco (San Francisco, 1980); Samuel L. Clemens, *Mark Twain's Autobiography* (New York, 1925); Herb Caen, *Baghdad by the Bay*, (Sausalito, 1949); Don Herron, *The Dashiell Hammett Tour* (San Francisco, 1991); Shirley Fong-Torres, *San Francisco Chinatown* (San Francisco, 1991); Allen Brown, *Golden Gate* (Garden City, N.Y., 1965); Charles Perry, *The Haight Ashbury: A History* (New York, 1984); Edward Halsey Foster, *Understanding the Beats*, (Columbia, S.C., 1992); and Herbert Gold, *Travels in San Francisco* (New York, 1990). The articles on San Francisco I used include Gina Arnold, "The Beats of San Francisco," *NYT*, August 16, 1992; John Krich, "San Francisco's Real Mission," *New York Times Magazine*, October 1, 1989; Stephen Jay Gould, "Counters and Cable Cars," *Natural History*, January 1990; Betty Fussel, "Bay Area Brewpubs: Beer at the Source," *NYT*, May 7, 1989; Jane Cross, "Alcoholism Battled at Gutter Level," *NYT*, June 16, 1989; James A. Martin, "Golden Gate, Silver Screen," *NYT*, January 7, 1990; Katherine Bishop, "What's Doing in San Francisco," *NYT*, September 8, 1991; Eloise Salholz, "Bracing for the Big One," *Newsweek*, October 30, 1989; Herb Caen, "Two Cities Wild for 'Baysball,' " *Newsweek*, October 23, 1989; Mark Helprin, "San Francisco, 1969," *Harper's Magazine*, October 1990; Don Freeman, "Sam Spade's San Francisco," *Saturday Evening Post*, March/April 1992; Mary Roach, "A Love Haight Relationship," *California*, July 1989; Richard Rodriguez, "Late Victorians: San Francisco, AIDS, and the Homosexual Stereotype," *Harper's Magazine*, October 1990. For a good short summation of Coltrane's career in music, see Martin Williams, *Jazz Masters in Transition 1957–1969* (New York, 1970). A great guidebook on Berkeley is Don Pitcher, *Berkeley Inside/Out* (Berkeley, 1989). For a brief explanation of London's Beauty Ranch, see Homer L. Haughey and Connie Kale Johnson, *Jack London Ranch Album* (Stockton, Calif., 1985). Great thanks are in order to Dr. Earle Labor of Centenary College of Louisiana and Russ Kingman of Jack London Books in Glen Ellen, California, for preserving the real Jack London for future generations. The suicide article that elicited my angry response was in the November 1991 issue of *American Heritage*. For information on Mendocino, I used Dorothy Bear and Beth Stebbins, *A Tour of Mendocino* (Mendocino, Calif., 1992); Mariah Zellerbach, "The Magic of Mendocino," *Town & Country*, May 1989; and Jeff Phillips, "Mendocino," *Sunset*, February 1993.

CHAPTER 17

Ray Riegert's *California: The Ultimate Guidebook* (Berkeley, 1991) and Mark Williams's *Northern California: Off the Beaten Path* (Chester, Conn., 1989) were the most useful guidebooks. The following books and articles were useful in obtaining a better understanding of the environmental issues of Mendocino and Humboldt counties: Trip Gabriel, "If a Tree Falls in the Forest, They Hear It," *New York Times Magazine*, November 4, 1990; Elliot Norse, *Ancient Forests of the Pacific Northwest* (Seattle, 1990); Christopher Manes, *Green Rage* (Boston, 1990); David Clary, *Timber and the Forest Service* (Lawrence, Kans., 1986); Greg King and Mark Mardon, "Last Stand for the Redwoods," *Sierra*, July/August 1990; John G. Mitchell, "War in the Woods II," *Audubon*, January 1990; and Joshua Mendes, "A Raider's Ruckus in the Redwoods," *Fortune*, April 24, 1989. Thanks to Judi Bari for helping me better understand the mission of Earth First! For information on Bigfoot, I used Janet and Colin Bord, *Bigfoot Casebook* (Harrisburg, Penn., 1982); John Green, *Sasquatch: The Apes Among Us* (Seattle, 1978); John Napier, *Bigfoot: The Yeti and Sasquatch in Myth and Reality* (New York, 1972); David George Gordon, *Field Guide to the Sasquatch* (Seattle, 1992); and Robert Gray, "Sasquatch: Fact or Fancy?" *Boys Life*, July 1991. For Ohio Bigfoot spottings, see Dana Milbank, "A 'Bigfoot' Tracker is Hot on the Trail in the Buckeye State," *Wall Street Journal*, February, 24, 1992. For information on Avenue of the Giants and Humboldt Redwoods State Park see Whit Bronaugh, "The Fall of the Dyerville Giant," *American Forests*, January/February 1992; and Jerry Rohde and Gisela Rohde, *Humboldt Redwoods State Park* (Eureka, Calif., 1992). The *Eel River Current*, an annual publication of regional state parks interpretive associations, was also useful. For information pertaining to the Ferndale earthquake I relied on issues of the *Humboldt Beacon* from April and May 1992. For information about Paul Bunyan I consulted Maria Leach, *American Folk Tales and Legends* (Cleveland, 1958).

CHAPTER 18

Anybody interested in finding out about Ken Kesey should of course read Tom Wolfe, *The Electric Kool-Aid Acid Test* (New York, 1969). Other colorful evaluations of Kesey as writer and Prankster include Suzie Boss, "Ken Kesey: Gonzo in Oregon," in Win McCormack, ed., *Profiles of Oregon* (Portland, 1986); M. Gilbert Porter, *The Art of Grit: Ken Kesey's Fiction* (Columbia, Mo., 1982); Chip Brown, "Ken Kesey Kisses No Ass," *Esquire*, September 1992; Alan Reder, "Ken Kesey Raves Again," *New Age Journal*, December 1992; Robert Lipsyte, "Alone with Ken Kesey, Talk Turns to Buses," *NYT*, November 29, 1991; and Ed McClanahan, "Ken Kesey's Latest Trip," *Esquire*, February 1991. Ken Kesey's new novel, *Sailor's Song* (New York, 1992), is an instant classic. For books on Kesey's bus, see Ken Kesey, *The Further Inquiry* (New York, 1991), and Paul Perry and Ken Babbs, *On the Bus: The Complete Guide to the Legendary*

Trip of Ken Kesey and the Merry Pranksters and the Birth of the Counterculture (New York, 1991). For books and articles on Oregon and Portland, see Ralph Friedman, *Oregon for the Curious* (Caldwell, Ore., 1987); Linda Lampman and Carolyn Wieks, *The Portland Guidebook* (Portland, 1989); Robin Will, *Beauty of Portland* (Portland, 1990); Leslie Rule, *Portland* (Wilsonville, Ore., 1989); Robin Garr, "Portland Prefers to Quaff Its Own," *NYT*, March 24, 1991; Thomas J. Meyer, "What's Doing in Portland, Ore.," *NYT*, May 31, 1992; and Suzie Boss, "What's Doing in Portland, Ore.," September 23, 1990. For the history of Nike see J. B. Strasser and Laurie Becklund, *Swoosh: The Unauthorized Story of Nike and the Men Who Played There* (New York, 1991). For information on Josephine Humphreys, I looked at *Contemporary Authors*, vol. 127, and Josephine Humphreys, "Inhabited by History: Charleston, S.C.," *New York Times Magazine*, March 12, 1989. She read from her novel *The Fireman's Fair* (New York, 1991). Chuck William's *Mount St. Helens National Volcanic Monument* (Seattle, 1988) was most useful in studying the park. Over the years I've read everything written on Bob Dylan. The best books are Sam Shepard, *Rolling Thunder Logbook* (New York, 1977); Larry Sloman, *On the Road with Bob Dylan: Rolling with the Thunder* (New York, 1978); Bob Spitz, *Dylan: A Biography* (New York, 1989); and Robert Shelton, *No Direction Home: The Life and Music of Bob Dylan* (New York, 1986). All of Paul Williams's writing on Dylan is first-rate. Your best bet, however, is to listen to any of Dylan's forty-plus albums. For information on Seattle grunge, I've been clipping articles from alternative papers and magazines for the past few years. Two deserve special mention: Grant Alden, "Grunge Makes Good," *Spin*, September 1992, and Steven Daly, "The Sub Pop Culture," *The Face*, August 1992. The most consistently updated articles about grunge rock are in the *Seattle Weekly*. For Seattle history see Jack R. Evans, *Little History of Pike Place Market* (Seattle, 1991); Archie Satterfield, *The Seattle Guide Book* (Chester, Conn., 1991); and Fodor's 1992 *Seattle and Vancouver*. A useful road book is Ruth Kirk and Carmela Alexander, *Exploring Washington's Past* (Seattle, 1990). For a beautifully written book about the Pacific Northwest, read Sallie Tisdale, *Stepping Westward* (New York, 1991).

CHAPTER 19

The best brief introduction to the Battle of the Little Bighorn is Robert M. Utley, *Custer Battlefield* (Washington, D.C., 1988). For a good history of Montana, see Joseph Kinsey Howard, *Montana: High, Wide, and Handsome* (Lincoln, Neb., 1983). A good introduction to the subject of the buffalo is Michael S. Sample, *Bison: Sample of America* (Billings, Mont., 1987). Anybody interested in finding out more about Theodore Roosevelt and the Badlands should read Edmund Morris, *The Rise of Theodore Roosevelt* (New York, 1984), and James F. Vivian, ed., *The Romance of My Life* (Fargo, N. Dak., 1989). George Bush on Theodore Roosevelt comes from the March 29, 1989, *NYT*. For information pertaining to the park, see Henry A. Schoch, *Theodore Roosevelt National Park: The Story Behind the Scenery* (Las Vegas, 1987), and David Harmon, *At the Open Margin* (Medora, N. Dak., 1986). Thanks to Harold and Sheila Schafer for giving me an armful of pamphlets and articles about Medora; they are the kindest, most generous people I know. For information on the Schafers I relied on profiles in the spring 1992 and winter 1993 issues of *North Dakota Horizons* magazine. Anyone interested in North Dakota should read the fiction of Larry Woiwode. For discussions on Mount Rushmore, see Dan O'Brien, "The Giants of the Black Hills," *NYT*, May 19, 1991; Alex Hoard "Mount Rushmore: the Real Story," *New Republic*, July 15 and 22, 1991; Rex Alan Smith, "Shrine of Democracy," *History Illustrated*, July/August, 1991; and William Zinsser, *American Places* (New York, 1992). For the carving of Crazy Horse in Black Hills granite, see David Grogan and Christopher Phillips, "The Ziolkowskis Are Honoring Chief Crazy Horse by Blasting Out a Mountain of a Sculpture," *People*, December 4, 1989. For articles pertaining to the battle over Hornell Brewing Co., see Ira Teinowitz, "Crazy Horse Brew Incenses Sioux," *Advertising Age*, April 6, 1992, and James Bovard, "The Second Murder of Crazy Horse," *Wall Street Journal*, September 15, 1992. A useful history of the state is John R. Milton, *South Dakota* (New York, 1977). Thanks are due in part to Dr. John Gable, director of the Theodore Roosevelt Association, for helping me with this chapter.

AFTERWORD

Writing is a lonely endeavor, and late at night, music becomes your only companion. The following albums and songs constantly inspired: Leonard Cohen, "Chelsea Hotel #2" and *The Future*; Bob Dylan, "Going, Going, Gone"; Talking Heads, "Nothing But (Flowers)"; John Cale, *Fragments From a Rainy Season*; and The Band's "It Makes No Difference."

PERMISSIONS AND CREDITS

ABOUT THE AUTHOR

Douglas Brinkley is director of the Eisenhower Center for Leadership Studies and associate professor of history at the University of New Orleans. A graduate of Ohio State University (1982), he obtained his M.A. and Ph.D. in diplomatic history from Georgetown University (1989) and subsequently taught at the United States Naval Academy, Princeton University, and Hofstra University. At thirty-three years old, he is already considered one of America's most prolific and outstanding scholars, authoring such award-winning books as *Dean Acheson: The Cold War Years, 1953–1971* (1992) and *Driven Patriot: The Life and Times of James Forrestal* (with Townsend Hoopes, 1992), as well as editing six scholarly volumes on American foreign policy. Professor Brinkley is currently writing a biography of Jimmy Carter and a short polemic entitled *Stop Making Sense of Generation X*. A published poet, he will soon be making his novelistic debut with *Mississippi Lightning Done Burned My Apple Pie*. Meanwhile his Majic Bus journeys across America continue.